Learn Mac OS X Snow Leopard

Scott Meyers and Mike Lee

Apress®

Learn Mac OS X Snow Leopard

Copyright © 2009 by Scott Meyers and Mike Lee

ISBN-13 (pbk): 978-1-4302-1946-0

ISBN-13 (electronic): 978-1-4302-1947-7

Printed and bound in the United States of America 9 8 7 6 5 4 3 2 1

Trademarked names may appear in this book. Rather than use a trademark symbol with every occurrence of a trademarked name, we use the names only in an editorial fashion and to the benefit of the trademark owner, with no intention of infringement of the trademark.

Lead Editors: Clay Andres, Joohn Choe
Technical Reviewer: Joe Kissell
Editorial Board: Clay Andres, Steve Anglin, Mark Beckner, Ewan Buckingham, Tony Campbell, Gary Cornell, Jonathan Gennick, Michelle Lowman, Matthew Moodie, Jeffrey Pepper, Frank Pohlmann, Ben Renow-Clarke, Dominic Shakeshaft, Matt Wade, Tom Welsh
Project Manager: Sofia Marchant
Copy Editors: Nicole Abramowitz, Kim Wimpsett
Associate Production Director: Kari Brooks-Copony
Production Editors: Laura Cheu, Kelly Winquist
Compositor: Kinetic Publishing Services, LLC
Proofreader: Linda Seifert
Indexer: John Collin
Cover Designer: Kurt Krames
Manufacturing Director: Tom Debolski

Distributed to the book trade worldwide by Springer-Verlag New York, Inc., 233 Spring Street, 6th Floor, New York, NY 10013. Phone 1-800-SPRINGER, fax 201-348-4505, e-mail orders-ny@springer-sbm.com, or visit http://www.springeronline.com.

For information on translations, please contact Apress directly at 233 Spring Street, New York, NY 10013. E-mail info@apress.com, or visit http://www.apress.com.

Apress and friends of ED books may be purchased in bulk for academic, corporate, or promotional use. eBook versions and licenses are also available for most titles. For more information, reference our Special Bulk Sales–eBook Licensing web page at http://www.apress.com/info/bulksales.

The information in this book is distributed on an "as is" basis, without warranty. Although every precaution has been taken in the preparation of this work, neither the author(s) nor Apress shall have any liability to any person or entity with respect to any loss or damage caused or alleged to be caused directly or indirectly by the information contained in this work.

The source code for this book is available to readers at http://www.apress.com.

Contents at a Glance

PART 8 ■ ■ ■ Cross-Platform Solutions

PART 9 ■ ■ ■ Appendixes

Contents

PART 1 ■ ■ ■ Getting to Know Snow Leopard

PART 2 ■■■ Customizing and Administering Leopard

PART 3 ■■■ Communications and the Internet

PART 4 ■■■ Working with Applications

PART 5 ■■■ Getting to Know Darwin

PART 7 ■■■ Snow Leopard Development and Scripting

PART 8 ■■■ Cross-Platform Solutions

PART 9 ■■■ **Appendixes**

About the Authors

**SCOTT MEYERS** got his start with computers as a kid hacking around TRS-80s and Apple IIs (his first computer was an Apple IIe that served him well until he got his second computer . . . a shiny new Macintosh). Professionally, after college and after bartending for a few years, Scott took a job as an Apple sales specialist and consultant for a Midwestern computer retailer that was long ago bought out by another company. Since then, Scott has had many titles including Web Developer, Senior Development Editor, Marketing Product Manager, Information Systems Specialist, and Acquisitions Editor—all revolving around the computer industry and often alongside one of his trusty Macs (currently a MacBook Pro).

Scott lives in Carmel, Indiana (just outside of Indianapolis), with his wife, two kids, an old fat cat, and a crazy mutt of a dog. When not working or writing, Scott likes building and modifying tube amplifiers and then making loud guitar noises through them, traveling, photography, and watching FCB beat Real Madrid.

Scott can be contacted at scott@beyondmac.com. Answers, updates, and errata for this book can be found at www.beyondmac.com.

**MIKE LEE**, the world's toughest programmer, is the founder and CEO of United Lemur, a philanthropic revolution disguised as a software company. Mike has had a role in creating many popular iPhone applications, including Obama '08, Tap Tap Revenge, Twinkle, and Jott.

Prior to the iPhone, Mike cut his teeth—and won an Apple Design Award—at the Seattle-based Delicious Monster Software. Mike is a popular blogger and occasional pundit and has been seen on Twitter as @bmf.

Mike is originally from Honolulu but currently lives in Silicon Valley with two cats. Mike's hobbies include weightlifting, single malts, and fire.

Mike can be contacted at mike@unitedlemur.org.

About the Technical Reviewer

 **JOE KISSELL** is the senior editor of TidBITS, a web site and weekly e-mail newsletter about the Macintosh and the Internet, and the author of numerous print and electronic books about Macintosh software, including the best-selling *Take Control of Mac OS X Backups*. He is also a senior contributor to *Macworld*. Joe has worked in the Mac software industry since the early 1990s and previously managed software development for Nisus Software and Kensington Technology Group. He currently lives in Paris, France.

Acknowledgments

A great deal of love and thanks go out to my family: Sara Beth, Ethan, and Isabel—writing sucks away a lot of time and occasionally makes me cranky, and I couldn't do this without their support (and I often wonder why I still get it).

A big thanks to everyone who worked on this book with me: Mike, Joe, Sophia, Nicole, Laura, Kim, Kurt, Joohn, Clay, and everyone else I missed. Bringing a book to market requires a lot of people doing a lot of work, and I appreciate it all.

Thanks also goes out to the folks at Apple who continue to amaze us with great products and great support for their products.

Finally, a shout-out to all the great people I've worked with at the old Apress office in Berkeley, California. They made this, and countless other Apress books, more than just possible; they made them great. I wish them all the best of luck.

Scott Meyers

In addition to the teams at Apress and Apple without whom this book could not exist, I have to acknowledge three groups of people who have accompanied me on this ride.

First, I have to thank the mentors who have given so freely of their time and knowledge to make me the engineer I am today. I can only hope to live up to your lessons.

Second, I have to thank the trail of broken engineers and designers who have followed me into the madness in which great software is forged. You've earned your success.

Finally, I have to thank the crazy people who should know better than to set aside their perfectly adequate lives to pursue their passions armed with little more than a book and a dream. You are the reason we write.

Mike Lee

Introduction

Whether you're new to the Mac or just new to Snow Leopard, we wrote this book for you.

We didn't say new to computers. That's what makes this book unique. Maybe you're an infrequent upgrader or a programmer from another platform who bought a Mac to write software for the iPhone. We talk to you, without talking *down* to you.

We don't explain to you what a mouse is, but we do tell how using a mouse on a Mac is different from using a mouse on Windows. We give detailed summaries of every part of Mac OS X, from the Finder to Terminal.

We give you a tour of the Applications folder, with chapters dedicated to Snow Leopard applications and iLife, Apple's digital lifestyle suite. We get you connected, with chapters on Safari, iChat, and MobileMe, as well as on the productivity trio of Mail, Address Book, and iCal.

We don't stop at the consumer stuff. We point out the Pro versions and link to the documentation. We provide generous screenshots and actual, usable sample code. We talk about the UNIX layer that lives beneath Aqua's candy shell. We show you how to master your Mac with shell scripts, AppleScripts, and Automator.

We show you how to install the Xcode developer tools. We take you on a tour of the Cocoa frameworks and get up close and personal with Objective-C, the native programming language of both Mac OS X and iPhone OS.

Whether you want to learn how to produce a podcast with GarageBand or become the next App Store millionaire with Xcode, we get you started. With the power that we help you unlock from your Mac, this book doesn't just pay for itself; it beats the returns on Wall Street.

PART 1

■ ■ ■

Getting to Know Snow Leopard

■ ■ ■

## CHAPTER 1

Working in Snow Leopard: The Aqua Interface

Whether you are new to OS X or just new to Snow Leopard, the first step to getting the most out of your computer is to learn a bit about Aqua. Apple has designed what many people think is the most attractive, user-friendly interface of any popular computer operating system today; however, if you come to OS X after years of using Windows or some other operating system, you will likely encounter a number of features that are different and perhaps even confusing. Also, if you are just making the upgrade from Tiger or an earlier Mac OS X version, you will immediately notice a number of differences in Snow Leopard; even if you're upgrading from Leopard to Snow Leopard, you may notice a few refinements to the interface. This chapter will go over the interface basics of Snow Leopard and show you how to get the most out of it, specifically:

- The menu bar
- The Finder and the desktop
- The Dock

The Menu Bar

The menu bar may seem like an odd choice as the first topic to cover in this book; however, it is one of the primary user-interface (UI) elements for both controlling and getting information in OS X. It is also the UI element that is most unique to OS X (and actually the Mac OS since its inception). The menu bar (shown in Figure 1-1) is divided into three primary areas: the Apple menu, the application menus, and the status menus.

Figure 1-1. *The OS X menu bar in Leopard*

The Apple Menu

The Apple menu on the far-left side of the menu bar (shown expanded in Figure 1-2) is a special menu containing a number of system-level commands and resources that are particularly handy to have easily accessible. This includes the About This Mac command; shortcuts to Software Update; the System Preferences command; shortcuts to Dock preferences; the Recent Items command (including shortcuts for applications, documents, and servers); the Force Quit command that allows you to immediately quit an application; the Sleep, Restart…, and Shut Down… commands; and the Log Out *User*… command. Most of these are fairly obvious as to what they do; however, some additional information about some of these items may be helpful.

Figure 1-2. *The Apple menu*

The About This Mac command opens a window (shown in Figure 1-3) that gives you some fairly self-explanatory information about your computer. Clicking the light gray text under the large Mac OS X that reads Version 10.6 will cycle through additional information, including the exact operating system build number and the computer's serial number (this is a much easier way to get your serial number than searching around for it on your actual computer). The More Info button in the About This Mac window launches the System Profiler application that contains all sorts of information about your computer and the software installed on it.

Figure 1-3. *About This Mac window*

The Recent Items command opens a submenu that by default shows you the last ten applications, documents, and servers you accessed (for a total of up to thirty items). You can adjust these defaults in the Appearance panel in System Preferences (we'll talk about System Preferences in depth in Chapter 4). You'll also see an option here to clear all items if, for whatever reason, you don't want that information to display.

The Force Quit command opens a new window that shows all the currently running Aqua applications. From this window you can select any of those applications to quit immediately. By immediately, we mean right away—no saving files or anything. The application will just quit. About the only times you may find yourself needing this is if an application freezes up (or in Apple lingo, *stops responding*) or if you need to *relaunch* the Finder (if you force quit the Finder, it will start back up, so in Apple lingo, rather than force quit the Finder, you relaunch it).

■**Tip** You can also force quit any item from the Dock by Control-Option-clicking on the desired item in the Dock and selecting Force Quit from the contextual menu (if you apply this to the Finder instead of Force Quit, you will see Relaunch). If all else fails, holding down Command-Option-Shift-Esc for a few seconds will force quit the foreground application.

■Note You may notice that some menu items have an ellipsis (…) after them, and some don't. According to Apple's Human Interface Guidelines (`http://developer.apple.com/documentation/userexperience/ Conceptual/AppleHIGuidelines/XHIGIntro/XHIGIntro.html`), items with the ellipsis require some additional user interaction to complete a task. In general, this means an item will either prompt you or open a window with additional options. Another item common in menus is the sideways triangle on the far right, which indicates the menu item will open a submenu, and of course keyboard shortcuts are viewable for a number of menu items.

Application Menus

Moving just to the right of the Apple menu begins the application menus. This is where people new to Macs tend to get thrown off; you see, in OS X, there is only one application menu bar, and this is it. The application menus, however, are dynamic in the sense that the information in one menu bar reflects the application running in the foreground. So if Microsoft Word is the active foreground application, the menu bar will provide the menu items provided by Microsoft Word (see Figure 1-4). If you bring the Finder or another application to the foreground, the menu bar will change to provide menu items for that application.

Figure 1-4. *The menu bar's application menu presents Microsoft Word's menus when you're using Microsoft Word. Compare this to the Finder's menus in Figure 1-1.*

■Note While Mac OS X runs many applications concurrently (i.e., it multitasks), it assumes that the user is generally actively using one application at a time. The application that is currently being used is referred to as the *foreground* application; other applications are said to be running in the *background*. Sometimes the foreground application is also called the application that has *focus*.

In keeping with standard Mac UI guidelines, many menu items are the same from one application to another; additionally, the general arrangement of the menus should be fairly consistent from one application to another (however, developers can create applications that deviate from this in sometimes minor and sometimes major ways). The first menu to the right of the Apple menu, called the *application menu*, should always reflect the name of the current foreground application. In addition to the application menu, almost all proper Aqua applications have at least the following additional menus: File, Edit, Window, and Help. Interface Builder, part of the Xcode tools, sets up the following application menus by default: New Application, File, Edit, Format, View, Window, and Help. Everything between the Edit and Window menus tends to vary from application to application.

■**Note** Strangely, while Interface Builder defaults to an order of menus that puts Format before View, many applications (including Microsoft Word, and even Apple's own Mail application) tend to switch that order.

The five most common menus tend to serve the following purposes:

Application menu: This menu identifies the application and usually contains the option to access the application's preferences and other options. This also contains the Services menu item, one of the most overlooked features of OS X.

■**Tip** The Services menu is a powerful way to leverage the power of external services inside any application. By default, Apple provides a number of services. (One of the most interesting services, Summarize, takes a large block of text and attempts to summarize it into a shorter block of text with surprisingly good results.) However, many applications also make some of their features available through the Services menu. We encourage you to play around with this, because it's a powerful feature that too few people take advantage of. If you have used Services in the past you may notice that this menu has undergone some changes in Snow Leopard. The most significant change is that rather than expand all installed services, the improved Services menu will only show relevant available services.

File: This is the menu where you generally create new documents or open, save, and print existing application documents.

Edit: The Edit menu contains standard menu items such as the Cut, Copy, Paste, Select All, Undo, Find, and Replace commands as well as Spelling and Grammar submenu items. The actual list of items here varies from application to application, as some of the default items are commonly removed from certain types of applications, and some applications add a few items of their own.

Window: The Window menu manages multiple open windows from an application. Certain applications are designed to run in only one window and therefore may remove this menu.

Help: The Help menu (Figure 1-5) contains a list of help documentation for the application and for OS X in general. The help search feature, introduced in Mac OS X Leopard, provides an immediate dynamic contextual help system to help you find just the right information or item you need to find.

Figure 1-5. *Snow Leopard's help system can help find an application's menu items.*

■**Note** One unique feature of OS X applications that relates to the menu bar is that since the menu bar is separate from the application window, the application can (and usually does) run even if no windows are open. This is one of those big WTF (Wow That's Fascinating) moments that people have when coming to the Mac from Microsoft Windows. With Windows, when you close a window (usually by clicking the X button on the far-right side of the title bar), the application closes along with the window. This is not so for many applications in OS X. In OS X if you close a window (usually by clicking the X button on the far-left side of the title bar), then the window will close, but the application itself will probably still be running. To actually close an application in Mac OS X, you generally must explicitly quit it from the application menu (or by using the Command-Q keyboard shortcut or selecting Quit from the application's Dock item contextual menu).

■**Note** Contrary to the previous note, sometimes applications do quit when you close the window. This is one of those further head-scratching moments in OS X. The reason is that in OS X, there are different application types. Document-based applications usually follow the previous rules, while other applications don't (always). The general rule is that if you can have multiple windows open, then you can have none, even while the application is running. However, if your application provides only a single window, then when that window is closed, the application usually quits. Examples of default Apple applications that quit when the windows are closed are System Preferences, Dictionary, and Font Book. Keep in mind that if an application is running, this will be indicated in the Dock.

Status Menus

On the far right of the menu bar is where you will find a number of status menus (a.k.a., menu bar icons, menu bar items, or menu bar extras). These special menus are available at all times and can provide information as well as quick access to certain functions. The magnifying glass icon on the far right is the Spotlight icon where you can access the Spotlight search feature of Mac OS X (covered in depth in Chapter 3); this icon is ever-present and immovable. You can usually move the other status menus around by Command-dragging them with your mouse. If you drag an icon out of the menu bar, it will be removed from it. Most of the status menus that are available by default in Snow Leopard are tied to System Preferences, so if you accidentally remove one, you can usually add it again in the appropriate System Preferences panel.

Besides the status menus available from System Preferences, additional status menu items are available from various applications and third-party utilities. A couple of examples included with Snow Leopard are the Script menu that can be added from within the AppleScript Utility and an iChat menu available from the iChat preferences.

Note The Script menu makes a large number of useful prewritten AppleScripts available from the menu bar (and of course you can add your own AppleScripts to the menu). This is a wonderful menu to include if you use even a few AppleScripts on a frequent basis.

The Finder (and the Desktop)

The Finder is a key application that provides the interface for navigating your file system, opening files and applications, and many more of the features that provide the Mac OS X its famed ease of use. It is designed to allow you to find whatever you are looking for on your Mac and then get out of your way so you can work (or play, create, or whatever you do on your computer). Most of the work done with the Finder is done in the Finder window, shown in Figure 1-6.

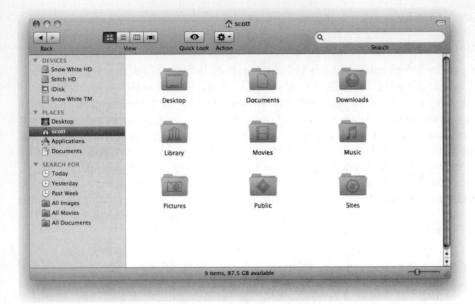

Figure 1-6. *The Finder window showing a typical home directory*

As you can see, the Finder window is divided into three areas: the toolbar on top, the sidebar along the left of the window, and the main viewing area that takes up most of the window.

The Finder's Toolbar

The toolbar (Figure 1-7) provides some buttons and a search field for working in the Finder. The arrows on the far left move you forward and backward through your Finder history in the same way as in most web browsers. The four buttons grouped together alter how the Finder displays items. The button with the eye icon opens the selected Finder item in Quick Look. The button with the gear icon opens a menu with some Finder options in it, and all the way on the right side is a search box that helps you find any item on any connected hard drive (using Spotlight). We'll talk about the different Finder views and Quick Look later in this chapter.

Figure 1-7. *The Finder's default toolbar*

■**Note** Most toolbars in Aqua applications, including the Finder's, can be customized by Control-clicking the toolbar and selecting Customize Toolbar from the contextual pop-up menu.

■**Note** A Control-click is commonly known as a *right-click* in Microsoft Windows speak (since by default, a right-click on a two-button mouse is set up to Control-click). Due to tradition (Macs used to come with one-button mice, and Apple notebooks still only have a single button, if they have a button at all) and to the fact that mouse buttons can generally be programmed differently, we will be using Control-click throughout the book. Still, by default, clicking the right mouse button (as well as the two-fingered trackpad click) will have the same effect.

The Finder's Sidebar

The sidebar in the Finder window (Figure 1-8) is divided into four areas:

Devices: This is where any attached file systems will show up. This includes connected disk volumes, your iDisk, and any attached network volumes.

Shared: This is where any shared network files or devices will appear, including Back to My Mac shares.

Places: By default, this contains a list of your personal directories. You can add or remove any files or folders here that you want.

Search For: This area contains some common search parameters and saved Spotlight searches. Saved searches in the Finder are similar to smart folders; however, rather than the folder showing up in the file system, the saved searches show up only in this part of the Finder sidebar.

Figure 1-8. *The Finder's sidebar*

The Finder's Views

The most important part of the Finder window is the viewing area; it is here that you actually access what you want to find. Depending on your needs, the Finder has four ways to view the items available to your computer: as icons, as a list, in columns, and in Cover Flow view.

Using the Finder's Icon View

Icon view is the more traditional Mac OS view of folders, files, and applications. This view shows the contents of one folder at a time, allowing you to traverse into other folders by double-clicking them (or selecting them and using the Open command or Command-O keyboard shortcut). To move up the directory path in Icon view, you can use the Go ➤ Enclosing Folder command (or the much easier Command-↑ keyboard shortcut). The Icon view defaults are generally fine for most things; however, like many other views, you can tweak this view to look or behave differently using the view options presented when you select Show View Options from the View menu or contextual menu (or when you press the Command-J keyboard shortcut). Figure 1-9 shows the Finder's Icon view along with the view's Options window open beside it.

Figure 1-9. *The Finder's Icon view with the view's Options window open beside it*

The options available to tweak Icon view include the following:

Always open in icon view: This causes the folder to always open in Icon view, overriding any system-wide defaults.

Icon size: This makes the icons in the view bigger or smaller.

Grid spacing: This adjusts the amount of space between the icons.

Text size: This adjusts the font size of the label text.

Label position: This moves the label text either below or to the right of the icons.

Show item info: This toggles extra information about items (that is, how many items are in folders, how much space is available on a storage system, how big an image file is in pixels, and so on).

Show icon preview: This toggles whether to show a thumbnail of certain files or to use the generic icon for the recommended application.

Arrange by: This selects how items are arranged in the view; Name is the default and arranges items alphabetically, but at times other options may be preferable. None (which means files will be where you put them), Date Modified, Date Created, Size, Kind, and Label are other options.

Background: This allows you to change the view's background to a different color or even an image file.

Use As Defaults: This final option becomes available if you make any changes. Clicking this button effectively makes the changes carry over to all noncustomized folders; otherwise, the changes you make are reflected only in the current folder.

Using the Finder's List View

The next view in the Finder is List view (Figure 1-10). This view has a number of advantages over the standard Icon view in that it presents more information about each Finder item, and it allows you to expand folders to see their contents without leaving the current folder. You do this by clicking the sideways-triangle symbol to the left of a folder item.

Figure 1-10. *The Finder's List view with the view's Options window beside it*

The view options for List view differ somewhat from the options in Icon view; the different options available in List view are as follows:

Always open in list view: This causes this folder to always open in List view.

Icon size: Rather than scaling the icons as in Icon view, in List view you can choose only Large or Small.

Show Columns: This allows you to choose which columns should be shown.

Use Relative Dates: When selected, the date columns can use terms such as *Today* and *Yesterday* rather than the actual date all the time.

Calculate All Sizes: This causes the computer to calculate the sizes of all items, even other folders (by adding up all its contents). In many cases, this can be a time-consuming process.

Show Icon Preview: This toggles between using a generic icon for files shown in this view and showing a preview of the files' contents. When viewing a large number of items, unchecking this box increases performance.

■**Tip** To sort the Finder items in List view, you can click any column header, and the column will determine the sort order. For example, to sort items by the date they were last modified, just click the column header Date Modified.

Using the Finder's Column View

The third view is Column view. This view was introduced in the first version of OS X and is the descendant of the File Viewer used in NeXTSTEP and later in OPENSTEP (from which OS X descends). Column view (Figure 1-11) is nice in that it reveals the whole file system path that leads to the Finder item you are viewing. Additionally, when you select a nonfolder item in Column view, the last column reveals a preview of the selected item along with some general information about it.

The view options for Column view are fairly limited, and the only new option is Show Preview Column. When the Show Preview Column option is checked, then a preview as well as information about the selected file or application appears in the last column. For certain file types, such as supported audio and video files, you can actually play these files in this preview.

Figure 1-11. *The Finder's Column view with the view's Options window beside it*

Using the Finder's Cover Flow View

The final Finder view is the new Cover Flow view. Cover Flow view (Figure 1-12) presents a split window with a standard column view on the bottom; the top, however, provides a scrollable display that allows you to "flip through" previews of all the items shown in the Column view below. Sometimes, when dealing with a large number of files, this is a helpful tool for visually identifying the file you want to find.

The Cover Flow view options mimic the options presented in List view since that is the view provided beneath the Cover Flow view area.

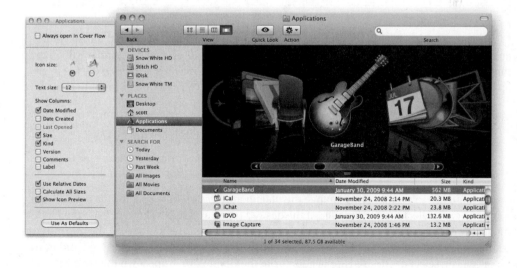

Figure 1-12. *This is Cover Flow view in the Finder; most of the view options are the same here as in List view.*

Common Finder Tasks

Although the Finder is a great tool for browsing around your computer, to be a useful file management tool in a modern operating system, the Finder needs to perform a number of additional tasks. Luckily, the Finder in Mac OS X performs all the basic tasks necessary plus a few handy extras.

■**Note** Many of the relevant commands in the Finder's application menu are available from a contextual menu that pops up when you Control-click a Finder item or Finder window. The contextual menus present different options depending on what options are available for any given item you Control-click. This includes most of the relevant menu commands, as well as some special commands that may not be available from the Finder's menu, because some applications install a special "contextual menu item" that allows special features of that application to become available in contextual menus. Using contextual pop-ups should be very familiar to users of Microsoft Windows.

Viewing and Opening Files and Applications

Double-clicking any item icon (or using the Command-O keyboard shortcut) in the Finder opens it. If the item is a folder, the Finder will open that folder in the current Finder window. If the item is an application, then that application will launch. If the item is a file, then the Finder will try to open that file with its preferred application.

■**Tip** If you want to open a folder in a new Finder window, you can hold Command while double-clicking the folder.

The preferred application with a file is usually the application that created the file. If the creating application is unknown or not present on your computer, then the Finder will try to make a guess based on the type of file it is. Occasionally you may want to open the file in an application other than the one the Finder thinks is best, and you can do this in numerous ways:

- Open the file from within the desired application.
- Drag the file onto the desired application icon in the Finder or on the Dock.
- Right-click the file to open the pop-up contextual menu, and choose an alternate application from the Open With menu.

If you'd like to permanently change the default application for a specific file or all files of a specific type, select the file (or a file of the desired type), and select Get Info from the Finder menu, the Action toolbar item (the menu with the gear icon on the toolbar), or the pop-up contextual menu by Control-clicking the file. This opens the Info window (Figure 1-13), and from there you can select the desired application from the Open With drop-down menu. If you'd like to make all files of the same type open in this alternate application, click the Change All button.

Figure 1-13. *The Info window, opened by selecting Get Info from a menu*

Sometimes you might just want to preview a file without opening any application. Snow Leopard includes a feature called Quick Look that allows you to do just that. To activate Quick Look, just select the desired file in the Finder, and hit the spacebar (or click the Quick Look button in the Finder's toolbar or press Command-Y). This immediately opens any supported file type in a hovering window for your viewing pleasure. You can even select a full-screen view (Figure 1-14) that causes the file to fill the screen for distraction-free viewing.

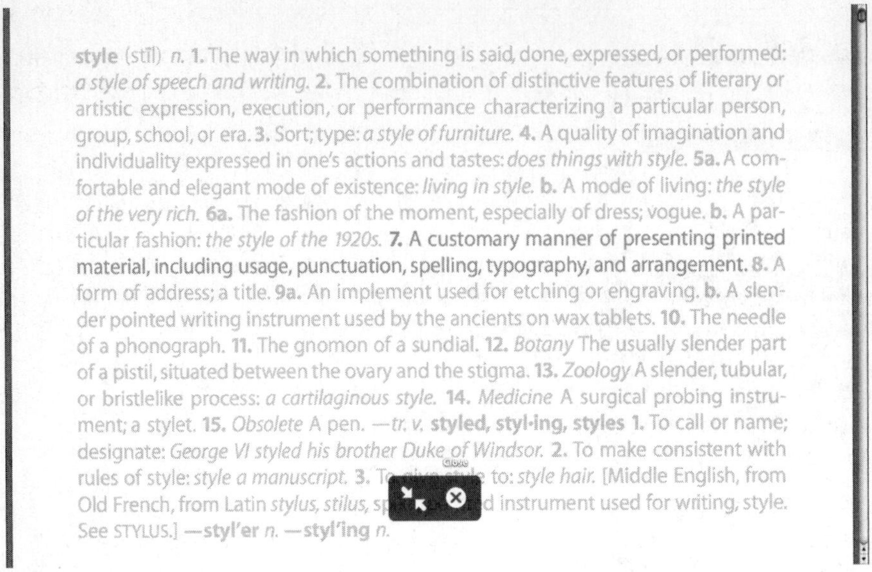

style (stīl) *n*. **1.** The way in which something is said, done, expressed, or performed: *a style of speech and writing*. **2.** The combination of distinctive features of literary or artistic expression, execution, or performance characterizing a particular person, group, school, or era. **3.** Sort; type: *a style of furniture*. **4.** A quality of imagination and individuality expressed in one's actions and tastes: *does things with style*. **5a.** A comfortable and elegant mode of existence: *living in style*. **b.** A mode of living: *the style of the very rich*. **6a.** The fashion of the moment, especially of dress; vogue. **b.** A particular fashion: *the style of the 1920s*. **7.** A customary manner of presenting printed material, including usage, punctuation, spelling, typography, and arrangement. **8.** A form of address; a title. **9a.** An implement used for etching or engraving. **b.** A slender pointed writing instrument used by the ancients on wax tablets. **10.** The needle of a phonograph. **11.** The gnomon of a sundial. **12.** *Botany* The usually slender part of a pistil, situated between the ovary and the stigma. **13.** *Zoology* A slender, tubular, or bristlelike process: *a cartilaginous style*. **14.** *Medicine* A surgical probing instrument; a stylet. **15.** *Obsolete* A pen. —*tr. v.* **styled, styl·ing, styles 1.** To call or name; designate: *George VI styled his brother Duke of Windsor*. **2.** To make consistent with rules of style: *style a manuscript*. **3.** To give style to: *style hair*. [Middle English, from Old French, from Latin *stylus, stilus,* spiked instrument used for writing, style. See STYLUS.] —**styl'er** *n.* —**styl'ing** *n.*

Figure 1-14. *Quick Look's full-screen viewing*

■**Note** The previewed file is not actually opened in the creating application but rather in a separate preview generator; therefore, occasionally you'll see some differences between the Quick Look preview and how the file will appear when opened in its actual application.

Moving, Copying, and Creating Aliases of Finder Items

Besides opening and viewing files, the Finder is also used for managing your documents and applications. Simply drag and drop items around where you want them.

■**Caution** One issue that may occur when you move an application from its original, installed location is that occasionally it's expected to be there. This is especially true with (but not limited to) some of Apple's own applications that won't update correctly if they are not located in the same folder in which they were installed. This doesn't mean you can't organize your applications into subfolders in the application folder; however, if you notice issues with an application that you've moved around, then you may want to move it back. Also, it's best to leave Apple applications where they are.

If, rather than just moving a file, you want to make a copy of the file, you can do this by using the Option-drag keyboard+mouse shortcut. (You should notice a green button with a plus sign appear while you are dragging to indicate you are making a copy.) Command-Option-drag creates an alias of the Finder item you are dragging.

■**Note** If you are moving a file from one volume to another, the Finder will, by default, create a copy rather than simply move the file. You can override this behavior by holding the Command key while moving the item.

If you want to create a copy of an item in the same folder as the original, you can use the File ➤ Duplicate command from the Finder's menus or use the Command-D keyboard shortcut (or select Duplicate from the item's contextual menu). You may also create aliases by selecting File ➤ Make Alias or pressing the Command-L keyboard shortcut. One final way to create a copy of a Finder item is to use a standard copy-paste operation; select Edit ➤ Copy (or press Command-C) to copy an item, and select Edit ➤ Paste (or press Command-V) to paste it wherever you want.

■**Note** Aliases are the OS X equivalent of shortcuts in Microsoft Windows. Rather than creating a copy of an item, OS X creates a link that points to the original Finder item. This is used when you want to keep one original Finder item, yet you want to access it from different places in the file system.

Renaming Finder Items

To rename a Finder item, you need to first select the item and then click the name of the Finder item. If you do this too quickly, though, the system may recognize this as a double-click and open the item. Once the item is selected for editing (the name will become highlighted in a rectangular edit field), you can edit the text as desired. Alternately, you can just select a Finder item and then hit the Return key; this toggles the name for editing without the need to time your second click.

■**Caution** When the name is selected for editing, the entire name minus the file extension is selected, so any typing will immediately overwrite the original name. If you want to just tweak the name, you can use the arrow keys or your mouse to position the cursor where you want to insert or delete text without overwriting the whole name.

You can also rename Finder items in the Info window (shown back in Figure 1-13).

■**Caution** Certain Finder items, such as applications and default system folders, should not be renamed. Renaming the default folders can cause all sorts of unexpected and undesirable results, and renaming applications can cause them to stop working correctly. As a general rule, you can rename any of your files and any folders you create, but you may want to think twice about renaming other items. If you do happen to make a mistake, you can use the Undo command (Command-Z) to reset the name to its previous state.

Creating New Folders and New Smart Folders

Sooner or later it's likely you'll want to create new folders to help organize your files or other Finder items. The easiest way to create a new folder is to select File ➤ New Folder from the Finder's menu or use the Shift-Command-N keyboard shortcut (or the contextual menu item). This creates a new folder with a rather generic name, so you'll probably want to rename it right away, and then it will be ready to go.

To create a smart folder (a special dynamically populated folder covered more in Chapter 3), select File ➤ New Smart Folder from the Finder's menu, or use the Option-Command-N keyboard shortcut. This opens a New Smart Folder window (Figure 1-15) that allows you to set the search parameters for your smart folder using steps similar to defining mail rules. The process of creating a smart folder is a subset of the Spotlight feature, so we'll cover this in more detail in Chapter 3 where we cover Spotlight.

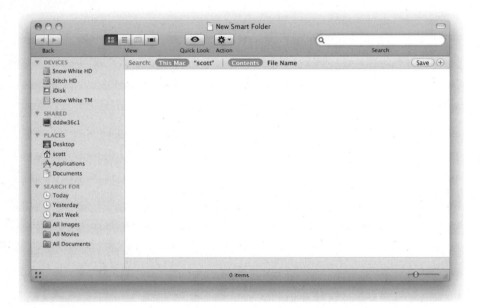

Figure 1-15. *The New Smart Folder window. Notice the Search text field is highlighted awaiting your input.*

Getting (and Altering) Information About Finder Items

If you want to get more information about a particular Finder item, then the Info window (shown in Figure 1-13 earlier in the chapter) is the place to go. The Info window allows you not only to view information about a Finder item, but also to add or alter information and attributes about the item. To open the Info window, select an item in the Finder, and then select File ➤ Get Info from the Finder menu (use the Command-I keystroke or the contextual menu item). At the top of the Info window, the name, size, icon, and last-modified date for the item appear. Table 1-1 describes the basic structure of the Info window.

Table 1-1. *Sections of the Get Info Window*

Section	Description
Spotlight Comments	This is a text field that allows you to add any comments about the item. These comments are searchable in Spotlight.
Kind	This tells the item's type: Folder, Application (for applications, it lets you know whether the application is universal, Intel, or PowerPC), or Document.
Size	This gives the size of the item (including the number of items in folders).
Location	This gives the directory path of the item's location (including the original location for aliases).
Created	This is the date when the item was created.
Modified	This is the date when the item was last modified.
Label	This shows the item's label, which is editable, allowing you to set the label of an item to one of seven predefined Finder labels (discussed later in this chapter).
Share Folder	This check box allows you to share a folder and its contents with other users of your computer and network (it appears only if Kind is Folder).
Stationery Pad	This check box for documents causes a selected document to always open as a copy of itself. This essentially sets up the document as a template.
Open using Rosetta	This check box allows you to run universal applications in PowerPC emulation mode if you are using an Intel-based computer.
Locked	This check box locks a file so it cannot be modified in any way as long as it remains locked.
Name & Extension	This is an editable text field that shows the item's full name (including the extension), which is immediately editable. OS X uses the file's extension as one way to choose which application can open a file, so changing the extension may change how a document is opened (possibly making it unreadable). A check box allows you to choose to show or hide the file extension in the Finder.
Open With	Discussed earlier in the chapter, this allows you to change the ownership of a document from one application to another application.
Preview	This shows a preview of the item (this plays back supported audio and video files).
Languages	For applications, this shows which localizations (that is, languages) the application can run in.
Sharing & Permissions	This allows you to view and alter the abilities of any users and groups to access the item. The ability to view and alter this information depends on the permissions you have. In general, you must be the file's owner or an administrator to edit this information.

■**Tip** If you want to replace the icon of any Finder item, you can do this by selecting the icon at the top of the Info window and then pasting any graphic in your clipboard over it. Should you ever change your mind, you can delete the custom icon, which will cause the item to return to its default icon.

Compressing (Zipping) Finder Items

Often, especially when you want to send files via e-mail to someone else, you may want to compress or archive a file. OS X allows you to create .zip files from within the Finder. You can do this easily by selecting the item (or items) you want to compress and selecting File ➤ Compress *Item Name* from the Finder's menu or using the Compress contextual menu item. If you want to create an archive of multiple items to be zipped into a single .zip file, just create a folder containing all the desired files and then compress the folder.

■**Note** These days, many files and media formats are already compressed, so compressing, say, a single .jpg or .mp3 file won't cut down on the file size much, if any (in fact, some will actually be a tad larger). Still, if you are sending lots of files, even if they are already compressed, it's a good idea to zip them up together anyway since, even though the total file size might not decrease much, it may leave more free space on your computer because of the nuances of how files are stored on your disk. Plus, a single archive is easier to manage than a bunch of separate files.

When you double-click a .zip file, the Finder automatically expands the compressed item.

■**Note** By default, the Finder uses the included Archive Utility to create and open compressed items. By default, Snow Leopard can handle many types of compressed items via Archive Utility; however, some compression and encoding types require third-party software to open. This includes the .sit format, which was once the most popular compression format for Macintosh systems prior to OS X Tiger. .sit files will require StuffIt Expander, available at http://my.smithmicro.com/mac/stuffit.html, or some other third-party compression application (including many decent free applications).

Backing Up and Burning Items to a Disc

We can't overemphasize the importance of backing up the data on your computer. The one truth of all storage devices is that someday they will fail, and when they do, they will likely take all the data stored on them along with them. Backing up data can be a bothersome task; however, Mac OS X's Time Machine makes the whole process much easier (almost pain free), provided you have an extra hard drive to which to back up your data. Still, sometimes you may want to burn some or all of your data to a CD or DVD for a more permanent "offline" backup.

■**Note** Chapter 7 is devoted to backing up and syncing data. There we will cover Time Machine in depth, as well as other backup strategies.

You can create backup data discs in the Finder in a few ways. First, you can simply select the data you want to back up in the Finder and select File ➤ Burn *X* Items to Disc… from the menu bar. This prompts you to insert a disc and upon doing so opens a burn disc window (Figure 1-16) to allow you to name the disc and set the burn speed. Then, simply clicking the Burn button starts the process.

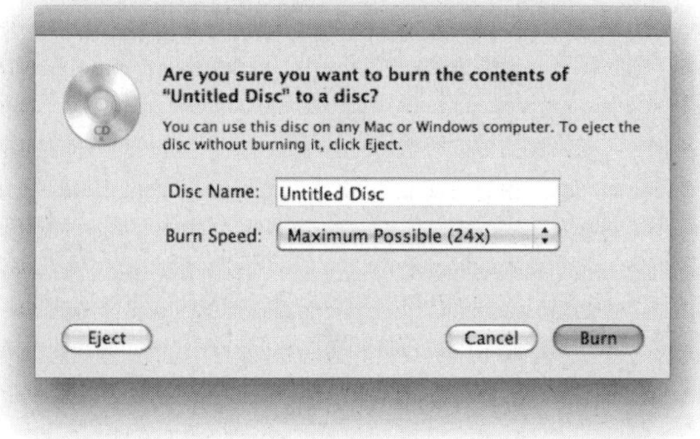

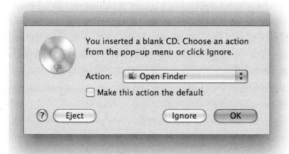

Figure 1-16. *The burn disc window*

Note If you select more data than will fit on the disc you insert, you will get a warning telling you that the data is "too large to fit on the disc." OS X will ask you then to remove some data and try again. You may need to use a larger disc (if you are using a CD-R, try using a DVD-R instead), or you may need to select less data at a time and make multiple burns.

Two other ways to burn data to a disc are very similar to each other. You can create a burn folder to collect items to burn at a later time, or you can just insert a blank, writable disc into the computer and select Open Finder in the Action drop-down menu (Figure 1-17) to mount the disk on your desktop. You can create a burn folder by selecting File ➤ New Burn Folder from the Finder's menu bar or from the Control-click contextual menu. Then you can drag any files you want to burn into this folder (which will automatically create an alias to the original). If you insert a writable disc and select the Open Finder action, the disc will mount, and you can then drag any items you want to burn on it onto the disc icon on the desktop. Either way, when you are done, you can click the special Burn button from either of these locations to start the burning process (see Figure 1-18).

Figure 1-17. *Pop-up window asking what action should occur when you open a blank, writable disc*

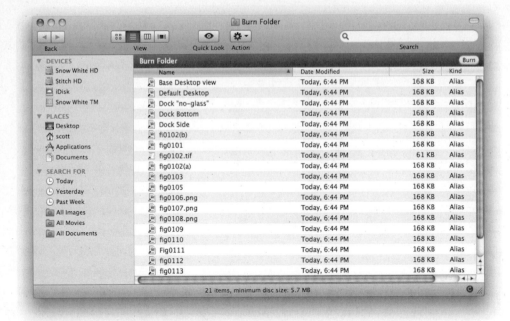

Figure 1-18. *The Burn button is in the upper-right corner of the Finder window. The information bar at the bottom keeps track of how much space you need on the disc to burn the items.*

■**Note** When you add items to a burn folder, you are really just adding an alias pointing to the actual item in the burn folder. This both saves space on your hard drive and allows you to safely delete the burn folder when you are done with it without deleting any actual items.

Labeling Finder Items

For many years, Mac OS has had the ability to label Finder items, and that tradition continues. Labels allow you to colorize Finder items as a way to sort them in the Finder; additionally, labels can have names associated with them (setting the names is covered later in this chapter), which may help you organize special items in the Finder. To label a Finder item, you can select it in the Finder and then select the appropriate label from the File ➤ Label item in the Finder menu.

In Icon and Column views, the label color highlights the item's name with the selected color; in List view, it highlights the item's entire row. Items in the Finder can then be sorted by label, and labels are an additional search parameter for smart folders and Spotlight.

■**Note** When sorting items by label in the Finder, the sort order is determined alphabetically by the label name, not by the color. This may be something to keep in mind when naming labels.

Choosing the Go to Folder Command

If you ever need to go directly to a specific folder in the Finder, you can use the Go ➤ Go to Folder… command in the Finder menu (or use the Shift-Command-G keyboard shortcut), which opens a dialog box prompting you for a directory path. Although sometimes it may be easier to navigate there through the Finder, this option can come in handy if you know where you want to go.

■**Note** As you will learn later in the book, many folders are usually hidden in the Finder. If you know about these folders, you can use the Go to Folder… command to take you to these hidden directories.

Choosing the Connect to Server Command

The Go ➤ Connect to Server… (Command-K) selection in the Finder menu is similar to the Go to Folder… command, but instead of opening a folder on your computer, it can open network resources using a variety of protocols including FTP, HTTP, NSF, SMB, CIFS, AFP, or others (including a user's iDisk). To connect, just enter the network resource's URL into the dialog box, and it will connect. If the resource requires login credentials (name, password, and so on), you will be prompted for that information.

The Desktop

The desktop (shown in Figure 1-19) is the main backdrop for Snow Leopard. Although it has some unique options, it works the same as any Finder window in Icon view. The items on it are in fact located in the Desktop folder in your home directory. Some of what makes the desktop unique is that the items placed on it are always there for easy access, it can automatically display mounted devices such as hard drives and removable media, and it can even show connected network resources on it. The view options available for the desktop are the same as those available to a Finder window in Icon view with the exception of selecting a desktop background. Setting the desktop background is handled through one of the System Preferences panes (covered in Chapter 4).

■**Note** Unlike past versions of Mac OS X, with a clean Snow Leopard install, the Finder by default will not display connected internal hard drives on the Desktop. If you are upgrading, however, your previous setting will remain.

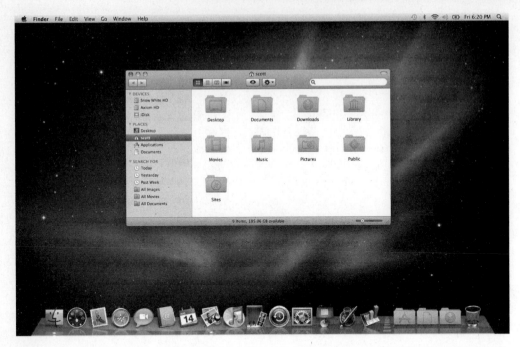

Figure 1-19. *Leopard's default desktop with the Dock at the bottom and the menu bar at the top*

Customizing the Finder

Besides altering the view options for each of the Finder's views, you can apply a number of additional preferences that affect the Finder as the whole. The Finder preferences (like most application preferences) are in the main application menu. In the case of the Finder, that's Finder ➤ Preferences (the default keyboard shortcut to open the preferences of any application is the Command-, shortcut). The Finder's preferences are divided into four sections, as covered next.

Setting General Options

Table 1-2 describes the Finder's General preferences (shown in Figure 1-20), which cover a few general Finder behaviors.

Table 1-2. *Finder's General Preferences*

Preference	Description
Show these items on the Desktop	This offers three check boxes to determine what sort of devices will show up automatically on the desktop.
New Finder windows open	This is a drop-down list that determines where a newly opened Finder window will start by default (this is where you begin when you open a new Finder window from the Finder's File menu or when you click the Finder icon in the Dock).
Always open folders in a new window	This check box, if checked, will cause all folders clicked in the Finder to open a new window rather than to open the contents of the folder in the existing window.
Spring-loaded folder and windows	This is a nice feature in OS X that helps in moving Finder items. When activated, if you drag and hold a Finder item over a folder for a period of time, that folder will spring open to reveal its contents. This way, you can move an item into a deep folder structure without first having to open the destination folder beforehand. The Delay bar indicates how long it takes for the folder to spring open.

Figure 1-20. *The Finder's General preferences*

Customizing Labels

The Labels tab in the Finder preferences (Figure 1-21) allows you to customize the names of the various colored labels. To change a label's name, just edit it in the text field next to appropriate color.

Figure 1-21. *The Labels settings in the Finder*

Customizing the Sidebar

The Sidebar preference tab (Figure 1-22) allows you to select what items automatically show up in the Finder's sidebar. Since you can drag in or drag out various folders anyway, most of these options include more dynamic, nonfolder items.

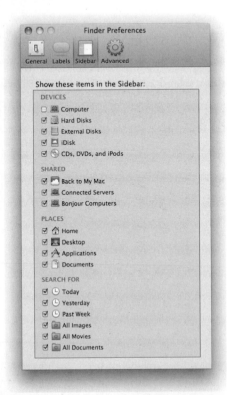

Figure 1-22. *The Finder's sidebar options*

Setting Advanced Options

The final Finder preferences tab includes advanced options (Figure 1-23) of which there are four fairly self-explanatory check boxes:

- Show all file extensions
- Show warning before changing an extension
- Show warning before emptying the Trash
- Empty Trash securely

Figure 1-23. *The Advanced Finder preferences*

Note The "Empty Trash securely" option actually writes over the disk space where the Trash items are located, making it nearly impossible to recover the items once they are deleted. This differs from a normal Trash empty procedure, which just lets the computer know that the space where the file exists is available for writing over, so until something overwrites that same area on your disk, that data could be recovered with the right software. The "Empty Trash securely" option takes more time to complete, especially if you are deleting a large amount of data. If you want to use this command selectively, you can select Finder ➤ Secure Empty Trash… from the Finders application menu, or select Secure Empty Trash… from the Dock's Trash icon's contextual menu using the special Control-Command-click.

The Dock

The final interface element we'll look at in this chapter is the Dock (shown in Figure 1-24). The Dock application allows you to keep your favorite applications a click away, manages the applications you have running, provides a place to access your favorite folders and documents, and also holds your Trash can for deleting Finder items you are done with.

Figure 1-24. *The Dock shown with Leopard's default items*

The items on the Dock are completely customizable; the only two elements that are bound to the Dock are the Finder item and the Trash item. The Dock is divided between application icons and other items by a faint dashed line resembling a crosswalk (called the *abbey road graphic*). We cover the types of items on the Dock in the next sections.

Favorite Application Icons

Beginning on the far left of the Dock are the application icons. The first one on the far left is always the Finder icon, but the ones that follow are entirely customizable. To add one of your favorite applications to the Dock, just select the application in the Finder and then drag the icon onto the Dock where you'd like it to be. You can also click and drag any icon already on the Dock to another location on the Dock or off the Dock entirely. To launch any of the applications on the Dock, just click them. Control-clicking any Dock icon opens a contextual menu that varies on the application, whether it's running or not.

Tip Option-clicking a running application in the Dock moves that application to the front while at the same time hiding all other running applications.

Applications that are open have a little bright blip under the icon (like a light shining up on the icon).

Note You can't remove the icon of a running application from the Dock; if you try, it will spring back to the Dock. This, however, will cause the item to leave the Dock when the application quits.

Open Applications

Anytime you open an Aqua application, the icon for that application will be added to the Dock just to the right of your other docked applications (provided that it isn't in the Dock already). By clicking any open application icon on the Dock, you make that the active application. Additionally, if that application has no open windows, then usually a new window will open when you make that application active. Upon closing any application not normally found in the Dock, the icon on the Dock will disappear.

Exposé from the Dock

New in Snow Leopard, Exposé is now built into the dock so that a click-hold on the icon of any running application will display all that application's open windows in Exposé form (Figure 1-25).

Figure 1-25. *Accessing Exposé from the Dock in Snow Leopard*

Folders and Stacks

In versions of OS X prior to Leopard (Mac OS X 10.5), you could add a folder to the Dock so that its contents would be easily available. This changed in Leopard; you could still add folders to the Dock, but the folders on the Dock were turned into stacks.

Stacks, as they were originally released in Leopard, at first received mixed reviews, as they seemed a step backward from the old folder-on-the-Dock behavior. However, with subsequent point releases of Leopard, stacks were refined and improved bit by bit, and today in Snow Leopard they have all the benefits of old and then some. To create a stack, just select the desired folder from the Finder and drag it into the area between the abbey road graphic (to the right of the application icons) and the Trash (being careful not to actually drag it into the Trash). Upon adding the folder to the Dock, it will, by default, change from a folder to what appears to be a stack of items contained in the folder. Clicking this stack in the Dock will expand it, making all its items accessible to you. By default, depending on the number of items in the stack, the stack will expand either to a single column of items, called the Fan view (Figure 1-26), or to a row of items, called the Grid view (Figure 1-27).

Figure 1-26. *A stack opened in Fan view*

Figure 1-27. *Traversing a stack in Grid view with the parent menu accessible from the upper-left corner*

From the contextual menu of any stack, you can make a few changes in how a stack looks and behaves. First, you can alter how the items in the stack are sorted when they are expanded (this may also alter what item is "on top" of the stack). These Sort By options are the same options available to sort items in the Finder (by Name, Date Added, Date Modified, Date Created, and Kind). Next, you can choose if you'd like the Dock icon to appear as the default stack of items or as a folder. Finally, you can override the default behavior of how a stack expands by setting each stack to open explicitly in Fan view, Grid view, or List view (Figure 1-28), which is very similar to the original folder behavior prior to Leopard.

Figure 1-28. *A stack opened in List view*

Note One of the biggest issues people had with stacks when they were first introduced was that you could not traverse through subfolders in stacks as you could in the old folder listings. Instead, selecting a subfolder in a stack would just open up that folder in the Finder. Later, Apple added the List view to stacks; this allowed you to browse through folders recursively. In Snow Leopard, the ability to traverse folders in stacks is kicked up another notch, for now you can browse through folders in Grid view as well (shown previously in Figure 1-27). In Snow Leopard, when you click a folder in Grid view, the new folder opens up in Grid view, clicking the arrow in the upper-left corner of the stack view allows you to return to the parent folder.

Note If you have more items in a stack than will fit nicely in Grid view, you can actually scroll down in Grid view to see the other items. If you wish to view the hidden items in Fan view, the view will switch to Grid view. For this reason, we generally recommend against explicitly using Fan view.

By default, OS X starts you out with your Download folder and your Documents folder placed as stacks on your Dock.

Minimized Windows

Occasionally you may have what seems to be too many application windows on your screen at one time. By clicking the Minimize button in the upper-left corner of any window, the window will shrink down into the Dock and out of the way. (By default, that's the yellow button that will reveal a "-" when you mouse over it; the three buttons at the left end of the title bar are commonly called the *window controls*.) Clicking the minimized window in the Dock will expand the window to its previous size and position on the screen.

The Trash

The final item on the Dock is the Trash. Rather than immediately deleting Finder items, in OS X you generally move an item to the Trash when you are done with it. Then when you are ready, you empty the Trash to permanently delete items. This two-step process adds a fail-safe to keep you from permanently deleting a file accidentally. You can drag any item into the Trash (or use Command-Delete), where it will remain until you empty the Trash. To empty the Trash, you can right-click (or Control-click) the Trash and select Empty Trash from the menu, or in the Finder you can select Finder ➤ Empty Trash from the application menu.

Tip One old feature that has resurfaced in Snow Leopard is the Put Back feature. If you select Put Back from the contextual menu of any item in the Trash (or select a series of items and use the Put Back item in the Finder's Action menu), the selected trash items will be returned automatically to the Finder location that they were in before being dragged into the Trash.

One advantage of emptying the Trash from the Finder's menu is that it also gives you the option to securely empty the Trash, which makes the items you delete nearly impossible to ever recover, even with the most sophisticated utilities.

One other, strange ability of the Trash is that if you drag any removable media, external hard drives, or network resources on to it, rather than delete those items, it will actually eject, unmount, or disconnect the resource. This is actually the traditional way to do this, though it's especially odd for people new to Macs.

Dock Preferences

The Dock preferences affect the Dock's behavior. The Dock's settings are located in System Preferences (Dock panel) but are directly accessible from the Apple menu by selecting Dock ➤ Dock Preferences. Table 1-3 describes the preferences available for the Dock (Figure 1-29).

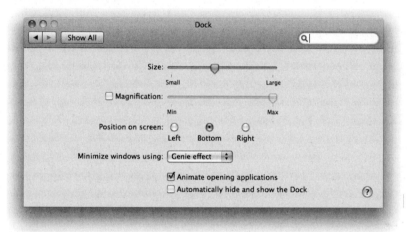

Figure 1-29. *The Dock System Preferences*

Table 1-3. *Dock System Preferences*

Preference	Effect
Size	This affects how big the Dock icons and the Dock will be.
Magnification	If selected, this affects how big Dock items will magnify to when the cursor moves over them. This is useful if you have many small items in the Dock. (You can trigger the magnification effect with the preference unselected by mousing over the Dock with the Control-Shift keys held down.)
Position on screen	This allows you to position the Dock on either side or the bottom of the screen. When the Dock is on either side, its appearance will change from the *glass* appearance (the default, translucent appearance where it appears as if the icons are sitting on a glass shelf) to a flatter appearance (Figure 1-30).
Minimize windows using	This allows you to choose between two different effects—the Genie Effect and the Scale Effect—when you minimize items onto the Dock. This really has no effect on anything practical and is purely an aesthetic thing.

(Continued)

Table 1-3. *(Continued)*

Preference	Effect
Animate opening applications	When selected, the application icons bounce up and down in the Dock while the application is starting up. (Some people count the bounces as a metric for how fast an application launches.)
Automatically hide and show the Dock	When selected, this causes the Dock to disappear and remain hidden until you move the mouse down to the area of the screen where the Dock would normally appear, at which time it will slide back into view to perform any regular Dock functions. This is nice in certain applications where you want to use the entire screen for the application and the Dock would normally get in the way.

Figure 1-30. *The Dock's appearance changes when it is placed on either side.*

Note You can select many of these Dock preferences by choosing the Dock item in the Apple menu, by right-clicking the space just to the right of the application icons on the Dock, or by clicking and dragging the Dock itself.

Tip If you prefer the appearance of the Dock while it's on either side (without the glass appearance) but still want the Dock located on the bottom, you can change its appearance by entering the following commands in the Terminal application (if command-line stuff intimidates you, you may want to read Chapter 18 before you do this): `defaults write com.apple.dock no-glass -boolean YES` followed by `killall` Dock. To reverse this, repeat the previous commands but change YES to NO.

Summary

This chapter explained all of the basics you need in order to work inside the Aqua interface. Even if at first it seems strange (and there are certainly parts of it that are), as you get used to it, you will find that it in fact serves its purpose extraordinarily well (more so in most cases than any alternatives). Coupled with some of the other features that will be revealed as the book progresses, you'll find the Aqua interface to be a great foundation for a fun and productive computing environment.

Next, we'll cover the file system and explain where everything is.

CHAPTER 2

■ ■ ■

The File System

This chapter will take you on a tour of the Snow Leopard file system to discover what items exist in what folders and why (and also what you can and shouldn't change and why). We'll cover in depth

- The overall file structure of Snow Leopard
- Your personal Home folder and its contents
- The top-level folders, including the System folder, the Library folder, and the Applications folder
- Other common folders
- Hidden folders

The Overall File Structure of Snow Leopard

The file system for Snow Leopard is pretty easy to understand. It starts at the root of your primary hard drive (the one that you boot Snow Leopard from). From there, a series of folders descends downward, each with their own purpose. Figure 2-1 shows a basic view of the default file system.

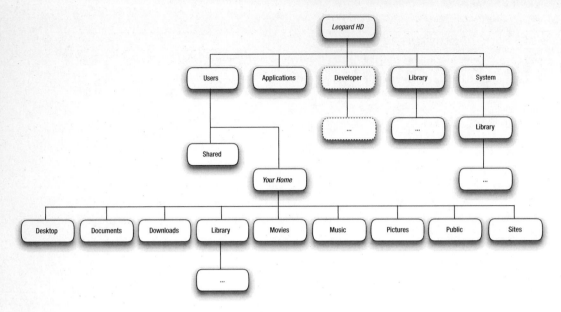

Figure 2-1. *A simple view of Snow Leopard's default file system*

The file system is devised so that certain items belong in certain folders. For example, most of your applications go in the Applications folder, and most of your personal documents go in the Documents folder within your home directory (which is titled with your short username).

The term *path* is often used to describe where something is located in the file system. A path usually begins with a /, signifying that it begins at the top level of the file system. It then lists the folder path with a / between each folder. The exception to this is a path that begins with ~. This indicates that rather than beginning at the top of the file system, the path begins from your home folder. For example, the path to my Documents folder could be written either as /Users/scott/Documents or just ~/Documents.

The Users Folder and Your Home

The Users folder located in the root (top level) of the file system in every Snow Leopard install is where each user's personal folder resides. This personal folder is usually referred to as the user's *home folder* (or just *home*). Inside of the Users folder is a home folder for each of the system's users (named after the short name chosen when the account was created) and a Shared folder. The Shared folder is a place where files may be kept that are shared among all users. Occasionally, this folder is used by some applications, but it can also be used by any users of the computer. Your home directory, however, is where you generally keep all of your documents and where all of your personal settings are stored.

Your home folder, by default, starts out with nine subfolders: Desktop, Documents, Downloads, Library, Movies, Music, Pictures, Public, and Sites. Table 2-1 explains the specific purpose of each of these folders.

Table 2-1. *Default Home Subfolders and Their Descriptions*

Folder	Description
Desktop	The contents of this folder are the items that appear on your desktop.
Documents	This is the primary folder for you to store all your document files. When you go to save or open a document from within an application, this is usually where it will start you out.
Downloads	This is generally the default location for files that are downloaded from the Internet via Safari or other applications. This folder was not present by default in Mac OS X prior to Mac OS X 10.5 Leopard.
Library	Most of your personal system and application settings are stored in this folder, including application preferences and data files, as well as a host of other items, such as plug-ins, caches, and preference panes. In general, this folder stores all that extra stuff your computer and applications need to function properly.
Movies	This is the default folder where imported videos and iMovie files are stored. It's worth pointing out that movies and videos that you buy from the iTunes Store are actually stored in the Music folder.
Music	This is where your iTunes, GarageBand, Logic Studio, Logic Express, and other musical files are stored by default.
Pictures	This is the default folder for most of your images. This is where iPhoto and other photo applications store their files by default.
Public	This is a special folder where you can store files that you wish to share with others on your computer or on your network. Inside of this is the Drop Box folder where others can leave you files as well. To share files with users on your network, file sharing must be enabled in the Sharing Preference pane.
Sites	This is the default folder for your personal web pages, if web sharing is turned on in the Sharing Preference pane. We cover web sharing in depth later in this book.

These default folders cover most of your personal folder needs (though subfolders are common in each of these). Occasionally you may want to add another folder for a specific need, and that's fine; this is your home, after all.

The Applications Folder

The Applications folder, as you may have guessed, is the recommended folder for installing applications. Keeping all your applications in this folder makes things fairly easy to find. However, if you find that you have many applications and this folder starts to get cluttered, you can create your own subfolders to organize types of applications. For example, you may create /Applications/Games for any games you install, or /Applications/Graphics for any graphic apps you install. This sort of organization makes it easy to find what you are looking for.

Tip One common practice is to drag your Applications folder onto your Dock. That way, you can easily access all of your applications from the Dock without having to dig through the Finder.

■**Caution** Some applications don't like to be moved from where they are installed. For the most part, any moved application functions just fine; the problem is that sometimes when it comes time to update your application, the update utility expects the original application to be in a specific location. This is especially true of Apple's default applications that are updated frequently with the Software Update utility. If you do move an application into a subfolder and something strange happens when you try to update it, you can usually move the application back to its original location and redo the update with no harm; it's just a bit inconvenient. As a general rule, if an installer installs the application, it's best to leave it where it installs (though often installers have an option to install in subfolders). If you can install the application manually by just dragging it into the `Applications` folder (as many let you), then it's probably safe to put it wherever you want.

The Library Folders

One thing you may notice about the file system is that it contains multiple `Library` folders. This is by design, and while many similarities exist between the contents of the `Library` folders, each folder is scoped differently.

■**Note** There are actually four `Library` domains, though generally you only see three `Library` folders. Some applications can contain their own application-specific `Library` folder to contain plug-ins or other information only they use.

The `Library` folders each contain the necessary support items for the applications on your system as well as the system itself. These library items include things like preference settings, cache items, scripts, screen savers, and much more. In practice, you almost never need to fuss with the contents of any `Library` folder; however, there are times when it may benefit you to do so (especially with the `Library` folder in your home directory). That said, there are certain rules for each `Library` folder. We'll first look at each of the three primary `Library` folders, and then we'll explore common subitems contained in `Library` folders.

The Library and System Library Folders

The primary `Library` folder (`/Library`), as well as the `Library` folder contained in the `System` folder (`/System/Library`) have a global scope. That is, their contents support every aspect of the system. Specifically, the `System Library` folder contains items necessary for the system to operate, and the primary `Library` folder contains the items necessary for most applications, third-party hardware, and other items that affect every user on the system.

As a general rule, `/System/Library` is sacred. Only necessary system-level items should be installed there, and only system-level events should affect them. As such, there is almost no reason for you (or me) to touch anything in there unless you are 100 percent sure you know exactly what you are doing and 100 percent sure that doing it here is the only way to solve your problem. Changing anything here can cause very bad things to happen (or even worse, cause nothing at all to happen . . . ever).

On the other hand, there are times when it may benefit you to make a few changes to items in the main `Library` folder. For example, you may want to install a screen saver that you want to make available to all users of your computer, or you may want to uninstall some old items left over from an old application or hardware device. That said, you should still be 100 percent of what you are doing before you do it. While any errors here might not render your system unusable, they could certainly make it less usable.

■**Caution** Sometimes you may want to clean out old unnecessary files that tend to build up in your `Library` folder, but first make sure that each item is no longer used. Sometimes an item installed by one item is used by another item as well (this is especially true with certain common frameworks and components). Often it's better to err on the side of keeping an unnecessary item rather than accidentally delete a necessary one.

Personal Library Folder

The `Library` folder inside your home directory (`~/Library`) is your own personal `Library` folder. This is where the system and individual application items that affect you are kept. This includes your personal system and application preferences, your Mail settings (and actual mail), your Safari bookmarks, your iCal data, and much more. This `Library` folder is the preferred one for adding personal items such as screen savers, desktop backgrounds, and add-on scripts. It's also in most need of an occasional cleaning; however, all the cautions mentioned previously still apply.

Table 2-2 describes the most common folders found in your `~/Library` folder and their contents.

Table 2-2. *Common Library Subfolders and Their Purpose*

Folder Name	Purpose
Application Support	This is the primary folder for applications to store any necessary support files, usually in a subfolder named after the application. Additionally, some companies, such as Apple and Adobe, store information here that different applications may share. Some of these files contain registration information and even saved data, so it's a good idea to include these files in any backup scheme you have. In general, if you delete an application, then the support files contained here will be safe to delete. Additionally, some application folders contain subfolders themselves, where users may add plug-ins, scripts, or other features.
Audio	The `Audio` folder contains subfolders for audio plug-ins, such as Audio Units, VST, and Digidesign, and other support items for audio applications. This includes all of your GarageBand loops and plug-ins.

Continued

Table 2-2. *Continued*

Folder Name	Purpose
Automator	The Automator folder contains Automator actions that are used within Automator to build more complex workflows. The ~/Library/Automator folder does not exist by default; however, you may create it if needed, or it may get created automatically when an installer wishes to place something here.
Caches	The Caches folder is where applications should store cached data (or data that they tend to refer to often). Rather than reforming the data from scratch, an application can use its cached data to save time and system resources. Some people clean out their Caches folders routinely, since the data there will be restored, but some of the data stored there could take some time and resources to regenerate (and they will be regenerated). Unless a cache file has grown to an excessive size or becomes corrupted, there is little use in cleaning it out except for deleting caches for applications that no longer exist on your system.
Calendars	Calendar information is stored in this folder. It is mostly used by iCal, but the information is available to other apps that may utilize iCal information.
ColorPickers	The ColorPickers folders are where you can install any third-party, color-picker plug-ins that you want to be available only to you (if you install them in /Library/ColorPickers, they will be available to all users). Color pickers are the various color-selection windows available to you when a standard Mac OS X application allows you to select a color. The default Mac OS X color pickers, installed in /System/Library/ColorPickers, include a few different color-picker plug-ins including Color Wheel, Color Sliders, Color Palettes, Image Palettes, and Crayons.
Compositions	The Compositions folder may contain movies or Quartz Composer files that provide animated backgrounds in applications such as Photo Booth and iChat.
Cookies	The Cookies folder is where Safari (and perhaps other web browsers and WebKit-enabled applications) stores cookies that are presented from web sites. The proper way to manage the contents of this folder is through Safari (the Show Cookies button in Safari's Security Preferences).
Favorites	Favorites is a carryover from older versions of OS X where aliases to your favorite folders could be added and thus displayed as your Favorites in the Finder. These days, the sidebar in the Finder window replaces this need (and is much more robust).
FontCollections	Font Book allows you to group fonts into various collections; that data is stored in this folder. A number of predefined font collections come with Mac OS X and are stored in /Library/FontCollections.
Fonts	The Fonts folder is where your personal fonts are stored. Keep in mind that fonts stored in ~/Library/Fonts are available only to you. Fonts stored in /Library/Fonts are available to all users. The /System/Library/Fonts folder contains all the fonts that your system absolutely needs. Font Book is aware of all these locations and is the preferred way to manage your fonts short of some heavy-duty, third-party, font-management applications.

Folder Name	Purpose
Fonts Disabled	When you disable fonts from within Font Book, they are stored in this folder. (To be specific, fonts disabled from ~/Library/Fonts are stored in ~/Library/Fonts Disabled, and fonts disabled from /Library/Fonts are stored in /Library/Fonts Disabled.)
iMovie	This folder contains iMovie plug-ins and sound effects.
Internet Plug-Ins	The Internet Plug-Ins folder contains the plug-ins for Safari and other applications. These allow the browser to display specific types of content inline, such as Flash, Java, QuickTime, and more.
iTunes	This folder may contain iTunes plug-ins, such as visualizer plug-ins, audio plug-ins, and other files, including iPod and iPhone updates.
Keychains	The Keychains folder in ~/Library contains your keychains. These are the system's built-in technology to store passwords and authentication information. These files are highly encrypted. The way to open and manage a keychain file here is through the Keychain Access utility.
LaunchAgents	This directory contains launched files that cause applications or services to activate when you log in to the computer.
Logs	Many of the applications and services in OS X generate log files that keep track of important events that occur during the execution of a particular service. These files are stored in the various Logs folders. All of these log files are accessible (to those who have proper permissions to read them) via the Console utility.
Mail	This folder stores most of your mail account information and your actual Mail folders for OS X's Mail application (this includes all locally stored mailboxes and messages).
PreferencePanes	This folder contains the individual preference panes that appear in the System Preferences window.
Preferences	The Preferences folder contains all of your personal saved preference data for the system and your applications. Deleting a preference file here usually causes the affected application to revert to its default state with all your personal settings gone (certain applications that require registration codes to activate will often need to be reactivated as well). Almost every application you launch creates a preference file, so you tend to acquire a large number of them. Feel free to clean out preference files from applications you no longer use.
Printers	This folder stores information about your selected printers as well as other important printing-system files.
PubSub	Many Apple applications use this folder to store data that is downloaded from RSS (Really Simple Syndication) feeds.
Safari	This folder keeps track of Safari information, including your bookmarks, history, values for forms, and more.
Saved Searches	This folder contains the saved searches you perform from within Spotlight.
Screen Savers	This folder contains your personal third-party screen savers.
Voices	This folder contains items that are used by the OS X speech system, including the various speech voices.
Widgets	The Widgets folder is where your personal Dashboard widgets are stored.

■**Note** Many of the folders found in your `~/Library` folder are also found in `/Library` and even `/System/Library`. The primary difference is scope; `~/Library` items only affect you (or some other user if we are talking about `/Users/SomeOtherUser/Library`), whereas items in `/Library` and `/System/Library` affect all users.

■**Note** The list of folders in Table 2-2 is by no means inclusive. Other `Library` folders likely exist in your `Library` folder, as both Apple and many third-party applications tend to create different folders here.

Other Library Items

Besides the `Library` items listed in Table 2-2, a number of other `Library` folders have special significance. These are listed in Table 2-3.

Table 2-3. *Other Special Library Folders*

Folder Name	Purpose
`[/System]/Library/ Contextual Menu Items`	These folders contain contextual menu plug-ins. These provide additional menu items for the pop-up contextual menus you get when you Control-click (or right-click) Finder items. Mac OS X includes a few of these in `/System/Library/Contextual Menu Items`. Third-party contextual menu items should be stored in `/Library/ Contextual Menu Items`.
`/System/Library/ CoreServices`	The `CoreSevices` folder contains a number of interesting utility applications that are used by the system. Things like the Dock, the Finder, and even Spotlight are in here (yes, they are all just individual applications). Obviously, we strongly encourage you not to remove any of these items.
`[/System]/Library/ Extensions`	Extensions are items that add functions to the system. They generally enable specific hardware features. Warnings about not messing with `/System/Library/` items apply doubly here.
`[/System]/Library/Filters`	This folder contains Quartz filters. These filters provide various means of manipulating images and are used by many graphic applications.
`[/System]/Library/ Frameworks`	Frameworks are the essential building blocks of most applications in Leopard. Most applications rely on a number of the native OS X frameworks in `/System/Library/Frameworks`. Additionally, some third-party applications and utilities require additional frameworks, which are installed in `/Library/Frameworks`.
`[/System]/Library/Image Capture`	This folder contains plug-ins and support devices that allow for the acquisition of images from external sources, such as scanners and digital cameras.
`Java`	The various `Java` folders contain the various core Java runtime libraries and extensions.
`[/System]/Library/ LaunchDaemons`	The contents here are similar to those in the `LaunchAgents` folder; however, items in `LaunchDaemons` activate when the system starts, whether or not a user has logged in.

Folder Name	Purpose
[/System]/Library/ Modem Scripts	The `Modem Scripts` directory contains a number of files that initialize various brands of modems.
/Library/ Receipts	The `/Library/Receipts` folder contains records of installed applications. OS X uses the contents of this folder as sort of an odd package-management system. The system uses this folder in many ways, so it's best to leave it alone. The exception is removing any receipts of applications you have removed.
/Library/Scripts	This folder contains AppleScripts that are accessible from various sources. If you plan on utilizing your own scripts, you should create a `~/Library/Scripts/` folder to contain them. Occasionally, individual applications install application-specific scripts in a subfolder of `Scripts`.
[/System]/Library/ ScriptingAdditions	This folder contains items that enhance the capabilities of AppleScript.
/System/Library/ ScriptingDefinitions	This folder contains dictionary documents that are available from within the Script Editor. It provides information about AppleScript syntax and usage.
[/System]/Library/ Services	This folder contains service applets that are available to most Aqua applications from their *Application* ➤ Services submenu. Many of the services that the system provides are kept here, while other applications may store services with the application bundles.
[/System]/Library/ Spotlight	This folder contains some Spotlight plug-ins that add to the search abilities of Spotlight.
/Library/WebServer	The `/Library/WebServer` folder is used by the Apache web server installed on Snow Leopard. This folder contains the default Apache root `Document` folder, as well as the `CGI-Executables` folder. We will talk more about this `Library` folder later in the book.

Other Common Folders

We've covered most of the default folders you'll interact with in Snow Leopard, but there are some other common folders you may encounter. One of the most common is the /Developer folder, which is present if you install the Xcode tools during or after your Snow Leopard installation. This folder contains all the developer applications, documentation, and other items necessary to develop your own Mac OS X applications.

A couple other common folders that may present themselves are the /opt and /sw folders. These special folders are used by certain popular projects such as MacPorts and Fink. We cover both of these projects later in this book, where you will learn more about these folders.

Hidden Folders

All the folders we've talked about so far barely scratch the surface of the whole file system on Leopard. The thing is, most of the other folders and contents are hidden from the Finder. These hidden files are mostly part of the underlying UNIX heritage of Mac OS X, which is largely referred to as the Darwin subsystem of OS X. Later (in Chapters 17 and 18) we devote large parts of this book to Darwin and the UNIX underbelly of Mac OS X.

If you're curious about these hidden files, the following AppleScript can toggle the visibility of hidden Finder items:

```
tell application "Finder" to quit
try
    do shell script "defaults read com.apple.finder AppleShowAllFiles"
    set OnOff to result
on error
    set OnOff to "0"
end try

if OnOff = "0" then
    set OnOffCommand to "defaults write com.apple.finder AppleShowAllFiles 1"
else
    set OnOffCommand to "defaults write com.apple.finder AppleShowAllFiles 0"
end if
do shell script OnOffCommand
delay 1
tell application "Finder" to launch
```

To run this script, open the Script Editor (found in /Applications/AppleScript/), type the script into the editor, and hit the Run button. Then have a look in the Finder and relish all the other folders and other items that appear. Run the script again to rehide the hidden items. Feel free to create a Scripts folder in your ~/Library/ folder, and save this little file there as Toggle Hidden or some other such name. It will be available to you later.

Note Most hidden files exist for a purpose and are likewise hidden for a purpose, usually to protect them from accidental disturbance by casual users. It's generally best to leave hidden files alone, at least until you learn what they do and how to work with them properly (some of which we'll teach you later in this book).

Summary

Now that you've had a glimpse of how everything is organized on your computer and know how to move around it, we're going to take a brief sidetrack in the next chapter to point out a few of the unique features in Mac OS X, including Spotlight, Dashboard, Spaces, and Exposé.

■ ■ ■

## CHAPTER 3

Using Spotlight, Exposé, Spaces, and Dashboard

Mac OS X has a few additional interface features that are definitely worth mentioning that we haven't covered yet in other chapters:

- Spotlight
- Exposé
- Spaces
- Dashboard

Searching with Spotlight

Spotlight, which was introduced in Tiger (Mac OS X 10.4), is a system-wide search tool that locates any items on your computer that match your search criteria. Spotlight not only allows you to search for items on your computer, but it also allows you to save your searches by creating *smart folders*. Smart folders are special folders that populate themselves dynamically based on your search criteria. They even allow you to search other computers and resources on your network (provided these resources allow such access).

Note When you first install Mac OS X, Spotlight is not immediately available. Before Spotlight is ready, it must index your entire system. This can take several hours to complete. While Spotlight is indexing, your hard drive will spin a lot, your system will get hot, and the computer's fan (if it has one) will probably start running at full speed. Oh, yeah, there will also be a pulsing black dot inside Spotlight's magnifying-glass icon in the upper-right corner of the menu bar that indicates Spotlight is indexing.

Performing a Basic Search in Spotlight

To perform a Spotlight search, you can either click the magnifying glass in the upper-right corner of your screen or press Command-Spacebar. This opens a simple drop-down text field for you to type your search (Figure 3-1). As you start to type, the drop-down field expands to reveal possible matches for your search (Figure 3-2). As you refine your search, the matches change dynamically to the most appropriate choices.

Figure 3-1. *Spotlight's search field*

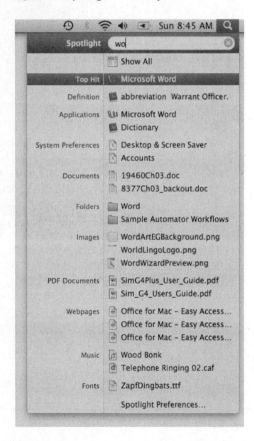

Figure 3-2. *Spotlight reveals top matches for your search as you type.*

Once you finish typing your search phrase, the top results matched are revealed for you, organized by type. Depending on how specific your search is, there could be only a few possible matches; however, often there are more matches than fit in the simple drop-down menu. Selecting the Show All item opens a special Finder search window containing all the results from your search (Figure 3-3). This window also allows you to further refine your search.

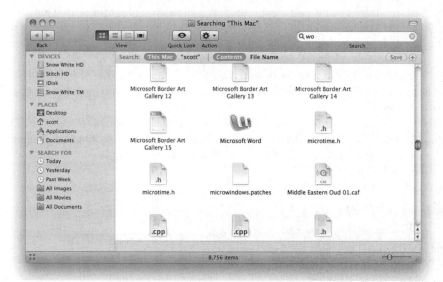

Figure 3-3. *Show All opens a special Finder window revealing every item that matches your search.*

Tip A number of keyboard shortcuts help you move around the list of search results without having to reach for your mouse or trackpad. The up and down arrow keys (as you may assume) move up and down one item at a time. Using the Command key with the up and down arrows moves up and down through the file types. Pressing Command-left arrow inserts a cursor at the beginning of your search term, and pressing Command-right arrow inserts the cursor at the end of your search term to edit or revise it. Finally, if Spaces is not active, pressing Control-up arrow will move to the top of the list highlighting Show All, and pressing Control-down arrow will move to the bottom of the list highlighting Spotlight Preferences. (If Spaces is active, it will by default use these shortcuts to switch from one space to another, and this function will override Spotlight. You may be able to duplicate this effect, though, with Function (fn)-arrow keys.)

Refining and Saving Your Searches

Whether you start with a simple Spotlight search and, as discussed earlier, choose the Show All option or you start a search directly in the Finder's search field, you're presented with a special Finder search window (shown in Figure 3-3) that allows you to refine and save your searches.

The Finder's search window and regular Finder window are different in two ways. First, since you are dealing with search results, the items shown are not necessarily located in a single folder but rather can be collected from all over your hard drive and attached file systems. Second, one or more special search toolbars present at the top of the Finder view area allow you to refine your search.

There is always one primary search toolbar at the top of a search window that allows you to generally refine the scope of your search; specifically, it allows you to set the search for your entire computer (This Mac) or limit the search to the specific folder from which the search began. (If you initiated the search from the Spotlight menu icon, this will be your home folder.) Furthermore, it allows you to choose whether to search just the File Name of Finder items or the Contents of individual files to match the search term. Occasionally, other search options will be listed here—for example, shared or network resources on which you have permission to perform searches may appear.

To the far right of the topmost search bar is a Save button that allows you to save your search for future use (as a smart folder). A + or - button allows you to add or remove additional search criteria. Each time you add criteria, a new bar appears that allows you to refine your search from a series of drop-down lists (Figure 3-4).

Figure 3-4. *Refining a search using search criteria*

Table 3-1 describes the general search criteria.

Table 3-1. *Search Criteria to Refine Searches*

Criteria	Description
What	This provides check boxes to determine whether the search should be limited to file names only and to system files. By default, the search excludes system files (special files that are specifically determined to be created by or used for the system itself). However, with all other files it attempts to find the search string in any metadata, text within the item, and Finder comments as well as the actual file name.
Kind	This can help narrow down your search to a specific kind of file and includes the following options: Applications, Documents, Folders, Images, Movies, Music, PDF, Presentations, Text, and Other. Certain options allow you to further refine the kind; for example, Images allows you to narrow search results to specific image formats.
Last opened date	This allows you to narrow search results to a date, or range of dates, when the item was last opened.
Last modified date	This allows you to narrow search results to a date, or range of dates, when the item was last modified.
Created date	This allows you to narrow search results to a date, or range of dates, when the item was created.
Name	This allows you to match additional search strings against the name of the file.
Contents	This allows you to match additional search strings against the contents of the file.
Other	This opens a window with a number of additional search criteria that you can add to your search (Figure 3-5); many of these items are common metadata items or other common possible search criteria. Your actual list may change because of third-party applications that add their own data here.

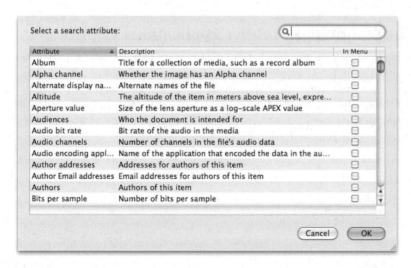

Figure 3-5. *The Other search option opens a window that contains a large list of other common metadata and search criteria.*

Once you have your search criteria set, you can select the specific item you are looking for in the Finder's Search view.

If you want to save your search, click the Save button in the top-left side of the view area. This will open a special Save dialog box (Figure 3-6) that will let you save your search and, if desired, add it to your Finder sidebar.

Figure 3-6. *The smart folder Save dialog box*

Setting Up Smart Folders

The default location for saving a search is in your ~/Library/Saved Searches folder. If you look there, you will see that saved searches are nothing more than smart folders. There is one subtle difference between the smart folder created out of a search and the smart folder created from the Finder's File ➤ New Smart Folder... (Option-Command-N). When you start with a search, the results always reflect the initial search term; when you create a smart folder from the Finder, there is no initial search term, so you can build your search based purely on other criteria (like file type and creation date).

Using Spotlight Technology in Other Applications

Spotlight is a key technology in OS X, and developers are able to include its features into their own applications as they see fit. For example, digital asset management (DAM) applications can use it to help organize and find specific digital media files in a large collection. The Mail app includes Spotlight technology to help locate mail messages, notes, and To Do items stored in Mail. Spotlight is even cleverly included in the default help system and can be used to find and highlight application commands in the application menus (Figure 3-7).

Figure 3-7. *Spotlight technology in the Help menu can help you find application menu items.*

Using Exposé and Spaces

Besides Spotlight, a number of other interesting features are built in to Mac OS X that can be summoned as necessary. Here we'll talk about the two remaining big interface features: Exposé and Spaces.

Exposé and Spaces help you find and manage open applications and application windows. Both Exposé and Spaces do this by manipulating your work area, but each of them does this in different ways.

Exposé

Exposé works within your current work area or desktop by moving, shrinking, and highlighting your current windows in ways that are incredibly useful, especially if you are working with many open windows at once.

Exposé provides three distinct views: an "All windows" view, an "Application windows" view, and a Desktop view. Each view provides certain benefits.

You can trigger the "All windows" view (Figure 3-8) by hitting the F9 key (by default). This view shrinks and arranges all the windows open on your current desktop so that they are all visible; from this view, you can mouse over and select the particular window you'd like to bring to the foreground.

■Note On Apple keyboards, the F# keys (a.k.a., *function keys*) are often used for controlling things such as the brightness of the screen and the volume. This is especially true with MacBooks and MacBook Pros, which by default have the F# keys set to control these features. On these computers, you may need to use Fn-*[F# key]* to activate the desired F# key. If you would rather have the F# keys work as the F# keys by default, you can set this behavior in the Keyboard & Mouse preference pane. Additionally, newer Apple keyboards actually have dedicated keys specifically to control Exposé and Spaces.

Figure 3-8. *Exposé's "All windows" view*

The "Application windows" view (Figure 3-9) is similar to the "All windows" view, but it affects only the open windows of the foreground application. Triggered by the F10 key by default, it causes the windows of all background applications to fade into the background while arranging and highlighting the windows of the current application. This is effective if you are working with many documents in a single application or if you have multiple Finder windows open.

The final Exposé view, triggered by the F11 key by default, is the Desktop view (Figure 3-10). This "slides" all the currently open windows off the screen, making the entire desktop visible so you can access any Finder items located on it that may be blocked by the current windows. This is especially nice for people who tend to collect a large number of items on their desktops.

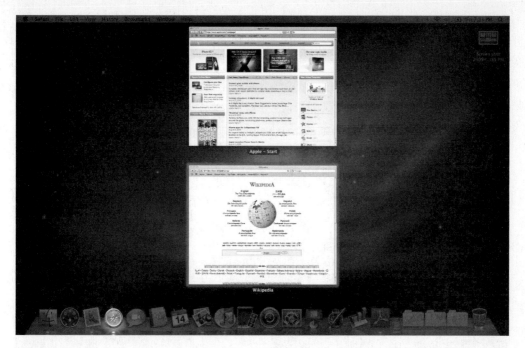

Figure 3-9. *Exposé's "Application windows" view highlighting only the open windows of the foreground application.*

Figure 3-10. *Exposé's Desktop view moves all the open windows to the side to reveal the entire desktop. The edges of the open windows remain slightly in view along the darkened edge.*

■Note As noted in Chapter 1, Exposé is now available from the dock to show all open windows of any open application just by click-holding the applications icon on the dock.

■Note The F# key defaults to control Exposé, Spaces, and Dashboard can all be changed in the Exposé & Spaces preference pane. Additionally, if you have a mouse with many buttons, you can easily map these features to mouse buttons.

Spaces

Spaces is a newer feature in Mac OS X (though there have been third-party applications available for a while that provide a similar experience) that allows you to set up multiple working environments, or desktops, and switch between them. This is commonly referred to as creating and managing virtual desktops.

By default, Spaces isn't enabled, but its icon is on the Dock. Clicking the icon on the Dock the first time prompts you to set up Spaces in the Exposé & Spaces preference pane (Figure 3-11). Clicking Set Up Spaces opens System Preferences to configure Spaces (Figure 3-12).

Figure 3-11. *If you attempt to use Spaces before it's set up, you will be presented with a dialog box asking you to do so.*

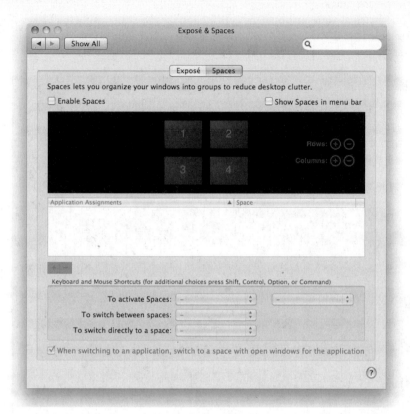

Figure 3-12. *Spaces is set up in the Exposé & Spaces pane of System Preferences.*

By default, Spaces is set up with a row of two spaces. To add a row or column, click the appropriate + in the preference pane. The preference pane shows you a small illustration of your current layout with a label on each space to designate its appropriate number. If you select the "Show Spaces in menu bar" option, it will use the designated number to display the active space and allow you to switch to other spaces via a drop-down menu.

Below the area displaying your spaces layout, you can set up applications so that they always open in a designated space. For example, you could have all your Internet applications open in one space and all of your office apps open in another. Switching to an application in the Dock, or opening an application, automatically takes you to the appropriate space.

Note Once you enable Spaces, a new item shows up in an application's Dock item contextual menu: "Assign Application To." This allows you to designate which space the application is assigned to. When an application is assigned to a space, it always opens in the space assigned (and upon opening it, you're moved to that space to begin working with it immediately).

To move from one space to another, you can "activate" Spaces by either using the F8 key (by default) or clicking the icon in the Dock. This presents a view of all your spaces shrunk down to fit on your screen, much like the "All windows" view in Exposé (Figure 3-13).

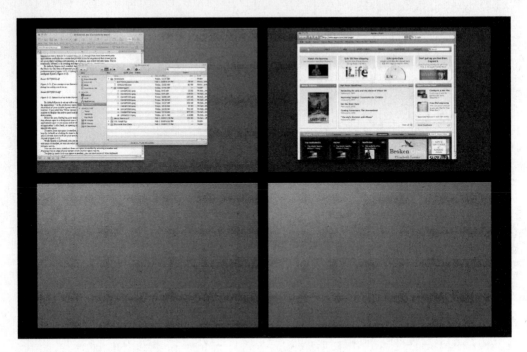

Figure 3-13. *Activating Spaces presents you with a live view of all your active spaces.*

While Spaces is activated, you can select any window in the view and move it from one space to another, or you can select any space to make that space active on your primary screen.

You can also move windows from one space to another by selecting a window and dragging it to an edge of your screen where another space may be.

To quickly move from one space to another, you can use a series of other keyboard shortcuts. By default, pressing Control and an arrow key at the same time moves you to the space in that direction. Specifically, pressing Control with the right or left arrow cycles through the spaces numerically, and pressing Control with the up and down arrows moves up or down only if there is a valid space above or below to move into. If you know the space's number, you can move directly to that space by pressing Control and the space's number (for example, pressing Control-4 moves to space 4). When you use these keyboard shortcuts, a small overlay graphic appears on the screen to illustrate where you are in the Spaces layout (Figure 3-14).

Figure 3-14. *A small overlay graphic appears when you switch to a new space using the keyboard shortcuts; it highlights the space you have just entered.*

■**Note** The maximum number of spaces is 16, a 4×4 grid. This should most likely be more than enough spaces, since in general it's probably best to utilize the fewest number of spaces necessary. If you were wondering, the keyboard shortcut doesn't work with spaces 10–16.

Using Dashboard

One final nifty OS X feature we'll talk about in this chapter is Dashboard. Dashboard is an interface feature that, when activated, brings forward a number of user-selectable widgets. A *widget* is a small, simple application that can do various things. Snow Leopard ships with a number of widgets that can display the current time, give you the latest movie schedule for your area, control iTunes, and do much more.

By default, you activate Dashboard with the F12 key (or, on newer Macs, you can use the dedicated Dashboard key). Alternatively, you can launch Dashboard by opening the Dashboard application (which is on the Dock by default). When you do this, the active widgets slide into view over your current Desktop view (Figure 3-15).

Figure 3-15. *Dashboard active with default widgets*

To add a widget to your Dashboard, you can click the + sign in the lower-left corner of the screen when Dashboard is active. This opens the widget bar across the bottom of the screen that contains all the Dashboard widgets currently installed (Figure 3-16). To add any of the installed widgets, select them and drag them off the bar onto the desktop. To remove a widget, click the X on the top-left of any widget when the widget bar is open. To move a widget, just click it and move it around to wherever you want. It reappears in your selected location each time you activate Dashboard.

■Note Holding the Option key while mousing over a widget also reveals its Close (X) button.

In addition to the widgets included with Snow Leopard, many, many other widgets are available to download and install. A good place to look is www.apple.com/downloads/dashboard/. If you download a widget in Safari, it will usually recognize the file as a widget and ask you whether you'd like to install it. To manually install a widget, just stick it in your ~/Library/ Widgets folder (you may need to create this folder if it doesn't exist). Once it's installed, it will be available from the widget bar. You can uninstall widgets by moving them out of the Widgets folder. You can also deactivate widgets using the Manage Widgets widget that presents a list of all the installed widgets with check boxes that you can uncheck to deactivate any widgets.

Figure 3-16. *Dashboard with the widget bar open at the bottom and the Manage Widgets widget open in the middle of the screen*

■**Note** Double-clicking a Dashboard widget in the Finder also installs the widget. If you are an administrator, when you do this, you will be prompted as to whether you'd like it installed for yourself or for everyone. If you are a regular user, this will simply install the widget in your `~/Library/Widgets` folder.

The use of each widget varies from widget to widget; however, many widgets have settings hidden in them. To check a widget's settings, mouse over the widget to see whether a small i appears (usually in one of the corners). Clicking this i causes the widget to flip over, revealing the widget information and settings.

In Snow Leopard, you can also add web clippings to your Dashboard from Safari. Web clippings are areas from any web page that you can select and have run as a stand-alone widget. This is most effective if the area of the web page you select is updated dynamically. If it is, your web-clipping widget will update automatically as well. We'll talk about web clippings more when we cover Safari in Chapter 10, but as far as Dashboard is concerned, they generally behave like any other widget.

■**Note** When Dashboard was first introduced, each widget ran in its own process, so running a large number of widgets could result in a performance hit on your computer. Today, all widgets run in the same process, so this isn't a significant issue anymore.

Summary

This chapter wrapped up our quick introduction to the interface basics of Mac OS X. The next part jumps into the basic administration of Mac OS X and explains how to customize your computer to suit your needs. We'll begin by going through System Preferences in the next chapter.

PART 2

■■■

Customizing and Administering Leopard

CHAPTER 4

■ ■ ■

System Preferences

Many of the configuration and administration options for Leopard are located in System Preferences (Figure 4-1). In Leopard, System Preferences is an application that presents a collection of individual items called *preference panes*. Each preference pane presents configurable options for one specific facet of the OS.

Figure 4-1. *System Preferences*

This chapter will give an overview of each of these preferences and explain what they all do. We will discuss them according to how they are categorized in System Preferences:

- Personal preferences
- Hardware preferences
- Internet & Network preferences
- System preferences

Some preferences will be touched upon only lightly, as they will be covered in depth later in this book.

■**Note** If you install any third-party system preferences, they will appear in a new Other category.

Personal Preferences

The first row of preferences in System Preferences contains the Personal preferences (Figure 4-2). These preferences together largely affect your personal environment and can be set differently for each user on your system.

Figure 4-2. *The Personal preferences in System Preferences*

Appearance

The Appearance preference pane (Figure 4-3) contains a number of options that control how certain aspects of your environment will not only look but also behave.

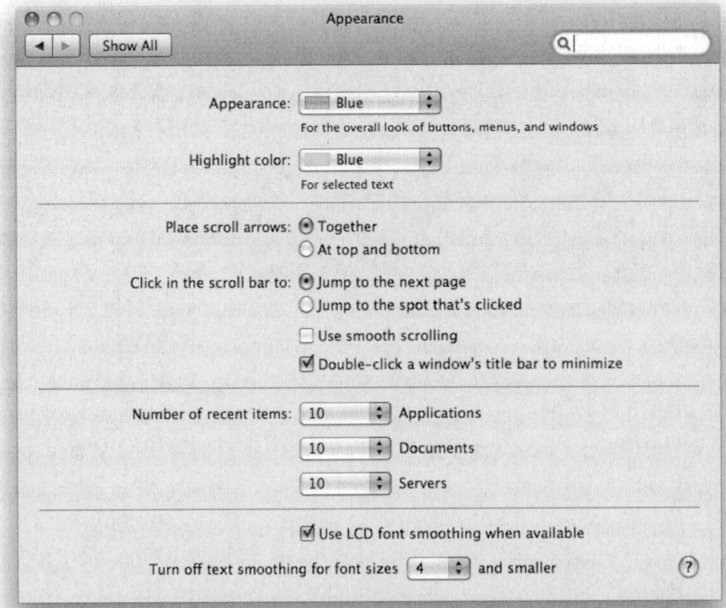

Figure 4-3. *The Appearance preference pane in System Preferences*

Table 4-1 lists each of the appearance options and describes them.

Table 4-1. *Appearance Options*

Option	Description
Appearance	This option allows you to change certain visual elements from blue to graphite (i.e., gray scale). These elements include the window widgets in the top left of the title bars (switching from blue to graphite causes the red, yellow, and green buttons to each change to become the same graphite color). The scroll bar handles and some other UI elements (e.g., the edges of the drop-down option menus) also change from blue to graphite.
Highlight color	This option allows you to change the highlight color of selected text in most applications.
Place scroll arrows	This option selects whether the scroll arrows in window scroll bars will be together (in the lower right of each scrollable window) or appear at each end of the scroll bar. This setting affects both vertical and horizontal scroll bars.
Click in the scroll bar to	This option affects the scroll behavior when you click an empty part of the scroll bar. Depending on your setting here, when you click an empty area of the scroll bar, the view will either scroll to the next page up or down (depending on where you click) or scroll directly to the relative location in the view where you clicked in the scroll bar.
Use smooth scrolling	Clicking this box increases the smoothness in which items scroll by. Because this forces the content to refresh on the screen faster, smooth scrolling comes at the cost of some system resources. On most newer machines, the effect of this is negligible.
Double-click a window's title bar to minimize	This option does what it says. When selected, it causes any window to minimize into the Dock when you double-click the window's title bar.
Number of recent items	These three drop-down menus select how many items of each type will appear in the Recent Items submenu in the Apple menu.
Use LCD font smoothing when available	This option controls font smoothing. Font smoothing rounds off fonts so the edges don't appear jagged, usually improving their appearance on the screen. Occasionally this can alter a font's intended look somewhat, and at very small font sizes it can cause them to become blurry—in which case, there is an option to turn off font smoothing for smaller fonts. It's worth pointing out that this option may vary if you are using an external display.

■**Note** Font smoothing (and onscreen font displaying in general) in Mac OS X is fundamentally different than in Microsoft Windows, and there are definitely proponents of each. In Mac OS X, the priority is preserving the look and spacing of the font so that the printed and onscreen text look identical. In Windows, the priority is placed on making the font most readable on the screen, even though that may mean that the onscreen font will be altered in unintended ways. As a result, the fonts in Mac OS X appear more accurate (in respect to their printed counterparts) but can seem a little soft or fuzzy, while the fonts in Windows look crisper, but the spacing and layout often don't appear necessarily as intended and might not match the final output.

Desktop & Screen Saver

The Desktop & Screen Saver preference pane is where you go to change your desktop picture or alter your screen saver and screen saver settings. This pane is divided into two tabs: one that sets the desktop image (Figure 4-4) and one that contains all of your screen saver options (Figure 4-5).

Figure 4-4. *The Desktop tab of the Desktop & Screen Saver preference pane sets your desktop background image.*

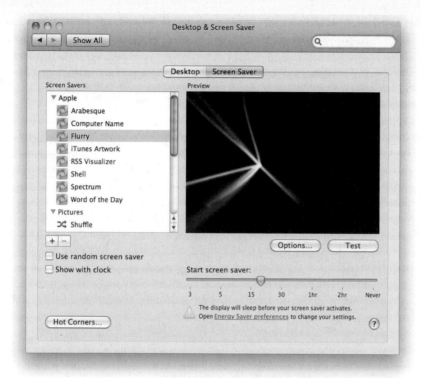

Figure 4-5. *The Screen Saver tab of the Desktop & Screen Saver preference pane*

The Desktop tab presents you with a selection of images to use as your desktop background. By default, Apple provides a wide selection of attractive backgrounds, classified into general categories. Clicking one of the folder items in the left column presents you with a preview of all the images in the right viewing area. Selecting an image in the viewing area automatically sets the image as your desktop background and puts the preview image in the top image space with the image's name besides it.

The default background images are set with preselected shape, position, and scale; however, if you choose one of your own images, a drop-down menu will appear that will allow you to alter the aspect of the image you choose. These aspects are described in Table 4-2.

Table 4-2. *Desktop Image Aspect Selections*

Aspect	Description
Fit to Screen	Fit to Screen scales the image so that the entire image fits your screen. This option doesn't change the aspect ratio of your image, so if your image is wider, empty space will appear above and below your image (the color of the empty space may be selected in the color swatch next to the aspect menu).
Fill Screen	This option scales your image so that it fills the entire screen. This option doesn't adjust the aspect ratio of your image, either; however, rather than fill the difference with empty space, it scales the image up to fill the empty space (possibly clipping off the edges of your image).
Stretch to Fill Screen	Stretch to Fill Screen scales the image to fill the screen, too. This option, however, adjusts the aspect ratio so that the entire image fills the screen. This may stretch your image's content oddly.
Center	This option doesn't scale your image; rather, it just centers your image on the screen. If your image dimensions are smaller than your screen dimensions, then empty space will appear around the image. If your image dimensions are larger than your screen dimensions, then the image will extend beyond the screen, effectively cutting off the edges. (You can select the background color that will be shown along the edges if visible.)
Tile	Like Center, this option doesn't scale your image at all; rather, it aligns the top-left corner of your image with the top-left corner of the screen. If the dimensions of the image are smaller than the dimensions of the screen, then the image will repeat itself to the right of and below itself over and over until it fills the entire screen.

This preference pane automatically reveals any top-level images in your Pictures folder; additionally, it shows items from your iPhoto and Aperture libraries so you can select images from them. You can also add your own image folders by clicking the + button and selecting the folder you wish to add. Also, if you'd like, you can set your preferences so that your background image will change at regular intervals.

One significant addition to the Desktop & Screen Saver preference pane is the "Translucent menu bar" option at the bottom. This check box toggles the appearance of the menu bar from translucent to opaque.

■**Note** The translucent menu bar allows you to view parts of your desktop background that were previously hidden behind the menu bar. If you wish to keep the menu bar translucent, keep in mind that high-contrast areas of images behind the menu bar can make the menu bar items difficult to read. Keep this under consideration when selecting your desktop backgrounds.

The Screen Saver tab presents a list of available screen saver modules on the left side of the window with a Preview area to the right. In addition to the individual modules, you can also select groups or libraries of images to be used as a screen saver.

To set up your screen saver, first choose the module you'd like to use. Some modules have settable options; if the selected module has options, the Options button will be active. Once you have chosen the module and set its options, you can test it by clicking the Test button. This activates the screen saver with your chosen module. To return, just wiggle the mouse or press a key.

Below the Preview area is the "Start screen saver" slider, which determines how long your system must be idle before the screen saver starts.

Note Certain computers, especially laptops, power down the screen after a certain amount of idle time. If this time is shorter than the screen saver start time, then the screen saver will never start. If this is the case, you will receive a warning to this effect in the Screen Saver preference pane, along with a link to the Energy Saver preference pane, where you can control the sleep setting.

The following are some other screen saver options:

Use random screen saver: This option randomly chooses a screen saver module when the screen saver starts.

Show with clock: This provides an overlay that presents the current time over the screen saver.

Hot Corners…: This button brings up the Hot Corner dialog, which allows you to assign certain functions to occur when the mouse cursor is moved into one of the corners of your screen. Two of the available options are Start Screen Saver and Disable Screen Saver (which prevents the screen saver from starting if the mouse cursor is in the selected corner).

While the screen saver modules included in Leopard are nice, there are tons of third-party screen savers also available for download (try `www.apple.com/downloads/macosx/icons_screensavers/`). To install a new screen saver, just download the screen saver file and then double-click it. This brings up a dialog box asking if you'd like to install the screen saver for just yourself or for all the users of your computer. If you select the option for just you, the screen saver file will be installed in `~/Library/Screen Savers/`; if you choose to install it for everyone, it will be installed in `/Library/Screen Savers/`.

Dock

The Dock preference pane (Figure 4-6) presents options for configuring your Dock behavior. These options were covered in Chapter 1 of this book.

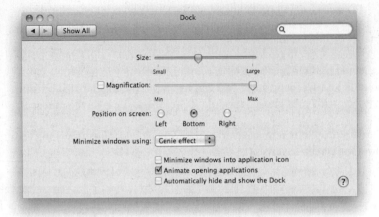

Figure 4-6. *The Dock preference pane*

Exposé & Spaces

The Exposé & Spaces preference pane (Figures 4-7 and 4-8) provides options for configuring Exposé and Spaces, as described in the previous chapter (Chapter 3).

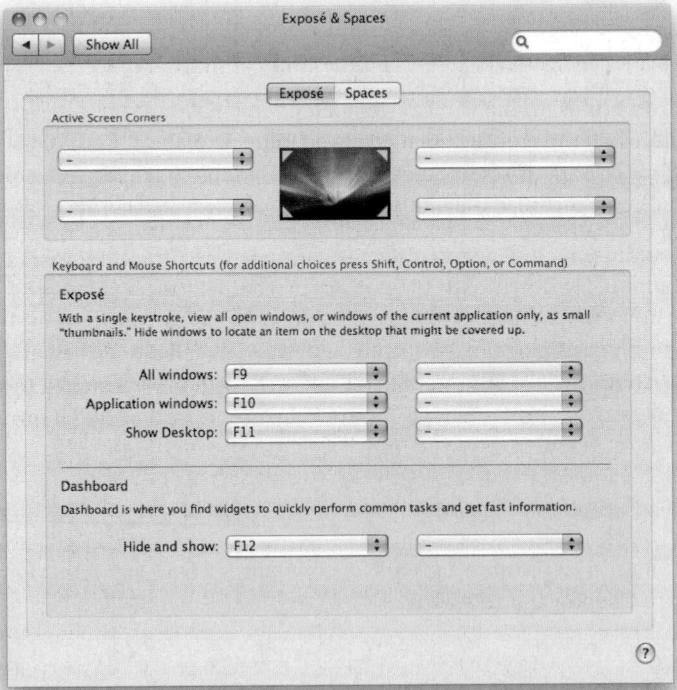

Figure 4-7. *The Exposé tab of the Exposé & Spaces preference pane*

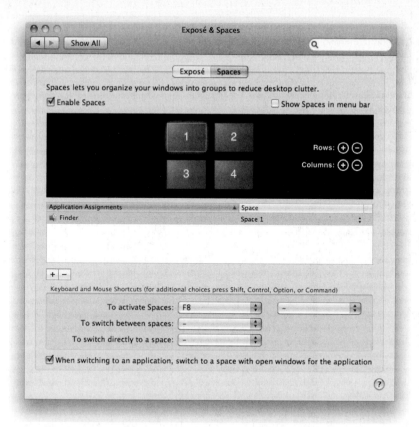

Figure 4-8. *The Spaces tab of the Exposé & Spaces preference pane*

Language & Text

The Language & Text preference pane in Snow Leopard replaces the International preference pane from previous versions of Mac OS X. These preferences control the language and regional display settings of your computer, as well as default text handling in OS X. This preference pane has four tabs that control various settings: Language, Text, Formats, and Input Sources.

The Language tab (Figure 4-9) allows you to set your preferred display language. The column on the left lists the activated languages, and you can drag them in the order of your language preference. For example, if you switch the order of English and Japanese so that Japanese appears first, then Japanese will become the default language for your system and all applications. If, however, an application weren't localized in Japanese (i.e., didn't contain Japanese translations), then the application would attempt to find your second choice (English, in this case). For the system or any application, the first available language will be used.

■**Note** *Localization* is a term referring to adding language information for a specific region in the world. Saying that an application is localized for the Ukraine means that Ukrainian language data was added to the application and is available to those who wish to use it. If you encounter an application that lacks a localization that you favor, you may want to contact the developer about this. You could even easily help implement the proper localization if you so desire.

Figure 4-9. *The Language tab of the Language & Text preference pane sets your default display language.*

You may notice that while the default list of languages covers many languages, many more are not covered. To add or remove languages from the list, click the Edit List... button. This brings up a dialog box with many more languages to choose from. Checking the box next to any of these languages will include that language in the default list.

The other option in this tab is an "Order for sorted lists" drop-down list. This selection determines the language used for sorting items in the Finder when you choose to sort items by name.

The next tab in the Languages & Text preference pane is the Text tab (Figure 4-10). Here you will find a number of options (many of which are new in Snow Leopard) for dealing with text, including a number of features to automatically substitute certain text with symbols, and options for smart quotes. All of these options are similar to AutoText features found in many word processors).

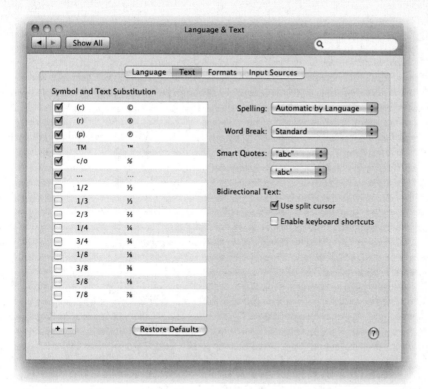

Figure 4-10. *The Text tab in the Languages & Text preference pane includes some system-wide options for dealing with text.*

Note Computer programmers may be interested in the "English (United States, Computer)" option under the Word Break list. This selection causes the computer to react more favorably to words in computer programs, specifically when it comes to common naming practices of variables. For example, if you have words separated by a colon (such as setName:aName), it will understand that these are separate words when selecting text.

The Formats tab (Figure 4-11) sets up default date, time, number, currency, and measurement unit settings for your computer. Selecting your region from the Region drop-down list generally sets these items accurately. For example, switching from United States to United Kingdom alters the order of the date, switches to a 24-hour clock, changes the currency from US Dollars to British Pound Sterling, and changes the measurement units to metric. If, however, the default settings for your region aren't exactly what you want, you can alter or customize most of them (e.g., if you work for NASA, on, say, a Mars Climate Orbiter project, you might want to switch to the metric system). If you don't see the region that you want in the Region menu, try checking the "Show all regions" selection.

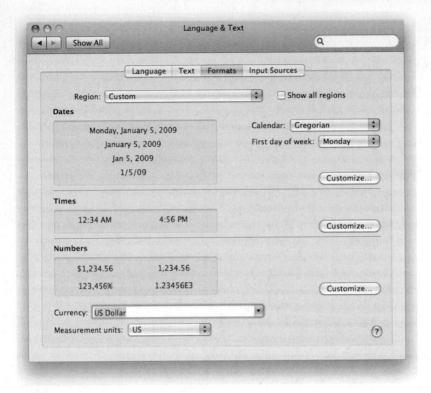

Figure 4-11. *The Formats tab in the Languages & Text preference pane sets how dates, times, numbers, currency, and measurements appear.*

■**Note** It seems that whatever region you choose, the Calendar setting will stay set to Gregorian, so if you wish to use a different calendar system, you will need to set that manually.

The Input Sources tab (Figure 4-12) is where you set up your input language and devices. It contains a long list of various items with check boxes. Each item represents an input palette, an input method, an input device (specifically, a keyboard), or a keyboard mapping. These items combine to allow a large number of languages to be used to input text in Mac OS X. Using the check boxes, you can select any number of languages and input devices that you commonly use. If you select more than one item, the "Show Input menu in menu bar" option will automatically be selected, allowing you to easily switch between inputting different languages at any time from the menu bar.

Figure 4-12. *The Input Sources tab in the Languages & Text preference pane sets the language input options for your systems.*

The input palettes in the list provide the ability to open up a couple of special dialog windows (Figure 4-13) that allow you to input characters by clicking them. The Keyboard Viewer (which becomes available from the menu bar if you select the Keyboard & Character Viewer option under the Input Sources tab) is particularly interesting, since it shows how your keyboard is mapped and responds dynamically as you type on the keyboard. For example, if you press the Option key, the Keyboard Viewer will change to reflect the symbols available with the Option-*key* combinations. Paying attention to changes while playing around with this can teach you new tricks. For example, if you look at the changes while you hold the Fn key, you may notice a number of interesting functions (e.g., Function-Delete deletes the characters in front of the cursor rather than behind). The Character Viewer provides a way to browse and input a wide array of symbols and characters from complex languages such as Chinese and Japanese.

Figure 4-13. *The viewers*

The input methods in the list affect the behavior of inputting text, primarily for languages with very large character sets. For such languages, you will commonly enter two or more key-strokes to input a single character. These varying input methods facilitate this.

Finally, the keyboard items affect the keyboard layout and language. In general, this is to accommodate different languages and the keyboards designed for them; however, you can use these options to remap any keyboard (even though in doing so, the letters on the keys will no longer match the inputted character). While some of the remappings are extreme, others are subtler—for example, switching to a Spanish key map will alter only a few symbol keys (making common Spanish symbols easier to access). In addition to changing the input character maps of your keyboard, changing to certain languages will alter the direction of input—for example, switching to Arabic or Hebrew will cause the input to flow from right to left rather than left to right.

In general, if you need to enter text, characters, or symbols and you are not quite sure how, selecting either the Keyboard Viewer or the Character Palette is a good place to start to help you find what you are looking for.

Security

The Security preference pane seems oddly placed in that most of its options affect the entire system rather than just your personal preferences. The Security preference pane provides three tabs: General, for general system security options; FileVault, for encrypting your personal home folder and all of its contents; and Firewall, which can help secure your system from network intrusion by limiting access to computer network services.

Chapter 8 is dedicated to system security, so these preferences and more will be covered there.

Spotlight

The Spotlight preference pane (Figure 4-14) helps you customize what types of items Spotlight will index and in what order you want the results of a search to be returned to you.

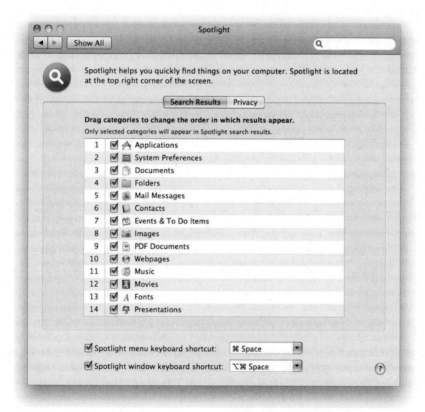

Figure 4-14. *The Spotlight preference pane with the Search Results tab showing*

The Spotlight preference pane has two tabs: Search Results and Privacy. The Privacy tab allows you to select folders that you want to prevent from being indexed. This can prevent information that you'd like to keep private from showing up in any searches of your system, or it can save system resources by indexing only the items that you are interested in indexing.

The Search Results tab provides a few more customization possibilities. First of all, it allows you to block certain types of files from appearing in a Spotlight search result. So, if you'd like to exclude mail messages from being returned in a Spotlight search, you can uncheck the Mail Messages item (this affects only system-wide Spotlight searches; messages will continue to be searchable from within Mail). Additionally, you can arrange the items in the Search Results list in the order that you'd like those items to be returned to you, so if you'd like all the matched images to appear before the matched contacts, just move the Images item above the Contacts item.

The options below the window allow you to alter the keyboard shortcuts for activating Spotlight. Should you decide to change these, consider that while most applications are aware of the default settings, custom settings may overlap with some applications' built-in shortcuts, so there may be times when the keyboard shortcuts you set do something unexpected.

Hardware

The row of preference panes below the Personal preferences contains the Hardware preferences (Figure 4-15). Here you will find settings for most of the hardware devices included with your computer.

Figure 4-15. *The Hardware preference panes*

▪**Note** Most third-party hardware, and even some software, includes its own preference pane. These non-Apple preference panes will be included together at the bottom of System Preferences, in the Other category.

CDs & DVDs

The CDs & DVDs preference pane (Figure 4-16) allows you to select what will happen when you insert certain media formats in your computer. The media formats that you can assign actions to include blank CDs, blank DVDs, music CDs, picture CDs, and video DVDs.

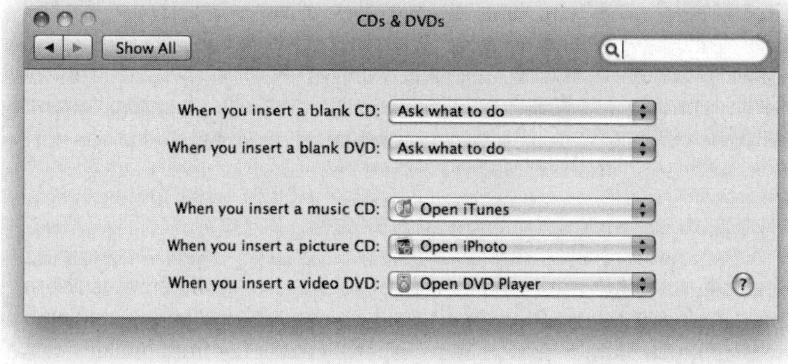

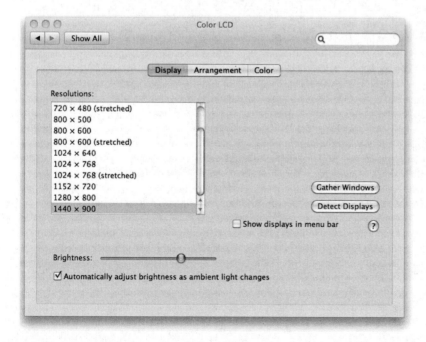

Figure 4-16. *The CDs & DVDs preference pane*

Displays

The Displays preference pane allows you to make adjustments to your computer displays. By default, there are two tabs in this preference pane: Display and Color.

The Display tab (Figure 4-17) allows you to set the display resolution and color depth for your display. Additionally, certain displays (predominantly CRT monitors) allow you to adjust the refresh rate, and others (predominantly Apple monitors) allow you to adjust the display's brightness from this preference pane. Finally, if your computer has ambient light sensors (as some Apple laptops do), you can set an option that will automatically adjust your screen's brightness according to the brightness of your environment.

Figure 4-17. *The Display tab of the Displays preference pane*

■**Note** These days, all the displays that Apple sells are flat-panel LCDs. These are generally easier to set up than the older CRT monitors, since you don't need to hassle with refresh rates. Also, LCDs are created to work best at specific resolutions (usually the highest resolution available), which makes choosing the best resolution easy as well, but you may notice a few different options available here when you attach an external display.

The Color tab (Figure 4-18) allows you to manage the display's color profiles. A *color profile* is a data file that contains color information about a device or color standard. ColorSync uses these data files to match up colors so that an item appears consistent from one device to another. All this allows an image from your digital camera to appear on your screen the way the camera intended and then allows the image you print out on your printer to match what you see on the screen. The trick, however, is to assure that your screen has the proper profile.

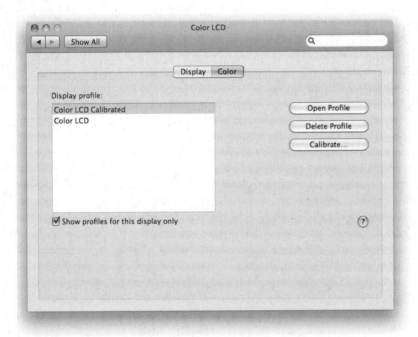

Figure 4-18. *The Displays preference pane's Color tab helps you manage your display's color profiles.*

Mac OS X comes with some generic color profiles for Apple displays as well as some others; however, it's likely that you will want to calibrate your monitor, creating a custom profile for your display.

Note Why calibrate your display? The generic color profiles that ship with Mac OS X are just that—generic. They are a decent average, but in reality each display is slightly different, so it's highly unlikely that the generic profile will match reality. Also, the generic profiles don't take into account your ambient lighting situation, which can have a big impact on how colors appear on your screen. Also, calibration allows you to adjust your display's gamma (see the "Gamma and Snow Leopard: Why Are Things Darker?" sidebar).

GAMMA AND SNOW LEOPARD: WHY ARE THINGS DARKER?

Gamma (or *gamma correction*) is a numerical value that determines the overall value, or brightness, of an image being displayed. The details of gamma could quickly divert into a discussion of complex algebraic equations and light physics, but in general terms, gamma represents a nonlinear relationship between the pixels of an image and the brightness of the monitor. This results in the variation of the brightness, contrast, and dynamic range of an image that appears onscreen. Lower gamma values create brighter images, and higher gamma values result in darker images. In general, the goal of adjusting gamma is to find a balance in the dynamic range of the display device, where whites are white, blacks are black, and all shades in between are accurately rendered. For a computer display, the ideal gamma number to make the best of the lights and darks usually falls between 1.8 and 2.5.

Now, traditionally, all Macs defaulted to a gamma of 1.8. This was determined to be ideal for working with all things destined for printing. Microsoft Windows computers, meanwhile, traditionally defaulted to a gamma *around* 2.2 (this really didn't have much to do with Microsoft per se; it just happened that most of the CRT monitors of the day happened to have a natural gamma value that ranged from around 2.2 to 2.5). This, of course, was a throwback to TVs (2.2 gamma is also known as TV gamma). As computer output transitioned from paper to digital, a problem occurred: images designed on a Mac looked dark and ugly on Windows computers, while things designed on Windows looked washed out and ugly on Macs. (There were other color space issues as well, but the whole gamma thing was the big elephant in the room.) Ultimately, the World Wide Web Consortium (W3C) (with help from HP and Microsoft) declared that the standard color space for the Internet would be sRBG (a color space devised by HP and Microsoft) and the default gamma would be 2.2. Now it's fairly easy to adjust the gamma on your Mac, but it's just not something most people would intuitively know to do, so in the past there were still imaging conflicts on the Web between Macs and Windows machines. Plus, most digital imaging devices, such as digital cameras and digital video recorders, also outputted images with a 2.2 gamma. Sooner or later, it seemed that Apple would have to come around.

The time has come. Beginning with Snow Leopard, Apple has changed its default gamma value for displays from 1.8 to 2.2. As a result, if you've been using the default color space on your Mac, things will seem a bit darker and higher contrast. Overall, this is good thing, and viewing images on the Web should be a bit better.

To create a basic profile, click the Calibrate… button in the Color tab. This opens up the Display Calibrator Assistant (Figure 4-19), which walks you through the process of calibrating your display.

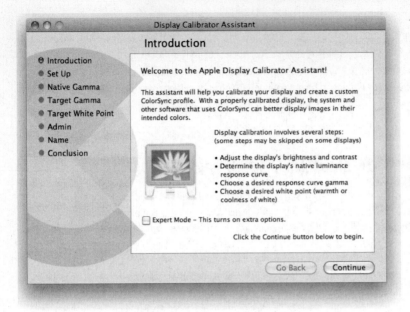

Figure 4-19. *The Display Calibrator Assistant*

Once the Display Calibrator Assistant is open, you can start a basic calibration by clicking the Continue button.

Note You may notice that an expert mode offering extra options is available. If you are calibrating an older CRT, then the expert mode might work for you reasonably, but many of the expert tests are extraordinarily difficult to get right if you are using a flat-panel display (since color shifts as your angle of view changes). If accurate color matching is really important to you, we recommend picking up a hardware device that will calibrate your monitor for you. Something like the Pantone Huey will do an excellent job for less than $100.

Clicking the Continue button takes you to the screen where you select your target gamma (Figure 4-20). There are only two options in basic mode: Gamma 2.2 (Standard) and Gamma 1.8. As stated previously, we generally recommend the 2.2 gamma option.

Note As you may have noticed, clicking Continue skips two steps: Set Up and Native Gamma. Certain displays (predominantly CRTs) require extra steps to create a baseline for the calibration. If you find yourself confronted with these steps, just follow the onscreen instructions to work through them.

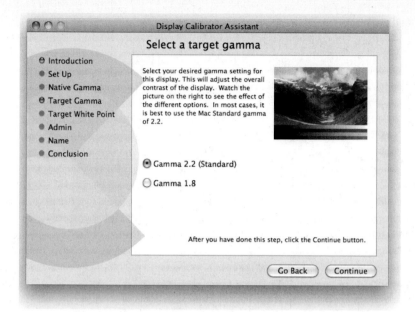

Figure 4-20. *Selecting the target gamma in the Display Calibrator Assistant*

Continuing on from the gamma selection, you're taken to the screen where you can set the display's white point (Figure 4-21). *White point* is the strangest and most difficult-to-grasp concept in color matching. Your eyes generally compensate for ambient light so that things that may not be white appear white. This makes setting the white point of your monitor a bit tricky to do manually. In general, depending on the ambient light surrounding your computer, you will find a comfortable white point around 6000 to 7500 K (Kelvin, which is how white point is measured). For most modern displays, this should be right about where the native white point is, so unless you really know you don't want to use your native white point, we recommend using it.

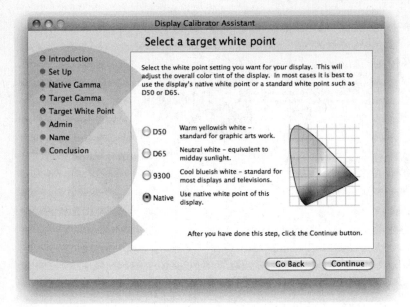

Figure 4-21. *Selecting a target white point for your display*

Note Besides measuring white point in Kelvin (commonly referred to as the *correlated color temperature*), there are other common names given to certain white points, such as D50 or D65. D65 is also known as the television white point and is the default sRGB color space white point.

Note If you use a hardware device to calibrate your monitor, it will have a weird effect on the white point of your display—it will look wrong, even though it's likely spot on. This is your eyes playing tricks on you again (this is temporary and lasts only until your eyes adjust to the new white point setting).

After you set the white point, click the Continue button. If you are using an account with administrator status, you will be prompted to choose if you'd like this profile to be available to users other than yourself; if not, you'll jump straight to the Name step, where you'll be asked to name your new profile (Figure 4-22). You can call your new profile anything you want, but we recommend using something sensible.

Once you are done, click Continue. You will be presented with one last screen, essentially telling you that you're done. Click the Done button. When the assistant goes away, you will see your new profile as an option in the Display Profile area, along with any other profiles.

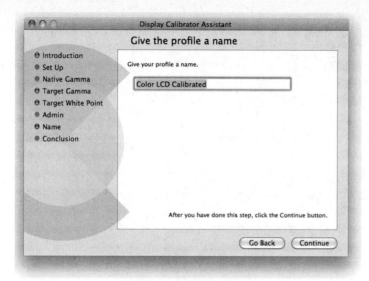

Figure 4-22. *Give your new display profile a name.*

If you happen to have two or more displays hooked up to your computer, a third Display tab called Arrangement will appear (Figure 4-23). This provides a view area that lets you arrange your monitors next to each other and a check box that allows you to mirror your displays. If the Mirror Displays option is checked, then both displays will have the same information on them. If the Mirror Displays option is unchecked, then the displays will act together as one large work area.

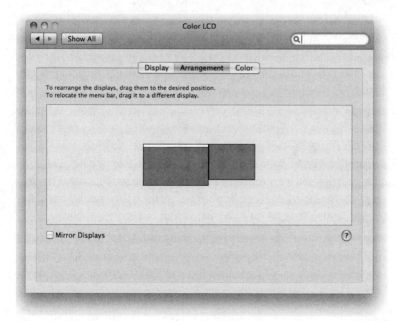

Figure 4-23. *When you have multiple displays attached to your computer, the Arrangement tab allows you to arrange the monitors into one large workspace.*

When you have multiple monitors attached, the preference pane opens separate preference windows in each display, allowing you to independently set each display's preferences.

Energy Saver

The Energy Saver preference pane (Figure 4-24) allows you to adjust some power-saving features for your computer. It does this by causing certain functions of your computer to sleep after a short idle period and by throttling overall performance of your system to conserve energy consumption.

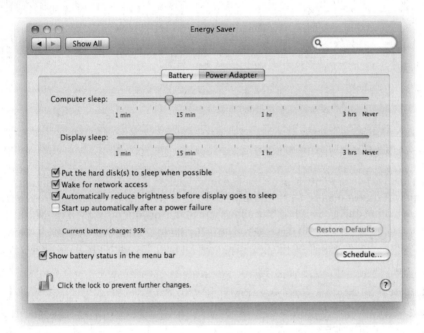

Figure 4-24. *The Energy Saver preference pane*

■**Note** The Energy Saver preference pane, like many System Preferences panes, may have different options depending on the type of computer you are using. If you are using an Apple notebook computer, you will have tabs at the top to set your preferences individually for when you are using the power adapter or for when you are running on batteries. Desktop Macs, on the other hand, provide only one set of options.

Table 4-3 lists the general options available in this preference pane and their effects.

Table 4-3. *Energy Saver Settings*

Setting	Description
Computer sleep	This slider allows you to set a value for how long the computer should remain idle before it automatically sleeps. (A computer is idle whenever it is not actively receiving user input. Even while it is processing some data or playing back a movie, the computer can be idle unless you are actively typing or moving the mouse around.) In sleep state, most computer processes stop, and most hardware is powered down (or placed in a low–power consumption mode). A minimal amount of power is consumed to keep the current state of the computer in memory so that it can quickly resume where it left off when it is woken up.
Display sleep	This mode is similar to the Computer Sleep setting, but it affects only the display (which is traditionally one of the most power-hungry components of a computer). Even when you have reasons not to sleep the computer, it's still a good idea to sleep the display after a period of time.
Put the hard disk(s) to sleep when possible	This check box tells the computer to power down the hard drives when it determines they are not being used. Powering down hard drives can save a bit of energy.
Wake for network access	This mode allows incoming network connections to wake up your computer. This option is not available when running under battery power.
Automatically reduce brightness before display goes to sleep	As it says, this mode dims the display before it actually puts it to sleep. This comes in handy if you are, for example, watching a movie on your computer; since you are not actively interacting with your computer, it will consider itself idle. By dimming the screen, you will be able to react to let your computer know you are still there before it just shuts down your screen.
Start up automatically after a power failure	This option is useful if you are running on a power adapter without a battery backup (primarily when using a desktop computer). If this option is selected, in the event of an unexpected power loss, your computer will restart automatically when power is restored.
Schedule…	This button opens up a dialog box that allows you to set a schedule for your computer to shut down or start up automatically at a predetermined time. For example, if you arrive at work every day at 8:30 a.m., you could have your computer start up and be ready for you at 8:15 a.m. every weekday morning.
Show battery status in the menu bar	This option adds a menu icon in your menu bar that indicates if you are running on the power adapter or battery power. It also tells you how much charge remains in the battery. This option is available only for notebook computers with a battery.
Slightly dim the display when using this power source	This setting is available under the Battery tab on notebook computers. It causes the brightness of the display to drop a few levels to conserve energy when running on battery power.
Restore Defaults	Clicking this button resets all preference options back to the default state.

One final option is the lock in the lower-left corner of the preference pane. This is the first time we've mentioned this in this book, although it's a common feature in many preference panes and applications. If you are an administrator on your computer, clicking this lock will lock the preference pane so that changes cannot be made to it until it is unlocked. Clicking the locked icon presents a standard authentication dialog box asking for your administrative password to unlock the preference pane. In general, if other people use your computer and you don't want them monkeying around with important settings, lock them.

Keyboard

The Keyboard preference pane controls the options for your keyboard. It is divided into two tabs: Keyboard and Keyboard Shortcuts.

■**Note** In previous versions of OS X, the keyboard and mouse preferences were combined, but beginning with Snow Leopard, they are separate, perhaps acknowledging that the mouse and keyboard may not forever be the two primary in/out methods for Mac OS X.

■**Note** Although the keyboard and the mouse preferences cover most standard hardware, they are mostly designed for Apple keyboards and mice. If you are using a third-party mouse or keyboard, they may have options not available with these preferences; additionally, some of the options here are specifically for Apple hardware features. For this reason, most third-party hardware comes with its own preference pane. There are also a couple of third-party drivers for mice and keyboards that offer different customization options that may suit you. For example, we tend to be fond of the Logitech MX Revolution mouse but find the included drivers . . . well . . . insufficient. For this reason, we use SteerMouse (`http://plentycom.jp/en/steermouse/index.html`) as the mouse driver.

The Keyboard tab (Figure 4-25) provides options for your keyboard. The basic options are the following:

Key Repeat Rate: This slider controls how fast a letter will automatically repeat if you hold down a key.

Delay Until Repeat: This slider controls how long you must initially hold down a key until the letter starts repeating.

Modifier Keys...: This button opens a dialog box that allows you to remap the modifier keys (for example, to switch the behavior of the Command and Control keys for a more Microsoft Windows–like experience). You can also turn these keys off (such as the dreaded Caps Lock key).

Show Keyboard & Character Viewer in menu bar: This option will turn on the Keyboard & Character Viewer along with the Input method menu item in the menu bar. (If you toggle this on and off, the Input menu is automatically turned on; to turn this off, you must deselect the option in the Input Sources tab of the Language & Text preference pane.

Other hardware-specific options include the following:

Use all F1, F2, etc. keys as standard function keys: On many Apple keyboards, the function keys control features such as volume, screen brightness, and other aspects of hardware by default. To use these function keys as standard function keys instead, you must hold down the Option key. Selecting this box reverses the default behavior.

Illuminate keyboard in low light conditions: This is for special Apple keyboards (like those found on many Apple notebooks) that allow the keyboard to light up. Selecting this box will cause the keys to light up in low-light conditions. You can use the slider to turn off the keyboard lights after a designated period of idle time.

Set Up Bluetooth Keyboard...: If you have Bluetooth available on your computer, this button will appear at the bottom of the preference pane. Selecting it will open a dialog box (Figure 4-26) that will walk you through the process of connecting a wireless Bluetooth keyboard to work with your computer.

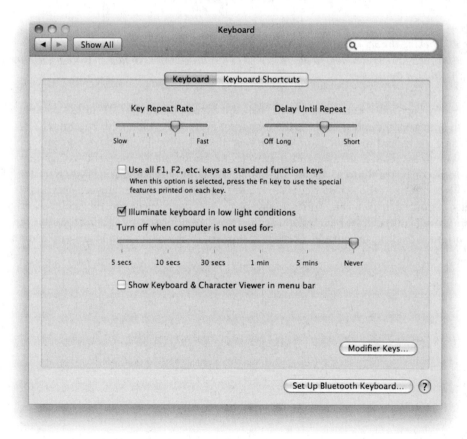

Figure 4-25. *The Keyboard tab in the Keyboard preference pane controls your keyboard.*

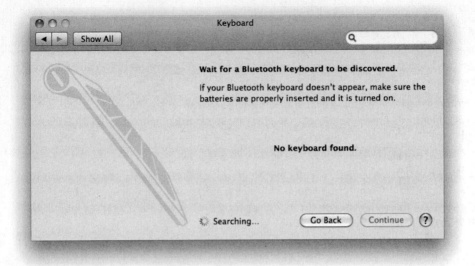

Figure 4-26. *Clicking the Set Up Bluetooth Keyboard... button will open a dialog box that will walk you through the steps needed to set up your wireless Bluetooth keyboard to work with your Bluetooth-enabled computer.*

Many years ago, one of the biggest fears we heard from people about Macintosh computers was that they felt they needed to use the mouse for everything, while with Windows there tended to be a keyboard shortcut for just about everything. (Ironically, the other big fear was people wrongly assumed that Macs work only with one-button mice.) The reality is that on a Mac there are keyboard shortcuts for all common tasks, along with some things you may not have thought of. The Keyboard Shortcuts tab (Figure 4-27) lists all the system-wide keyboard shortcuts, organized in useful categories, in one place. You can also change the default shortcuts here as well (although we recommend against this). Additionally, by clicking the + button at the bottom of the list, you can add a keyboard shortcut to any menu item in any application.

Figure 4-27. *The Keyboard Shortcuts tab on the Keyboard preference pane displays (and allows you to remap) a wide number of system-wide keyboard shortcuts.*

■Note The ability to add a keyboard shortcut for any menu item in any application is a powerful feature. It can, however, cause all sorts of messiness if used haphazardly. Feel free to take advantage of this—however, be careful not to override existing, common keyboard shortcuts.

Mouse

The Mouse preference pane provides different options depending on the mouse you have attached to your computer (provided you have a mouse attached at all). For most mice, it will provide a number of standard mouse options (Figure 4-28). These options include setting the mouse's tracking speed, double-click speed, scrolling speed, and depending on the mouse whether the left or right button is the primary click (which is nice for left-handers). The pane also includes options to use the scroll wheel to zoom (magnify) the screen.

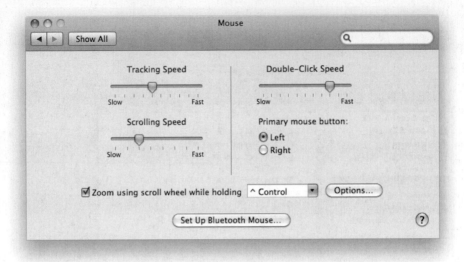

Figure 4-28. *The default Mouse tab on the Mouse preference pane*

If you happen to have an Apple Mighty Mouse attached to your computer (whether wired or wirelessly), the Mouse tab will be quite different and provide different options tailored specifically for this mouse (Figure 4-29). This special preference pane allows you to select special actions for the different buttons available on this mouse.

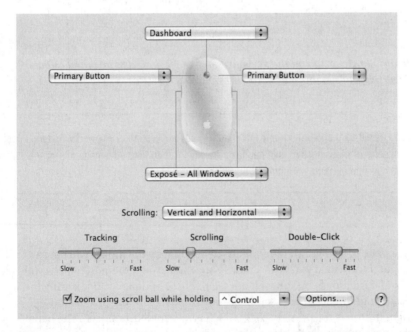

Figure 4-29. *The Mouse tab on the Mouse preference pane for Apple's Mighty Mouse*

Trackpad

The Trackpad preference pane is available on Macs that have a built-in trackpad (which includes all Mac laptops able to run Snow Leopard). Depending on the trackpad, however, this preference pane comes in one of two flavors. For trackpads with a separate button (as on any MacBook or MacBook Pro that doesn't have the new unibody aluminum design), you will see one set of features (Figure 4-30); for the newest Apple laptops with the larger glass trackpad (which is the button itself), you will see a different preference pane (Figure 4-31). Whichever trackpad you have, the primary differences between the Trackpad preference options and the preferences available for a standard mouse revolve around what are known as *gestures*. Gestures are specific taps or movements you make on the trackpad with one or more fingers (sometimes in conjunction with a button click) that cause specific events to happen. In addition to the Tracking Speed, Double-Click Speed, and Scrolling Speed options (which are equivalent to the Mouse preferences of the same name), the options for the single-button (non-glass) trackpads are as follows:

Use two fingers to scroll: This option allows you to scroll up and down in a window using two fingers on the trackpad.

Allow horizontal scrolling: This option allows the two-finger scroll to also work for scrolling right and left.

Zoom while holding [Control]: This option allows you to magnify the screen by dragging two fingers on the trackpad while holding a modifier key (by default, the Control key). The Options… button opens a dialog box that provides some additional zoom options.

Clicking: When this option is selected, a quick single-finger tap on the trackpad works as a click of the button.

Dragging: With this option selected (along with the Clicking option), a quick tap followed by a hold grabs a window, allowing you to drag it.

Drag Lock: With this option selected along with Dragging, you can continue a dragging motion even if you lift up your finger. To stop dragging, you need to tap the trackpad.

For secondary click, place two fingers on the trackpad then click the button (or *Tap trackpad using two fingers for secondary click when Clicking is selected*): These options are fairly self-explanatory. They provide an easy way to use a secondary click (or Control-click), even with just one button (or even no button at all).

Ignore accidental trackpad input: This option attempts to compensate for accidental trackpad touches. With the trackpad so close to the keyboard, keeping this option selected can prevent a number of accidental cursor movements (which can be extremely frustrating).

Ignore trackpad when mouse is present: If you often use a mouse with your notebook, and the above options aren't enough, this option lets the computer ignore the trackpad (and button) entirely when a mouse is connected to the computer.

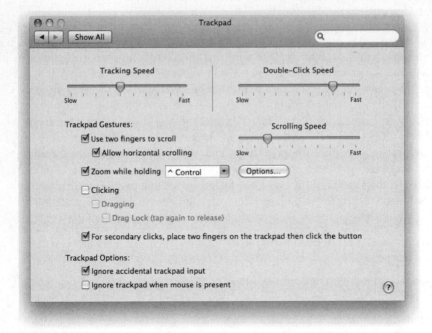

Figure 4-30. *The Trackpad preference pane for older non-glass trackpads*

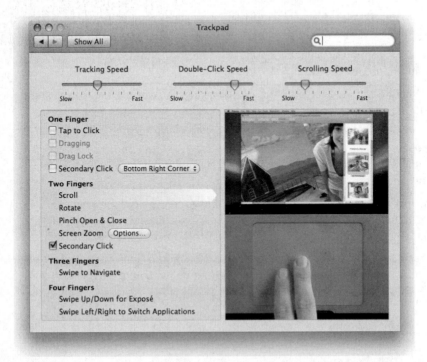

Figure 4-31. *The New Trackpad Preference pane for the new Multi-Touch glass trackpads*

Now if you happen to have a newer notebook with the glass trackpad, your options are different (though some are actually the same thing but phrased a bit differently). The glass trackpad options are organized by the number of fingers used. The One Finger options include the following:

Tap to Click: This is the same as the Clicking option described previously.

Dragging: This is the same as the Dragging option described previously.

Drag Lock: This is the same as the Drag Lock option described previously.

Secondary Click: This option allows you to assign a tap area on the trackpad so that when you tap in that area, it registers as a secondary click. The default location is the bottom-right corner of the trackpad.

Following the One Finger options are the Two Finger options. Although five items are listed, only one selection is possible (Secondary Tap, which allows you to toggle on and off two-finger tapping working as a secondary click). There is also only one Options… button, which brings up the previously mentioned dialog box to tweak some zoom options. Rather than providing an actual option, selecting one of the remaining items (including all the Three Finger and Four Finger items) causes a small movie to play in the right-hand view area demonstrating how the item works (in other words, rather than an option, you get a lesson). These are actually nice tools for learning how to take full advantage of Apple's new glass trackpad; however, in the future, it may be nice to have more control over what a gesture actually does.

Note The new glass trackpads add many of the Multi-Touch capabilities found on the iPhone and iPod touch. Some claim that these capabilities are not backward-compatible with the older trackpad hardware, and while a number of people are attempting to prove this wrong, as of this writing nobody has done so successfully. So, at least for the time being, there will be no four-finger swipes or two-finger pinches on the older trackpads. At the moment, this isn't a huge loss; however, Apple has made the Multi-Touch capabilities accessible through the glass trackpads available for developers, which could mean that in the not-so-distant future, some developer will create the coolest application ever, and it will work right only with an Apple computer with a Multi-Touch–capable device (which would not only keep people with older notebooks from using it but all desktops as well).

Print & Fax

The Print & Fax preference pane allows you to add and manage local and network printers, and if you have a modem, it allows you to set up fax capabilities. Setting up printers will be covered in detail in the next chapter (Chapter 5).

Processor

The Processor preference is not available by default. When you install the Xcode tools, the Processor preference pane is placed in the /Developer/Extras/PreferencePanes/ folder. If you double-click the Processor preference pane (or any uninstalled preference pane), a dialog box will pop up asking if you would like to install the preference pane and if you want this available

only to you or to everyone. Select one of the options and click Continue (if you selected everyone as an option, you may be prompted for the administrator's password). This will install the
new preference pane and open it in the System Preferences. The Processor preference pane
(Figure 4-32) provides information about your computer's processors. It allows you to tweak
some options (like disabling processor cores and other things that are of little to no use for most
people). In general, it's best to leave this alone unless you know what you are doing. While altering anything here won't destroy anything, your computer's processing power could suffer.

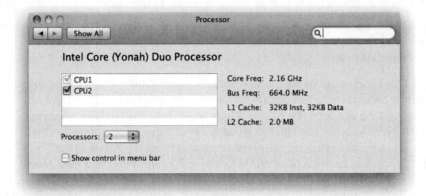

Figure 4-32. *The Processor preference pane is part of Xcode's performance and optimization tools.*

Sound

The Sound preference pane controls your sound input and output devices, and provides
options for system sounds and effects. The Sound preference pane has three tabs: Sound
Effects, Output, and Input.

The Sound Effects tab (Figure 4-33) allows you to set your alert sound (the sound your
computer plays when it tries to get your attention—usually when something bad happens).

The Output tab (Figure 4-34) allows you to select your primary output device (if more
than one is available) and set the setting for the selected devices. At the bottom of the Sound
preference pane is the "Output volume" slider, along with an option to show (and control) the
volume in your menu bar.

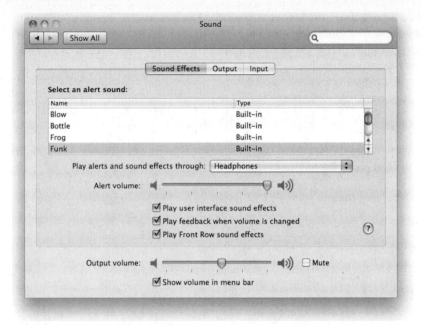

Figure 4-33. *The Sound Effects tab lets you choose your system alert sound and provides a few options for audio feedback.*

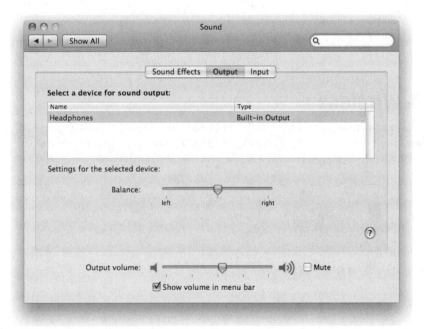

Figure 4-34. *The Output tab in the Sound preference pane*

The Input tab (Figure 4-35) in the Sound preference pane lists each of your available input devices and allows you to make level adjustments for the selected input device. Ambient noise reduction may help eliminate excess background noise; however, in some cases, it could also adversely affect the input sound quality.

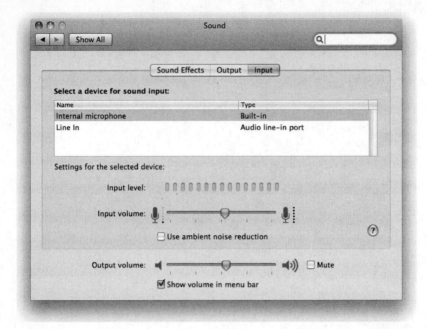

Figure 4-35. *The Input tab in the Sound preference pane controls your sound input devices.*

Internet & Wireless

The next section of System Preferences deals with Internet and network preferences (Figure 4-36). This contains your Bluetooth, MobileMe, Network, and Sharing preference panes. Each of these topics, along with relevant preferences, will be covered later in this book.

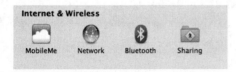

Figure 4-36. *Internet & Wireless system preferences*

■Note Bluetooth is covered in the next chapter (Chapter 5), MobileMe is covered in Chapter 13, network preferences are covered in Chapter 9 (and in more depth in Chapter 19), and sharing preferences are covered in Chapter 20.

System

The System section of System Preferences (Figure 4-37) contains the remaining preference panes that are installed with Leopard. The preference panes in the System section are Accounts, Date & Time, Parental Controls, Software Update, Speech, Startup Disk, Time Machine, and Universal Access.

Figure 4-37. *The System preference panes in System Preferences*

Accounts

The Accounts preference pane manages all the system's users, including some of their settings and their login options. When an existing user is selected, you will see two tabs—Password and Login Items—each containing information about that specific user.

The Password tab (Figure 4-38), as the name suggests, allows users to change their password by clicking the Change Password button. It also allows you to do the following:

- Change your user icon by clicking the icon image and selecting a new image from the drop-down list (or use the Edit Image selection to create a custom image)

- Change your user name by typing in a new name (this, however, doesn't change your short name)

- Add your MobileMe account information if you have a MobileMe account

- View and edit your address book card in the Address Book application

- Grant (or remove) administrator rights on the computer, provided that you are an administrator (you cannot remove administrator rights from yourself)

- Enable (or disable) parental controls for the user (provided that you have administrator rights)

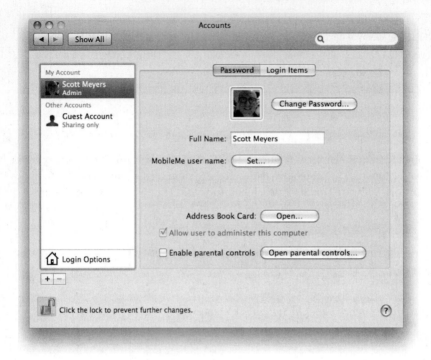

Figure 4-38. *When a user is selected, the Password tab allows that user to change his or her password and other user information.*

The Login Items tab (Figure 4-39) lets you manage applications, scripts, and other executable items that you want to start automatically when you log in to your computer. In general, what you will find listed here are background tasks that certain applications use to provide some sort of feature. You can, however, add your own items. For example, if you want the Mail application to start up immediately when you log in to your computer, you can add it to this list by clicking the + button and selecting Mail from the resulting dialog box.

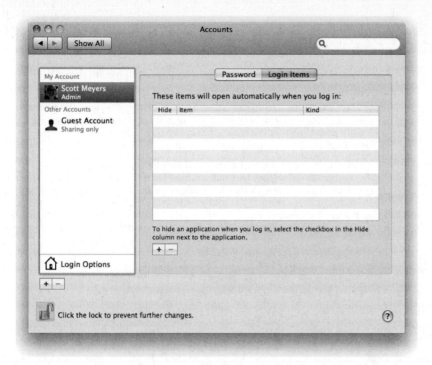

Figure 4-39. *The Login Items tab allows you to manage scripts and applications that will run automatically when you log in.*

Selecting Login Options (Figure 4-40) allows you to set options that govern login behavior. They are listed and defined in Table 4-4.

Table 4-4. *Login Options*

Option	Description
Automatic login	This option allows you to select a user who will be logged in automatically when the computer starts up. This is handy if you are the only user on a particular system. Disabling this option requires users to log in whenever the computer starts up. If "Automatic login" is set, a user can still log out, allowing others to log in.
Display login window as	This sets what a user sees at the login screen. The "List of users" option provides a list of all the users of the system. Clicking one of the user's names or icons prompts for a password. The "Name and password" option prompts for the user's name and password without revealing any of the usernames. The "List of users" option is faster and more user-friendly, but the "Name and password" option provides slightly better security.
Show the Restart, Sleep, and Shut Down buttons	This shows the Restart, Sleep, and Shut Down buttons on the login screen, allowing these options to be used when no user is logged in.
Show input menu in login window	This option provides a list to set different language options prior to logging in.
Show password hints	This shows the user's password hint after three failed login attempts. Obviously, there are security implications with this option.

Continued

Table 4-4. *Continued*

Option	Description
Use VoiceOver in the login window	This option enables VoiceOver at the login window. VoiceOver causes any text under the mouse to be spoken through the computer. This is useful for the visually impaired.
Enable fast user switching	This option adds a user-switching menu to the right side of the menu bar, allowing you to switch from one user to another without logging out first. Setting the "View as" option to Menu allows you to choose what information appears in this menu.
Server Connection	Clicking the Join… button allows you to select and open Directory Server, Active Directory Domain, or Mac OS X Server. These servers provide directory and network security services that allow organizations to manage users centrally across a wide array of computer and network services.

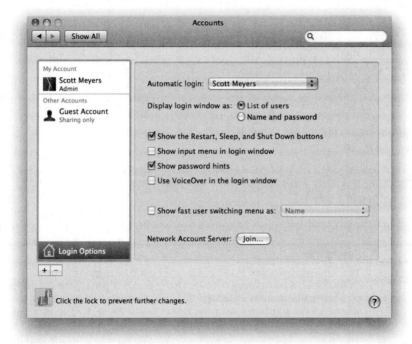

Figure 4-40. *Selecting Login Options from the bottom of the user list allows you to customize the login process.*

Adding New Users to Your System

To add a new user to your system from the Accounts preference pane, first make sure that the preferences are unlocked, and then click the + button at the bottom of the user list. This brings up a window (Figure 4-41) to enter the basic information for your new user.

Figure 4-41. *Information needed to add a new user*

This window requires some basic information. To the right of New Account is a drop-down menu prompting for what type of account you are creating. Options include the following:

Administrator: This grants users the ability to do just about anything they want on the system.

Standard: This allows users to work fairly normally on the system but won't let them do any tasks requiring administrator access.

Managed with Parental Controls: This allows the administrator to restrict users in various ways using parental controls (covered shortly).

Sharing Only: This only allows access for remote file sharing; these users cannot actually log in through the login window.

Group: This is a special option that, rather than creating a new user, creates a group that existing users can be part of. You can allow access to files, folders, applications, and other system services based on the groups a user belongs to.

After you select the account type, just enter the name of the account, the short name, the password (twice), and a password hint if you'd like. If you are having trouble coming up with a password, you can access a random password generator (Figure 4-42) by clicking the key icon.

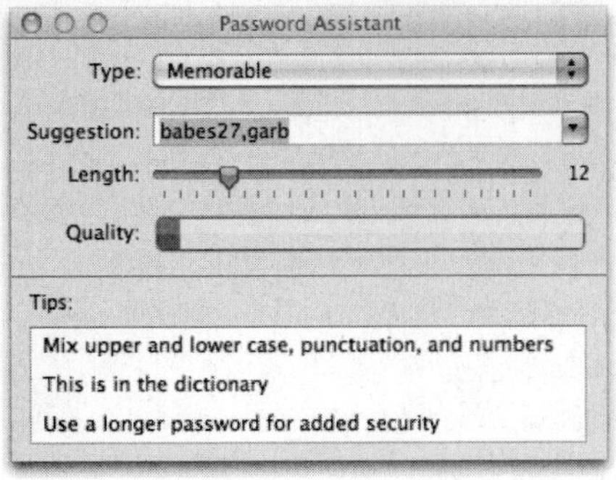

Figure 4-42. *Password Assistant helps you create a reasonably strong password for new accounts.*

■**Note** The short name, once selected, shouldn't be changed. For all practical purposes, the short name is your actual username for the system, and the name is just a familiar alias to it.

■**Note** As an administrator, if you Control-click any username in the Accounts preference pane and select Advanced Options…, an Advanced Options dialog will appear that will allow you to edit some user information used by the system. These options largely define user information that is stored in various system configuration files and provide basic information that is used throughout Mac OS X for many things, including file ownership and permissions. If you come from a UNIX/Linux background, many of these items may be familiar and even useful to you in some situations (especially when setting up special accounts). You can even change the short name (account name) here, but as the warning points out, this could damage the account.

If you set up multiple users, a Guest account will automatically be added to your user list. The Guest account is a limited account with its own options (Figure 4-43).

The Guest account can be configured in various ways. Selecting "Allow guests to log into this computer" allows guests to log in and use your computer as a sandbox of sorts. They will have access to most applications—however, all settings and files they create will be wiped out when they log off. "Allow guests to connect to shared folders" allows guests to access any shared folders on your system over the network. It's important to note that guests never need a password, so by allowing a guest access, you are essentially allowing anyone access to your system.

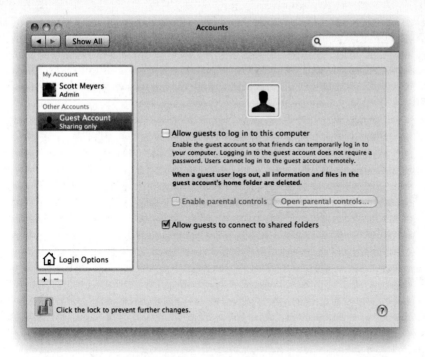

Figure 4-43. *Guest account options*

Date & Time

The Date & Time preference pane contains the system's date and time settings. These settings are broken up across three tabs: Date & Time, Time Zone, and Clock.

The Date & Time tab (Figure 4-44) simply allows you to either set the date and time of your system manually or set it automatically using one of Apple's timeservers. There are actually very few situations where you wouldn't want to set the time automatically (e.g., you have no Internet connection and thus the timeservers aren't available, or you want to fool your system into thinking the time is different than it actually is). If you choose to have the time set automatically, just select the closest Apple timeserver while connected to the Internet.

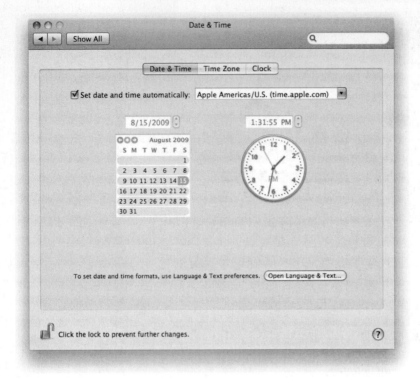

Figure 4-44. *The Date & Time tab of the Date & Time preference pane*

■**Note** There are other timeservers available besides the Apple timeservers that are listed. In fact, many organizations have their own timeserver on their network. You can utilize any available timeserver by entering its network address in the timeserver text field.

The Time Zone tab (Figure 4-45) allows you to select what time zone you are in. You can do this by entering or selecting a city from the Closest City drop-down menu/text field or by clicking your location on the minimap. It's important to accurately set your time zone, even if you are manually entering your date and time information—otherwise, you may get incorrect time information.

The Clock tab (Figure 4-46) provides a number of options that affect how the clock appears in your menu bar. There is a further option that causes your computer to speak out the current time at designated intervals. These options are fairly explicit and shouldn't need much elaboration.

Figure 4-45. *The Time Zone tab in the Date & Time preference pane*

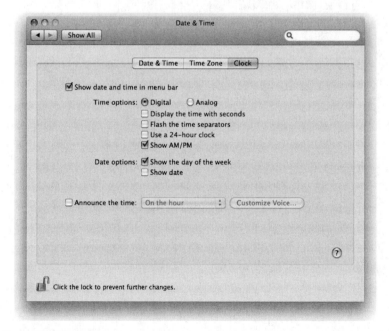

Figure 4-46. *The Clock tab in the Date & Time preference pane allows you to set options for the clock in the menu bar.*

Parental Controls

Parental controls allow an administrator to put in place a number of restrictions upon a user. These are generally thought of as a way for parents to limit the computing activities of their children but could be used in any situation in which you want to restrict or monitor a user's activity on the computer. The Parental Controls preference pane lets you tailor the controls for any user account that has parental controls enabled. To set the controls, first select the desired user from the user list (if the list is empty, then you have no accounts with parental controls enabled), and then work through the five tabs presented to configure them. The five tabs in the preference pane are System, Content, Mail & iChat, Time Limits, and Logs.

The System tab (Figure 4-47) provides options that control how a user can interact with the system itself. The Use Simple Finder option alters the Finder's appearance (Figure 4-48), removing many options and directories, and providing access only to a user's allowed applications and his or her documents. For old-school Macintosh users, this is similar to what At Ease used to provide.

Figure 4-47. *The Parental Controls preference pane with the System tab active*

Figure 4-48. *The Simple Finder*

The "Only allow selected applications" option allows access only to the applications (or groups of applications) selected in the following list. If you are using the Simple Finder, then only the selected applications will show up; otherwise, the user will be prompted for an administrator's password before launching an unselected application.

The remaining options, "Can administer printers," "Can burn CDs and DVDs," "Can change password," and "Can modify the Dock," are additional system actions you may choose whether to allow access to.

The Content tab (Figure 4-49) allows you to attempt to limit the content that the user has access to. The first selection limits access to words in the OS X dictionary. The Website Restrictions options offer three choices for attempting to manage web content:

Allow unrestricted access to websites: Does not block any web sites.

Try to limit access to adult websites automatically: Tries to filter out adult web sites using a variety of methods. While somewhat effective, this is not foolproof, and it may both block sites that you don't find objectionable and let some objectionable content through. The Customize button allows you to fine-tune this behavior a bit by manually entering acceptable and unacceptable web sites.

Allow access to only these websites: Allows you to specifically enter the addresses of acceptable web sites. Only those entered will be accessible. Obviously, this will likely block lots of valuable information, while at the same time this is really the only way to block objectionable content with some certainty.

Note Content filtering has proponents and detractors from both political and technical points of views. One of us is a parent of two who has mixed feelings about this sort of technology—currently we don't use any content filtering, but we reserve the right to change this if we notice the kids doing something that really concerns us. That said, these filtering technologies are not foolproof and should not be relied upon to protect your children or anyone else from unsavory elements of the Internet. The best advice we know of is to be honest with your kids about things they may encounter on the Internet, and explain what your values are and why. Most kids will get it.

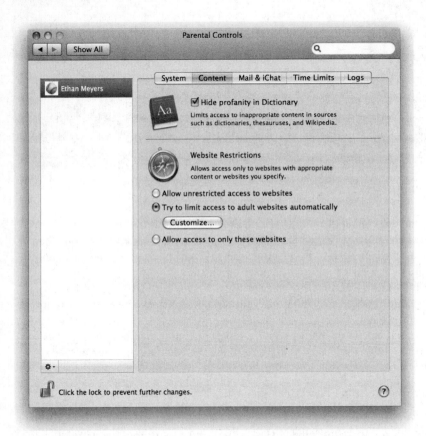

Figure 4-49. *The Content tab in the Parental Controls preference pane*

The Mail & iChat tab (Figure 4-50) allows you to specify addresses of select people who you allow the user to interact with through Mail and iChat. There is an option at the bottom that can be set to send a message to you every time the user attempts to contact someone who is not preapproved. This is a decent way to attempt to keep track of people who a user is interacting with online—however, this has no effect on web-based chats, or any other e-mail or messaging applications. As such, this is really only effective in combination with other controls.

Figure 4-50. *The Mail & iChat tab of the Parental Controls preference pane*

■**Note** While online content won't jump out of your computer and cause you any physical harm, people are a different thing altogether. It's important to discuss, especially with children, that people on the Internet are not always what they seem and are not all harmless. Personal information should not be shared with strangers, whether in chats, in e-mails, or on web sites. In our experience, knowledge and understanding are better at protecting our children and ourselves than depending on computer systems and blocking technologies.

The Time Limits tab (Figure 4-51) allows you to limit the time a user spends in front of the computer. It allows you to set daily limits for weekdays and weekends, as well as set specific times when the computer is off limits.

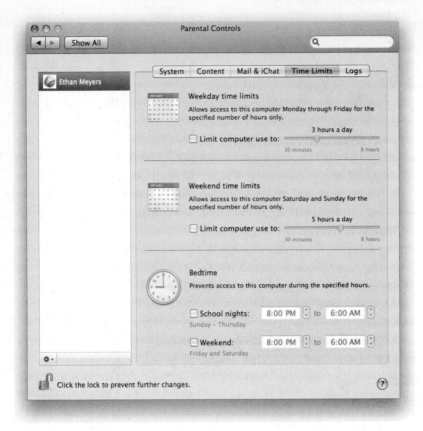

Figure 4-51. *The Time Limits tab in the Parental Controls preference pane*

Note You may have discovered from our previous notes that we're generally skeptical of most parental controls (especially the content-filtering stuff). This is because we've never seen one that worked well and couldn't be worked around by a clever kid wanting to break the rules (of course, maybe you actually want to train your kid to become a skilled hacker). That said, we think there is something to setting time limits. Seriously, there are days when we wish our computer would kick us out after a certain amount of time using it.

The Logs tab (Figure 4-52) provides an account of certain activities that a user is engaging in on the computer. If you are concerned that a user is up to no good, then this will often let you check. It's a little Big Brother–esque, yet sometimes it's the only way to know for sure. The Logs tab reveals what web sites a user is visiting (including ones that are blocked) and what applications are being used, and it keeps track of iChat chats.

Figure 4-52. *The Logs tab on the Parental Controls preference pane keeps track of a user's activities.*

Software Update

The Software Update preference pane (Figure 4-53) manages the Software Update features of Leopard. This allows you to set the frequency that updates are checked for automatically, and it also provides a Check Now button to check for new updates manually.

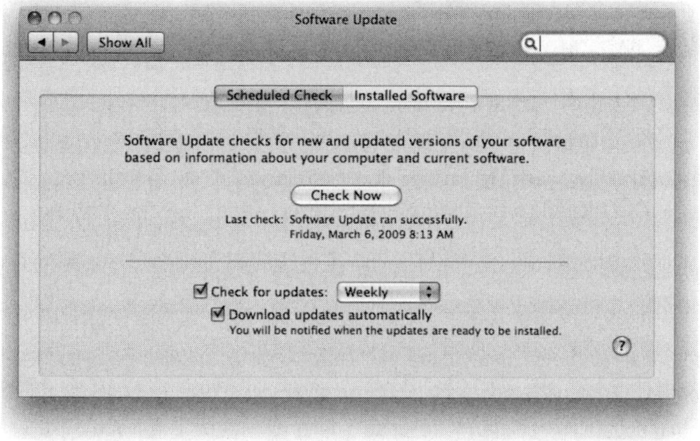

Figure 4-53. *The Software Update preference pane*

When you run Software Update (by clicking the Check Now button or using the Software Update item in the Apple menu), the Software Update window opens and checks for the availability of updated software. If updates are available, they will be listed in the window with a description of what the updates contain (Figure 4-54). To perform the updates, make sure the desired items are checked, and click the Install button in the lower-right corner of the window. This downloads and installs the updates. Certain system updates require authentication to install or require you to restart your computer to complete—in either of these cases, you will be prompted accordingly.

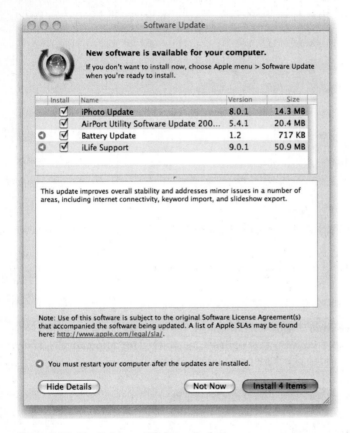

Figure 4-54. *The Software Update window*

The Installed Software tab of the Software Update preference pane lists all of your past software installs. Software Update tracks all the software listed here, but it's likely not all the software you have installed.

■Note If you have your Software Update preferences set to automatically check for updates (and you probably should), when new updates are found you will be presented with an abbreviated dialog box asking if you'd like to download and install that update immediately ("Continue"), later ("Not Now"), or if you'd like more info about the updates ("Show Detail").

Speech

The Speech preference pane contains two tabs: Speech Recognition, which contains options for responding to speech; and Text to Speech, which contains settings for controlling how the computer speaks back to you.

The Speech Recognition tab (Figure 4-55) contains settings that control how to set up the computer to receive and respond to speakable items. To enable this feature, you first must set the Speakable Items option to On. Once the Speakable Items option is switched on, a small, roundish floating window with a microphone in it will appear. This provides visual feedback for your speakable items. By default, to speak a command, first hold down the Esc key and then speak your command clearly into the microphone. If the computer accepts your command, it will carry out the command requested and provide you with acknowledgment as set up under the Upon Recognition setting. The Commands sub-tab provides a list of active command categories. Any time speech recognition is active, you click the small inverted triangle at the bottom of the small, round, hovering speech window, and select Open Speech Commands Window to view a list of available speech commands as well as a log of previous spoken actions.

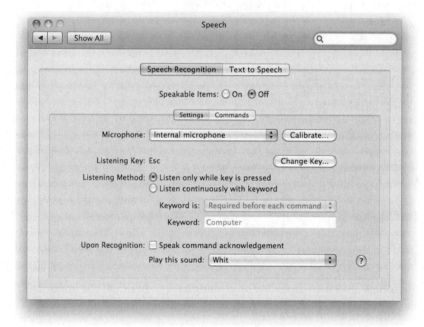

Figure 4-55. *The Speech Recognition tab contains settings that allow your computer to respond to spoken commands.*

■Note Apple speech recognition technology has been around for years and has progressively gotten better; however, our results have always been mixed. While we find this fun to play around with sometimes (the chess game included in Mac OS X responds to spoken commands), we don't find it particularly useful. Maybe we just have terrible voices. As they say, "Your mileage may vary."

The Text to Speech tab (Figure 4-56) controls how your computer speaks to you. Here you can change your computer's voice and the speed at which it talks. You can then set up options that will cause your computer to speak certain items:

Announce when alerts are displayed: Causes your computer to read any alerts that pop up

Announce when an application requires your attention: Causes your computer to tell you when an application is awaiting your input or has some message for you

Speak selected text when the key is pressed: Allows you to set a key that causes any selected text to be read back to you

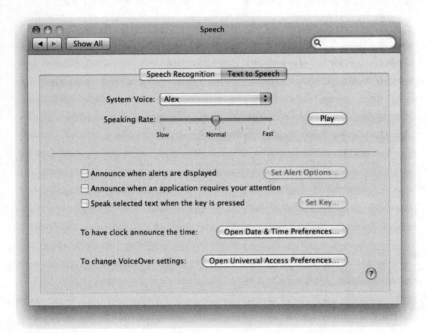

Figure 4-56. *The Text to Speech tab in the Speech preference pane*

Some applications have their own capability for reading back text as well. The important thing here is that the voice you pick on the Text to Speech tab will be the default voice used in all of the applications.

■**Note** Outside of some of the universal access uses of Text to Speech, this too tends to be more fun than useful. That said, speech has come a long way over the years—just compare the Fred voice (one of the original voices) to the Alex voice (a newer voice), and that's not even accounting for improvements in the underlying technology (of which there are many). (Zarvox, by the way, is still our favorite voice.)

Startup Disk

If you have multiple bootable volumes connected to your computer, the Startup Disk preference pane (Figure 4-57) will allow you to select which disk to default to when starting your computer.

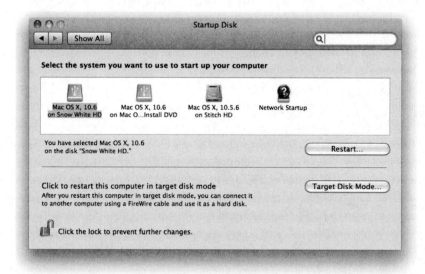

Figure 4-57. *The Startup Disk preference pane controls which bootable volume the computer uses by default when starting up.*

The startup disk selected here can always be overridden by special startup key commands (holding the Option key while starting your computer allows you to choose to boot from any connected bootable hard drive), unless you've set a firmware password (covered in Chapter 8).

One interesting option here is the Target Disk Mode... option. This allows you to set up your computer so that the next time it's started, you can connect to another Mac via a FireWire cable and use it as a hard drive. This is a handy option for copying files from one computer to another very quickly (this is covered in Chapter 20). (You can also boot your computer in Target Disk mode by holding the T key while starting your computer.)

Time Machine

Next is the Time Machine preference pane. This allows you to set up and configure Time Machine. (This is covered in Chapter 7.)

Universal Access

The Universal Access preference pane provides settings to assist people who have difficulty hearing, seeing, or otherwise working with their computer. This preference pane is divided into four tabs: Seeing, Hearing, Keyboard, and Mouse & Trackpad.

The Seeing tab (Figure 4-58) provides a number of options to assist people who have trouble seeing things on their computer screen.

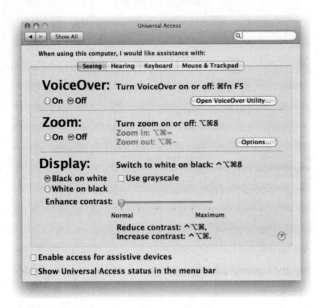

Figure 4-58. *The Seeing tab of the Universal Access preference pane*

VoiceOver, when activated, speaks out selected regions of the computer interface. First, it identifies the selected window, and then it allows you to tab through interface features, speaking the name of each as you tab through. VoiceOver itself has many options and can be fully customized via VoiceOver Utility (Figure 4-59), accessible in the /Applications/Utilities folder or by clicking the Open VoiceOver Utility… button in the preference pane.

■**Note** VoiceOver is a sophisticated piece of software, providing options for everything from minor audio assistance to full Braille output for the blind (and many options in between). VoiceOver Utility provides many options to customize this to whatever your needs are, and we encourage anyone needing this level of assistance to fully explore it.

Zoom allows you to zoom in and out of the screen. This is an extension of the zoom functions for the mouse and trackpad discussed earlier, but it provides a few additional options and methods of zooming.

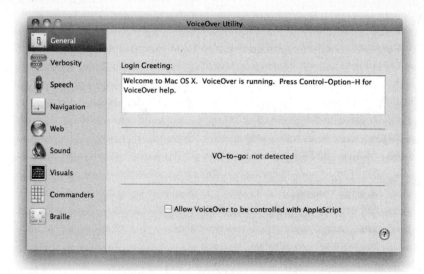

Figure 4-59. *VoiceOver Utility provides many options for customizing VoiceOver's capabilities.*

The Display section provides options that allow you to alter the display. This includes switching the display output to gray scale or color, adjusting the display's contrast, and even inverting the color scheme of the display (try Command-Option-Control-8).

The Hearing tab (Figure 4-60) provides a few options to aid people with hearing issues. The primary option here allows you to flash the screen when an alert occurs. This option can come in handy if you work in a very loud (or very quiet) environment.

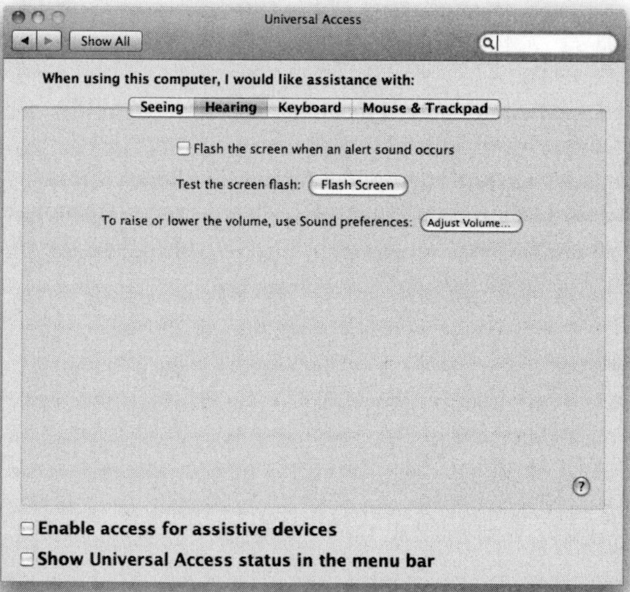

Figure 4-60. *The Hearing tab of the Universal Access preference pane*

The Keyboard tab (Figure 4-61) builds upon the keyboard options on the Keyboard & Mouse preference pane. Sticky Keys provides options for people who may have trouble holding multiple keys at once, so that they can more easily use keyboard combinations and shortcuts. The Slow Keys option helps the system ignore accidental key input.

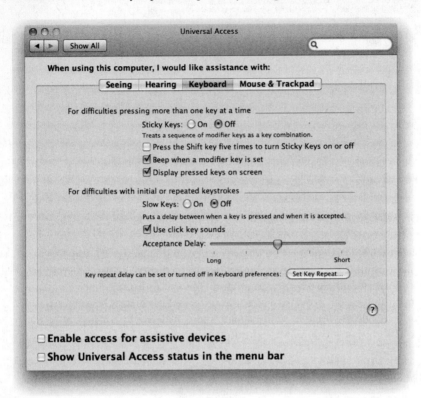

Figure 4-61. *The Keyboard tab provides some additional keyboard options.*

The Mouse & Trackpad tab (Figure 4-62) provides options for people who have trouble using the mouse or trackpad. Mouse Keys allows you to use the keyboard's keypad to move the cursor around on the screen instead of the mouse. There is also an option to increase the size of the mouse cursor so that it's easier to track on the screen.

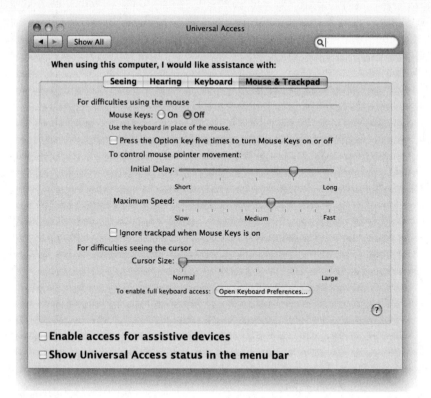

Figure 4-62. *The Mouse & Trackpad tab on the Universal Access preference pane adds additional mouse and trackpad options.*

Summary

We have covered a lot of ground in this chapter, and while we have saved a few things that need more elaboration than was possible here for later in the book, you have hopefully learned a number of ways to help set up your computer to work in a way that suits you. Next, as promised, we will look at connecting and using a range of external devices with your computer.

CHAPTER 5

■■■

Printing, Peripherals, and Bluetooth in Snow Leopard

Today more and more features are built into computers than ever before. Most new Macs (except the MacPro and Mac mini) include features such as stereo speakers, decent microphones, and even video cameras all built in and ready to use. Still, oftentimes you need something else or want to improve on what you already have in your computer. Luckily for you, a range of hardware devices exist that can work wonderfully with your Mac (commonly referred to as *peripherals*). Since you have a Mac, you just need to plug in most of these items, and they work (that is, they're plug and play, as it was intended). However, with the complexity and features available for some of these external devices, occasionally you need to do a little more to get the most out of them. Additionally, these days, many peripherals connect over a network or wirelessly, so rather than plugging something in, you often need to tell your computer to look for it. This chapter addresses all of this, including the following:

- Printing
- Bluetooth devices
- External storage
- Other external peripherals

Printing in Mac OS X

The world we live in is getting increasingly digital, and yet the paperless world isn't quite ready for primetime. Thus, sometimes you may need to resort to actually printing things. To do this, you need to connect to and configure a printer. You can connect your computer to your printer in a number of ways, ranging from physically through a USB cable to over a wireless network. If it's over a network, whether wireless or wired, many protocols (the ways that your computer talks to the printer) are available, and each handles printing a little differently. Luckily, Mac OS X makes all of this easy (or at least as easy as possible).

How "Print" Happens

In very general terms, when you hit the Print button in an application, a few things happen:

1. You are often presented with a Print dialog asking you to choose which connected printer you want to print to and what printing options (if any) you'd like to utilize. When you have made your selection, you click the Print button to print your document.

2. Once you hit Print, the printing system in Mac OS X (CUPS) takes your document and converts it to a language that your printer will understand. It does this using a translation file known as a *print filter*.

3. Once the file is translated, this translated file is put in a special block of memory called a *print spool* where the file is then streamed to your printer over whatever connection is being used.

4. The printer, as it receives this stream, usually starts printing the file as it receives it. Because your computer can usually feed information to your printer faster than it can print, a lot of communication is necessary between your printer and your computer to regulate the flow of information. If your printer runs out of memory (and many less expensive printers have very little to begin with) and your computer keeps sending the data, then data will get lost, and you'll end up with a garbled mess . . . not to worry, this rarely happens these days.

In a nutshell, that's it. It sounds like a lot of complicated stuff going on, and actually there is, but luckily for you, all you need to worry about is step 1 and occasionally adding more paper and ink/toner to your printer. Of course, before you can print, you need to set up your printer.

Setting Up a USB Printer

The most common printers, and the easiest to set up, are basic USB printers. In general, to set up a USB printer, plug in the printer power cord, and then plug in a USB cable from your printer into one of the USB ports on your computer. Unless your printer is a super-new model or a really strange off-brand, it's likely that's all you need to do. Your printer is ready to use. If in doubt, take a look in the Print & Fax pane of System Preferences (Figure 5-1); if you see the printer you just plugged in listed and correctly identified, you are good to go.

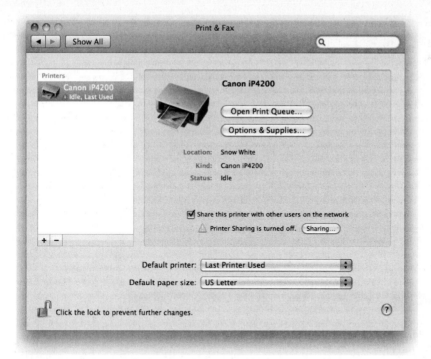

Figure 5-1. *The Print & Fax pane of System Preferences showing the Canon iP4200 printer we just plugged into a fresh Snow Leopard install; there's no need to add any drivers or software or anything.*

At this point, you may be skeptical that everything worked; in other words, that was too easy, right? You didn't even need to insert the CD that came with the printer. If you double-click the printer icon in the Print & Fax preference pane, the printer's Print Queue window (Figure 5-2) will open. This window provides information about your printer, including information about any documents currently printing or waiting to be printed (documents waiting in the print spool to be printed are called *print jobs*). If you want to test your printer, you can select the Printer ➤ Print Test Page command from the menu bar. If the test page prints, then all is well, and your printer is ready to use.

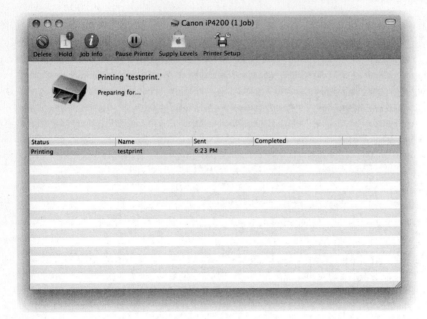

Figure 5-2. *The printer's Print Queue window provides information about a specific printer connected to your computer.*

So, what happens if things don't work or if your printer isn't recognized correctly when you plug it in? In this situation, you may need to install a driver for your printer.

Printer Drivers

The way printer drivers are handled in Snow Leopard has changed. When first you install Snow Leopard, by default it installs only a relatively small selection of printer drivers; they're mainly for USB printers that are currently attached, printers that were previously used by the old system (if upgrading), visible network printers using Bonjour, and a selection of drivers for the most common printers. If at a later date you attach or attempt to connect to a new printer for which the driver isn't installed, Snow Leopard will attempt to identify the printer and then automatically download the proper driver using the Software Update tool. In the rare case that this fails, you may need to go out to the printer manufacturer web site and see whether a Mac OS X driver is available for you to download and install.

Connecting to a Network Printer or Shared Printer

Printers in most companies as well as more and more homes are accessed through a network. These printers could be actual network printers, complete with network interfaces (either wired or wireless). Or they could be common USB printers attached to other computers on a network or a network print server (such as the ones built into Apple's AirPort and AirPort Express). The process of connecting to these printers ranges from almost as easy as connecting a USB printer to fairly easy if you know exactly what you are doing. We'll walk you through the general process using a real-life example of connecting to a networked Brother multifunction device (a fax/scanner/printer/copier).

The first step of adding a printer is to open the Print & Fax pane from System Preferences and click the + button at the bottom of the printer list. This opens a Printer Browser window (Figure 5-3).

Figure 5-3. *The Printer Browser window allows you browse and pick various types of printers to connect to.*

As we look in the browser, we see Brother HL-2040 listed, which happens to be the printer we want. When we select it in the list, our computer will try to find the name, location, and driver automatically. In this case, it succeeded (Figure 5-4).

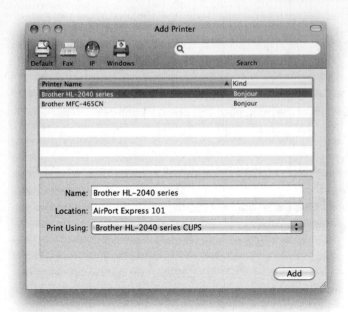

Figure 5-4. *After selecting the printer we want to add, Mac OS X automatically attempts to determine the name, location, and appropriate print driver.*

Note You may notice that the Location field is blank; this is because the printer is connected using Bonjour. *Bonjour* is a special networking technology (which is also known in some non-Apple circles as *zeroconf*) that allows systems on a network to identify themselves and the services they offer in a flexible way without a central name server. Since this allows the location to be dynamic, it is not listed.

If the print driver is not found automatically, then you will need to select an appropriate driver manually for the printer. To do this, click the Print Using drop-down menu, and there you should first try "Select a driver to use," which will provide a list of all the currently available print drivers. If your driver isn't listed but you have it on your system, you can select Other, which will open a standard Open dialog box for you to locate and open the appropriate driver.

When your printer is selected and set up with the proper driver, click the Add button, and your printer will be ready to use (Figure 5-5).

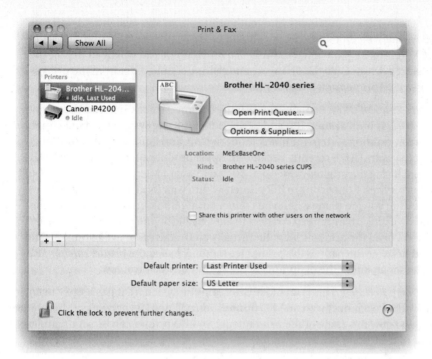

Figure 5-5. *Our newly added printer shown in the Print & Fax preference pane*

Ninety-nine percent of the time adding a printer is quite easy. But what about the other times—the times when your printer just doesn't get automatically recognized?

■**Note** There tends to be a few ways to think about network printers. Some printers broadcast their presence (such as Bonjour printers), and they usually just show up in the default options of the Printer Browser window. Other printers, like those that use Windows networking, are browsable; that is, you can navigate around the network to find available printers in the various Windows workgroups or domains. Finally, there are other types of network printers, and basically, you have to know where they are located on the network, and usually some more information about them, to connect to them.

When you are attempting to connect to a network printer at work or in a large computing environment or you are attempting to use a printer that is being shared by another computer, it might not just show up in the default printer listing in the Printer Browser window. When confronted with this situation, you need to find out what type of printer sharing is being used. The most common choice around homes and offices would be some sort of Windows printer sharing. Other less common network printer sharing protocols include the following:

Bluetooth: There just aren't that many Bluetooth printers available right now, but if you happen to have one, the Bluetooth printer should be easily discoverable from the Bluetooth System Preference pane if it's in range, at which point you will need to pair the device and select a driver. Only the discovery and pairing should differ from the process of connecting a USB printer or a Bonjour printer.

Internet Printer Protocol (IPP): Actually, this is fairly common since Common Unix Printing System (CUPS) is built around IPP and CUPS is the printing system used in Leopard and is the default printing system for many modern Unix and Linux systems. (Although an open source system, CUPS recently became an Apple product after acquiring the CUPS trademarks and hiring the original developer, Michael Sweet.) Microsoft also has IPP built into its printing services. Connecting to IPP printers within your local network is usually easy (in fact, that's what you are doing when you connect using Bonjour); however, occasionally the printer you are attempting to connect to isn't visible on the network, so in order to connect, you will need the printer's location (usually an IP address or even domain), and you may need to know the path to the printer (commonly called the *printer queue*). IPP printers can be set up under the IP options in the Printer Browser window.

Line Printer Daemon (LPD): This is an older Unix printing system that has largely been replaced by CUPS. To connect with an LPD printer, you will need its network address, and you will need to know the name of the print queue. An LPD printer can be set up under the IP options in the Printer Browser window.

Others: There is a handful of other, less common, mostly older, proprietary methods of connecting to a network printer. Leopard supports a number of these, including HP Jetdirect, Canon IJ Network, Epson FireWire, Epson TCP/IP, and HP IP Printing.

Note Some newer printers also have built-in Wi-Fi capability. In general, these printers, if set up properly, will appear just like any other network printer. As a bonus, since these printers are fairly new, almost all of them will use Bonjour, making connecting to the printer a snap.

If you are connecting to a Windows network printer (shared or otherwise), click the Windows button, and then browse through the network until you locate the printer you want. It's unlikely that a driver will be selected for you automatically, so you will need to select "Select a driver to use" from the Print Using menu. When you select the appropriate driver, click the Add button.

Printer Options and the Print Queue

Once a printer is set up and working properly, there isn't much you need to do, but some options are available to you in the Print & Fax preference pane. When you select a printer in the preference pane, the view area displays some brief information about your printer and also has one check box and three buttons. The "Share this printer with other users on the network" check box will allow you to share this printer with other users on your network (provided that printer sharing is enabled in the Sharing preference pane). If sharing is not yet configured, you can click the Sharing... button to take you to the sharing preferences to configure it. The other two buttons are the Open Print Queue button, which will open the print queue (just like double-clicking the printer icon), and the Options & Supplies button.

Clicking the Options & Supplies button will open a dialog providing three or four tabs (depending on the driver, there may or may not be a Utility tab), as shown in Figure 5-6. The General tab provides basic information about the printer and the driver. The Driver tab lists your current driver in a drop-down list and allows you to select a new driver if you want. The Supply Levels tab can show you how much ink or toner is left in your printer; however, this relies on a number of variables and may not work accurately (or at all). The Supplies button at the bottom of this tab will take you to a web site to buy more printer supplies. It's also possible that there will be a Utility tab that contains tools specific for you printer; this is dependent on the driver, though.

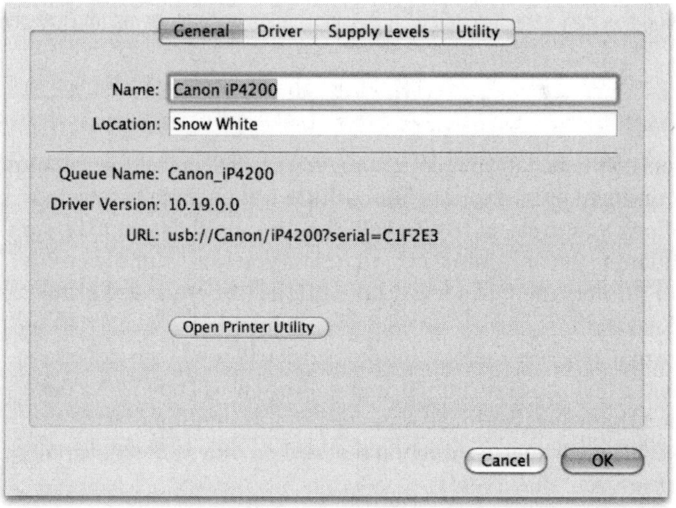

Figure 5-6. *The printer Options & Supplies dialog*

The Open Print Queue button will open the printer's print queue (shown earlier in Figure 5-2). As mentioned, this will provide information about what print jobs are being printed or waiting to be printed. This will also let you pause the printer, delete print jobs, and even rearrange the order of awaiting print jobs. The Supply Levels and Printer Setup buttons open the same dialog as the Options & Supplies button does.

In general, setting up a printer to work with your Mac is a fairly easy process. Even when it's not automatic, the features in Leopard tend to make it at least easier than may have been the case in the past (or is with other computer systems).

Printing from an Application

To use your printer, you usually just need to select File ➤ Print... from the menu bar (or press Command-P) in any standard application. This will open a standard print dialog box that walks you through the printing process. The default Print dialog (Figure 5-7) is simple, with only a few options.

Figure 5-7. *The simple default Print dialog box*

▌Note Some applications will open the Print dialog as an attached dialog box, while others will open it as a floating window. Also, the Print dialog box may vary depending on the application because some applications provide special printing options.

If you have multiple printers connected to your computer, you can select the one you want to print to from the Printer drop-down menu (your default printer will be initially selected for you). The Presets button allows you to select any preselected print options you may want to use. For most printers, Standard is the only initial option unless you save your own print options; however, many photo printers include a few other options (different size prints, borderless options, and so on).

Along the bottom of the Print dialog box are four buttons. Print will send your document to the printer. Cancel will close the dialog box without printing. Preview will open your document in the Preview application that will give you an onscreen representation of what the printed document will look like. PDF will open a submenu that will provide you with various options for creating a PDF file from your document.

▌Note All of Mac OS X's graphics are PDF based; as such, you will find that it can create a PDF out of any document from the Print dialog without any additional software.

For more options for your printing, you can extend the Print dialog by clicking the inverted-triangle button (the Disclosure button) to the right of the selected printer. This will provide many more printing options (Figure 5-8).

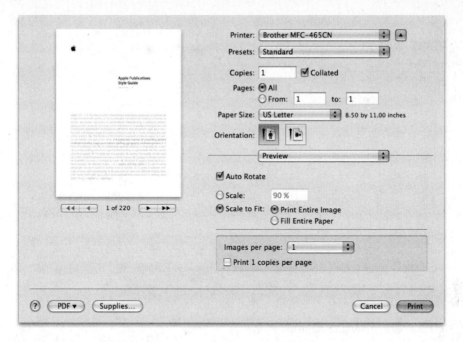

Figure 5-8. *An extended Print dialog box provides many more printing options, depending on the print driver and the application.*

The extended Print dialog provides a number of additional print options. The standard extended elements include a preview of the document, the ability to print multiple copies of the document, the ability to print only a range of pages rather than the entire document, the ability to adjust paper size and orientation, and the ability to scale the document up or down. However, numerous other options are available from the drop-down menu. This menu includes application options, options associated with your printer's features, color-matching options, advanced paper-handling options, scheduling options, fax options, and more.

Connecting Bluetooth Devices

Bluetooth is a technology that allows two devices, such as your mobile phone and your computer, to connect to each other. Unlike other common methods of doing this (USB and FireWire), Bluetooth does this wirelessly, and because of this, some additional work is necessary. The best place to begin connecting and setting up a Bluetooth device is from the Bluetooth preference pane in System Preferences (Figure 5-9).

Figure 5-9. *The Bluetooth preference pane, with no devices set up*

When no devices are set up, the preference pane will provide a Set Up New Device button right in the middle. There are various other areas in Snow Leopard where you can set up Bluetooth devices as well. When you begin to set up a new Bluetooth device, Snow Leopard will launch the Bluetooth Setup Assistant to help you through the process (Figure 5-10).

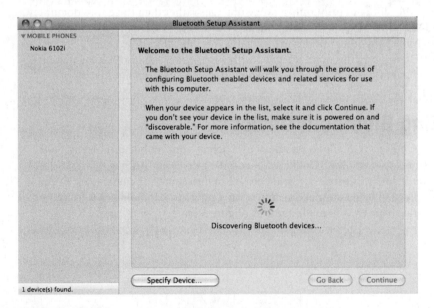

Figure 5-10. *The welcome screen of the Bluetooth Setup Assistant*

The first screen of the Bluetooth Setup Assistant is a welcome screen. Once the Bluetooth Setup Assistant launches, it will immediately begin scanning for any detectable Bluetooth devices. Any devices that are found will appear in the list in the left pane of the Bluetooth Setup Assistant window.

To continue setting up your device, simply select your device from the list and click Continue. If your device isn't recognized, make sure it is set up to be discoverable by other devices, and try again. Alternately, if you know the Bluetooth address of the device, you can click the Specify Device… button at the bottom of the window and manually enter the address there.

After you select your device and click Continue, the Bluetooth Setup Assistant will attempt to gather any information from your device to determine what services are available from your Bluetooth device. Once it has completed this, the assistant will walk you through pairing your device.

Note When the Bluetooth Setup Assistant first discovers a device, the initial name of the device may be a strange-looking string of digits. If you wait, this string will most likely become something a bit more familiar as the computer discovers more information about the device.

To pair your Bluetooth devices, you will usually be presented with a passkey to enter on your device (Figure 5-11), or alternately you will be prompted to enter a passkey that your device has generated. The theory behind passkeys is that since various types of information can be passed from one Bluetooth device to another, the connections between Bluetooth devices should occur only through paired devices. During the pairing process, each device must use the same passkey to assure a valid pairing. The complexity of the passkeys used to pair two devices tends to be consistent with the amount of risk involved with the pairing.

Figure 5-11. *Your computer provides a passkey to enter on your device; alternately, you may be prompted to enter a passkey that your device has generated.*

Note The default passkey for simple items such as headsets and mice is often 0000. The Bluetooth assistant, knowing this, will automatically attempt to pair with these devices using this passkey. If successful, the pairing will occur automatically, and you'll never need to enter a key. This also applies to most Bluetooth printers, which don't require a passkey at all.

Tip If you want to choose the passkey yourself, if you want to force pairings with no passkey at all (which is not recommended), or if the initial pairing didn't work (you have to be quick, because if the passcode isn't entered within a short period of time, the pairing will fail), a Passcode Options... button will appear. Clicking the button will open a dialog box (Figure 5-12), allowing you to choose many different options for selecting (or not selecting) a passcode.

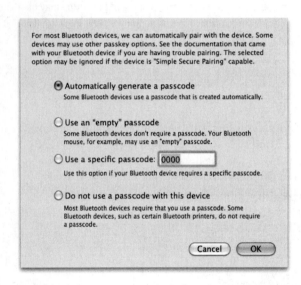

Figure 5-12. *The Passcode Options dialog box is available if the initial pairing is unsuccessful.*

Once the passkey is entered in to the appropriate device (if necessary), the assistant will continue making the connection, which results in a screen indicating that the pairing was successful (Figure 5-13).

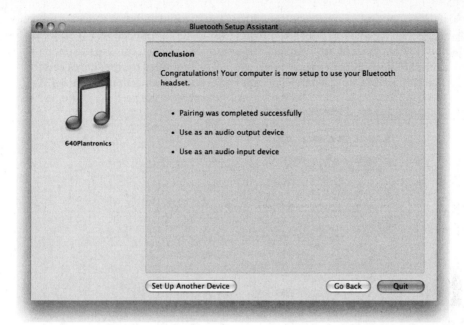

Figure 5-13. *Provided everything went well, you will be presented with a final screen indicating that the pairing was successful.*

Once you are done, when you take a look in your Bluetooth preference pane, you can see that it has changed to display your Bluetooth devices (Figure 5-14).

Figure 5-14. *The Bluetooth preference pane changes now that devices have been set up.*

Certain devices, once set up, may require additional configuration during the setup process to take advantage of all the features available through the Bluetooth connection. For example, certain Bluetooth phones can be *tethered*, or used as modems, so you can use the phone's network to connect to the Internet. In such a case you will be prompted to enter the necessary information that your mobile service providers requires for such a connection (Figure 5-15).

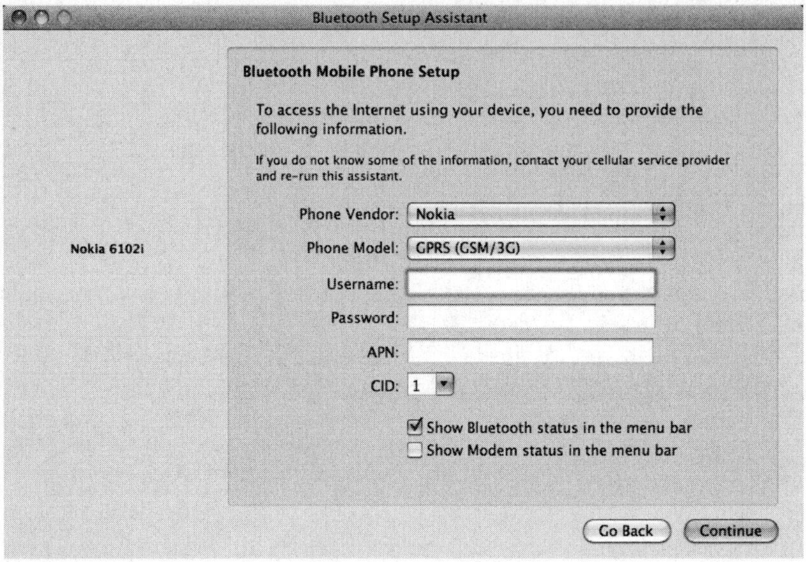

Figure 5-15. *Certain Bluetooth phones (not the iPhone as of yet) can be used as modems or "tethered" so that you can connect to the Internet using your mobile phone's network.*

Connecting External Storage

Ever since the advent of the floppy disk, and even the magnetic tapes before that, external storage has been a popular way of backing up and moving files, adding extra system storage, or even running entire operating systems. These days with the cost of large external hard drives dropping, the rampant use of thumb drives, and even media devices such as iPods being used for storage, this trend continues.

Like most things, connecting to external storage in Mac OS X is easy. In fact, you just plug in the external storage, and it shows up on your desktop alongside your primary hard drive and any other storage media you have connected to your computer. To remove it, you first tell your computer to "eject" the media and then unplug it. Still, a few things are worth knowing about: what the differences are between the different types of storage media and what all the available interfaces are and their advantages.

■**Caution** To eject media in Mac OS X, you can either select Eject from the item's contextual menu, click the Eject button next to the item in the Devices section of a Finder window, or drag it into the Trash (to name a few ways you can do it). It's important to do this before you unplug the device, especially with external hard drives. If you forget to "eject" the device and you just abruptly unplug the external storage device, you may have unplugged the device while it was still writing data, thus causing data loss and corruption.

Storage Media

The storage media is that actual mechanism that stores your data, of which there are three popular types: magnetic, optical, and flash.

Magnetic media includes hard drives, as well as tape drives and floppy drives. Today that primarily means hard drives, though high-end tape drives are still in use for large-scale backup and archive purposes by many organizations and institutions. Magnetic media is generally fast, is stable, can store very large amounts of data, and, these days, is relatively inexpensive. On the downside, it can be fragile and susceptible to damage from outside radiation and magnetism; it also isn't the most energy-efficient media, since moving parts are used in almost all cases.

Optical media includes CDs, DVDs, and an array of both newer, emerging and older, deprecated media types. Advantages of optical media include the cost of storage and the durability and flexibility of the media. Because of this, optical media is perhaps the best, cost-effective media for archival for most users. On the downside, optical media is traditionally slower in both reading and writing data, and most optical media is write-once media, meaning once the data is written, it can't be manipulated. There are today a number of rewritable optical formats; however, they tend to lose reliability after a number of rewrites. Optical media tend to require more power than other media types. Finally, although the technology exists (and is constantly under development) to increase the storage capabilities of optical media, the capacity is significantly less today than what is available with magnetic media.

Flash media is becoming more and more popular. Flash media is popular in many electronic devices for digital storage, including digital cameras, media players, iPods, mobile phones, PDAs, and more. It's also more and more popular as external computer storage for moving files from place to place with thumb drives. It's fast, durable (no moving parts to break), energy efficient (no moving parts, just shuffling electrons), and small. Despite all the advantages, it's expensive and limited in capacity; in addition, since it's newer, its long-term reliability is still in question. Still, technologically it has made the most gains of any storage media over the past few years. Capacity has increased, and costs have dropped dramatically.

Storage Interfaces

Besides the different types of storage media, several interfaces are available. When choosing an external storage device, it's important to pick one with an interface that will fit your needs. Table 5-1 lists the common interfaces.

Table 5-1. *External Storage Interfaces*

Interface	Description
USB	The USB interface is one of the most common interfaces, not only for storage but for many external peripherals. USB comes in three flavors (or versions really): USB 1.0, 1.1, and 2.0 (alternatively referred to as low speed, full speed, and high speed). These provide maximum data speeds of 1.5 Mbit/s, 12 Mbit/s, and 480 Mbit/s. (Note the "bit" part! There are 8 bits per byte, so USB 2.0 really provides speeds up to 60 MB/s, for example.) Most USB ports, as well as most USB storage devices today, provide USB 2.0, but you really should check to be sure. USB 1.1 is sufficient for smaller thumb drives, but for hard drives the performance would be excruciatingly slow. Also note that older PowerPC (PPC) Macs will not allow you to boot from a USB device. Finally, USB 2.0 ports and devices are backward compatible with older USB ports and devices.
FireWire 400 (IEEE 1934a)	FireWire 400, also known as IEEE 1934a and as i.Link by Sony, is a technology originally invented by Apple to provide an alternative to SCSI for high-speed data transmission. It was quickly adopted as a standard A/V interface for sending digital A/V data from one device to another (camcorder to computer). Because of its cost and simplicity, it's also quickly replaced SCSI as the external storage interface of choice for all but a few situations. FireWire 400 provides up to 400 Mbit/s transmission speeds, which in theory makes it similar to USB 2.0. However, FireWire, in the real world still tends to be faster than USB 2.0 devices, and it can support more devices on a single node than USB.
FireWire 800 (IEEE 1934b)	FireWire 800 doubles the performance of FireWire 400. The only issue with FireWire 800 is that while technically FireWire 800 is backward compatible with FireWire 400, they use different connectors, which makes the physical connection incompatible. So, although today only the new MacBooks, the MacBook Air and Mac minis lack FireWire 800, the original MacBook Pros and iMacs prior to the new aluminum ones didn't have it either. If you have FireWire 800, it's a great choice.
FibreChannel	FibreChannel connections are available as an option only on Mac Pros and Xserves, but they provide a blazing 4 GB/s transmission (for comparison, that would be 32,000 Mbit/s). This is used for Apple's discontinued Xserve RAID system and other high-end storage systems. It's awesome if you can afford it.
eSATA	External Serial ATA (eSATA) is a technology that extends the SATA bus for external use. SATA is what all new Macs use on the inside to connect hard drives. For external connections, though, although eSATA promises high-speed throughput of data. eSATA is not included with any current Mac, though expansion cards may be available.

The goal in choosing an interface is to pick the fastest one that provides what you want. If your new iMac supports FireWire 400, FireWire 800, and USB 2.0 but you also have an older iMac that supports only FireWire 400 and USB 1.1, then a FireWire 400 port may be the best common denominator (though you could get the FireWire 800 drive and buy a FireWire 800 ➤ 400 adapter to be prepared for your next computer). That said, there is recent uncertainty regarding the use of FireWire on many future Apple computers (for example, the newest MacBook's don't have FireWire of any kind, just USB 2.0), so to be safe, it may be best to get devices that support both FireWire and USB.

Note Many external hard drives available today will include multiple interfaces. This is nice for maximum performance and connectivity, especially if you have computers of various ages.

Note Many newer Apple computers don't have a FireWire 400 port at all; some rely on USB for all connections, and others come with just FireWire 800 connections. If you have FireWire 400 devices, there are relatively inexpensive adapters that will allow them to connect to FireWire 800 ports; however, these devices will not work with USB.

No matter what interface or media is being used, it's important to remember that as long as the interface on your device matches up with an interface on your computer, you are good to go.

Note When you get a new hard drive, you may want to partition or format it before you use it. We'll cover this in Chapter 6.

Connecting Other Peripherals

Besides printers, extra storage, and general Bluetooth devices, lots of other things are available to plug into your computer for various reasons. Although it's impossible to cover each possible device here, we'll end this chapter with some general advice as well as a few specific instances where something unique will happen that relates to Snow Leopard.

Whenever you connect a device to your computer, your computer must be able identify and communicate with the device. Most of the time your Mac OS X system will at least be able to identify the device; however, it may have no idea how to communicate with the device or how to make it work. A driver generally handles this communication process, and although Mac OS X ships with a large number of drivers and knows how to communicate with a large range of products, a large number of items will need you to install a driver for them to work correctly. Usually, any device you purchase will include not only any necessary drivers but also supporting software and instructions on how to get your device working with your computer.

Occasionally there will be a product that will work well without an additional driver but certain features won't work (common among certain multifeatured mice and keyboards). In such a situation it's up to you whether to install the manufacturer's driver; in general, if you bought something for the features, then you probably want them to all work.

Tip If you happen upon a really nice mouse with lots of features, yet you find the drivers provided with the mouse to be lacking, there are a couple of third-party mouse drivers that are extremely flexible and that work with a large number of different brand of mice. My personal favorite is SteerMouse available from http://plentycom.jp/en/steermouse/.

The following types of devices generally require a driver to function properly:

- Scanners
- Input tablets
- Audio/MIDI interfaces and controllers
- Screen calibration devices
- Multifunction mice and keyboards
- Certain video interfaces
- Some printers

On the other hand, a large number of devices should work immediately after plugging them in (though some configuration or special software may be needed to do much with them):

- Digital cameras
- Video camcorders with a FireWire link
- Most Apple hardware
- Speakers and microphones (including USB headsets)
- Some USB/MIDI keyboards and adapters
- Storage devices
- Many standard mice and keyboards (including multibutton mice with a scroll wheel)
- Many printers

Occasionally some special action occurs when you connect a particular type of device.

Digital Cameras

Mac OS X has always recognized every digital camera we've ever plugged in. What you need to decide, however, is how you would like your computer to respond when you attach a digital camera. In Snow Leopard the standard application for dealing with importing images, Image Capture, has changed, and so has the default behavior when you plug in your camera. In Snow Leopard, when you first plug in your camera, your camera will mount as a new drive on the desktop, and that's it (unless you have already set a preference in some other application such as iPhoto to open automatically when camera is attached)! If you don't have iLife and thus iPhoto, you can browse and download the images on your camera using Image Capture (Figure 5-16). Image Capture provides an easy way to preview and download images from your camera to your computer (by default it will download images to your Pictures folder.)

■**Note** The new version of Image Capture that ships with Snow Leopard has a new streamlined interface and is very easy for most people to figure out with just a quick glance. After all, its only purpose is to facilitate the transfer of images from your camera (or in some cases a scanner or other imaging device) to your computer. One notable omission with the new version of Image Capture, however, is that ability to launch an application or script after it's done downloading the images. This seems to be another case of ease of use trumping useful (but occasionally confusing) features (like with iMovie '08).

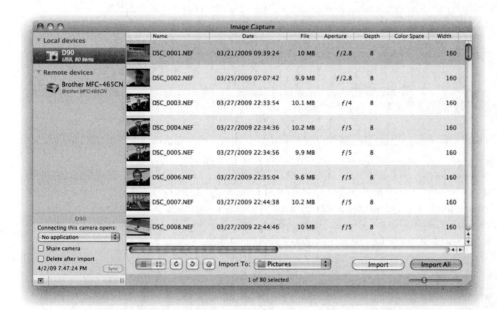

Figure 5-16. *The Image Capture application is a standard part of Mac OS X and is always available for importing images from a digital camera.*

■**Note** You can also use Image Capture to import images from devices other than cameras. In fact, in Snow Leopard, you can use Image Capture to import images from a wide range of scanners without installing any additional software or drivers (Figure 5-17).

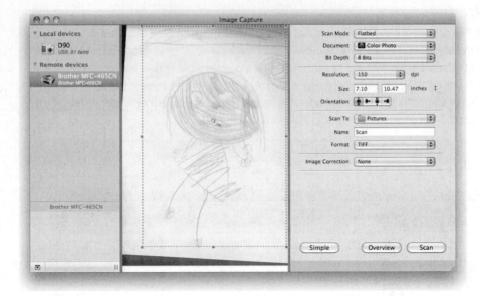

Figure 5-17. *The Image Capture application also provides basic scanning tools for supported scaners.*

If you've installed iPhoto (Figure 5-18) or Aperture, you can choose to have these automatically launch to import images when you connect your camera. (In fact, when you first launch iPhoto '09, it will ask you whether you would like to do this. If iPhoto is your primary image application, then it's probably a good idea to do this.)

Figure 5-18. *If installed, iPhoto can also be used to import images from your digital camera.*

What you do with your images once they are imported is entirely up to you, though we will talk a bit about iPhoto '09 later in this book.

Input Tablets

Input tablets are another interesting input device, although they're generally used by graphic designers and artists with graphic applications. When you plug an input tablet into your Mac OS X computer, you will find that a new preference pane appears in System Preferences: Ink.

The Ink preference pane (Figure 5-19) provides options for the Inkwell feature introduced in Tiger (Mac OS X 10.4). Inkwell is a handwriting recognition technology that allows you to write text with your input tablet, which the computer will then (attempt to) convert into editable type:

this is an example oftext entered withinkwell .

As you can see, it's still not perfect (though it does get significantly better with each release), but it's fun to play around with (and your handwriting may be better than ours).

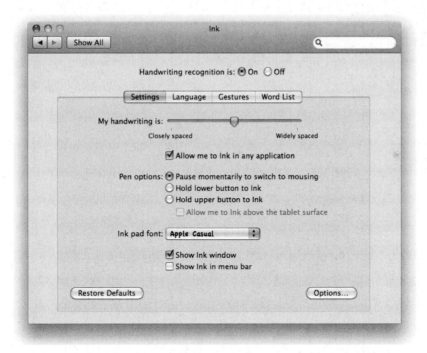

Figure 5-19. *The Ink preference pane appears when you have an input tablet connected to your computer.*

Note The Inkwell preference will not work until the proper driver is installed for your input tablet and the tablet is plugged in.

Summary

Now you shouldn't have too much trouble getting any external peripheral to work with your Mac (provided it was designed to work with your Mac . . . getting non-Mac-compatible devices to work goes beyond the scope of this book). Next we will move on to some general administration tasks for Snow Leopard.

■Note A number of devices that don't make claims to work with a Mac will in fact work just fine, so if you have something laying around, give it a shot.

CHAPTER 6

∎∎∎

Common Mac OS X Maintenance

Mac OS X tends to do a pretty good job of taking care of itself; however, there are a few things that occasionally need attention or that Mac OS X leaves up to you to take care of. The issues that we will cover in this chapter include the following:

- Disk setup and maintenance
- Application management
- Font management

Disk Setup and Maintenance

▌Note The most important thing about hard disks is that they will all fail in time. Sometimes it is a slow death where they start making a loud clicking that gets progressively worse until they just stop working; other times there is no warning. If you want to keep your data, back it up. Buy an external hard drive (or two) and use Time Machine or some other utility. Really. As the saying goes, "Pay now or pay more later."

Hard drives—both the primary hard drive that came in your computer and any extras, either internal or external—are an essential part of your computer. If things go wrong with a hard drive, your system may stop functioning, or more importantly, you may lose data. Luckily, apart from the very real worry that your hard drive may (and someday will) eventually physically stop working, Mac OS X tends to take care of things on your drive, limiting the amount of routine maintenance needed to keep your file system and hard drive (and thus your data) healthy. Still, occasionally there are routines that you may want to run to verify that everything is OK. Additionally, someday you may want to format, partition, or utilize a specific file system on one of the hard drives connected to your system. To manage your hard drives and take care of all these functions, Mac OS X includes the Disk Utility application (located in /Applications/Utilities/).

■**Note** Two primary things can go wrong on a disk: there's physical damage, which is when the disk mechanism fails and possibly crashes, and there's file system damage, which is when the data on your disk gets mixed up or damaged. Tools like Disk Utility can often detect and repair file system damage before it causes data loss. Physical damage to the disk is more permanent and often irreparable (although in some cases the data can be recovered by special hardware and/or software).

■**Note** The term *disk crash* refers to the event when the arms that pass over the disk surface to read the data fall and literally crash into the disk's surface, causing irreparable damage. This used to happen with older disk mechanisms that would rely on the air force of the spinning disk to keep the arms up, so if the disks quit spinning suddenly before the arms could move back off the disk's surface (e.g., in a power failure), the arms would fall. Disk crashes like this don't happen with today's hard drives, but mechanical issues still arise, and disks do get old and eventually wear out (usually after years of service, though).

Disk Utility divides its abilities into five panes: First Aid, Erase, Partition, RAID, and Restore. First Aid provides a couple of general maintenance tools that can help identify and repair both file system damage and issues in which the system's file permissions become altered. The Erase tab provides the necessary tools to partition and format a disk using various supported file systems. The Partition option appears if you select an entire disk, rather than just a volume in the list of devices on the left. The Partition tab allows you to split a single disk into multiple volumes (or create a single volume from multiple volumes). The RAID tab allows you to configure multiple disks to behave as one in various ways. The Restore tab lets you restore a disk image onto a disk. We'll cover each of these in the following sections.

■**Note** A disk is a physical device, whereas a volume is a file system written to a disk. The physical space on a disk can be divided up into different volumes (or even left as empty space). These divisions are referred to as *disk partitions*.

Performing First Aid

The First Aid tab (Figure 6-1) allows you to run a few tasks to help identify and fix certain problems with your disk's file system. If you seem to be having issues with your disk or notice anything unusual about how it's running or storing data, this is the first place to go to try to solve the problem.

Figure 6-1. *Mac OS X's Disk Utility repairing permissions on a volume using one of the First Aid tools*

In the lower-right corner are two buttons: Verify Disk and Repair Disk. Clicking Repair Disk will scan the disk to identify and repair many common file system errors. Although most of the errors it may find are in themselves minor, they can often cause bigger issues down the road. One gotcha here is that you can't repair the boot volume—you can, however, click the Verify Disk button to see whether there are any problems with it, and if so, you can utilize the Repair Disk function from the Disk Utility application included with your Snow Leopard install DVD. Just boot from your install DVD and run Disk Utility using the Utilities ➤ Disk Utility… command from the menu bar (you may need to quit the installer to access this—don't, however, start a new install unless things are really hopeless). On occasion, the Repair utility will come across an issue it cannot repair. At this point, you have two primary options (well, three if you are the type of person who can just ignore a problem until it's too late). Before you decide what you want to do, you should first make backup copies of everything you value on your hard drive. Even if you already have a copy, make another one. (We've had a primary disk and a backup disk fail simultaneously, and it was not a happy moment. Luckily, we had another backup and lost only about a month of work; now we use a mirrored RAID so we don't lose any data if a drive fails.) Once that's done, you can do either of the following:

- *Erase, reformat, and reinstall everything on your disk*: This option takes a long time and will likely cause a few frustrating moments—and nothing will ever be quite the same. However, it should fix any file system problem, plus it can clean out some other gunk that can creep into your computer as you use it over a long period of time.

- *Purchase and try some other disk utility software*: There are three very good, easily obtainable disk utilities out there for Macs: TechTool Pro by Micromat (`www.micromat.com/`), DiskWarrior by Alsoft (`www.alsoft.com/DiskWarrior/`), and Drive Genius by Prosoft (`http://prosofteng.com/products/drive_genius.php`). Each of these come on a bootable CD or DVD (you can even get a special bootable thumb drive with TechTool Pro), so you can boot them up and use them right away. The downside it that any of these will set you back about $100 (at least).

Note Before you break out that checkbook, check whether you got AppleCare with your new computer (you did, didn't you?). If so, check the box it came with—inside is a CD with a special version of TechTool. It doesn't have all the features of the Pro version, but it might solve your problem, and at the very least, you can use this version to save some money when upgrading to the full Pro version ($59 vs. $98 on the web site).

So, what happens if nothing works? Sadly, in that case it may be time to replace your hard drive. If it's your original internal hard drive and your computer is covered under warranty or AppleCare, you should be taken care of. Otherwise, you'll either have to order a new hard drive and install it yourself (easy with a Mac Pro; not so easy, but doable, with a portable or an iMac) or have to take it in and have someone else do it (a nearby Apple Store is a good choice, or ask around . . . just make sure if you pay someone to do it that they are Apple certified).

Note You may wonder whether replacing a hard drive in your computer will void the warranty or interfere with Apple Care. The answer is no. However, especially with Apple portables, it's not a trivial task, and the hard drives are often tucked in close to other components. If you are not careful, you could cause some collateral damage that would void your warranty. Also, we should mention that the replacement drive (or any damage it may cause, however unlikely) will not be covered under your warranty (though it may come with its own).

The other pair of buttons on the First Aid tab, Verify Disk Permissions and Repair Disk Permissions, do what they say. In OS X, each item in your system has a set of permissions that determine who can do what with the item and, in return, what that item can do (you can find a deeper look at Unix-style permissions in Chapter 17). Occasionally, for a variety of reasons, permissions get changed, and sometimes this causes applications to behave poorly or not work at all. In such a case, setting the permissions back to their defaults usually fixes the problem. To do this, just run Repair Disk Permissions and see whether that fixes the problem.

■**Note** The Repair Disk Permissions option resets the permissions of certain Apple software back to its original state. This can cure some runtime issues that occur when an application can't complete a task because of insufficient permissions. We've never seen this fix anything; however, especially in the early days of Mac OS X, there is evidence that it has successfully fixed some issues. It's a fairly painless exercise, so if you are having issues, it's worth a try. It could just be the magic you need to solve your problem.

Erasing and Formatting a Volume

The Erase tab (Figure 6-2) allows you to erase all or part of a disk.

Figure 6-2. *The Disk Utility's Erase tab lets you erase and format disk volumes.*

You will use this in the following scenarios:

- If you just want to zap all the data on your disk and start over
- If you want to change how a disk is formatted
- If you actually want to wipe the data on your hard drive clean

In the case of the first two scenarios, you basically do the same thing: choose a format from the Volume Format list (formats are explained in a moment), choose a name for your new volume, and click the Erase button. This effectively reformats your drive. A simple format, however, does not actually erase your disk; it just erases the existing directory information. With the directory information cleared, your computer has no record of anything stored on it, so it just assumes it's empty and starts writing over old content, keeping track of the new directory information.

If you want to actually erase the content on your hard drive so it cannot be recovered, you have two options. If you just want to assure that any files you have deleted in the trash are actually gone, then you can use the Erase Free Space button. If you want to assure that the entire volume is erased when you format it, click the Security Options button prior to formatting it. Each of these buttons will allow you to choose between three different modes: zero out, 7-pass, or 35-pass of data. Each additional pass will assure that the data will be unrecoverable; however, it will also add a significant amount of time to the process (7 or 35 times the amount of time, to be specific).

Partitioning a Disk

Partitioning a disk is a similar process to formatting a volume; however, it allows you to create and format multiple volumes on the same disk at the same time. The Partition option (Figure 6-3) appears when you select a disk from the list at the left.

Figure 6-3. *The Partition tab allows you to create and format multiple volumes on a single disk.*

To partition a disk, first select the number of partitions you'd like to create on the disk from the Volume Scheme drop-down list. This will split the disk into the chosen number of partitions, each with approximately an equal size. To resize partitions, simply drag the separator between two partitions in the visual disk partition view below the Volume Scheme menu, thus shrinking one while increasing the size of the other. Alternately, you can select a partition and enter a size in the Size text field to the right (this will also change the size of surrounding partitions). When you have your partition sizes correct, you may enter a volume name in the Name field and choose a file system from the Volume Format list. If you are sure you are ready, click the Apply button, and your selected partitions will be created and formatted as you selected.

Note The file system you choose to install on a partition determines some of the types and capabilities of the systems that can be run on them. This is especially true when it comes to booting the computer. For example, through fancy software like VMware Fusion or Parallels, you can run Windows on an HFS partition, but you can only boot your computer into Windows (via Boot Camp) from an MS-DOS or NTFS-formatted partition.

The various file systems available in the format fields are the following:

- *Mac OS Extended (Journaled)*: This is Mac OS X's current default file system (HFSJ or HFS+ Journaled).

Note Journaled partitions keep track of what the disk is doing at all times. In the event that a disk transaction fails, a journaled partition may be able to piece together what was going on when the failure occurred so you don't lose any data.

- *Mac OS Extended*: This is Apple's previous default file system (HFS+).
- *Mac OS Extended (Case-Sensitive, Journaled)*: This is the same as HFSJ, but it adds case sensitivity to the file system (so, for example, *Apple* and *apple* would be recognized differently in the file system).

Note Although case sensitivity sounds like a good thing, it's not always. It can make certain applications and computer functions behave poorly and therefore should be used only in situations where it's essential. The normal HFS+ file system, while it ignores case, preserves it, and that is generally sufficient, even in cases where case is important.

- *Mac OS Extended (Case-Sensitive)*: This is the same as HFS+ with added case sensitivity.

- *MS-DOS*: This will use the FAT32 format, which is useful if you intend to physically share the volume with Windows systems.

- *Free Space*: This will leave the partition empty and unusable until you reformat it later.

There are some additional file systems that are possible to utilize; however, at this stage they are considered experimental.

Resizing Partitions

One other feature that Disk Utility recently added is the ability to resize partitions. To shrink an existing partition, grab the lower-right corner of the partition in the Partition pane of the Disk Utility, and drag it to the new desired size (or use the Size text field to enter the new size). When you click Apply, the partition will be resized, creating empty space on the drive for a new partition or for expanding an existing one. To increase the size of a partition, you can use the same technique, but instead of making the existing partition smaller, you can grow it into adjacent empty space.

While doing this, keep the following in mind:

- You can shrink only a partition's unused space, so if you have 2GB of data on a 3GB partition, you'll be able to reclaim (at most) 1GB of disk space.

- You can grow a partition only into empty disk space that is physically adjacent to the partition you want to grow.

- This isn't magic, and it won't create new space that didn't exist. Often the only way to effectively repartition a disk is to erase the existing ones. Still, in some situations, this is exactly what you need.

Using RAID

The RAID tab (Figure 6-4) allows you to configure multiple hard drives into a single volume (or RAID set name).

Figure 6-4. *The RAID tab allows you to combine multiple hard drives into a single volume.*

Disk Utility allows you to create three different types of RAID configurations:

- *Mirrored RAID set (a.k.a. RAID 1)*: This will configure two hard drives of the exact same size in a mirrored array. This means that any data you store on the resulting volume will be physically stored separately on each drive, thus assuring that the data will be safe in the event that one of the drives fails.

- *Striped RAID set (a.k.a. RAID 0)*: This option will take two hard drives of the exact same size and combine them into one larger volume (equal to the size of both of them together). It will do this in such a way that alternating data is fed to each physical drive (i.e., *striping*), thus greatly increasing overall disk read and write speeds. This is very popular with people who work with large amounts of data and large media files. On the downside, if either drive fails, it will be difficult to recover any data from either drive.

- *Concatenated disk set*: This will take any number of hard drives and combine them into a single volume spanning all the drives.

Besides these options, there are many other types of RAID configurations that are possible using third-party software or hardware. Many external drive enclosures that support multiple drives include hardware that makes different types of RAID configurations much more efficient.

■**Note** The RAIDs created in Disk Utility are *software* RAIDs. In this case, Mac OS X does the work in the background to accomplish the desired effect. Although this is highly effective, it's not as effective as a *hardware*-based RAID where the device in question has dedicated resources to create and manage the RAID.

■**Note** Hardware-based RAIDs, though they are physically separate volumes, will many times appear as a single volume even in Disk Utility. Most software-based RAIDs, on the other hand, will show up as different devices in Disk Utility, even though they will appear as a single volume in the Finder.

Creating and Restoring Disk Images

A popular way of transmitting large files or applications from one computer to another, especially over a network, is to create a disk image. A disk image is essentially an archive of a disk volume that can be mounted like a disk. You can create a disk image using the Disk Utility application in a number of ways. If you know you want to create a disk image of a certain size, you can click the New Image button on Disk Utility's toolbar (or select File ➤ New ➤ Blank Disk Image… from the menu bar or use the Option-Command-N shortcut). This will open a dialog box that allows you to name the image file, name the volume that the image file will expand into, and choose the size of the volume. Once you've filled out the information in the dialog box, click Create, and the system will create and mount the image. At this point, the image is writable, so you can copy any data you want to this image. When you unmount the disk, the data is still stored in the image file, so when you remount it, it will be available. The other way to create a disk image is from an existing folder. To create an image this way, use the File ➤ New ➤ Disk Image From Folder… command from the menu bar (Shift-Command-N). This will open a dialog for you to select a folder. Once you select the desired folder, click the Image button, and a new dialog box will pop up asking you where to save the new image along with some other options.

■**Note** If you select one of the encryption methods for your disk image, you will be prompted to create a password to decrypt the image before it is created. You will be prompted for this password before you can mount or restore this image file. If you forget it, your data will be lost.

■**Tip** If you work with sensitive data, you can create a secure disk image containing this data and mount the disk when you need to work with the data. Then you can unmount the image when you are done with it, returning the data into a state of blissful encryption.

Clicking an image file will mount it to your desktop (you may need to enter the password for an encrypted image file first). Occasionally you may want to restore an image file to a disk or a partition. The Restore tab (Figure 6-5) allows you to re-create the image file onto a disk volume simply by selecting a disk image, selecting an available volume that the image will fit in, and then clicking the Restore button. You should be aware that this will often overwrite the destination volume entirely.

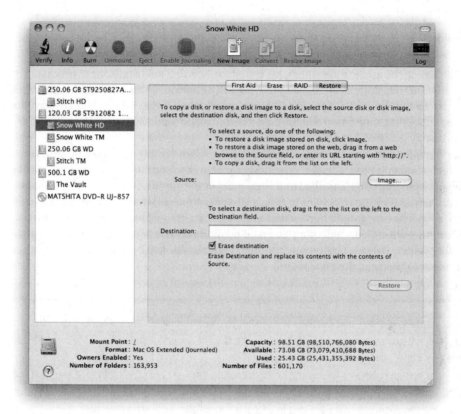

Figure 6-5. *The Restore tab allows you to restore a disk image to a disk volume.*

Burning an Image File to a CD or DVD

Certain disk images are actually images of CDs or DVDs, and as such, they (or any other appropriately sized image file) can, rather than be restored to a disk volume, be burned to a CD or DVD. To accomplish this, select Images ➤ Burn from the Disk Utility menu (or use the Command-B keyboard shortcut). This will first prompt you to select the appropriate image file from the standard open dialog, and then it will prompt you to insert the appropriate writable disk into your disk burner. It will then burn the image to disk.

Managing Applications

A computer without applications is like a car without tires—you can turn it on, but you can't go anywhere. As far as managing applications, there are three primary tasks that may require some thought: installing, updating, and removing them. Although none of them is complicated, there tends to be different ways of doing each of these, and there are some extra things to look for when doing them.

Installing

Generally there are two ways that applications are installed on your computer: either by dragging and dropping the applications into your system or by using an installer application.

You can install most simple apps just by moving them into your system (for a disk or mounted disk image) or by simply downloading and uncompressing them. There really couldn't be anything easier—just move that application where you'd like it (usually somewhere in the Applications folder), and use it.

Other applications come with an installer, which when double-clicked will walk you through the installation process, often providing you with some options as to where you'd like the application (and its parts) installed and what parts of the application you'd like to install. In general, there is nothing tricky about this, and often it makes what could be a complex task really easy. The one gotcha here is that often an installer will install more than just the application—other items will often be installed along with it in places other than your Applications folder. This isn't inherently bad, but it is something to consider (especially when the time comes to uninstall the application).

Note Occasionally, updaters and installers will prompt you for an administrator's password to install an application. This is usually when the application has to install some support items in the /Library folder or somewhere else where privileges are necessary to install items. (If you aren't an administrator, that's pretty much the entire system outside of your home folder, including the Applications folder). If you trust the source of the application, then you should have no worries; however, if you are not sure about the source of what you are installing, it might be a good idea to cancel the installation until you know more.

One thing to think about when installing an application is exactly where you want it. As mentioned, it's likely that you will want to install most of your applications in the Applications folder, but if you have lots of applications, it's not uncommon to create a number of subfolders in your Applications folder for certain types of applications. For example, you may want to put all of your graphics applications in one folder and all of your Internet applications in another. This organization is entirely up to you; Mac OS X should have no problem running an application wherever you install it. Since Mac OS X doesn't care too much where the application is, occasionally you may want to install an application elsewhere. It's not uncommon to keep a few personal applications somewhere in your home folder, and this is perfectly fine.

■**Caution** Although Mac OS X doesn't care where an application is installed, it possible that some other application does. For this reason, if you plan on moving an application from its default location, it's a good idea to keep in mind where it started should some issues arise.

Updating

Like everything else in the computer industry, things are always changing, including the applications you use every day. For this reason, you will likely have to update them from time to time. There are different methods of updating applications that closely mirror the installation options. Sometimes, you just download an updated application and drag it into the same folder as the older version. This will usually cause the Finder to pop up a dialog that says that you are about to replace an older item with a newer one and asks you whether this is OK (Figure 6-6). In this case, just click Replace if you'd like to continue.

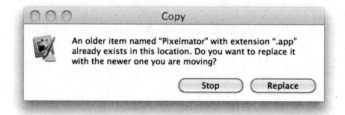

Figure 6-6. *A dialog box warning you that you are about to replace an older item with a new one*

Other times you may need to use an updater application to update an application (you'll usually use these if you used an installer in the first place). An updater will search your system for the older version of the application and then update it.

■**Note** For whatever reason (usually lazy programmers), certain updaters will not seek out the proper location of older versions of applications and will instead install the update files where they assume the program to be (usually in the top level of the Applications folder). This may even create a new application item that contains only half the application (the new half), resulting in two items claiming to be the application: one broken and one outdated. The only fix for this is to delete the new item, move the original item where the installer thinks it should be, and then rerun the installer. Or at worst, delete everything, reinstall the original application, and then update it.

These days, many applications will include their own update functions that will either allow you to check for updates yourself or even notify automatically if a new update is available, at which point it can automatically download and install the update on its own.

One other method of updating applications (and the system) is Apple's Software Update function. This will automatically check for updates and install them for most Apple-branded software (including system updates). Setting up and running Software Update is covered in Chapter 4.

■**Note** Where do you look for software updates? Some applications have options that will allow the application to check for updates when you launch them, and others don't. Either way, a good way to keep up on updates is to routinely check software update sites like MacUpdate (http://macupdate.com/) or Version-Tracker (www.versiontracker.com/). If you subscribe to either of their RSS feeds, you can easily keep track of new applications and application updates as they are released.

Uninstalling Applications

Uninstalling applications, and by that we mean completely uninstalling applications, is a bit more complicated than installing them. Certain applications include an uninstaller application (and certain installer applications likewise include an uninstall option). If this is the case, then using the uninstaller should be your first step. Otherwise, the first step is simply moving the application to the trash and emptying it. Either of these steps generally removes the application effectively; however, applications tend to leave behind some additional traces that you may want to get rid of.

■**Note** AppZapper (http://appzapper.com/) is an application that can help remove old applications completely. When you want to uninstall an application, simply drag the application file into AppZapper, which will then look through your system for all those other pesky parts and related files.

Cache Files, Preferences, and Support Files

The first place to look for leftover files is in your ~/Library folder, particularly in the Caches folder, the Preferences folder, and the Application Support folder.

The Application Support folder is a common place for applications to store all sorts of items that help them function. This should be stop one. Just take a look and see whether the application you are removing has a support folder here (it will usually have the same name as the application itself). If so, you may delete it.

■**Note** Before you delete support files, make sure you back up any information that the application was storing for you.

■**Note** Some applications will create their own support folder in your ~/Library folder rather than in the Application Support subfolder.

After you clean out any application support files, check the `~/Library/Caches` folder. Here, many applications (especially network-enabled apps) store temporary cache files. These can take up lots of space, so you don't want to leave any unused cache files lying around.

■Note It's not a bad idea to delete the caches of all applications every now and then. Just make sure that the application isn't running when you delete the folder. The application should just create a new cache the next time it needs one. Cleaning out these folders can add a fairly significant amount of disk space.

The next place to look is your `~/Library/Preferences` folder. This folder keeps track of all your personal preferences for all your applications and many other system features; and every application, even if just launched once and closed, is likely to have created a file here. Finding the appropriate preference file is a bit tricky. Traditionally, there was no specific naming convention for preference files, so they were usually named after the application. Additionally, certain software developers would (and still do) create a folder here to store the preferences for all their applications (because some applications share preferences among similar applications). Today, however, there is a specific naming convention for most preference files that uses a reverse top-level domain for the developer, followed by the name of the application, followed by some sub-information if needed. So, for example, all the preference files for Apple products would follow the format `com.apple.appname.subpref`. Usually, these will end with a `.plist` extension indicating the type of file is a property list. Once you locate the appropriate preference for your deleted application, you may likewise delete it.

■Note Preference files are interesting to view. If you installed the Xcode tools, then a special application, `/Developer/Applications/Utilities/Property List Editor`, was installed that makes browsing and editing these `.plist` files easy. Most `.plist` files are written in XML, which can be viewed in any text editor as well. Although you should exercise some caution with preference files, you may discover preferences for certain applications that aren't otherwise accessible (hidden preferences).

■Note It's not recommended that you regularly delete a preference file, but if you do mistakenly delete one, it essentially resets the application back to the first time you used it. With some apps, this may cause no noticeable difference; with others, you may need to go through the setup or registration process again. While this may be inconvenient, it's rarely a big problem.

■Note Occasionally, an application may create some of these files in the `/Library` folder as well. Feel free to delete these as well.

Frameworks, Components, Receipts, and Contextual Menu Items

Besides the extra items mentioned previously that are installed and created by applications, a number of applications may install some additional support files. These include special development frameworks, special components, and contextual menu items. Most of these items can be safely deleted; however, you should use care when doing so.

Contextual menu items (which are often installed in the `Contextual Menu Items` subfolder in one of the `Library` folders) are items that enable some application-specific behavior to be accessible from a contextual menu. If you delete the application that the item is attached to, then it will cease to function; so obviously, if you find these "dead" items, you should delete them.

Components (found in the `Components` subdirectory of a `Library` folder) are generally not needed when you remove the application they are associated with either. The only problem is that these items are often named in such a way that it's hard to determine what component is attached to what application, and deleting the wrong one can cause an existing application to fail. In general, if in doubt, leave it alone. If, however, you are sure that you no longer need a component, you may remove it.

Frameworks are trickier. One application may install a third-party framework, and a subsequent application you install may also use that framework, so even if you delete the initial application that installed the framework, by removing the framework you could damage another application. As such, we generally recommend against uninstalling any frameworks unless you are absolutely sure that it's safe. Other than taking up some disk space, an unused framework won't interfere with your system in any way.

Finally, most installer packages leave behind a *receipt* (which is a copy of the package file) in the `/Library/Receipts` folder. When you delete an application, it's safe to delete any package files here associated with it. Removing receipts for existing applications could, however, affect the ability to upgrade the application in the future—and many update packages use receipt data to determine the necessity or eligibility for an upgrade.

Other Hidden Application Files

Hidden or obscure files are the last type of file that may be installed along with the application. These files are installed for one of two reasons. First, some applications install files that are accessible from the command line—while these files are not normally viewable from the Finder, they are not specifically hidden from you (often applications will check with you before installing command-line tools). The other reason applications install hidden or obscure files is specifically so you don't find them; this is usually for licensing reasons and to prevent you from pirating the software or reusing timed-out demo versions of software.

The "hidden" command-line tools (which really aren't hidden; they just aren't immediately visible) can easily be removed from the command line (this is covered later in the book, beginning in Chapter 18). The other files—the ones that are actually intentionally hidden—are problematic. While they generally don't affect your system in any way (other than restricting the use of a particular application), the idea of them lying around bothers people.

There are no specific instructions for finding and removing all of these intentionally hidden files, but there are some suggestions:

- Look around your file system using the command line (see Chapter 18). Lots of files that are hidden from the Finder are easily revealed in the command line. If you find files in a Library folder or subfolder in the command line that you don't see in the Finder, they are probably being hidden.

- If you are really stumped, have an extra hard disk that you can use and some time on your hands. Create two partitions on the disk, and install a clean system on each. Then install the suspected application on one partition, and compare the resulting file systems. If you do this correctly, then any additional files on the application partition belong to the application. (There are a number of ways of creating directory lists, including all files, and then comparing the lists using a variety of command-line and text-based tools.)

- Finally (and this should probably be the first step you try), search the Internet for information about the application and hidden files. Like most things, it's unlikely you are the first person to encounter this situation, and perhaps the answers you are looking for are already out there.

Note Even though you might not want these hidden files around once you remove the associated application, if you are currently using the application, it's likely that you need these files for it to work correctly, so use caution here and don't delete hidden files just because they are hidden—it's likely you won't like the results.

Managing Fonts

Fonts may not seem like things that need to be managed too much, and in OS X, fonts don't tend to cause many of the issues that have been attributed to them in the past. Still, if you tend to accumulate lots of fonts, you may want to manage them for a number of reasons:

- To be able to find the exact type of font you are looking for quickly and easily from a large list of installed fonts

- To "turn off" unused fonts, since many applications (especially graphics apps and word processors) load all active fonts into memory when they launch (slowing up launch time and consuming memory)

Mac OS X, beginning with Panther, included an application named Font Book that helps you manage your fonts. Font Book (Figure 6-7) provides the ability to find, preview, organize, and switch on or off all the fonts installed on your system.

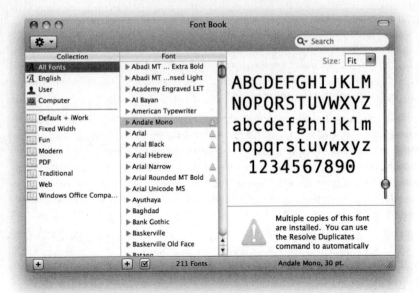

Figure 6-7. *The Font Book application is included in Mac OS X to help manage fonts on your system.*

The Font Book application is organized with two columns and a preview window. The first column, Collection, allows you to select and create sets, or *collections*, of fonts. The set you select in this column determines the specific font families that are displayed in the Font column. Selecting a font family or specific font from within a family will display that font in the view window.

Tip The version of Font Book included in Snow Leopard has the ability to identify and resolve duplicate copies of the identical font files that may be stored in different locations. (This commonly happens when applications, especially word processors and graphics apps, install font files that are already present.) If you have duplicates of a certain font, Font Book will identify it with a yellow caution icon next to the font name. You can then use the Edit ➤ Resolve Duplicates command to automatically correct this issue. To rectify this all at once, use the Edit ➤ Select Duplicate Fonts menu and then run the Resolve Duplicates command.

To create your own collection, click the + button at the bottom of the Collection column, and give your collection a name. Then you can drag fonts displayed in the Font column into your new collection. When you select your set, only the fonts you added to it will appear in the Font column.

To add a new font, click the + button at the bottom of the Font column, and select the font file(s) to add.

To deactivate a font or collection of fonts, right-click the font or collection, and select the Disable option from the contextual menu. Alternately, you can select fonts in the Font column and toggle them with the small check box button at the bottom of the column.

When you deactivate a font collection, it will deactivate any fonts in that collection that are not present in any other activated collection. This prevents fonts from an active collection becoming inadvertently disabled.

Fonts may be reactivated in the same manner.

One nice thing about creating groups of fonts, beyond the ability to activate and deactivate entire groups easily, is that the groups appear in the standard Cocoa font selection dialog box (Figure 6-8), making it easy to find specific fonts that exist within a particular collection.

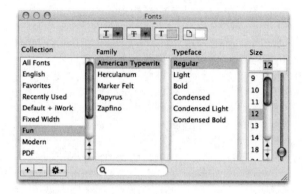

Figure 6-8. *Font collections appear in the standard font selection dialog box, making finding a particular font easy.*

Summary

This chapter has covered a few basic housecleaning tasks that you are likely encounter at some point. The next chapter will focus on a more specific maintenance task touched upon in this chapter: keeping your data backed up and current.

CHAPTER 7

■ ■ ■

Backup, Synchronization, and Recovery of Data

Most people who have been around computers for a long time have horror stories of disk crashes and data loss. And even if your story isn't horrific, you probably have an "Oh, $#!*!" moment or two when things go wrong and you lose an hour's or a day's (or more) worth of work. The thing is, the minute your hard drive was created, it started a countdown toward its *mean time before failure* (MTBF—a rating that measures the average amount of time before a hard drive fails); of course, more frequently, we tend to occasionally make mistakes (either as a user or a developer), so we must make sure we have effective ways of backing up and syncing our data.

■**Note** An interesting article explaining MTBF and drive failure from *eWeek* can be found at www.eweek.com/ article2/0,1895,2099467,00.asp.

This chapter is dedicated to backing up and syncing data, not because it's a terribly long and complicated thing to explain (in fact, Mac OS X makes it relatively easy these days), but because it's such an important topic that it deserves to be treated on its own. In this chapter, we will cover the following:

- The difference between backup and synchronization and what's appropriate in what circumstances

- Keeping your computer's data backed up using Time Machine

- Syncing your data with iSync and MobileMe

- Other methods of backup, syncing, and data recovery

The Difference Between Backups and Synchronization

Before we go too far, it's important to make some general differentiations between a backup and a sync. In overly simple terms, suppose you have two disks: disk A and disk B. When you *backup* disk A to disk B, you make an exact copy of disk A's data onto disk B. This assures that in the event that something undesirable happens to the data on disk A (or if disk A fails altogether), you can revert to the backup data on disk B. When you *synchronize* disk A with disk B, the information on each disk is usually copied to the other so that the data on each drive matches. One special feature of some backup applications is that they archive old information that has been deleted or changed. This can be known as an *archived backup* or *versioned backup*, but whatever it's called, it allows the added benefit of looking "back in time" to find files that may otherwise have been deleted (this is how Time Machine works). If you are more of a visual thinker, these differences are illustrated in Figure 7-1.

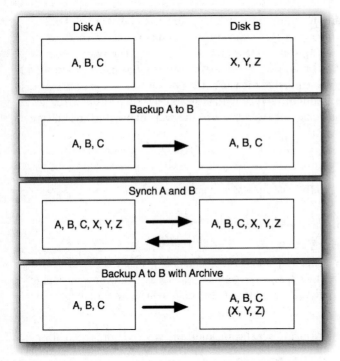

Figure 7-1. *Differences between backups and synchronization*

■**Note** These descriptions of a backup and a sync, along with Figure 7-1, are meant to provide a simplified (perhaps overly simplified) differentiation between backups and synchronization. The reality can be much more nuanced. For example, while a backup only provides a one-way transfer of data (i.e., backing up one data source to another), synchronization can provide both a one-way and/or a two-way transfer of data, depending on settings. (In fact, when you first sync data, you're often asked if you want to copy source A to B, copy source B to A, or synchronize A and B. If data changes on both sources, most sync programs will ask you which change you want to use.)

DEFINING AN ARCHIVE

The word *archive* is a bit of a semantic battlefield and can mean different things in different applications. First the verb, *to archive*: some backup applications may ask, "Would you like to archive your data?" While this seems like a simple question, it could have two different results. In one scenario, the system could start keeping track of old files (this is the definition we're using and could—perhaps should—be referred to as *versioning*). In another situation, the system could ask you to insert a CD or DVD. In this case, the application is offering to help you create an offline archive or snapshot of your current data.

An *archive* (noun) could be many things: the physical CD or DVD you created when you made your archive, a single large file containing archived data in some proprietary format, a more general collection of files organized in a means for software to easily identify and retrieve it, or some combination of all of the above (or something in between). Archives aren't always backups, either (though often there is that connotation); they more generally are large collections of somehow related data. Confused yet? Don't worry, it's really not that bad. Generally, in any given situation, an archive means whatever makes the most sense for that situation, and if not, it's not too difficult to find out.

Generally, when you want to keep an extra copy of your important data in case something happens to your primary data store, then what you want is a backup. When you have two data stores that you need to keep current with each other, then what you want is synchronization. Either way, you are creating a redundancy that is important should one data source fail. One important note, though: creating a backup with archiving is the only way to effectively protect against file corruption. If you synchronize or simply back up a corrupted file, then you are just creating a new copy of a corrupted file, often overwriting an old, noncorrupted file.

Backing Up Your Data with Time Machine

Snow Leopard includes a fantastic little backup utility called Time Machine. Time Machine provides data backups of all your information complete with a historical archive of data. The best thing about this is that Time Machine does all of its work automatically in the background, making it painless. However, like any good backup utility, in order to take full advantage of Time Machine, you will need an extra hard drive connected to your computer for Time Machine to back up data to.

■**Note** When deciding whether to invest in an external hard drive for Time Machine to use, ask yourself how much the data you keep on your computer is worth. You can easily find a nice-sized external hard drive these days for less than $100, and in our opinion, our data is worth at least that.

■**Note** If you are desperate, you can set up Time Machine to back up to a different partition on your primary hard drive. Although this provides some protection of your data as well as a nice historical archive of data, this will do nothing if your hard drive fails or your computer is lost or stolen.

Note Time Machine will eventually use all the free space on the drive or partition you set for it. So, if you want to use a hard drive for both Time Machine and anything else, then you'll most likely want to partition the drive, dedicating one partition to just Time Machine. (We covered how to partition drives in the last chapter.)

To set up Time Machine:

1. Open the Time Machine pane in System Preferences (Figure 7-2).

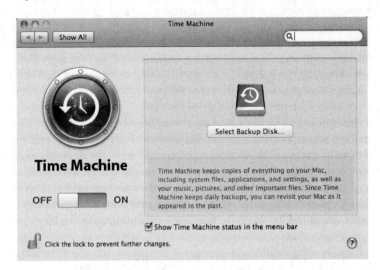

Figure 7-2. *The Time Machine preference pane prior to setting up Time Machine the first time*

2. Click the Select Backup Disk… button, which opens up a dialog box (Figure 7-3) allowing you to select the desired backup disk. Select the desired device and click the Use for Backup button. This selects the device automatically, turns Time Machine on, and starts a 120-second countdown until your first back up. Time Machine is now ready to go.

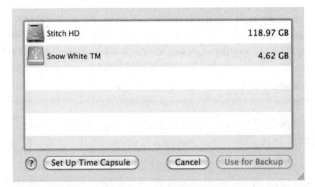

Figure 7-3. *The dialog box asks you which device you wish to dedicate to Time Machine.*

■**Note** If you haven't set up Time Machine already, when you first connect an external hard drive, you will be asked if you'd like to use that drive as a Time Machine backup. If you choose Yes, then you can bypass the previous steps.

■**Note** If you are using one of Apple's Time Capsule network devices for back up, you may select the Set Up Time Capsule button. This launches the AirPort Utility to allow you to select the appropriate Time Capsule device to use.

Once you've selected a backup device, the Time Machine preference pane changes to offer more information and options (Figure 7-4). Selecting the Options... button opens a dialog box (Figure 7-5) that allows you to tweak a few options, the most important of which is the ability to select any folders or attached devices that you want Time Machine to ignore (and thus not back up). This is particularly useful if you have large files or archives that are backed up with other methods, if you don't care whether they are backed up, or if you have folders containing sensitive data that you don't want archived.

■**Note** You also may want Time Machine to ignore very large files that change often—for example, virtual disks from Parallels, VMware Fusion, or your Entourage database. However, if you do have Time Machine ignore these files, you may want to back them up manually (especially your Entourage database, if that's your primary e-mail and contacts tool). If you don't ignore these every time you make even a small change (which happens constantly when, in the case of the previous examples, a virtual machine is running or Entourage is open), then Time Machine will detect a change, back up the entire file, and archive the old. Not only will Time Machine be running constantly, but its drive will fill up with lots of large, slightly changed, archive files.

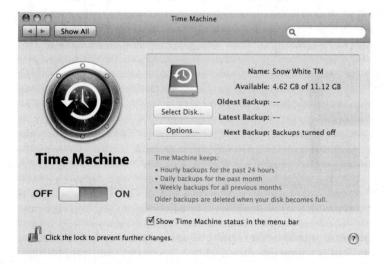

Figure 7-4. *The Time Machine preference pane changes to offer more options once you choose a Time Machine device.*

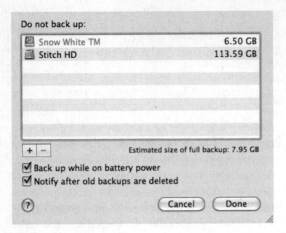

Figure 7-5. *The Options… dialog box provides some added options that affect how Time Machine works.*

■**Note** When you initially set up Time Machine or select a new Time Machine device, the initial backup may take a long time to complete. Once it completes, Time Machine will only back up new or altered items on your hard drive. These backups are generally quite fast unless you're doing manual or infrequent backups.

When Time Machine is active, it makes automatic backups every hour. This keeps a rather complete record of changes to your system should anything minor or major occur, from the accidental deletion of a file to a dreaded hard-drive failure. If, however, you would like to forgo this level of detail and control your backups manually, simply turn Time Machine's OFF-ON switch to OFF. If you wish to use Time Machine manually, it's handy to have the "Show Time Machine status in the menu bar" option selected. This allows you to select Back Up Now from the menu bar at any time and create a backup manually (Figure 7-6). Alternately, you can select the Back Up Now option by Control-clicking the Time Machine icon on your Dock.

Figure 7-6. *The Time Machine icon in the menu bar allows you start a Time Machine backup manually.*

Once Time Machine is set up, it should begin keeping an up-to-date archive of the data on your system. Through the Time Machine interface (Figure 7-7), you can use Time Machine to recover past files that have been altered or deleted. Additionally, should your primary hard drive ever crash and you need to do a clean install of OS X (or you just wish to do a clean install of OS X because you have some extra time on your hands), you can recover all of your data from your Time Machine backup either during the install process (covered in Appendix B) or at a later time using the Migration Assistant application.

Figure 7-7. *Time Machine browsing Finder items as they were backed up through time*

You can enter the Time Machine interface by clicking the Time Machine icon, just as you would launch any other application. Alternately, you can select the Enter Time Machine option from the Time Machine menu icon (unless you've disabled it). To recover any data from the Time Machine archive, you may navigate through the single Finder window normally and then simply use the arrows or the timeline along the right side of the interface to navigate "back in time" and select the item you wish to recover. Once you select the desired item, click the Restore button in the lower-right corner. This brings you out of the Time Machine interface and places the recovered file in its original Finder location. If an item of the same name already (or still) exists in that place, then you will be prompted to keep either or both files.

■**Note** Time Machine assumes that the selected Time Machine disk or partition exists solely for Time Machine archives. It continues to fill up this drive with archives until the drive is full. When the Time Machine device is full, Time Machine begins to delete the oldest archived files to make room for the newer ones. If the "Warn when old backups are deleted" option is selected, you will be prompted before Time Machine overwrites old files.

If you want to leave Time Machine without restoring any items, just click the Cancel button in the lower-left corner of the Time Machine interface.

When you launch Time Machine, it usually opens up in the active Finder location; however, certain applications are also Time Machine–aware. One example of this is Apple's Mail application. Opening Time Machine with Mail active provides a Mail window in Time Machine so you can go back and find old deleted messages (unfortunately, you can't use Time Machine to go back and not send old sent messages).

■**Note** Time Machine goes beyond just backup and actually provides a personal version control system as well. Version control tracks changes of items over time so that you can recover older versions if something critically wrong happens in a new version. For developers, version control (or source code management [SCM]) is essential for creating stable software, and support for a number of version control systems, including CVS, Subversion, and Perforce, are built into Xcode. For more general project version control, Versions (www.versionsapp.com/) provides an easy-to-use interface for taking advantage of the Subversion version control system. One significant difference between Time Machine's version control and professional SCM is that the SCM tools are designed to keep track of changes made by a large number of different users, while Time Machine just tracks changes, not necessarily who's making them.

Synchronization

Besides backup, Snow Leopard provides a number of options for you to keep important information synchronized across multiple devices. One of Apple's most comprehensive synchronization methods is through MobileMe, Apple's online service; we will discuss this in detail in Chapter 13. The other synchronization method included with Snow Leopard is the iSync application.

iSync allows you to sync your calendars and your contacts with many common non-Apple mobile devices such as Nokia, Sony Ericsson, and Motorola. So if you are out and about and meet an old friend and enter his or her contact information in your phone, the next time you sync your phone using iSync, that contact information will be added to your Address Book. At the same time, if you add a number of events in iCal, when you sync your phone with iSync, those events will get entered into your phone's calendar.

■**Note** Apple devices, including the iPod and iPhone, sync from within iTunes. We will cover this with iTunes in Chapter 15.

When you first launch iSync, you are presented with a simple window with a single toolbar listing the devices you have set up and a Sync Devices button. If you haven't set up any devices, then you'll just see the Sync Devices button (Figure 7-8).

Figure 7-8. *iSync, before you've added any devices*

To add a device, select Devices ➤ Add Device… from iSync's application menu or use the Command-N shortcut. This opens the Add Device window and immediately tries to detect a device. By default, iSync connects to devices using Bluetooth, so it must be active on both your computer and your device. After scanning, iSync provides a list of detected devices (Figure 7-9). Double-clicking the device you wish to add launches the Bluetooth Setup Assistant, which walks you through the process of pairing your device. We covered this process in Chapter 5.

Figure 7-9. *Devices iSync discovered that may be used to sync information with your computer*

■**Note** You can find an up-to-date list of devices that iSync supports at `http://support.apple.com/kb/HT2824`.

Once a device is added and recognized, it shows up as an item in iSync's toolbar. Selecting a device in iSync's toolbar allows you to set up the sync options (Figure 7-10). Here you can choose which contact and calendar items you want to synchronize, what calendar iSync should associate new calendar items you've added to your device with, and how to handle the initial sync. Additionally, the More Options… button opens a dialog box that provides a few options to fine-tune what gets synced (Figure 7-11). To start the synchronization process, hit the Sync Devices button in the top-right corner. If your device is found and ready to receive (you may need to allow syncing on the receiving device as well), then the sync will begin, and a progress bar will indicate the progress as your computer and devices sync up (Figure 7-12).

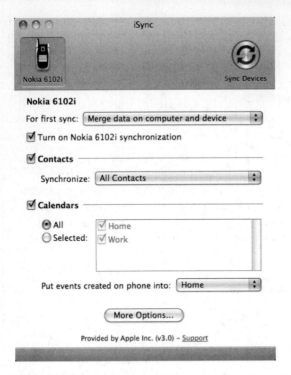

Figure 7-10. *The basic options for syncing a device with your computer*

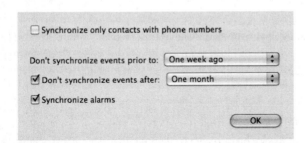

Figure 7-11. *The More Options… button for syncing your device*

Figure 7-12. *A progress bar indicates when a sync is in progress.*

When the sync is completed, you will be notified of any errors as well as how many items have been synchronized successfully. Additionally, iSync will occasionally detect changes on both your device and your computer and will prompt you to indicate which one is correct.

Note Prior to Leopard, iSync also managed the syncing of data with .Mac (the precursor to Apple's MobileMe online service). Today, MobileMe syncing is set up in the MobileMe System Preferences pane. We'll cover more about MobileMe syncing in Chapter 13.

Other Methods of Backup, Sync, and Recovery

Besides Time Machine, iSync, and the other backup and sync features that are part of Snow Leopard, you can use a range of other utilities, applications, and methods to protect your data. Some applications, such as Apple's Aperture, provide an integrated means of backing up and archiving their data.

If, however, Apple's backup tools don't quite fit your needs (or for whatever reason, you just don't like them), these other applications are worth a look:

- Decimus Software (www.decimus.net/) makes three different backup applications depending on your needs: Synk Backup, Synk Standard, and Synk Pro. These apps range in cost from $25 to $45. Although the Standard version handles most common backup and synchronization tasks, the Pro version adds some nice features, and at $45, it offers the best bang for your buck.

- Intego (www.intego.com) has, for the last ten years, consistently provided an ever-expanding array of high-quality Mac utility software, including virus protection, spam guards, and, of course, file backup. Its Personal Backup software provides a full range of configurable options in a fast and easy-to-use package for $49.99.

- EMC Insignia (www.retrospect.com), a division of storage powerhouse EMC, recently acquired Retrospect, a highly regarded backup solution for Macs. EMC Retrospect for Macintosh comes in four versions. The Express version, which is distributed only with hard drives from some manufacturers and resellers, provides basic backup capabilities. The Desktop version (about $120) provides everything you could want in a desktop backup solution. The Workgroup version (about $500) is designed to keep up to 20 networked computers all backed up. The Server version (about $800) provides backups for up to 100 desktop clients (this version supports clients running Mac OS X, Windows, and Red Hat Linux).

Note Two other backup utilities worth considering are SuperDuper! (www.shirt-pocket.com/SuperDuper/SuperDuperDescription.html) and Carbon Copy Cloner (www.bombich.com/software/index.html). What sets these apart from the others is their ability to keep up-to-date *clones* of your system; in other words, these backup utilities maintain a fully *bootable* copy of your system that can be swapped in for your primary system drive at a moment's notice, should the need ever arise.

What's most important—whether you use Time Machine, use Retrospect, or copy all your data onto thumb drives manually—is that you do *something* to back up your data. Just pick a system that works for you and go with it.

Summary

Now that you know how to protect your data from hard drive failures and accidental data loss, we'll move on to protecting your data and your computer from other threats.

CHAPTER 8

■ ■ ■

Mac OS X Security

Besides protecting your data from hardware failure and accidents, in today's world, where computers tend to be always connected, it's also important to protect your data from other users—both on your computer and outside of it. This chapter deals with security, including the following topics:

- Passwords and keychains

- Data encryption and FileVault

- Other security features

Passwords and Keychains

Passwords are used time and time again on your computer: logging in to your account, checking your e-mail, visiting certain web sites, logging in to connected servers, and more. You probably have so many passwords that it becomes a chore to keep track of them all. To help manage all your passwords, security certificates, and encryption keys, OS X includes a keychain feature to keep track of all this information.

The Keychain Feature

Whenever you enter a password into an application that takes advantage of the OS X keychain, you will be asked whether you want to save the username-password combination in your keychain. If you select yes, then the next time you log in, rather than getting a prompt to enter your username and password, the application will automatically use what's already saved in your keychain. Now, your keychain will use the passwords stored in it only under certain circumstances:

- The keychain will use data saved in the logged-in user's keychain only, so your keychain is protected from all other users (excepting shared keychains).

- By default, passwords associated with a particular application allow only that application to access the password item in your keychain. Often when you update your application and attempt to use it, you will be prompted to update the key to work with the updated application (you will need to authorize the update).

- The key in the keychain is valid and unexpired. Although this usually isn't a big problem for passwords, security certificates and encryption keys (which are also stored in the keychain) are generally set to expire after a certain amount of time.

The keychain data itself is stored in a number of keychain files located in various `Library` folders. For example, the System Roots keychain files are stored in `/System/Library/Keychains`, and the actual System Keychain is stored in the `/Library/Keychains` folder. The keychain files of most interest to you as a user are the ones stored in your `~/Library/Keychains` folder. It's in your personal keychain file that all of your sensitive data is stored (safely encrypted from prying eyes). Should you ever need to view your keychain (or other keychains you have access to), Mac OS X includes the Keychain Access utility (in the `/Applications/Utilities` folder). The Keychain Access utility (Figure 8-1) provides a way for you to view, edit, and configure individual entries stored in your keychain.

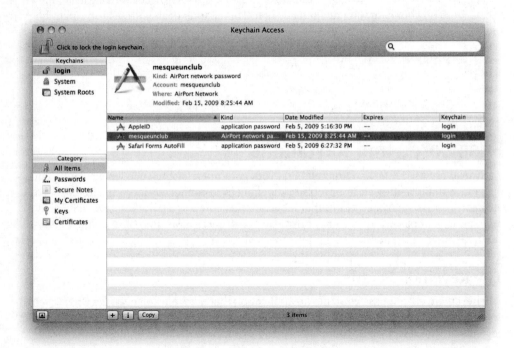

Figure 8-1. *The Keychain Access utility provides a way to view and alter your keychain items.*

The Keychain Access utility provides a column on the left where you can select the keychain you'd like to view (any available keychains will be listed there; your default keychain is the login keychain). Below the list of keychains is a list of categories of items that are stored in the keychain. Table 8-1 describes the categories and their descriptions. On the right side is the view area, where, at the bottom, the individual items stored in the keychain are listed. Above that is a view that provides some basic information about the selected item.

Table 8-1. *Categories of Items Stored in Your Keychain*

Category	Description
Passwords	These are your passwords, which are broken into three subcategories: AppleShare: These are your passwords associated with file servers and other people's computers that you have accounts on. Application: These passwords are associated with specific applications. They can be used for just about anything, including Internet sites, but rather than being associated with the site, they are associated with the application. Internet: These are your Internet passwords, which include certain web site login information, as well as mail accounts and other Internet server credentials.
Certificates	Certificates provide a method of verifying a site's credentials, certifying that a service on the Internet (or network) is who it says it is. This is based on a method of trust: there are a number of certificate authorities who issue certificates—assuming you trust the authority, then you can trust all the certificates issued by that authority. A number of certificates from reputable issuing authorities are included with Snow Leopard (these are viewable from the System Roots keychain). Occasionally you may be prompted by a web site to approve a new certificate, which is of course at your discretion (Figure 8-2). If the certificate checks out, it will be categorized here.
My Certificates	The My Certificates category also stores certificates, but rather than certificates that verify others to you, these certificates verify you to others. Using certificates to verify you are who you say you are is becoming more common, especially in situations where data integrity is essential. These sorts of certificates can be used in lieu of a password or, more often, used in conjunction with a password. (If someone walks up to your computer, the certificate is available, but they may not know your password; on the other hand, if someone has your password, then they need physical access to your computer [or certificate] to do anything with it.)
Keys	Keys are used for encryption and digital signatures. In general, many forms of encryption use keys, but the essential idea is that communication on one end of the network uses one key to encrypt data that only a specific (and different) key on the other end of the network can decrypt. This is important because most bits of information passing through the Internet or a network can usually be viewed by many other computers and systems in between.
Secure Notes	Secure notes are different from most of the other items stored in your keychain, in that they are generally not used outside the keychain. Rather, they just provide a way for you to store confidential notes in your keychain. The information here could contain credit card information or any other personal information to which you decide to limit access.

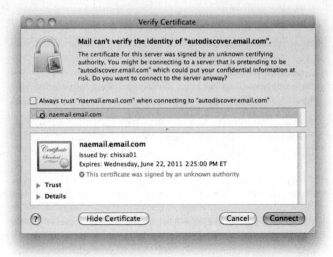

Figure 8-2. *When your system encounters a new certificate that it cannot verify, it will prompt you about whether you want to accept the connection. Selecting the "Always trust..." check box will add the certificate to your keychain.*

Note Cryptography and encryption are very big, complicated topics. A great book that does a good job of introducing them, including keys and certificates, is *Cryptography Decrypted* by H. X. Mel and Doris Baker (Addison-Wesley Professional, 2000).

Double-clicking any of the items in your keychain will open a window providing detailed information about that item. For items such as passwords and secure notes, some details will be hidden, specifically the password and the actual content of the note.

The password items have a number of options spread out over two tabs: the Attributes tab and the Access Control tab.

The Attributes tab (Figure 8-3) provides the following information:

- *Name*: This is just the name of the keychain item.

- *Kind*: This is the category to which the item belongs.

- *Account*: This is the name associated with the account. Usually this field contains the username, but occasionally, especially for application passwords, it is used to represent something used similarly by the application.

- *Where*: This identifies where the password is valid; this is commonly a URI pointing to the online resource for which the item is valid, but occasionally it is something else (a protocol, for example, or just something that has meaning to an application).

- *Comments*: This field contains any comments associated with the item.

- *Show password*: This is where the password is shown. However, by default it is empty to protect the password. To view the password, you will need to select the "Show password" option and then authenticate yourself. The key icon to the right of the password text field opens the Password Assistant, which can help you create strong passwords.

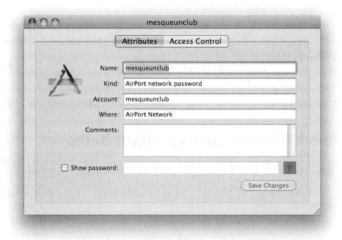

Figure 8-3. *The Attributes tab of a password keychain item*

Note All the fields in the Attributes tab are editable. If you are storing items here for your own reference, you can certainly edit these—however, if the item is being used by an application, altering this information may interfere with the normal operation of the application.

The Access Control tab (Figure 8-4) allows you to delegate what applications can access the keychain item and whether you'll be prompted to approve any new application that wants to use the information.

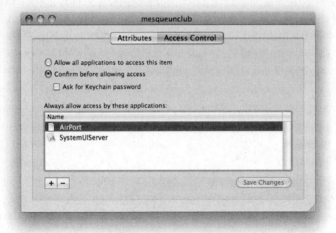

Figure 8-4. *The Access Control tab controls how the information in the item can be accessed.*

Creating Your Own Keychains and Keychain Items

While the keychain feature is designed to mostly run in the background to seamlessly manage passwords, keys, and certificates, it will also allow you to store your own information inside of it. You could store your own passwords and notes and even keep track of serial numbers for registered applications.

■Note Besides using the keychain, you can securely store password and application data using solutions provided by third parties. Some interesting applications include the $39.99 1Password (www.agilewebsolutions. com/products/1Password), which not only stores passwords and other encrypted information but also integrates with your web browsers to make using strong web passwords a snap (it even has a version for your iPhone, which allows you to keep your password data in sync and at your fingertips when you are away from your computer); the donationware Pastor (www.mehlau.net/pastor/), which is a lightweight, easy-to-use password storage application; and the $15 info.xhead (www.xheadsoftware.com/info_xhead.asp), which is an all-purpose utility for storing passwords and other sensitive information.

To add a keychain item, you click the little + button at the bottom of the keychain window, and a dialog box will open so you can enter your information. By default, the dialog box will be geared toward passwords. If you want to create a note, select the Note group in the left column, and then click the + button. This will open a dialog box for entering your note. Alternately, you can select File ➤ New Password Item or File ➤ New Secure Note Item directly from the menu bar.

The password dialog box (Figure 8-5) is fairly straightforward; you enter a name for your item, the account name, and your password. There are some interesting points here, though. For one, the keychain item name determines what the type of item will be. If you enter a URL, the item will be created as an Internet password; otherwise, the item will be created as an application password. Finally, the bar at the bottom will extend to the right and change from red to green as you enter your password to indicate its strength.

Figure 8-5. *The password dialog box allows you to enter a password into a new keychain item.*

The strength of a password is determined by how hard it would be for a malicious user to crack it using various methods. This determination consists of many variables, including the length of the password, the uniqueness, and the type of characters used. Common names and words found in dictionaries are very weak, because a modern computer can run through a dictionary list of common words and passwords in a few minutes. Beyond that, short passwords take a relatively short amount of time to crack using brute-force methods (which basically means using every possible combination of every letter, number, and symbol for each space). The difficulty of brute-force cracking increases dramatically with each additional character. It's good practice to attempt to mix uppercase and lowercase letters, numbers, and, if possible, symbols, into your passwords. Additionally, passwords should be at least eight characters long.

Note Apple's Password Assistant (Figure 8-6) can help you craft secure, unique passwords based on various criteria. This utility will present itself as a dialog box when you click the key icon next to many password text fields in Mac OS X.

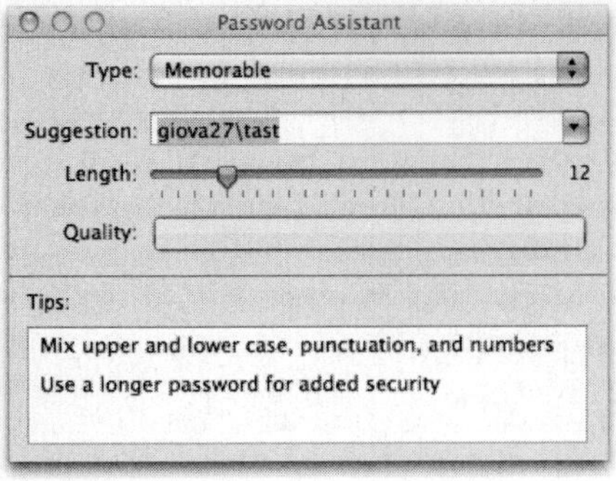

Figure 8-6. *The Password Assistant is available in many places throughout Mac OS X to help you create secure, unique passwords.*

Note Ten years ago, an eight-character password was considered strong. Today, that would be the minimum acceptable in most situations. As computing power increases, passwords become increasingly less effective, since as password lengths increase, it becomes increasingly hard to remember them and therefore less practical. For this reason, a number of password alternatives have been developed and are gaining in popularity. These alternatives may be used to complement a password system or eliminate passwords altogether. These alternatives include smart cards and other hardware authentication devices, as well as biometric security measures (such as fingerprint readers).

Besides storing passwords and security certificates, you can also securely store notes containing any information you choose in your keychains. If you select Secure Notes under the Category pane and click the + button, a dialog box will open (Figure 8-7) asking for a name for your note item and showing a large text field for the contents of your notes.

If you intend to store lots of personal information in a keychain, you may want to create a keychain separate from your login keychain to store information; you can easily do this by selecting File ➤ New Keychain... from the Keychain Access menu.

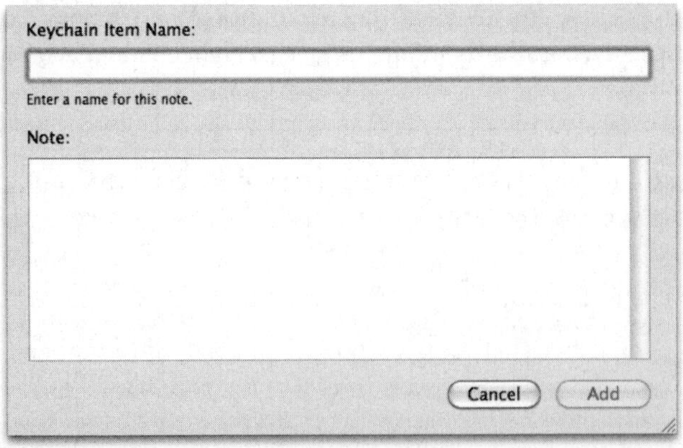

Figure 8-7. *The keychain dialog for entering a secure note item*

Other Keychain Options

A few other features associated with keychains are available from the Keychain Access utility. These are described in the following sections.

Keychain Passwords

By default, your keychain password (the password you will need to unlock data such as passwords and notes in your keychain) is the same as your login password. You can change this password for each keychain using the Edit ➤ Change Password for Keychain "*keychain*"… command.

■**Caution** When your keychain password is the same as your login password, your keychain is automatically unlocked when you log in. That means if you step away from your computer while you are logged in, someone could walk up and view your keychain contents fairly easily.

Keychain Settings

The Edit ➤ Change Settings for Keychain "*keychain*"… menu item allows you to access some additional options for a particular keychain. These include the ability to lock your keychain after a certain amount of time or when your computer goes to sleep (you will need to enter your keychain password each time you or an application attempts to access a locked keychain). This also provides an option to synchronize your keychain with Apple's MobileMe service, allowing you to share a keychain across multiple computers utilizing MobileMe's sync features.

Keychain First Aid

If your keychain gets mucked up to the point that it no longer functions correctly (for example, because of data or file corruption), the Keychain First Aid selection under the Keychain Access application menu can help solve a number of problems. Depending on what options are set on the First Aid tab in the Keychain Access utility's preferences, running Keychain First Aid will rebuild your keychain file and reset most settings to the defaults, including setting the keychain passwords back to the login password and setting the login keychain back to the default keychain.

Data Encryption with the FileVault

The keychain feature protects your passwords while keeping them easily accessible, and FileVault protects your data from others. FileVault, accessible from the FileVault tab in the Security preference pane (Figure 8-8), encrypts the contents of your home folder, protecting them from anyone who attempts to access anything stored there.

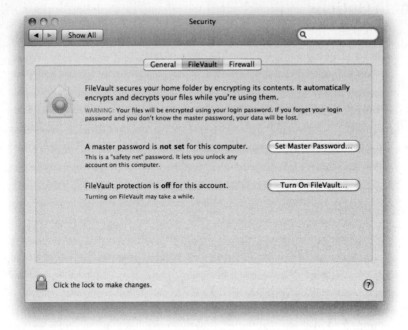

Figure 8-8. *The FileVault tab of the Security preference pane lets you turn FileVault on and off.*

The first step in enabling FileVault is to choose a master password by clicking the Set Master Password button. This will open a dialog (Figure 8-9) for you to enter a master password that can be used to decrypt any of your computer's FileVaults. The reason for this is that if a user forgets their login password, then an administrator can use this master password to reset the user's password, allowing them to regain access to their home data.

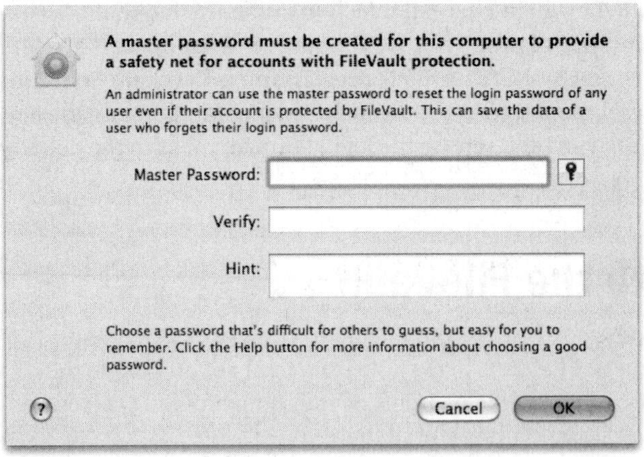

Figure 8-9. *A master password is a safeguard that allows an administrator to reset a user's password. Without this, the entire contents of the user's home directory could be lost.*

Once you've set the master password, click the Turn On FileVault button, and you'll be asked for various forms of authentication, including administrator and user passwords. Then you'll be presented with a dialog box containing some final warnings about the limitations of FileVault-protected accounts and a couple more options (see Figure 8-10).

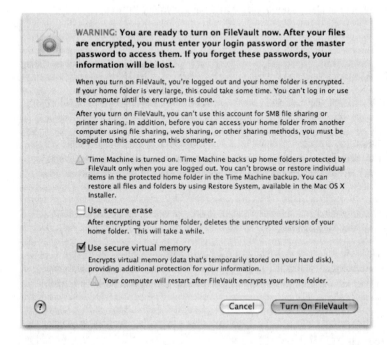

Figure 8-10. *Last warnings and two more options before turning on FileVault*

The "Use secure erase" option will cause the Secure Empty Trash option to be used by default when the trash is emptied. The "Use secure virtual memory" option will additionally overwrite any memory traces that may be on your hard drive to further protect all your data. If you are ready to go, click the Turn On FileVault button.

When you initially turn on FileVault, you will be immediately logged out, because the system encrypts all your data. Depending on the amount of data you have in your home directory, this process could take some time and will require a restart when it's completed.

Once FileVault is set up, using your protected account will be pretty much the same, because your home directory data will be decrypted when you log in.

As mentioned, using FileVault has some disadvantages:

- File sharing of all types will be disabled for the FileVault-enabled account.

- Remote access will be disabled.

- Time Machine will have limitations. Primarily, you will no longer be able to use it to restore single files; you will be able to restore only an entire vault.

- There will be some minor performance issues, especially the time required to log in (as necessary data is decrypted) and log out (as new data is encrypted and traces are cleaned up). Additionally, other minor delays for various tasks will occur.

■**Note** FileVault provides some very serious data protection, and despite conflicting with some other features of OS X, if you must work in an entirely secure environment and data security is extremely important, this will help provide that. On the other hand, for most users, this will be overkill. If you simply want to keep a handful of files encrypted, a number of utilities are available that will accommodate you.

FILEVAULT CONSIDERATIONS: THE GOOD AND THE BAD

Besides what's already been mentioned, there are some serious considerations you should think about when deciding to use FileVault:

- Although, in general, passwords are required to access a user's data on a running system, there are ways to work around this, such as booting the computer in Target Disk mode. When using FileVault, your data is still encrypted, so even though someone may have access to it, they can't easily do anything with it.

- Since FileVault encrypts your entire home directory, it tends to encrypt lots of things that just don't need to be encrypted (e.g., the iTunes library).

- If you use FileVault, you should also keep in mind that any backups should be encrypted as well. It doesn't do any good to protect your information on your computer if your backups aren't equally protected. (Although Time Machine will store your information encrypted, it's important to keep in mind that it will not allow you to simply restore individual files.)

- If you occasionally need this sort of protection, it may be a good idea to create a separate account specifically for this purpose.

- If you need to protect only a limited amount of data, it may be a better idea to just utilize an encrypted disk image that contains the protected data, because this provides quite a bit more flexibility.

If you should change your mind, you can turn off FileVault by repeating the same steps used in turning it on.

Other Security Features

In very general terms, computer security is divided into physical security and network security. Physical security represents the security of your computer when someone is sitting right in front of it, and network security protects your computer from a potential threat that could be halfway around the world. The trouble with these simple distinctions is that these days they tend to blur a bit, especially with multiuser systems like OS X. For example, remote desktop technologies (such as Apple Remote Desktop and VNC) allow many users to essentially have physical access to the system, even over a network.

Many of the common security features for protecting Mac OS X are in the Security preference pane. The Security preference pane contains three tabs: General (Figure 8-11), FileVault (which we talked about in the previous section), and Firewall (which we'll talk about in detail in Chapter 20).

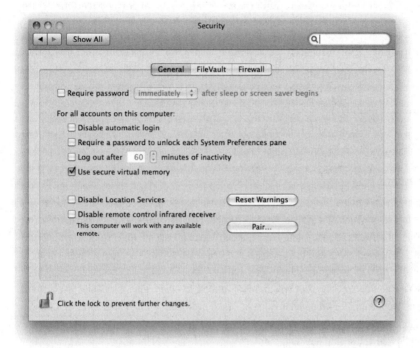

Figure 8-11. *The general security options in the Security preference pane*

The general security options cover a wide range of options normally associated with physical security. Table 8-2 describes the options covered on the General tab of the Security preference pane.

Table 8-2. *General Security Options*

Option	Description
Require password X after sleep or screen saver begins	This option will prompt for a password when the computer is awoken from a period of inactivity. This protects your system if you step away for a bit, leaving your computer on but unattended.
Disable automatic login	This option requires a user to log in when the system is turned on.
Require a password to unlock each System Preferences pane	This will require an administrative password whenever someone attempts to adjust any system preferences (specifically the Mac OS X preferences listed under the System heading in System Preferences).
Logout after X minutes of inactivity	This will log out any user who is inactive for a certain period of time.
Use secure virtual memory	This will overwrite any disk space used for virtual memory when the memory is no longer used.

Continued

Table 8-2. *(Continued)*

Option	Description
Disable Location Services	Location Services are new in Snow Leopard and allow applications to utilize your location in them. Selecting this option will prevent location information from being passed to any applications. Hitting the Reset Warnings button will remove any previously stored location information as well.
Disable remote control infrared receiver	If your system includes a remote control (e.g., portables and iMacs), which is commonly used to control Front Row and other features, this option will disable this functionality. Additionally, the Pair button will allow you to set up your system to work with a specified (paired) remote control only.

The Firewall tab is associated with network security and, combined with sharing options, can control what sort of network activity your computer will allow. This is covered in Chapter 20.

■**Note** Snow Leopard ships with the firewall allowing all incoming and outgoing connections—however, all network services are turned off. This effectively eliminates most potential network security issues from the outside since no individual services are accepting any incoming communications. However, certain applications may open their own network ports and run services on them. Usually, if they're from a trusted source, you'll be OK; but if they're from an untrusted source, look out! Also, since no outgoing connections are being blocked, you should have no trouble using your web browser, e-mail, or other network-enabled applications unless you are on a network with its own dedicated firewall (and even most home cable and DSL routers have built-in firewalls these days). Again, caution should be used when using untrusted applications, since by default they would be free to transmit anything.

Finally, Mac OS X includes a range of additional features built in to the system and various applications that will allow you to provide any level of data security you want. For example, another way to protect your data is to put it on an encrypted disk image. You can do this by creating a blank disk image in Disk Utility and selecting one of the encryption options for it. This will prompt you for a password that will be necessary every time you attempt to mount the image.

■**Note** One other password option is setting a firmware password, which provides low-level system protection. To set a firmware password, you must boot up your computer using the Snow Leopard install DVD and then select Utilities ➤ Set Firmware Password Utility... from the Mac OS X Installation menu. This will walk you through the process to set a password. Once a firmware password is set, it will be required for most special boot sequences, including booting your computer in Target Disk mode and selecting an alternative boot device at startup.

Summary

Mac OS X is built upon a naturally secure foundation and, coupled with a range of features, makes maintaining a secure system easy and without lots of the headaches and pain associated with security. This chapter covered mostly user-centric and basic system security, and later in the book we will cover network security in more detail. Additionally, we will continue to provide added security tips where applicable throughout the book.

The next part of the book will begin covering more of the day-to-day usability of OS X, beginning with utilizing the Internet.

## PART 3

Communications and the Internet

■ ■ ■

## CHAPTER 9

Connecting to the Internet

One of the first things most people want to do today once they get their computer set up is to get it connected to the Internet. Depending on your connection, this could range from ridiculously easy to just fairly easy . . . at least as far as configuring Mac OS X goes. Essentially, there are two common ways to connect to the Internet today, and we'll cover each of them in this chapter:

- Connecting via dial-up
- Connecting via a broadband, high-speed Internet connection

We'll also cover how to set up networking profiles for different locations.

Connecting to the Internet Using Dial-Up Networking

Dial-up networking, once the king of Internet connections, seems to be fading away as broadband networks reach out across the world. Still, for some people in some situations, it's the best or only option available.

■**Note** It should be obvious that to use dial-up networking, you'll need a modem. Many slightly older Macs have internal modems, but the currently shipping Macs don't. Apple, however, offers an external USB modem as an option with all Macs that you just need to plug into a USB port. One other option for dial-up networking is that some mobile phone services offer network services that can be accessed via a Bluetooth connection. If you have a phone (and mobile service) that supports this, you may utilize this connection just about anywhere you get mobile service.

Setting Up Your Dial-Up Connection

Setting up your dial-up connection is usually done in three simple steps:

1. Make sure your hardware is connected and set up. An internal modem should be ready to go as soon as you connect an active phone line to it. An external Apple modem should be ready as soon as you plug it in. If you are using a Bluetooth phone for dial-up, you will need to make sure you have set up your phone as a Bluetooth device.

   If you are using one of Apple's external USB modems, when you plug it in once your computer is already on, a dialog box will pop up (Figure 9-1). This lets you know that the computer has recognized the new modem and prompts you to set up dial-up networking.

Note When we talk about modems for dial-up, we are talking about a traditional plain old telephone service (POTS) modem. Cable modems do not require this setup, because most cable modems are simply routers. We will cover cable modems later in this chapter.

Note Not all phone lines are POTS lines. Many companies these days have installed Voice over Internet Protocol (VoIP) telephone systems. Although these systems look like pretty normal telephones and telephone plugs (RJ11), they send a digital signal rather than an analog one. Additionally, some telephone companies have begun to install fiber-optic telephone lines, replacing the copper POTS lines. In either of these cases, a traditional modem will not work and could possibly be damaged if connected.

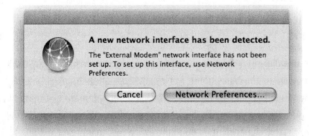

Figure 9-1. *A dialog box pops up letting you know that the system has detected a new network device (in this case, the external modem).*

2. Collect the information you need to connect to your dial-up account. Usually you need three items:

   - The phone number for your access provider
   - Your account username
   - Your account password

For a Bluetooth connection utilizing a mobile network, you will also need the access point name (APN), along with a number of other details that should be provided by your mobile network provider.

3. Open the Network panel in System Preferences, select the appropriate device (Figure 9-2), and fill in the appropriate information.

Figure 9-2. *To set up a dial-up connection, you just need to attach a modem and fill in the appropriate information in the Network preference pane.*

Usually these three steps should get you connected (just click the Connect button and try it). Occasionally, though, your ISP will require you to set up some additional advanced options. Clicking the Advanced… button provides a sheet containing five tabs for setting advanced options. Of these five tabs, unless you have specific networking needs, you most likely will need to adjust the settings on the Modem tab if you are having trouble connecting.

Note For dial-up connections using your mobile phone's data connection, the phone number can vary from something like 99# to the APN used by your mobile access provider.

The Modem tab provides different information depending on your dial-up device. For a POTS modem (Figure 9-3), you may need to adjust the Model list that selects the proper modem script to initialize your modem. Ideally this should be set to Apple Modem (v.92) for an external Apple modem or to Internal 56K Modem (v.92) if you have an internal modem. However, your ISP's modem must be v.92-compliant for this connection (most today are). If you are having trouble connecting, you may need to fall back to an older modem protocol, so try the v.90 option, the v.34 option, and so on. Also, the "Enable error correction and compression in modem" option may affect the connection. This option, when selected, provides added performance, but this must also be supported on your ISP's modem for it to work.

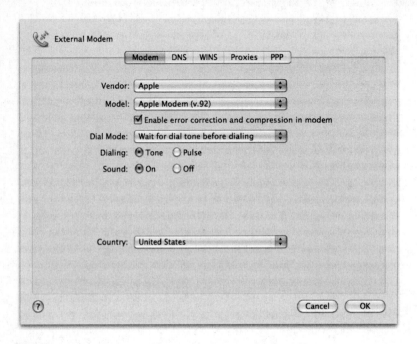

Figure 9-3. *The advanced Modem options for a POTS modem*

If you are setting up a Bluetooth dial-up modem, then the Modem options will be different (Figure 9-4). The model you select must correspond with your Bluetooth device; thankfully, Snow Leopard adds support for most popular Bluetooth-enabled modems. Additionally, there is a place to enter your APN here.

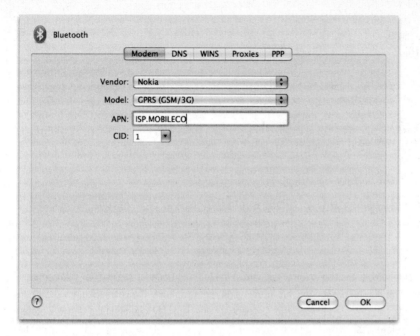

Figure 9-4. *The advanced Modem options for a Bluetooth data connection*

■**Note** The exact configuration for a Bluetooth data connection varies slightly for each model of phone and varies even more from one service provider to another (there are even different services for each service provider). This makes setting up this sort of connection a bit difficult to get right. Unfortunately, many mobile phone companies aren't too helpful with these matters either—that is, unless you are specifically paying for this service.

Initiating Your Dial-Up Connection

Once you have your dial-up connection set up, you'll still need to make the connection when you want to access the Internet. Apple has a couple of ways to do this besides hitting the Connect button in the Network panel in System Preferences each time you want to initiate a dial-up connection. One way is to simply select the "Show modem status in menu bar" option in the Network preference panel. This provides a menu item (Figure 9-5) that allows you to initiate your modem connections quickly and easily from the menu bar.

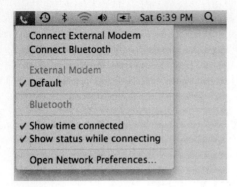

Figure 9-5. *You can add a menu item that allows you to initiate your modem connections from the menu bar.*

Note One application notably missing in Snow Leopard is the Internet Connect application. This application, originally designed for dial-up networking, has grown a bit redundant over the years. Beginning with Mac OS X 10.5 (Leopard), all the features of Internet Connect are now sensibly located in the Network preference pane of System Preferences.

Setting Up Multiple Dial-Up Configurations for a Modem

If you use dial-up frequently, you may want to set up different configurations. Say, for example, you use one number to connect from home, another to connect when you are visiting your mother-in-law, and another when you travel elsewhere. To add a new configuration, simply select Add Configuration from the configuration menu in the Network panel in System Preferences, select a name for this configuration, and then fill in the details for this connection. When you are done, click Apply, and that configuration will be saved. Then you can select that, or any other saved configuration, from the Configuration menu in the Network preference pane; additionally, all of your configurations will appear in the modem status menu item.

Note Many ISPs provide software to manage dial-up connections. Although using this software usually provides easy setup and use, they are often unnecessary and may not be 100 percent compatible with all versions of OS X. As with many things, there seems to be a trade-off. We recommend trying to set up dial-up networking as outlined earlier in the chapter.

Note One potential exception to the previous note applies when dealing with mobile service data providers. As mentioned, these are not straightforward to set up, so if your service provider provides software or if you choose some third-party connection software, such as nova media's launch2net (www.novamedia.de), you may save yourself some time and aggravation.

■**Note** Many mobile phone companies now offer mobile broadband data plans that utilize dedicated network devices (usually PC ExpressCards or USB devices) that can connect your computer directly to the Internet. Using one of these devices is synonymous with tethering a mobile phone via Bluetooth or cable and using that as a modem; however, the setup, configuration, and overall user experience with these devices is much, much better. Today there are even computers that come with the ability to connect to a mobile data network out of the box (well, after you sign up for the service). Of course, with all great things comes a downside. Right now the plans attached to these devices are quite pricey and usually provide limited amounts of data transfers (and hefty fees for exceeding the limit). Still, if you've got an extra $50 or so a month to burn on bandwidth (or you work somewhere that's willing to reimburse you), these sure are nice.

Broadband (High-Speed) Network Connections

Broadband networking has come a long way over the years. Today broadband access is available almost everywhere, and the cost, on the lower end, rivals the cost of dial-up access. Many types of broadband connections are available; Table 9-1 covers some of the currently prominent technologies.

Table 9-1. *Common Broadband Networking Technologies*

Technology	Description
DSL	Digital subscriber line (DSL) is, along with cable, one of the most popular broadband technologies used today. DSL sends a digital signal over traditional phone lines, making it easily available to many existing phone customers. There are a number of variants of DSL; the most common today is asymmetric DSL (ADSL). The big drawback to ADSL is that its speeds start to diminish over distance, making this technology less effective for rural areas. ADSL also provides fast download speeds while limiting its upload speed; this makes it suitable for most home users but less useful for businesses. Symmetric DSL (SDSL), on the other hand, provides the same upload and download speeds. ADSL is commonly referred to as residential DSL, while SDSL is usually referred to as business DSL.
VDSL	Very high bitrate DSL (VDSL) is a newer DSL technology that is beginning to be rolled out all over the world. This DSL technology, which relies on fiber cable rather than traditional copper wire, is currently able to provide up to 100 Mbps upload and download speeds over traditional POTS copper wiring. As with DSL, this speed diminishes over distance; still, VDSL provides higher speeds and longer distances than earlier versions of DSL. (In the United States, AT&T is rolling out VDSL as U-verse, and Verizon calls its implementation FiOS.)
Cable	Cable broadband is another big broadband technology used today. This provides access over existing cable TV lines. Unlike DSL, cable broadband does not lose its effectiveness over distances and traditionally has been able to provide faster data speeds than DSL; on the other hand, cable is also generally more expensive, and most cable companies provide cable broadband only to cable TV subscribers, raising the costs associated with cable even higher.
ISDN	Integrated Services Digital Network (ISDN) is one of the original broadband technologies available to consumers. It provides faster-than-dial-up speeds; however, there are lots of higher costs associated with it. ISDN has for the most part been replaced with other less expensive, faster technologies today.

Continued

Table 9-1. *Continued*

Technology	Description
T1	T1 lines (also called DS1 and E1) are the traditional broadband, high-speed connections that are common in many commercial offices. Originally, T1 connections were special telephone lines designed to carry voice communications for large organizations; however, early in the expansion of the Internet, digital T1 lines were used to provide high-speed Internet connections. T1 lines are still in use in many businesses for both voice and data. The downside to T1 lines is that even today they are regulated and require special lines to be run to connect the provider with the user. This makes their costs high. There are also T2 and T3 lines, which are similar yet faster than the traditional T1 lines.
SONET	Synchronous optical networking (SONET) technologies are slowly replacing T1 as the commercial data connection of choice. Using fiber-optic lines to carry the digital information allows OC-*x* technologies to provide extremely high-speed data throughput over long distances (though at a very high cost).
Wi-Fi	Wi-Fi is a blanket term that covers wireless 802.11 technologies, including Apple's AirPort technologies. Although the range of Wi-Fi is relatively low, it is quite popular in high-density and commercial areas. (Being short range, Wi-Fi is usually used in conjunction with a hardwired broadband technology such as DSL, cable, T1, or OC-x.)
WiMAX	WiMAX is a new emerging wireless broadband technology that attempts to provide faster speeds and, more important, greater range than traditional Wi-Fi technologies.
LTE	Long Term Evolution (LTE) is another emerging contender for high-speed wireless networks. Many mobile phone companies, including AT&T, T-Mobile, Vodafone, and Verizon, have announced plans or are currently testing LTE as their next generation (4G) of mobile technology.
Satellite	Satellite broadband provides high-speed access utilizing satellites to provide the communication over great distances. Satellite broadband is generally slightly more expensive and slightly slower than other methods of broadband; it is a viable alternative especially in rural areas where other technologies are unavailable or prohibitively expensive. The big disadvantage of satellite broadband is a latency problem, where a delay of 500 to 900 milliseconds is added to any other network latency transmitting the signal into space and then back again. Although this is not a big deal for casual Internet usage, such as web browsing and e-mail, it's a burden for real-time Internet activities such as VoIP (and it's a real killer for online gaming).

Besides the technologies listed in Table 9-1, a range of other technologies is available, and new ideas and technologies are constantly being developed. What's interesting about almost all of these, though, is the following:

- They all carry Internet Protocol (IP) packets from point A to point B.

- In a broadband environment, most of these technologies (except in most cases wireless technologies) usually just bridge a gap between the Internet and a router on your end.

Because of this, the actual broadband technology has little to do with how you set up your computer to take advantage of it. When the broadband connection enters your home, office, or company, it is usually run into an Ethernet or Wi-Fi router, which in turn you connect to with your computer using standard Transmission Control Protocol over Internet Protocol (TCP/IP) networking.

TCP/IP NETWORKING

TCP/IP networking consists of a collection of networking protocols collectively known as the Internet Protocol (IP) suite. In very general terms, Transmission Control Protocol (TCP) is responsible for application data carried over the Internet, and Internet Protocol (IP) is responsible for communication data. So although TCP carries the message, IP makes sure the message gets where it needs to go. When you configure your networking, you are essentially setting up your computer as a uniquely identifiable destination on the Internet for IP to successfully deliver TCP data to your computer.

The current IP protocol being used today is version 4. IPv4, in theory, addresses each computer on the Internet with a unique address made up of four series of numbers, called *octets*, that range from 0–255. A typical IP address may look like 153.29.250.112.

For those of you keeping count, this means IPv4 can address, in theory, only a bit more than 4 billion devices. When this was conceived in the early 1980s, a device was a computer, and 4 billion seemed like a lot. Today not only are there a lot more computers, but there are other devices such as phones, watches, automobiles, and more that use TCP/IP. In addition, a significant chunk of those 4 billion addresses are reserved for special uses, and you may notice a problem . . . we are running out of IPv4 addresses.

According to the Internet Assigned Numbers Authority (IANA) (the organization responsible for assigning IP addresses), the current projected date when all IPv4 addresses run out will be around 2011 or 2012. This won't matter much if you go by the Mayan calendar, which says the world will end then anyway, but for the rest of us, it's a problem. Although there are a number of ways to extend IPv4 (IP masquerading, NAT, and other technologies that are common today), a new version of IP, IPv6, has been defined and is currently being deployed. (The US government was pushing for deployment for all civilian and defense vendors by the summer of 2008, but clearly that has passed and IPv4 is still very much in use.) For comparison, IPv6 supports approximately 3.14 undecillion addresses. Undecillion is 10 to the 36th power (or add 36 0s) . . . either way, it's a big number.

Configuring Your Mac for a Broadband Connection

For your Mac to function on the Internet, it must have the following information:

A qualified IP address: IP addresses are discussed in the "TCP/IP Networking" sidebar. An IP address is a unique address that identifies your computer on the Internet so that all information being sent to your computer actually makes it there. You cannot (usually) just make up an IP address; it must be assigned, or else it will likely not work.

A subnet mask: A subnet mask is used to separate the network address from the host address. This can be further used within a network to create subnets; breaking up a host address into subnets allows more effective routing of IP traffic. An example of an IPv4 subnet mask is 255.255.255.0, and any IP address that shares the first three octets in the IP address is part of the same subnet. If all that sounds foreign to you, don't worry; just use the subnet mask your ISP or network administrator gave you.

A gateway address (or router): The router address (also known as a gateway address) is the IP address of the next upstream router.

A DNS server address: The Domain Name System (DNS) server is the primary server for your subnet that is responsible for providing DNS services. A DNS server is responsible for translating a domain name (that is, `apple.com`) into an IP address (in other words, `17.254.3.183`). You can list multiple DNS servers if you would like, and if the first one is unable to resolve a domain name, then the next one listed will be consulted.

Search domains (optional): Search domains are an optional list of domains to search if a domain address cannot be resolved by any of the DNS servers. This can provide a shortcut on some networks as well, since it will allow you to address a computer by the hostname alone.

■**Note** IPv4 has set aside a number of IP address blocks as private addresses (`10.x.x.x`, `172.16.x.x`, and `192.168.x.x`). These private IP addresses are for the creation of private networks that utilize IP. Many routers (and firewalls) take advantage of these private IP addresses to perform network address translation (NAT, a.k.a. network masquerading). This allows the router to be assigned a valid Internet IP address yet assign all the computers behind it private IP addresses. The router can then act as a gateway between the private network and the Internet, providing each computer connected to the router with full Internet access without a dedicated IP address. Although initial implementations of NAT often carried with them some side effects, most current implementations of NAT provide Internet clients with complete functionality. Server processes running behind NAT, however, need special considerations and are limited. This can be used advantageously from a security point of view, and in fact, many firewalls use NAT combined with port forwarding to hide the actual server from the Internet.

■**Note** Port forwarding allows the router or firewall facing the Internet to masquerade as a server while server requests are actually being passed along to other systems on the private network. This can be set up so specific services, which use specific ports, can be passed to specific systems. So, all e-mail traffic using ports 25 (SMTP), 110 (POP3), and 143 (IMAP4) could point to one server behind the router, while all web traffic using port 80 (HTTP) would be directed to another.

There are two primary ways to connect your computer to a broadband connection: Ethernet and Wi-Fi.

Making an Ethernet Connection

Prior to Wi-Fi, the most common way to make a high-speed connection was through Ethernet, and this remains popular today, since it's easier to control and is capable of much faster speeds. Currently all shipping Apple computers have a high-speed Ethernet port installed, with the exception of the MacBook Air.

An Ethernet connection is a physical connection in which a cable runs from a router or modem into your computer. Depending on your broadband service and your local area network (LAN) setup, configuring your connection through Ethernet could be handled automatically through Dynamic Host Configuration Protocol (DHCP) or Bootstrap Protocol (BOOTP), or the configuration may need to be done manually. Additionally, some service providers (especially ADSL) use a connection called Point-to-Point Protocol over Ethernet

(PPPoE) that, while creating a high-speed connection over Ethernet, is configured a bit more like a dial-up connection.

If you know you need to use PPPoE or configure your network connection manually, then you can get the proper configuration information from your service provider or administrator. Otherwise, just plug in the Ethernet cable and turn on your computer; a surprisingly large amount of the time, DHCP is used and configures your network information automatically. To check, take a look in the Network panel in System Preferences and see whether you are connected (Figure 9-6).

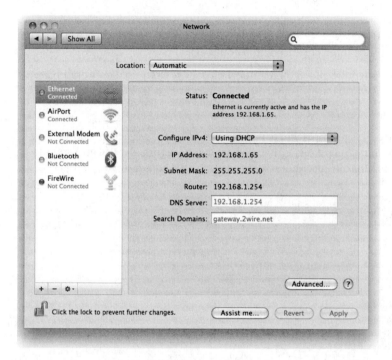

Figure 9-6. *This Ethernet connection is configured and connected automatically using DHCP.*

If the little bubble next to the connection in the left column of the Network preference pane is green, then your connection is successful. If it is yellow, then the computer has detected that a cable is plugged in, but there is problem with either the physical connection or the configuration. If the bubble is red, then that service is not currently connected.

If DHCP doesn't work, then you will need to choose another way to configure your network. The configuration drop-down provides a list that includes the following:

Using DHCP: DHCP is more and more common these days in almost every environment. Not only does it make setting up a system incredibly easy from the user end, but it also allows reuse of IP addresses and increased manageability from the administrative perspective.

Using DHCP with manual address: Usually DHCP automatically assigns a computer that connects to it the next available IP address it has at its disposal. It leases this address to that particular system for a period of time (and usually continues to renew that lease as long as the system remains connected); however, after a period of time, it may issue the system a different IP address. For most situations, this is fine; however, occasionally a system needs a static IP address that won't change. This option allows you to pick a static IP address.

■Note IP addresses need to be unique; even on a private network, every IP address needs to be different than every other IP address on that network. Because of this, when you manually assign an IP address, you should be careful that it doesn't belong to the block of IP addresses being dynamically assigned and that it isn't being used by another system on the network.

Using BootP: BOOTP is an older technology that was created to allow diskless workstations or thin clients to receive an IP address automatically from a server. DHCP is based upon BOOTP but is much more advanced (and complex).

Manually: This option requires that you manually fill in all the required networking information. In this case, you will likely be given specific information to use (Figure 9-7).

Off: This turns off the interface.

Create PPPoE Service: This prompts you to create a new PPPoE interface for configuring the PPPoE service (Figure 9-8). If this is required, your service provider will give you the necessary information for this (username, password, and perhaps a service name).

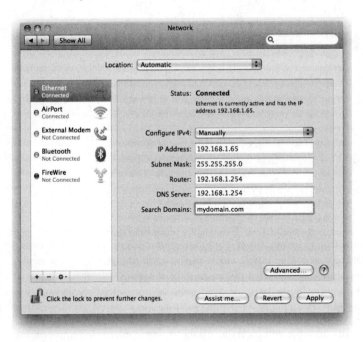

Figure 9-7. *If you must configure your network manually, you will need to fill in all the required information.*

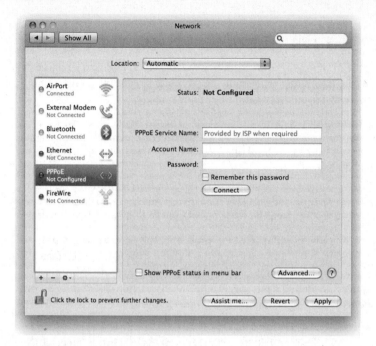

Figure 9-8. *A PPPoE connection works much like a dial-up connection; however, it creates a much faster connection when active.*

Making an AirPort Internet Connection

Today every computer Apple sells comes equipped with what Apple calls AirPort technology. What Apple calls AirPort, most everybody else refers to as Wi-Fi, or more properly 802.11.

■**Note** 802.11 or IEEE 802.11 is the proper name of the WLAN technology we are talking about here. Apple calls its implementation of this standard AirPort, and an industry group has formed outside the IEEE called the Wi-Fi Alliance. This group was created to help certify new incarnations of 802.11 before the IEEE officially approves them. Either way, in the big picture, whatever it's called, it usually refers to the same technology.

802.11 is a point-to-point networking technology that is used to create LANs that work like a traditional wired network without the wires. These are commonly referred to as *wireless LANs* (WLANs).

802.11 networks handle the network configuration in the same manner as wired networks; in fact, almost all 802.11 networks use DHCP to make this configuration automatic. The tricky part comes during the process of joining or connecting to the WLAN to begin with. This is because there are a number of different types of 802.11 networks; also, there are a number of types of security schemes available to limit who can join an 802.11 network and to encrypt the network data once the connection is made.

Types of Wi-Fi Networks

Currently, four common variations of 802.11 networks are in use today:

802.11b: This was what the original AirPort technology was based on and also what most people associate with Wi-Fi. It provides reasonably fast transfer speeds over a reasonably large area. It operates in the 2.4 to 2.5 GHz radio frequency range.

802.11a: 802.11a came out about the same time as 802.11b, provided faster transfer speeds, and used radio frequencies in the 5 GHz range, which cut down on interference from cordless phones, Bluetooth devices, and microwave ovens. However, 802.11a products started shipping late, by which time the industry was already implementing 802.11b. As such, 802.11a never really caught on to the extent of 802.11b. (An ironic twist on this is that although Apple has never supported 802.11a, the current AirPort chips included with Intel-based Macs do support 802.11a.) 802.11a is not compatible with 802.11b or 802.11g.

802.11g: This is currently the most popular 802.11 variant. It is 100 percent compatible with 802.11b, but when used with 802.11g devices at both ends, it provides much faster transfer speeds and a slight boost in distance. Apple's AirPort devices (both in computers and base stations) quickly switched from 802.11b to 802.11g (Apple called this AirPort Extreme). The downside with 802.11g is that it still operates in the crowded 2.4 to 2.5 GHz radio frequency range.

802.11n: 802.11n is the newest version of 802.11. 802.11n increases transfer speeds up to 5 times over 802.11g and doubles the range of 802.11g, when used in 802.11n mode with other 802.11n devices. It can work in either the 2.4 to 2.5 or 5.0 GHz radio frequency range. 802.11n devices also can operate in three modes: Legacy, which supports 802.11 b/g and 802.11 a; Mixed, which supports 802.11 b/g, 802.11 a, and 802.11n; and then a pure 802.11n mode, which is necessary to take advantage of the increased speed and distances offered by 802.11n. Apple's newest AirPort Extremes, as well as all new Core 2 Duo and newer Macs, support a draft of this technology.

Wi-Fi Security Schemes

Besides the different types of actual networks, there are also different security mechanisms used to protect 802.11 networks. These include the following:

WEP: Wired Equivalent Privacy (WEP) was written as part of the 802.11 standard to provide access control and data security to WLANs. Standard 64-bit WEP uses a 40-bit encryption key; however, today 128-bit WEP is prevalent and supports a 104-bit encryption key. Although WEP is quite popular and does provide at least some protection from casual eavesdropping, from a security standpoint it is considered broken. Not only are the keys vulnerable (a WEP key can be cracked in a few minutes using readily available software from the Internet), but there are other inherent flaws in WEP that makes it unsuitable for situations where security and data integrity are a priority.

WPA/WPA2: Wi-Fi Protected Access (WPA) was created in response to flaws discovered with WEP, and it was quickly implemented and is based upon the IEEE 802.11i standard (WPA2 fully implements 802.11i, while WPA implemented most of it). WPA uses an improved encryption key, making cracking the key significantly more difficult than a WEP key, and improves data integrity checks lacking in WEP. WPA2 further increases the strength of the encryption key. WPA and WPA2 offer two modes of use: a Personal mode and an Enterprise mode. Personal mode works similarly to WEP in that there is a single preshared encryption key (PSK) used. In Enterprise mode, a user must first log into a RADIUS server that assigns a dynamic key to that user. Not only does this provide excellent user access control, but by providing a unique key for each user, it provides excellent data security as well.

802.1X: This is an IEEE standard that is part of the same group as 802.11 (though it is not directly related). It is a method of authentication often used in conjunction with WPA2 Enterprise mode when authenticating the user to the RADIUS server.

LEAP: Lightweight Extensible Authentication Protocol (LEAP) was developed by Cisco for Cisco wireless routers. This requires the user to first log in with a username and password to receive a WEP key. Beyond the login, this operates similarly to WEP; as such, it is not used much anymore.

None: It is of course possible to have no security on a WLAN. This is referred to as an *open network*. Most public Wi-Fi access points are open networks (though some require registration and perhaps fees to access the Internet). The most important thing to keep in mind about using an open network is that there is no wireless encryption, so everything you send over the network is potentially viewable by those around you. As such, it's important to use encrypted connections to services you are accessing whenever possible.

Joining a Wi-Fi Network

You can join a wireless network either from the Network preference panel (Figure 9-9) or from the AirPort menu item (Figure 9-10).

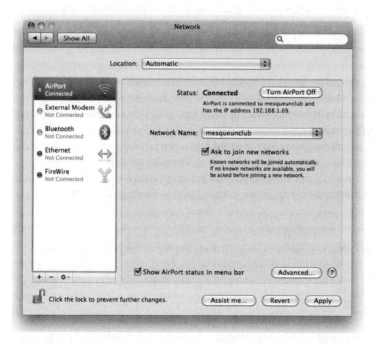

Figure 9-9. *Connecting to an AirPort in the Network preference panel*

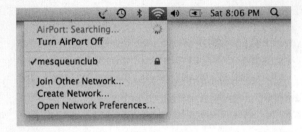

Figure 9-10. *The AirPort menu item allows you to view and select any of the Wi-Fi networks in your location.*

The first thing you need to do is ensure you have powered on the AirPort in your computer. Once the network is on, you can click the Network Name drop-down list, which lists all the advertising Wi-Fi networks in range of your computer. Select the network you want join from the list, and then click Apply. If the selected network requires authentication or a password (key), you will be prompted to enter that information. If your password or authentication information is correct, then you will be connected immediately. If for whatever reason you want to adjust the network settings, you can access them by clicking the Advanced button.

A much more convenient way to join a Wi-Fi network is by selecting the "Show AirPort status in menu bar" option and using the menu item.

Tip If you access the AirPort menu icon while you hold down the Option key, detailed information about all of the detected wireless networks will be shown.

The AirPort menu item provides some additional information about your current connection as well as other available WLANs in your area. First, the icon in the menu bar will signify the relative strength of your current network signal; four bars is great, and one bar (which looks more like a dot) is not so good. In the list provided from the AirPort menu item, you can see a list of all the available networks divided by secured and open networks. If you hold your cursor over one of the network names, a tool tip will pop up showing the type of security used as well as the relative signal strength. Selecting a network from the menu will prompt you for any security passwords or authentication and then connect you to that network.

Note WEP passwords are generally hexadecimal strings 10 digits long for 40-bit and 26 digits long for 104-bit keys. Apple, however, tends to use common "password" strings for passwords (which are then converted to hexadecimal strings). The thing is, if you are connecting to a WEP-secured WLAN and are given the hexadecimal key, when you type it into the Password text box, Leopard will by default assume you are entering a text password and convert the string you enter from a normal text string to a hexadecimal string. To prevent this from happening, you must start the hexadecimal string with a $ character. So if you are given 3B-2D-98-AA-32 as a hexadecimal string, you should enter $3B2D98AA32 in the Password box.

■Tip If you select the Advanced… button in the Network Preferences with the AirPort network selected, it will open up an special AirPort pane that will list all of your preferred wireless networks (by default, networks that you have connected to in the past). Among other options, here you can set the order of preference for your preferred wireless networks, and you can also modify or delete them.

Creating Separate Networking Profiles for Different Locations

If you rely on DHCP for everything or you never move your computer around, then you can set up your network and live just fine with it. However, if you are using a portable computer and you need to connect multiple networks that use different settings, then you may want to take advantage of the Location feature. At the top of the Network preference pane, there is a drop-down list that by default is set on Automatic. While Automatic is selected, any changes you make to any of your network interfaces are saved in the Automatic location.

If you need to have multiple network configurations—one at home that is basically the same as the Automatic setting and one for work where you are assigned specific networking information—then you can add a location from the drop-down list and configure the networking for that location as needed. Once you have multiple locations set up, a Location item will appear in your Apple menu that will allow you to switch your networking preferences from one location to the next.

Summary

This chapter covered what you need to get your computer connected to the Internet with your Mac. We attempted to skirt around some of the more complex networking issues, saving most of those for Part 6 of this book, which is dedicated to networking. The point of this chapter was to get you up and running so you can follow along with the next chapters that cover Safari, Mail, and other Internet-related applications.

CHAPTER 10

■■■

Browsing the Web with Safari

Snow Leopard includes the latest version of Apple's web browser, Safari 4. Safari is a fast, standards-compliant web browser loaded with lots of useful features for getting the most out of the Web. This chapter will take a look at Safari and its capabilities, including the following:

- Safari basics
- Adding and managing bookmarks
- Tabbed browsing
- Downloading content from the Web
- Viewing PDFs
- Auto-filling form data
- Security
- Advanced browsing features
- RSS and syndication feeds
- Plug-ins and inline content
- Web clippings

Safari Basics

Safari is Mac OS X's default web browser, but you can install and use any other available Mac web browser as well. (Firefox, Camino, OmniWeb, Opera, and many more exist. You could even whip up your own in Xcode without writing a single line of code!) However, most people who start using Safari tend to stick with it. Like most Apple software, Safari packs in a lot of useful features while still providing a clean, easy-to-use interface.

■**Note** If you've been using Snow Leopard for any amount of time now, you may notice that it runs quite a bit faster than previous versions of Mac OS X. Similarly, Safari 4 has seen significant performance gains over previous versions of Safari. Not only does Safari 4 benefit from the underlying performance gains of Snow Leopard, but it also hosts a new, faster version of WebKit (the component that renders web pages) and a new JavaScript interpreter (called Nitro or SquirrelFish, depending on whom you ask). Together with these new features, web pages load faster and respond faster—a lot faster in Safari 4 than in any other current browser out there (as of this writing anyway . . . eventually, others will likely catch up and play leapfrog for awhile).

The Basic Interface

Safari 4 (Figure 10-1) appears and works like most other popular web browsers, with a few twists that set it apart from most other browsers (even previous versions of Safari). By default, its toolbar is sparse yet functional, with only a handful of items (Back, Forward, and Add Book-mark buttons; an address field; and a web search field). Below the toolbar is the Bookmarks Bar, which provides easy access to your favorite bookmarks or bookmark collections. It also provides buttons to open your Collections (Figure 10-2) and Top Sites (Figure 10-3). Below the Bookmarks Bar (if visible) is the Tab Bar, and below that (if visible) is the Find Banner, which appears when you use the Edit ➤ Find ➤ Find... (or Command-F) command. This allows you to find text within a web page. Below that is the main browser pane where the web pages are rendered, Collections are browsed and organized, and the Top Sites window appears. Finally, at the very bottom is the Status bar (if enabled, which by default it is not), which provides some information about loading pages and hyperlinks.

Figure 10-1. *Safari with expanded view options*

Figure 10-2. *Safari's Collections view is where you can view and manage your browsing history, bookmarks, and more.*

Figure 10-3. *The Top Sites view is new in Safari 4. This view dynamically presents small representations of the web sites you visit the most. (Clicking one of the small windows loads the site.)*

■**Note** By default, only the toolbar and Bookmarks Bar are shown. You must select View ➤ Show Status Bar (or Command-/) to activate the Status bar.

Secondary-clicking (or Control-clicking) the toolbar and selecting Customize Toolbar... from the resulting contextual menu opens a dialog containing other buttons and items that you can drag to your toolbar (Figure 10-4). Some popular items that users add are the Home and Print buttons. From the Customize Toolbar dialog, you can add, remove, or reorganize any of these items on your toolbar. At the bottom of the Customize Toolbar dialog is a default toolbar, which you can use to return your toolbar to its default state.

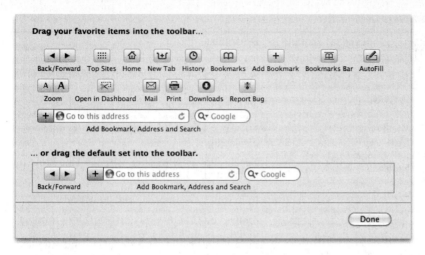

Figure 10-4. *You can customize your Safari toolbar in a number of ways to suit your needs.*

■**Note** What happened to the Stop and Reload buttons? They were removed and replaced with a small icon on the far right side of the Address field. Clicking the icon either stops loading a page that is loading or reloads a page that is already loaded. The icon itself changes between a Loading X icon and a circular arrow icon to indicate which action will occur when clicked.

Besides the options viewable in the window, like most applications, there are many menu items in the various menus provided. Table 10-1 provides a list of Safari menu items that are unique or particularly useful to Safari.

■**Note** Many menu items (as well as their keyboard shortcuts) are common among all Mac OS X applications. Occasionally, though, even common items have unique behavior in some applications and situations. For Safari, we will go over all the default options, but as we progress through the book, we will only cover options that are unique to the product or that haven't been covered previously.

Table 10-1. *Useful Safari Menu Items*

Menu/Submenu Item	Keyboard Shortcut	Description
Safari		
Block Pop-Up Windows	Shift-Command-K	Toggles Safari's ability to block those mostly unwanted pop-up windows that spring up automatically when you load some web pages. This doesn't prevent requested pop-up windows (ones that you initiate when you click a link) from displaying.
Private Browsing...		Toggles Private Browsing. When Private Browsing is activated, none of the pages you visit are added to your browser history, and items are removed from your browser cache and downloads.
Reset Safari...		Allows you to selectively reset (clear) a number of items that Safari stores all at once. These include the history, cache, cookies, and AutoFill information.
Empty Cache...	Option-Command-E	Empties your browser cache.
File		
New Window	Command-N	Opens a new browser window in Safari.
New Tab	Command-T	Opens a new tab in the current browser window.
Open File...	Command-O	Opens a file dialog box, allowing you to open a file located on your computer in Safari.
Open Location...	Command-L	Highlights the Location text field in the toolbar, allowing you to type in a URL of a web resource you wish to open. (Pressing Return will then take you there directly, without needing to move your hands from the keyboard.)
Close Window	(Shift-)Command-W	Closes the current browser window. If multiple tabs are open in the window, the default keyboard shortcut will change, as Command-W will only close the front tab. Also, if you are closing a window with multiple tabs, you will be prompted to verify your action.
Close Tab	Command-W	Closes the current tab. The Command-W keyboard shortcut will close the window if there are no tabs (or only one tab).
Save as...		Brings up a save dialog, allowing you to save the current web page. You can save the page as a web archive, which will create a special file that includes all images and other data that can be viewed in Safari on Mac OS X or Windows (however, only Safari 4 or later on Windows), or as a source file, which will only save the text source of the page (however, you will be able to view the HTML file in any browser).

Menu/Submenu Item	Keyboard Shortcut	Description
Mail Contents of This Page	Command-I	Opens the contents of the web page in a new Mail message so you can send it to others who can view HTML messages.
Mail Link to This Page	Shift-Command-I	Opens a new Mail message with the link embedded to facilitate the e-mailing of the link to your recipients.
Open in Dashboard...		Allows you to select a region of the current web page to be added as a web clipping to your Dashboard (this is covered later in this chapter).
Import Bookmarks...		Allows you to import a bookmark file from another location on your computer (including bookmarks from some other browsers).
Export Bookmarks...		Exports your Safari bookmarks into a separate file for archiving or for importing into a different browser. The bookmark file you export will be a properly formatted HTML file, so you can use it in various interesting ways.
Print...	Command-P	Opens the Print dialog so you can print out the current web page. Since you can print to PDF, this provides another option for saving web content.
Edit		
AutoFill Form	Shift-Command-A	Attempts to fill in a web form using data from the AutoFill feature in Safari. This feature is sometimes triggered automatically when you begin to fill out a form.
Find		Opens a submenu of the following items (i.e., the items from Google Search to Jump to Selection).
Google Search	Option-Command-F	Moves the focus to the Google search box in the toolbar so you can enter a term to search with Google.
Find...	Command-F	Opens up the Find Banner at the top of the web page so that you may search the web page for specific text.
Find Next	Command-G	Cycles forward through the web page revealing the next match to your Find search string in the web page.
Find Previous	Shift-Command-G	Cycles back through the page finding previous search matches.
Hide Find Banner	Shift-Command-F	Hides the Find Banner if opened.
Use Selection for Find	Command-E	Copies the selected text into the Find field (even if the Find Banner is hidden). You may then use the Find Next or Find Previous commands to cycle through matched or selected text.
Jump to Selection	Command-J	Automatically scrolls the web page up or down (if necessary) to recenter the page on the selected region.

Continued

Table 10-1. *Continued*

Menu/Submenu Item	Keyboard Shortcut	Description
View		
(Show|Hide) Bookmarks Bar	Shift-Command-B	Toggles the visibility of the Bookmarks Bar.
(Show|Hide) Status Bar	Command-/	Toggles the visibility of the Status bar.
(Show|Hide) Tab Bar	Shift-Command-T	Toggles the visibility of the Tab bar. This only has an effect when no tabs are currently open (or if there is only one tab).
(Show|Hide) Toolbar	Command-| (Shift-Command-\)	Toggles the visibility of the main toolbar.
Customize Toolbar...		Opens the Customize Toolbar sheet as described previously.
Stop	Command-.	Stops loading the currently loading page.
Reload Page	Command-R	Reloads the current page. This causes the page to fully reload, overwriting any information in the cache.
Actual Size	Command-0	Adjusts the browsing area to display its contents at its normal size.
Zoom In	Command-+ (Command-=)	Zooms into the web page, making its contents bigger (by default, this does more than just increase the text size; it increases the size of all the elements and graphics).
Zoom Out	Command--	Zooms out, decreasing the size of all the elements in the web page.
Zoom Text Only		When this option is selected, the Zoom Out command only impacts the text on the web page.
View Source	Option-Command-U	Opens the web page's source in a separate window.
Text Encoding		Opens a submenu providing different text encoding options for different language sets. This is useful if the default language isn't properly recognized automatically.
History		
Show Top Sites	Shift-Command-1	Opens the Top Sites view in the current browser window or tab.
Back	Command-[	Returns you to the last page you visited.
Forward	Command-]	Returns you forward after going backward.
Home	Shift-Command-H	Takes you directly to your home page as configured in your preferences.
Search Results SnapBack	Option-Command-S	Returns you to your last Google web search results page. This feature even works with searches performed directly from the Google web page.
Reopen Last Closed Window		Reopens the last window you closed. The window opens with any tabs that were closed with it as well.

Menu/Submenu Item	Keyboard Shortcut	Description
Reopen All Windows From Last Session		Reopens all previously opened windows from the last session (and returns Safari to the state it was in the last time you closed it).[1]
Show All History		Opens a window, allowing you to view all your previous browsing history. By default, this includes the browsing history as set up in Safari's general preferences.
Clear History		Clears your browser history.
Bookmarks		
(Show|Hide) All Bookmarks	Option-Command-B	Toggles open the bookmark window in the main viewing area. This is the same view as the Show All History view. This view allows you to view and organize all of your bookmarks.
Add Bookmark...	Command-D	Opens a small sheet that allows you to add a bookmark to the current web page to any of your bookmark folders.
Add Bookmark For These Tabs		Allows you to add bookmarks for all the open tabs in a window at once.
Add Bookmark Folder	Shift-Command-N	Creates a new unnamed folder selected in the Bookmarks view.
Bookmarks Bar		Opens a submenu containing the bookmarks that you have on your Bookmarks Bar (this may be turned off in Safari's preferences).[2]
Open in Tabs		Opens each bookmark stored in your Bookmark Menu collection in a separate tab at the same time. This could be a whole lot of bookmarks (Safari seems to have a limit of 200), so use this with care.
Window		
Select Next Tab	Command-}	Cycles to the next tab.
Select Previous Tab	Command-{	Cycles to the previous tab.
Move Tab to New Window		Opens the active tab in a separate window.
Merge All Windows		Consolidates all open browser windows into one window using tabs.
Downloads	Option-Command-L	Opens and brings to the foreground the Downloads window.
Activity	Option-Command-A	Opens and brings to the foreground the Activity window.
Bring All To Front		Brings all of Safari's open windows to the foreground.[3]
Help		
Installed Plug-Ins		Opens a window listing all of the browser plug-ins currently active in Safari.

[1]*Following the Reopen All Windows From Last Session item, Safari will provide the last 20 history items (or bookmarks from the last 20 web pages stored in its history), followed by submenus containing your browser history over the last week.*

[2]*After the Bookmarks Bar item, there will be list of bookmarks that are part of your Bookmark Menu collection.*

[3]*Following the Bring All To Front item, each open window will be listed.*

That covers the basics of the interface, including the menu items. Now we'll take a closer look at how to perform certain tasks in Safari.

Setting Your Home Page

Your home page is the default web page that Safari goes to when it is initially launched. Out of the box, this is set for the Apple Start page (`www.apple.com/startpage`), which provides Apple news and links to other Apple products and features. If, however, you'd like to open a different page (or no page) when you start Safari, then open the Safari preferences, click the General button (Figure 10-5), and set a few options:

New windows open with: This drop-down list allows you to select if new windows open with Top Sites, the home page (Figure 10-5), an empty page, or the same page (i.e., the page that was last opened in Safari), or if they open in Bookmarks view.

Home page: This text field allows you to enter the URL of any web page that you'd like to use as your home page.

Set to Current Page: Clicking this button automatically enters the URL of your current web page into the "Home page" text field.

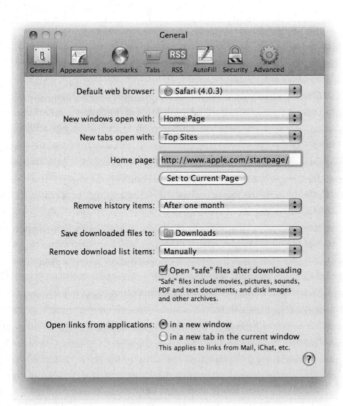

Figure 10-5. *You can select your own home page on the General tab of Safari's preferences.*

Searching the Web

If you'd like to perform a search on the Web, Safari by default provides a search field in the top right of the toolbar to enter a search string, which opens a page of search results from Google.

Bookmarks

Bookmarks provide a way for you to keep track of the web sites you visit that you'd like to return to (or keep track of for some other reason). Safari has a very nice bookmark system in place that allows you to keep an extensive collection of bookmarks well organized in folders and collections.

Adding Bookmarks

To add a bookmark of a page you are visiting, you can select Add Bookmark from the Bookmarks menu, use the Command-D keyboard shortcut, or click the Add Bookmark button on the toolbar. Any of these actions open a dialog allowing you to name and choose a location for storing your bookmark. You can also add a bookmark by selecting the URL from the Address field in the toolbar and drag it down to the Bookmarks bar, a specific bookmark folder, or a bookmark collection in the Collections view.

Managing Bookmarks

When you are in the Collections view, you can organize your bookmarks in a way that makes the most sense to you. To enter the Bookmarks view, select the Show All Bookmarks item from the Bookmarks menu, use the Option-Command-B keyboard shortcut, or click the Show All Bookmarks button on the far left of your Bookmarks bar (the icon that looks like an open book).

Note When viewing the items in the Bookmarks Bar collection, you may notice a column called Auto-Click, which contains a check box next to each folder item. When the Auto-Click feature is selected, rather than providing a drop-down list of bookmarks contained in that folder, all the bookmarks contained in the folder open in individual tabs when you select this item in the Bookmarks bar.

In the left column of the Collections view, there are two areas: Collections and Bookmarks. *Collections* are special groupings of bookmarks or other related items. The Bookmarks Bar and Bookmarks Menu collections provide a place for you to store bookmarks so they are easily accessible from Safari; the contents in these two collections are fully customizable. Other collections provide access to links that are collected automatically. The Address Book collection contains all the URLs associated with contacts in your Address Book. The Bonjour collection contains a list of web sites on your network that take advantage of Bonjour. The History collection provides links to your browsing history. All RSS Feeds is a collection of links that lead to RSS feeds rather than traditional web pages.

Below the collections are your primary Bookmarks folders. Here you can add, remove, and move around folders, and store any bookmarks within them. This is a great way to store large amounts of bookmarks in an organized manner. It's important to note, though, that the bookmarks stored here are only accessible from this view. If you need quicker access to particular bookmarks, it's best to store those in the Bookmarks Bar or Bookmarks Menu collections.

Bookmark Preferences

The Bookmarks tab in Safari's Preference window (Figure 10-6) provides a few options: primarily, how to treat certain collections, but also a sync option.

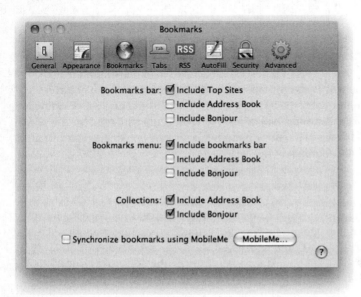

Figure 10-6. *The Bookmarks options in Safari's Preference window*

The Bookmarks bar and Bookmarks menu options allow you to select from a list of collections. Any selected collections then appear as items in the selected element. The Collections options let you choose whether to include the Address Book or Bonjour collections at all.

The last option, if selected, will keep your bookmarks in sync with your MobileMe account (and thus, in sync with other computers you use that also sync with MobileMe). This is handy if you use many different computers and want to keep all your bookmarks handy from any of them. Also, enabling this provides you with an up-to-date backup of all of your bookmarks.

Tabbed Browsing

The Safari browser fully supports tabbed browsing, which allows you to open up and view multiple web pages at one time all in one window. For those of us with a history of browsing many sites at once, this is a massive improvement over shuffling around many separate browser windows.

The ability to use tabs is always present in Safari—however, setting a few options in the Tabs tab in Safari's preferences (Figure 10-7) can make using tabs more convenient.

■**Note** When you adjust the Tabs preference options, the actions associated with common keyboard shortcuts also change. At the bottom of the Tabs window, a list of the keyboard shortcuts and their resulting actions updates dynamically, depending on your selections.

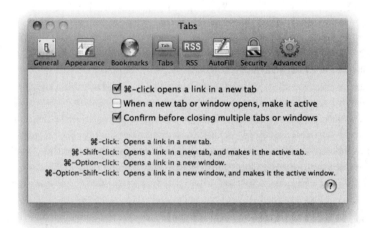

Figure 10-7. *The Tabs options in Safari's preferences*

One other option in Safari's preferences that has a direct impact on the use of tabs, but isn't in the Tabs section of the preferences, is the "Open links from applications" option on the General preference tab. This option allows you to configure Safari so that when you click a link in another application, it opens that link in a tab in the current Safari window instead of opening a new window each time (if no Safari window is currently open, then of course a new window will be created).

Creating New Tabs

To create an empty tab in a Safari window, select New Tab from the File menu (or use Command-T). Otherwise, depending on your preferences, new tabs can be created when you Command-click a hyperlink in a web page or when you click a link in an external application.

■**Note** By default in OS X, mouse click 3, which is commonly the middle mouse button (or the scroll wheel when clicked), opens up new links in a new tab as well. Some mice (e.g., Logitech MX Revolution) have other default actions when you click the scroll wheel, though, so this behavior can vary both in hardware and third-party mouse drivers.

Moving Tabs

Occasionally, especially when you have a bunch of tabs open, you may want to move the tabs around into a different order in the title bar (or even into a different browser window). To move a tab, just grab (click and hold) the tab, then drag the tab across the tab bar to reorder it. If you drag the tab out of the tab bar, though, the tab will change into a thumbnail of a browser window. If you release the window in this state, you will have moved the tab into a new window. This works the other way around too; if you grab the shaded corner of a stray browser window, you can drag it into the tab bar of another window to convert it into a tab. (And yes, you can use this to move a tab from one browser window into another as well.)

■**Tip** To quickly consolidate any number of open browser windows into tabs in a single browser window, use the Window ➤ Merge All Windows command in Safari's menu bar.

Closing Tabs

To close a tab, you can either click the small x located on the left side of any tab or use the Close Tab menu option in the File menu (or the Command-W keyboard shortcut).

Downloading Content from the Web

Besides browsing the Web, Safari can also easily download content that it encounters on the Web. When you click a link in Safari that leads to a file that Safari doesn't display, Safari will automatically start to download the selected item, and the Downloads window will open up to display the download progress.

■**Note** Safari doesn't support all the popular protocols used today to download files, including BitTorrent, Gnutella, and others. If you wish to utilize this type of file download, you will need to get a third-party application like Acquisition (www.acquisitionx.com) or Transmission (http://transmission.m0k.org).

■**Note** Chapter 20 covers all sorts of ways to transfer files from one location to another in more depth.

■**Note** The first time you attempt to launch an application or open a file that you have downloaded from the Internet, Mac OS X will always warn you that you are about to open an application you downloaded from the Internet and that you should do so only if you downloaded it from a trusted source. Due to an issue with some copies of iLife '09 that some people downloaded from some unknown torrent (a BitTorrent stream), this advice should always be heeded. (Oh, and you should probably buy your software rather than steal it from the Internet.)

On the General tab of Safari's preferences, a few options affect how Safari downloads items:

Save downloaded files to: This option allows you to choose a folder to save all downloads in. By default, this is the Downloads folder in your home directory.

Remove download list items: This option allows you to choose whether downloaded items remain listed in the Downloads window until you remove them manually (using the Clear button), or whether this list should be cleared automatically when the download is complete or you quit Safari. Private Browsing overrides this option. Additionally, failed or canceled searches are never cleared automatically.

Open "safe" files after downloading: When this option is selected, items deemed safe will launch automatically when they have completed downloading. Not only does this include opening items like images and movies in Safari, but when this option is selected, archives will be uncompressed and disk images will be mounted automatically. This will not in any situation cause a newly downloaded application to launch automatically, though (that would be considered unsafe).

Viewing Image Files and PDFs in Safari

When Safari downloads certain types of files that it can display, it will (depending on the "safe" file option) open that item in Safari. When that item is a stand-alone image, if the image is larger than the Safari window it is opening in, then Safari's will scale the image so it fits in the window. If you click the scaled image, it will scale back to its original size, allowing you to scroll around to view it.

■**Note** One nice thing about this feature is that when you click a large image to zoom in on it, the image will zoom into the region you clicked in.

Besides images, Safari displays PDF files from the Internet for easy viewing (Figure 10-8). Additionally, Safari provides a nice toolbar overlay (Figure 10-9) that appears when you move your mouse toward the bottom center of the PDF view. This toolbar allows you to zoom in and out of the PDF, open the PDF in the Preview application, and save the PDF file to disk.

■**Note** Besides the visible options, additional options are available for both images and PDFs from the contextual menu.

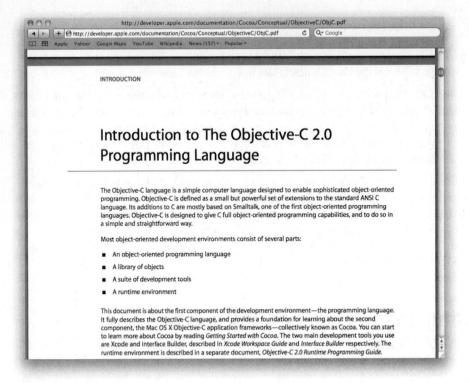

Figure 10-8. *Viewing a PDF file in Safari*

Figure 10-9. *A small toolbar appears at the bottom of the Safari view window when you are viewing a PDF to provide the ability to zoom, open in Preview, or save the PDF to disk.*

Web Forms and AutoFill

Many functions of many web sites require that you fill out forms with data ranging from simple web site login information to shipping information and other contact info. While none of this is very hard, sometimes you wish this information would just fill itself in. Safari provides a feature called AutoFill that can help.

The AutoFill options are located under the AutoFill tab in Safari's preferences (Figure 10-10). Here you can select what type of information you would like Safari to save and fill in when you access many forms in a web site.

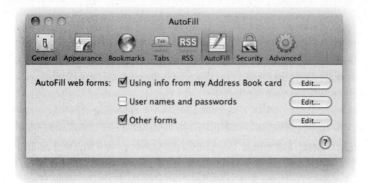

Figure 10-10. *The AutoFill options in Safari's Preference window*

Checking the "Using info from my Address Book card" option enables you to use the contact information about you stored in your Address Book card to fill in that information when it is requested in an online form. This detects fields like "Address," "email," and so on, and fills in the appropriate information. Clicking the Edit... button next to this option opens up the Address Book application to your Contact information.

The "User names and passwords" option, which is off by default, stores usernames and passwords for various web sites. It ties a specific username/password combination to a particular web site and only fills in the specific username/password combo for that specific site. This data is stored safely in your keychain so that it would be difficult for someone to discover your password using devious means. However, if this is active, any user who has access to your account will be able to access any web sites protected by information stored here (unless you do not unlock your keychain). The Edit... button allows you to view and edit web sites and usernames associated with those web sites that are stored in AutoFill. Passwords are not shown (however, you can view them in your keychain with the Keychain Access utility).

If you check the "Other forms" option, data will be collected from forms on various web sites, and that information will be stored for reuse the next time you visit those sites. You can view what web sites AutoFill is storing data for by clicking the Edit... button.

AutoFill is clearly one of those things that, if enabled, adds a lot of convenience but at the cost of some security.

■Note A number of third-party applications are available that let you store your web passwords and related content in a more secure way. One particular product, 1Password (`http://agilewebsolutions.com/products/1Password`), even plugs into Safari and other browsers, providing a single safe storage mechanism that can work in multiple browsers.

Security

As more and more services and activities shift over to taking place on the Internet, and particularly on the Web, browser security becomes more and more important. Since its inception, Safari has proven to be one of the more secure browsers out there, and the version of Safari that ships with Mac OS X seems to uphold that level of security.

■**Note** Safari isn't without its security flaws. In the past, there was a potentially critical flaw that could cause some security headaches if a user had the "Open 'safe' files after downloading" option selected. Also, there were some potential issues discovered with the first public beta of Safari for Windows. While there are no reports that any of these things actually resulted in a security breach, it underlies the importance of keeping your software up to date, as issues like these are usually quickly resolved after they are discovered. Additionally, besides Safari itself, certain plug-ins may possess their own security flaws.

Secure Browsing

To support a secure environment, Safari has built-in support for an array of protocols that assure the information you send and receive from a web site is encrypted. Safari supports the standard Secure Sockets Layer (SSL) versions 2 and 3, as well as Transport Layer Security (TLS, a newer, potential replacement for SSL). Whenever you have a secure connection between your browser and a web site, Safari will display a small lock icon right next to page title in the browser's title bar (or appropriate tab). Clicking the lock will provide information about the security being used, as well as the certificate information assuring that the web site is indeed what it claims to be.

■**Caution** It's not advisable to send any information you deem private or important over the Web unless you know who is on the receiving end and the connection is secured. This rule generally applies beyond the Web as well, and should be followed for all network communication. A secure connection doesn't guarantee the information you submit will be secure once it reaches its destination.

Blocking Web Content

Safari can also block certain types of web content, specifically any pop-up windows that are not only annoying but may contain undesirable content. To enable pop-up blocking, you can select Block Pop-Up Windows from the Safari menu (or use Shift-Command-K). Safari tries to block only non-requested pop-ups, but if for some reason Safari blocks a desirable pop-up window, then you may need to toggle off this protection temporarily.

Besides blocking pop-ups, you can block other web content as well. On the Security tab of Safari's Preference window (Figure 10-11), you can disable JavaScript, Java, and plug-ins to further block potentially harmful content. Also, at the very top of the Security Preference tab, a new option warns you when you are visiting a potentially fraudulent web site. This option will notify you if you are about to visit a site that may be used in phishing scams. *Phishing* refers to when one site pretends to be another site to acquire personal information such as credit-card information or usernames and passwords to sensitive sites. (Banks, eBay, and PayPal are common sites that phishers attempt to mimic.)

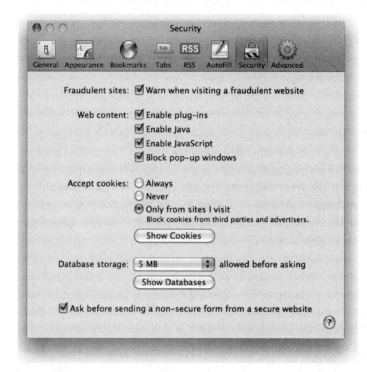

Figure 10-11. *The Security options in Safari's Preference window*

■**Note** Disabling plug-ins, Java, and JavaScript may make for a safer and perhaps less distracting web browsing experience, but by disabling these things, you will also be losing a great number of features, and some web sites may become unusable. It comes down to your own personal security vs. hassle priorities.

Private Browsing

Another way to protect your information when browsing is to utilize the Private Browsing feature of Safari. When Private Browsing is enabled (by selecting Private Browsing... from the Safari menu), Safari will not save any of your browsing activity in the browser history or cache. This assures that people can't go into your computer and poke around at places you've been and items you've been browsing.

■**Caution** Private Browsing may overlook items in your Downloads window, specifically any canceled or incomplete downloads, as well as any data cached by plug-ins (i.e., Flash).

Cookies

HTTP is a stateless protocol, so when you connect to a web site, there are complications in carrying out complex transactions, since the protocol doesn't keep track of one particular user vs. any other user. There are, of course, many ways to work around this, but the most popular method today is to use a cookie to keep track of session data as well as other data (web site preferences and other information can be stored in cookies as well). As such, cookies are an important part of using the Web today, and while you can disable them, you will be losing out on a great deal of web functionality doing so.

Note Since cookies became popular, there has been a large amount of paranoia about them, most of which is unfounded. Cookies can track your movement around a web site, and they can contain personal information, but a cookie is only valid for the originating web site, so any personal data stored in the cookie is data that you willingly submitted to that web site to begin with. That said, you may not want to leave cookies lying around on a computer in a user account that others have access to—but beyond that, they are perfectly safe and make the Web a much more interesting place to visit. Like plug-ins and so many other computing features, it comes down to a security vs. ease issue.

Safari has a number of options available to you regarding the accepting of cookies. In the Security tab of Safari's Preference window, you select when you wish to accept cookies: never, always, or only from sites you navigate to (which is the default and most sensible option). Additionally, the Show Cookies button opens up a window providing information about each cookie you have stored in your system. This view also allows you to selectively remove individual cookies or choose if you'd like to remove them all.

Emptying the Browser Cache

The browser cache stores most of the content you encounter on the Web locally to help improve the browser's response time when revisiting a web site. While this is fantastic from a performance point of view, you might not want to leave all the items you were browsing lying around in your computer, as they may contain sensitive or private information (they can also take up a good amount of disk space, although that's not as big of a problem today as it was a few years ago). Either way, you may wish to occasionally empty your browser cache. To do this, just select the Empty Cache... item from the Safari menu or use the Option-Command-E keyboard shortcut. This opens up a dialog to confirm you want to empty the cache. Click the Empty button to empty it.

Tip It is possible to disable the cache entirely. In Safari's preferences, navigate to Advanced ➤ Develop (Figure 10-12), then select Disable Caches. You can select from a number of other advanced features as well.

Caution The Develop menu has lots of fun and useful options (launching the Web Inspector is awesome for debugging web sites), many of which can be useful if used in the proper context. However, used poorly, these options can cause all sorts of problems with Safari and have an unfortunate effect on your web browsing experience. If you don't know and understand what you are doing here, it's best to leave these options alone.

Advanced Safari Features

Safari has a few Advanced options located in its preferences (Figure 10-12) that are useful in certain situations.

Figure 10-12. *The Advanced Safari preferences*

Universal Access

The Universal Access options on the Advanced preference tab allow you to adjust the minimum font size for readability and to select between using Tab or the default Option-Tab to cycle through links *and* form items on a web page.

Note The difference between the default Tab and Option-Tab is that, unless you set the "Press Tab to highlight each item on a webpage" option, Tab will only cycle through form items (as well as the address field and search field on the toolbar), while Option-Tab will cycle through form items and hyperlinks.

Setting a Default Style Sheet

The Advanced Safari preferences also include the ability to use a specific style sheet that will affect every web page you visit. It's important to note that only text settings are imported from this style sheet to help improve readability, so the layout of each web site shouldn't be affected (unless large text settings cause items to wrap funny, which is really the fault of an inflexible web design(er), not Safari or the style sheet).

RSS Feeds in Safari

RSS is a way for web sites to syndicate their content. This allows users to subscribe to a web site's RSS feed, which contains any updates to the web site. This is great if you like to visit a large number of web sites frequently, because with RSS, instead of going to each site to see what's new, you can get a list of new items from all of the web sites and filter out what items interest you.

Note   When is RSS not RSS? When it's some other type of syndication standard. RSS has always had a few things that others found as weaknesses. This has resulted in two things: first, people adding content to RSS feeds that weren't covered by the RSS standard (Apple, for example, does this for iTunes podcast feeds); and second, people getting together and inventing new syndication standards, like ATOM. Most RSS clients, including Safari and Mail, support ATOM along with RSS—however, they still tend to refer to it all under the blanket of RSS.

Note   Occasionally, a particular web site will have more than one RSS feed available. This is especially true of larger web sites, like news sites or even Apple. This allows subscribers to only receive information that they find interesting (for example, a sports site may allow you to subscribe to an RSS feed that only relays stories about a particular sport or a specific team).

Safari contains the ability to subscribe to RSS feeds as easily as adding a bookmark, and it makes a suitable RSS reader with some nice features.

Note   Apple has also added the ability to handle RSS in Mail, which provides a nice alternative to Safari's RSS feature. While some items referring to this will come up here, we will focus on how Safari handles RSS here, and how Mail handles RSS in the next chapter.

Note Even though Apple provides a couple of good options for viewing RSS feeds, a number of other third-party applications specifically handle RSS feeds (called news aggregators) that add some additional or unique features or that help you organize a large number of feeds in a more suitable way. One such reader is NetNewsWire (`www.newsgator.com/NetNewsWire.aspx`). NetNewsWire is a free, full-featured RSS aggregator that makes managing and reading a large number of RSS feeds a snap. If you manage lots of RSS feeds, NetNewsWire is definitely worth checking out.

Adding Feeds

When you are browsing the Web in Safari, whenever you visit a site with an RSS feed, a blue RSS icon will appear on the far right side of the Address field in Safari's toolbar (Figure 10-13).

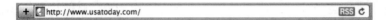

Figure 10-13. *A web site that has an RSS feed associated with it will display a blue RSS box in Safari's address bar.*

Clicking the RSS icon either opens the RSS feed in your browser or opens a list of all the feeds available if more than one feed is available. Select the feed you wish to subscribe to from the pop-up, and the news feed will open up in Safari (Figure 10-14).

Note When you select an RSS feed from within Safari, the RSS feed opens up in the default RSS news reader. If your default news reader is not Safari (e.g., Mail or a third-party RSS reader), then something else will happen than what is described here.

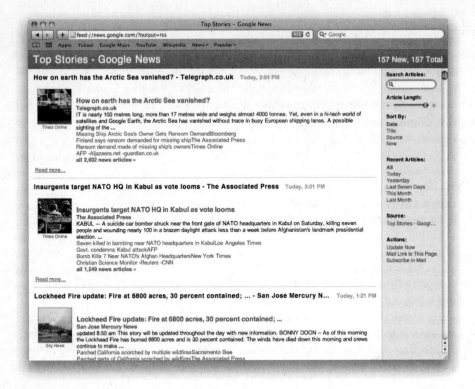

Figure 10-14. *An RSS feed open in Safari*

Once the feed is open, you can add the feed just as you would any bookmark (Command-D). Adding a feed saves the feed's location but doesn't necessarily update the feed automatically (which is usually the desired result). Depending on your RSS options, you must add the bookmark to either your Bookmarks Bar collection or your Bookmarks Menu collection for the feeds to update automatically. (You may want to create an RSS folder in one of these locations to store your favorite RSS feeds.)

Note The Bookmarks view provides an All RSS Feeds collection that contains all the RSS feeds you have bookmarked. You can use this to view all your RSS feeds in one place.

Note When you go to add the bookmark, you will notice an option to add the bookmark to Mail. This is provided if you wish to subscribe to the RSS feed in Mail as well.

Reading Feeds

Reading RSS feeds is pretty straightforward in Safari. If you select a specific feed, all of the current articles will appear in the Safari view area. If you select a collection of feeds by clicking

View All RSS Articles in the Bookmark menu or from a folder list in the Bookmark bar, then all the articles from all the feeds will be displayed.

On the right side of the view area are some RSS options that apply to the feed(s) you are viewing. The Search Articles text field allows you to search for specific strings within all the visible articles. Below the Search Articles text field is the Article Length slider. This limits how much of the feed summary to show. (RSS feeds themselves vary in how they summarize articles. Some feeds give no summary at all, while others send the entire article.) The Sort By options adjust the order in which the articles appear in Safari. The Recent Articles option adjusts which articles appear in the view. For example, if you select Today, then only the articles that were updated today will be shown. The Source item shows where the feeds come from: if you select an individual feed, then the feed's name will be shown (and will open the source site if clicked); if you select a collection of RSS feeds, then the name of that collection will be shown. Finally, there are some actions available: Mail Link to This Page opens up a new mail message in Mail containing a link to the news feed or feeds being shown; Subscribe in Mail subscribes to all the feeds in Mail (which is handy if you use Mail as your primary RSS reader).

Feed Options

The Safari preferences include an RSS tab containing some options for RSS feeds (Figure 10-15).

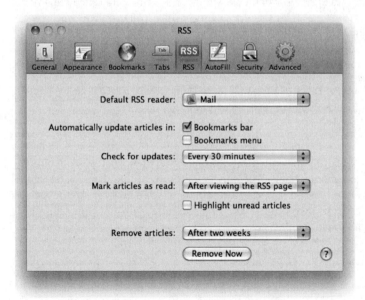

Figure 10-15. *The RSS options in Safari's Preference window*

The "Default RSS reader" option provides a list of all the known RSS readers installed on your system. The application chosen here is the primary one that Safari will use to open RSS links in.

The "Automatically update articles in" options allow you to select whether you would like all the RSS feeds in your Bookmarks bar, Bookmarks menu, or both to be updated automatically. The "Check for updates" list determines how often these feeds get updated.

The "Mark articles as read" option allows you to choose if an article should be counted as read when it's opened in a page or only after it's been clicked on. You can also select to highlight unread articles.

Finally, while RSS feeds themselves often limit the number of articles that are contained in the actual feed, Safari will keep track of all the articles once downloaded until they are removed. The "Remove articles" list allows you to determine when Safari should automatically remove older articles.

Safari Plug-Ins

Safari in Snow Leopard comes equipped with the most commonly used browser plug-ins, including Shockwave and Flash plug-ins, Java plug-ins, and a QuickTime plug-in that supports a wide variety of image, audio, and video media formats. Occasionally, however, you may come across some content on the Web that requires some other type of plug-in. Depending on the web site, you may be prompted to download and install the plug-in, or you may just be told that you are missing the required plug-in (and usually told which one you are missing). Two common plug-ins not installed by default are plug-ins for Real Media and for Windows Media. To get the Real Media plug-in, visit `www.real.com` and download the free RealPlayer for the Mac. This includes the browser plug-in. Things for Windows Media are a bit trickier, as currently there is no up-to-date version of Windows Media Player for OS X. However, a program called Flip4Mac WMV, from `http://www.telestream.net/flip4mac-wmv/overview.htm`, will install the necessary plug-ins to allow most Windows Media files to be played back both in Safari and QuickTime.

Note Another useful QuickTime plug-in that allows a wide range of media to be played back in a web browser (or stand-alone in QuickTime) is Perian, available from `http://perian.org`.

Beyond that, there are some other infrequently used plug-ins. Often when you encounter these, there will be information about what is necessary to view the content. Luckily, though, the days of plug-in madness have passed (i.e., the dot-com days when every wannabe tech company had its own plug-in for its own proprietary format). Today, most of your plug-in needs should be fulfilled by the included plug-ins.

Web Clippings

Web Clippings is a feature in Safari that allows you to select regions of a web page and add those regions to your Dashboard. The type of content can be anything that is contained in a web page, so this feature can be really interesting. For example, say you've been waiting and waiting for the people over at `www.homestarrunner.com` to release a Dashboard widget. With the Web Clippings feature in Safari, you can head over to `www.homestarrunner.com`, select the File ➤ Open in Dashboard... command, select the area of the page you want to move into the Dashboard (selectable areas will highlight as you mouse over them), and click the Add button (Figure 10-16). This will add the selected region to your Dashboard (Figure 10-17). Once placed, you can click the small i button on the clipping to add a border around it.

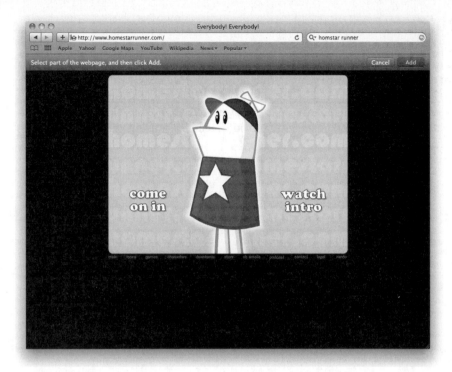

Figure 10-16. *Selecting a region in a web page to add to your Dashboard*

Figure 10-17. *You can have your very own fully functioning,* Homestar Runner *Dashboard widget.*

Summary

Since Apple introduced Safari, it has been a quite capable web browser, but with Safari 4, Apple has introduced what is clearly one of the best (and fastest) web browsers available on any platform today. Combined with its tight integration with Mac OS X, it's a clear winner. Of course, there is much more to the Internet than the Web—in fact, for many people, e-mail is the most important feature of the Internet—so next, we'll talk about Mail, along with iCal and Address Book, which now all work together to provide a seamless way to manage your e-mail, news feeds, To Do lists, notes, and more.

CHAPTER 11

■■■

Mail, Address Book, and iCal

In today's digitally connected world, where more and more of our planning and communication are facilitated with our computers, people increasingly rely on e-mail, contact management, and calendaring to help facilitate their planning and communication needs both at work and at home. These three tasks tend to go hand in hand, so much so that many e-mail/contact-management applications combine them all in a single application (like Microsoft's Outlook and Entourage). While a number of single applications include all of these services, in Snow Leopard (as with previous versions of Mac OS X), Apple ships three separate applications. However, because of the nature of Mac OS X, these three applications work together seamlessly, providing the advantages of separate applications with the conveniences of a single application. In this chapter, we will cover all three of these default applications:

- Mail
- Address Book
- iCal

Mail

Mail is Apple's e-mail application that has been part of OS X from its start. With each new release of OS X, Apple refines the Mail application a bit. With Snow Leopard, this trend continues. The most significant addition to Mail is full, native compatibility with Microsoft Exchange Server. This eliminates many headaches for both users and administrators using Macs in corporations that rely on Exchange.

Working in Mail's Interface

If you've used Mail in Leopard (OS X 10.5), then you'll find that the Mail application in Snow Leopard looks and acts very much the same on the surface. If you are entirely new to Apple's Mail application or have used only a version prior to the version that shipped with Leopard, then you may need a quick overview of the interface of the Mail application in Snow Leopard (Figure 11-1).

By default, Mail's main window is the message viewer window. It is presented in a traditional three-pane layout. The column on the left provides a hierarchical list of your mailboxes, folders, and other items. The top-right pane lists all the items contained in the mailbox or folder selected on the left, and below that is a view area to view any selected item in the top area. Basically, it's a traditional mail layout that is common among many mail clients and many other applications.

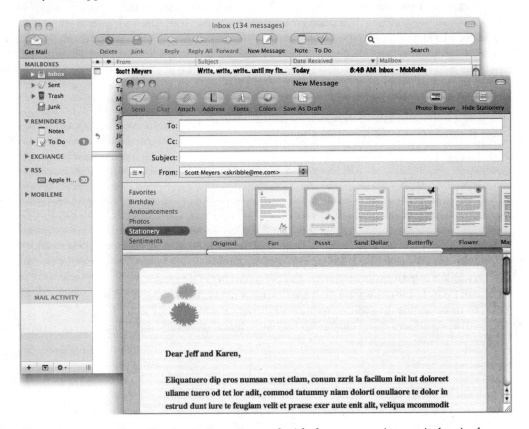

Figure 11-1. *The Mail application in Snow Leopard with the message viewer window in the background and the New Message window in the foreground*

Like many applications you've seen (including Safari and the Finder), Mail has a single toolbar that you can customize with a wide array of optional buttons. Besides the toolbar, many commands and options are located in Mail's menus in the menu bar (Table 11-1).

Table 11-1. *Select Menu Bar Items for Mail*

Item	Keyboard Shortcut	Description
Mail[1]		
File		
New Message	Command-N	Opens a New Message window to create and send an e-mail.
New Note	Control-Command-N	Opens a New Note window.
Add To Do	Option-Command-Y	Switches to your To Do list and adds a new To Do item.
New Viewer Window	Option-Command-N	Opens a new view window, which is the default Mail window.
Open Message	Command-O	Opens selected message(s) in a new window.
Close	Command-W	Closes the active window.
Save	Command-S	Saves new or edited notes or current e-mail messages as drafts.
Save As…	Shift-Command-S	Allows you to save a message or note as a separate file in a variety of formats.
Save as Stationery…		Saves an e-mail message you create as a template for other future e-mail messages.
Attach File…	Shift-Command-A	Opens a browser dialog box to select a file to attach to an e-mail message.
Save Attachments…		Saves incoming e-mail attachments to a location chosen by you (or you could just drag the attachments out of the message to your desired location).
Quick Look Attachments	Command-Y	Opens the attachment in Quick Look if the attachment is a supported type.
Add Account…		Opens a window to walk you through adding a new mail account.
Import Mailboxes…		Aids you in importing e-mail messages from other Mail mailboxes or even other e-mail clients.
Add RSS Feeds…		Opens a dialog box to add URLs of RSS feeds you want to subscribe to in Mail.
Edit		
Delete	Command-Delete	Deletes the selected item; if the item is a message or note, the item will be moved immediately to the trash. For a To Do item, the item will be deleted immediately. (Command-Shift-Delete deletes an item immediately and permanently, bypassing the trash.)
Complete	Option-Esc	Opens a list of possible words for the word you are typing.
Paste as Quotation	Shift-Command-V	Pastes the text in the clipboard into a new mail message formatted as quoted text.

Continued

[1]*The Mail menu contains the standard Application menu items.*

Table 11-1. *Continued*

Item	Keyboard Shortcut	Description
Paste and Match Style	Option-Shift-Command-V	Pastes any text in the clipboard in a message matching the currently selected message text style.
Append Selected Messages	Option-Command-I	Appends any selected e-mail messages into a new message.
Add Link…	Command-K	Opens a dialog box to enter a URL to create a hyperlink in a mail message, which will either link the selected text or insert the URL if no text is selected.
Attachments		Opens a submenu, allowing you to select one of three options for dealing with attachments in mail messages.
Attachments ➤ Include Original Attachments Reply		Includes in replies any attachments that are included with an original message.
Attachments ➤ Always Send Windows Friendly Attachments		Creates attachments included in a manner that is compatible with most Windows mail clients.
Attachments ➤ Always Insert Attachments End of Message		Always inserts attachments at the end of the message rather than allowing attachments to be inserted inline.
Speech		Opens a submenu, allowing you to have the default system voice start and stop reading your mail message aloud.
View		
Columns		Opens a submenu containing a list of message properties that can be viewed as columns in the message list area of Mail's viewer window.
Sort By		Includes a list of potential column items. Selecting one causes your messages to sort themselves based on the selected field (alternately, you can just click the column header to sort your messages by that field).
Organize by Thread		Keeps messages that are part of the same message thread (which is a series of messages related to the same subject) together in the e-mail list view.
Expand All Threads		Reveals all messages in all threads.
Collapse All Threads		Collapses threads so that only the most recent message is shown (you can expand or collapse each thread individually as well).
Cc Address Field		Toggles the visibility of the Cc address field for a new message.
Bcc Address Field	Option-Command-B	Toggles the visibility of the Bcc address field for a new message.

Item	Keyboard Shortcut	Description
Select		Opens a submenu of options for easily selecting messages that are part of the same thread.
Select ➤ All Messages in this Thread	Shift-Command-K	Highlights all the messages in a specific e-mail thread.
Select ➤ Next Message in this Thread		Selects the next message in the current e-mail thread.
Select ➤ Previous Message in this Thread		Selects the previous message in the current e-mail thread.
Message		Provides a submenu containing view options for individual messages. Some of these options are only available when a message contains alternate formats (i.e., some messages contain both rich-text and plain-text versions.)
Message ➤ Long Headers	Shift-Command-H	Reveals additional header information about each e-mail message.
Message ➤ Raw Source	Option-Command-U	Reveals the entire contents of an e-mail message in plain text, including all header information and all formatting.
Message ➤ Plain Text Alternative	Option-Command-P	Views a message in plain text if it's sent with a plain-text alternative message.
Message ➤ Previous Alternative	Option-Command-[	Displays the previous alternative format for the selected e-mail message.
Message ➤ Next Alternative	Option-Command-]	Displays the next alternative format for the selected e-mail message.
Message ➤ Best Alternative		Selects the best alternative text format for viewing the message in Mail (this is the default).
Display Selected Messages Only		Hides all messages in the message list except those that you have selected (which is useful if used in combination with Select ➤ All Messages in this thread).
(Hide|Show) Mailboxes	Shift-Command-M	Toggles the visibility of the left column in the message view area, which contains the list of mailboxes and folders.
(Show|Hide) Deleted Messages	Command-L	Toggles the visibility of deleted messages in your Inbox. This option depends on both the type of server and your account settings.
(Hide|Show) Toolbar		Toggles the visibility of Mail's toolbar.
Customize Toolbar…		Opens a sheet allowing you to customize your toolbar with various alternate commands and options.

Continued

Table 11-1. *Continued*

Item	Keyboard Shortcut	Description
Mailbox		
Take All Accounts Online		Takes all of your e-mail accounts online.
Take All Accounts Offline		Takes all of your e-mail accounts offline.
Get All New Mail	Shift-Command-N	Checks for and retrieves any new messages from all online accounts.
Synchronize All Accounts		Synchronizes all IMAP and Exchange accounts, updating both remote and local mailboxes with any changes.
Online Status		Displays a submenu allowing you to view and toggle the online status of each account individually.
Get New Mail		Displays a submenu allowing you to choose a specific account to check for new mail messages.
Synchronize		Displays a submenu allowing you to choose a specific account to synchronize.
Erase Deleted Messages		Displays a submenu that presents options for removing deleted (trashed) messages permanently, including each individual account separately as well as a few other options.
Erase Deleted Messages ➤ In All Accounts	Command-K	Erases all deleted items in all accounts, including expunging messages from IMAP and Exchange servers (though server settings may override this).
Erase Deleted Messages ➤ On My Mac		Deletes any trashed messages stored in the local trash; this won't erase any messages stored on remote servers (such as IMAP and Exchange).
Erase Junk Mail	Option-Command-J	Permanently removes any junk e-mail messages stored in the Junk mailbox. For this option to be available, you must activate the "When junk mail arrives: Move it to the Junk Mailbox" option in Mail's preferences.
New Mailbox...		Opens a dialog box allowing you to name and choose a location for a new mailbox.
New Smart Mailbox...		Opens a dialog box to allow you to name and configure a new smart mailbox. Smart mailboxes are similar to smart folders for searching and sorting e-mail.
Edit Smart Mailbox...		Opens a dialog box allowing you to alter the selected smart mailbox's rules.
Duplicate Smart Mailbox		Creates a new smart mailbox with the same rules as the selected smart mailbox.
New Smart Mailbox Folder		Opens a dialog box to enter the name of a new smart mailbox folder for organizing smart mailboxes.
Rename Mailbox...		Highlights the name of the selected mailbox or folder to be renamed.

Item	Keyboard Shortcut	Description
Delete Mailbox…		Deletes the selected mailbox. Depending on the type of mailbox, this may delete all the messages the mailbox contains as well. You will be prompted to verify this action.
Archive Mailbox…		Saves an archive file of the selected mailbox, allowing you to import the mailbox and data back into Mail at a later date. This is useful both as a way of creating emergency backups when moving old mail from one computer to another, and as a way of creating archives of old mail prior to cleaning out you mailbox.
Go To		Opens a submenu of common mailboxes and folders. Selecting an item here will take you to that mailbox.
Go To ➤ In	Command-1	Takes you to Mail's Inbox.
Go To ➤ Out	Command-2	Takes you to Mail's Outbox.
Go To ➤ Drafts	Command-3	Takes you to Mail's Drafts folder.
Go To ➤ Sent	Command-4	Takes you to Mail's Sent Items folder.
Go To ➤ Trash	Command-5	Takes you to Mail's Trash folder.
Go To ➤ Junk	Command-6	Takes you to Mail's Junk folder.
Go To ➤ Notes	Command-7	Takes you to Mail's Notes folder.
Go To ➤ To Do	Command-8	Takes you to Mail's To Do items.
Use This Mailbox For		Opens a submenu that allows you to designate the specific purposes of mailboxes, such as storing mail drafts, trash, junk, and so on. This is nice if, for example, your IMAP server has a Junk mailbox named Spam. With this command, you can tell Mail to use the Spam folder for junk mail to keep all of your junk mail in a single folder (and so Mail won't create an extra Junk folder).
Rebuild		Rebuilds your selected mailboxes. This can help fix potential (or real) corruption and can help save space by reorganizing your mailbox files. It's good to use this every once in awhile.
Message		
Send (Again)	Shift-Command-D	If you are writing a new message, this option will be Send and will send the current new message. Otherwise, this option will be Send Again, which will allow you to resend the selected message from your Sent mailbox.
Reply	Command-R	Opens the New Message window all set up to send a reply to the sender of the selected message.
Reply All	Shift-Command-R	Behaves like Reply, but in addition to sending your reply to the initial sender, the reply will also be sent to everyone included in the original message.

Continued

Table 11-1. *Continued*

Item	Keyboard Shortcut	Description
Reply With iChat	Shift-Command-I	Allows you to start a chat with the sender of a message if the sender has a known iChat (or AIM) account and is currently available online.
Forward	Shift-Command-F	Opens a New Message window with the current selected message pasted in it so you can easily forward that message to another recipient.
Forward as Attachment		Allows you to forward a message, but rather than pasting the original message in the New Message window, it attaches the original message.
Redirect	Shift-Command-E	Redirects a selected message to another recipient. This is useful if you were sent an e-mail by mistake and you wish to forward it to the intended receiver. Using this option causes replies to go back to the original sender as opposed to you.
Bounce	Shift-Command-B	Bounces a message you receive back to the original sender as if your account doesn't exist. Although in theory this sounds like a good way to make spammers think your e-mail address is no longer valid, the most annoying spammers probably don't use their own return addresses, so it's likely using this will just end up spamming some other poor random soul with a bunch of bounced messages.
Mark		Opens a submenu to provide options for marking or labeling e-mail messages in your mailboxes.
Mark ➤ As (Unread|Read)	Shift-Command-U	Toggles selected messages as being unread/read.
Mark ➤ As (Flagged|Unflagged)	Shift-Command-L	Toggles a flag for the selected messages, which is a common way to mark e-mail messages for follow-up.
Mark ➤ As (Not) Junk Mail	Shift-Command-[J]	Toggles the current message as junk mail or as not junk mail.
Mark ➤ As Low Priority		Marks the selected message as low priority.
Mark ➤ As Normal Priority		Marks the selected messages as normal priority.
Mark ➤ As High Priority		Marks the selected messages as high priority.
Move To		Opens a submenu containing a list of all of your mailboxes, allowing you to move selected messages into a different mailbox.
Copy To		Marks a submenu containing a list of all your mailboxes, allowing you to copy selected messages into a different mailbox.
(Move|Copy) To "x" Again	Option-Command-T	Moves another message into the mailbox used in the last Move To command.
Apply Rules	Option-Command-L	Applies your mail rules to selected messages.

Item	Keyboard Shortcut	Description
Add Sender to Address Book	Shift-Command-Y	Adds the e-mail address (and name if available) of the sender of selected messages to your Address Book.
Remove Attachments		Removes the attachments of a selected message.
Format[2]		
Make (Plain|Rich) Text	Shift-Command-T	Toggles the formatting of the text in a message from plain text (which is no formatting) to rich text (which is actually formatted using HTML and allows formatted text and images). Traditionally, e-mail was all plain text, and today some people and e-mail clients still prefer it that way.

Note When sending a message using rich text from Mail, the Mail application will also include a plain-text version of your message for people who prefer plain text or can't or won't except rich text.

Window		
Message Viewer		Selects the message viewer window (Mail's default window).
Photo Browser		Opens Mail's Photo Browser window, allowing you to browse iPhoto libraries for images to include in your messages.
Address Panel	Option-Command-A	Opens a window containing an abbreviated view of contacts from your Address Book, displaying only their names and e-mail addresses.
Previous Recipients		Opens a window to keep track of all your previous message recipients. Whenever you start to type an e-mail address in a To, Cc, or Bcc field, the Mail application uses this list to attempt to autocomplete the name.
Activity	Command-0	Opens the activity viewer window showing any background activity taking place in Mail. Although this is still available, there is now an option to toggle mail activity in the left column of the message viewer window.
Connection Doctor		Opens a window that checks all the network connections used by Mail. This helps determine whether a network failure is on your end or on one of your mail servers. This also helps verify that all of your accounts are set up and working properly.

[2]*Most of the standard text formatting options are contained here; however, their availability will be based on whether you are sending a rich-text or plain-text message.*

Note The Help menu contains fairly standard help items for using Mail, so it isn't covered in this table.

Adding Mail Accounts

The easiest and most effective way to add a new e-mail account is to use the File ➤ Add Account menu option, which walks you through adding a new e-mail account step by step. You can also access this account setup walk-through when you add an account from the Accounts tab in Mail's System Preferences. The information you'll need to know varies with the type of account and the mail service you use.

The first bit of information you will need to know for all e-mail accounts is your e-mail address and your password (Figure 11-2). Once you enter this information, Mail contacts the server and attempts to autoconfigure the e-mail account. This is effective for a large number of e-mail services, including Gmail, Yahoo, MobileMe, and even many Exchange 2007 servers with the autoconfigure option set on the server. If you get the option to set up an account automatically, select that option, and let Mail do the rest.

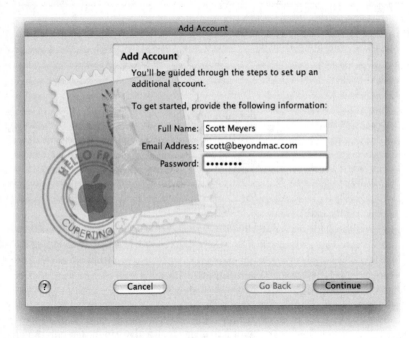

Figure 11-2. *The first step in adding a new e-mail account is entering your name, e-mail address, and password.*

If your account isn't set up automatically, then you'll need some more information to set up both your incoming and outgoing mail servers. To configure your incoming server (the one you receive your e-mail from), you'll need to know the following information (Figure 11-3):

- The type of server or protocol you are using: POP, IMAP, Exchange 2007, or Exchange IMAP.

- The address of your incoming mail server.

If you are configuring an Exchange IMAP server, you'll also be asked for the address of the Outlook Web Access (OWA) server. You are also asked for a description, which is the name by which this account will be referred to in Mail.

■**Note** Mail in Snow Leopard fully supports Exchanges 2007's autodiscover feature. If you are connecting to an Exchange 2007 server that has this feature enabled then most of the setup will be handled automatically for you.

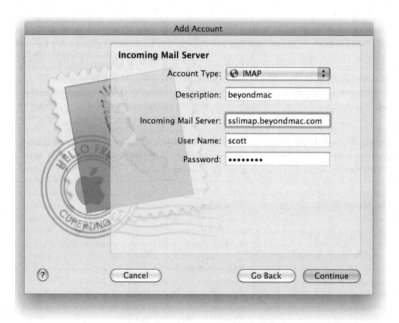

Figure 11-3. *Initial configuration of an IMAP mail account*

■**Note** Figure 11-3 shows us configuring an IMAP account. This dialog box will look the same when you configure a POP account, but for an Exchange server, it will appear a bit different. For an Exchange 2007 server, it will provide a couple of check boxes asking you if you'd like to configure iCal and Address Book. If you check these, you will be able to access your Exchange Contacts in Address Book, and your Exchange Calendar items in iCal. For an Exchange IMAP connection, you will need to know the web address of your OWA server.

■**Note** Beginning with Snow Leopard, Mail natively supports connections to Exchange 2007, so setting up your account should be trouble-free; however, many companies require a connection to the internal corporate network either physically or by using a VPN to connect to the Exchange server.

Note If you are attempting to connect to an older Exchange server, you must connect using the Exchange server's IMAP services. However, these services are not always available; they must be activated explicitly by the Exchange administrator. Also, this type of connection only allows you to get your e-mail, not your contacts or calendar items.

Once you've entered all your information and hit the Continue button, Mail will try to connect to the server and determine the best means of connecting to it. If this fails, then you will get a pop-up message warning you that Mail was unable to connect to the mail server. This usually means something was entered incorrectly, the mail server is down or not accepting connections, or the server is unreachable (perhaps behind a firewall that requires a VPN connection). If you are sure everything is correct, you can click Continue again to move on.

At this point, depending on what happened when Mail contacted your incoming server, you may or may not be prompted to select your security settings (Figure 11-4). If you are, you should enter them here. We strongly encourage you to select SSL encryption.

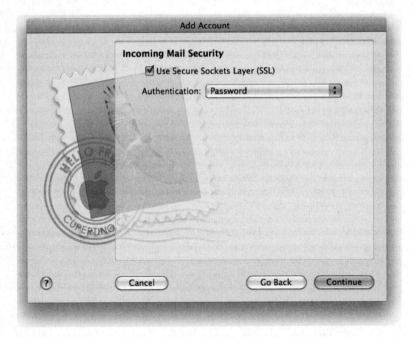

Figure 11-4. *If prompted to choose an SSL connection, you should do so.*

■Note SSL encryption encrypts the data being passed between your computer and the server at the other end. Some services, for whatever reason, don't accept SSL encryption (or any other encryption) for e-mail. If this is the case, we strongly urge you to find another e-mail provider and not use the account lacking encryption. Checking your e-mail over an unencrypted connection and sending your username and e-mail address across the Internet in easy-to-read plain text that anyone with a little know-how can intercept is very, very bad. If you don't want to fork over money for a MobileMe account or some other e-mail provider service that offers good, secure e-mail, you can always get a free, permanent, secure Gmail account at www.gmail.com (which may redirect you to Google—it's OK, Gmail is synonymous with Google Mail), so you have no excuses.

The next step is selecting your outgoing mail server for this account (Figure 11-5). Here you can either choose an existing outgoing mail server (one from an existing account) to use when sending mail from this account or enter the details of a new one. Usually you will want to enter the outgoing account information associated with the account you are setting up.

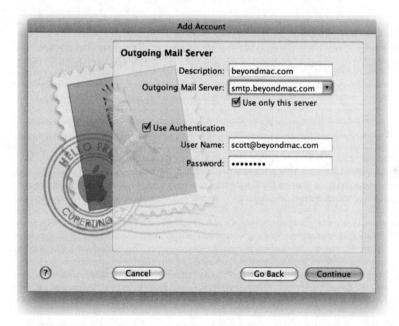

Figure 11-5. *Configuring your outgoing mail server*

■**Note** Almost all outgoing servers will be Simple Mail Transfer Protocol (SMTP) servers. SMTP is what makes e-mail work by moving your message from SMTP server to SMTP server until your message reaches its destination. Unfortunately, as the name implies, it is very simple, but it is also very old. It was written for a day long ago when the Internet, and e-mail, was used mainly by educational, government, and research institutions. Spam wasn't a problem. Today, most SMTP servers have evolved to provide some checks in an attempt to limit spam, but the fundamental design of SMTP is to accept and route all e-mail as quickly and effortlessly as possible. As such, spam gets through. This presents some issues for non-spammers (well, spammers too, but the more "issues" they have, the better, right?). Certain public Internet connections routinely block SMTP traffic, so if you find yourself attempting to send an e-mail from a public place or even from work or a hotel room, you may find it doesn't work. In some cases, there is a special SMTP server you can gain access to (Mail will present you with the opportunity to change or add an SMTP server when it fails to connect to the default SMTP server tied with a particular account); other times, it's just not going to work. About the only real solution I've found in some of these situations is to send my message through a webmail interface.

■**Tip** Since many service providers block the standard SMTP ports, many e-mail services offer up port 587 as an alternative SMTP port. If your service allows this, you will need to change the port number in your account preferences.

Just like when you configure your incoming account, when you enter new outgoing account information, Mail will attempt to contact the server to acquire additional information about the server and to verify the connection when you click the Continue button. If Mail can't connect to the server, you will get a warning asking whether you'd like to continue. After you click Continue, you may or may not get the Security Options screen to set up a secure connection for outgoing mail.

■**Note** If you want to encrypt a mail message, a number of utilities can allow this, each with its own pros and cons (including Mail, provided you get the proper certificate). One of the most popular is Pretty Good Privacy (PGP) encryption. This is a public key encryption system that is widely distributed. In this system, each user has a private key and a public key. Any information encrypted using the public key can be decrypted using only the private key. Commercial versions (www.pgp.com) and open source variations based on OpenPGP are available.

Upon completion of entering your outgoing mail information, you will be presented with a summary of your new account information (Figure 11-6). If everything is correct, hit the Create button to create your new account.

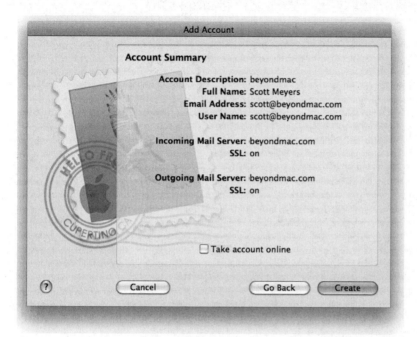

Figure 11-6. *Preview your e-mail account information, and hit Create to create your new account.*

Once your accounts are set up, you can edit or delete an account in Mail's Preferences under the Accounts tab (Figure 11-7). By selecting an account in the Accounts pane, you can edit that account using one of the three sub-tabs: Account Information, Mailbox Behaviors, and Advanced. The Account Information pane allows you to edit the server information, user-name, and password (essentially the same stuff you used to set up the account, unless your account was autoconfigured). The Mailbox Behaviors pane allows you to select how messages are stored and how Mail should deal with specific types of messages (including notes, trash, and suspected junk mail). The options provided here, as well as the specific behavior, will vary depending on the account type. The Advanced tab contains a number of other options for your account, including the ability to disable the account in Mail or to toggle SSL for connecting to the incoming server.

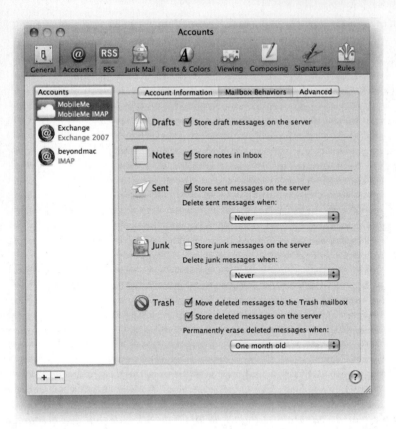

Figure 11-7. *Mail's Accounts preferences allow you to revisit the configuration of your mail accounts, plus make a few additional choices about how Mail will work with a specific account.*

Note If you configure an IMAP account manually (or sometimes even if it's autoconfigured), and everything connects OK, but you notice a number of strange mailboxes popping up in Mail (and possibly no mail), it's likely that you will need to set the IMAP Path Prefix under Mail's Advanced Accounts preferences. What specifically needs to be set here will vary with your account, but if one of those strange folders that pops up says something like Mail, that's a good place to start. (Of course, the most effective thing would be to ping the server's support people or administrator and ask.)

Tip If you have more than one e-mail account in Mail, the order in which the accounts are listed in the Accounts preferences is important. Mail considers the account listed first as the default mail account. When you create a new message, it generally associates that message with this account. To reorder your accounts, you can simply select and drag them up or down in the Accounts pane.

Receiving and Managing E-mail

Receiving, reading, and managing e-mail messages are the main tasks that most people are occupied with when using their mail clients. Mail provides some nice features for this whether you deal with a few messages from a single account every day or you deal with hundreds from multiple accounts.

Checking and Reading New E-mail

Mail is set up, by default, to automatically check for new e-mail in each of your active, online accounts every five minutes. This interval is adjustable on the General tab of Mail's System Preferences (Figure 11-8) from the "Check for new messages" drop-down list. Of course, you are always free to check your e-mail manually by clicking the Get Mail button in Mail's toolbar or by using one of the Get Mail options in the Mailbox menu.

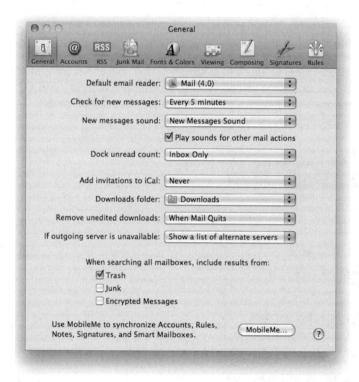

Figure 11-8. *The General tab of Mail's preferences provides many of the common options you may want to adjust.*

By default, when Mail discovers new messages for one of your accounts, the new messages are downloaded into the Inbox associated with the account, and the "new mail" sound will play, notifying you of new mail. Additionally, the number of unread messages in your Inbox will appear on the Mail icon in the Dock (known as *badging*), as well as next to your Inbox. Unread messages in the message list area of the message viewer window will be flagged with a small blue dot that will go away when you select the message to read.

■**Note** In the Mailboxes area along the left side of Mail's message viewer window, Mail provides a single Inbox that expands into separate Inbox folders for each account. This allows you to view your messages from different accounts either together by selecting the Inbox item or separately by account by selecting one of the subitems under Inbox.

When you select a message, its contents appear below the message list area in the message view area of the message viewer window. You can scroll through it there, or if you double-click the message item in the message list area, the message will open in a separate window.

Dealing with Junk E-mail

Mail has a built-in system to help you identify and deal with junk mail, or *spam*. This system is actually quite good and, with proper training, can rival many other spam/junk filters out there. The key point is that it must be trained. By default, Mail's junk filter is pretty average as far as filters go, but as you mark missed messages as Junk and mislabeled good mail as Not Junk, Mail will learn over a fairly rapid period of time what you consider to be junk and what you don't.

Most of the configurable options regarding how junk mail works are contained on the Junk Mail tab of Mail's preferences (Figure 11-9).

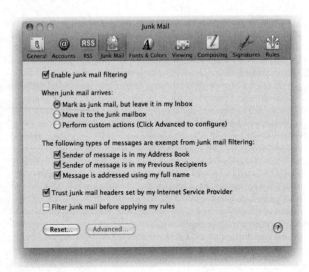

Figure 11-9. *The Junk Mail tab provides options regarding how Mail deals with mail it considers to be spam.*

The first option on the Junk Mail preferences tab is to enable junk mail filtering. Below that are options for what Mail should do with e-mail it considers junk. The "Mark as junk mail, but leave it in my Inbox" option is the best choice when you are first training Mail as to what you consider junk and what you don't. When you think Mail is identifying junk mail at a good rate, you can alter this setting. The "Move it to the Junk mailbox" option creates a new mailbox called Junk where, when this option is activated, Mail will store junk mail rather than in your

Inbox. The final option, "Perform custom actions," allows you to set up a custom mail rule for dealing with junk mail when you click the Advanced… button. We cover setting up mail rules in the "Creating Mail Rules" section.

■Note The Erase Junk Mail menu item in both the Mailbox menu and the contextual menu available from the mailbox area of the message viewer window causes any messages stored in your Junk mailbox to be immediately deleted—not stored in the Trash, but gone. This is both a handy way to rid yourself of trash and an easy way to accidentally rid yourself of an important message that was flagged as Junk by mistake.

Next you can choose certain criteria for messages that should never be marked as Junk. You can exempt mail from people in your Address Book or people in your Previous Recipients list, or e-mail that is addressed using your full name. Exempting people listed in your Address Book and Previous Recipients list is usually safe; however, we find that for whatever reason, lots of junk mailers tend to know our full names, so this option is bit more questionable.

The "Trust junk mail headers set by my Internet Service Provider" option allows Mail to look at certain e-mail headers that are commonly used by ISPs and mail servers to rate the probability that a message is junk. The results of using this option are mixed depending on your mail server.

■Note We leave this option checked since it covers all our accounts; however, one of our primary e-mail accounts has its own junk mail quarantine, and we find that when we release a message from this quarantine, Mail will flag it as Junk when it hits the Inbox, since the headers identifying it as Junk on the mail server are still intact.

The "Filter junk mail before applying my rules" option identifies mail as junk before looking at any other rules. This option could prevent rules from running on messages that Mail considers junk. If this option in unchecked, then, unless you specify a custom junk mail action, the junk filter will work after your mail rules are run, thus allowing them to affect all messages.

The Reset button resets all of your junk mail options and resets all the junk mail training you have done.

Creating Mailboxes and Folders to Store E-mails

Besides your Inbox and other special-purpose mailboxes and folders that Mail creates for you, it's likely you'll want to create your own to organize any saved messages, as well as notes you store in Mail.

■Note In Mail, folders are synonymous with mailboxes. Mailboxes you create will actually appear as folders, and although you can store both mail and notes in them, they are still generally called mailboxes in Mail.

To create a new mailbox, simply select Mailbox ➤ New Mailbox from the menu bar or select New Mailbox from the menu that appears when you click the + button in the lower left of the message viewer window. This opens a dialog box with a text field to enter the name of your new mailbox and a drop-down list for you to choose where you want the mailbox to be created. In general, new mailboxes are stored On My Mac (that being your Mac), which means they are kept locally. If you have access to an IMAP mail account (which includes MobileMe as well as many older Exchange servers you have added), then you can also create folders on the remote mail server this way (since IMAP stores your mail remotely). This makes those mailboxes and the items stored within them accessible from any computer you have set up to access that account.

Once you create a mailbox, if you want to change its location, you can do so by selecting and dragging the mailbox where you'd like it. To further add to the flexibility, you can nest mailboxes (that is, mailboxes can reside in other mailboxes).

In addition to your standard mailboxes, you can also create smart mailboxes in Mail that will dynamically contain messages based on the rules you define for your smart mailbox. Setting up a smart mailbox in Mail is similar to setting up a smart folder in the Finder. It's good to know that like smart folders, messages added to smart mailboxes aren't moved there; the message will still remain in its regular mailbox as well.

Creating Mail Rules

Mail rules can help you deal with large amounts of e-mail by automatically performing tasks on individual messages that meet certain specified criteria. To view your rules, go to the Rules tab in Mail's preferences (Figure 11-10).

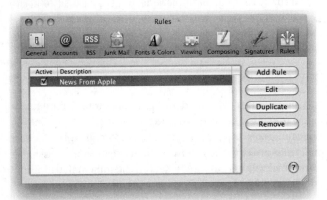

Figure 11-10. *The Rules tab shows you your existing rules and allows you to edit them or create new ones.*

The Rules preference tab allows you to view your existing rules, activate or deactivate each of them, and reorder them. There are also four buttons that allow you to create new rules (Add Rule), edit an existing rule (Edit), create a copy of a rule as a starting point for a new rule (Duplicate), or delete a rule (Remove).

The activated rules will be applied in the order they are listed on either each new message as it arrives or on selected messages when Message ➤ Apply Rules (Option-Command-L) is applied. The order of the rules is significant since the last-run rule will have precedence over previously applied rules. Additionally, each rule has the option of preventing further rules from being executed. To reorder your rules, simply drag them in the order in which you want them executed.

■Note Rules are generally applied to mail in a certain folder, so if one of your rules happens to move a message into a different folder, the following rules will not be processed for that message.

To create a new rule, click the Add Rule button, and a sheet will open for you to begin creating the rule (Figure 11-11).

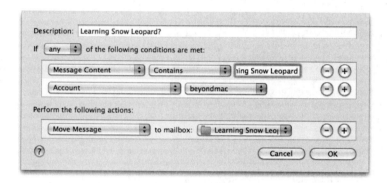

Figure 11-11. *The rule sheet allows you to fill in the criteria for new rules or allows you to edit existing rules.*

A rule has three parts: the description (or name), the conditions when the rule's actions are applied, and the actions that will occur when the conditions are met.

The description can be any name you want to use to identify the rule.

You can set the conditions so that the actions will trigger when any of the conditions are met or all of the conditions are met. To add a condition, click the + button next to any existing condition, and a new blank condition will appear below. To remove a condition, click the - button next to the condition you want to remove.

You can add and remove actions the same way as adding and removing conditions (the + and - buttons). Some special actions available are Run AppleScript, which allows you to run any AppleScript, making the possibilities of what you can do here rather immense, and "Stop evaluating rules," which immediately halts running all further rules for the current message.

Adding iCal Events from Mail

Often people will e-mail you important dates that you'll want to add to one of your iCal calendars. Mail makes this easy.

You can receive an event in two ways. First, if the event is sent to you as an iCal event attachment, just double-click the attachment, and iCal will open the event and ask you which of your calendars you'd like to add the event to.

More interesting, though, is that Mail can now recognize dates in the text of a message. If you hold your mouse over a date listed in a message, the date will become outlined and act as a small drop-down menu, allowing you to add the date to iCal (Figure 11-12).

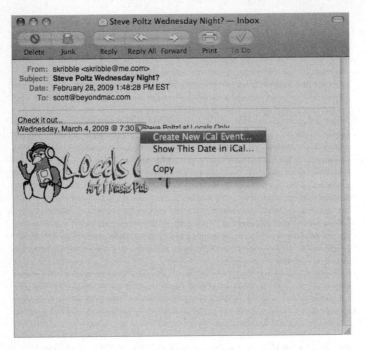

Figure 11-12. *You can click any date in a message's text to add a new iCal event.*

When you select Create New iCal Event…, a small pop-up sheet appears for you to fill in the details of the event (Mail will try to fill in some information based on the information it can get from the message), as shown in Figure 11-13.

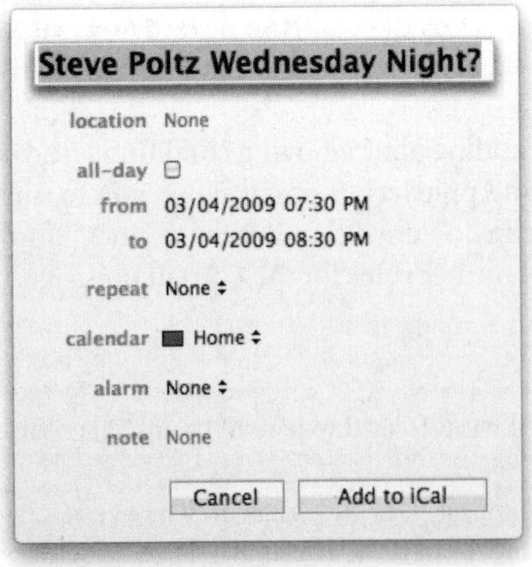

Figure 11-13. *Mail opens a sheet allowing you to fill in the details of your new event.*

When the details are correct, click Add to iCal, and your new event will be added.

Sending E-mail

Sending e-mail is a pretty straightforward task: you create a new message; type your recipients, subject, and message; and hit Send. Mail adds a few options that you can take advantage of, such as the ability to use stationery to apply a theme to your message.

Creating a New Message

To start a new message, select File ➤ New Message (Command-N) from the menu bar, or click the New Message button on Mail's toolbar. This opens a blank New Message window (Figure 11-14).

To start, you must first fill in the To and Cc (and/or Bcc) fields with the names of your recipients and fill in the Subject field with the subject of the message.

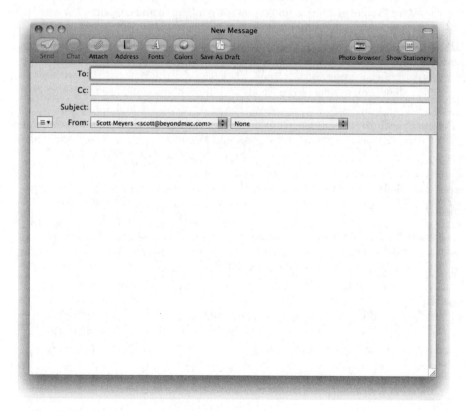

Figure 11-14. *Mail's New Message window*

Note The To field is traditionally for the primary recipients of a message. The Cc (which stands for *carbon copy*) field is for including anyone else you want to "keep in the loop." The Bcc field (which stands for *blind carbon copy*) is where you can add recipients that will be unknown to all other recipients, including other Bcc recipients.

Note By default, certain fields, including Bcc, Reply-To, and Priority, are hidden. The small drop-down menu to the left of the From field allows you to reveal these fields as well as any other header information you'd like to add (via the Customize option).

As you fill in the recipient information, Mail will attempt to autocomplete the names or addresses you are typing using information from your Previous Recipients list, your Address Book, and any LDAP or Exchange address books that are configured and connected. If you enter a name in the one of these fields that Address Book has multiple e-mail addresses for, you can click the name to select which e-mail address(es) you'd like to use. Additionally, if you click the Address button in the New Messages toolbar, you will get a list of all the names and e-mail addresses contained in your Address Book.

The From field allows you to select from which of your accounts you'd like the message to be sent. The initial account listed will be the one belonging to your default e-mail address. However, if you are viewing e-mail in a mailbox other than the default mailbox, then selecting New Message will use that account instead of the default. This has the effect of ensuring that any message you reply to will come from the account to which it was sent. You can alter this behavior in the Composing section of Mail's System Preferences.

After you have filled in the required fields, you can start typing your message in the large text area. By default, the message text is formatted using rich text (which in Mail is HTML). This allows you to style your text using different font styles, colors, and sizes (accessible from the Fonts and Colors buttons on the toolbar or from the various options in the Format menu bar's submenus). Additionally, you may include inline images in your message.

To add an image to your message, you can drag and drop the image file from the Finder into your message, or you can use the Photo Browser built into Mail to browse your iPhoto library for an image to insert.

To add an attachment to your message, you can drag and drop the file in your message, or you can select the files you want to be attached from the dialog that appears when you click the Attach button on the toolbar (or you can select File ➤ Attach File... or press Shift-Command-A).

Note There is a preference to use Windows-friendly attachments. This option is selected by default, and it is likely that you will want to keep it selected unless you are 100 percent sure the person you are sending an attachment to is using a Mac.

When you are done with your message and are ready to send it, just click the Send button in the toolbar, or select Message ➤ Send (Shift-Command-D) from the menu bar, and your message will be sent using the outgoing server set up for the chosen account.

If, for some reason, your outgoing mail server is unreachable, Mail will prompt you to either try again later or try sending the message using one of the other outgoing mail servers you have set up for other accounts. If you want to try again later (maybe you have limited Internet access or SMTP is being blocked), the message will be saved, and Mail will attempt to send the message later.

If you are working on a message and you aren't ready to send it, when you close the message, Mail will ask you whether you'd like to save the message as a draft. If you select Yes, the message will be saved in your Drafts mailbox (if one doesn't exist, it will be created). You can select the message from your Drafts mailbox later to finish and send it or delete it.

Using Mail Stationery

The Mail application in Snow Leopard has the ability to apply themes to your e-mail messages using what Apple calls *stationery*. When you are creating a new message in Mail, if you click the Show Stationery button on the toolbar, a special area will slide open between the header fields and the message text to reveal a selection of stationery.

As you select specific stationery, the stationery will be previewed in the message area. Usually stationery consists of a background, image area, and text area. The text area is where you type your message. In general, the photo areas may be replaced with your own images. To replace the placeholder image with your own image, just drag a new image from the Finder or the Photo Browser into the image area, and the placeholder image will immediately be replaced with your chosen image. Besides the images, some of the backgrounds (such as Birthday Daises) have different options that are available by clicking the background.

Note Stationery items are really just bundles of specially formatted HTML documents and images. Therefore, it's possible to create your own. However, the exact process of packaging them is a bit complex. Mail does allow you to save new messages as stationery so that you can use them as the basis for future messages.

Replying To and Forwarding a Message

Besides creating a new message from scratch, you can also send mail by replying to or forwarding existing messages. The primary difference between a reply and a forward is that a reply will be, by default, directed to the initial sender (and other original recipients if you choose Reply All), whereas a forward is usually addressed to someone not part of the initial e-mail thread.

When you reply or forward a message, the original message is usually included (or quoted) in the reply. The original message(s) are usually indented and formatted in a special way (formatted as quoted text), leaving room at the top of the message for you to add your own text to the e-mail thread.

■**Note** When you redirect a message, you are not adding to or continuing the thread so much as you are just passing the message on to someone else as you received it.

Creating Notes and To Dos

Mail also has the ability to store notes and To Dos. Notes are a fantastic way to keep track of just about anything and can be stored right alongside your mail in any mailbox. To Dos, on the other hand, are a bit more restrained and exist only in the To Do "mailboxes" in your Reminders area. The neat thing about the To Do list in Mail is that it is the same To Do list used in iCal, so you can create a To Do item in Mail and view it in iCal, and vice versa.

To create a new note, just click the Note button on the Messages View toolbar, or select File ➤ New Note (Control-Command-N) from Mail's menu bar. This opens a New Note window (Figure 11-15), which is ready for you to start entering your information.

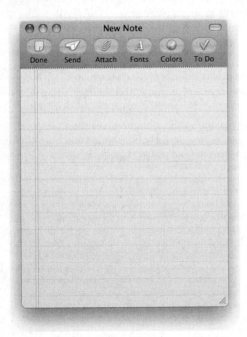

Figure 11-15. *A New Note window in Mail waiting for information*

One super-nice feature is that notes can contain any images or attachments; additionally, you can add To Do items to individual notes (which will then appear in Mail's To Do list and in iCal's To Do list). Once you have completed your note, hit the Done button or save it by selecting File ➤ Save (or pressing Command-S). The name of the note that will appear is the first line of your note.

Each saved note is an individual item that can be moved into any other mailbox. You can even drag copies of your note from Mail into the Finder.

To create a new To Do item, click the To Do button on the toolbar, or select File ➤ New To Do (Option-Command-Y). This creates a new item in your To Do list and asks you for the title, due date, priority, calendar, and whether you want to set an alarm for it (pretty much the same information you are asked in iCal).

> **Note** Interestingly, by default the keyboard command to create a new To Do item in Mail (Option-Command-Y) is different from the keyboard shortcut in iCal (Command-K). This is a rarity in the Mac world, and it wouldn't be surprising if in the future one of these changes so they are the same.

Reading RSS Feeds in Mail

Another new feature in Mail is the ability to subscribe to and read RSS feeds. If you set your default RSS reader to Mail (either in Mail or in Safari's RSS preferences), then whenever you select an RSS link, you will be prompted to add the news feed in Mail. Otherwise, you can use options in Safari to subscribe to a feed in Mail or add the URL of an RSS feed in the dialog box that appears when you select File ➤ Add RSS Feeds… in Mail's menu bar.

When you initially subscribe to an RSS feed in Mail, it will appear in the RSS area in the Mailbox column; however, when you select a feed, an arrow will appear to the right of it that will bump the feed up to your Inbox. This will not only add new RSS items to your Inbox but will also notify you when new RSS items are downloaded.

In general, feed items appear and behave as messages, while feeds behave as individual mailboxes. You can even sort your feeds into separate mailboxes to help keep them organized (and read many feeds at once).

If you want to unsubscribe to a feed, you can select Mailbox ➤ Delete Feed… from the menu bar (or Delete Feed from the feed's contextual menu), which will delete the feed and remove any items.

Address Book

Address Book (Figure 11-16) is Mac OS X's primary tool for managing contact information. It allows you to add contact information about individuals and organizations, create groups, and even access networked directory services.

The Address Book in Snow Leopard provides a three-column view by default (but also has a view that contains just the address card). The first column (Group) is where you can create groups to contain multiple contacts, the second column (Name) contains the names of individual contacts, and the last column contains the address card for the selected individual.

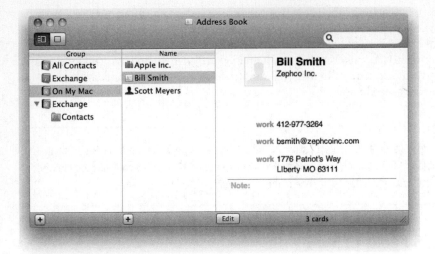

Figure 11-16. *Snow Leopard's Address Book*

Adding and Editing Contacts

You can get new contacts into your Address Book in a few ways. One way is to simply import them from another device or file. Another way is to enter them manually.

You can import contacts to Address Book by syncing your Address Book through MobileMe, by using iSync to sync Address Book to a mobile device, or by syncing your computer with your iPhone or iPod. Additionally, if you have access to an Exchange Server 2007, LDAP server, or an Address Book server, you can access the contacts stored there.

You can also import contacts from various files, including vCards (which are a standard way of sharing contact information among many contact management clients), LDIF files (which are a standard format for exchanging LDAP data), or even comma-separated value (CSV) or tab-delimited text files. Finally, you can also import contact data from Address Book archive files. Any of these can be imported using the File ➤ Import submenu on the menu bar; additionally, you can drag vCard files into Address Book to import them or simply double-click them in the Finder, provided that Address Book is the default application for dealing with vCards. (Additionally, if you drag a contact from Address Book, it will be exported as a vCard.)

If you need to add a new contact from scratch, either click the + button at the bottom of the Name column, select the File ➤ New Card menu, or press Command-N. This will create a new empty contact card ready to edit in the card view area (Figure 11-17).

■Note The card view area has two modes: an edit mode and a view mode. By default, Address Book opens with cards in view mode that will hide empty fields and restrict the editing of the contact fields (clicking a field name in view mode will generally open a menu with options pertaining to the type of field it represents). Address Book will switch to edit mode when you create a new contact. In edit mode, clicking a field will select it for editing; additionally, all default template fields will be visible even if they are empty, and you will be able to add new fields. To toggle between the modes, click the Edit button beneath the card view area.

Figure 11-17. *Address Book with a new contact card waiting to be filled in*

When the new card is created, it will reveal all the fields set up in the template. To fill in a field, simply click the grayed-out text describing the field, and type the proper information. Most fields include a drop-down list (or lists) that describes the nature of the field, generally whether the information is associated with home or work and other descriptive information that can help differentiate between similar information. Additionally, in edit mode many fields will be preceded with a red - and or green + field, which allows you to add or remove fields of similar data. For example, if you fill in all the e-mail address fields available, you can click the + button to the left of the last e-mail field to add a blank e-mail field below the last one.

If you are looking for a specific field that is currently not listed in the card, you can add a number of fields from the Card ➤ Add Field menu. This includes fields such as birthdays and other dates (which can be added to iCal) and other common contact fields.

If you find you are consistently adding information fields that are available but aren't listed in the default contact card template, then you can change the card template on the Template tab of Address Book's preferences.

If you'd like to associate an image with a contact, you can drag an image into the image field of a contact (the gray shadow of a head next to the name).

If the contact is primarily a business or organization, selecting the Company option will list the company name in the Name column rather than the person's name associated with the card (if there is one).

Learning About My Card

One special card in the Address Book is the card that represents you and your information. This information is used for all sorts of things in the system and various applications, so it's good to keep it up to date. If you'd like to set a different card, for whatever reason, as My Card, you can use the Card ➤ Make This My Card option in the menu bar.

Creating Groups

You might want to create contact groups for several reasons: to create mailing lists, to make it easier to find particular contacts, or to just keep things organized. To create a group, just click the + button beneath the Group column, and a new group will be created. To add contacts to the group, you can drag existing contacts from the Name column to the group item in the Group column, or you can create new contacts from within the group.

Once you create the group, you can right-click the group name to export the vCards of the group, send an e-mail to each member of the group, or edit the group distribution list, which determines which e-mail addresses are used when you send a group e-mail.

Sharing Contacts

Address Book allows you to share your contacts with specific people through MobileMe. To enable this feature, you must turn on sharing on the Sharing tab of Address Book's preferences, and then you must select which other MobileMe member you are allowing to view (and optionally edit) your contacts.

Viewing Shared Contact Lists

If you have permission to view a shared Address Book through MobileMe, select File ➤ Subscribe to Address Book from the menu bar, and then enter the MobileMe member information of the person whose Address Book you'd like to share. If you have permission to view these contacts, then they will show up as a group in your Address Book.

Besides MobileMe address sharing, Address Book can also display contact information being shared through LDAP or any network directory service to which your computer has access. If you have access to an LDAP server, you can fill in the appropriate information on the LDAP tab of Address Book's preferences. To configure other directory services, you will need to use the Directory Utility in the `Applications/Utilities` folder. Any of these resources will appear under the Directories item listed in the Group column.

■Note Names for directory services will appear only in response to a search string, occasionally a very specific search string. Ideally, if you find you need to contact certain people listed in a directory service often, drag their information from the directory service section into a group or the All item to add that person to your local Address Book. If you really must browse a directory that you have access to, you can use the Directory Utility application in the `Applications/Utility` folder.

Printing Labels and Envelopes

One nice hard-to-find feature of Address Book is the ability to print labels or envelopes for a specific contact or a group of contacts. To find this feature, select the contact or group you want to print labels or envelopes for, and then select File ➤ Print (Command-P) from the menu bar.

Make sure to expand the Print dialog (Figure 11-18), and select Address Book from the Print Options menu. This reveals a number of options to not only print labels and envelopes but also to print nicely formatted contact lists or small Address Book pages.

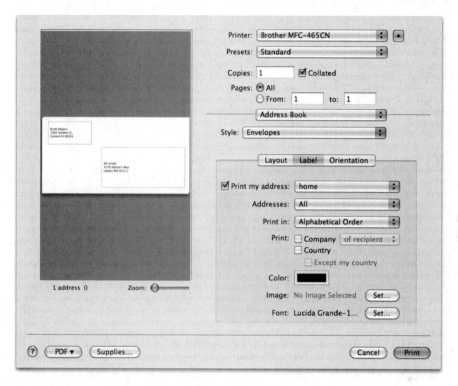

Figure 11-18. *Address Book has print options that automatically print envelopes, labels, and contact lists.*

iCal

The iCal interface (Figure 11-19) has become extremely streamlined as it has evolved, while at the same time adding some nice new features. The iCal window by default has a simple tool-bar that allows you to scroll forward and backward through time, change your calendar view, center the view on the current day, and search text in your calendar. The calendar view by default has a column on the left that contains your Calendar list at the top and a Mini Months calendar at the bottom, and to the right of the column is the main calendar view. At the bottom of the view area is a group of buttons below the Calendars list column that adds new calendars, toggles the Mini Months view, and toggles the Notifications view. In the lower-right corner is a button to toggle the To Do list, which, when visible, appears as a column to the right of the main calendar view.

Unlike some older versions of iCal (pre-Leopard), there is no information sidebar; now event information pops up when you double-click the event item in the calendar view. This pop-up window reveals event details and lets you edit the event information.

Figure 11-19. *ICal's Week view*

The view buttons in the toolbar (and the associated menu bar items) control the calendar view and whether it will display a single day, a week, or a whole month. The Day view (select View ➤ by Day or press Command-1) provides the most information, at a glance, about any events that are occurring that day, and if you have a very crowded calendar, it's about the only view that will help you make sense of it. In the Month view (select View ➤ by Month or press Command-3), there is limited space to provide much information about a single event, but it does give you a nice view of future and past dates (and makes scrolling to a future or past date much quicker, though the Mini Months calendar could serve this purpose as well). The Week view (select View ➤ by Week or press Command-2) provides a nice compromise between the two. In the end, you will likely find the view, or combination of views, that generally works best for how you work.

Adding Calendars to iCal

A nice feature of iCal is the ability to add and display multiple calendars at the same time within iCal. This feature is not only useful as a way to organize your events, but it also allows you to selectively share and view certain types of events.

By default, iCal starts you out with two sensible calendars: Home and Work. However, if you'd like to add another, simply click the + button below the Calendars List area, select File ➤ New Calendar (Option-Command-N) from the menu bar, or select New Calendar from the contextual menu that appears when you right-click in the Calendar list. This creates a new calendar and highlights the name for editing. If you select Get Info from a calendar item's contextual menu, then you can add a description for that calendar and select a display color that all events associated with that calendar will appear in.

If you'd like, you can also organize calendars into calendar groups. To create a calendar group, select File ➤ New Calendar Group (Shift-Command-N) from the menu bar or New Group from the Calendar list area's contextual menu. Then you can drag individual calendars into that group.

Adding and Editing Events

You can add an event in a number of ways. Selecting File ➤ New Event (Command-N) adds a new event item to the selected date in the calendar, and in month view you can double-click a date or select New Event from the contextual menu. In any of those cases, you will likely need to double-click the event and edit it. In the Day or Week view, you can actually click and drag across a time frame to create a new event for that time.

Note Initially, all events will be created in the calendar selected in the Calendar List area; like most other properties, you can edit this later if you desire.

Once your event is created, it's likely you'll want to edit it. To edit an event, double-click it to open the Event Information pop-up, and click the Edit button to put the window into edit mode (Figure 11-20). The edit window allows you to change the date and times associated with an event, change the calendar the event is associated with, set an alarm to go off reminding you of the event, and make the event repeatable.

This mode also allows you to tag the event as an all-day event, which will list the event differently in the calendar view and allow the event to span multiple days. Finally, you can add attachments, notes, and URLs to the event to help you keep associated files and information tied to the event. When the event information is complete, just click Done.

If an event gets rescheduled or needs to be moved for any reason, rather than having to go into edit mode, you can change the date and time of the event by dragging the event from one time slot in the calendar to another.

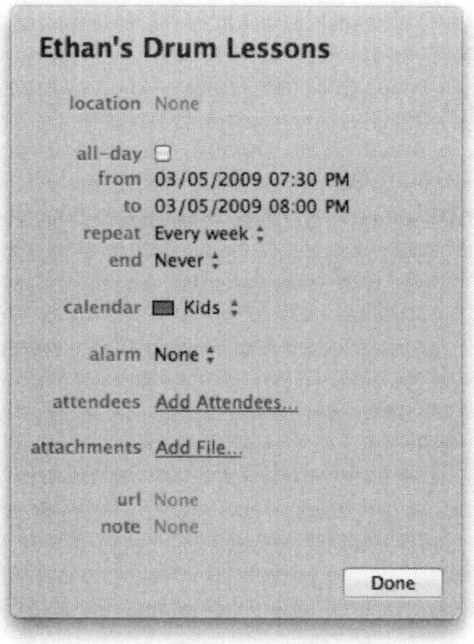

Figure 11-20. *Editing an iCal event*

Using To Dos

Besides events, iCal (now in tandem with Mail) also keeps track of To Do items. To view your To Do items in iCal, either click the button in the lower-right corner of the iCal window or select View ➤ Show To Do List (Option-Command-T). This opens your To Do list along the right side of your calendar view (Figure 11-21). To Do items in iCal are essentially the same as they are in Mail (though the keyboard shortcut to create a new To Do item in iCal is different—Command-K).

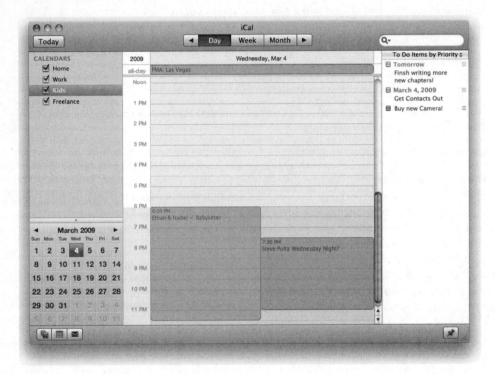

Figure 11-21. *iCal's Day view with a To Do list shown*

Inviting Others to Events and Appointments

In an event's edit mode, there is also a section for adding attendees. By clicking here, you can add any number of people you want to add as attendees for your event. Any attendees who are listed in your Address Book are automatically sent an invitation to the event.

■**Note** Attendees whom you are inviting need to be in your Address Book for them to get an invite, so if an attendee isn't listed there, it's best to add the information to your Address Book before you send out the invite.

Adding Time Zone Support

iCal has a nice time zone support feature that is not activated by default, but if you often travel or deal with people in other time zones, then this is a fantastic feature to use. Activating time zone support is as easy as selecting the "Turn on time zone support" option on the Advanced tab in iCal's preferences. Once the support is turned on, you will notice that a small time zone drop-down list will appear in the upper right of iCal's main window above the search field. You can alter this field to reflect the time zone that iCal is in. Additionally, events will gain a time zone setting. With time zone support enabled, iCal will automatically alter event times based on the time zone of the event and the time zone of iCal.

Subscribing to Other Calendars

Sometimes you may want to subscribe to a calendar other than your own. For example, you may want to subscribe to a calendar that provides the schedule of your favorite baseball team's games, or you may want to subscribe to a calendar that contains all the common UK holidays.

Often, organizations post calendar links on their web sites where you can just click a link and iCal will automatically open and add the calendar. Other times you may need to use the Calendar ➤ Subscribe menu bar option (Option-Command-S), which opens the dialog box and allows you to enter the URL in the calendar file.

To get started, select the Calendar ➤ Find Shared Calendars option from the menu bar. This opens your web browser to an Apple web site where Apple makes available a number of common shared calendars (including MLB baseball schedules and UK holidays).

Sharing Your Calendars

Besides subscribing to other calendars, sometimes you may want to share one of your calendars. To enable other people to subscribe to your calendar, you must have access to MobileMe or a CalDAV server to publish your calendar. If you have access, then you can select a calendar and select Calendar ➤ Publish from the menu bar. This will open a sheet asking for information about where and what you want to share. Once the calendar is shared, you can pass the URL to anyone whom you want to view it.

Learning About iCal and CalDAV

There are lots of issues with sharing calendars, as outlined previously, but the biggest one is that it's a little too static; in other words, calendar information doesn't freely flow back and forth. Many calendaring systems avoid these issues, but most of them are fairly proprietary systems, so there are interoperability problems. To solve this, Apple and a number of other organizations have joined together to create the CalDAV standard, which provides a standard way to handle calendaring systems in a client/server environment.

In this system, calendars are stored on a central calendar server that makes everyone's schedules available to everyone else (with the security frameworks in place at the organization). The big advantage to this is that it facilitates scheduling and even planning in a much more effective manner.

It just so happens that iCal in Snow Leopard supports CalDAV (and Snow Leopard Server provides a nice CalDAV-based calendar server called iCal Server). If you have access to a

CalDAV server, you'll need to set up the account information on the Accounts tab in iCal's preferences. This will add a calendar to iCal representing the calendar on the server.

Once this is all set up, then you can select Window ➤ Availability Panel to view the availability of other users of the calendar server. Using this makes scheduling meetings with a number of others a snap; in fact, iCal can use this to automatically find the next time that everyone is available for a meeting.

Summary

Mail, Address Book, and iCal have worked well at their respective tasks since their inception, but in Snow Leopard, they reach new levels of functionality and, more important, seamless integration. Next we'll cover Apple's instant message client, iChat, which is, in some circles, replacing e-mail as the Internet communication method of choice.

CHAPTER 12

■■■

iChat

Instant messaging (IM) has been gaining popularity over the last few years as the Internet communication method of choice for many situations. iChat is Apple's default instant messaging client in Snow Leopard and has lots to offer. First, it's compatible with AIM as well as Google Chat, two of the biggest instant messaging networks out there. Second, it adds lots of cool features that go beyond simple text chat, including voice and video chat. Finally, it's easy to use and well integrated with other Snow Leopard applications. In this chapter we'll cover the following:

- Getting an iChat account
- Logging in with your account
- Adding and managing buddies
- Text chat and instant messaging
- Voice and video chat
- Using iChat with other programs
- Customizing iChat
- iChat Theater
- File transfers

Getting and Setting Up an iChat Account

Since iChat supports various IM services, there are many ways to get an account that will work with iChat. AIM and MobileMe usernames are the easiest to set up from iChat. To get an AIM account from AOL, you'll need to go to http://aim.com, select the Get a Screen Name option, and go through the registration on that site. Being a faithful Mac user, you may opt to get a MobileMe account instead.

There are two reasons to go the MobileMe route instead of the AIM route. First, Snow Leopard can take advantage of MobileMe in many ways, and if you wish to take advantage of all these, you'll need a MobileMe account anyway. Second, AOL has been around for a very long time, and all usernames must be unique, so you stand a much better chance of getting a username that doesn't resemble scdmeye27653 or some other unrecognizable mess if you go through MobileMe, where there are likely more sensible screen names available. MobileMe has a 90-day trial offer, if you'd like to give it a try.

To get a MobileMe username, you just need to sign up at http://me.com. Once you have an account, go to the Accounts tab of iChat's preferences, as shown in Figure 12-1. Click the little + button beneath the Accounts column. This will open up a sheet for you to enter your account information, as shown in Figure 12-2.

On the Account Setup sheet, you first must pick your account type. This will either be a MobileMe account, Mac.com (.Mac) account, AIM account, Jabber account, or Google Talk account. Below that, you will be asked for your username (Member Name, Account Name) and password. Additionally, if you are using a Jabber server, you will be prompted to enter the server information. The Get an iChat Account… option will take you to the MobileMe registration page in your web browser.

When you have entered the required information, click Done, and your new account will appear in the Accounts column of the Accounts tab in iChat's preferences.

Note There is one other type of account that iChat can use that does not need to be configured—that's Bonjour. The Bonjour account will automatically use your Snow Leopard account info to identify you and will find any other iChat users on your LAN who have their Bonjour account activated. Bonjour is a great way to IM people in your organization a few offices away, or one of your children upstairs in their room blaring music loudly with their door closed.

Figure 12-1. *iChat's Accounts preferences*

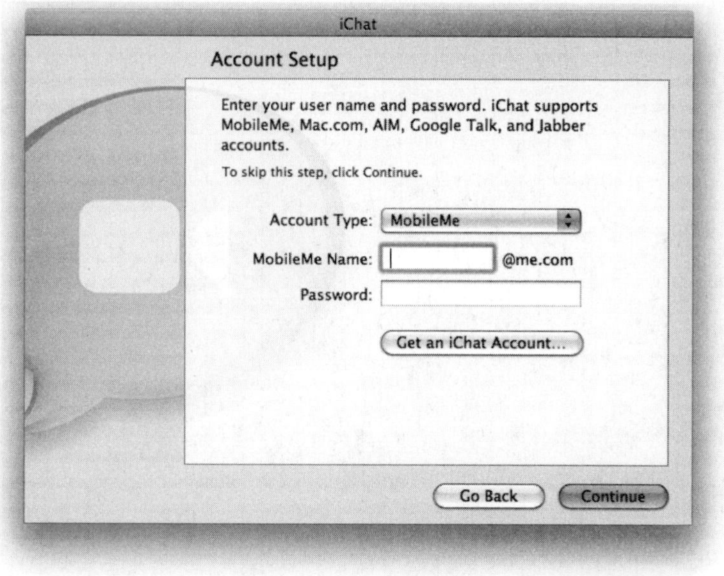

Figure 12-2. *The Account Setup sheet used to add new iChat accounts*

Depending on the account type for each account listed in your Accounts column, there will be some additional configuration options. The key options you'll want to know about are the "Use this account" and "When iChat opens, automatically log in" options. "Use this account" enables the account and lists it in the File ➤ Accounts submenu. The "When iChat opens, automatically log in" option is fairly obvious: when you launch iChat, iChat will automatically attempt to log in to the account.

Some accounts also have security options associated with them; these options generally enable you to restrict how other people view your status when you are online.

Logging In to Your iChat Account and Setting Your Status

Logging in to your iChat account(s) is a fairly easy process. Obviously, if you have selected the option to have your account automatically log in when iChat launches, then you really don't have anything to do. However, to manually log in and log out, all you have to do is toggle your account in the File ➤ Accounts submenu.

When you log in, an account window opens up that allows you to access account IM features for that account and view your buddy list, as shown in Figure 12-3.

Figure 12-3. *An iChat account window, with a buddy list*

The top of the account window provides your account status. The top line provides the name you have associated with the account, or your *handle* (which is another way of saying your screen name, or account name). You can toggle between the two by clicking the name/handle. To the left of your name is your online status: a green dot means you are online and accepting IMs; a red dot means you are online, but you are not accepting incoming IMs; a faint gray circle means you are online, but are invisible (people can't see you are online); and no dot means you are offline.

Below the name is your online status message. Your status message and current online status will be visible to anyone (unless you limit the visibility of your status in the account's security preferences). To change your status or message, click the status message and select a new status from the pop-up menu. You can set a custom status message by selecting Custom Available... or Custom Away... from the menu and then typing in anything you want. Selecting Edit Status Menu... opens a sheet where you can create, edit, or delete the status messages that appear in the pop-up, and change whether and how iChat remembers your custom status messages.

To the right of your name is your picture, also known as your buddy icon. Your initial picture is the same icon you have associated with your account and your contact info in Address Book. To change your picture, drop an image on the current picture, or click it to bring up a list of recent pictures. From the Recent Pictures sheet, you can also select Edit Picture... for more options, including taking a snapshot with iSight.

If you have audio or video chat enabled, a green audio or video icon will also be visible.

Adding and Managing Buddies

Each account maintains a buddy list to keep track of friends, family, and associates who have IM accounts. To add a buddy, click the + button at the bottom of your account window and select the Add Buddy... option or select Buddies ➤ Add Buddy... (Shift-Command-A) from the menu bar. This opens up a sheet for you to fill in information about your new buddy, as shown in Figure 12-4.

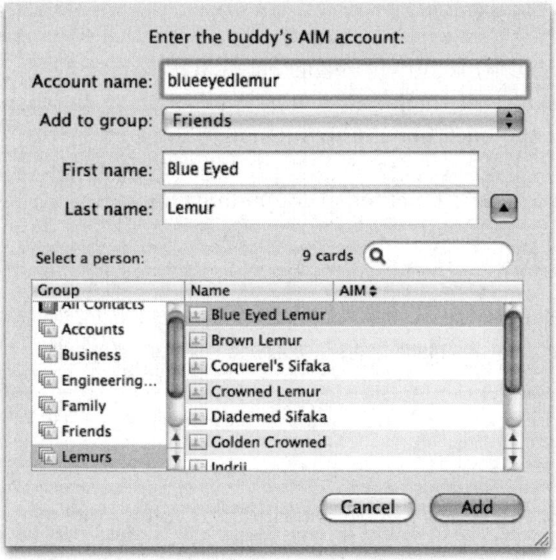

Figure 12-4. *The Add Buddy sheet in iChat*

Address Book is integrated with iChat. If your buddy is already listed in your address book, iChat will autocomplete the Add Buddy form as you type. Clicking the blue disclosure button to the right of the Last Name field expands the sheet into a people picker. Selecting an Address Book card associates it with that buddy. You can also drag contacts from Address Book into your buddy list to add them.

To help you keep track of your buddies, you can organize them into groups. To create a group, click the + button at the bottom of the account window and select the Add Group... option. A small sheet will open up and ask for the name of your new group. Enter the name and click Add to add the group. To change or delete groups, select the Edit Groups... option from the Account + menu.

When you add a buddy, you are asked what group you'd like that person to be in. If you'd like to change the group, simply select and drag your buddy into a new group. If you'd like to rearrange the order in which your groups appear, grab their headers and drag them around.

In iChat's View menu, there are a number of options about how to display offline buddies. You can hide them, display them in their regular groups, or coalesce them into a special offline group.

The View menu also lets you choose whether to use groups at all; whether to display your audio or video status; whether to display buddies by full name, short name, or handle; and whether to sort buddies by name, availability, or not at all.

■**Note** For more options, see the "Customizing iChat" section, which follows.

Communicating with iChat

While iChat started as a fancier version of AOL's Instant Messenger client, it has evolved into a multi-protocol communication powerhouse. The traditional features are still there, but they are joined by advanced audio and video chat modes, and are augmented by integration with other programs on the system. Right- or Control-clicking a name on your buddy list reveals a long list of options, each one representing a different method of communicating.

■**Note** In addition to the buddy list's contextual menu, you can also initiate communications with selected buddies from the Buddies menu on the menu bar, or by the menu items' associated keyboard shortcuts.

Text Chat

Invite to Chat... is the first option. Selecting this opens a new chat window. Typing a message and pressing Return cause a window to pop up on your selected buddies' screens inviting them to chat. If they accept, you will be able to type messages back and forth, forming a conversation, as shown in Figure 12-5.

Figure 12-5. *Multiple-participant chat room in iChat*

The chat window displays your conversation as it happens, with the users' buddy icons and text balloons indicating who said what. To enter a message, just type your text in the text field at the bottom of the window. When someone is typing, a gray thought balloon appears next to their buddy icon, so you know they're formulating a response and not just ignoring you.

■**Note** The thought balloons only appear in one-on-one chats. It would be entirely too annoying if a ten-person chat window was constantly full of thought balloons.

That the chat option is first on the list suggests it's iChat's preferred method of communication. This is a not a coincidence, as the chat mode offers several conveniences over traditional IM.

Chats can involve more than two people. Selecting multiple buddies when initiating a chat will send invitations to everyone. Anyone who joins that chat will be able to participate in the conversation.

Chat mode uses a chat room metaphor, similar to Internet Relay Chat (IRC). That means people can be invited to join at any time and leave as they please. As long as one person remains in the chat room, the conversation will remain open.

Even if you're only talking to one person, chat is still a good mode because you always have the option of inviting more people—more like a natural conversation. Imagine if you were in a coffee shop talking to a friend when another friend came in. How silly it would be to have to leave the coffee shop and come back for them to join you!

■**Note** You can chat without using your buddy list. To start a chat with someone who isn't on your buddy list, select File ➤ New Chat... (Command-N) from the menu bar and fill in the information in the pop-up dialog box. To join a chat room by name, select File ➤ Go to Chat Room... (Command-R) and type the name of the room. If a room by that name does not exist, it will be created.

Instant and Direct Messaging

Instant messaging is hardly a new invention. Indeed, its limited person-to-person connection could be called a step backward, as it has more in common with the old UNIX `talk` command than with the sophisticated chat rooms of IRC. Still, what it lacks in features, IM makes up for in simplicity and ubiquity.

In iChat, selecting Send Instant Message... or Send Direct Message... works almost identically to Invite to Chat...; in fact, the window will still say you are "chatting with" your buddy, as shown in Figure 12-6. Don't be fooled; IM has fewer options than a true chat. While you can hold multiple IM conversations, you can't have three or more people talking at a time, nor can you add participants as you can with a chat.

Figure 12-6. *Direct messaging over Bonjour in iChat*

To add to the confusion, if you try to send an instant message to multiple buddies at once, you will actually start a chat session, even though you selected Send Instant Message…, not Invite to Chat…!

Direct messaging is identical to IM, with one subtle behind-the-scenes difference. Whereas IM uses a central server to route messages, direct messaging establishes a direct connection between two computers.

The main advantage of direct messaging is enhanced privacy, but IM has its own advantages. It's older and more common, so it's more likely to be understood by chat clients other than iChat. It's also less prone to interference from network settings and firewalls.

Caution Direct messaging enhances privacy, but it cannot be considered secure, because it doesn't use encryption to protect the content of your messages. To read more about secure chatting, see the "Customizing iChat" section, which follows.

Ironically, the IM central server also provides an advantage over both direct messaging and chatting. Since instant messages are directed to a single person, the server can store them until that person logs on. Thus, you can send instant messages to people who are offline.

Note Double-clicking names on your buddy list will always start a conversation, but the mode used depends on the situation. If multiple buddies are selected, double-clicking always launches a chat. If a single buddy is selected, double-clicking will start an IM session, unless you are communicating via Bonjour, in which case double-clicking will use direct messaging.

Audio and Video Chats

Like you, people in your buddy or chat participant lists with video chat enabled will display a camera icon. Clicking this icon invites them to video chat and present you with a video preview window, giving you a last chance to get the spinach out of your teeth. If they accept, you will see a picture-in-a-picture video screen.

■**Note** Not every type of account has audio and video chat capabilities. Google Chat clients, for example, only have access to text chat. If your buddies can only support audio chats, they will have a telephone icon. Clicking this icon invites them to audio chat instead. If your buddies can't support either, they will not have an icon. If, however, they have an icon, but it's grayed out, that means they are already in a video chat.

As with text chat, video chat can support multi-way conferencing, as shown in Figure 12-7. Depending on the speed of your computer's processor, you can video chat with as many as three people simultaneously. Chat participants can be selected when you start the chat, or they can be invited late by pressing the + button.

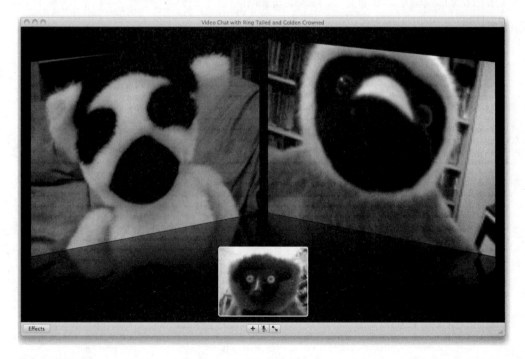

Figure 12-7. *Three-way video conferencing in iChat*

Adjacent to the + button is a mute button, which disables the audio portion of the chat. To the right of the mute button is a button for going into full-screen mode. To the far left is the Effects button, which toggles a menu of real-time effects you can apply to your video, as shown in Figure 12-8.

Figure 12-8. *The Video Effects window in iChat*

You can also summon the Video Effects window by selecting Video ➤ Show|Hide Video Effects (Shift-Command-R) from the menu bar. To select an effect, click it. To remove the effect, click the original effect in the middle of the page.

There are a few pages of effects, which you can navigate by using the arrow buttons on either side of the panel. There are also several blank spots on the last page where you can insert your own effects by dragging pictures, videos, or Quartz Composer compositions into the blank spots.

Background Effects

Video effects that have an outline of a person in them are background effects. If you select one, iChat will ask you to step out of the frame while it analyzes the background. It will then replace the background with full-motion video. When you step back into the frame, it will appear that you're standing in front of the new background, as shown in Figure 12-9.

For best results, select an even, neutral background. If you happen to have a high-tint green or blue chroma-key screen, use that. Otherwise, a white wall works well. Make sure your clothes have sufficient contrast from the background (unless you want to look like a floating head). If you see spots where the background shows through, select Video ➤ Reset Background (Option-Command-R) from the menu bar and try again. It also helps if you don't move around too much.

All in all, the background effects are probably not going to convince your boss you're hard at work at the office while you sip margaritas on the beach, but it may certainly add a fun flare to your Friday meetings.

Figure 12-9. *The results of applying background effects in iChat*

Variations on Video Chat

Clicking a buddy's video icon always launches video chat, even if all you want is audio chat. Fortunately, there are several other ways to launch audio and video chats, the most obvious of which is to select Invite to Video Chat or Invite to Audio Chat from the buddy list's contextual menu, or from the Buddies menu in the menu bar.

If a buddy does not have audio or video chatting enabled, these menu items will become Invite to One-Way Video Chat and Invite to One-Way Audio Chat. That means, for example, you can still originate a video chat with them, and they will be able to see you, but you won't be able to see them.

You can also click the telephone and camera buttons on the bottom of your buddy list to launch that type of chat with the selected buddies. Pressing the text button is equivalent to double-clicking; it will launch some kind of text-based communication, depending on context.

iChat also works with other AIM video chat clients, most notably AOL Instant Messenger for Windows, assuming the users have the appropriate hardware.

Mobile Text Messaging

Most mobile phones support text messaging via the Short Message Service protocol, also known as SMS, or simply *text messaging*. iChat has two ways to participate in text messaging. First, you can send a text message to a buddy by selecting Send SMS… from the buddy list contextual menu, or Buddies ➤ Send SMS… from the menu bar.

In order for the Send SMS... command to be enabled, you must have a phone number set for your buddy in Address Book, and that number must be labeled as "mobile." If the number is labeled as anything else, including home, main, pager, or a custom label, it will not work in iChat.

■**Caution** Support for SMS only works on phone numbers from the United States, Canada, and other members of the ten-digit North American Numbering Plan. The same is true for AIM mobile forwarding, discussed as follows.

Sending an SMS message launches a chat window, just like sending an instant message. If your buddy sends a response, it will show up in the chat window, as expected. If you have since closed the window, iChat will open a new one. However, this is not a true instant message, so if your buddy tries to respond after you've closed iChat or logged out, that person will receive an error message.

Another way to communicate with iChat from your mobile phone is to enable mobile forwarding on your AIM account. This is done online, but you can get to the appropriate web page by clicking the Configure AIM Mobile Forwarding... button in iChat's account preferences. The process is simple; you enter your phone number and AOL sends a confirmation code to your phone. Enter the code on the activation page, and you're done.

With mobile forwarding enabled, you will never go offline. If anyone sends you an instant message, it will be converted to an SMS text message and sent to your phone. Your responses will be returned in the chat window, much like the Send SMS feature.

In iChat, buddies who are receiving their messages via mobile forwarding will have a gray "broadcasting" symbol next to their names, as shown in Figure 12-10. Their availability dot will be clear to light gray in color, and they will have the status message they had when they logged out.

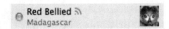

Figure 12-10. *A buddy using mobile forwarding in iChat*

■**Caution** Most mobile plans limit the number of SMS text messages subscribers can send and receive, and some even charge a fee for each message. Keep this in mind before using mobile messaging features from iChat.

File Transfers

One nice feature of iChat is the ability to send a file to someone you are chatting with. If you'd like to send a file, select Buddies ➤ Send File... (Option-Command-F), which will open a file dialog to select the file you wish to send. Once the file is selected, the person you are sending the file to will get prompted to accept the file. When that person accepts, the download will begin.

Likewise, if you are being sent a file, you will be prompted in your chat window to accept or decline the item. If you accept, the file will be downloaded to your system.

You can also drag files from within the Finder to names in your buddy list, or into the input field of an open chat. Certain types of files, such as images and PDFs, will be rendered in place, as shown in Figure 12-11.

Figure 12-11. *Pictures are usually rendered in place in iChat.*

To save the image, drag it from the chat window to the Finder. If the image is large, it will be scaled down in the chat window; but when you drag it, you will save the original file as if you had just transferred it.

Since moving files around in iChat has become so common, Snow Leopard has a File Transfers window, much like the one found in Safari. This window contains a list of files, their transfer status, and a magnifying glass icon you can click to jump to the file in the Finder. The File Transfers window will launch automatically as needed, but you can also summon it from the menu bar by selecting Window ➤ File Transfers (Option-Command-L).

■**Caution** Macs don't have the virus problems of other operating systems, but that doesn't mean you should be careless. Don't accept files from people you don't know.

Screen Sharing

Screen sharing allows you to view and control another user's computer from a window on your own machine. It's a great way to show something to a friend, collaborate with a colleague, or provide technical support for a family member.

You can initiate screen sharing from within iChat by selecting Share My Screen... or Ask to Share Remote Screen... from the buddy list contextual menu or the Buddies menu bar item. You can also click the Screen Sharing button on your buddy list. That's the one on the right side that looks like one rectangle overlapping another.

Screen sharing is actually one of Snow Leopard's Sharing networking features, so it's discussed in much more detail in Chapter 20.

■**Note** The Share My Screen... and Ask to Share Remote Screen... menu items will change to reflect the buddy you have selected, so don't be surprised if you actually have to click Share My Screen with Alice... or Ask to Share Bob's Screen....

Integrating with Mail

Mail and iChat represent two different ways of communicating that are nevertheless complementary. You might start writing an e-mail message and realize it would be better said over iChat. Or you might want to iChat someone, but that person isn't online.

For situations like these, iChat and Mail both make it easy to use the other. In iChat, selecting Send Email... from the buddy list context menu or the Buddy menu bar item will launch Mail with a new message to that buddy, assuming you have that person's e-mail address in Address Book.

If you are reading or composing mail to a buddy who is available in iChat, that person's name will display a green availability dot. Mail includes Reply With iChat among the options available from the message contextual menu, the menu bar, and an optional toolbar icon.

Advanced Status Messages

Despite their name and original purpose, iChat's status messages have become a handy way to announce things to your friends without having to specifically address them. Since status messages can't be too long, it's often handy to just set your status to a link, which your friends can follow if they want to know more.

In iChat, friends with URLs in their status messages will display a small gray circle with an arrow on it, as shown in Figure 12-12. Clicking the arrow launches the URL in Safari. You can also launch the URL by selecting Open URL from the buddy list contextual menu.

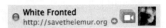

Figure 12-12. *A buddy with a URL status message in iChat*

■**Note** If a buddy is selected, the Open URL menu item will change to reflect the name of the URL—so in the example in Figure 12-12, the menu item would actually read "Open http://savethelemur.org."

Another popular use for the status message is displaying the current song you're listening to in iTunes. You can set this to update automatically by selecting Current iTunes Song from the status message pop-up menu. If your buddy is taking advantage of this feature, his or her status message will have the same gray circle and arrow as with a URL, except clicking it will take you to that track in the iTunes Store.

Note You might expect the Open URL menu item to take you to a buddy's home page, assuming it's listed in Address Book, but it does not. It also doesn't work with the Current iTunes Song feature.

Customizing iChat

A lot of options are packed into iChat's Preference window. While you can certainly use iChat without going through the preferences, you'd be missing out on a lot of functionality. Here is a quick tour of what you can do from the various preference panels.

General

- Change the default IM application, allowing you to use iChat to facilitate not using iChat.

- Optionally show your iChat status in the menu bar by adding a miniature version of iChat to the menu bar as a menu bar extra, from which you can monitor and change your status, watch your buddy lists, and launch chats.

- Set options to auto-reply when you are away, which basically functions as an answering machine for iChat. You can let people know what you're doing, and they can continue chatting, effectively leaving you a message for when you get back.

- Set "Animate buddy pictures," which restores one of the more polarizing features of AIM: the use of animated GIFs as buddy icons. This was absent for a long time in iChat, because a lot of people find them annoying.

- Automate your status changes, such as changing your status to "available" when you wake your computer from sleep, automatically logging out of iChat when you use Mac OS X's fast user-switching feature, and keeping IM accounts logged in even when iChat is closed.

Accounts

- Add and remove accounts, as well as activate and deactivate accounts without actually removing them from the list.

- Allow iChat to automatically log in to your accounts when you open iChat.

- Allow your account to be logged in to from multiple machines. If you log in to an account from a second machine (or session or client), AOL will prompt you to log out of the existing session remotely.

- Use a special "recent buddies" group to remember people who chat with you but are not in your buddy list.

- Configure mobile forwarding to receive instant messages on your phone, as discussed previously.

- Set privacy options, including the ability to block specific people, preventing them from seeing you online or sending you messages.

- Enable encrypted chats, so MobileMe and .Mac connections are automatically protected by 128-bit encryption.

Messages

- Change the color of your word balloons and the font used in your text chats. You can also override other people's word balloon and font choices.

- Set a keyboard shortcut to immediately bring iChat into focus, which is handy if you always keep iChat running in the background so people can get in touch with you. This is particularly useful combined with iChat's Dock icon, which displays a badge showing you the number of pending unread messages.

- Automatically save chat transcripts to a folder, which is handy if you need to remember things you talk about in your chats. This is discussed in more detail in the "Nifty iChat Features" section later in the chapter.

- Collect chats into a single window, also known as tabbed chatting. This is also discussed in more detail in the "Nifty iChat Features" section.

- Remember open chats when you close iChat, so you can pick up where you left off the next time you open iChat.

- Watch for your name in incoming messages, automatically highlighting your name in chats. This is quite useful if you hang out in a chat room where the conversation doesn't necessarily revolve around you.

Alerts

- Set custom alerts so you can keep watch on iChat when it's in the background without actually having to switch to it.

- Play sounds, use the speech synthesizer to make announcements, or bounce the Dock icon in response to specific events.

- Run AppleScripts, so you can do cool things like send commands to control iTunes on another machine via iChat.

Audio/Video

- Preview your video window prior to starting a chat, or just use your computer as a really expensive mirror.

- Set the microphone you're using, or set up a Bluetooth headset for better sound quality and privacy during audio or video chats.

- Set a bandwidth limit to prevent performance problems on your network.

Nifty iChat Features

In addition to being a versatile chat client and communication center, iChat has several additional features to add utility and a bit of fun to your conversations.

iChat Theater

iChat Theater lets you use iChat's video chat feature in conjunction with external applications. For example, you can give a Keynote presentation or present an iPhoto slideshow from within iChat, as shown in Figure 12-13.

The effect is not unlike starting a video chat and pointing the camera at the screen while running an application, except that the application feeds video directly to iChat, so neither you nor the person you are chatting with have to have a video camera in order to use iChat Theater. The application you share is your only video source.

Our personal favorite use of iChat Theater is true to its name: watching a movie with a spouse even though one person is traveling. Depending on your network connection, your mileage may vary.

Figure 12-13. *Sharing an iPhoto slideshow in iChat Theater*

The one big caveat of iChat Theater is that applications you share have to implement the functionality. It's not something that comes for free. Fortunately, many of Apple's applications already work with iChat Theater, so you can get some use out of it while third-party developers catch up.

The easiest way to use iChat Theater is to drag a file onto the window of your video chat. You can also select File ➤ Share a File With iChat Theater... from the menu bar. iChat does a pretty good job of parsing many files you'd like to share without having to invoke another application.

You can also enter iChat Theater from within other applications. For example, in Keynote, you can select View ➤ Play in iChat Theater from the menu bar. This presents the current presentation in iChat Theater.

Tabbed Chat

The nice thing about iChat vs. the telephone is that you don't have any awkward silences. If you don't have anything to say, you can just not type anything. Then, if something comes to mind, you can send it along and it will be appended to the conversation as if no time had passed (except, of course, for the telltale timestamp).

That means you can have several chats happening at once, potentially causing a lot of clutter, and making it difficult to know which window needs your attention. In Snow Leopard, tabbed chats collect all your chat windows into one, as shown in Figure 12-14. This is great for people for whom iChat is their primary communication tool for friends, family, and clients.

The tabs are actually a list of chats, not unlike a buddy list. If someone has something to say, a miniature word bubble will appear, making it clear which tab needs your attention. To switch chats, just click the appropriate tab.

Figure 12-14. *Tabbed chat helps you manage multiple conversations.*

Saving Your Chats

Another advantage iChat has over the telephone is the ability to save your chats. If someone gives you a To Do list, or you have a late night trans-Atlantic brainstorming session with your colleagues in Amsterdam, you can save the chat by selecting File ➤ Save a Copy As (Command-S) from the menu bar.

Alternately, if you have a really bad memory and you just want to automatically save all chats, you can set this in the preferences. This is good for business users who need to keep track of conversations. Like e-mail, chat transcripts are discoverable information in American court proceedings.

To open a chat, just select File ➤ Open... (Command-O) from the menu bar and navigate to the saved file, or, if it happened recently, find it in the File ➤ Recent Items submenu.

Smileys

One of the biggest problems with text chat is that you can't convey emotions. The best accepted solution to this problem was invented in 1982 by a computer scientist at Carnegie Mellon University named Scott Fahlman. His simple proposal, known today as *smileys*, or *emoticons*, are small text drawings representing facial expressions. For example, a statement meant to be taken as tongue-in-cheek can be followed by a smiley face, rendered as =-).

In iChat, text smileys are replaced with small pictures. Hence, typing =-) will insert a yellow smiley face graphic. If you're a traditionalist, or if you frequently use iChat to discuss programming code or other sources of nontraditional punctuation, you might find this feature annoying. Luckily, you can turn it off by selecting View ➤ Messages ➤ Hide Smileys from the menu bar. You can also insert smileys by clicking the smiley face icon in the input field of a chat window, or by selecting Edit ➤ Insert Smiley from the menu bar.

Alternatives to iChat

While iChat is great, it's not the only game in town. There are several other competing IM applications, each with their own protocols, features, strengths, and weaknesses. Most of these have Mac clients you can download and use, including Windows Live Messenger and Yahoo Messenger.

Another popular solution is to use a multi-protocol communication tool that understands all the major chat protocols. Adium is by far the best of these. Adium is Mac-only and open source, and the guys who work on Adium are really cool, to boot.

Adium supports AIM, Google Talk, Windows Live Messenger, Yahoo Messenger, Jabber, Bonjour, and several other protocols we've never even heard of. It has a slick interface, it's easy to use, and best of all, it's free. You can get Adium at www.adiumx.com.

Finally, for those who like what iChat has done for their long-distance bill, but miss the whole telephone experience, there's Skype. Unlike iChat, Skype can actually place voice calls to standard phones. Skype also handles text chat. Skype has a nice Mac client, which you can download from www.skype.com.

Summary

iChat is a fun and useful tool for keeping in contact with people all over the world instantly. While there are still times when e-mail is preferable to IM, this is becoming a more important means of communicating on the Internet.

Now that we've covered most of the Internet tools that come with Snow Leopard, you should be all set for about 90 percent of what most people use computers for these days. Of course, you probably didn't buy a Mac just to surf the Internet (although it's a good choice if you did). The next section of this book will deal with some of the other applications that come with Snow Leopard, as well as touch upon iLife and iWork.

■ ■ ■

## CHAPTER 13

MobileMe

MobileMe (an evolution of .Mac) is an online service provided by Apple that not only provides basic features such as e-mail, file sharing, and web site hosting, but also provides a link between many OS X applications and computers. However, to take advantage of MobileMe, you'll have to shell out for a yearly subscription (currently $99 per year in the States). Is it worth it?

That's a question you'll have to answer yourself, but it helps to know what MobileMe is all about. First of all, if all you want is an e-mail address (which MobileMe offers quite nicely), Google, Yahoo, and others will give you one for free. However, if you are looking for a complete integrated service that provides added utility to your system and applications, as well as a host of other online services, then MobileMe may be just what you need.

In this chapter, we'll outline how to set up MobileMe and then outline just a few of the its features, including the following:

- E-mail

- Web hosting

- iDisk

- File sharing

- System syncing

- The Back to My Mac feature

- Application integration

Setting Up MobileMe

You set up MobileMe from the MobileMe System Preferences pane (Figure 13-1). You're first prompted to enter your MobileMe member name and password (if you maintained a .Mac account in the past, that member name and password will carry over to MobileMe). If you don't have an account, you can sign up for a free trial by clicking the Learn More... button, which will take you to `www.apple.com/mobileme`, where you can click one of the Free Trial buttons to sign up for a 60-day free trial.

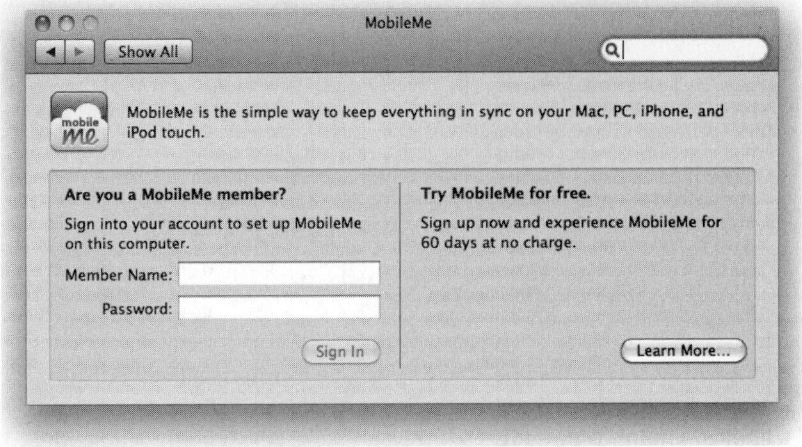

Figure 13-1. *The MobileMe System Preferences pane before you sign in*

If you are signing up for the first time, you will be led through a couple of screens during the sign-up process. The first screen will ask you to enter your desired MobileMe member name and password, your real name, a valid e-mail address, and your date of birth. Finally, it will ask you to make up a security question that you will need to remember should you ever forget your password. The next screen will prompt you for your credit-card and billing information to activate your account. Your credit card will not be charged until after the first 60 days, after which time you will be billed $99 for the first year.

■**Caution** If you don't wish to keep your MobileMe account active after the first 60 days, make sure you cancel your account before the 60-day trial period is up; otherwise, Apple will charge your credit card for the first year of service. Also, Apple will continue to use this information to renew your MobileMe account automatically as long as the credit card is valid. However, Apple will send you notice prior to charging your credit card, so you will have plenty of notice to cancel or change the information.

■**Note** If your desired member name is already used, you will be prompted to choose a different username when you try to move on from the first screen. Apple will provide you with a few options based on the member name you entered initially as well as your real name.

Once you set up your account, one of the first things you may want to do is enter your member name and password into the appropriate area in the MobileMe control panel. Once your information is entered and verified, your computer will be able to communicate with MobileMe. Also, the MobileMe System Preferences pane will change to provide you with a number of options for using MobileMe with your computer (Figure 13-2).

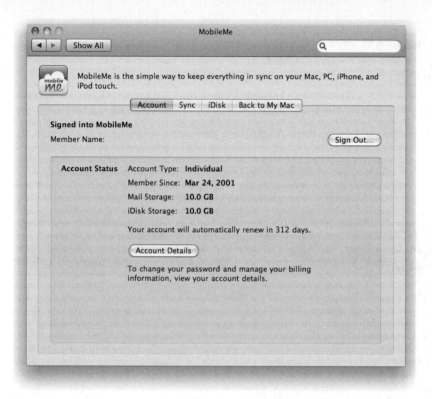

Figure 13-2. *The MobileMe System Preferences pane after you sign in*

MobileMe E-mail, Contacts, and Calendars

In its humble beginnings, prior to its evolution into MobileMe, .Mac was thought of primarily as an e-mail service, and while it has branched out to provide much more, it still of course provides top-notch e-mail services. What's particularly nice about MobileMe's e-mail is that it not only works seamlessly with Apple's Mail app, but it also works with any other e-mail client that supports IMAP. MobileMe also provides a fantastic webmail application that allows you to work with your MobileMe e-mail from any modern web browser (Figure 13-3).

■**Note** You can access MobileMe's webmail in any browser from www.me.com/mail. If you haven't already signed in to MobileMe, you will be prompted for your member name and password.

Caution When accessing MobileMe's webmail from a browser on a computer other than your own, you should be careful not to save your member name or password on the computer or browser. If you are using Safari on someone else's computer, you can do this by selecting the Private Browsing option (just be sure to turn it off when you are done). If you are using another browser, it's a good idea to close the browser when you are done. If it's a public computer, you might also clear the history and cookies before you quit the browser just to be safe (although if you do this on a friend's computer, you might delete some things that he wants).

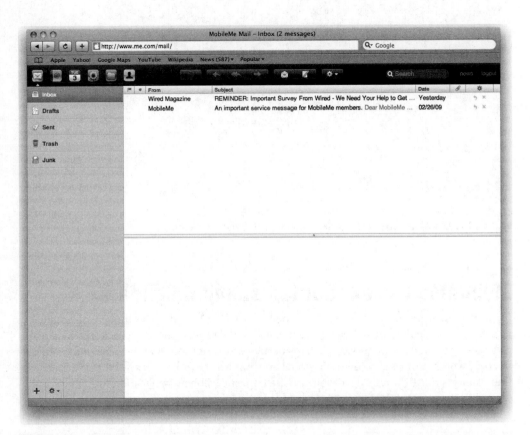

Figure 13-3. *MobileMe's webmail (shown here in Safari) looks and acts very much like the Mail app on your computer.*

MobileMe's Mail Preferences pane (located in webmail's toolbar under the Action menu—the button that has a gear icon on it) offers a number of options (Figure 13-4). The General, Viewing, and Composing tabs in the MobileMe webmail preferences generally allow you to set options that affect how the webmail interface looks and operates. The Aliases and Other tabs, however, provide some nice extra features.

Note If you access your MobileMe account from the Mail app and enable junk mail filtering in the MobileMe webmail preferences, then you should also select the "Store junk mail messages on the server" option under the MobileMe mail account options in the Mail app. This will ensure that all of your junk mail will be stored only in one common folder rather than two separate folders (and junk mail is bad enough without having to deal with two folders full of it).

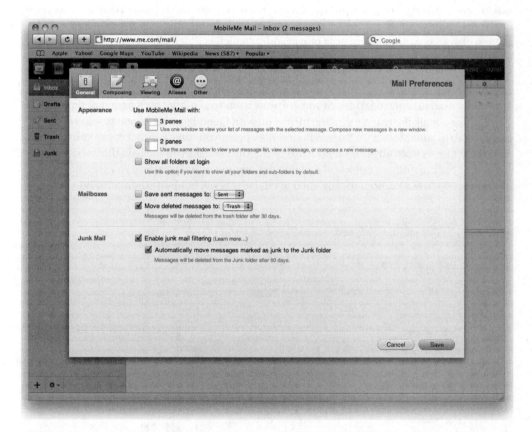

Figure 13-4. *MobileMe's webmail preferences provide all sorts of options for working with webmail and some nice other options for MobileMe's mail in general.*

The Aliases tab allows you to set up aliases for your MobileMe mail account. An *alias* is an alternate username that points to your real name. For example, if you want to create a new e-mail address such as learnosx@me.com that would send e-mail to your existing MobileMe mail account, then you could go to the Aliases tab, and if that username is available, you could set it up as an alias. You could even make e-mail addressed to an alias show up in a different color for easy sorting and viewing.

■Note Just like your member name, aliases must be unique. Any alias you choose is no longer available to any MobileMe users as a member name or alias, even if you delete the alias. It's not a good idea to go crazy here, because Apple limits the number of aliases you can use at one time to five, and if you delete one of your five, you'll have to wait a week before you can add a new one.

The Other tab provides two more nice options: "Checking email from an external account" and Mail Forwarding. The first option allows you to set up MobileMe mail to check and receive mail from a different POP account. This is useful if you have another POP e-mail account but want to check your e-mail from only one account (which is especially useful if you are away and want to check all your mail from a single webmail account). Mail Forwarding, on the other hand, forwards e-mail received by your MobileMe account to another e-mail address. Also in the Forwarding section is an "Automatically reply to email when it is received" option, which is commonly used to reply to senders if you are away from your e-mail for a period of time.

Besides e-mail, if you have syncing turned on with Calendars and Contacts selected under the Sync tab in your MobileMe System Preferences pane, you can easily access all your calendar and contact items from any browser (Figure 13-5). Any changes you make in the web interface are synced back to Address Book and iCal on your computer the next time you sync (if you have the sync set up to work automatically, then of course this will happen automatically).

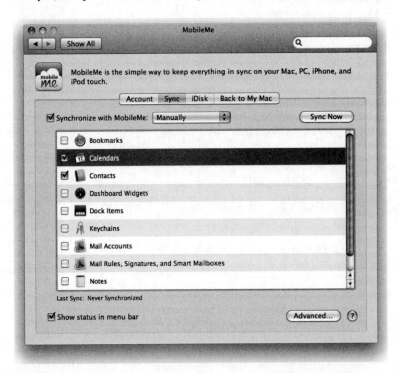

Figure 13-5. *The Sync tab in MobileMe's System Preferences pane allows you to set up the syncing of information between your computer and MobileMe. (This also facilitates the syncing of information from one computer to another.)*

Web Hosting and Gallery

MobileMe, combined with iLife '09 (which we will talk about in Chapter 16), provides a couple of interesting ways to publish your own content to the Web. First, with iWeb and MobileMe, you can easily create your own web sites that users can view at `http://web.me.com/yourmembername`.

Note If, rather than have your web site hosted at `http://web.me.com/yourmembername`, you'd like it hosted at `http://www.mydomain.com`, MobileMe has included a feature called Personal Domain, where you can set up any of your registered domains to be hosted through MobileMe. You can set this from the MobileMe web site by selecting Personal Domain under the Accounts tab (or go directly there at `www.me.com/account`).

Besides posting entire web sites, MobileMe has a Gallery feature that works with iPhoto to allow you to easily upload your photos to share with friends and family. Others can then view your Gallery at `http://gallery.me.com/yourmembername`.

Note In addition to iPhoto, your MobileMe Gallery can also be set up to sync with Aperture if that's your photo-management application of choice. Also, you can create a Gallery directly at `www.me.com` without the aid of any other photo applications.

---

iDisk

Another feature provided by MobileMe is your own iDisk, which is an online storage system that is tightly integrated into OS X (and Apple provides iDisk access tools specifically for Microsoft Windows as well). iDisk allows you to store, back up, and share files that are then accessible from any other computer connected to the Internet either by using a MobileMe web interface, by using the Windows iDisk utility, or by using the OS X Finder.

Note MobileMe currently provides 20 GB of storage that can consist of any content on your iDisk, your web pages, and your MobileMe e-mail. This total storage limit has been steadily increasing, and it is conceivable that the storage limit will continue to increase in the future. You can view your current and available storage space on the iDisk tab in the MobileMe panel of System Preferences.

To share files using iDisk, you simply need to place them in the `Public` folder on your iDisk (all other folders are visible only to you on your iDisk). You can configure the access you give to others from the iDisk tab in the MobileMe pane of System Preferences. The access can range from a free-for-all, allowing anyone to freely read and write to your iDisk (not the recommended option), to setting up a password to grant access to your iDisk to only those with the proper password. Your `Public` folder is accessible at `http://public.me.com/yourusername`.

> **Note** Apple recently created a new way to share a file from your MobileMe account. From within MobileMe's web interface under the iDisk tab, select the item you wish to share. In the File Info pane to the right, click the Share File… button. This opens a dialog box where you just need to enter the e-mail address of the person (or e-mail addresses of the people) you wish to share the file with, along with a message. Then click the Share button; an e-mail will be sent to the people you indicated, along with your message and a link to the file. If you'd like, you can password-protect each file, and you can set the amount of time the link will be active (the default is 30 days).

Data Syncing

We touched upon syncing your data from your computer and MobileMe when we talked about syncing your contact and calendar items. However, MobileMe does more than just sync a few items with your computer and MobileMe. The sync feature of MobileMe also allows you to keep items synced from one computer to another. For example, if you set up your MobileMe system preferences to sync your contacts, calendars, and bookmarks on one computer (say your notebook) and then select the same settings on another computer (say your desktop), you can use MobileMe as the "middle man" to sync all of the information on both computers (and MobileMe's web applications). As a super-cool extra, this feature is built in to iPhones, and Apple even has a MobileMe control panel available for Microsoft Windows computers, so you can even keep things synced up across different platforms and devices.

Back to My Mac

Imagine a situation in which keeping data in sync isn't enough, and what you really need is actual access to some file or other information on your computer that's halfway across the country. Well, MobileMe provides a solution for that as well—it's called Back to My Mac. Back to My Mac combines your MobileMe account with file and even screen sharing, allowing you to access or control a remote computer. To enable Back to My Mac, you must turn on the feature in the MobileMe System Preferences pane under the Back to My Mac tab for each computer you want to connect with. Each computer must also have file and screen sharing enabled in the Sharing System Preferences pane. Also, if this wasn't obvious, each computer needs to be configured with the same MobileMe account. Once you enable all of this, each computer will appear in the Finder's sidebar of all the other configured computers. To connect with the remote computer, select it from the Finder's sidebar.

All this is fairly easy; however, as a warning, lots can go wrong. There are two top problems that prevent this from working (provided everything is set up correctly):

- The networking magic that makes all of this work requires certain protocols, so if a computer is behind a router that doesn't support NAT-PMP or UPnP (or if these services aren't enabled), then this won't work.

- The computer you are attempting to connect to may be turned off or asleep.

Beyond that, there are a number of other possible issues. The Apple Tech article, "Using and troubleshooting Back to My Mac in Mac OS X 10.5" (available at `http://support.apple.com/kb/HT1109`) offers the best source of possible issues along with some solutions.

Application Integration

Finally, Apple has added nice little features into many of its applications (even beyond what we have covered here). Apple has made much of this information available to developers so that they can add MobileMe services into their apps as well. A couple of third-party applications take advantage of MobileMe:

- *Plasq's Comic Life* (`http://plasq.com/comiclife`): Allows you to save your completed comics to MobileMe for instant sharing. Many of Plasq's other applications also provide MobileMe integration, including Comic Life Magiq and Skitch, its forthcoming image-sharing application.

- *Delicious Monster's Delicious Library* (`http://delicious-monster.com`): Allows one-click publishing of your library to your MobileMe web site.

■**Note** Recently, as part of iWork '09, Apple announced plans for iWork.com, an online component of iWork. iWork.com is planned as being a separate entity from MobileMe and will be focused more specifically on sharing and collaborating with documents. At the time of this writing, iWork is still in beta.

Summary

Besides what we covered in this chapter, Apple and third-party developers continue to expand the types of services and application integration that make MobileMe a useful part of the Mac experience. Next, we are going to back away from the Web and the Internet and focus on Mac OS X applications in general.

PART 4

■ ■ ■

Working with Applications

CHAPTER 14

■■■

Application Basics

You've already worked with a number of applications in this book, and although each application is unique in many ways, they all tend to share some commonalities. In this chapter, we will cover some of these common features that aren't covered elsewhere in the book so that whatever application you are using, you will have a good grasp of how to do certain tasks (and have a good starting point for figuring everything else out). These tasks include the following:

- Installing an application with a standard installer
- Using the file dialog (opening and saving files)
- Choosing a document's default application
- Using the Services menu

■**Note** Most of these tasks are the same across applications, because they all rely on the same common frameworks to perform these functions. That said, some applications will not work in all the ways described in this chapter because the developer decided, for whatever reason, to do things differently. In those cases, we can only hope that the developer came up with something so obviously easy that it doesn't need description or that the developer documented the differences sufficiently.

Installing an Application Package

In Chapter 6, we covered the basic ways of installing an application; some applications you can just drag onto your hard drive and they are ready to go, while others come in packages that walk you through an installation. Applications are generally packaged either when they require more complex installations than simply moving an application bundle where you want it or when multiple options are provided when you install the application. If you just click through the installer, though, you may miss these options. Although every package you install will be slightly different, the general process is similar, so the best way to show how this works is to walk you through some of what you may encounter.

Starting the Installer

An installer package is usually distributed on a disk image or even a CD or DVD. Upon opening the disk (image), you will usually see one or more packages (Figure 14-1). Double-clicking the package will begin the installer.

Figure 14-1. *The iLife '09 installer package*

■**Note** There are two similar-appearing types of package files; some have the .pkg extension, and others have the .mpkg extension. The .mpkg files are special metapackages that generally contain a number of smaller .pkg files. The installation of both types is similar; however, the .mpkg file often has more available options.

When you double-click the installer package, Mac OS X's Installer application starts the installation process. One of the first things the Installer may do is check your system to verify it is suitable for installing the application (Figure 14-2).

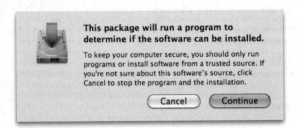

Figure 14-2. *Some packages must check your system before they can begin the installation.*

After the system check (if necessary), the Installer usually presents you with a few screens of information about the application. This generally includes up to three items: an Introduction screen, a Read Me screen, and a Software License screen.

The Introduction screen generally just welcomes you to the installation application and summarizes the software you are installing. The Read Me screen contains more in-depth information about the application(s) you are installing. Often readme files contain some important last-minute information about the software, so they're worth the read. Following that, you may be presented with a software license, which when you click Continue will prompt you with a sheet asking whether you agree or disagree (you have to agree if you want to install the software).

Customizing Your Installation

After you've clicked through the informational screens and accepted any licensing agreement, you will be presented with the Standard Install screen (Figure 14-3). Here you can choose either to proceed with the standard install in the default location on the default drive or to customize your install.

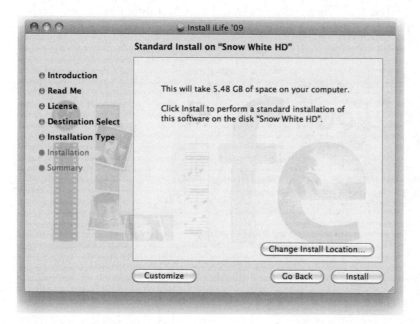

Figure 14-3. *The Standard Install screen allows you either to proceed with the standard install or to choose to customize your install.*

■**Note** Most of the time, a standard install (which used to be called an *easy install*) installs the application, along with the most popular options, in the Applications folder (occasionally in a special subfolder just for the particular application and components).

■Note Many applications use an installer rather than allow you to simply copy the application in place, either because they require more than a simple application bundle or because they have special install options. Many times, these applications require additional components to be installed in locations other than the Applications folder, and the installer does its best to simplify this process for the user. However, this also means that unless an uninstaller application is also included, removing all the components manually will require more than just dragging the installed application into the Trash.

There are two ways to alter the standard install, should you choose to do so. First, if you select the Change Install Location… button, you may be able to choose a different volume to install the software onto (Figure 14-4). This option is only available if you have more than one drive or partition available, and even if you do, certain software (including, as you can see in the image, iLife '09) will only allow you to install on drives that meet certain criteria. Second, you can choose which specific components get installed, and occasionally you can choose where they will be installed. If you choose to go this route, click the Customize button, which takes you to another screen (Figure 14-5) that provides you with the ability to fine-tune your install.

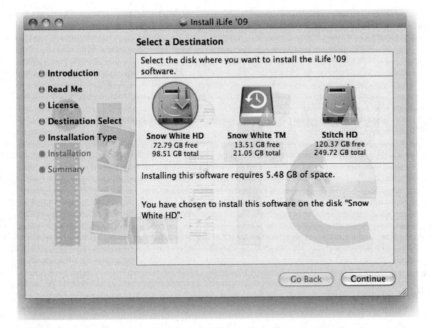

Figure 14-4. *The Select a Destination screen may allow you to install your software on an alternate volume (drive or partition). This also identifies which volumes are unavailable for your install.*

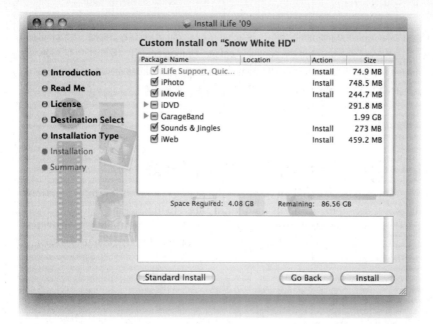

Figure 14-5. *The Custom Install screen allows you to manually select which components of your software will get installed. Occasionally, this screen lets you choose what folder the software should be installed to (an option that isn't available here).*

■**Note** Most people are aware that iLife '09—our example here—is a combination of a few separate applications, so it's not unexpected that you have lots of options in the Custom Install screen. This is not uncommon even for "applications," which you might at first assume refers to just a single application. In general, if given the option, we always like to click the Customize option just to see what's getting installed and what our options actually are.

Depending on the package, the custom options available to you will vary greatly, but generally the Custom Install screen will let you add or remove optional components to/from your install and may also provide a column to customize the installation folder on the selected install volume (otherwise, the default install will be either directly in the Applications folder or in a subfolder in the Applications folder).

Whether you choose the standard install or custom install, once you click the Install button, the installation will begin (though often you will be prompted to enter an administrator password before the install will begin).

When the installation is complete, you will often be presented with a screen letting you know that your installation was successful (and depending on the install, you may be asked to restart your computer).

■**Note** An application package, like many applications, is actually a bundle of various pieces. To look inside a package, select Show Package Contents from the contextual menu. One particularly interesting file you will find inside is the BOM file (usually called `Archive.bom`). What's interesting about this is that it contains a listing of all the application parts and where they go. To view this information, use the `lsbom` command-line tool.

File Dialogs: Opening and Saving Files

One common feature found in most applications is the file dialog. This window and variations of it are used throughout the system, primarily for opening and saving files.

The simplest file dialog is often used to open a file (Figure 14-6). Essentially, this provides a mini-Finder view to browse the system and select the item you want to open, along with a few application-specific options.

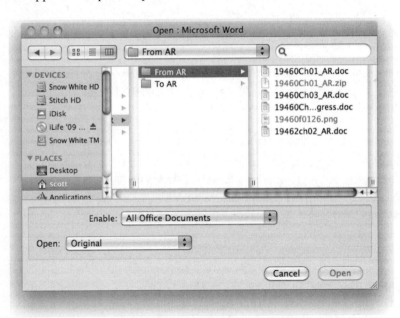

Figure 14-6. *An Open file dialog from Microsoft Word 2008*

When you want to save a file, the file dialog is a bit different and has greater variations between applications. Additionally, even the most simple Save As… dialog boxes tend to have both a simplified view (Figure 14-7) and an extended view (Figure 14-8).

Figure 14-7. *The simplified view of a basic Save As… dialog (from TextEdit)*

The simple Save As… dialog asks what you'd like the name of the file to be and provides a drop-down menu of common and recent folders into which to save the file. Beneath that is an area with application-specific save settings. Clicking the disclosure triangle to the right of the Save As text field expands the dialog into an expanded view, which includes the Finder view and occasionally other save options not available in the simplified view.

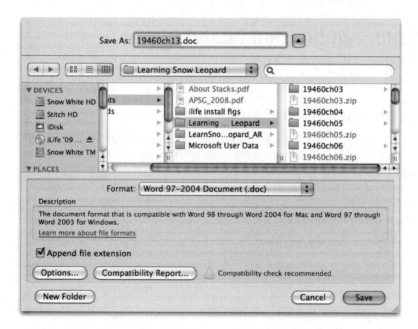

Figure 14-8. *This expanded Save As… file dialog from Microsoft Word offers many more options (including an Options… button that can provide even more options for saving).*

■Note The Save option saves an existing file with changes, overwriting the old file. Save As…, on the other hand, prompts you for a new file name (and location), so you can save a duplicate or updated copy of the file while preserving the original. If the file doesn't exist yet, Save will work the same as the Save As… option. In the past, occasionally Save would sometimes tack on new information to a file in an inefficient manner, creating larger-than-necessary files, and it was recommended that you use Save As… to save a fresh file every once in a while to correct this bloat. However, this behavior is no longer common.

■Note Some applications also offer Import… and Export… options that are similar to Open… and Save As… options, except they generally provide additional options for opening or saving files in formats other than the application's native format, or they alter one file format into another. A good example of this is when you wish to save an image file of one type to another—for example, let's say you want to save a raw image file from your digital single-lens reflex (DSLR) camera to a JPEG for viewing on a web site.

Other Common Application Features

Besides what we've covered previously in this chapter and elsewhere in the book, there are a few other useful things to know about when working with applications in Mac OS X.

Choosing a Document's Default Application

When you double-click a document, the document opens automatically in the default application for that document. This application is usually the same as the one that created the document, but not always. If you want to specify what application a document will open in, you can select from a list of compatible applications from the Open With submenu from the document's contextual menu. The default application will be listed first, followed by any other application the system identifies as being able to open that type of file.

■Note Dragging a file over an application's icon in the Finder usually causes the application to launch and attempt to open the file or files you dragged onto it. If the application can't open that particular file type, unexpected results could occur.

If you'd like to change the default application associated with a specific file, or even all files of the same type, you can select the new application in the Open with section of the file's Get Info window. Selecting the Change All… button makes that application the default for all files of that type.

▮Note OS X looks at a few things when determining what application to use to open a particular file: the file's extension (which may be hidden) and certain Finder metadata or attributes associated with the file. Some files that are received from another computer or created in a non-Aqua application may have none of these. In this case, you will be prompted to find a suitable application to open that file.

▮Note Occasionally you will not be able to open a file if the creating application doesn't exist on your computer. In that case, you may be able to import the document from within another application. However, if the application is not compatible, you may get strange results.

Using the Services Menu

The Application ➤ Services menu provides a way for the system, and other applications, to offer features that are accessible from within any other application. A number of these services even have system-wide keyboard shortcuts. For example, if you are reading some text in an application, you can select a word or phrase from that text and hit Shift-Command-L to automatically open a Google search on that phrase.

▮Note The Shift-Command-L Services shortcut is the default shortcut set up in the System's Keyboard Shortcuts preferences in the Keyboard & Mouse preference pane. This is fully customizable and apt to change—in fact, in previous versions of Mac OS X, the default shortcut for this command was Shift-Control-F. Also, in the event that there is an overlap of keyboard shortcuts between services and applications, the Applications shortcut should take precedence.

There are all types of useful features in the Services menu, and many new applications add services of their own to this.

▮Note Services are not available from all applications, even though the Services menu is present. In general, Cocoa applications support the Services menu out of the box, but Carbon apps (of which a few still are prevalent) don't. If you find yourself using one of these applications and missing this feature, you should let the developer know how you feel and perhaps they will update their application someday.

Using AppleScript and Automator

Most OS X Aqua applications expose at least some of their abilities to AppleScript and Automator to allow savvy users to extend the functionality of the application or to utilize the features of the application in an automated workflow. This ability can be put to some very powerful uses and is covered in much depth in Chapter 22.

Summary

Most of what we have covered in this chapter applies to most of the applications you will use on your Mac. That said, developers have a lot of freedom to change the behavior of any or all of the features covered in this chapter. Next, we'll cover some common applications that are included with Snow Leopard.

## CHAPTER 15

Snow Leopard Applications

If Snow Leopard came preinstalled on your new computer, then you'll find all sorts of software, including iLife and some third-party applications, already installed. If you purchased the Snow Leopard DVD and did a clean install of it on your computer, you won't find quite as much software, but you will find a number of applications that are important and useful. This chapter is going to highlight some of these applications that you may want to know about, yet aren't covered in depth elsewhere in this book, including the following:

- QuickTime Player
- iTunes
- Preview
- Photo Booth

QuickTime Player

QuickTime itself falls into two general areas: there's all the QuickTime technologies that exist behind the scenes in the system that make the music play and the videos go, and then there's QuickTime Player (Figure 15-1), which provides an application for viewing QuickTime media.

By default, QuickTime Player is simply a viewer for various media types, including, of course, QuickTime movies, but also a wide range of other video, audio, and image formats. Generally, when you double-click a media file that QuickTime Player is set to play back, it will open automatically and start playing the file.

■**Note** QuickTime Player is only one way to play back QuickTime media. QuickTime can also be embedded in web browsers and integrated into other applications (for example, iTunes is essentially a special-purpose media player based upon QuickTime).

QuickTime also provides the means to extend its capabilities with special plug-in files (called *codecs*) that allow QuickTime to play back other media formats.

Figure 15-1. *A video playing in QuickTime Player*

QuickTime and QuickTime Player have seen some changes in Snow Leopard. First, the features of QuickTime Pro are now included in QuickTime by default, so you no longer need to pay an extra $20 to add some of the more advanced features that QuickTime is capable of. Second, now you can actually create and record new media files right from QuickTime Player by using either File ➤ New Movie Recording (Control-Command-N) or File ➤ New Audio Recording (Option-Control-Command-N) from QuickTime Player's menu bar. This opens a record window to record the media. While this isn't as nice as some other software that you may have available (especially if you have GarageBand or iMovie from iLife '09 installed), these options are quick and easy and always available.

iTunes

iTunes (Figure 15-2), originally designed as a simple music library and playback application, has since moved beyond just music. Today, combined with the iTunes Store, iTunes can download and play back Internet streaming radio, movies, and TV shows. You can even use it to purchase, download, and install applications on your iPhone or iPod touch. Combined with an Apple TV or one of many Apple AirPort products, you can even use iTunes to stream music and video around your network.

While iTunes is feature-rich, it's still easy to use. The iTunes toolbar provides the basic controls to start, stop, and control the media playback, while the main window area is designed to select and manage your media.

The main window provides a column along the left side to select your media libraries (sorted by type) and your playlists, along with a selection to take you to the iTunes Store. The main window area to the right is where you can view your media in a number of different views: List view (Figure 15-3), Grid view (Figure 15-2), and Cover Flow view (Figure 15-4).

■**Tip** In List view, you can also show a browser by selecting View ➤ (Show|Hide) Browser (Command-B). The browser makes it easy to find the music you're looking for by allowing you to search by artist, genre, and album at the same time.

Figure 15-2. *An iTunes music library shown in Grid view*

Figure 15-3. *Viewing your iTunes library by album in List view, with the browser visible*

■**Note** Version 8.1 of iTunes replaced the Party Shuffle feature with iTunes DJ. While the new iTunes DJ feature randomly creates a playlist that updates itself continually from any selected iTunes library just like Party Shuffle did, iTunes DJ adds a new fun new twist to this. If you have an iPod touch or iPhone that is connected to the same network as your iTunes library, you can enable iTunes DJ to use the Remote application from the App Store to request and even vote on what songs should be added to the playlist. When a song is requested, it gets added to the playlist as the next song, unless you enable voting as well, in which case the song with the most votes gets played next.

Figure 15-4. *The Cover Flow view lets you "flip through" album covers to find what you're looking for. Also, in certain modes like the iTunes DJ mode, it can provide visual cues to what artists are coming up next.*

Importing Media into iTunes

To take advantage of iTunes, you must first import your media into it. The way this is done depends on what sort of media you are starting with. If you already have a collection of supported digital media files—including MP3, AAC (Advanced Audio Coding), and MOV—then you can just use the File ➤ Import... command from the menu bar.

■**Note** The Advanced tab in iTunes preferences contains a number of options that are relevant to importing media. For example, under the Advanced ➤ General tab, you may want to select "Copy files to iTunes Music folder when adding to library" and "Keep iTunes Music folders organized," which will keep all of your iTunes media organized in its own location without affecting any of the original files you import.

If you are importing your music from a CD collection, iTunes will automatically convert your audio CDs into MP3, AAC, or other formats, and import them into your library. The options available to you are located on the Advanced ➤ Importing tab in iTunes preferences.

Note Which settings are best for importing your CDs is mostly a personal choice. If you are a true audiophile with lots of hard drive space, then of course Apple Lossless format is your best choice (it makes an exact copy of the audio with no loss in quality whatsoever, yet still occupies only half the space as a CD audio file). For everyone else, it becomes a space, quality, and compatibility issue. AAC and MP3 are both compatible with most digital media players; however, MP3 would still be the default if maximum compatibility is an issue. Many people feel that AAC provides better playback quality at the same compression over MP3 (and at higher compression, we tend to agree). We find that 256 Kbps AAC provides excellent audio files while saving considerable disk space over uncompressed (or lossless) formats, while 128 Kbps AAC provides good enough sound quality for most situations and allows you to cram lots of music on your iPod. For MP3s, we find 192 Kbps files to be good enough, but we find 128 Kbps MP3s to have quite noticeable audio issues.

Once you have your import preferences set up, when you insert an audio CD into your computer, it will show up in your iTunes library, and (at least the first time) a pop-up window will appear asking you if you'd like to import the CD into your iTunes library. If you send away the pop-up window (either momentarily or permanently), you can still import your CD by clicking the Import CD button in the lower right-hand corner of iTunes.

Note When you insert your CD, if you are connected to the Internet, iTunes will seek out information about the CD you inserted and automatically fill in the CD and track details (unless you turned this feature off on the Advanced ➤ Importing tab of iTunes preferences). If for some reason the details are wrong or you'd like to change them, then select the track (or tracks) you wish to alter and select Get Info from the contextual menu. The Get Info box will not only reveal more information about the tracks and album, but will allow you to freely edit the information.

The other way to get music into your iTunes library is to buy it from the iTunes Store (Figure 15-5) (known formerly as the iTunes Music Store before it started selling videos and applications, too).

The iTunes Store, which now ranks as one of the leading music retailers in the world, provides a huge selection of music both new and old, along with an ever-increasing selection of movies, TV shows, music videos, and audiobooks. Most of this is for sale, although there are occasionally freebies available for download.

To buy music from the iTunes Store, you must first sign in with your Apple ID (if you have a MobileMe account, your MobileMe account ID is also your Apple ID unless you've previously registered using some other information).

Figure 15-5. *The iTunes Store in iTunes*

ITUNES STORE FILES, DRM, AND ITUNES PLUS

Traditionally, all the files you purchased from the iTunes Store were "protected" using a method of digital rights management (DRM) called FairPlay. As far as DRM goes, FairPlay is fairly lenient, allowing any purchased files to be transferred and played on five different computers (the same five for all purchases, and each computer must be authorized). It also allows a playlist with that song to be burned to seven audio CDs, allows unlimited syncs to iPods and iPhones, and allows the ability to stream the items to Apple AirPort Expresses and Apple TVs.

However, over time, Apple started distributing some items not only free of DRM, but also of a higher quality than traditional iTunes music files. These files are called iTunes Plus files and are common 256 Kbps AAC files. Today, all music (but not video) purchased from Apple's iTunes Store is distributed in the iTunes Plus format. Also, Apple has made it possible (for a small fee) to upgrade your old FairPlay files to iTunes Plus, though if you choose not to, the FairPlay files will continue to work as they always have.

By the way, the iTunes Plus files do contain embedded information about who purchased the file, which should not bother anyone who wishes to use the files legitimately, but could be used to help identify people who are taking their purchases straight to The Pirate Bay or some other file-sharing system.

■**Note** While you can easily export your own iMovies and other QuickTime movies so that they will appear in iTunes (and sync with your iPod/iPhone), Apple doesn't provide a way to import DVDs into iTunes. This could be because Apple sells movies on the iTunes Store, but it's unlikely. More likely is that importing movies from DVDs is somewhat legally ambiguous. From a technical standpoint, it's perfectly legal to make a copy of a movie you own—however, to make a copy of a DVD, you must unencode the content, which is actually encrypted on the disk. This may run afoul of the Digital Millennium Copyright Act (DMCA—a sloppy little law passed by government officials who either were getting big money from the MPAA, or more likely just weren't paying attention). Most right-minded people would agree that it's fine, but the movie industry and some others tend to disagree. Either way, if you wish to do this, it's usually a two-step process: ripping the DVD (or converting it for use from your hard drive), and then converting the video. We tend to find that using HandBrake (`http://handbrake.fr`) to convert a DVD to M4V format ready for an iPhone works just fine. However, the newest version removes the ability to rip DVDs natively. To rip a DVD, we currently recommend RipIt (`http://ripitapp.com`), but only you can decide if the $18.99 licensing fee is worth it to you.

Creating Playlists

Once you have some music in your iTunes library, you may want to create playlists of your favorite tunes for specific occasions. iTunes provides a number of interesting ways to create playlists. The most basic playlist is one you create yourself by selecting each song from your library and then adding it. To create one of these playlists, simply click the + button in the lower left-hand corner of the iTunes main window. This creates a blank playlist for you to name and add any songs you wish.

iTunes also has the ability to create Smart Playlists. These are like smart folders in that you select some search criteria, and iTunes will automatically populate the Smart Playlist with songs that match the criteria. iTunes comes with a number of common Smart Playlists already (Recently Played, Recently Added, My Top Rated, and more). To create your own, hold down the Option key, and the + button you would use to add a regular playlist will turn into a gear icon. Click this gear icon to open up a dialog box for you to name and define your own Smart Playlist.

Finally, you can create a playlist using iTunes' Genius feature. The iTunes Genius feature attempts to analyze your music collection. When you pick any song to base a playlist on, iTunes will use the Genius feature to attempt to create a playlist of songs that mesh well with the song you started with. (This feature is also used to provide you with a list of music on the iTunes Store that you may want to purchase.)

Note iTunes Genius doesn't just create playlists; it also analyzes your entire library. The iTunes Store uses this information to help make recommendations for music you may wish to buy and to help feed the data that devises the Genius results in the first place. This means two things: first, you will need an iTunes Store account for this to work (you'll also need an account if you want iTunes to attempt to download album covers for you automatically); and second, the information you send will be used to help sell you stuff. Now, since the personal data is restricted to your own account, there really isn't an immediate privacy issue here, but if you don't want people collecting marketing information about your music likes and dislikes and then using it to try to sell you stuff (though really in a noninvasive way), then you may not want to activate this feature. (Personally, we use it and find it fairly interesting.)

Sharing and Streaming iTunes Media

iTunes allows you to share your iTunes library with anyone else on your network. You can enable this from the Sharing tab in iTunes preferences. This allows your library to show in the iTunes libraries of any other people on your network. Likewise, you can view and play songs from other users on your network who are sharing their libraries.

Note DRM-protected iTunes Store files can't be shared unless the receiving computer is one of the five computers authorized to play back your iTunes DRMed files. In fact, if you attempt to play one from an unauthorized computer, the music will stop.

Besides sharing your files, you can also stream your files. Music files can be streamed to AirPort and AirPort Express devices equipped with speakers, as well as Apple TV systems. Video can be streamed to Apple TV systems. To stream your files, select the output source from the drop-down menu in the lower right-hand corner of iTunes.

To fully take advantage of Apple TV with iTunes, you must also set up Apple TV in the Apple TV iTunes preferences.

Syncing iPods and iPhones

When you connect an iPod or iPhone to your computer, the device shows up as a device in your iTunes library. Selecting the device allows you to configure the settings, which range from simple for an old iPod shuffle (Figure 15-6) to more complex for an iPhone (Figure 15-7). After you set your settings, click the Apply button to resync your device with the new settings.

Figure 15-6. *Device settings allow you to update and apply settings to iPods and iPhones. For an iPod shuffle, there aren't too many options.*

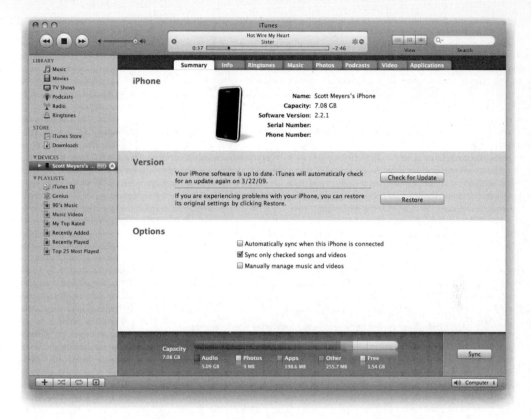

Figure 15-7. *Due to its enhanced capabilities, iTunes displays quite a few more options when an iPhone is connected to it vs. an iPod shuffle.*

Preview

Preview (Figure 15-8) is to PDF and image files what QuickTime Player is to video. It provides an excellent alternative to Adobe Reader for viewing PDF files, complete with support for performing text searches, copying and pasting text from a PDF, viewing encrypted PDFs, creating bookmarks, page previews, and annotation capabilities. Beyond that, it's a multiformat image viewer allowing you to quickly open a wide range of image formats.

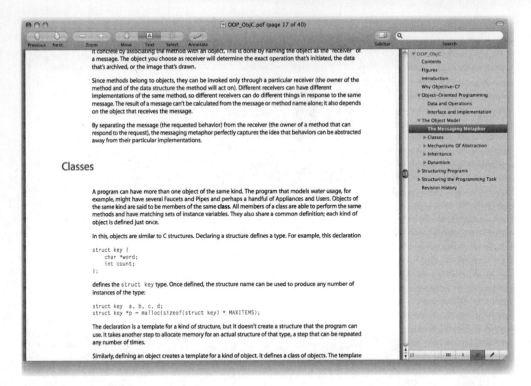

Figure 15-8. *A PDF document open in Preview*

Besides viewing images, Preview also has the ability to do some minor image editing, including image color adjustments, cropping, resizing, and saving in an array of image file formats.

Photo Booth

Photo Booth is a fairly silly yet highly entertaining application that takes advantage of the iSight camera that is attached to most new Macs (except Mac Pros and Mac minis). When you launch Photo Booth, it automatically fires up the camera built into your computer and allows you to capture photos or videos.

Once Photo Booth is launched, you can switch between a single picture, four quick pictures (just like a real photo booth!), and a video mode using the button on the left below the preview area. You can also apply effects to the images or video by clicking the Effects button and scrolling through the effect previews. All the images and videos shot with Photo Booth will scroll across the bottom. Selecting an existing image opens it up in the preview area (Figure 15-9), allowing you to send the image to someone through Mail, add the image to iPhoto, or use the image as your iChat or Account icon.

Figure 15-9. *A four-picture image previewed in Photo Booth*

Other Default Snow Leopard Applications

Snow Leopard comes with a number of other applications for various purposes that aren't covered elsewhere in this book. These applications are described in Table 15-1.

Table 15-1. *Other Applications Installed with Snow Leopard*

Application	Description
Calculator	This application provides not only a simple calculator mode, but also advanced scientific and programming modes. It also provides conversions to and from many systems of measurement.
Chess	This application provides a 3D chess set that pits you against the computer. It also supports voice recognition, which makes it interesting to play around with.
Dictionary	This handy application provides dictionary, thesaurus, and Wikipedia references for a word or term either individually or together.

Continued

Table 15-1. *Continued*

Application	Description
DVD Player	This application provides a great experience for watching DVDs on your Mac.
Front Row	Coupled with an Apple remote, this application provides a nice interface for controlling and viewing media on your computer from across the room.
Stickies	This application allows you to create sticky notes that appear on your desktop.
TextEdit	This is a simple text editor with some basic word-processing features.

Summary

Besides these basic applications, which range from indispensable to at least sort of interesting, Apple provides a number of other common applications, many of which we talk about in other areas of this book. Next, we're going to discuss one of Apple's extra software suites, iLife '09.

CHAPTER 16

■ ■ ■

iLife '09

Apple's iLife '09 is the latest version of Apple's bundle of digital lifestyle applications. It is included with all new Macs from the Mac mini up to the Mac Pro. If you have a previous version iLife, you can purchase '09 for the bargain price of $79. Included are applications for photo management and workflow (iPhoto), digital video editing (iMovie), audio and music production (GarageBand), and web site creation (iWeb), as well as an application to take your media and create DVDs (iDVD).

This chapter will go over the individual applications contained in iLife '09 and discuss some of the new features in the latest version. We will cover the following:

- iPhoto '09

- iMovie '09

- GarageBand '09

- iWeb '09

- iDVD '09

iPhoto '09

iPhoto (Figure 16-1) has always been one of the premier consumer photo-management tools available on any computer platform, and the latest version improves on almost every aspect of it.

iPhoto '09 is a complete photo workflow tool, allowing you to import and organize your photos, edit them, and then export and share them in a number of ways.

Photo Management

When you connect a digital camera to your computer and launch iPhoto (you can set iPhoto to launch automatically when you connect a digital camera in iPhoto's general preferences), your camera will show up as a device in iPhoto and give you a number of import options. By default, iPhoto will import all the images into a single event (an *event* in iPhoto is one method of categorizing photo collections, sort of like folders). However, you can select an option that will split up your photos into multiple events based on time if you choose.

Figure 16-1. *iPhoto's main browser window allows you to browse, organize, and work with your photos quickly and easily.*

Note iPhoto actually manages video as well as photos, which is significant since many digital cameras these days also shoot video. If you import from your camera directly to iPhoto, your videos will be imported safely along with your photos. You can then work with these videos in iMovie from the iPhoto Video library in iMovie.

Events are one of the traditional ways that iPhoto divides and organizes your photos. They serve a similar role to rolls in previous versions of iPhoto—however, events are much more flexible, as you can move images from one event to another and can reorder entire events in your library.

iPhoto '09 also adds some new ways to organize photos: Places and Faces. *Places* organizes your photos by the location that the picture was taken, using GPS data embedded in a photo's metadata. A wave of new cameras that include GPS systems (including, of course, many mobile phone cameras) can add this GPS data automatically. If your images aren't *geotagged*—that is, embedded with the location data—out of your camera, then you can add the location data automatically from within iPhoto. Just bring up a photo's information dialog by clicking the small i button that appears in the lower-right corner of a thumbnail when you mouse over it. In the dialog, click the Enter Photo Location text to bring up a list of previously entered locations to choose from. If the location is new, click New Place…, which will open the Edit My Locations dialog containing a searchable Google maps view. Use this view to locate the desired location on the map and then click the Drop Pin button to place a pin in the exact location. You can then name this location in the locations view on the left side of the dialog. Once the location pin is in place, you can move it around on the map to the precise location. You can also expand and contract the shaded circle around the pin to increase or decrease the location's area. Once you have defined your locations, you can easily add them to your photos automatically. Any geo-tagged photos from a defined location will be added to that location automatically.

Faces is another great feature to help you organize your photos based on the people captured in your photos. To take advantage of this, first select a photo that contains one of the people you wish to select, and then click the Name icon in the toolbar at the bottom of iPhoto's browser window. This expands the photo, and Faces attempts to identify any faces in the photo. iPhoto then creates a box around all the faces found. If iPhoto thinks it can identify the people in the photo, it will ask to confirm the face. Any unidentified faces will be identified as "unknown face." Clicking the unknown face text makes it editable for you to enter the name of the person (Figure 16-2). (A list of possible matches shows up in a drop-down menu as you type. If the person you are identifying is listed here, you should select their name from the list so iPhoto knows this is the same person.)

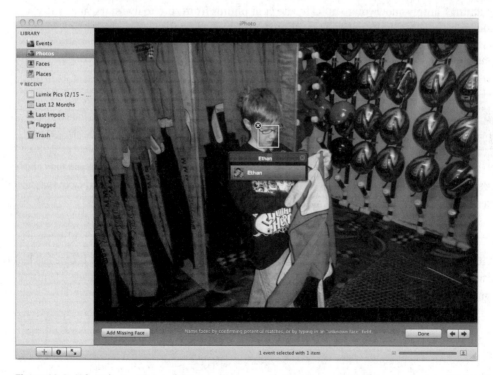

Figure 16-2. *iPhoto's new Faces feature allows you to identiy people's faces in photos. iPhoto then tries to find all the photos in its library that belong to that person.*

Once you've identified a face or two in iPhoto, iPhoto automatically attempts to find the identified faces in every photo in your library. When you select a person from the Faces library, iPhoto may show you two areas: one that contains the confirmed photos of the selected person, and one that contains faces that iPhoto thinks may belong to the identified person.

Note The Faces feature is quite sophisticated in identifying people's faces in your library. However, as of yet, it's not foolproof and often misses a number of photos of an identified person. It also occasionally identifies the wrong face as an identified person (with occasionally bizarre and often entertaining results).

Albums and *smart albums* provide another way to organize your photos. The key difference between albums and events is that a single photo can only reside in one event, while it can be placed in many albums.

Another feature included in iPhoto is the ability to tag individual photos with titles, ratings, and keywords. Titles allow you to provide easily recognizable names to images without renaming the actual image file. This is very useful for those who use specific naming schemes for files (such as time and date information) that may not be very descriptive of the image content. Ratings simply allow you to quickly rate your photos from zero to five stars, allowing you to find your very best (four- or five-star) photos quickly at a later time. Keywords allow you to add searchable words that help describe your images; they can range from very specific names to general categories.

Tip Keywords aren't very useful if you aren't somewhat consistent with them. If you use different words for every photo, then they quickly become out of control. However, if your keywords aren't specific enough, then they don't serve much purpose either. One suggestion is to jot down some general keyword categories (for example, you can start out with People, Places, and Things as your top-level keywords) and then add some subcategories (e.g., under People, you might have Family, Friends, Celebrities, etc.) and more specific information under that (specific names of people). The most important rule is to be consistent.

Note As a general rule, keywords should be no more than 64 characters long. This length is based on the maximum length for IPTC (International Press Telecommunications Council) data. This is a standard format of transmitting image data along with digital images (either embedded or as "sidecar" XMP files).

■Note iPhoto keeps track of all your keywords. To view them, open the Keyword window (Command-K). You can use this window to add keywords to selected photos by clicking the keyword. You can even set up common keywords with their own keyboard shortcut to apply them quickly to any photo. This not only makes adding popular keywords easy, but is also a good way to keep keywords consistent.

Once all the data (titles, ratings, and keywords) are set up for your images, you can really take advantage of the search and smart album tools in iPhoto to find just the right image or images you are looking for.

Photo Editing

iPhoto includes a range of easy-to-use image editing tools. To switch into Edit mode, click the Edit icon in the lower left-hand corner of iPhoto. In Edit mode, a number of editing tools are listed along the bottom toolbar:

Rotate: Rotates the image 90 degrees counterclockwise. You may need to use this more than one time to rotate an image that needs it.

Crop: Allows you to select and crop an image.

Straighten: Allows you to slightly rotate a photo where the subject is slightly off skew.

Enhance: Provides some automatic image adjustments to attempt to improve the image.

Red-Eye: Provides a tool that can help eliminate red-eye in photos.

Retouch: Provides tools that can help mask blemishes or strange anomalies in photos (including dust specks).

Effects: Opens a window that provides a number of effects that you may apply to the photo.

Adjust: Opens up a window with a number of very high-quality image-enhancement tools that give you precise control over levels, contrast, exposure, color, sharpening, and other sophisticated image-editing features.

Any edits you make will be applied the image—however, iPhoto will preserve the original image so you can revert back to it at any time in the future if necessary.

When switching into Edit mode, all of the editing tools are available from the lower pop-up toolbar in iPhoto's full-screen mode (Figure 16-3).

Figure 16-3. *The image-editing tools in iPhoto are easily accessible in full-screen mode, which provides an uncluttered way to view and edit your images.*

Printing and Sharing Your Photos

Taking and organizing your photos is nice, but ultimately you'll likely want to share them with others, and iPhoto provides a number of ways to do this, both digitally and physically.

If you just want to share some photos with a minimum of fuss, you can select the desired images in your library and e-mail them to the desired recipients, print them from your own printer, or order professional prints using Kodak Print Service.

■**Note** The first time you order prints, you will need to set up an account for yourself. This is fairly easy, as iPhoto will walk you through the process.

For those who wish to share photos with a bit more flair, iPhoto has a number of ways to satisfy this desire. This ranges from creating simple slideshows of photos that can be played back in iPhoto or exported and played as QuickTime movies, to sending a selection of photos to iDVD to create a photo DVD to share with friends and family.

For those who wish to publish photos to the Web, iPhoto comes ready to publish photos directly to your MobileMe web galleries, your Facebook account, or your Flickr account, all at the click of a button. Also, your iPhoto library is accessible from many other applications, including iWeb and iMovie; they provide a number of other ways to view and share your photos.

Finally, if you want a nondigital, interesting hard copy of your images, iPhoto allows you to create and order amazing photo books, cards, and even calendars from your photos.

iMovie '09

iMovie '09 (Figure 16-4) is a significant upgrade to iMovie '08 (which many people felt was a significant downgrade from previous versions of iMovie). While iMovie '09 retains some of the uniquely easy paradigms for creating digital video introduced in iMovie '08, it adds a number of powerful editing features that allow you to put an extra polish on your videos.

Figure 16-4. *iMovie '09*

■**Note** iMovie '09 packs in a lot of power that was previously missing from iMovie '08; however, it still lacks many features found in more traditional, nonlinear digital-editing solutions. As some of our digital video-editing roots are back in the now-defunct Digital Origin's EditDV, we generally find ourselves more comfortable working with Apple's more expensive Final Cut Pro or Final Cut Express editing applications, which each provide quite a bit more editing capabilities in a more traditional video-editing environment. That said, once we accepted the paradigm shift from the traditional way of building videos to how iMovie '09 works, we've found that iMovie '09 does 90 percent of everything we'd ever want to do, and it does it a whole lot faster and easier.

To begin using iMovie, you simply import your video. iMovie detects many types of digital video cameras, from traditional MiniDV camcorders to the newer hard drive– and flash-based camcorders, when they are plugged into your computer. iMovie then brings up the Import

From: *Camera* window (Figure 16-5), which helps you import your videos from your camera into iMovie's Video library. If your camera is connected when you launch iMovie or doesn't pop up automatically when you plug your camera in, you can open it by clicking the Import From Camera button on the far-left side of iMovie's toolbar or by selecting File ➤ Import From Camera (Command-I) from iMovie's menu bar. Depending on how the videos are stored on your camera (either on linear media like MiniDV tapes or on nonlinear media like hard drives or flash media), you may be able to select individual video files (nonlinear media) to import, or you may be able to control the camera to stream the video into iMovie (linear media). Either way, when you go to import the video, you will be prompted about where you want to save your video and whether you want to add it to an existing or new iMovie event (Figure 16-6). iMovie '09 also provides you with an option to analyze and apply video stabilization after the import is complete. This is a new feature of iMovie '09 that attempts to detect and remove camera shake from videos.

Figure 16-5. *iMovie's Import From: Camera window allows you to view and select video to import.*

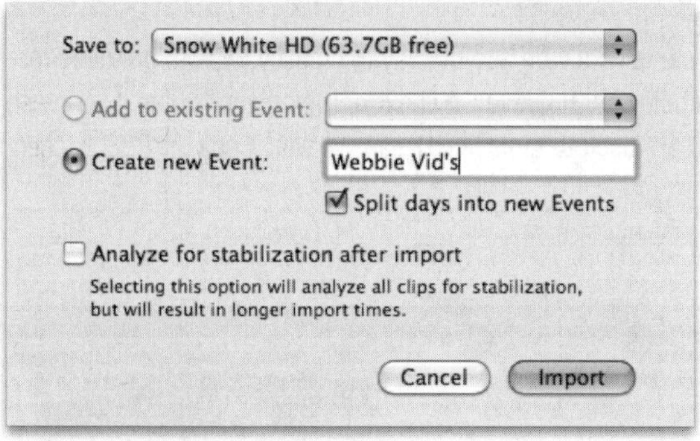

Figure 16-6. *Before you import the video, you must choose a location and event to save the movie into. You can also select an option to stabilize your video.*

■Note If you anticipate creating a lot of video, it may be a good idea to think about getting an external hard drive for your video. Digital video can consume a large amount of disk space. This is especially true of raw DV or HDV, but even new digital video formats such as AVCHD, which manages to significantly compress video while still retaining high quality, can fill up disk space fairly quickly.

Once the video is imported, you can select your movie files from iMovie's Event Library, scrub through them, select the sections of video you want to include in your final movie, and drag them up to the project area in the order you want them. If desired, you can select and place transitions between clips, and add background sounds or sound effects to save to your new video—nice and easy with surprisingly wonderful results.

When you have finished creating your new movie, iMovie allows you to share your finished video in a number of ways, from exporting the video to a DVD using iDVD, to uploading it directly to your YouTube or MobileMe accounts for all to view online.

If you dig around, there are a number of additional tweaks you can make, but really this is designed for quick-and-easy movies. If you crave more control, your iMovie projects can be imported into Final Cut Pro or Final Cut Express for additional touches.

iWeb '09

iWeb '09 is an application that allows you to easily create theme-based web pages and web sites with a WYSIWYG, layout-based interface (Figure 16-7).

To begin creating a web site with iWeb, you first select a theme from one of the many available themes in iWeb. Each theme also contains a number of page templates, including a Welcome page (usually the first page you want to start with), and special templates for blogs, movies, photos, podcasts, and more.

Note iWeb is a great tool for people who wish to build a web site quickly and easily without the need for learning HTML, CSS, and other web-creation technologies. However, it is extraordinarily inflexible if you wish to build a truly customized web experience. If you are used to tools like Dreamweaver, Coda, or BBEdit, then iWeb probably won't be of much interest to you.

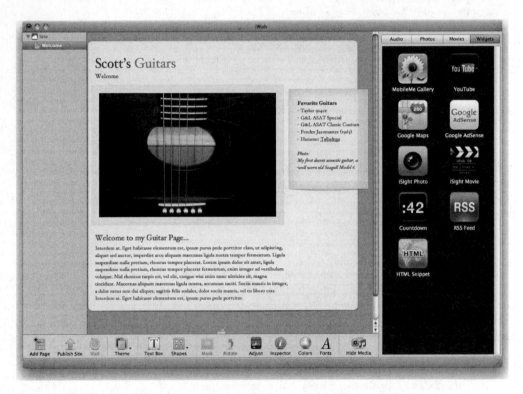

Figure 16-7. *Building a Welcome page from a template in iWeb '09*

Once you select a theme and a template to begin with, you simply start editing the template with your content, replacing the placeholder content as you go. To replace images, you can select any image from the Media Browser or the Finder and drag it over an image placeholder. To replace text, just select it and start typing. Most of the image and text boxes on the page can be selected and relocated by clicking an item and moving it where you want it to go. If you'd like to insert additional content, iWeb provides a number of interesting and useful ready-made widgets, including Google AdSense, Google Maps, MobileMe Gallery, and RSS feeds. If you're inclined, you can insert any HTML code into your page, allowing you quite a bit of flexibility. As you add pages to your web site, iWeb keeps track of the new content and automatically updates the links on all the related pages on your web site.

When you have done what you want, iWeb publishes your web site automatically, either directly to your MobileMe account or to a folder on your computer that you can host from your computer or upload to another web site. iWeb '09 now even includes the ability to upload your iWeb web site to any web site that you have FTP access to.

GarageBand '09

GarageBand (Figure 16-8) is Apple's entry-level DAW (digital audio workstation). GarageBand
lets you record, mix, and edit multiple audio and MIDI tracks together and then save them
as audio files in a variety of formats. While GarageBand lacks some features of Apple's other
DAWs (Logic Express and Logic Studio), it provides a number of professional-quality software
instruments and effects coupled with reasonable track-editing abilities (including volume,
panning, and new track-automation abilities) that can easily create professional-sounding
recordings.

Figure 16-8. *GarageBand '09 with a couple of guitar tracks*

Each track can contain either a software instrument track or a real instrument track. The software tracks contain MIDI information that is translated into sound based on the software instrument associated with it. Real instrument tracks contain actual sound files that can come from prerecorded music or loops, or can be recorded on the fly in GarageBand through an audio interface (including the built-in audio inputs if necessary).

■**Note** If you are serious about recording, you should probably look into purchasing an audio interface for your computer. A decent two-channel USB2 or FireWire audio interface can cost less than $200 and will provide you with much better sound quality than using your Mac's built-in audio port. Obviously, there are more expensive audio interfaces as well that include more features. Some companies that make good audio interfaces include TASCAM, Mackie (or TAPCO), M-Audio, Digidesign, PreSonus, and MOTU (Mark of the Unicorn).

When you first start up GarageBand '09, either it will automatically open the last project you were working on, or it will open a dialog box allowing you to choose the type of project or activity that you want to use GarageBand for (Figure 16-9). The following options are available:

New Project: This option is for when you plan to begin a new recording or project. GarageBand provides a number of common options to help you get started, based on the type of instrument you plan on playing or type of recording you plan on making. (No matter what you choose, though, all options are available, so if you choose the piano, you can still record guitars, use MIDI loops, and more).

Learn to Play: This new feature in GarageBand '09 contains a series of interactive lessons that teach you how to play certain songs and certain instruments. GarageBand '09 ships with two sample lessons, but more are available.

Lesson Store: The lesson store provides you the opportunity to add Learn to Play lessons to GarageBand. Many of the basic lessons are free to download and use, but there are also Artist Lessons that teach you how to play a song by the song's actual performer. Most of these lessons will set you back $4.99.

GarageBand Magic: GarageBand Magic allows you to form a virtual band to play along with. You can choose a musical genre, select the instruments, and then play along with them. The selections here are a bit basic, but it's a fun way to practice nonetheless.

iPhone Ringtone: The iPhone Ringtone project is similar to the New Project option; however, it is set up specifically to help you create ringtones that you can then use with your iPhone.

Recent Projects: This brings up your recent projects to continue working with.

Figure 16-9. *What shall we do today in GarageBand?*

Once you have finished with a song in GarageBand, GarageBand will allow you to export it to a number of different audio formats. Normally you would export it to iTunes, where you can use iTunes to play it back and then burn a selection of your songs to CD.

iDVD

There's more to creating a DVD than just having a great movie. You need menus and transitions and chapters and special features. iDVD gives you the power to create amazing, professional-looking DVDs with very little effort. However, iDVD (Figure 16-10) seems to have reached "forgotten stepchild" status in iLife '09, and other than a few interface tweaks, little if anything separates this version of iDVD from the previous version.

Figure 16-10. *iDVD is easy to use; just set up the menus, drop in the media, and burn (or using Magic iDVD, just add the media and let iDVD do the rest).*

Despite the fact that lots of sharing of movies and photos and such is being done now more than ever on the Internet, iDVD is still a great way to create DVDs for sharing or archiving your content (plus, sometimes it's preferable to crash down on the sofa in front of your big-screen TV than to huddle around a computer).

Summary

There's only so much room in an OS X book to cover things like iLife, but we wanted to give you a quick look at what's there. Most of these applications are fairly easy to pick up and use after just a little guidance, although you'll find as you dig deeper into each of these iLife applications that they offer quite a bit of power behind their easy-to-use exterior. In the next section, we are going to leave our pretty interfaces behind and look at the powerful features of Darwin, Apple's UNIX runtime.

## PART 5

Getting to Know Darwin

CHAPTER 17

■ ■ ■

Introducing Darwin and the Shell

Running behind the slick Mac OS X Aqua GUI is Darwin, the POSIX-compliant operating system that forms the foundation of Mac OS X. Included in Darwin is a collection of many powerful tools that are not only used by many functions of Mac OS X, but are also available for you to use. The most direct way to interact with Darwin and take full advantage of all these wonderfully powerful UNIX tools is through the use of the Terminal application (/Applications/Utilities/Terminal). When Terminal is launched, it opens up a terminal window running a shell program, as shown in Figure 17-1.

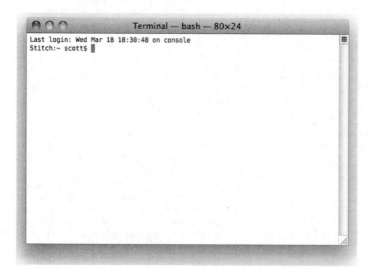

Figure 17-1. *The Terminal application running in Mac OS X*

Darwin Basics

The first thing you need to know when working with Darwin is some of the common language used, in order to avoid confusion. Second, you need to know how files are organized; and finally, you need to know how to move around the file system.

■**Note** When we talk about files here, we are not just talking about the last text file you created; Darwin treats everything as a file. For example, a directory (a.k.a., folder) is a file that contains other files. Each file has a number of properties that determine how the shell treats that specific file; if it's an application, the shell will launch it; if it's a directory, the shell will know that it can access other files contained in it. We'll cover file properties a bit later.

Darwin Semantics

To avoid confusion as the chapter proceeds, we should quickly go over some of the important terms used in Darwin and how they compare with terms used in the Finder. Table 17-1 defines a handful of terms used commonly in Darwin (and other UNIX systems), gives the Finder equivalent or alternate term, and adds any relevant notes. While there are many other terms you'll come across, these basics will be used repeatedly, so they are good to know.

Table 17-1. *Darwin Terms Explained*

Darwin Term	Finder or Alternate Term	Notes
File	File (and others)	Darwin treats all items, documents, directories, and applications as files; in the Finder, when we talk about a file, we are generally talking specifically about a document.
Directory	Folder	Folders are generally referred to as directories.
Root directory, or /	Top level of hard drive	Not to be confused with the root user, the root directory, which is represented by the / symbol, is the highest level of the Darwin file structure.
Root (user)	Administrator	In addition to the root directory, there is also a root user. The root user (also known as the *superuser*) has the ability to do just about anything in the Darwin environment, including irreparably destroying it. To maintain a secure system and avoid devastating problems, certain files require root privileges to read, write, and execute. While the administrator is the closest thing to root in Aqua, it's not quite the same, as root actually has more abilities.
Link (specifically a symbolic link)	Alias	A link in Darwin functions the same way as an alias does in the Finder (and appears as such when viewed in the Finder). While the function of a symbolic link and an alias are the same, it's worth knowing that they are implemented differently.
Alias	N/A	An alias in Darwin is a simple command set up in the shell that can trigger more complex commands or allow you to override the behavior of an existing command.

Darwin Term	Finder or Alternate Term	Notes
Directory path	N/A	The directory path is a representation of where you are in the file system, beginning from the root directory. For example, if your username is scott, then the path to your home directory would be /Users/scott/ (your home directory can also be abbreviated to ~, as you will see later). The leading / represents the root directory.
Executable command	Application or script	Any command that's issued at the command line and causes something to happen can be referred to as an executable.
Command arguments, arguments	N/A	Arguments are additional, sometimes necessary information added to commands. Arguments don't affect how the command is run in the way options do; instead, they generally target the command to affect specific items.
Command options or flags	Switches (DOS)	Command options are special arguments (usually preceded by a - and immediately following the command) that can change how a command is run. This is similar to setting command preferences for an Aqua application, but more flexible, as different preferences can be issued at runtime. For Windows and DOS users, these are like switches issued with a DOS or Windows command prompt command.
Process	N/A	A process is a running application or daemon (also known as a background process). In Mac OS X (and in fact most modern systems), there can be (and often are) hundreds of processes running at any one time.
Pipes	N/A	Pipes, represented by the | symbol, provide a way of stringing two or more commands together. Piping one command into another is a powerful way to accomplish some otherwise complex tasks. Pipes, along with redirection, are covered in more depth later in this chapter.

The File System

The Darwin file system shares the same folder structure found while navigating through the Finder. However, while navigating through Darwin, you will notice a few differences. First, there are quite a few more visible items in the Darwin view. Second, you will find that your additional volumes (added hard drives, CD/DVD drives, flash drives, etc.) are found a little differently.

The Darwin file system starts from root, which is symbolized by /. This is the highest level of the file system and is essentially the same as viewing your primary hard drive in the Finder. A quick look in our root directory reveals the following items (the trailing / and @ symbols that follow have special meaning and are only visible when you use the ls with the -F flag: / indicates that the item is a directory [or folder], and @ indicates that the item is a link [or alias]):

```
Applications/   Network/      cores/      net/        var@
Desktop         DBSystem/     dev/        private/    Desktop DF
Users/          etc@          sbin/       Developer/  Volumes/
home/           tmp@          Library/    bin/        mach_kernel
usr/
```

As you can see, all the basic Finder folders—Applications, Library, System, Users, and Developer (provided you've installed the Xcode developer tools)—are there, along with a slew of other items. Some of these are merely system files that are of little interest to most people. Table 17-2 shows some common directory paths and describes what sorts of files are located in them.

Table 17-2. *Common Darwin Directories and Their Contents*

Directory Path	Contents
/bin	The /bin directory contains the core user executables that are necessary for the OS to function normally.
/etc (/private/etc)	The /etc directory contains the primary configuration files for much of OS X and its services.
/sbin	The /sbin directory contains the core administrative executables necessary for the OS to function normally.
/tmp (/private/tmp)	The /tmp directory is where the OS and many services and applications store data that is only used briefly and then discarded.
/usr	The /usr directory is a metadirectory that contains a number of sub-directories. Traditionally, these directories contain files that, while not necessary for the basic functioning of the system, are still often necessary for a system that functions the way one would expect it to. The truth is that these days, while the system would technically function without these files, most people would find it unusable.
/usr/X11 (/usr/X11R6)	X11 is UNIX's traditional graphical interface. While it's seldom used in Mac OS X, some people may have uses for specific applications that rely on it. This is an optional install when you install Snow Leopard, but if it is installed, this is where most of the parts of X11 live.
/usr/bin	Like /bin, /usr/bin contains user-level command-line executables. Many of the most common commands you will use are found in this directory.
/usr/libexec	This directory contains a number of special executables. This includes files that control tasks related to printing, networking, security, and the built-in web server.
/usr/local	This is yet another metadirectory. In the traditional UNIX way of doing things, this is where one would install any add-ons to the system that didn't come with it by default. Many third-party additions will still install themselves here.
/usr/sbin	Like /sbin, this is a directory that contains administrative executables.

Introducing the Shell

The Terminal application (go ahead, fire it up) is essentially an empty window that can display and accept text input. In order for you to actually do anything, Terminal must run a shell program inside of itself. A shell is a specialized application that helps you interact with Darwin; it shares the same relationship to Darwin that the Finder shares with the Aqua interface. By default, Mac OS X includes five of the most common UNIX shells: Bash, Korn, Bourne, Tcsh, and Zsh (the C shell is also listed as a shell—however, it is actually a link to Tcsh). Of the five, the shell Snow Leopard uses by default is Bash.

Note Originally, Mac OS X used Tcsh by default, but switched to Bash with the release of OS X 10.3 Panther. If you are new to working with UNIX shells, I'd recommend sticking with Bash, at least while you are learning. The lessons in this book, unless specifically noted, are all given using the Bash shell.

The first time you launch Terminal, you'll be greeted by some text similar to this:

```
Last login: Wed Mar 18 18:30:48 on console
Snow-White:~ scott$ _
```

The first line tells you when you last logged in to Darwin (even if you've never logged in to Darwin before intentionally, you'll still get a message saying you did); the second line is the default prompt for Bash. The default prompt (which, like most everything else in Darwin, can be changed) gives you some important information. First, it gives you the name of your computer, which is either assigned by your network or taken from the Computer Name field in the system's Sharing preference pane. Next, following the :, the prompt gives you your location in the file system (the ~ is a shortcut representing your home directory). Then the prompt gives you the username you are logged in as, followed by the $ prompt (which will change to a # if the user is logged in as the root user, otherwise known as the superuser). Finally, you get the cursor anxiously waiting your command.

As you will soon see, shells possess some hidden powers that can make your interactions with Darwin more pleasant and add a new level of power and flexibility to the command line. Before you look at the shell in more depth, though, you should first learn a bit about the Darwin file system as well as a few basic Darwin commands (walk before flying and all that).

Moving Around Darwin

One of the first things you need to learn about the shell is how to move around and view the file system. To do this, there are three basic commands to start with: ls, cd, and pwd.

ls

ls is the "list" command, and by default, lists all the visible files in a directory. If you're familiar with DOS, it would be the replacement for dir. By default, the ls command looks something like this:

```
Snow-White:~ scott$ ls
Autosaved Information  Library      Public
Desktop                Movies       Sites
Documents              Music        bin
Downloads              Pictures
```

The first thing you may notice is that by default all directories (folders), files, and executables (applications) look the same when using the ls command (of course, in this example, they all are directories). That's because, as we mentioned previously, Darwin treats everything as a file. To differentiate between the different types of files, there are two primary options:

- ls -F: Appends special files with a symbol to determine their type. It adds a / to directories, a * to executables, a @ to symbolic links (aliases), and a few other symbols for other special file types.

- ls -G: Colorizes the output using different colors for different file types as well as other file options. For example, by default most directories will appear blue; however, world-writable directories will appear black with a yellow background. Likewise, most executables will appear red, and most symbolic links will appear purple—however, if certain attributes are set, this will not always be the case.

■**Note** One thing immediately noticeable to users moving to Darwin from Linux is that certain command-line commands are slightly different. For example, to colorize your output in Linux, one would traditionally use ls --color, and in some cases the output colors are different. This difference exists because UNIX comes in many different flavors and occasionally there is slight deviation in commands from one to the other. For example, some UNIX tools are derived from the traditional BSD (Berkeley Software Distribution) camp, and they differ in some subtle ways from tools from the GNU camp. Linux almost always chooses its tools from the GNU camp, while Darwin tends to favor the BSD camp. While in general the tools will work the same, there are a few cases where there are minor differences—colorizing ls is one of those differences.

Like most command-line commands, the options can be combined. For example, you can use -F and -G together:

```
Autosaved Information/ Library/     Public/
Desktop/               Movies/      Sites/
Documents/             Music/       bin/
Downloads/             Pictures/
```

Other important `ls` options include the following:

- `ls -l`: Prints out a long list that provides additional information about each file. We'll cover what everything here means later in the "File Permissions and Attributes" section of this chapter, but for now the results appear to be something like this:

```
Snow-White:~ scott$ ls -l
total 0
drwx------    2 scott   staff     68 Mar  6 15:48 Autosaved Information
drwx------+   5 scott   staff    170 Mar 18 18:35 Desktop
drwx------+   9 scott   staff    306 Mar  6 16:48 Documents
drwx------+  14 scott   staff    476 Mar 15 15:43 Downloads
drwx------+  36 scott   staff   1224 Mar 15 15:25 Library
drwx------+   4 scott   staff    136 Mar 15 12:33 Movies
drwx------+   4 scott   staff    136 Mar 15 12:43 Music
drwx------+   6 scott   staff    204 Mar 15 15:46 Pictures
d---------+   5 scott   staff    170 Mar  6 08:09 Public
drwxr-xr-x+   5 scott   staff    170 Mar  6 08:09 Sites
drwxr-xr-x    4 scott   staff    136 Mar  7 15:47 bin
```

- `ls -a` and `ls -A`: Print out a file listing that includes hidden dot files. There are two main types of files hidden on your computer—some that are hidden by default from the Finder but show up normally in Darwin; and others (the dot files) that are generally hidden in Darwin. These dot files (called that because they always begin with a .) are often preference or configuration files. They are usually hidden to reduce clutter and not for some nefarious purpose (although you may find that some Aqua applications utilize these hidden files to hide something they really don't want you to find). The main difference between `ls -a` and `ls -A` is that using `ls -a` will show two special files found in almost every directory—the . and the ..—which represent the current directory and the directory immediately above, respectively (these act the same as the . and .. files shown when issuing a `dir` command in the Microsoft Windows command prompt). A common `ls -a` on a home directory will produce quite a few more files than just a vanilla `ls` (three times as many or more is not uncommon):

```
Snow-White:~ scott$ ls -a
.                       .viminfo              Movies
..                      Autosaved Information Music
.CFUserTextEncoding     Desktop               Pictures
.DS_Store               Documents             Public
.Trash                  Downloads             Sites
.bash_history           Library               bin
```

While there are significantly more options available for the `ls` command, those are the most common and should get you started on the right path. You may learn a few other options as you go along, and later you'll learn about the `man` command, which will allow you to learn more about the `ls` command (and most others) than you care to know.

Listing a Directory Other Than Your Current Directory

Besides ls's many options, ls will also accept a directory or file name as an argument. This allows you to view the contents of any directory without actually moving into that directory, or explore a single file's attributes (using the -l option). For example, if you're in your home directory but want to view the files in your Documents folder, your can do this by adding Documents as an argument—for example:

```
Snow-White:~ scott$ ls -G
Autosaved Information/ Library/          Public/
Desktop/               Movies/           Sites/
Documents/             Music/            bin/
Downloads/             Pictures/
Snow-White:~ scott$ ls -G Documents
CDC Baseball/    Personal/       Stuff/     CDCrosters.pdf
Projects/        Work/           Rails/     Writing/
eBooks/          Microsoft User Data/
```

Furthermore, if you want to find out more about a specific file, you can enter a command like this:

```
Snow-White:~ scott$ ls -l Documents/CDCrosters.pdf
-rw-r--r--   1 scott  scott  25739 Apr 24 09:39 Documents/CDCrosters.pdf
```

Now that you know how to list other directories, the next thing you may want to learn is how to move into them (virtually anyway).

cd

The cd command allows you to move from one directory to another (or as the command implies, it allows you to change directories). The cd command doesn't have any options, and it only accepts a path name as its single argument.

■**Note** cd is kind of special in that, unlike ls, it is not an executable file—rather, it is a special type of command referred to as a built-in command. This command, along with a few others you will learn about, is a function of the shell and not traditionally a separate executable file. Although most common built-ins like cd exist in all common shells, it is possible that a built-in command in one shell will behave slightly differently than one in another (cd isn't one of these—it behaves the same way in every shell we've used over the past 20 or so years).

To issue the cd command, simply type cd followed by your destination, like so:

```
Snow-White:~ scott$ cd /
Snow-White:/ scott$
```

If no argument is given, then cd will take you back to your home directory:

```
Snow-White:/ scott$ cd
Snow-White:~ scott$
```

Finally, if cd doesn't recognize the argument as a file or directory, it will tell you so:

```
Snow-White:~ scott$ cd /blah
-bash: cd: /blah: No such file or directory
Snow-White:~ scott$
```

This is an error statement, and most well-written functions and executables will provide some sort of error message if the information you provide doesn't make sense to them.

Caution Just because well-written commands often give you an error message when you do something wrong, it's important to note that this only happens when the command has no idea how to parse the information you've given it. However, this will not prevent all erroneous commands from executing. If a command is recognized as valid, even if the information you enter isn't, the command will execute. While this is often harmless, it can have disastrous consequences (the rm command, as you will soon learn, deletes files immediately and permanently and can cause all sorts of badness if used poorly).

---

pwd

The final command in this section is the pwd command. The pwd command returns your current working directory, as this information is available by default in your prompt (after the :). You may not need to use this command too often—however, it is useful in illustrating the file structure of the system and can come in quite handy when you need to pass your current path into a script. Also, it's possible that you may find yourself stuck in a foreign shell on a foreign machine, where you may actually need this. The basic pwd command looks like this:

```
Snow-White:~ scott$ pwd
/Users/scott
```

In this case, pwd returns the absolute path of your home directory rather than the abbreviated ~ in the command prompt. This can come in handy on a foreign machine where you may not know where the home directory is located, or one where the path info isn't part of the prompt.

Being a rather simple command, pwd only offers two extra options:

- pwd -L: Prints the logical path to your working directory.

- pwd -P: Prints out the physical path to your working directory, resolving any symbolic links. This is the default behavior of pwd.

Wildcards

Before moving on to more Darwin commands, we should have a quick lesson on wildcards and pattern matching. Wildcards are special symbols that, when used with other commands, can help limit or expand the results. Table 17-3 shows the three major wildcards and what they represent or match.

Table 17-3. *Darwin Wildcards*

Wildcard	Definition (Matches)
?	The ? used on the command line matches any single character.
*	The * matches any one or more characters in a file name.
[ ]	The [ ] matches any characters listed between the brackets; this can include a series of characters as well—for example, [l-p] would match l, m, n, o, and p.

To put this to use using what you learned previously, if you cd to /usr/bin and list out the contents using ls, you are struck with a rather large list of files (in this case, mostly executable commands). Wildcards allow you to selectively list out the directory contents in more manageable chunks. For example, if you just wanted to list the files that begin with v, you could use ls v*, like so:

```
Snow-White:/usr/bin scott$ ls v*
vers_string* vi@        vim*        vimtutor*    vm_stat*
vgrind*      view@      vimdiff@    vis*         vmmap*
```

If, for whatever reason, you wanted to expand the search to include b and v, you could use ls [bv]*:

```
Snow-White:/usr/bin scott$ ls [bv]*
b2m*       bg*            bzcat*         bzless*        vimtutor*
banner*    biff*          bzcmp*         bzmore*        vis*
basename*  bison*         bzdiff*        vers_string*   vm_stat*
bashbug*   bridget*       bzegrep*       vgrind*        vmmap*
batch*     bsdmake*       bzfgrep*       vi@
bbdiff*    bspatch*       bzgrep*        view@
bbedit*    bspatch_apple@ bzip2*         vim*
bc*        bunzip2*       bzip2recover*  vimdiff@
```

Note Like most things in Darwin, the characters used within the square brackets are case sensitive, so [bv] would not match any Bs or Vs.

Finally, if you wanted to list all files with two-letter names that begin with any letter in the alphabet from b to v, you could use ls [b-v]? and get the following:

```
Snow-White:/usr/bin scott$ ls [b-v]?
bc* cc@ ci* dc* ex@ fg* ld* m4* nc* nm* pl* ri* su* ul*
bg* cd* co* du* fc* id* lp* md* nl* od* pr* rs* tr* vi@
```

Working with Files and Directories

While most people are perfectly happy and comfortable working with files and directories in the Finder, there are some times when it's either necessary or advantageous to work with files in Darwin. Of course, like all things, before you are able to unleash the power of Darwin, you need to learn a few basic commands for working with files and directories. These basics are shown and described in Table 17-4.

Table 17-4. *File and Directory Management Commands*

Command	Usage	Description
cat	cat filename	The cat command lists the contents of a file. This command was originally written to perform concatenation functions, so if used improperly, this could have unexpected results.
head	head [-n #] filename	The head command allows you to display just the beginning of a long file using the -n option followed by the number of lines you wish to view.
tail	tail [-n #] filename	The tail command allows you to display just the end of a long file using the -n option followed by the number of lines you wish to view.
cp	cp filename filecopy	cp creates copies of files.
mv	mv filename newfilename	mv is interesting in that it is used both to move files from one location to another and to rename files.
rm	rm filename	rm permanently and immediately removes a file (or files).
mkdir	mkdir newdirectory	mkdir is used to create new directories.
rmdir	rmdir directory	rmdir is a special command used to delete directories. It's a safer option than rm in that it will not delete a nonempty directory (which at times makes it more frustrating as well).
touch	touch filename	touch creates a new empty file. (However, if the file already exists, touch will merely alter the date it was last accessed.)

■**Caution** Irresponsible uses of rm can result in very bad things happening—for example, if you happen to be utilizing root privileges (which, in general, you probably shouldn't) and happen to type rm -R /* at the command line, your system will immediately begin to delete itself and everything contained within it until it deletes enough of itself that it can't continue . . . ever. (By the way, the -R option stands for recursive, a handy option found in many commands.)

To illustrate how all of these work, we've created a test file named soliloquy4 in a directory named Shakespeare.

First, you can use the cat command to view the file:

```
Snow-White:~/Documents/Shakespeare scott$ cat soliloquy4
Tomorrow, and tomorrow, and tomorrow,
Creeps in this petty pace from day to day
To the last syllable of recorded time,
And all our yesterdays have lighted fools
The way to dusty death. Out, out, brief candle!
Life's but a walking shadow, a poor player
That struts and frets his hour upon the stage
And then is heard no more: it is a tale
Told by an idiot, full of sound and fury,
Signifying nothing.
```

Now if you weren't sure what this file was (or how long it was), you could use head to view just the first three lines:

```
Snow-White:~/Documents/Shakespeare scott$ head -n 3 soliloquy4
Tomorrow, and tomorrow, and tomorrow,
Creeps in this petty pace from day to day
To the last syllable of recorded time,
```

Likewise, you could use tail to view the last three lines:

```
Snow-White:~/Documents/Shakespeare scott$ tail -n 3 soliloquy4
And then is heard no more: it is a tale
Told by an idiot, full of sound and fury,
Signifying nothing.
```

Note Like many OSs these days, OS X keeps rather long log files about many of the things happening on the system. While there are many dedicated viewers for many of these files, these files are often very, very long. For such files, tail can be a godsend. For example, if you ran a busy web server for which you wanted to see the details of the last 50 hits, you could use tail -n 50 /var/log/httpd/access_log.

To make a copy of the file, you would use the cp command:

```
Snow-White:~/Documents/Shakespeare scott$ ls
soliloquy4
Snow-White:~/Documents/Shakespeare scott$ cp soliloquy4 macbethsolo
Snow-White:~/Documents/Shakespeare scott$ ls
macbethsolo  soliloquy4
```

You could then create a new subdirectory:

```
Snow-White:~/Documents/Shakespeare scott$ mkdir Macbeth
Snow-White:~/Documents/Shakespeare scott$ ls
Macbeth/    macbethsolo  soliloquy4
```

and then move one of the files into the new directory:

```
Snow-White:~/Documents/Shakespeare scott$ mv soliloquy4 Macbeth/soliloquy4
Snow-White:~/Documents/Shakespeare scott$ ls
Macbeth/     macbethsolo
Snow-White:~/Documents/Shakespeare scott$ ls Macbeth/
soliloquy4
```

You can also use the mv command to rename a file:

```
Snow-White:~/Documents/Shakespeare scott$ mv macbethsolo tomorrow
Snow-White:~/Documents/Shakespeare scott$ ls
Macbeth/  tomorrow
```

Next, you could try to remove the Macbeth directory:

```
Snow-White:~/Documents/Shakespeare scott$ rmdir Macbeth/
rmdir: Macbeth/: Directory not empty
```

Oops, first you need to remove any files in there:

```
Snow-White:~/Documents/Shakespeare scott$ rm Macbeth/*
Snow-White:~/Documents/Shakespeare scott$ rmdir Macbeth
Snow-White:~/Documents/Shakespeare scott$ ls
tomorrow
```

Next, you can create an empty file with touch:

```
Snow-White:~/Documents/Shakespeare scott$ touch nothing
Snow-White:~/Documents/Shakespeare scott$ ls
nothing    tomorrow
Snow-White:~/Documents/Shakespeare scott$ cat nothing
Snow-White:~/Documents/Shakespeare scott$
```

More Essential Commands

There are literally hundreds of commands available at the command line, and it would take far more space than we have in this book to cover them all; however, as you progress through the rest of the book, you will learn a number of new commands when they are applicable to the topic at hand. In the meantime, there are a number of essential, or at least very useful, commands that you may want to know about that don't fit nicely in a future discussion in this book. They are covered here.

man

The man command is the command that explains all others. If you want to learn more about the ls command, enter man ls, and your terminal will open into a special mode (called a pager) for reading man pages, which will look something like this:

LS(1)   BSD General Commands Manual   LS(1)

NAME
    ls -- list directory contents

SYNOPSIS
    ls [-ABCFGHLPRTWZabcdefghiklmnopqrstuwx1] [file ...]

DESCRIPTION
    For each operand that names a file of a type other than directory, **ls**
    displays its name as well as any requested, associated information. For
    each operand that names a file of type directory, **ls displays the names**
    of files contained within that directory, as well as any requested, asso-
    ciated information.

    If no operands are given, the contents of the current directory are dis-
    played. If more than one operand is given, nondirectory operands are
    displayed first; directory and nondirectory operands are sorted sepa-
    rately and in lexicographical order.

    The following options are available:

    -@ Display extended attribute keys and sizes in long (-l) output.

:

   Now this is just the first page of the man page—you can scroll through the rest using
either the arrow keys (to move up and down one line at a time) or the spacebar (to move
through one page at a time). When you are done, you can exit the man page by pressing Q on
the keyboard.

■**Tip** Computers have come a long way since the man page system was created, and while reading a
man page in the terminal is relatively easy for short and simple commands, it isn't ideal for more complex
commands that can scroll through 100 or more screens. One neat trick you can use is man -t command |
open -f -a /Applications/Preview.app, which will open the entire man page of the command in
Preview as a PDF file for immediate reading, printing, or saving. (The -t option converts the man page into
a PostScript file, which you can then pipe into your Preview application, which converts the PostScript file
into a PDF file as it opens it. Pipes are covered later.)

---

grep

The grep command searches through files or results for a specified string and then prints out
the lines that contain a match. For example, using the preceding text file, you could print out
all lines that contain "to" using the command grep to tomorrow. This is shown here:

```
Snow-White:~/Documents/Shakespeare scott$ ls
nothing    tomorrow
Snow-White:~/Documents/Shakespeare scott$ grep to tomorrow
Tomorrow, and tomorrow, and tomorrow,
Creeps in this petty pace from day to day
The way to dusty death. Out, out, brief candle!
```

ln

ln is the command-line utility for creating links. While there are different ways of linking files, what we are most concerned with are symbolic (a.k.a., soft) links (more commonly referred to as aliases, or shortcuts in Windows). To create a symbolic link, you use ln with the -s link, followed by the name of the source file and then optionally the name of the linked file.

Note ln by default creates a hard link, which is most likely not what you want, so it's important to remember the -s option. For the technically curious, a *hard link* essentially creates a new file that shares its data with another (the source). If you edit one, the data will change in the other. If you delete one, the other will still remain with all the data intact. A *symbolic link*, on the other hand (like an alias or shortcut), creates a special "path" file that always refers to the original. If this original is deleted, the path is broken unless a new file of the same name replaces the original. A big difference in use is that a symbolic link can refer to a directory or a file on a different file system, while a hard link cannot.

Let's look at ln in action:

```
Snow-White:~/Documents/Shakespeare scott$ ls
macbeth/ nothing
Snow-White:~/Documents/Shakespeare scott$ ls macbeth/
soliloquy4
Snow-White:~/Documents/Shakespeare scott$ ln -s macbeth/soliloquy4 tomorrow
Snow-White:~/Documents/Shakespeare scott$ ls
macbeth/   nothing    tomorrow@
Snow-White:~/Documents/Shakespeare scott$ cat tomorrow
Tomorrow, and tomorrow, and tomorrow,
Creeps in this petty pace from day to day
To the last syllable of recorded time,
And all our yesterdays have lighted fools
The way to dusty death. Out, out, brief candle!
Life's but a walking shadow, a poor player
That struts and frets his hour upon the stage
And then is heard no more: it is a tale
Told by an idiot, full of sound and fury,
Signifying nothing.
```

who

The who command tells you who else is logged in to the computer. Traditionally, this would just be you, since most personal computers would only allow one person to be logged in at a time (and this is how we still tend to use them). However, if you've turned on the Remote Login option in the Sharing control pane, it's possible for multiple users to actually be using one Mac OS system at a time. who also has a related command, whoami, which also tells you your username if you ever forget. (By the way, your Darwin username is the "short" username you picked when you created your account.)

To see these in action on your system isn't always that exciting:

```
Snow-White:~ scott$ who
scott     console  May 20 19:39
scott     ttyp1    May 20 20:17
Snow-White:~ scott$ whoami
scott
```

■Note who may be considered dangerous by many systems administrators who feel it's a potential security breach to disclose too much information about the system or its users; for this reason, on many of today's servers, systems are in place to keep you from finding out who's really online at any time. Of course, the real cool (or if you're a systems administrator, real bad) command that is similar to who is finger. Traditionally, finger would allow you to find out all sorts of personal information about any user, not only those on your local machine, but you could actually "finger" anyone on any UNIX-type machine (and most other multiuser systems of the day). The finger command still exists on some computers and is even installed on your Mac (go ahead, finger another user or yourself)—however, it's unlikely that you'll be able to find many machines on your network or on the Internet that will allow you to finger them or any of their users (for aforementioned security and even privacy fears). By default, Mac OS X will not allow any remote machine to finger you.

---

ps

ps allows you to view what processes are running at any given time on your system. By default, it shows limited information about all the services running from the terminal you are using (i.e., only the current Darwin process that you've started from your current terminal session). Until you really start digging into the power of Darwin, ps will likely just return your shell as your only process:

```
Snow-White:~ scott$ ps
  PID  TTY TIME CMD
  310  p1 0:00.12 -bash
```

The important pieces of information here are the PID (process ID) and the COMMAND. However, with a few options, ps can give you lots of information about every command running on your system. The most common options are -a, -j, and -x (so common, in fact, that you can issue them without the -). The ps command will most likely give you a long scrolling list of processes:

```
Snow-White:~ scott$ ps ajx
USER               PID  PPID  PGID   SESS JOBC STAT   TT      TIME COMMAND
root                 1     0     1 3e62e78   0 Ss     ??   0:02.29 /sbin/launchd
root                10     1    10 3e62c08   0 Ss     ??   0:00.56 /usr/libexec/kext
root                11     1    11 3e62ad0   0 Ss     ??   0:00.81 /usr/sbin/notifyd
root                12     1    12 3e62998   0 Ss     ??   0:03.16 /usr/sbin/syslogd
root                14     1    14 3e62860   0 Ss     ??   0:04.54 /usr/sbin/ntpd -n
root                15     1    15 3e625f0   0 Ss     ??   0:02.79 /usr/sbin/httpd -
root                16     1    16 3e624b8   0 Ss     ??   0:17.14 /usr/sbin/update
root                17     1    17 3e62110   0 Ss     ??   0:00.01 /sbin/SystemStart
root                20     1    20 3e62728   0 Ss     ??   0:00.28 /usr/sbin/securit
root                22     1    22 3e619c0   0 Ss     ??   0:10.30 /System/Library/F
_mdnsresponder      23     1    23 42f1fd8   0 Ss     ??   0:04.70 /usr/sbin/mDNSRes
scott               24     1    24 3e61c30   0 Ss     ??   0:08.08 /System/Library/C
root                25     1    25 3e61af8   0 Ss     ??   0:00.00 /usr/sbin/KernelE
root                27     1    27 3e61d68   0 Ss     ??   0:00.01 /usr/libexec/hidd
root                28     1    28 3e61270   0 Ss     ??   0:01.92 /System/Library/F
...
```

■**Note** Traditionally, ps aux is one of the most popular ps commands. However the -u option in the version of ps shipped in Mac OS X performs a different task. That said, if you are in the habit of typing ps aux, it will still work, but you won't be able to use it with any additional options.

This gives you much more information besides the PID and COMMAND (which is the full path, and as shown, is often truncated by the width of the terminal), including what USER is responsible for the process. By default, the information is sorted by the process ID. If you want to filter this a bit to show only what tasks a specific user is running, you can use the -u option. For example, if you just wanted to see how many processes you are personally responsible for, you could use the following:

```
Snow-White:~ scott$ ps -jxu scott
USER    PID  PPID  PGID   SESS JOBC STAT   TT      TIME COMMAND
scott    74     1    74 442aaf8   0 Ss     ??   0:00.11 /sbin/launchd
scott    93    74    93 442aaf8   1 S      ??   0:00.02 /System/Library/CoreSe
scott    99    74    99 442aaf8   1 S      ??   0:00.78 /usr/libexec/UserEvent
scott   101    74   101 442aaf8   1 S      ??   0:01.90 /System/Library/CoreSe
scott   102    74   102 442aaf8   1 S      ??   0:01.82 /System/Library/CoreSe
scott   103    74   103 442aaf8   1 S      ??   0:09.80 /System/Library/CoreSe
scott   112    74   112 442aaf8   1 S      ??   0:00.01 /usr/sbin/pboard
scott   113    74   113 442aaf8   1 S      ??   0:00.13 /Applications/iTunes.a
scott   117    74   117 442aaf8   1 S      ??   0:11.70 /System/Library/Framew
scott   130     1   130 4be7ad0   0 SNs    ??   0:00.73 /System/Library/Framew
scott   153    74   153 442aaf8   1 S      ??   2:02.94 /Applications/Microsof
scott   157    74   157 442aaf8   1 S      ??   0:00.59 /Applications/Microsof
scott   160    74   160 442aaf8   1 S      ??   0:00.03 /Library/Application S
```

```
scott    193    74    193 442aaf8    1 S      ??    0:03.19 /Applications/Utilitie
scott    250    74    250 442aaf8    1 S      ??    0:12.83 /Applications/Preview.
scott    195   193    195 442afd8    0 Ss   s000    0:00.77 login -pf scott
scott    196   195    196 442afd8    1 S    s000    0:00.02 -bash
scott    258   196    258 442afd8    1 R+   s000    0:00.01 ps -jxU scott
```

■**Note** A similar command to ps is top. The primary difference between the two is that ps takes a snapshot of processes when you run the command, while top stays active and continually updates itself. The Activity Monitor application in the Utilities folder provides a nice GUI to the top command (and presents some additional information as well, including disk usage, memory usage, and CPU usage).

kill

kill is used to stop a specific process. This can be necessary if you have a task that is running amok and you can't figure out how else to stop it (perhaps you are attempting to write your own application or script, and it gets caught in a nasty loop).

To see this in action, you can intentionally create some nasty background tasks using the yes command, which you will then kill.

■**Note** The yes command by default prints out y indefinitely as fast as possible. If you want to find out just how hot your computer will get before a fan kicks in, you can open up a few terminal windows (or tabs that were added to the Terminal application in Leopard) and run yes in each one. We're not sure we'd recommend this if you are using a portable while it's sitting on your lap, though . . . you might not like the burning sensation it causes. To stop yes from running the "correct" way, just press Control-C, and it should stop.

To do this, first start running yes in the background twice, and then find out what the PID of each yes process is and kill it:

```
Snow-White:~ scott$ yes > /dev/null &
[1] 480
Snow-White:~ scott$ yes > /dev/null &
[2] 481
Snow-White:~ scott$ ps u
USER    PID %CPU %MEM     VSZ    RSS  TT  STAT STARTED      TIME COMMAND
scott   481 96.8 -0.0   27376    476  p1  R    10:38PM   0:03.25 yes
scott   480 93.4 -0.0   27376    476  p1  R    10:38PM   0:05.20 yes
scott   473  0.1 -0.0   27728    784  p1  S    10:35PM   0:00.02 -bash
Snow-White:~ scott$ kill 481
Snow-White:~ scott$ kill 480
[1]-  Terminated               yes >/dev/null
[2]+  Terminated               yes >/dev/null
Snow-White:~ scott$ ps u
```

```
USER    PID %CPU %MEM    VSZ    RSS  TT  STAT STARTED    TIME COMMAND
scott   473  0.0 -0.0  27728    788  p1  S    10:35PM  0:00.02 -bash
```

There are a few things we should explain. The yes command you entered, yes > /dev/null &, takes the output of yes and redirects it to /dev/null, which is a special device in most UNIX systems that is a black hole of sorts. Everything sent to /dev/null just goes away. The > is the redirect command, and the & tells the terminal to run this in the background. We will cover background tasks and redirections later.

Finally, you may notice the ps command shows that one yes process is using 96.8 percent of the processor, and the other is using 93.4 percent, and these numbers don't seem to add up. The reason for this is that the %CPU shows the percentage for a single processor. Most Apple computers these days include at least two processing cores (including ours shown here), so in this case, one yes command is using 96.8 percent of one, while the other is using 93.4 percent of the other (your mileage may vary).

Occasionally, a simple kill still won't stop a process; in that event, you'll need to use kill -9 to stop the process. The -9 signal runs kill in KILL mode, which means that the process will force stop immediately. Common kill signals include the following:

1: HUP (hang up)

2: INT (interrupt)

3: QUIT (quit)

6: ABRT (abort)

9: KILL (unstoppable killing of process)

less (more)

less is a pager, which allows you to scroll through large amounts of text that may normally scroll right by you in the terminal. You learned how pagers worked with the man command, which automatically runs in a pager (which by default in Mac OS X is actually less)—however, sometimes it's useful to use a pager with other commands as well. For example, when you use the ps aux command, you are presented with lots of information scrolling right by; however, if you pipe the ps aux command into less, then you can scroll around the output just as you scrolled around the man pages. An example of this is the following:

```
Snow-White:~ scott$ ps aux | less

USER      PID %CPU %MEM    VSZ    RSS  TT  STAT STARTED    TIME COMMAND
scott     304  5.9 -8.1 795272 170688  ??  S    8:15PM  24:06.93 /Applicati
root       39  0.7 -0.3  30440   6192  ??  Ss   4:14PM   0:05.56 /usr/sbin/
windowse   62  0.1 -2.2 902716  45600  ??  Ss   4:14PM   5:30.36 /System/Li
scott     307  0.1 -0.6 372104  12548  ??  S    8:17PM   1:10.59 /Applicati
root       31  0.0 -0.1  27840   2408  ??  Ss   4:14PM   0:00.03 /usr/bin/W
root       32  0.0 -0.4 303152   7440  ??  Ss   4:14PM   0:01.47 /Library/A
root       33  0.0 -0.1  27824   2052  ??  Ss   4:14PM   0:00.01 /System/Li
root       34  0.0 -0.1  27844   2328  ??  Ss   4:14PM   0:00.02 /usr/sbin/
root       35  0.0 -0.1  28564   2696  ??  Ss   4:14PM   0:00.82 /usr/sbin/
root       36  0.0 -0.1  27580   1088  ??  Ss   4:14PM   0:00.47 /usr/sbin/
```

root	37	0.0	-0.0	27288	1016	??	Ss	4:14PM	0:00.08	/usr/sbin/
root	40	0.0	-0.3	31852	5772	??	Ss	4:14PM	0:00.23	/usr/sbin/
root	41	0.0	-0.1	27776	2780	??	Ss	4:14PM	0:00.12	/usr/sbin/
root	42	0.0	-0.1	28324	1716	??	Ss	4:14PM	0:00.02	/usr/sbin/
root	44	0.0	-0.3	29268	5316	??	Ss	4:14PM	0:00.27	/usr/sbin/
root	46	0.0	-0.0	27864	880	??	Ss	4:14PM	0:00.15	/usr/sbin/
root	50	0.0	-0.0	27252	708	??	Ss	4:14PM	0:20.84	/usr/sbin/
root	54	0.0	-0.3	30744	6768	??	Ss	4:14PM	0:00.32	/usr/sbin/
root	55	0.0	-0.1	27676	2184	??	Ss	4:14PM	0:00.37	/usr/sbin/
root	63	0.0	-0.3	37828	5512	??	S	4:14PM	0:00.18	/usr/sbin/
root	64	0.0	-0.5	37028	9752	??	Ss	4:14PM	0:00.53	/System/Li
scott	69	0.0	-0.4	82936	8332	??	Ss	4:15PM	0:02.26	/System/Li

:

Using the arrow keys, you can now scroll through your output, and when you are done, you can quit the pager and return to the prompt by pressing Q.

■Note Another older yet extremely popular pager was called more. Although more was very popular, it was lacking in many ways—for instance, it would only allow you to scroll down (e.g., you couldn't go back once you scrolled past something). Because of this, less has largely replaced more; however, for backward compatibility, the more command has been linked with less, so the more command still works (although it will actually run less).

---

find and whereis

find and whereis are two commands that work very differently, yet are both used to the same ends: finding something in the Darwin file system.

find, by default, takes a path variable and presents a list of matches. Additionally, if a match is a directory, find will traverse that directory as well (find / will return every visible file on your hard drive!). Using regular expressions and wildcards can effectively narrow (or broaden) your search as needed. A simple find example may be something like this:

```
Snow-White:~ scott$ find ~/Documents/Shakes*
/Users/scott/Documents/Shakespeare
/Users/scott/Documents/Shakespeare/macbeth
/Users/scott/Documents/Shakespeare/macbeth/soliloquy4
/Users/scott/Documents/Shakespeare/nothing
/Users/scott/Documents/Shakespeare/tomorrow
```

Listing directories is nothing new, but find becomes very useful with its ability to search for matches of specific file properties, the most popular being the name of the file. To use find this way, you give find the directory you wish to traverse, and then enter the -name option, followed by your search string. For example, if you were looking for the soliloquy in your Documents folder, you could use the following:

```
Snow-White:~ scott$ find ~/Documents -name "sol*"
/Users/scott/Documents/Shakespeare/macbeth/soliloquy4
```

Other properties that you can use as search parameters for find include the file's owner and its group.

■**Note** When using find, it's best to have a good general idea of the location of the file you are looking for. While it's perfectly acceptable to do something like find / -name "sol*", find is not a fast command, so in addition to getting a number of false hits and warnings (mostly Permission Denied warnings from sub-directories that find isn't allowed to look in), it would take a relatively long time to perform such a search.

Unlike find, whereis is tailored specifically for finding executable files. It does this by specifically searching the common places where programs live (primarily the various bin and sbin directories for a specific program name you enter). For example, if you wanted to see where the whereis command is located, you could do this:

```
Snow-White:~ scott$ whereis whereis
/usr/bin/whereis
```

While this may seem trivial on a certain level, there are a couple of good reasons to use this. First, if you occasionally compile or install your own Darwin software (which we'll talk about in the next chapter), at some point you may end up with two copies of the same program, and whereis will help you find them so you can deal with it. Second, scripts written in languages like Perl, Python, or Ruby often want to know where the language executable is, and whereis is a quick way to determine that.

■**Note** Two other commands worth mentioning here are locate and mdfind. locate searches its database for matches to your query, which makes it quite a bit faster than find—however, it's possible that what you are looking for isn't in the database. mdfind is a command unique to Mac OS X that actually searches on Spotlight's metadata. This makes it very fast and powerful—however, there is one minor setback in that Spotlight doesn't always index items until they are opened in the Finder. So, for example, our soliloquy4 text file may not show up in an mdfind search (or Spotlight search), at least until it is accessed by a non-Darwin application. As such, mdfind wouldn't be a first choice for looking for something in the Darwin file system on the whole (however, it's an excellent choice if what you are looking for is visible in the Finder).

---

lipo

lipo is a command that has special meaning to Mac OS X universal binaries. When Apple switched hardware platforms from the PowerPC architecture to the Intel architecture, it introduced the universal binary, which allows the application to run natively on both platforms. Whether you are running an older PowerPC Mac or a newer Intel Mac, you probably don't need both types of code in your application. lipo allows you to take a universal application and "thin" it so that the resulting application will only run on one architecture. The advantage of this is that you can free up significant amounts of space on your hard drive by thinning your application. For example, if you delve into iDVD.app (which in Darwin will appear as a directory, since most OS X applications are actually application bundles, or special directories containing all the pieces of the application) to the actual executable (/Applications/iDVD.app/Contents/MacOS/iDVD), you can see that its default size is 7492 KB. If you run lipo using the -thin i386 option (if you're using an Intel machine; if you are on a PowerPC computer, you would replace the i386 with ppc), you can shrink this file down to around 3884 KB. That's a 50 percent savings of disk space by stripping away parts you don't need and will never use on your computer! lipo will thin a file by taking the initial universal binary executable, followed by the thin option, followed by the output option and the name of the output file. lipo always makes a copy of the original, and it's not a bad idea to back up the original file until you are sure that the thinned file works without error. An example of running lipo on iDVD could look something like this:

```
Snow-White:~ scott$ cd /Applications/iDVD.app/Contents/MacOS/
Snow-White:/Applications/Sherlock.app/Contents/MacOS scott$ ls
iDVD
Snow-White:/Applications/Sherlock.app/Contents/MacOS scott$ du -hsk iDVD
7492    iDVD
Snow-White:/Applications/Sherlock.app/Contents/MacOS scott$ lipo Sherlock -thin i386
-output iDVD.i386
Snow-White:/Applications/Sherlock.app/Contents/MacOS scott$ du -hsk Sh*
7492    iDVD
3884    iDVD.386
Snow-White:/Applications/Sherlock.app/Contents/MacOS scott$ mv iDVD ~/Documents/
Snow-White:/Applications/Sherlock.app/Contents/MacOS scott$ mv iDVD.i386 iDVD
```

■**Note** The du command is a simple "disk usage" command. When used with the -hsk option, it simply shows you how big a file or directory is from the command line.

■**Note** The savings with lipo only apply to the executable portion of the application. The resources, which make up a large part of the application's total size, are not affected by this.

■**Note** Since Snow Leopard is written specifically for Intel processors, most of the applications that ship with it are already compiled specifically for Intel, and there is no PowerPC code to remove.

Now you can run iDVD to make sure everything works, and once you verify that it in fact does, you can run rm on the original iDVD executable and gain back close to 3 MB of precious disk space.

Note What happens if something goes wrong? Well, that's why you back up the original, which you can then just put back in place with no ill effect at all. By design, this should work without issue—however, as companies transition from PowerPC-only applications to universal applications, it's prudent to expect that somewhere, somehow, something important could get lost in this process. It's never happened to us, but it's better to be safe than sorry.

Note `lipo` is actually used to create and get information about universal binaries, not to break them apart. The use of `lipo` to thin out universal binaries is more of a useful side effect than an intention.

Pipes, Redirection, and Background Tasks

A few more things we should cover before we move on are the ability to pipe one command into another, the ability to redirect output (or input) to and from a command, and the ability to run tasks in the background. We've actually done each of these things in some of the preceding examples, yet as they are quite powerful tools, we'll give a bit more depth here.

Pipes

Piping one command into another is a great way to make even the simplest Darwin tools do powerful things. You saw this previously when you piped the `ps` command into the `less` command. The pipe symbol is the | (which is the tall line that lives above the \ on a normal US Mac keyboard). In practice, this takes the first command and sends the output into the second. Commands like `less` rely almost entirely on the ability to pipe one command into it, and other commands become much more useful with this ability. For example, the ability to take commands that produce large amounts of output and pipe that content into a filter (like the `grep` command) can save lots of time and headaches.

Redirects

A redirect allows you to alter what happens to the output of a command, or alternately direct the content of a file into a command. The symbols for redirection are < and >. A very simple use of a redirect is to create a text file using `echo`, like this:

```
Snow-White:~ scott$ echo "Hello my name is Scott" > name.txt
Snow-White:~ scott$ cat name.txt
Hello my name is Scott
```

The `echo` command normally would just print out whatever you feed into it back to your terminal, but here we redirected the output to `name.txt` (which may or may not have existed).

Caution If you are redirecting data into an existing file, the entire contents of that file will be replaced with the new data. So be very careful with this command.

If you wanted to redirect additional data into an existing file (rather than replace the content, which the > always does), you could use >> to append the new data to the old:

```
Snow-White:~ scott$ echo " Hello Scott" >> name.txt
Snow-White:~ scott$ cat name.txt
Hello my name is Scott
 Hello Scott
Snow-White:~ scott$ echo "Ooops" > name.txt
Snow-White:~ scott$ cat name.txt
Ooops
```

Background Tasks

Any Darwin command can be issued to run in the background with the & symbol tacked onto the end of the command. This is particularly useful when you want to start a command that may take a long time to finish, or when running a task that you want to keep running indefinitely. For example, if you wanted to use the find command to find something with the name motd somewhere on your system, knowing that this may take some time, you may want to run it in the background. Here's an annotated example of this:

```
Snow-White:~ scott$ find / -name "motd" > found 2> found_err &
[1] 358
```

Here you start the find command in the background. You are redirecting the output to a file named found. Also, the 2> found_err will redirect any error messages to a file named found_err; otherwise, even though the command is running in the background, error messages would still spam the terminal (2> is a special redirect in Bash that only redirects error messages).

```
Snow-White:~ scott$ jobs
[1]+  Running              find / -name "motd" >found 2>found_err &
```

The jobs command gives you a list of all of the background tasks and tells you their state (in this case, your only task is running).

```
Snow-White:~ scott$ fg
find / -name "motd" >found 2>found_err
```

The fg command (fg for foreground) brings forward the first running task (which for now is your only task). Since the command is running in the foreground, you can no longer use the terminal unless you pause the process. You can do this using the Control-Z key combo.

```
^Z
[1]+  Stopped              find / -name "motd" >found 2>found_err
```

When you use Control-Z, you are giving the message that your task has stopped. You can now resume this task in the background using bg.

```
Snow-White:~ scott$ bg
[1]+ find / -name "motd" >found 2>found_err &
```

While this task runs, let's start another background task.

```
Snow-White:~ scott$ (sleep 30; echo "done")&
[2] 359
Snow-White:~ scott$ jobs
[1]-  Running                  find / -name "motd" >found 2>found_err &
[2]+  Running                  ( sleep 30; echo "done" ) &
```

Now you have two jobs running in the background, your find command is still chugging along, and you have the new command (which will wait, or sleep, 30 seconds, and then run the echo "done" command). Notice that each job has been given a number. The find command is [1], and the sleep command is [2]. To pull the sleep command into the foreground, you must specify that you want job 2.

```
Snow-White:~ scott$ fg 2
( sleep 30; echo "done" )
done
```

Eventually, the sleep command will complete and echo "done" to the terminal. At this point, you can continue to use your terminal, and eventually you will get a message that your find command has completed.

```
 [1]+  Exit 1                  find / -name "motd" >found 2>found_err
Snow-White:~ scott$ cat found
/private/etc/motd
```

Working As Root

In Darwin, the root user is synonymous with the administrator, superuser, or all-knowing, all-doing, grand poobah. Working as root is sort of like splitting the atom: great potential for good, great potential for total destruction . . . in the case of root, that which gets destroyed can vary from an important file to all of your data and the OS itself. Traditionally, root has no boundaries and no restrictions, and it can override all the security safeguards on the system. As such, you should never use it. (Sometimes, though, if it's your personal computer, and you really want to do certain things, you may have to.)

■**Caution** With root comes lots of responsibility. Nothing short of a very powerful magnet sitting on your hard drive can mess up your system quite like a misplaced root command. As such, we cannot stress enough that root should be used sparingly and only when absolutely necessary.

So, when should you run a command as root? When there is no other way to run it. For example, when we ran our find command on the whole hard drive, we received a number of Permission Denied warnings. If we in fact wanted to search those protected files and directories, we would have to do so as root (or as the owner of the specific protected files or directories). Additionally, while you may be allowed to see and use many of the files and directories in Darwin, you won't be allowed to alter them or add new files to the directories. If you need to alter a configuration file, or install a new Darwin application in a specific location, or do one of the many other related tasks, you will often have to do so as root.

When the time comes to run a command as root, one generally doesn't log out and log back in as root (which Apple goes to great lengths to make very difficult to do anyway). Instead, the recommended way is to utilize the sudo command.

sudo

The sudo command (which means *substitute user do*) allows selected users (only users with administrator privileges, by default) to run any other command as the root (or any other) user, as specified in the sudoers file (located at /etc/sudoers).

To run a command as root (which is sudo's default nature), merely precede the command with sudo—for example, if you wanted to manually run the weekly maintenance script, you would do so like this:

```
Snow-White:~ scott$ sudo periodic weekly

WARNING: Improper use of the sudo command could lead to data loss
or the deletion of important system files. Please double-check your
typing when using sudo. Type "man sudo" for more information.

To proceed, enter your password, or type Ctrl-C to abort.

Password:

...
```

As you can see, the first time you use sudo, you are given a stern warning about the dangers of using sudo, followed by a prompt for your password. Upon entering your password, the command will execute. The preceding warning will only appear the first time you use sudo—however, each time you use sudo, you will be prompted for a password, with one caveat: by default, sudo will save your password for a period of time (five minutes is the default), so you won't have to reenter it for any subsequent sudo commands within that time period.

Note The weekly maintenance scripts are among three script collections the system runs to maintain your computer. The other two are daily and monthly. These scripts are meant to run at their indicated intervals. However, this is based on the premise that your computer is always on! If you frequently turn off your computer (especially common for laptops), then it's possible that these scripts and their subsequent commands may never run. Thus, it may be beneficial to run these commands manually as indicated previously to help clean up and maintain your system. (The weekly and monthly scripts may take a few minutes to complete.)

By default, sudo allows root and any user in the admin group to utilize it. If a nonadmin user attempts to use sudo, instead of his or her chosen command being executed, that person will be presented with the following warning:

```
user is not in the sudoers file.  This incident will be reported.
```

To run a command as a user other than root, sudo offers the -u option, which you would use as follows:

```
sudo -u username command
```

On the slight chance that you really must execute a series of commands as another user and you'd like to maintain the user state for an extended period of time, sudo offers the -s option, which in effect starts the shell as the specified user. Since this command starts a shell as the specified user or root, no additional command is necessary. By default, this is the equivalent of using the older su command. If you must use this (and it's recommended that you don't), it's important to remember to quit (i.e., type exit) as soon as you are done—otherwise, you will remain in root state and are more likely to do something regrettable (or forget you are logged in as root and walk away from your computer for a cup of coffee or something and allow someone else to do something perhaps even more regrettable)!

■**Note** Before there was sudo, there was su (substitute user). Rather than taking a command, su just dropped you into a shell as root or the specified user. For whatever reason, many old-time UNIX users still swear by the su command, and while these are generally intelligent people who can perform amazing computer tasks in their sleep, their stubbornness in regard to su is misplaced. You shouldn't use su on the Mac (and yes, it is there). su was written in a time of relative innocence, when mail servers didn't require passwords and spam filters didn't exist, when virus protection wasn't a billion-dollar industry, and when *god* was an appropriate (and sadly all too common) password for the root user. Anyway, those days are gone, and su just doesn't provide the features and, more importantly, the security that sudo provides (such as fine-grained per-user and per-group customizability, sophisticated checks on timestamps and files to assure that nobody has tampered with the file, and more).

---

sudoers

The sudo defaults are sensible and appropriate for most computer uses. However, for servers or other computers with many users, sudo can be coaxed into providing very specific, fine-grained privileges to individual users or groups. To do this requires editing the /etc/sudoers file. The catch is that to edit this file, you must have root privileges and you must use a special editor named visudo. visudo is really a special mode of the Vi editor—or more specifically, Vim, which stands for *Vi improved*, and is installed on Mac OS X in place of Vi. The easiest way to accomplish all this is to merely use the following:

```
Snow-White:~ scott$ sudo visudo
Password:
```

This immediately opens up the sudoers file to be edited (assuming you understand how Vi works, which if you don't right now, we will explain in the next section).

Sadly, a discussion of the many specific tweaks that can be made to this file would extend far beyond the confines of this book. However, typing man sudoers brings you to the man page for this particular file and explains in detail things like the extended Backus-Naur form, what exactly it means, and how to put it to use.

Editing Files

Editing files in Darwin is just one of those things that you'll eventually have to do to get the most out of it. For the most part, using a normal Mac OS X text editor like TextMate (€39, about $54), BBEdit ($125), TextWrangler (free), or Smultron (free, donations accepted) may be your best bet—however, at times it may be handy or necessary to edit a file on the command line. Mac OS X ships with four command line–based text editors in Darwin: Ed, Vim, Emacs, and Nano. Ed is the original text editor for UNIX, but many newer text editors have surpassed it in both usability and features. Despite this, it is still included in most UNIX distributions, since it has found a small niche within certain shell scripts. Each of the remaining three have their advantages, and what it comes down to for most people is a matter of taste and habit (i.e., once you start using one, it becomes a bit frustrating to use another, since they vary quite a bit).

Note Since we mentioned some GUI text editors previously, it's worth noting that many of these come with a command-line executable as well, so that you may open any file in them from the command line. Specifically, BBEdit allows you to install the `bbedit` command-line executable, and TextMate allows you to install the `tm` command-line executable. Each of these will open the file in the GUI application, but it's handy to do so from the command line. However, these applications won't help you much if you are accessing the machine remotely through a terminal window.

Vim

Vim is, as the name suggests, an *improved* clone of Vi (Visual Editor), which in turn is based on Ex, which is based on the aforementioned Ed (which was based on an even older text editor called QED). Vim is interesting to people new to command-line editors because, like its predecessors, it is a dual-mode text editor. To get things done, you must switch between an insert or edit mode and a command mode. While this way of working with a text editor takes some getting used to, it's fairly easy once you get the knack of it. Also, Vim, Vi, or one of its clones is installed by default on almost every version of UNIX or Linux, so once you learn it, you can count on something like it to be installed on any UNIX (or UNIX-like) system you encounter.

Note Vim specifically has a special third mode—visual mode—which can be toggled by typing v in command mode. Once in visual mode, you can move the cursor around normally—however, the text you move over will be selected. This mode is very handy for selecting text for precise copying and pasting.

When you launch Vim, you can either open an existing file, create a new file, or just jump into the editor without creating a file. The syntax is fairly straightforward:

```
vim [filename]
```

where `filename` is either an existing file or one you wish to create.

Note In Darwin, `vi`, `view`, `vimdiff`, and `ex` all point to `vim`—however, they each cause Vim to exhibit different default behavior. `vi` and `vim` both launch in normal mode, `view` opens a file read-only, `vimdiff` allows you to open multiple files at the same time so that you can compare them, and `ex` opens Vim in `ex` mode (the `:vi` command returns you to normal mode).

Vim begins in command mode when opening a new or existing file; so, if you open the soliloquy file you've been working with earlier in the chapter, you will be presented with the following:

```
Tomorrow, and tomorrow, and tomorrow,
Creeps in this petty pace from day to day
To the last syllable of recorded time,
And all our yesterdays have lighted fools
The way to dusty death. Out, out, brief candle!
Life's but a walking shadow, a poor player
That struts and frets his hour upon the stage
And then is heard no more: it is a tale
Told by an idiot, full of sound and fury,
Signifying nothing.
~
~
~
~
~
~
~
~
~
~
~
~
~
"soliloquy4" 10L, 409C
```

Some things to note here are the following:

- The cursor begins on the first letter of the first line.

- Lines on the screen beginning with ~ indicate that the line is empty (not just blank, but empty—in other words, it's not there).

- The line at the very bottom of the screen is the informational display. Initially, it displays the name of the file, how many lines the file contains, and how many characters the file contains.

In command mode, the keys and key sequences have special meanings. For example, you can move your cursor around the text using the arrow keys, or the H, J, K, and L keys (old UNIX keyboards didn't all have arrow keys). If you are searching for a particular word (for example, *candle*), you could use the search function, which is / followed by your search term. /candle followed by the Return key moves the cursor to the first letter of the first instance of *candle* that it finds. If you want to continue to search for the next occurrence of your search term, you can use an empty / and then press Return. In this particular case, since there is only one occurrence of *candle*, the informational line at the bottom tells you search hit BOTTOM, continuing at TOP. If there were more occurrences of your search term, / would continue to search forward in your text for them. To search backward, replace the / with ?.

■**Note** Searching in Vim is case sensitive. Also, in its search, Vim has its own special characters—for example, the . character is a wildcard, so if you were to search for, say, the period at the end of a sentence, you would need to escape the . with a \ (backslash). Otherwise, it would match every character in the document.

To actually enter text, you need to enter insert mode. You can do this by typing i, which starts inserting at the point where your cursor is. Alternately, typing I begins inserting text at the beginning of the line you are on, and o starts you at the beginning of a new line immediately below the line your cursor is on. In insert mode, you can type as you would normally. To exit insert mode and return to command mode, press the Esc key.

■**Note** If in doubt about which mode you are in, you can always press the Esc key to return to command mode (pressing Esc in command mode has no effect). Additionally, the informational line at the bottom will present you with a big, bold -- INSERT -- message when you are in insert mode.

When you are done editing your file, you can save it (while in command mode) using :w followed by Return if you wish to save it with the name that you initially opened the file with. Alternately, you can use :w filename to save the file with a specific name.

■Tip To save some typing when saving files, you can use the % symbol to represent the initial file name. For example, if you opened a file named `supertext`, you could save it as `supertext.new` using `:w %.new`.

When your file is saved and you are ready to quit, you can quit using `:q`. Alternately, you can save and quit in one shot using either `:x`, `:wq`, or (our favorite) `ZZ`.

■Note Occasionally you will find that Vim won't let you simply save a file or quit for certain reasons— most commonly when you wish to quit and your file is unsaved, or you are attempting to save a file that was opened as read-only. In either of these cases, the informational line will tell you why Vim is acting ornery and give you the option of overriding its warnings by appending `!` to the end of your command. For example, to force quit an unsaved file, you need to use `:q!` rather than just `:q`.

Once you get used to working with two modes in Vim, the next thing you'll want to do is explore the features of the command mode. To help, Table 17-5 lists common command-mode keystrokes and what they accomplish (this is by no means a complete list).

Table 17-5. *Vim Command-Mode Keystrokes Quick Reference*

Keystroke	Action
Moving Around	
k or up arrow	Move cursor up one line
j or down arrow	Move cursor down one line
h or left arrow	Move cursor one space to the left
l or right arrow	Move cursor one space to the right
e	Move to end of word
b	Move to beginning of word
$	Move to end of line
0	Move to beginning of line
(	Move back one sentence
)	Move forward one sentence
{	Move back one paragraph
}	Move forward one paragraph
:n	Move to line n
nG	Move to line n
G	Move to last line in document
1G	Move to first line in document
Control-f	Scroll forward one screen
Control-b	Scroll backward one screen

Continued

Table 17-5. *Continued*

Keystroke	Action
Inserting Text	
i	Insert text before cursor
a	Insert text after cursor
I	Insert text at beginning of line
A	Insert text at end of line
o	Create blank line below cursor and insert text
O	Create blank line above cursor and insert text
r	Overwrite one character and then return to command mode
R	Begin overwriting text at cursor
Deleting Text	
x	Delete character under cursor
X	Delete character before cursor
dd or :d	Delete entire line
Searching and Replacing Text	
/pattern	Search forward for pattern
/ or n	Search forward for previous pattern
?pattern	Search backward for pattern
? or N	Search backward for previous pattern
:s/orig/repl	Replace orig with repl on current line
:%s/orig/repl	Replace orig with repl throughout entire document
Copying and Pasting Text	
yw	Copy word
yy	Copy line
y	Copy selected text (from visual mode)
dw	Cut word
dd	Cut line
d	Cut selected text (from visual mode)
p	Paste text
:w [filename]	Save file as file name (if no file name is specified, the file will be saved with the current name)
:q	Quit Vim
:x, :wq or ZZ	Save file and quit
:w!	Force save read-only file (if you have proper permissions)
:q!	Force quit changed file without saving

Keystroke	Action
Other Commands	
Esc	Return Vim to command mode
u	Undo
J	Join two lines into one
:.=	Display current line number

Emacs

Emacs (or GNU Emacs, as the faithful like to refer to it) is another popular text editor (perhaps it may be best described as a powerful runtime system with text-editing capabilities). Emacs can do wonderful things provided you take the time to learn a rather large number of mystical key combinations (and learning a little Lisp helps too). In fact, people who love and use Emacs (who really should have a name to describe them—like Trekkies or something, since they tend to share the same sort of devotion) won't settle for anything less.

Unlike Vi, Emacs is a single-mode text editor; so, in that way, it's probably similar to most GUI text editors you may have used. However, since it lacks a GUI, you can't use your mouse to access the fancy features. That's where the crazy keystrokes come into play. In general, these keystrokes take the form of either the Control key or the Meta key plus some other key (in Emacs, the shorthand for this would be something like C-k for Control-K, or M-k for Meta-K). Usually, you would hold these keys at the same time. The gotcha here is that the Mac keyboard doesn't have a Meta key. You can fix this by selecting the "Use option as meta key" option in Terminal's Settings preferences (on the Keyboard tab, as shown in Figure 17-2).

Figure 17-2. *The "Use option as meta key" option selected in Terminal's Settings preferences*

As with Vi (described previously), you can either open an existing file, create a new file, or just start with a scratch buffer when you launch Emacs using the emacs [*filename*] command. Opening the soliloquy file produces the following output:

```
Tomorrow, and tomorrow, and tomorrow,
Creeps in this petty pace from day to day
To the last syllable of recorded time,
And all our yesterdays have lighted fools
The way to dusty death. Out, out, brief candle!
Life's but a walking shadow, a poor player
That struts and frets his hour upon the stage
And then is heard no more: it is a tale
Told by an idiot, full of sound and fury,
Signifying nothing.
```

```
-uu-:---F1  soliloquy4    All L1    (Fundamental)----------------------------
For information about the GNU Project and its goals, type C-h C-p.
```

Once the file is open, it's immediately ready to edit. To move around in the file, you can use either the arrow keys or some C-n keystrokes (C-f, C-b, C-p, and C-n). The Delete key works as you would expect, and you can enter text at the cursor just by typing.

To save the file, you can either use C-x C-s to save the file as its existing name, or C-x C-w file name to save the file as file name. C-x C-c quits Emacs (it prompts you to save any changed files first). If you need to edit an additional file, you can use C-x C-f to open or create another file without quitting Emacs. Table 17-6 provides a handy list of a few common keystrokes and their effects.

Table 17-6. *Common Emacs Keystrokes and Their Effects*

Keystroke	Action
Moving Around	
C-f or right arrow	Move one character to the right
C-b or left arrow	Move one character to the left
C-p or up arrow	Move one line up
C-n or down arrow	Move one line down
M-f	Move one word to the right

Keystroke	Action
M-b	Move one word to the left
C-a	Move to the beginning of the current line
C-e	Move to the end of the current line
C-v	Page down
M-v	Page up
M->	Go to the end of the document
M-<	Go to the beginning of the document
C-u n C-n	Move ahead n lines
M-g g n	Go to line n
Searching and Replacing Text	
C-s pattern Ret (Return)	Search forward for pattern
C-r pattern Ret	Search backward for pattern
C-s Ret Ret	Search for next occurrence of previous pattern
M-% orig Ret repl Ret	Replace orig string with repl string (Emacs will prompt you for confirmation; press y to continue)
Copying and Pasting Text	
C-Spc (spacebar)	Set mark at cursor, which allows you to move the cursor anywhere in the document, thus "selecting" text between mark and cursor (called a *region* in Emacs lingo)
C-w	Cut region
M-w	Copy region
C-y	Paste last cut or copied region
Saving and Quitting	
C-x C-w filename	Save file as file name
C-x C-s	Save file under current file name (will prompt to confirm overwrite of existing file)
C-x C-c	Quit Emacs (will prompt to confirm if current document has changed)
Other Commands	
C-x C-f filename	Open existing or new file in current buffer
C-h t	Start a built-in Emacs tutorial
C-x u	Undo

Nano

Nano is another handy command-line text editor in Mac OS X. What makes Nano special is that, compared to the others, it is relatively easy to figure out and use. The trade-off is that it lacks some of the more advanced (esoteric) features of Vim or Emacs, and while it's installed by default with Mac OS X (since Tiger), it's not as pervasive as Vim or Emacs.

■**Note** Nano is a clone of the Pico text editor, which is part of the fabulous command-line mail reader Pine. If you've used Pine in the past (or still do), you will find Nano immediately understandable. As an additional bonus, while many UNIX and Linux systems may not have Nano installed, it's just possible that they do have Pine installed, which will mean you may find Pico available where Nano isn't. Before Tiger, OS X included Pico, and today the `pico` command is still there, it's just aliased to `nano`.

One advantage of Nano is that the most common commands along with the keystrokes to invoke them are listed at the bottom of the screen (and the ones that aren't listed are easily looked up with the short yet concise built-in help). While the keystrokes may seem similar to Emacs in practice, the actual keys are different. Also, the common shorthand is different— while in Emacs, Control-X is represented as C-x, in Nano, it's represented ^x (the ^ [caret] symbol means Control).

Opening files in Nano is the same as opening them in Vi or Emacs. Just type `nano filename` at the cursor, and it will open up. Once again, opening the soliloquy, you would see the following:

```
GNU nano 1.2.4    File: Documents/Shakespeare/macbeth/soliloquy4


Tomorrow, and tomorrow, and tomorrow,
Creeps in this petty pace from day to day
To the last syllable of recorded time,
And all our yesterdays have lighted fools
The way to dusty death. Out, out, brief candle!
Life's but a walking shadow, a poor player
That struts and frets his hour upon the stage
And then is heard no more: it is a tale
Told by an idiot, full of sound and fury,
Signifying nothing.
```

```
^G Get Help   ^O WriteOut   ^R Read File ^Y Prev Page ^K Cut Text   ^C Cur Pos
^X Exit       ^J Justify    ^W Where Is  ^V Next Page ^U UnCut Txt ^T To Spell
```

As you can see, at the top of the window Nano identifies the open file, and at the bottom it provides a list of common actions. The action list at the bottom will change based on circumstance—for example, when you go to save a file (using ^o), you will be prompted for the file name you wish to save your file as. The action list will also provide some other saving options (creating a backup, appending this file to another, etc.). With the short help file included with Nano, plus the adaptive action list shown, we're going to forgo the table of commands since it would largely be redundant.

File Permissions and Attributes

File permissions are a central concept found in traditional UNIX systems. They allow one user to share files with everyone else on the system while still maintaining control of those files. The easiest way to view these permissions and attributes is with the `ls -l` command. For example, one line from an `ls -l` command may look like this:

```
-rw-r--r---   1 scott  scott    409 May 17 10:44 soliloquy4
```

The first string of 11 characters represents the permissions. Also of interest here are the file's owner (scott) and the file's group (also scott).

The first ten characters are broken down as follows:

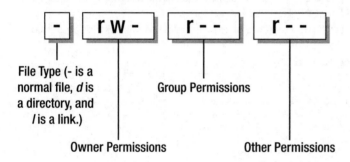

Each of the permissions are r, w, or x, signifying the ability to read, write, or execute (these are often referred to as bits). In the case of a directory, the execute bit signifies the ability to open the directory. The owner of any file can set these permissions as he or she sees fit using the `chmod` command. Additionally, the owner can reset the group the files belong to to any other group the owner belongs to using the `chgrp` command.

The `chmod` command can be used one of two ways to set the permissions (also referred to as setting the mode): either literally or symbolically. The literal way is to specify the permissions as a string of numbers such as the following:

```
chmod nnnn filename
```

where nnnn is the combined value of permissions based on Table 17-7.

■ **Note** The 11th character is special and indicates additional file attributes or security applied to the file. We'll cover this in the "ACLs and Extended File Attributes" section.

Table 17-7. *chmod Literal Number Values*

Value	Description
Basic Permissions	
400	Allows read by owner
200	Allows write by owner
100	Allows execute by owner
040	Allows read by group
020	Allows write by group
010	Allows execute by group
004	Allows read by everyone
002	Allows write by everyone
001	Allows execute by everyone
Advanced Mode Selectors (Optional, and Generally Not Recommended to Use Unless You Really Know What You Are Doing)	
4000	Sets UID on execution bit (execution of file will run with permissions of file's owner)
2000	Sets GID on execution bit (execution of file will run with permissions of file's group)
1000	Sets sticky bit

For example:

```
chmod 755 filename
```

would result in the `filename` having permissions `-rwxr-xr-x`.

The other, symbolic, way of setting permissions is to use `chmod` in the following way:

```
chmod [u][g][o]+/-[r][w][x] filename
```

where u stands for owner, g stands for group, and o stands for other (everyone); followed by + (for adding) or - (for denying) permissions (r, w, and x).

For example, if you had a file with the permissions `-rwxr-xr-x`, but you wanted to allow anyone in its group to also write to the file, you could just use the following:

```
chmod g+w filename
```

This would effectively just add write permissions to the group for `filename`.

Suppose you create a file and then wish to give special permissions to a group of people. By default, any file you create will have both the owner and group listed as you. You can change the group file to any other group that you belong to using the `chgrp` command with the following syntax:

```
chgrp group filename
```

To find out what groups you belong to you (and thus what's available to you), you can use the `id` command, like so:

```
Snow-White:~ scott$ id
uid=501(scott) gid=501(scott) groups=501(scott), 81(appserveradm),
79(appserverusr), 80(admin)
```

So in this case, if you want to allow anyone in the admin group to be able to write to your `soliloquy4` file, you could do the following:

```
Snow-White:~/Documents/Shakespeare/macbeth scott$ chgrp admin soliloquy4
Snow-White:~/Documents/Shakespeare/macbeth scott$ ls -l
total 8
-rw-r--r---   1 scott  admin  409 May 17 10:44 soliloquy4
Snow-White:~/Documents/Shakespeare/macbeth scott$ chmod g+w soliloquy4
Snow-White:~/Documents/Shakespeare/macbeth scott$ ls -l
total 8
-rw-rw-r---   1 scott  admin  409 May 17 10:44 soliloquy4
```

ACLs and Extended File Attributes

ACLs (access control lists) and extended attributes were introduced to OS X in Tiger (OS X 10.4), but while they used to simply be an option available to those who wished to use them, they are now used by default.

Note ACLs will only be available on your system locally if you are using the HFS+ file system. For network shares, they can be used over AFP and SMB/CIFS.

ACLs allow fine-grained control of a file's access far beyond UNIX's traditional owner-group-everyone permissions. With ACLs you can control specific permissions for specific users or groups, and you can treat each user and group differently.

Specifically, each file on your system has one ACL, and each ACL may contain an ordered list of entries. Each entry sets specific permissions for a single user or group.

Note If you have a user and a group with the same name, and you must differentiate these in an ACL, you may prefix the name with either `user:` or `group:` to specify which entity you are referring to.

Files with entries in their ACL will include a + in the 11th character in the permission listing when you use `ls -l`. If there are no ACL entries, but there are other file attributes for the given file, then the 11th character will contain an @. If there are no ACL entries or attributes, then the 11th character will be left off.

To view the ACL associated with a file, use the `-e` option with the `ls` command—for example, here's what one of our home directories looks like:

```
Snow-White:~ scott$ ls -le
total 0
drwx------   2 scott  staff     68 Mar  6 15:48 Autosaved Information
drwx------+ 6 scott  staff    204 Mar 18 19:32 Desktop
 0: group:everyone deny delete
drwx------+ 9 scott  staff    306 Mar  6 16:48 Documents
 0: group:everyone deny delete
drwx------+ 14 scott  staff    476 Mar 15 15:43 Downloads
 0: group:everyone deny delete
drwx------+ 36 scott  staff   1224 Mar 15 15:25 Library
 0: group:everyone deny delete
drwx------+ 4 scott  staff    136 Mar 15 12:33 Movies
 0: group:everyone deny delete
drwx------+ 4 scott  staff    136 Mar 15 12:43 Music
 0: group:everyone deny delete
drwx------+ 6 scott  staff    204 Mar 15 15:46 Pictures
 0: group:everyone deny delete
d---------+ 5 scott  staff    170 Mar  6 08:09 Public
 0: group:everyone deny delete,file_inherit,directory_inherit
 1: user:scott allow list,add_file,search,add_subdirectory,delete_child,readattr,
writeattr,readextattr,writeextattr,readsecurity,file_inherit,directory_inherit
 2: group:staff allow list,search,readattr,readextattr,readsecurity,file_inherit,
directory_inherit
 3: group:everyone allow list,search,readattr,readextattr,readsecurity,file_inherit,
directory_inherit
drwxr-xr-x+ 5 scott  staff    170 Mar  6 08:09 Sites
 0: group:everyone deny delete
drwxr-xr-x  4 scott  staff    136 Mar  7 15:47 bin
```

When you look at the ACLs attached to the default folders in your home directory, you'll see that they are set to deny everyone from deleting them. Don't be afraid to try it; if you try a `rmdir`, you'll get a `Permission Denied` warning, and if you try to drag the folders into the trash, you'll get a warning telling you that that directory can't be modified or deleted.

To view a file's attributes, use the -@ option with ls.

Note Most of the file attributes are strictly there for application and Finder support. You can add your own attributes for whatever reason you want, but for the most part in OS X they are there to support the Finder.

To add entries to or delete entries from an ACL, you use the chmod command with +a (to add an entry) or -a (to remove an entry). When you are adding an entry, the new entry will be added to the ACL. To remove an entry, you need to specify the entry number using # n directives. Here are some examples of working with ACL entries:

```
Snow-White:macbeth scott$ ls -l
total 8
```

```
-rw-r--r--  1 scott  staff  401 Sep  7 07:47 soliloquy4
Snow-White:macbeth scott$ chmod +a "staff deny write,delete" soliloquy4
Snow-White:macbeth scott$ ls -le
total 8
-rw-r--r--+ 1 scott  staff  401 Sep  7 07:47 soliloquy4
 0: group:staff deny write,delete
Snow-White:macbeth scott$ chmod +a "scott allow read,write,delete" soliloquy4
Snow-White:macbeth scott$ chmod +a "nobody deny read,write,delete" soliloquy4
Snow-White:macbeth scott$ ls -le
total 8
-rw-r--r--+ 1 scott  staff  401 Sep  7 07:47 soliloquy4
 0: user:nobody deny read,write,delete
 1: group:staff deny write,delete
 2: user:scott allow read,write,delete
Snow-White:macbeth scott$ chmod -a# 1 soliloquy4
Snow-White:macbeth scott$ ls -le
total 8
-rw-r--r--+ 1 scott  staff  401 Sep  7 07:47 soliloquy4
 0: user:nobody deny read,write,delete
 1: user:scott allow read,write,delete
Snow-White:macbeth scott$
```

The types of actions you can control in ACLs depend on the type of file. The following actions are settable for any file:

- delete
- readattr
- writeattr
- readextattr
- writeextattr
- readsecurity
- writesecurity
- chown

The following actions are settable for folders/directories:

- list
- search
- add_subdirectory
- delete_child

Finally, the following are available for nonfolder/directory items:

- read
- write

- append

- execute

More details about ACLs and controlling them are available in the chmod man page.

Customizing Terminal and the Shell

Once you start getting into using Darwin, you may want to make a few tweaks to both the Terminal application and your shell environment to streamline how you work. Before we leave this chapter, we feel we must cover these last few issues of customizing your Darwin experience.

Terminal Setup

The Terminal application that Apple ships with Mac OS X is a nice, feature-rich application. It includes a number of features such as tabbed windows, which are handy for those who work with multiple shells or must access many remote terminals at the same time. It also includes the ability to save different window settings that control the appearance and behavior of your terminal.

One of the first things you may want to do when working with Terminal is adjust how it looks and make a few other tweaks (such as remapping the Meta key if you are a big Emacs user). The options to control your terminal settings are listed under the Settings tab of Terminal's preferences (Figure 17-3).

Figure 17-3. *The Settings tab of Terminal's preferences*

The Terminal settings preferences provide a number of different possible terminal settings listed in the column on the left. In the preferences, you can set options for each setting individually using the five tabs: Text, Window, Shell, Keyboard, and Advanced.

The Text settings control the font size face and colors. They also allow you to set the options for the terminal's cursor.

The Window tab allows you to set options for controlling the background color, title bar information, initial window size (set in character width and line height), and scrollback buffer.

The Shell tab allows you to set special shell startup commands as well as options about what happens when you exit the shell or try to close the window while a shell is still running.

The Keyboard tab allows you to set up key bindings, and it lets you toggle the option to use the Option key as the Meta key.

The Advanced tab allows you to set a few other miscellaneous options pertaining to terminal emulation, bell actions, and text encoding options for foreign languages.

The other main Terminal preference tabs include the Startup tab, which allows you to select the default settings to use when Terminal launches, as well as what type of shell Terminal should use upon launching; the Window Groups tab, which allows you to save the behavior of multiple Terminal windows together as a group; and the Encodings tab, which allows you to select which text encoding should be made available to Terminal's settings.

Setting Up Your Shell Environment

Every shell has what is referred to as an environment, which is basically made up of customized variables and commands that make the shell work the way you want it to. The Bash shell stores this info in a number of places. The variables that apply to everyone are stored in /etc/profile and /etc/bashrc. Additionally, you can make your own personal configurations to ~/.bashrc and ~/.bash_profile. As a general rule, things that affect your environment should go in the .bash_profile file, and things that affect the shell specifically should go in the .bashrc file.

Note Traditionally, things in the profile files would get read when you logged into a terminal, and things in the bashrc files would get read each time you launched a new shell. This isn't exactly how these things work anymore, but it's still nice to keep the content of each separate.

One common environmental variable that you may want to set is the $PATH variable. The $PATH variable describes where your shell will look for executables when you attempt to launch one from the command line. By default, your $PATH is set to include /bin, /sbin, /usr/bin, /usr/sbin, /usr/local/bin, and /usr/X11/bin (in the /etc/profile file). However, if you begin to install new executables, or even write your own, you may find that you need to add additional directories to your $PATH. The syntax to add a directory to the $PATH is as follows:

```
$PATH=/new/directory:/another/new/direcotry:"${PATH}"
```

■**Note** Whether you add your own paths before or after the default $PATH is significant, since each path in $PATH is checked in order. When you enter a command, the first match found will execute.

You can add as many directories as you need, separated by a colon. The "${PATH}" at the end represents your existing path; without it, any of the default $PATH directories will be removed from your $PATH. To have your path updated each time you launch a shell, it's best just to put this info in your .bash_profile. For example, the common .bash_profile may look like this:

```
###  .bash_profile  ###

# a good place for environmental variables #

### $PATH ###

if [ -d /usr/local/bin ] ; then
      PATH=/usr/local/bin:"${PATH}"
fi
if [ -d /usr/local/mysql/bin ] ; then
      PATH=/usr/local/mysql/bin:"${PATH}"
fi
if [ -d ~/bin ] ; then
      PATH=~/bin:"${PATH}"
fi
if [ -d /opt/local/bin ] ; then
      PATH=/opt/local/bin:"${PATH}"
fi


### include .bashrc if one exists ###
if [ -f ~/.bashrc ]; then
      . ~/.bashrc
fi
```

Any line beginning with # is a comment. Here some of the built-in scripting functionality is used to check if common executable directories exist—if they do, then they are automatically added to the $PATH.

The last part checks to see if the .bashrc file is present, and if it is, it includes that as well.

The .bashrc files generally contain variables and commands that are specific to the shell. For example, the default /etc/bashrc file sets the prompt variable. Other things that are generally included in the bashrc files are common aliases and shell functions.

For example, a .bashrc file may contain the following:

```
###   .bashrc file   ###

#  This file is for shell-specific stuff                         #
#  $PATH and other env variables should go in the .bash_profile  #
```

```
### aliases ###

alias ls="ls -FG"
alias la="ls -FGA"
alias ll="ls -FGAl"

### functions ###

function pman() {
    man -t "${1}" | open -f -a /Applications/Preview.app/
}
```

Again, the lines that begin with # are comments.

Creating Commands with Aliases and Functions

The preceding sample .bashrc file shows a few aliases and a function. Essentially, these are both
ways to create simple command-line commands that carry out more complex commands. In
general, an alias is a way of creating a shortened version of a single command, while a function
creates a command out of an actual shell script that may consist of many commands and simple
logic.

Aliases are incredibly handy when you find you are using the same commands over and
over and want to simplify them; you can even use them to essentially overwrite the default
behavior of a command. Take the first alias listed previously:

```
alias ls="ls -FG"
```

This command creates the ls alias from the ls -FG command, effectively overwriting ls
so that it will, by default, provide colored output and the benefits of the -F flag as well. The
other two aliases in the previous .bashrc file example also create aliases to other common ls
options.

■**Note** You can create aliases at the command line using the alias command as well—however, if you
don't save these to your .bashrc file, they will be gone once you exit that particular shell.

Functions, on the other hand, are more complex, as they are essentially simple shell
scripts. Here's an example from the preceding .bashrc file:

```
function pman() {
    man -t "${1}" | open -f -a /Applications/Preview.app/
}
```

The first line defines pman as a function accessible from the command line, and everything
between the curly braces defines what happens when we use the pman command. So, if you were
to enter pman ls at the command line, the function would take the first argument, ls, and run
man -t ls | open -f -a /Applications/Preview.app/, thus allowing you to simply open the
man page of any command in the Preview application in one simple command.

Summary

Whew, there was lots of info in this chapter. While the aim wasn't to teach you everything about working with Darwin (which would be an entire book in itself, just to scratch the surface), hopefully you now know enough to get around comfortably in Darwin, and more importantly, have a good base to build upon where you see fit. We will be using the info in this chapter to build upon in various upcoming parts of this book, beginning with the next chapter, where we will take a quick look at adding to the abilities of Darwin by creating our own simple scripts and adding new programs from other sources.

CHAPTER 18

■ ■ ■

Extending the Power of Darwin

After the previous chapter, we hope you are at least somewhat comfortable working at the command line. In this chapter, we'll move on and show how to extend the power of Darwin by covering the following:

- An introduction to shell scripting

- An overview of Perl, Python, and Ruby, which are three powerful scripting languages included with Snow Leopard

- How to find and install a range of additional applications using MacPorts and Fink

- How to custom-compile a Darwin application from the source code

Getting Started with Shell Scripting

Shell scripting has been a staple in Unix since the first shell was launched. In its most basic form, a shell script allows you to add a series of shell commands to a file so that these commands can be easily run over and over. You can see an example of the value of this by examining the startup process of Snow Leopard. During the startup, the shell script /etc/rc.common is started; this file begins a series of processes that effectively start up, configure, and maintain many of the necessary OS and networking functions that occur during startup.

■Note The rc.common file is a holdover from previous versions of OS X and has a strong Unix heritage. Beginning with Mac OS X 10.4 Tiger, Apple introduced launchd, a startup daemon that standardizes the way processes start on OS X. With Snow Leopard, most of the old rc, xinit, and initd startup systems are gone or are no longer used very much, and it's likely that in future updates to Mac OS X they will be gone completely.

Writing a shell script can be as easy as just listing a series of any of the commands you may enter at the command line; however, shell scripts can also accept external variables and may contain simple if...then logic and loops. We'll briefly explain all of these things, but first let's take a look at a sample shell script (the line numbers are for reference and shouldn't be typed into your script):

```
 1:  #!/bin/sh
 2:
 3:  # togglevis
 4:  # A shell script to toggle the visibility of hidden files in the Finder
 5:
 6:  set `ps acx | grep Finder`
 7:
 8:  show=`defaults read com.apple.finder AppleShowAllFiles`
 9:
10:  if [ $show -eq 1 ]; then
11:      defaults write com.apple.finder AppleShowAllFiles 0
12:      kill $1
13:  else
14:      defaults write com.apple.finder AppleShowAllFiles 1
15:      kill $1
16:  fi
```

Note For those of you who really hate line numbers in programs because they prevent you from copying the text out of an e-book and running it, later in this chapter there will be a Perl script that you should be able to tweak (when you are done with this chapter) to strip them out automatically.

This handy script will toggle the visibility of hidden items in the Mac OS X Finder, which is done by setting the hidden Finder preference AppleShowAllFiles to 1 (to show all files) or 0 (to hide hidden files) and then restarting the Finder to immediately enact the change.

Note Truth be told, this script doesn't restart the Finder. The script instead just kills the Finder, and since OS X depends on the Finder, it will automatically restart it.

The first line, #!/bin/sh, often referred to as the *interpreter line,* is important for all scripts because it points the shell to the executing script interpreter. This is often referred to as the *shebang line* for the #! combination that begins it. (The # resembles a musical sharp, so "sharp" + "bang" for the ! = "shebang.")

Note Most shell scripts in OS X (and generally in Unix) were traditionally written for the Bourne shell (sh) for compatibility across various Unix platforms (of which almost all have the Bourne shell installed). The Bash shell itself (a.k.a. Bourne Again SHell) is 100 percent backward compatible with the Bourne shell, with some extra features borrowed from the C shell and Korn shell. The general scripting syntax we are covering in this chapter is mostly Bourne shell compatible; however, there may be certain commands issued inside a script that are specific to OS X.

Note There is no Bourne shell by default in Mac OS X; rather, /bin/sh is actually a Bash executable.

Lines 3 and 4, like all script lines beginning with # (except the shebang line), are comments. These are included to provide a clue about what's going on for anyone reading the script. Comments have no effect on how the script runs and in this respect are purely optional elements. It is a good habit to use comments, not only for others who may be looking at your script but also for yourself should you have to look at a script weeks, months, or even years after you wrote it. Here the first comment line gives the name of the script, and the second comment describes what the script does.

Line 6 shows us two things, the use of the set command and the use of backticks (`) in scripts. In a shell script, anything within backticks is executed, and the result is passed to the script (this is called *command substitution*). The set command sets the arguments used in the script just as if they were entered at the command line. So, line 6 takes the results from the ps acx | grep Finder command (which would be something like 261 ?? S   0:00.93 Finder) and makes them our arguments (of which there would be 5). The importance of line 6 for the rest of the script is that it specifically assigns the PID of the Finder to our first argument that can then be accessed as the variable $1.

Line 8 sets the variable show to the result of the defaults read com.apple.finder AppleShowAllFiles command. defaults provides a way to access and alter Mac OS X user default settings from the command line. In this case, we use it to read the AppleShowAllFiles value stored in the com.apple.finder preference to determine the existing setting (0 or 1) so we can then toggle the setting. If the AppleShowAllFiles value doesn't exist yet in your Finder preference file, you will get an error similar to this:

```
2007-06-26 12:24:00.175 defaults[1180]
The domain/default pair of (com.apple.finder, AppleShowAllFiles) does not exist
togglevis.sh: line 10: [: ==: unary operator expected
```

In this case you can ignore this, since the script will continue and actually create this value. However, if you continue to get errors after this (or if you get a vastly different error), then something else is wrong, and you should check your script closely.

Lines 10 through 16 provide a conditional if...then...else statement and provide the expected actions based on the condition. First, in line 10 we check to see whether the show variable (which is the set value of com.apple.finder AppleShowAllFiles) is 1; if it is, then we move on to line 11 where we change com.apple.finder AppleShowAllFiles to 0. Then in line 12 we kill the Finder using $1, which we set in line 6. If the condition in line 10 is false (the show variable is not 1), then we move on to the else part of the script, and in line 14 we set com.apple.finder AppleShowAllFiles to 1 and then kill the Finder. Line 16 ends the if...then...else statement with fi (that's if backward).

The script ends when it runs out of things to do.

There are a few ways to run this script: one is to pass the script to the shell executable as an argument, and the other is to make the actual script executable. Passing the script as an argument to the shell looks like this:

```
Snow-Leopard:~/bin scott$ sh togglevis
```

If you want to have access to the script easily from anywhere, though, you must first make the script executable and make sure it's in a directory that is included in your $PATH (as discussed in the previous chapter). For example, we've placed this file in our own bin directory, which you can see is set in our path with the following statement:

```
Snow-Leopard:~/bin scott$ echo $PATH
/opt/local/bin:/Users/scott/bin:/usr/local/bin:/bin:/sbin:/usr/bin:/usr/sbin
```

To make it executable, we use the chmod command:

```
Snow-Leopard:~/bin scott$ chmod u+x togglevis
```

Now provided the script is in your path, you can use togglevis as you would any command from the command line.

Variables

Variables in shell scripts are generally reserved for use from within the script itself unless they are explicitly exported as environmental variables. Environment variables (which include things like $PATH) are variables that are available to all shell scripts and programs, where shell variables are available only within your script.

Setting a variable is quite easy; just create a variable name, and set its value like this:

```
aVariable=Value
```

■**Note** The possible names a variable can have are virtually endless, but there are some rules. First, although the name can contain letters, numbers, or underscores, it's best that they begin with a letter (and they can't begin with a number, since that is reserved for command-line argument variables). Second, variables obviously can't share a name with a reserved word, which is one of the many words that have special meaning to the shell. Finally, by convention, environmental variables are often written with all capital letters, and shell variables are traditionally written in all lowercase letters, but of late many people use CamelCase, which starts out lowercase but uses a capital letter where a new word begins. An example of camel casing is aVeryLongVariable.

■**Note** Here's a list of standard shell reserved words (separated by spaces): ! case do done elif else esac fi for function if in select then until while { } time [[ ]].

It is important not to include spaces around the = when declaring your variables; if you do, you will get an error.

If you want to make your variable an environmental variable, then you must export it using the export command. Usually this is done immediately after the variable is declared, which can be done all on one line like this:

```
ENVVAR=Value; export ENVVAR
```

After the shell exports the variable, it will be immediately available for any program or shell script until the parent shell process exits. (In other words, every time you launch a new shell, you will need to redeclare and export the variable to use it again.) If you are planning on using an environmental variable over and over, it may be best to declare it in your `.bash_profile` file so it gets declared each time you launch your terminal or a shell.

Argument Variables

Some of the most commonly used variables are ones you don't need to declare at all. These are variables passed to the script as arguments from the command line when the script is called. For example, if you were to run an executable script called `ascript`, you could pass arguments to the script when you call it, like this:

```
Snow-Leopard:~ scott$ ascript arg1 arg2 arg3
```

Here the `arg1`, `arg2`, and `arg3` values are automatically assigned to variables $1, $2, and $3 so they can be used as needed in the script.

■**Note** In many computer languages, counting begins with 0, not 1. Command-line arguments in scripts are no exception. In scripts, $0 is always the script itself and will return the complete path name of the executed script.

These special variables don't have to be passed in from the command line, though. Occasionally it may be advantageous to create and control these arguments from within the script. This can be done by using the `set` command (as we did in our example shell script earlier). The `set` command will replace all command-line arguments with the arguments provided.

■**Note** `set` is a fairly complex command in Bash with lots of different capabilities. If you use `set` alone on the command line, it will list every environmental variable and function available to you in a nice, readable format. Used with options, `set` allows you to toggle many shell attributes. If you are interested, the gory details of all the possibilities for this command begin on page 51 of the Bash man page and continue until about three-quarters of the way through page 53. Also of note, `set` behaves differently in other shells; for example, in `csh` you would use `set` in place of `export` to create environmental variables. You can find a brief description of the `set` built-in as it relates to Bash at `http://www.gnu.org/software/bash/manual/html_node/The-Set-Builtin.html`.

Command Substitution

Another way to assign a variable is through command substitution. This allows you to work with the result of any shell command by enclosing the command with backticks (the ` charac-ter below the Esc key on most Mac keyboards). This allows you to take advantage of any shell command, making up for most of the shell's natural shortcomings. For example, the Bourne shell doesn't have built-in capabilities for simple arithmetic; however, using command substitution, you can take advantage of command-line executables that do this for you anyway, like this:

```
#!/bin/sh
x=2
y=3
z=`expr $x + $y`
echo $z
```

This little script uses the expr executable to do the math for you and then prints 5, which is what you'd expect.

■**Note**   The Bash shell actually does have built-in arithmetic capability facilitated by the let built-in, so if you were so inclined, you could replace the z=`expr $x + $y` line with let z=$x+$y and get the same results. (let specifically carries out arithmetic operations on variables.)

Controlling the Flow

The ability to control the flow of a script makes it much more adaptable and useful. There are two primary ways to control the flow of a script: conditionals, which will execute commands if certain conditions are met, and loops, which can repeat commands over and over a predetermined number of times.

Conditional Statements

Two common conditional statements are available in shell scripts: if statements and case statements. An if statement checks to see whether a condition is true or false. If the condition is true, then a block of code is run; if it is false, an else block is run (if else exists; otherwise, nothing else happens in the block). The whole thing looks something like this:

```
if [ condition ]
then
    condition is met block
else
    condition not met block
fi
```

The fi at the end signals the end of the if statement.

One other thing that can be added to respond to multiple conditions is the elif (else-if) condition. This allows you to create logic like this:

```
if [ condition1 ]
then
    condition1 block
elif [ condition2 ]
    condition2 block
elif [ condition3 ]
...
else
    no conditions met block
fi
```

One thing to keep in mind is that once the condition is met, the script will execute that block and then exit the if block entirely, so if condition1 is met, the script will not check for condition2 or run the code in that block.

There are a number of ways to create conditional statements; one of the most common is to use a mathematical test condition as listed in Table 18-1 (the Bash alternate expressions will work only with Bash and not a traditional Bourne shell).

Table 18-1. *Mathematic Test Expressions for sh and Bash*

Expression (sh)	Bash Alternate	Result
$x -eq $y	$x == $y	True if $x is equal to $y
$x -ne $y	$x != $y	True if $x is not equal to $y
$x -lt $y	$x < $y	True if $x is less than $y
$x -gt $y	$x > $y	True if $x is greater than $y
$x -le $y	$x <= $y	True if $x is less than or equal to $y
$x -ge $y	$x >= $y	True if $x is greater than or equal to $y

Another common conditional statement is to check on the existence of a file or directory. This is especially handy if you are creating workflow or other scripts that interact with the file system. An if statement that checks for the existence of a particular file would look like this:

```
if [ -e /path/to/file ]
then
    If file exists do this
else
    If file doesn't exist do this
fi
```

Here the -e option checks for the existence of the file. Table 18-2 lists some possible options.

Table 18-2. *Common Options for Testing File Attributes in Shell Scripts*

Option	Result
-e file	True if the file exists at all
-f file	True if file exists and it is a regular file
-d file	True if file exists and it is a directory
-r file	True if file exists and it is readable
-w file	True if file exists and it is writeable
-x file	True if file exists and it is executable

Note In the Unix landscape where everything in the file system *is* a file, a regular file is most easily defined by what it isn't. Specifically, it's not a *block special file*, a *character special file*, a *directory file*, a *pipe*, a *FIFO special file*, a *symbolic link*, or a *socket*. Those are special files, while regular files (which generally contain binary or text data) are, well, not special.

It is also possible to test multiple conditions using logical and/or statements. This allows you to check either whether multiple statements are all true or whether one of many statements is true. This is done using either && or || (that's the long bar over the \ key) between the conditions. [condition1] && [condition2] will return true if both conditions are true, while [condition1] || [condition2] will return true if either condition is true.

One final common conditional is to utilize the exit status of a command. Every command you run will provide an exit status; that's usually a 0 if everything ran as expected and some other number if something special happened. Using the special $? variable (which contains the exit status of the last command), you can do some interesting stuff. For example, if we wanted to periodically see whether a user was running any processes on our computer, we could use the following:

```
#!/bin/sh

ps U scott >> /dev/null

if [ $? = 0 ];
then
    echo "Scott is working on something."
else
    echo "Scott's not doing anything here right now"
fi
```

The ps U scott >> /dev/null command simply lists all the processes being run by the user scott. Since we are not interested in the output of the command (just the exit status), we send the output to /dev/null. If there are any processes, the exit status will be 0. If the user doesn't exist or the user isn't running any processes, the exit status will be 1 (different commands may provide different exit statuses for different reasons). Although this example was fairly simple, with a few tweaks it could do some more interesting things. For example, if we replaced the user scott with the user www, we could check to see whether the default Apache web server was running. If it's not, we could use the else block to restart it.

Another way of dealing with multiple potential conditions is the use of the case statement. A case statement looks at a variable and responds differently depending on its value.

A case statement is generally much easier to use then an if statement; however, it's a viable alternative only if you are dealing with multiple similar outcomes that may be stored in a singe variable. For example, if we wanted to check for different exit statuses using a case statement, we could write the following:

```
#!/bin/sh
shutdown
case $? in
    0) echo "Returned 0: The command executed successfully...goodbye.  ;;
    1) echo "Returned 1: The command or shell returned an error." ;;
    127) echo "Returned 127: The command couldn't be found." ;;
    *) echo "* is a wildcard, I'm not sure what happened" ;;
esac
```

As you can see, using case you can easily check for and respond to many different outcomes.

Loops

Now that you've learned a bit about how to selectively run or not run a command based on a condition, we will cover how you can run a command over and over with loops. There are three main types of loops for shell scripting: while, until, and for loops.

The while and until loops are similar in idea, but they do the opposite in practice. Each of them takes a condition (similar to the if statement); however, where the while loop will run a block of code as long as the condition is true, the until loop will run as long as the condition is false.

■**Caution** Poorly written loops can have the adverse effect of running forever. If you are running a script from the command line, it's easy enough to stop such a runaway script with Control-C, but if this is part of a background or startup script, things can get more complicated. Therefore, it's a good idea to test your scripts from the command line before you place them in startup files and such.

A simple while loop could look like this:

```
#!/bin/sh
x=1
while [ $x -le 10 ]
do
    echo $x
```

```
    x=`expr $x + 1`
done
```

This script will simply go through the `while` loop, printing the value of $x and then increasing the value of x by 1 as long as the value of $x is equal to or less than 10. If we switched `while` to `until`, the loop would skip entirely since our declared value of x (1) would immediately be less than or equal to 10.

■**Note** Like `if` statements, `while` and `until` loops can also evaluate multiple conditions using logical and (&&) and or (||) statements.

The other common loop is the `for` loop. Rather than relying on a true/false condition like the `while` and `until` loops, a `for` loop iterates over all the elements in a list. For example, a simple script to echo back the command-line arguments could look like this:

```
#!/bin/sh

echo "The command line arguments given to $0 are: "
for x in $@
do
    echo $x
done
```

■**Note** When you run the previous script, any arguments you add will be echoed back to you. So, if you run it, make sure to add some.

■**Note** $@ is a special variable that contains each command-line argument together in a single variable.

You may find that there is situation where you need to get out of a loop before it completes, which is accomplished with either the `break` or `continue` command. The `break` command will immediately stop the current loop pass and exit the loop process entirely (that is, the script will continue immediately following the loop). The `continue` command will cause a halt in the current pass through the loop but will continue the loop process if the conditions are still met.

Input and Output

Many scripts you write will need to provide output, and often you may want a script to prompt for input as well. In the previous chapter, you learned most of the basics you need in order to output text either to the terminal or to a file using the `echo` command (with redirection if you want to write the output to a file), but there is also the `printf` command that provides more options in how your output is presented. To get information into a script, you can use the read command, which will provide a prompt at the command line for input.

The following script (enhanced from previously) shows how read and printf work (line numbers have been added for reference):

```
 1:  #!/bin/sh
 2:
 3:  printf "Please enter your input here: "
 4:  read input
 5:  set $input
 6:  c=$#
 7:  printf "You entered the following: "
 8:  for x in $@
 9:  do
10:  c=`expr $c - 1`
11:      if [ $c -gt 0 ]
12:      then
13:          printf "\"$x\", "
14:      else
15:          printf "and \"$x\".\n"
16:      fi
17:  done
```

When you run this script, you get something along the lines of this:

```
Please enter your input here: hello goodbye dogcow
You entered the following: "hello", "goodbye", and "dogcow".
```

The first thing you may notice is that unlike the echo command, printf does not automatically add a linefeed to each statement. By using printf in line 3, the prompt for the read statement appears on the same line rather than the line below.

The read statement is on line 4, and it's fairly easy: the read command followed by a variable to contain our input (cleverly called input).

In line 5 we set the input as our primary script arguments.

Line 6 starts a counter and starts it with $#, which is a special variable that tells the total number of arguments assigned by set in line 5.

Line 7 provides some text for our output.

Line 8 begins a for loop that will iterate through each of the arguments set in line 5. The $@ is another one of those special variables that contains all of our arguments in a single variable. In this case, $@ and $input will contain the same values.

Line 9 starts the for loop.

Line 10 decreases the value of our counter by 1.

Line 11 uses an if statement to see whether our counter, c, is greater than 0. The counter is set up so that when it hits 0, the loop will be on our final input argument, so we continue the loop on line 13 until we reach the last of our inputs and then switch over to line 15.

Line 13 uses the printf statement to print one of our arguments surrounded by quotes. To get the quote to print, rather than get interpreted as the closing or opening of the text we are printing, we need to escape the ". We do this by preceding the quote symbol with a backslash (\). printf knows a number of these formatting escape characters (which are actually borrowed from the C programming language) and will automatically expand them into their proper form when printing. Table 18-3 lists the common escape characters.

Table 18-3. *Escape Character Expansion*

Escape Character	Name	Output Result
\a	Alert (bell)	Activates the terminal's bell. Depending on your Terminal preferences (set on the Advanced tab of the Terminal Inspector), this will either flash the terminal screen or make an audible noise (or both or neither). By default the terminal window will flash.
\b	Backspace	Moves the cursor back one space.
\f	Form feed	Clears the screen. Traditionally this would eject the current sheet of paper and start a new sheet.
\n	Newline	Moves the input to the beginning of the next line, like hitting Return.
\r	Carriage return	Moves the cursor back to the beginning of the current line; any further input would overwrite what's already there.
\t	Tab	Moves the cursor one tab space to the right.
\v	Vertical tab	Moves the cursor down one line; however, unlike \n, it will not return to the beginning of the line.
\\	Backslash	Prints the backslash character.
\'	Single quote	Prints a single quote character.
\"	Double quote	Prints a double quote character.

If our counter is set up properly (and there aren't any other glitches in our script), line 15 will run on the last of our input values, also printing it surrounded by quotes, but then instead of placing a comma (as if to continue the list), it will print out a . and then a newline character.

Line 16 then ends the if statement, and line 17 ends the loop and thus our little script.

One thing not shown here is that the read command can actually assign different variables to the input, where, for example, each input value would be assigned its own variable . . . well, that is if we assume that the number of variables and the number of words are the same. If we had the following read statement:

```
read a b c
```

and entered this:

```
one two three
```

then $a would be assigned the value one, $b would be assigned the value two, and $c would be assigned the value three. In the event we set read to accept three variables and we get four or more input terms, the last read variable will absorb all the remaining values.

■**Tip** If the integrity of your `read` variables is important and you want to protect against additional input, you could assign an additional `read` variable to suck up all the extra data. So, if you really wanted only three input values, you could set up `read` with four variables and then just use the first three, thus essentially ignoring all the excess input.

One final useful related tidbit is the ability to merge an entire file into a script. This is done quite easily with the dot (that is, period) command. If you paid attention, you saw this in our sample `.bash_profile` file toward the end of the previous chapter where we used this:

```
if [ -f ~/.bashrc ]; then
        . ~/.bashrc
fi
```

Here we first check to see whether our desired file (`.bashrc`) exists and is a normal file. If so, we include it with the `. ~/.bashrc`. And that's it. This is a handy way to create complex scripts where you can write entire parts as separate files and then include them all together to effectively run as one.

■**Caution** If you do combine scripts together, be careful with your variables. If two different script files use the same variable names and are then included together, unexpected (often bad) things can happen since the values of the named variable may get unexpectedly changed.

Advanced Scripting with Perl, Python, and Ruby

Shell scripting is very useful and fairly powerful for many things; however, there are a number of languages more powerful than the shell for writing scripts. Snow Leopard comes with three of the biggest and most powerful scripting languages in use today: Perl, Python, and Ruby. Given the breadth of these languages (which are often referred to as *interpreted programming languages* or *very high-level languages* [VHLLs], rather than just scripting languages), it would be impossible to properly teach you how to use them in all their glory in this chapter. Although these languages are fairly easy to learn to use (some perhaps more so than others), the space (and time) needed to cover all of this goes beyond what is available in this book. Still, for those of you who are familiar with these or those of you looking to expand your programming repertoire, we would be remiss not to talk a bit about these languages and how they work within OS X.

Each of these languages shares a number of benefits vs. more traditional compiled languages such as C, C++, Objective-C, and Java, including ease of use, portability, and immediate feedback (since there is no compilation). Since they are scripting languages, all you need to write them is a text editor, and each of these languages is free and well supported across a wide range of platforms and devices. The other side of this coin is that interpreted languages such as Perl, Python, and Ruby (and shell scripts, for that matter) have a few disadvantages vs. their compiled brethren: they lack the performance of a well-optimized compiled program; they are not as well suited for low-level programming tasks; and if you choose to distribute your script, you are also revealing all your source code, which makes scripting languages less inviting for commercial applications.

■**Note** Performance is a tricky matter. Although a well-optimized compiled program will always outperform an interpreted program (at least on the initial execution of the program), because of caching, the advanced subsequent execution of interpreted programs can easily match that of the compiled programs. Additionally, because of hardware advances, the real-time difference between the two is rapidly diminishing (though never quite reaching equality). Interestingly, certain programming technologies such as Java and some .NET technologies are both compiled and interpreted. This could lead one to assume that these would share the faults of both compiled and interpreted languages such as added development complexity and time and less than optimal performance. Although this may be true, they also gain a few benefits such as portability and source code obfuscation. (That's not to say that if a language can be portable, it actually is.)

Perl

Perl (which stands for Practical Extraction and Report Language) is currently the leading interpreted language used today (though Python and Ruby have been gaining on it over the past few years). Perl, as its name seems to imply, was initially designed to work with large chunks of text: to read in information and to parse it and/or manipulate it in meaningful ways. Thus, when the World Wide Web came into being with all of its marked-up text, Perl, combined with CGI, was uniquely suited to work with all of this data and manipulate it in fun, interesting, and useful ways. As a web language, Perl's popularity began to grow rapidly.

As a language, one of Perl's greatest assets, and also one of its greatest weaknesses, is its fantastic flexibility. It prides itself on providing multiple ways to solve any given task—Perl's motto is T.M.T.O.W.T.D.I. ("There's More Then One Way To Do It"). In the hands of a skilled programmer, this flexibility can unleash wonderful things, but it can also create a lot of unintelligible, unmaintainable code (thus giving Perl the unflattering reputation of a "write-only" language). The truth is that although Perl allows you to write some very ugly code, you can also write very clean, understandable code in Perl. Most important, though, when you have a problem, Perl usually can provide a way to solve it. For example, let's say we wanted to simplify numbering lines in source code (you know, because we're writing a book and sometimes it's nice to refer to line numbers). Rather than going through each code listing and manually entering numbers, we could easy whip together the following script in Perl:

```perl
#!/usr/bin/perl -w

foreach my $file ( @ARGV ) {
    my $n = 0;
    open (OFILE, $file) || die "Sorry, $file can't be opened: $!";
    open (NFILE, ">num_$file");
    while ( <OFILE> ) {
        $n++;
        print NFILE sprintf("%3d: ",$n), $_;
    }
}
```

```
    close OFILE;
    close NFILE;
}
```

This script allows us to enter any number of scripts as arguments at the command line, and it will go through each one of them numbering every line and formatting the output back into another file with the same name prefixed with num. If we ran this script on itself, we'd get this:

```
 1: #!/usr/bin/perl -w
 2:
 3: foreach my $file ( @ARGV ) {
 4:     my $n = 0;
 5:     open (OFILE, $file) || die "Sorry, $file can't be opened: $!";
 6:     open (NFILE, ">num_$file");
 7:     while ( <OFILE> ) {
 8:         $n++;
 9:         print NFILE sprintf("%3d: ",$n), $_;
10:     }
11:     close OFILE;
12:     close NFILE;
13: }
```

One other fantastic feature of Perl, which may be its ultimate strength, is that because of its maturity, it has built up a large collection of code libraries (called *Perl modules*) that can help you solve almost any task you can think of. Additionally, it has created a system around these libraries, the Comprehensive Perl Archive Network (CPAN), that provides an effective way of accessing these modules for your code. For the OS X user, included in CPAN are a number of modules for using Perl to manipulate Apple applications such as iTunes and iPhoto, as well as for accessing Apple Events from Perl and more.

For the ultimate in OS X/Perl programming, the Camel Bones project (http://camelbones.sourceforge.net/index.html) brings together a range of OS X/Perl–specific libraries, frameworks, and modules, allowing you to perform tasks such as create Aqua interfaces for Perl scripts and use Perl instead of Objective-C in Cocoa applications.

Snow Leopard ships with version 5.10.0 of Perl, which, as of this writing, is the latest official version of Perl. Somewhere on the horizon is Perl 6, a complete rewrite of Perl that promises not only a new and improved interpreter but also many updates to the language. For more information about Perl, the best place to start is the official web site: www.perl.org. If you'd like a book on Perl and you are completely new to programming, we recommend *Beginning Perl, Second Edition* by James Lee (Apress, ISBN 1590593912), which, despite being the same publisher as this book, we had nothing to do with. For a slower, gentler introduction, try *Teach Yourself Perl in 24, Third Edition* by Clinton Pierce (Sams Publishing, ISBN 0672327937), which, despite being from a different publisher, one of us had a hand in editing.

Python

Python, although not as well known as Perl, has been around for almost as long, but while Perl got to ride on the web wave because of its text-processing abilities, Python, being designed as a general-purpose scripting language, was often overlooked. Because of its more general-purpose beginnings, in many areas, especially surrounding math and science, Python was just the thing developers needed.

Python possesses a number of features that differentiate itself from Perl. First, Python was designed as an object-oriented scripting language (Perl gained reasonable object-oriented capabilities in version 5; however, on the whole, Perl is still used very much as a procedural programming language). Second, unlike Perl, Python script writing style is very strict. Proper indentation of code, whitespace, and line breaks have specific, essential meaning to Python. This often makes existing Python code much easier to understand than most Perl code, but dictating a strict style has also caused a few issues through Python's evolution (and of course has caused a few "free thinking" individuals to shun the language).

Python has been around on the Mac for a while (beginning with MacPython even before OS X). Today, like Perl, it's a standard part of Darwin. Unlike Perl, Python is developed as a framework, rather than a traditional Darwin application, making Python available for Cocoa programming as well as Darwin development right out of the box.

Learning Python is fairly easy with lots of books and online tutorials available. One of the best places to start is the Python tutorial at http://docs.python.org/tut/. One nice part about learning Python is that it comes with its own interactive interpreter, which will start when you type python at the command line without arguments. Not only is this a great tool for learning the language, but it can be very handy for unleashing the power of Python for common tasks. We use the Python interpreter all the time as a calculator (we find it much faster and more flexible to use than the GUI calculator for most things). A session with the Python interpreter could look like this:

```
Snow-Leopard:~ scott$ python
Python 2.6.1 (r261:67515, Feb 18 2009, 19:11:02)
[GCC 4.2.1 (Apple Inc. build 5641)] on darwin
Type "help", "copyright", "credits" or "license" for more information.
>>> x=2
>>> for y in range(11):
...     y*x
...
0
2
4
6
8
10
12
14
16
18
20
>>>
```

> **Note** Remember, Python uses tabs to indent code, not spaces. In the previous code sample, there is a singe tab between the first . . . and y*x. There is simply a hard return after the second . . . .

As you may surmise from this, you can accomplish a lot of stuff with very little code. Once programmers learn the nuances of Python, they generally find themselves creating code at a significantly faster pace than with most other languages.

Ruby

Ruby is the new kid in the family, but it's making quite a showing, largely because of the buzz surrounding Ruby on Rails (RoR). RoR, which is included in Snow Leopard, is a very nice web application framework written in Ruby. Ruby shares many similarities with Python in general and on Snow Leopard. Both are object oriented (in Ruby everything becomes an object), both are relatively easy to pick up, and both include an interactive interpreter for playing around with code (Ruby's interactive interpreter is not built into the language in the same way that Python's is; to get to the Ruby interactive interpreter, you use the `irb` command). For OS X developers, the most important similarity is that they are both compiled as Cocoa frameworks, which makes them available for Cocoa development as well as Darwin development. Despite the similarities, Ruby is different from Python most noticeably semantically but also syntactically.

Because Ruby is a newer language, it seems to have learned to avoid a number of issues and perhaps shortcomings that Perl and Python have had, while at the same time incorporating new ideas that weren't mature when Perl and Python were conceived. On the other hand, because of its relative newness, Ruby has not been tested as much as Perl or Python and as such may not be as hardened as them. For example, there are those who think Ruby does not scale (in a performance sense) as well as Perl or Python.

> **Note** Much of the performance talk about Ruby may be because, in the past, its use on a large scale was fairly limited. Today, you need only point to Twitter or Hulu to see that Ruby can in fact scale quite well, and as it matures, we can imagine it improving in this area.

To learn more about Ruby in general, check out *Beginning Ruby* by Peter Cooper (Apress, ISBN: 1590597664). If you are looking for specifics on developing Ruby Cocoa applications, documentation is included with the Xcode Tools installation (`/Developer/Documentation/RubyCocoa/`).

Installing New Darwin Software

Although scripting is a good solution for simple problems, or new problems, often it's easier to just use a program that someone else has already written. Unix and related operating systems (such as Linux) have been around for a very long time and continue to be popular, so for many of the tasks you may want to accomplish, an existing application or program may already be available. Best of all, many of these programs are available for free and are waiting for you to install them. Some are available simply by downloading an OS X installation package and installing it like any other OS X app (MySQL is a popular database that is available in many formats, including an official OS X installation package), but many more are available either as a precompiled binary (that is, a ready-to-run program) or more commonly (and often preferably) as a source package. This gives you some options; you could download the source package, configure it for your specific needs, and then compile the source code into an application optimized for your computer. You could try to locate a precompiled binary and install that (and hope that it works right). Or you could take advantage of either Fink or MacPorts (formally known as DarwinPorts), which are two systems of finding, installing, and maintaining third-party Darwin applications. This ultimately boils down to preference, but if you haven't already formed your own, we suggest you try things in this order:

1. An official binary release, if available, would be the first choice. This should make installation trivial and effective and should make for easy upgrades if needed. Additionally, any other applications that may rely on the application would probably assume the official release.

2. If an official version is not available, check either Fink or MacPorts (you'll most likely want to pick one and stick with it) to see whether the application you are after is available. Both Fink and MacPorts, once properly set up, will provide you with a way then to download and install the application. These systems will also assure that any other applications or libraries that the application depends on are installed as well and will provide an effective way to upgrade the apps or uninstall them if you no longer need them.

3. If you need a highly customized version of an app, or want to sidestep Fink or MacPorts for whatever reason, then you can download the source code and compile the application yourself. This will assure that the app is good to go; however, if you go this route, you will need to manually assure that all dependencies are covered, and all further maintenance of the package will need to be made manually.

4. Installing a random precompiled binary should be a last resort and should generally be avoided unless it comes from a trusted reliable source and it was compiled for your specific system; that is, an application compiled for Tiger (OS X 10.4) might not work right on Snow Leopard (OS X 10.6). There are very few cases where this is recommended.

Note A good source of finding official binaries, or at least reputable ones, is Apple's web site at `www.apple.com/downloads/macosx/unix_open_source/`. Here Apple provides lots of Unix and open source software and utilities to download.

___

■Note Much of the software available for Darwin has come it from other Unix and Linux roots; however, binary applications from Linux or other Unixes will not just work in Mac OS X. First they must be specifically compiled and occasionally significantly changed to work correctly (if at all).

___

MacPorts and Fink

As mentioned, the preferred way to get a large amount of Darwin goodness is through either Fink or MacPorts. To take advantage of one of these, though, you first must choose which one to use. In a side-by-side feature comparison, both of these come out pretty similarly. Fink, however, offers binary installation and source installations, where MacPorts uses source installs all the time. Fink also includes a GUI to install packages called Fink Commander. The main difference, though, is how these programs actually do what they do. The Fink project is based on the Debian packaging system from the Debian Linux Projects, while MacPorts is loosely based on FreeBSD's ports system.

Fink

Fink (`http://finkproject.org/`) was designed to bring the world of Unix to Mac OS X using tools provided by the Debian Project. Fink is designed to keep everything it does relegated to the `/sw` directory where it won't interfere with any of the default Mac OS X settings or applications.

The easiest way to get started with Fink is to download the binary installer package from its web site and install it. During installation, Fink will prompt you for the administrator password so it can add some paths to your `$PATH`. Once the installation package is done with its installation, you should open your Terminal and issue the following commands to initialize Fink:

```
fink scanpackages; fink index
```

Once those two commands are finished running, before you start installing, you should make sure Fink is up-to-date. If you have installed the Xcode Tools package (that is, Apple's developers tools), the best way to do this is to issue the following command:

```
fink selfupdate
```

When prompted, select the rsync option (option 1). This will start a process of downloading, compiling, and installing the latest version of Fink. Once it's done, you're good to go.

Table 18-4 lists some handy commands to work with Fink.

Table 18-4. *Fink Commands (Assumes Xcode Tools Are Installed)*

Command	Action
fink list	Gives you a list of all the available packages. This is a long list, so you might want to do something like fink list > finkapps to create a text file called finkapps (or whatever you want to call it) containing the package list that can be perused in a text editor, Preview, or even Quick View.
fink describe someapp	Prints a description of *someapp*.
fink install someapp	Downloads and installs *someapp*.
fink --use-binary-dist someapp	Downloads and installs the binary version of *someapp*, thus skipping the install phase.
fink remove someapp	Removes *someapp* from your system. The -r option will remove all dependencies as well.
fink purge someapp	Removes *someapp* from your system, along with all the configuration files.
fink cleanup	Removes obsolete and temporary files, freeing up disk space. By default this includes any old .deb files as well as any existing source files.
fink update-all	Updates all your installed Fink packages to their latest versions.
fink selfupdate	Updates the actual Fink package to its latest version. Upon its first use you will be prompted to select either rsync or CVS; rsync is the recommended option.

If you don't have the Xcode Tools installed for some reason and you still want to use Fink, you certainly can, but rather than using fink at the command line, you would be best served using either the apt-get command or dselect. dselect will allow you to scroll through a text listing of packages and manually select the ones you want to install. apt-get works more like the fink command and can be used as described in Table 18-5.

Table 18-5. *apt-get Commands (for Binary Package Management in Fink)*

Command	Action
apt-get update	Updates the listing of binary packages. This command must be run to initially get a list of packages for apt-get. After that it should be run periodically to keep the list updated.
apt-get install someapp	Installs *someapp*.
apt-get remove someapp	Removes *someapp*.

Note Most packaging applications will require you to use sudo to install and remove packages.

MacPorts

MacPorts (www.macports.org) originated as the DarwinPorts project at Apple as the quasi-official way to manage additional Darwin applications. As such, it was rumored that sooner or later DarwinPorts would be integrated into Mac OS X. As of yet this has not happened; instead, recently, the project was renamed to MacPorts. MacPorts is part of Mac OS Forge (http://macosforge.org), which is a larger project that hosts many of the open source projects specific to OS X. Other Mac OS Forge projects include Bonjour, the Darwin Streaming Server, WebKit, xnu (Darwin's Kernel), and Calendar Server. Apple sponsors all of these projects.

From a user perspective, MacPorts works similarly to Fink from the command line. Unlike Fink, MacPorts does not have an option to install precompiled binaries, so to use MacPorts, you must have the latest version of the Xcode Tools installed. Many MacPorts applications also assume you have installed the X11 packages and the X11SDK.

MacPorts by default installs itself, and all the packages you install with it, in the /opt/local directory, so to effectively use MacPorts, you'll need to add /opt/local/bin and /opt/local/sbin to your $PATH. Additionally, if you decide at some point to use any of the X11 applications from MacPorts, you should add the line export DISPLAY=:0.0 to your .bash_profile as well.

Once all of that's out of the way, you can download the latest MacPorts binary installer from macports.org.

Like with Fink, once the installation is complete, the first thing you should do is to make sure everything is up-to-date. To do this, run the following command in the terminal:

```
sudo port selfupdate
```

■**Note** Why would you need to update something you just downloaded? Well, binary installer is packaged together only at certain intervals, while the updating of software is constant. By performing a self-update, you ensure that you are catching any new packages that have been added since the binary package was assembled.

This will update the entire ports system. Once you start using MacPorts, you should continue to periodically run this command to make sure you are working with a current version of MacPorts and that you have a list of all the current applications.

Once your environment is set up and you have the latest updated version of MacPorts installed, it's quite easy to use MacPorts with the commands listed in Table 18-6.

Table 18-6. *MacPorts Commands*

Command	Action
`port list`	Returns a list of all available ports.
`port search` *searchstring*	Returns a list of available ports whose name matches *searchstring*.
`port info` *appname*	Returns information about the port named *appname*.
`port variants` *appname*	Occasionally a port will have multiple options; if so, this command will list the additional port options available for the port *appname*.
`sudo port install` *appname*	Installs the base *appname* port.
`sudo port install` *appname* + *option1* +*option2*	Installs the port *appname* with *option1* and *option2*.
`port installed`	Returns a list of installed ports.
`sudo port selfupdate`	Updates the base port package as well as list of ports.
`sudo port outdated`	Lists outdated installed ports.
`sudo port upgrade` *appname*	Upgrades port *appname*.
`sudo port upgrade outdated`	Upgrades all outdated installed ports.
`sudo port uninstall` *appname*	Removes the port *appname*.
`sudo port clean` *appname*	Removes the build files for *appname*, which is a good way to free up disk space after you install a port.

■**Note** So, you may ask, what's really better, Fink or MacPorts? The answer is that it probably doesn't matter much these days. We use MacPorts since it's familiar to us and because of some historical reasons that have no significance anymore. Today, as far as we can tell, they are both equally good at doing what they do, and either of them is better than none of them.

Compiling Software from the Source Code

With the maturity of Darwin in Snow Leopard combined with the availability of most popular open source software through either MacPorts or Fink, it's rare that you would ever need to compile software from source code (unless of course you are actively developing software, in which case you probably know all the information we're about to relate, plus a good bit more). Still, if you really want to try a bleeding-edge program that hasn't found its way to Fink or MacPorts or you think you must compile an application with just the right options, then you want to compile your own application from source code.

■**Caution** Compiling your own software from source code is not for the weak. Things will often just not work as they should, and it could take some time and research to figure out how to get something built correctly on your computer. Sometimes, things won't work at all (unless of course you want to dig into the code yourself and tweak it). If you are easily frustrated, then we suggest that the benefits of compiling your own program might not outweigh the mental anguish you could be setting yourself up for.

Compiling your application from source code generally requires three steps: configuring, building, and installing. Usually these steps are fairly automated and, with the exception of the configure stage, are usually pretty much the same.

■**Note** To be honest, there is often a fourth step: figuring out what went wrong when one of the three primary steps fails. We'll talk about this too.

Before you start any steps, though, you need to get the source code. This can usually be found on a project's web site or through a source repository such as SourceForge (www.sourceforge.net).

Step 1: Configure

For the user building an application for their own use, the configure stage is the most important part of the whole build process. This is where you can customize the application for your specific needs and your specific system. The first part of configuring your build is to see what configure options are available. You do this by going into the primary source folder and typing the following:

```
./configure --help
```

which will return a whole list of configure options. Most of these options either have sensible defaults or are automatically set during the configure stage. The things you want to look at are the optional features to see whether any of them would be useful to you.

■**Note** Certain programs require that your system provide specific libraries or other applications to compile correctly, and this is especially true for certain options you may want to build into your application; these are what are referred to as *dependencies*. MacPorts and Fink will usually solve dependency issues automatically when you install apps using them, but when you are compiling things yourself, you need to make sure these dependencies are satisfied.

If you think you don't need any options, you can usually configure your build by just typing this:

```
./configure
```

If you want to include options, then you would type something like this:

```
./configure --with-option1 --with-option2 --enable-feature-x [...]
```

Either way, when you press Return, the configure script will run and attempt to create a makefile, which will guide the actual build and install process (together referred to as the *make process*). For a complex program, the configure script can take a few minutes or even longer to do its work, during which time lots of text will scroll by, letting you know what's happening. Upon successful completion, the text will often issue a message saying that the configure completed successfully and perhaps giving some additional build advice. If something goes wrong, the text may or may not give you a clue as to what needs to be fixed.

■**Note** If something goes wrong, it's not always going to be easy to fix. Scrolling through the configure text may reveal a missing library, or it may indicate it cannot figure out what to do with your system. A missing library can usually be found and installed (sometimes it's there, but the configure can't find it, in which case you may need to specify the library path as a configure option). Sometimes there is a specific issue and if you poke around support forums, you can get an answer. Sadly, sometimes it's just not going to work on your system.

Step 2: Build

If the configure stage went without issue, the next step is to build the app. This should be as easy as typing the following:

```
make
```

Yep, that's it. Now go get a cup of coffee, stretch your legs, play a game on your Wii, or whatever, while your computer compiles your program. OK, although these days it could take your computer anywhere from a few seconds to a few hours to compile a program, for a moderately complex application it usually takes only between 5 minutes to 30 minutes depending on your computer.

If you have a newer Intel-based Mac, there is a trick to significantly speed up this process. Since even the lowliest Intel-based iMac has at least two processor cores, to use them both, just add -j 2 to the end of make. make -j 4 will work if you have four cores (a quad G5 or two dual-core Intel chips), and so on.

> **Note** Again, occasionally things will go wrong. Unfortunately, an error during the build process is usually even more difficult to track down than during the configure stage. If you notice the build failing in a specific area of the build that you identify with a configure option, you may try not enabling (or disabling) that particular option. If you really aren't using any strange options (or none at all) and this is a fairly popular program, then it's likely someone else is having the same issues, and if enough people are having these issues, then it's possible someone out there has a solution.

Step 3: Install

Usually, if you are dealing with a stable version of a popular application, things go smoothly and your configure and build stages happen without issue (or without major issues anyway), after which it comes time to install your program. This is also a very easy process; just type the following:

```
sudo make install
```

That should do it.

Most software compiled this way will install software in the /usr/local/ directory. By default this directory doesn't exist in Snow Leopard, so you may want to create it. If, however, you want to install your software (or parts of it) somewhere else, this can usually be configured as a configure option.

To sum up, the quick and easy way to compile a program you downloaded as source code is often as easy as this:

```
./configure
make
sudo make install
```

Summary

We covered a whole lot of stuff in this chapter, from writing to shell scripts to compiling an application from source code. The point here wasn't to make you an expert at any of these things, but more so to familiarize you with some of the power that Darwin brings to the Mac world. The most important parts of this chapter were the ones on MacPorts and Fink, though, so pick one of these and install it. Then should you ever need to install and use something like, say, figlet, you'll be just a few commands away from being able to do this:

```
stich:~ scott$ figlet Neat huh?
```

## PART 6

Snow Leopard Networking

CHAPTER 19

■■■

Snow Leopard Networking

The Mac is known for making it easy and safe to get online. Under the hood, Mac OS X has all the networking power of UNIX. The Internet and UNIX go way back, growing up together. You might even say they were made for each other. Like any UNIX system, Mac OS X comes with a full set of networking tools built in:

Firewall software: For keeping your computer safe on the Internet in an effective, easy-to-use way

Monitoring tools: For keeping an eye on what your computer is doing, online and off

Network utilities: For inspecting your packets from the UI or the command line

AirPort utilities: For setting up and managing wireless networks and shared resources

---

■**Note** This chapter assumes you've already managed to connect your computer to the Internet. If you haven't gotten that far, see Chapter 9.

Setting Up the Firewall

The Mac has a well-deserved reputation for being safe on the Internet, but that doesn't mean you should be careless. The simplest thing you can do is set up the built-in firewall.

The firewall in Mac OS X arbitrates incoming connection requests based on the requested port, the source, and the intended recipient. It's not unlike a lobby security guard in that it doesn't limit the ability of packets to leave; it cares only about things trying to come in from the outside.

To change your firewall settings, launch System Preferences by selecting System Preferences... from the Apple menu. Then click the Security preference pane, and select the Firewall tab, as shown in Figure 19-1.

In order to be effective, security has to be simple. The firewall in Mac OS X is about as simple as a firewall can be, but it's backed by Snow Leopard's solid UNIX underpinnings.

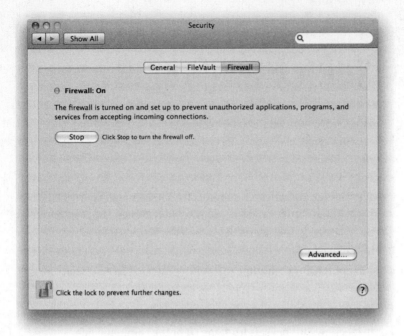

Figure 19-1. *Firewall settings in System Preferences*

On the BSD level, Mac OS X uses `socketfilterfw`. This is both simpler and more effective than older port-based filters. Aside from eliminating the hassle of manually configuring ports, the socket filtering method is more accurate, because it filters packets based on where they are going, rather than which port they are coming into.

Networking gurus might argue this approach is less flexible, and therefore less effective, than `ipfw`'s rulesets. With rulesets, it's easy to block a specific protocol from a specific IP address.

As is typical of Mac OS X, the majority simple case prevails. The minority edge case is left to its own device. If you're smart enough to care, you're smart enough to install your own firewall.

■**Note** There are a few times when it might be necessary to leave your firewall down. If you're behind a dedicated firewall, it might be redundant. If you're having trouble connecting to another machine, you might need to temporarily disable the firewall. Finally, your network administrator, who has the last word on network configuration, might ask you to keep it open.

Snow Leopard's firewall requires no configuration. If you enable a network service on the Sharing panel in System Preferences, that service will automatically be added to the firewall's list of allowed applications. Applications that have been code signed to prevent tampering are also allowed to access the network. Applications that have not been code signed will ask permission the first time they try to access the network, as shown in Figure 19-2.

Figure 19-2. *Automated firewall management dialog*

The nice thing about building the list on the fly like this is that you don't have to spend a bunch of time building a list of abstract applications whose usage you may not have put that much thought into yet. You can still view and edit the list by clicking the Advanced... button on the Security panel. This will pop up a sheet, as shown in Figure 19-3, from which you can add and remove applications, as well as switch between allowing and denying connections.

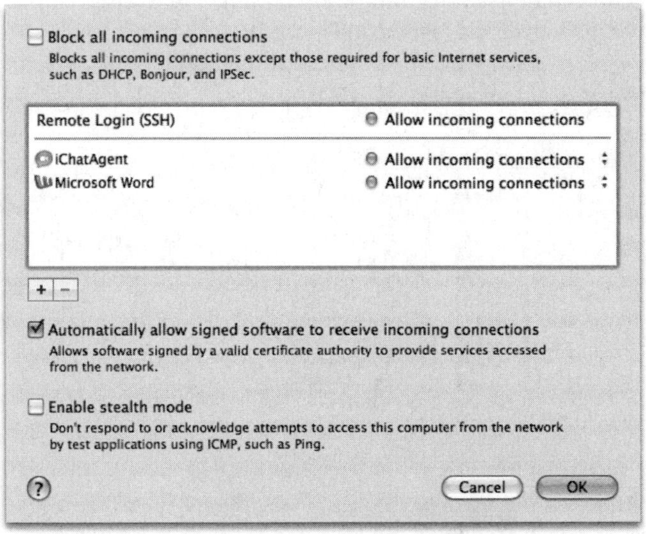

Figure 19-3. *Advanced firewall settings sheet in System Preferences*

In addition to the firewall's application list, several check boxes are available. You can choose to simply deny all connections, to disable trusting signed applications, and to enable "stealth mode."

Stealth mode means your computer ignores pings, giving it the appearance of being off or disconnected from the network. Logic dictates this should make you some percentage safer.

Some people say that stealth mode won't make you any safer, and certainly it makes your computer uncooperative with the protocols of the Internet. Since none of those people is named Bruce Schneier, we generally ignore them.

That is to say, we run stealth mode. People don't need to ping our computers, regardless of the way the Internet is supposed to work. If you find yourself running network diagnostics or have your machine set up as a server, you'll probably want to disable stealth mode.

Note Machines on a local network that uses network address translation (NAT) aren't usually visible to the Internet, but depending on your network, you might want to run stealth mode anyway. The people on a home network are probably trustworthier than the people on the open Wi-Fi at a coffee shop.

Monitoring Network Traffic

Raising the firewall is a good first step, but nothing beats basic situational awareness. If your computer were infected with malware and participating in zombienet denial-of-service attacks or sending out spam, would you know?

We like to know what our computers are doing, which is why we love Activity Monitor, located in /Applications/Utilities. Activity Monitor lets you know what's running and how much memory and CPU it's taking up. It also lets you monitor when things are writing to disk or sending and receiving traffic over the network, as shown in Figure 19-4.

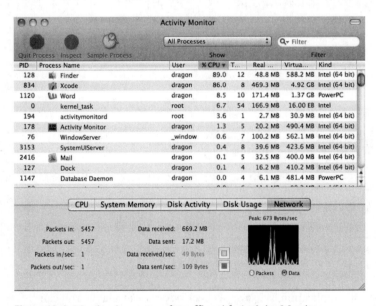

Figure 19-4. *Monitoring network traffic with Activity Monitor*

Activity Monitor has a convenient animated Dock icon, so even when the monitoring window is not open, we can keep an eye on packets traveling over the network. If you see a lot of activity and you're not actively using the network, you'll want to know why. Within Activity Monitor, select View ➤ Dock Icon ➤ Show Network Usage to enable this feature.

Tip A lot of root and system programs have arcane invocations that can make it hard to tell what a given program in Activity Monitor actually is. You can google the program name, or you can look it up on such convenient lists as Amit Singh's Mac OS X Hacking Tools: www.kernelthread.com/mac/osx/tools.html.

If you want to take network monitoring to the next level, you need to check out Little Snitch by Objective Development. Little Snitch complements your firewall by letting you know when applications try to send data from your machine.

Why might an application send out packets? If it's iChat or Mail or Safari, it probably has a legitimate reason. On the other hand, there are a lot of other reasons you might not be in total agreement with, such as phoning home with personal information the developer thinks it's OK to take without asking.

You can also use Little Snitch to selectively allow or block individual servers. For example, you might allow Safari to connect to a web page you are trying to view but not allow it to connect to a site hot-linked from that page, such as an advertising or tracking network.

Like the firewall, Little Snitch has a list of rules you can build on the fly via notifications, as shown in Figure 19-5. Unlike the firewall, Little Snitch has a lot of configuration options, being designed for more advanced users. Even so, it's still a Mac application; you can install and run it without bothering with any of that stuff.

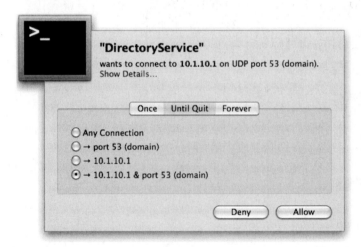

Figure 19-5. *Little Snitch noticing an application sending out packets*

Unlike the built-in firewall and Activity Monitor utility, Little Snitch costs $25. Like all good software, it comes with a free demo mode. Download it from the developer's site (www.obdev.at) and give it a try. We think you'll agree it's well worth the price.

Network Utilities

Every UNIX distribution comes with a full complement of networking tools, and Mac OS X is certainly no exception. Generally you have to go to the command line to use UNIX tools, but Apple has bundled the most common network utilities into a graphical application aptly named Network Utility, which lives in /Applications/Utilities.

Network Utility encompasses eight areas of functionality. Each lives in its own tab, with several subfeatures delimited with pop-up boxes, as shown in Figure 19-6.

Info

Chances are your computer has several network interfaces. Most Macs have an Ethernet port, an AirPort card, and a FireWire bus, all of which are capable of connecting to the Internet.

The Info panel lets you get statistics on all your network interfaces, such as their hardware (MAC) and Internet (IP) addresses, their make and model, whether they're active, and at what speed they are connected. You can also see how many packets they've sent and received and how many errors and collisions they've logged.

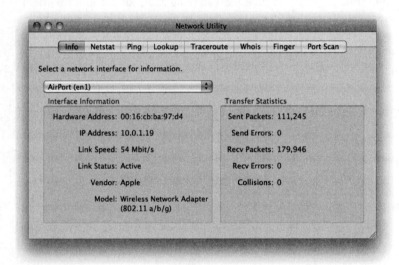

Figure 19-6. *Exploring the Net with Network Utility*

Netstat

Netstat, as its name implies, provides network statistics in four varieties.

- *Routing Table*: This is a map of known nodes from which your packets can begin their long trek across the Internet. This is not unlike a list of your local post offices.

- *Statistics*: This is a comprehensive list of statistics by protocol. This is the long version of the simple numbers displayed by Activity Monitor and the Info tab. If you're curious to know how many inbound IPsec/IPv6 packets failed because of insufficient memory, here's where you can find out.

- *Multicast*: This many-to-many communication protocol is used primarily by enterprise networks, though it's also used by mDNS, peer-to-peer technologies, and Internet Relay Chat (IRC). If you want to monitor your multicast memberships or packet statistics, Netstat is there for you.

- *Socket States*: Every connection on the Internet uses a socket, which is the combination of your computer's IP address and a port. It's not a bad idea to see who's connecting to your machine and what they're doing.

Ping

Ping is a diagnostic tool that uses the Internet Control Message Protocol (ICMP) to determine your ability to reach a given IP address, be it another computer or something like a router. The theory behind Ping is that any machine that receives a ping is supposed to echo it back. Unfortunately, Ping has been abused by malware in the past—hence stealth mode.

To use Ping in Network Utility, enter an IP address or domain name. Ping will then list the pings as they return, along with how long it took them to traverse the network. This is useful in any number of ways.

For example, if your web site goes down but your web host responds to pings, you can deduce that the host program crashed but that the server is OK. If the server does not respond to pings, you can assume something is wrong on a hardware level.

Similarly, if your server responds by IP address but doesn't respond by domain name, you can deduce that something is wrong with the Domain Name System (DNS). Further investigation would be needed to determine whether the domain name has expired or whether there is something else going on. These can be determined elsewhere in Network Utility.

Lookup

The Lookup tab combines the `nslookup` and `dig` tools to query DNS, which converts human-readable web addresses to the numerical IP addresses used by computers. The information returned by Lookup varies by host, but at the very least you can use it to get the IP address of a given server name.

Traceroute

Traceroute maps the path of packets as they travel to a given server address. Aside from being kind of interesting, it's a useful diagnostic tool. When a server is unreachable, you can use Traceroute to figure out where the packets are being stopped and whom you need to call to get traffic flowing.

Like Ping, Traceroute has been abused by nefarious forces, so some servers will block Traceroute requests. Even so, you can usually get to the outer bounds of a given network, which will certainly tell you something, so Traceroute remains a good thing to have in your toolbox.

Whois

As opposed to the tools in Lookup, which convert domain names into IP addresses, Whois queries domain registries to determine who owns them. There are a couple of reasons why you might want to know this.

If your site is down and your server is reachable by IP address, but not by domain name, one possibility is that your domain name has expired or has been stolen. Checking the Whois information will let you know for sure. If Whois checks out OK, you can begin suspecting something is wrong with the name server itself.

Should you find your packets are being stopped at a certain node via Traceroute, Whois will tell you whom you need to call about it. It's also a good way to see whether a domain name is available and, if it's not, to see when it expires. There's no sense putting up good money for a domain-watching service if the registration is not going to expire for another five years.

As with many parts of the Internet, Whois registries have been abused. Putting your name, e-mail address, home address, and telephone number where anyone can get them is a potential privacy concern.

As such, some registrars now offer anonymous registration, whereby they will register the domain in their own name on your behalf, preventing people from getting any useful information about you. As with any such tactic, this certainly improves security by some degree, while breaking the Internet by another.

Finger

In the halcyon days of yore, when spam was just a delicious luncheon meat and the Internet was just a military research project, a computer scientist named Les Earnest wrote a program that would take an e-mail address and "point out" who it belonged to by giving you the person's name, whether they were logged on, and where their home directory was.

When the Internet opened for general use, people soon found less earnest uses for Finger, and the protocol was eventually abandoned. The tool still exists but mainly as a way to generate the words the connection refused.

Port Scan

You should probably be noticing a theme with Internet tools. That is, they can be used for good or evil. Of all the tools in Network Utility, nothing fits this profile as well as Port Scan.

In a nutshell, Port Scan tries every port on a given machine and reports which ones are open. This is handy information for potential attackers, which makes it handy information for potential victims.

It's also useful for figuring out, say, why a particular Internet service is not working, because having its port closed will render any Internet application silent.

Advanced Networking with Darwin

As discussed in Chapters 17 and 18, the underlying BSD system, accessible from the Terminal application, is the place to go for advanced hacking. The following listing shows a handy shell script for rerouting a web address to your local machine.

```
#! /bin/sh

if [ -f "/etc/hosts.old" ] ; then
sudo mv -f /etc/hosts.old /etc/hosts
fi
```

```
new_host=$1
if [ "$new_host" = "" ] ; then
exit
fi

sudo cp /etc/hosts /etc/hosts.old
cat /etc/hosts > hosts.new
echo "127.0.0.1    $new_host" >> hosts.new
sudo mv -f hosts.new /etc/hosts
```

Say you were working on a local copy of your web site. All your absolute links would still point to your server, until you ran the localize script:

```
./localize.sh mywebsite.com
```

When you were done editing your site, you would run the localize script with no argument to return things to normal:

```
./localize.sh
```

Many networking utilities have more options than are available from within Network Utility. There are also esoteric, specialized, and third-party tools that don't have graphical versions and, as such, can be run only in Terminal. Even simple utilities like Ping are at your disposal, as shown in Figure 19-7.

Figure 19-7. *Running network tools from the command line in Terminal*

So, while Network Utility is a good place to start, when you're really ready to become a network power user, open Terminal and start reading man pages.

■**Note** Some good Darwin network utilities to read up on would be `ifconfig`, which lets you configure your network interfaces, similar to the Network panel in System Preferences; and `tcpdump`, which lets you examine the contents of network packets and replaces the popular `tcpflow` application.

Wireless Networking with AirPort

We would be remiss not to mention a very important networking tool that comes in a pretty graphical package—AirPort Utility—which lives in `/Applications/Utilities`.

AirPort Utility replaces the old AirPort Setup Assistant and AirPort Admin Utility programs with a single, attractive, easy-to-use application. AirPort Utility also adds several new features and makes it easier to manage multiple AirPort base stations.

At its most basic, AirPort Utility will show you which AirPort base stations are operating in your area, their names, and their IP and AirPort addresses, as well as which standards and firmware versions they support, as shown in Figure 19-8.

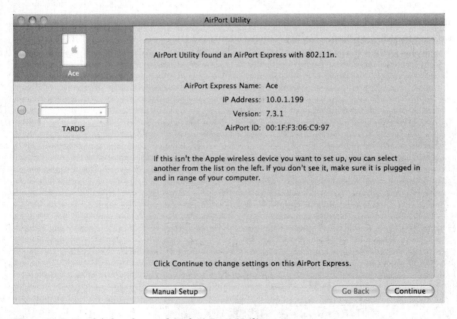

Figure 19-8. *Apple's lovely graphical AirPort Utility*

If one or more of the base stations in range belong to you, you can rename them and change their settings.

The availability and usefulness of settings in AirPort Utility will vary depending on which model of AirPort base station you have, its firmware version, and the peculiarities of your Internet provider. There are, however, a few notable groups of settings you should pay particular attention to:

- *Profiles (Base Station ➤ Manage Profiles)*: These are groups of settings you can easily switch between. This is handy if you travel with an AirPort base station so you can, say, share an Internet connection, as discussed in the next chapter.

- *Identify (Base Station ➤ Identify…)*: This convenient menu item tells the base station to flash its status light, alternating amber and green. That way, you can figure out which base station you're dealing with, without having to figure out people's cutesy naming schemes.

- *Wireless Security (Airport ➤ Wireless)*: Unless you're intentionally running an open access point, you need to protect your network by setting up encryption and a password from the Wireless tab of the AirPort panel. Several encryption standards are in common use, but you should probably choose one based on Wi-Fi Protected Access, such as WPA2 Personal. AirPort's recommended setting is WPA/WPA2 Personal, which supports the older version of WPA for backward compatibility. If you have machines that do not support WPA2, you can use this setting, but in general, you want to limit the abilities of your AirPort base station to those needed by machines you own.

■**Caution** If at all possible, avoid using a standard based on the Wired Equivalent Privacy (WEP) protocol. It's better than nothing, but at this point, even a moderately competent attacker can crack a WEP key with ease. If you have to use WEP to support older hardware, make it habit to frequently change your password. You should also steer clear of WPA2 Enterprise, which requires a special RADIUS server far beyond the means and needs of the everyday user.

- *Radio Mode (Airport ➤ Wireless)*: This single setting resides right above the security options on the Wireless tab. Because an AirPort base station will support up to four wireless standards, you should check this to ensure you're using the smallest, fastest set of standards that will meet your needs. For example, if all your machines have an 802.11n AirPort card, supporting the a, b, or g standards could needlessly slow the network down, besides making it all the more usable by uninvited guests.

- *MAC Access Control (Airport ➤ Access)*: This panel lets you filter access by hardware ID. This can be used to close a network to guests or to impose time limits on certain machines. This should be used only for convenience, not security. Unlike a password, a MAC address is easily spoofed.

- *DHCP (Internet ➤ DHCP)*: From this panel, you can limit the range of IP addresses DHCP uses, limit the length of a DHCP lease, and set a custom message displayed when people log in to your base station. You can also reserve IP addresses, which is particularly useful with port mapping.

- *Port Mapping (Advanced ➤ Port Mapping)*: Typically your AirPort base station will have a single public IP address shared among the private addresses of your network. In order to reach a service on an individual machine from outside the local network, you have to map it to a port on your AirPort base station in a process known as *port forwarding*. We'll come back to this in a moment.

- *Logs and Statistics (Advanced ➤ Statistics)*: AirPort Utility lets you monitor your network usage. For example, you can see a list of all the computers connected to the base station, including their MAC and IP addresses.

- *Remote Printing (Printers)*: By connecting a printer to your AirPort base station, you can allow any machine on the network to use the printer. This is an improvement over standard printer sharing because it doesn't require a host computer.

- *AirPort Disks (Disks)*: Similar to printer sharing, you can connect USB hard drives to your AirPort base station, which will allow them to be shared by people on your network.

Sharing a disk connected to an AirPort base station—known generically as *network-attached storage* (NAS)—is a really cool feature, particularly if you have a laptop. Shared disks host files that can be accessed over your network or, used in conjunction with MobileMe's Back to My Mac feature, the Internet. See Chapter 13 for more information about MobileMe.

Unlike a printer, hard drives contain personal data, which raises privacy issues. Apple lets you set up user accounts, password protection, and permissions on shared drives. That way, multiple people can use the same drive without having access to each other's data.

Port Forwarding

A typical home or small office network will have a single machine, usually a router, connected to the Internet by a public IP address. That machine, in turn, will share its Internet connection with other machines on the network. Rather than having public IP addresses, the machines on the local network use local addresses. Aside from saving the significant expense of having multiple IP addresses, this gives the network added security, since machines without reachable addresses are essentially invisible to anyone outside the network.

Normally this is a good thing, but not always (such as if you decide to use your computer to serve web pages, which is the topic of Chapter 21). Invisibility is not a good trait for a public web server. In order to receive requests and send out pages, your web server must be reachable by the outside world. The best way to deal with this problem is to set the router to forward any incoming packets on a certain port to the web server, which can then fulfill the requests and send out the necessary data. This process is known as *port forwarding*.

Of course, the router can't forward packets if it doesn't know where to find the server, so the first step is to give your machine a static IP address. You can either use a hybrid method such as DHCP with a manual address, or you can just set the entire address manually.

To set up a static IP address, open the Networking panel of System Preferences. Select the network interface your machine will use to connect to the Internet. Since servers need to stay in one place in order to effectively serve, this will probably be a desktop machine connected by Ethernet.

That said, there's no technical reason why you can't serve your pages over another interface, such as AirPort. In fact, we're going to use AirPort in this example. Click the Advanced... button to reveal the Advanced Settings sheet, and then click the TCP/IP tab, as shown in Figure 19-9.

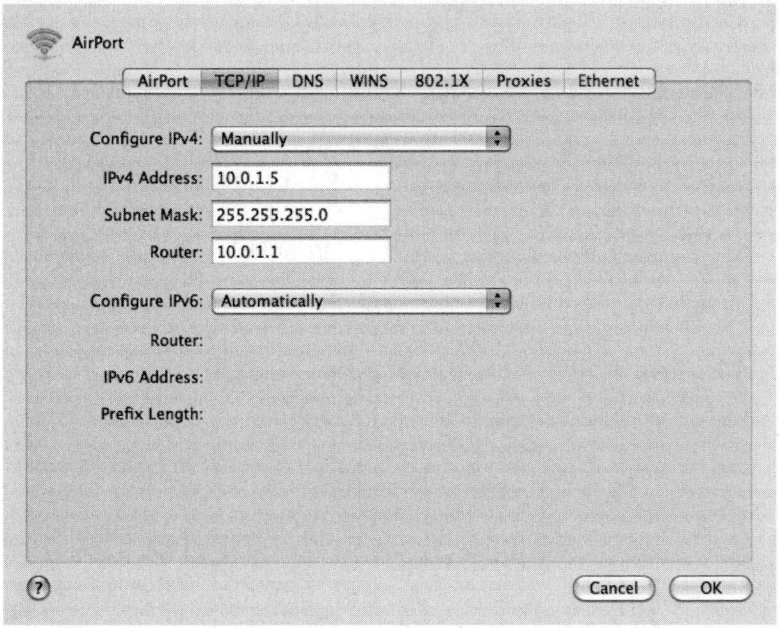

Figure 19-9. *Setting up a static IP address in System Preferences*

Make a note of your IPv4 address, subnet mask, and router address, as well as which ports you're trying to access. In the case of serving web pages, the default is 80, so if you changed it earlier, make a note of that. It's not a bad idea to confirm from within the local network that the socket you will be forwarding to works, which will make testing the forwarding that much easier.

Once you have the IP address set and the ports open and tested, configure your router to forward messages on the appropriate ports to your machine's IP address and local port. Every router is different, so you'll have to read the manual or search the Internet for the exact information. That said, Apple's AirPort base stations are DHCP-enabled routers, so we'll show how to set one up as an example. Open AirPort Utility, and sign in to the base station that connects your web server to the Internet.

Click the Manual Configuration button, select the Advanced panel, and then select the Port Mapping tab. You can also reach this tab by clicking the Configure Port Mappings... button on the NAT tab of the Internet panel. Either way, the port mappings are just a list of ports. To add yours, click the + button, and then fill out the form, as shown in Figure 19-10. The Public Port Number(s) field lists the ports you want forwarded. In this example, we're assuming our ISP blocks port 80, so we're mapping port 8080. Of course, there's no reason we couldn't map them both, just in case.

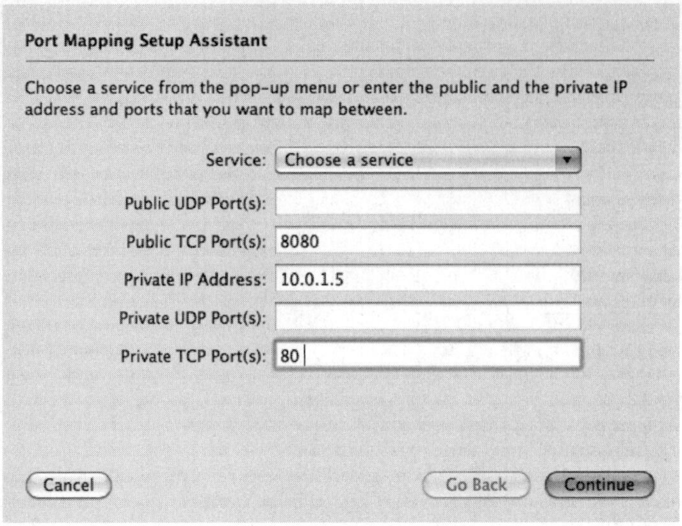

Port Mapping Setup Assistant

Choose a service from the pop-up menu or enter the public and the private IP
address and ports that you want to map between.

Service: [Choose a service ▼]

Public UDP Port(s): [   ]

Public TCP Port(s): [8080   ]

Private IP Address: [10.0.1.5   ]

Private UDP Port(s): [   ]

Private TCP Port(s): [80 |]

(Cancel)   (Go Back) (Continue)

Figure 19-10. *Setting up port forwarding in AirPort Utility*

The Private IP Address field lists the IP address of the machine receiving the packets,
which is to say your web server. Enter the IP address you gave it in System Preferences. Finally,
enter the port you want to receive the packets on in the Private Port Number(s) field. Click the
OK button to dismiss the sheet, and then click the Update button to commit your changes.
After the base station reboots, test your forwarding by accessing your web site using the outside IP address.

Summary

From the Finder to the command line, Leopard's built-in tools give you the power to monitor
every aspect of the network. Third-party tools extend those abilities even further. Apple also
includes specialized tools for dealing with AirPort networks and the specialized resource sharing they can provide.

Of course, connecting to a network is only of limited use unless you can actually connect to other machines. In the next chapter, we'll explore ways to connect your Mac to other
machines, whether they're next door or on the other side of the world.

## CHAPTER 20

Working with Remote Servers and Networks

Chances are you connect to remote servers and networks every day without really thinking about it. When you open your favorite web browser to read the news, check the weather, or catch up on the blogosphere, you're sending out packets of information requesting data. Those packets adhere to a particular protocol, in this case the Hypertext Transfer Protocol, and they traverse networks around the globe seeking the particular port at the particular address of the particular server that has your requested content.

The server will consider your request and, if all goes well, package the information you've requested and send it flying through the vast network of networks until it ends up back at your machine. Most people probably never realize how much work they're doing just by slacking off on the Web!

Making the Connection

The Web is just one part of the Internet, which is in turn just one type of network. There are as many ways to connect to another machine as there are reasons to do so, which has resulted in an alphabet soup of capabilities, methods, and protocols. Fortunately, Mac OS X has integrated, easy-to-use networking built right in. In fact, it's quite possible that, as with surfing the Web, you won't even have to think about the fact you're using a remote machine.

Navigating in the Finder

The easiest way to browse your local network is in the Finder. Machines that have enabled an appropriate type of sharing, such as file sharing, will be listed in the Finder window under the Shared category, as if they were part of the system.

Selecting the machine in the Finder will display a visual representation of that system's options. If you can connect to the system remotely, a Connect As… button will let you do so. The available folders, including any public folders, will be listed by user account, as shown in Figure 20-1.

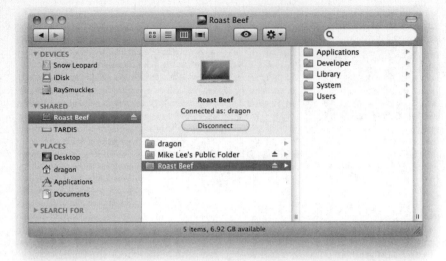

Figure 20-1. *Browsing the local network in the Finder*

If the machine has screen sharing enabled, the Share Screen… button will let you activate it. Screen sharing descends from the Apple Remote Desktop application, which has roots going all the way back to Mac OS 8. The upshot is Snow Leopard's screen-sharing feature can connect to machines running previous versions of Mac OS X. Even Tiger (10.4) and Panther (10.3) come with the necessary client software already installed.

When you make a screen-sharing connection, the system will launch an application named Screen Sharing. Its main window will contain a live, interactive image of the remote computer's desktop. Depending on the remote computer's settings, you can take control of the cursor, launch and use applications, and manipulate files.

The Screen Sharing application has a few preferences worth checking out. By default, the remote screen is scaled to fit your screen, data is minimally encrypted to improve network performance, and drawing quality is adjusted on the fly depending on the quality of your connection. You can instead elect to view the screen at full size, to encrypt all data, or to draw the screen at full quality regardless of performance.

■**Note** This section deals only with connecting as a client to machines that already have a network service available. We'll discuss how to enable your machine as a server in the "Sharing" section later in this chapter.

Connecting Directly

The Finder's network browsing is limited to machines on your local network, but the Finder can address any machine, local or remote. As long as you can resolve an IP address or a domain name to it, you can connect to it directly using the Finder's Connect to Server window, as shown in Figure 20-2.

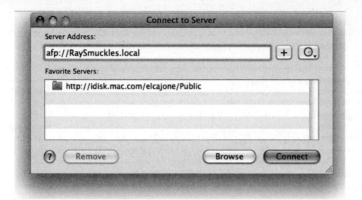

Figure 20-2. *Connecting to a server by name in the Finder*

Launch the Connect to Server window from the Finder's menu bar by selecting Connect to Server from the Go menu, or press Command-K. To connect to a machine, type its address in URL form into the Server Address text field. If you intend to connect to the machine on a regular basis, click the + button to add it to the Favorite Servers list.

Earlier, we connected to a machine using the Connect As... button in the Finder. We could have also established that connection directly by typing the machine's URL, like so:

`afp://10.0.1.5`

Connecting to a machine in the Finder will use the default protocol. Connecting directly allows you to explicitly specify the protocol. Valid protocol declarations include the following:

afp: The Apple Filing Protocol is the standard protocol used for addressing remote volumes in the Finder. Although it is Apple's standard, AFP support is available for many operating systems, including Windows, NetWare, and several flavors of UNIX and Linux. If you do not specify a protocol, afp is assumed.

at: AppleTalk is an obsolete networking protocol that is included for backward compatibility. Previous versions of AFP used AppleTalk behind the scenes, but modern AFP uses the Virtual Network Computing (VNC) standard on top of standard TCP/IP.

nfs: The Network File System protocol is a remote file access protocol developed by Sun Microsystems. It is similar to AFP and is available for several flavors of UNIX, as well as for operating systems such as NetWare, Windows, and, of course, Mac OS X.

smb: The Server Message Block protocol is the Windows equivalent to AFP. From within Windows, it's referred to simply as Microsoft Windows Network. The SMB protocol is sometimes called Samba, though technically Samba is a free reimplementation of SMB and not simply another name for the same thing.

cifs: The Common Internet File System, despite its name, is actually just a rebranding of SMB to reflect changes Microsoft made to the protocol since its invention at IBM. It was submitted, but not accepted, as an Internet standard. It can be considered to be the same as SMB.

http: The Hypertext Transfer Protocol is the standard protocol of the World Wide Web. Taking advantage of the ubiquity of the Web, HTTP is used for transporting more than web pages. For example, the WebDAV standard is used to mount remote file systems over HTTP. This is the same standard used when connecting to iDisk, which we'll discuss in the "Connecting to MobileMe" section of this chapter.

https: The secure version of HTTP is not a true protocol. Instead, it simply refers to the use of standard HTTP over a connection that has been encrypted by either the Secure Sockets Layer (SSL) or Transport Layer Security (TLS) protocol.

ftp: The File Transfer Protocol is a very old standard for moving files from one computer to another. Because of its age and that it's compatible with every known operating system, it's in widespread use all over the Internet.

ftps: Analogous to HTTPS, FTPS refers to the use of regular FTP over an SSL or TLS connection.

The list of protocols supported by the Finder's Connect to Server window is impressive but not all-encompassing. Absent are sftp, the Secure Shell File Transfer Protocol; svn, the Subversion file transfer protocol (although Subversion can be transacted over other protocols, such as HTTP); and file, as used in standard file URLs. The absence of file URLs is notable not because they have much meaning in a dialog intended for connecting to servers but because they are used extensively throughout the system. Using them in the Connect to Server window simply returns an error.

Connecting in Darwin

Although using a computer's graphical interface via screen sharing is relatively new, the concept of using one computer to log in to and control another computer remotely is anything but. UNIX is, by its very nature, a remotely controllable operating system, and old-fashioned shell-to-shell networking is very much alive in Terminal, as shown in Figure 20-3.

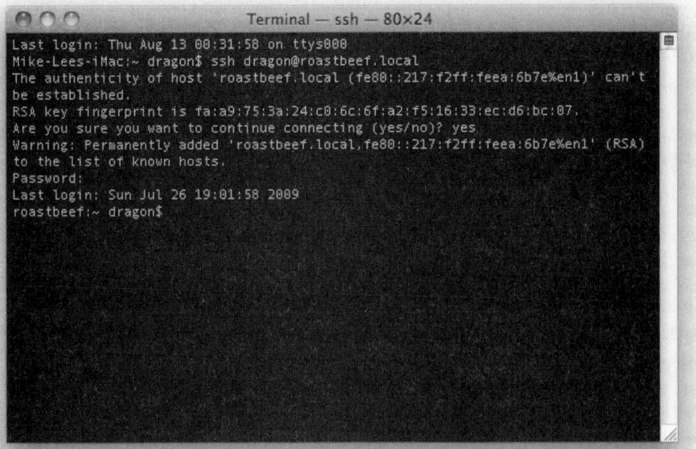

Figure 20-3. *Remote computing by Secure Shell in Terminal*

To connect to another machine, open Terminal from /Applications/Utilities. From the command line, invoke ssh with the username and address of the machine you want to connect to, separated by the "at" sign. For example, to connect to a machine at the local IP address 10.0.1.5 with the username booksystem, you would type this:

ssh booksystem@10.0.1.5

■**Note** You don't have to use a local IP address or an IP address at all. Anything that can be resolved on the Internet is valid, including standard and local domain names.

If you are connecting to a machine for the first time, you will be asked whether it is safe to proceed. Confirm this by typing yes. Unlike most UNIX programs, you have to type the entire word. You will then be prompted for a password, and then, assuming you can authenticate properly, you'll be presented with a welcome message and the command prompt.

From this prompt you can create, delete, and alter files and folders, as well as list, run, and kill processes. You can even launch new shells and Secure Shell sessions in other servers. It's the same as if you were sitting at the remote machine typing into a Terminal window.

This can have unexpected consequences. For example, any DNS resolution will be in terms of the remote machine. If you have domains listed as default, a custom hosts file, or discrepancies in the closest name server's routing table, the remote machine might behave differently than would your local host.

To log out of the remote server, type exit. This is the same as exiting any shell, so bear in mind that if you've launched a new shell from within Secure Shell, typing exit will not log you out. Fortunately, when you log out of a Secure Shell session, Secure Shell will let you know the connection is closed. If you don't get that confirmation, assume you are still logged in.

Remote login via Secure Shell can be enabled from System Preferences, as discussed in the "Sharing" section later in this chapter.

■**Note** Secure Shell replaces the older Telnet application. Both programs accomplish the same thing, but ssh uses encryption to ensure an attacker cannot view your data in transit. Most machines do not allow insecure access, but Telnet remains in the UNIX toolbox for backward compatibility.

Darwin also includes an ftp program for using the File Transfer Protocol to move files between machines. As opposed to shell access, which allows for all manner of shenanigans, FTP access is much more limited, restricting user privileges to basic file operations.

To use FTP from the command line, simply type ftp. Unlike Secure Shell, FTP can be invoked without actually opening a connection. To connect to a remote machine, type open, and then, when prompted, enter the address of the machine, your username, and your password.

Unlike the Finder's Connect to Server menu, Darwin does not have an ftps command, but it does have an sftp command, which works just like the regular ftp command. However, although opening a connection and supplying your username at invocation time are optional in `ftp`, they are required in `sftp`.

```
sftp booksystem@10.0.1.5
```

Enter your password when prompted, and then proceed as normal.

Whatever the advantage to using `sftp`, moving files back and forth in the terminal is almost too complicated to make it worthwhile, but if you really want to know, type `man ftp` or `man sftp` in the terminal to read all about it. A much better idea would be to use a dedicated FTP client.

Third-Party Solutions

The Finder was designed to be a file browser, so it's a great way to take advantage of remote file protocols, such as AFP, SMB, and WebDAV. However, just as you wouldn't use the Finder to surf the Web, it's also ill-suited for dealing with the peculiar needs of FTP and related protocols. Instead, it's best to turn to third-party solutions.

Transmit

We've used a lot of FTP clients on a lot of different platforms, but one application stands head-and-shoulders above any other: Transmit (`www.panic.com/transmit/`). This award-winning application is available only on the Mac and was written by Panic, a Portland-based, Mac-only software company held in the highest esteem by developers and users alike.

As shown in Figure 20-4, Transmit has a simple, native drag-and-drop interface that belies its power. Under the hood Transmit has a robust file transfer engine that works with all manner of protocols, including FTP, FTPS, SFTP, WebDAV over HTTP and HTTPS, and Amazon S3. It also deals with such vagaries as proxies and passive mode.

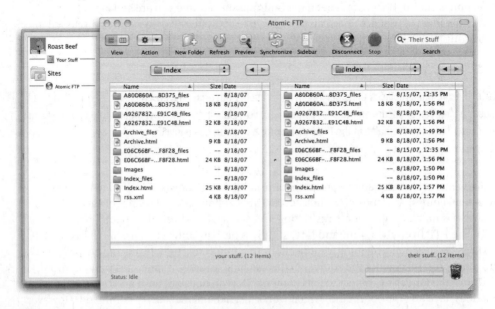

Figure 20-4. *Connecting to an FTP server with Transmit*

Other features in Transmit include directory synchronization, bookmarks, and remote viewing and editing. What really makes it worth the price is the level of integration it has with Mac OS X, including the Dock, iDisk, Bonjour, Dashboard, AppleScript, and Automator. It also works with MobileMe's syncing feature, so your bookmarks are always backed up and in sync.

Transmit is available for $29.95. You can download it from Panic's web site and try it free for 15 days, after which time certain features are limited.

Note Several free and open source FTP clients are also available for the Mac, such as NcFTP (`www.ncftp.com`) and CyberDuck (`http://cyberduck.ch/`). Fans of Mozilla Firefox can also check out the FireFTP plug-in (`http://fireftp.mozdev.org`).

BBEdit

One of the most common uses of FTP and other file transfer protocols is for uploading content to a web server. Some applications have file transfer capabilities built in to streamline your workflow.

Bare Bones Software's BBEdit (`http://barebones.com/products/bbedit/`) is probably one of the oldest and most respected text editors on the Mac. It has the kind of understated interface over tremendous power beloved by veteran users of the great UNIX text editors Emacs and Vi. But it also has the convenience and easy approachability of a graphical application, as shown in Figure 20-5.

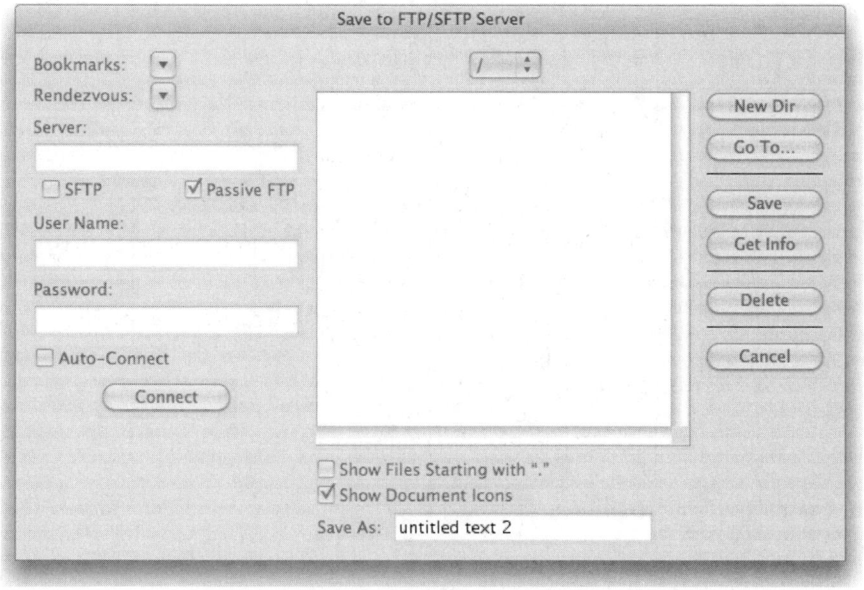

Figure 20-5. *Saving a file directly to a server in BBEdit*

BBEdit's features are too numerous to enumerate, but suffice it to say it's not only a great text editor but also a great web page editor. Germane to the subject at hand, BBEdit can open and save files to a remote server via FTP or SFTP, eliminating the need for a separate file transfer protocol.

BBEdit is $125 but has a demo mode and significant discounts for students and users of previous versions. Bare Bones Software also makes a free "lite" version called TextWrangler. Although it lacks the most advanced features of BBEdit, TextWrangler has BBEdit's best features, including the FTP functionality.

Connecting to MobileMe

As Transmit and BBEdit demonstrate, integration is the order of the day for many native Mac applications. As the Finder's built-in networking demonstrates, this is also true of the system in general. However, when it comes to simplicity through integration, nothing compares to Apple's MobileMe.

Note If you're not familiar with MobileMe, check out Chapter 13.

Connecting to MobileMe is easier than connecting to other Internet hosts. You don't have to access it with Terminal or Transmit, because the interface is built into Mac OS X. You also don't have to deal with online control panels or configuration files because all that is handled from within System Preferences, as shown in Figure 20-6.

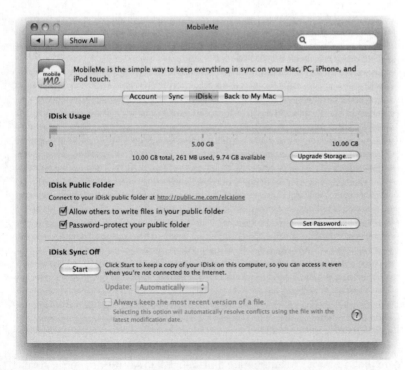

Figure 20-6. *Setting up MobileMe in System Preferences*

iDisk

If you create a web site in iWeb, which is part of iLife and included free on every new Mac, you can publish your home page to MobileMe with one click. If you use another program to create your web pages, you can just mount your MobileMe server space, known as iDisk, and copy, move, or delete files in the Finder.

If you have a bunch of pictures in iPhoto and you want to share them with your family, you can publish them straight to MobileMe. You can also use MobileMe to share movies you make in iMovie or music and podcasts you make in GarageBand. Using MobileMe is all about putting things on the Web without ever having to actually deal with the Web.

Much like your home account, your MobileMe account contains a public folder. If you want to put something online for a friend or co-worker, you just copy it to your public folder. If you have a friend who puts something in their public folder for you, you can mount their public folder in the Finder as well.

To access your iDisk, click its icon in the Devices section of any Finder window. The Finder's menu bar also contains an iDisk submenu under the Go menu. You can use that to connect to your iDisk, another user's iDisk, or another user's public folder. You can also jump to your iDisk by pressing Shift-Command-I.

If your friends don't have a Mac, let alone MobileMe, that's OK. With a few clicks, you can set up a file exchange site so people can download and upload files to your public disk from their web browser, as shown in Figure 20-7. If you'd rather not have your public disk be entirely public, you can password protect it.

Back to My Mac

When you turn Back to My Mac on, the MobileMe server keeps track of where on the Internet your computer is. Should you find yourself at work or school having left your big presentation sitting on your desktop, no worries. With Back to My Mac, you can log into your machine remotely and access the missing files.

To use Back to My Mac, select the MobileMe pane in System Preferences, and then choose the Back to My Mac tab. Click the Start button to make your computer accessible from the Internet. Then, click the Open Sharing Preferences button to move to the Sharing pane. From here, enable screen sharing, file sharing, and other services you'd like to be able to access remotely.

Figure 20-7. *Navigating an iDisk in the Finder and Safari*

■**Note** For more information on the various sharing services, see the "Sharing" section later in this chapter.

Third-Party Integration

A platform is only as strong as its third-party development. Even though Apple writes a lot of great software and bundles most of it for free with every new Mac, what really makes the platform amazing is how much great third-party software there is. Development on the platform is strong, competitive, and innovative.

It's the same story with MobileMe. Apple doesn't hog it all to itself. Rather, Apple has opened it up for development and encouraged developers to incorporate MobileMe into their applications. Many developers do, and why not? Customers love being able to use MobileMe, and providing a great user experience is what makes great software.

Third-party software can (and does) take advantage of MobileMe to back up and sync the data on all your machines. For example, Panic's Transmit uses MobileMe to sync bookmarked FTP servers, and Bare Bones Software's Yojimbo uses MobileMe to sync bookmarks, notes, and other stored data. Third-party developers also take advantage of MobileMe's ability to get your stuff on the Web with little to no effort on your part.

We'll give you a personal example. One of us worked for a company that makes a piece of software for organizing your personal media collection called Delicious Library. In Delicious

Library 2, we added a feature called Web Publishing. This is probably the number-one requested feature, and it's definitely the biggest selling point of the new version. When we won the Apple Design Award for Best Leopard Application, this was the feature the judges showed off.

When you publish a collection, you can send it to iWeb to deal with it as you will. If you have a server, you can set up an FTP account and upload it that way. You can also publish your collection to a folder and use Transmit to deal with it. In any case, it's pretty easy, but it takes a few steps and some configuration—that is, unless you have MobileMe, as shown in Figure 20-8, in which case, you don't have to configure anything because all your MobileMe account information is already known to the system. You can just hit the Publish button, and your collection will be turned into a web page and uploaded to your MobileMe account. When it's done, you can visit your collection online and send the link to your friends to check it out.

Figure 20-8. *Publishing to MobileMe in Delicious Library 2*

If your friends are using Delicious Library as well, your collection will automatically be added to their computers so they can browse your media from within Delicious Library. You don't have to take any additional steps. All of that stuff is handled automatically by MobileMe.

Informal Networking

It wasn't that long ago when there was no Internet to which regular people could connect. Back then, setting up a local area network in your house was far too expensive to be feasible, and wireless networking wasn't even something most people could fathom. Yet, whenever two people had a file they wanted to exchange that wouldn't fit on a 1.44 MB floppy disk or they wanted to play some head-to-head Doom, they were always faced with the same problem: how the heck do we connect these two computers?

Even when the Internet was well established and routers were cheap, creating a small, informal network between two or three computers was always a big challenge. Fortunately, the modern Macintosh makes these arrangements, known as *ad hoc networks*, extremely easy to set up and use.

Target Disk Mode

The first question you have to ask yourself is, why would I want to connect two computers? A lot of times it's to exchange files. Whether it's to copy some work from a laptop to a desktop or to move some videos from a desktop to a TV server, people are forever connecting two machines just to facilitate getting files from computer A to computer B.

In this case, a network is not actually necessary. Any two Macs with FireWire ports can take advantage of a special FireWire trick called Target Disk mode. To put a computer into Target Disk mode, hold the T key while booting, or select Target Disk mode from the Startup Disk pane of System Preferences. The machine will start, but instead of a login screen, the computer's monitor will display the FireWire symbol.

When it's in Target Disk mode, a computer is treated as just another FireWire peripheral. That means if you plug it into another computer, that machine will mount the targeted machine's drives as if they were regular external drives, as shown in Figure 20-9. This includes the hard drive, as well as connected drives such as the DVD drive.

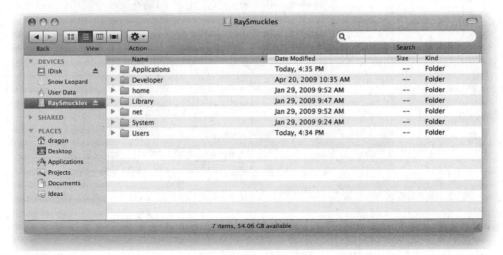

Figure 20-9. *Mounting a machine in Target Disk mode in the Finder*

To copy, move, or delete files, just do so in the Finder as you would with an external drive. You can also read or eject removable media in the usual way. Even with gigabit Ethernet, which is theoretically faster, a direct connection with a FireWire 800 cable is pretty much as fast as it gets when it comes to moving files.

■**Note** Somewhat counterintuitively, the proper way to bring a computer out of Target Disk mode is to hold down its power button until it shuts down. However, like any other external drive, you must remember to eject it from your machine first.

Target Disk mode can do some pretty interesting things. Since Mac OS X can boot from a FireWire drive, you can boot your computer as a different machine by putting that machine in Target Disk mode. That means you could put your laptop into Target Disk mode and boot your Mac Pro from its drive so you'd be using your laptop, except it would be your Mac Pro. Then you put the Mac Pro into Target Disk mode and use it from your laptop.

Why would you ever do that? Well, maybe your laptop got run over by a car and the screen is busted but the mechanics are still good. That sounds far-fetched, but it's actually a documented occurrence. Or maybe your friend brings over a Mac mini, and you want to boot it up but you don't have a monitor. As long as you have your laptop, Target Disk mode is all you need.

AirPort

If both machines have AirPort cards, it's easy to connect them. One machine can create an ad hoc AirPort network if you simply select the Create Network option from the AirPort menu bar item, as shown in Figure 20-10. After you give it a name and an optional password, other people can join the network from the AirPort menu bar item as well.

Figure 20-10. *Creating an ad hoc network with AirPort*

If you don't use the AirPort menu bar item, you can accomplish the same thing through the Network pane of System Preferences. Simply select the AirPort icon on the sidebar, and then, from the Network Name drop-down menu, select Create New Network. Other AirPort users can connect the same way.

We've never had a lot of luck setting up Wi-Fi on non-Macintosh computers, but since AirPort is just Apple's brand of Wi-Fi, it's at least theoretically possible to connect to Windows machines the same way.

■Note Unfortunately, AirPort's ad hoc networking doesn't support WPA, so you're stuck with easily cracked WEP encryption instead. Try not to talk about too many state secrets over an ad hoc network.

FireWire and Ethernet

If you don't have AirPort or want a faster way to connect, you can always plug the two machines together with FireWire. Aside from Target Disk mode, FireWire is actually a full network interface. After connecting the two machines, open the Networking pane of System Preferences.

You will have a self-assigned IP address. It doesn't really matter what it is, as long as the other person's self-assigned address is not the same. If it is the same, one of you should edit the last number so it's different.

Ethernet works the same way. Connect two machines, check the IP addresses, and change one if necessary. With Ethernet there is a trick, however. Some types of Ethernet cables are specially designed for connecting two machines directly. These so-called crossover cables are typically green in color.

If you're both using Macs, it doesn't matter whether you're using a crossover cable. If you connect two Macs with a standard cable, they will automatically cross over their Ethernet connections, so it makes no difference at all. If you're trying to connect to a machine that isn't a Mac, or a Mac too old to run Mac OS X, be aware that you might need the special cable.

Assuming you have the latest versions of each and the proper cables, there's no particular advantage between FireWire and Ethernet as network adapters. There is, however, an advantage to having two network adapters.

You can connect your computer to another computer using one and then connect your computer to a different computer using the other. By switching off between the two, you can chain together any number of computers into an arbitrarily long daisy chain.

Bonjour

Once your machines are connected, you can do any of things you would be able to do on a local area network, including connecting via the Finder and addressing each other directly by IP address or the .local name setup in the Sharing pane of System Preferences.

More important, Bonjour will work. If you need to exchange a file or communicate in some way, iChat's Bonjour window will enable you to do that, as shown in Figure 20-11. Many networkable Mac applications provide support for Bonjour, so if you're connecting your machines to go head-to-head on some network-enabled game, check to see whether it supports Bonjour. If it does and you can manage to somehow connect one machine into the other, you're good to go.

Whether you're connected directly, via a LAN, or by the Internet itself, there's a lot more you can do than pass files back and forth in iChat, share a printer, or play a game of Quinn. To enable most of it, though, you'll have to learn to share.

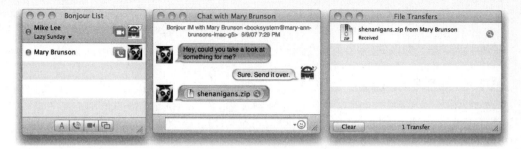

Figure 20-11. *Simple file transfer with Bonjour in iChat*

Sharing

If this chapter has taught you anything, it should be that there are a lot of different ways to connect to another computer. Even though the standard version of Mac OS X is called the client version, in UNIX the line between client and server is tenuous at best. With Mac OS X, if you can be a client, you can probably be a server. To see this for yourself, open the Sharing pane in System Preferences, and read the long list of services you can offer, as shown in Figure 20-12.

Selecting a service from the list on the left will open status and preference information on the right. To activate or deactivate a service, toggle the check box next to its name. System changes, such as opening the relevant port and making necessary adjustments to the firewall, are done for you.

Figure 20-12. *Many ways to share your Mac in System Preferences*

Although each type of sharing has a description, it's not necessarily obvious exactly to which protocols or services they relate. Make sure you have the right service before you check the box and run out the door, or you might be in for an unpleasant surprise.

DVD or CD Sharing

Optical drives are such anachronisms, or so the MacBook Air would have you believe. For people who use only the DVD drive to install updates of Mac OS X that come knocking, Snow Leopard provides DVD or CD sharing. You wouldn't want to use this to watch a movie, but for installing software once in a while, it gets the job done.

Screen Sharing

This allows people to connect to your machine using Snow Leopard's built-in screen sharing, but not Apple Remote Desktop. It bears noting that screen sharing is more than just being able to see your machine. People who share your screen can actually use your computer as if they were sitting at it, as shown in Figure 20-13. It's the graphical equivalent of logging in with ssh.

Options include explicitly naming which users can connect using this protocol, whether people can request to control the screen, and whether to protect screen control with a password. Note that turning on screen sharing will cause your computer to become browsable from your local network, so don't turn it on unless you need it.

When might you use screen sharing? Traditionally, its primary purpose is administrative. Apple Remote Desktop is, above all, a tool to help system administrators manage a network of machines. By bundling screen sharing with Snow Leopard, Apple is expanding it to more informal uses. For example, if your mom calls you for tech support, you can just show her how to update her web page in iWeb instead of trying to describe it over the phone.

Figure 20-13. *Controlling a remote computer with screen sharing*

File Sharing

When you connect to another machine in the Finder, you are using file sharing. In some previous versions of Mac OS X, different protocols were listed separately. In Snow Leopard, AFP, FTP, and SMB are all covered by the same service. You can decide which protocols are allowed by clicking the Options button.

In addition to the protocol list, you can decide which folders you'd like to share and explicitly list which users should be allowed to connect to your machine. As with screen sharing, enabling file sharing will make your machine visible on the local network, so make sure you need it before activating it. Also, SMB requires storing passwords in a less-secure way than Mac OS X prefers, so make double sure you need to let people connect to you with SMB before activating it.

Access to folders and files on your machine is determined by the permissions and access lists you've already set up. If you'd like to exchange files with other people on the network without having to worry about all that stuff, you can use the default `Public` folder, which is set up automatically on each new account.

By default, people who connect to your machine can read files from the `Public` folder, but they cannot edit or delete them, and they cannot put files in the `Public` folder itself. Within the `Public` folder, there's a folder called `Drop Box`, which works in the opposite way. People can put files in the `Drop Box` folder, but they cannot open the `Drop Box` folder to access the files it contains.

If you have a file you want people to access, simply put it in the `Public` folder. If someone else needs to give you a file, they can simply drop it in the `Drop Box` folder. It doesn't get much easier than that!

Printer Sharing

When printer sharing is enabled, printers connected to your machine are also connected to the network. Other machines on the network can see the printer in the printing system and negotiate the protocol on their own, typically via Bonjour. If you have a desktop machine hooked up to the printer, this a great way to print from your laptop.

Scanner Sharing

Many, if not most, of the printers sold these days are multi-function machines that also serve as scanners. Snow Leopard brings improved support and additional functionality for scanning, as Leopard did for printing. Expect to see a lot of references to printing in Snow Leopard to be followed with references to scanning. Scanner sharing is a case in point. It's just like printer sharing, but for scanners.

Web Sharing

This simple, ambiguous name covers a lot of ground—so much ground, in fact, the entire next chapter is devoted to it. In a nutshell, though, web sharing means you will host web sites from your machine.

Remote Login

Unlike file sharing, which covers all manner of file transfer protocols, Remote Login specifically enables Secure Shell. Although Remote Login is conceptually similar to screen sharing
(and sounds similar to Remote Desktop), as far as the Sharing pane is concerned, they are
completely unrelated. The only option is an access control list.

Remote Management

Not to be mistaken for Remote Login or screen sharing, Remote Management controls whether
people can connect to your machine using Apple Remote Desktop. Options are almost identical to screen sharing.

Traditionally, a given protocol used a given port, so enabling access to a particular service
was an all-or-nothing affair. As discussed in the previous chapter, Snow Leopard's firewall is
able to route or block requests at the application level. As such, even though Apple Remote
Desktop and screen sharing use the same protocols, they can be enabled, disabled, and configured separately.

Remote Apple Events

The Apple Events system underlies inter-application communication, as used by AppleScript.
To control a remote machine with AppleScript, therefore, a machine would have to respond to
remote Apple Events. This would be useful if you were trying to use AppleScript to automate
some administrative task over a network.

For example, if your remote machine were at IP address 10.0.1.5, you could make it sleep
with the following bit of AppleScript:

```
tell application "Finder" of machine "eppc://10.0.1.5"
    sleep
end tell
```

You can scale this technique to do amazing things with scriptable applications such as
iTunes. For an example, check out the remote access section of Doug's AppleScripts for iTunes
(http://dougscripts.com/itunes/itinfo/remcontrol.php). We talk more about Doug, and
AppleScript, in Chapter 22.

Xgrid Sharing

If you have a bunch of Macs and a copy of Snow Leopard server, you have a supercomputer.
Mac OS X includes Xgrid, the same cluster computing software used in university supercom-
puters. The Xgrid Admin application bundled with Mac OS X Server makes it easy to set up
computing clusters using Bonjour. You can also purchase the application separately from
Apple, but you need only one copy. The other machines simply enable Xgrid sharing with
this setting.

Internet Sharing

Contrary to what you might be led to believe by its ambiguous name, enabling Internet sharing does not allow you to connect to your computer from other computers on the Internet. Rather, it allows you to share the Internet from your computer with other computers.

The typical Mac has at least three network interfaces: Ethernet, FireWire, and AirPort. At any moment, only one of those interfaces is usually connected to the Internet, while other interfaces could be connected to another computer or even an entirely different network. By enabling Internet sharing, you're able to let the computers on one network interface connect to the Internet on another.

For example, a typical setup might have the Internet coming into your home via a cable or DSL modem, which, in turn, is connected to an AirPort base station. All the computers in your home would then be connected to the AirPort base station, sharing its Internet connection.

With Internet sharing, you could instead plug one computer directly into the modem via Ethernet and then use that machine's AirPort card to create an ad hoc network that other computers could use to share the Internet connection, eliminating the need for the AirPort base station altogether.

This kind of setup is particularly convenient when you are away from home. If your hotel room has an Internet connection via Ethernet, several people can share that connection without having to pack an AirPort base station or other network hardware.

Bluetooth Sharing

Although it's usually associated with headsets and other simple gadgets, Bluetooth is a general short-range wireless standard that can connect two machines with file systems, such as two computers, or a computer and a phone. To move files around over a Bluetooth connection, you'll need to enable Bluetooth sharing, though connecting a Bluetooth device will usually activate Bluetooth sharing for you.

Summary

When it comes to connecting to remote machines, you have a lot of options. Networking is built into the Finder, and MobileMe takes this even further, integrating the entire web publishing experience into the Mac's legendary interface. Third-party applications expand this integration by offering direct connections to the Internet, either through MobileMe or by directly incorporating Internet technology such as FTP and Secure Shell.

Networking is no longer a one-way street with clients and servers having immutable, predefined roles. Any Mac has the pedigree of a server built right into System Preferences, whether it's to simply share a file, to allow remote access to the machine, or to take on a more permanent role.

In the next chapter, we'll explore a particularly common sharing scenario: setting up a web server on your Mac. Whether creating an intranet, building a test platform for development, or hosting a web site from your home or office, you'll see that serving web pages on Mac OS X is easy to do but endlessly configurable.

## CHAPTER 21

Snow Leopard As a Web Server

Snow Leopard makes doing everything with the Web as easy as doing it on Mac OS X. We talked about surfing the Web with Safari in Chapter 10, publishing to the Web with MobileMe in Chapter 13, and generating content for the Web throughout the book. There's one thing left to do: become a part of the Web itself by hosting a web server.

To some that might sound complicated, but it doesn't have to be. Getting started is as easy as clicking a button. For the hardcore Net geeks, don't be fooled by the Snow Leopard's cuddly appearance. When you want to get fierce, there are fangs and claws to go around.

So, whether you'd like to host a home page for your neighborhood bridge club, build an intranet for your home or office, or develop and stage web applications for production and profit, keep reading. It's time to get your web on.

Apache

Snow Leopard's built-in web server traces its lineage to an undergraduate working at the National Center for Supercomputing Applications named Rob McCool. As part of the Mosaic web server project, McCool wrote a web server named NCSA HTTPd. The incongruous name, like the program itself, was named after the first web server, CERN HTTPd, developed by Sir Tim Berners-Lee on a NeXT cube.

Rob McCool, and his twin brother Mike (who joined the Mosaic team to port Mosaic to the Macintosh), graduated, leaving NCSA HTTPd orphaned. As many a young engineer discovers, software has a way of outliving its creator's interest. People continued not only using the web server but also writing improvements that could be patched over the original code.

In 1996 this crazy quilt of code became known as the Apache web server, a nod both to the Native American people famed for their endurance and to its roots as a "patchy" web server. Apache has since become the world's leading open source web server. Its current incarnation, Apache 2, stands ready to host your personal home page, as shown in Figure 21-1.

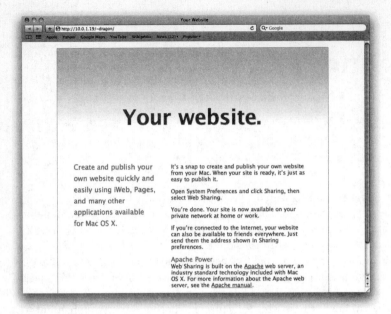

Figure 21-1. *The default personal home page in Safari*

To enable all this goodness, you need to turn on web sharing in the Sharing preference pane in System Preferences. Select the Web Sharing box, and you may imagine your computer shuddering slightly as Apache rumbles to life. Once the check box is tamed, the dialog helpfully explains where everything is, as shown in Figure 21-2.

Figure 21-2. *Activating web sharing from System Preferences*

■**Note** If your site doesn't show up, see the "Tips and Tricks" section later in this chapter.

■**Caution** Turning on web sharing is an all-or-nothing proposition. If you turn web sharing on for one account, it will be on for all accounts. To change this behavior, see the "Configuring Apache" section later in this chapter.

Customizing Your Site

As the panel explains, your personal home page is kept in your user `Sites` directory. Visiting the address it gives you will load the content in that directory. Using your favorite web design tool, publish your content to your local `Sites` directory, and then reload the page; your new site should be there, as shown in Figure 21-3.

Figure 21-3. *A customized local home page in Safari*

In addition to the user sites located at `~username`, your machine also has a site, as shown in Figure 21-4. This site's content is located in the Apache server's document root. Unlike the logical `~/Sites` location, the default document root is `/Library/WebServer/Documents`. On a single-user machine, these two sites can be combined, as discussed in the "Tips and Tricks" section later in this chapter.

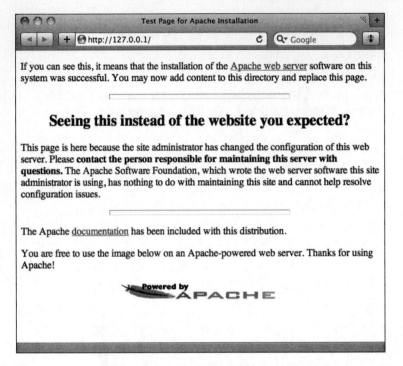

Figure 21-4. *The site at Apache's document root*

Accessing Your Site

The IP addresses provided by the Web Sharing panel are sufficient for most tasks. You can use them to access your machine from the local network. That's enough for testing web applications, participating in an intranet, or testing an iPhone application.

That said, several other addresses refer to your site. Some may be more or less appropriate than the suggested addresses, depending on your needs and network configuration.

Your computer is also known by the name localhost and the IP address 127.0.0.1. These are *loopbacks*, meaning they always refer to the current machine. In other words, if another user on your network were to try to access your site at 127.0.0.1, they would get their own machine.

Your machine also has a domain name in the .local domain, based on the machine name you set in the Sharing preferences. Domain name services for .local are provided by the multicast DNS functionality that underlies the zero-configuration networking feature, Bonjour.

If you want to serve web pages to the world at large, things get a bit more complicated. As explained in Chapter 19, most machines aren't directly accessible from the Internet. A typical network uses NAT and DHCP to dynamically map local, private IP addresses—typically starting with 10, 169, or 192—to an external IP address that connects to the Internet.

It's certainly possible to get your external IP address by visiting a web site like whatismyipaddress.com, whatismyip.com, myipaddress.com, whatsmyip.org . . . the list goes on. Or, just google *My IP Address*. Then you can use the port mapping technique, again covered in Chapter 19, and set your computer to use its reserved address via the Network pane of System Preferences, as shown in Figure 21-5.

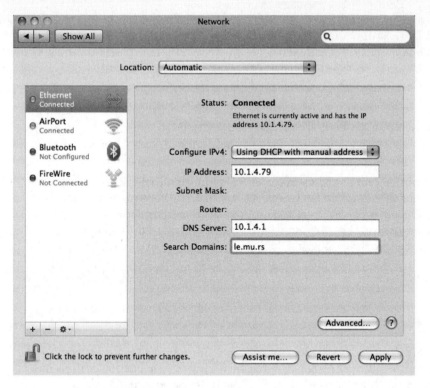

Figure 21-5. *The Network pane of System Preferences*

■**Tip** Which network interface is the appropriate one? Chances are, you have only one active interface, which will have a green light next to it. If you have multiple active network interfaces, pick one that's connected to the network from which you are trying to access the machine.

It's certainly possible, using techniques such as port mapping, to provide technical solutions that may not jive with your ISP or local IT department. For most people, hosting a production web server is like sewing your own clothes. You're not going to beat the professionals on quality or price, but you have the hobbyist's satisfaction of doing things your own way.

Configuring Apache

Since Apache is a UNIX application, it doesn't have a convenient GUI preference pane, and it doesn't use a standard Macintosh property list. Rather, it has its own configuration file in its own directory using its own peculiar scheme.

Fortunately, the configuration file, like everything else about Apache, is well documented and, honestly, not that complicated. The default home pages all contain links to the Apache manual, as does the dire warning that begins the configuration file itself. You can always just go straight to Apache's documentation home page: http://httpd.apache.org/docs/.

Apache's configuration files live in the directory /private/etc/apache2. Unless you've turned on the ability to see invisible files in the Finder, you'll have to navigate there in Terminal. Listing the contents of the directory shows the file we've come here to see: httpd.conf.

■**Note** Although it's called Apache, the name of the UNIX executable is httpd, which reflects its role as a background process (daemon) that serves the Hypertext Transfer Protocol.

Open httpd.conf in your text editor of choice. We recommend using BBEdit or its free alternative, TextWrangler. With BBEdit, you can use the disk browser to easily navigate here, since it can see the hidden folders. It will also take care of overwriting the old file, which is read-only. That said, you can also use Nano, Emacs, or Vi, as detailed in Chapter 17.

The configuration file is very long, but don't be scared. Lines that start with the pound sign are comments, which is to say they are ignored. The file mainly consists of hints explaining what the various sections do. There's very little actual content here, and even less you have to worry about.

ServerRoot

Much as UNIX considers ~ to be a shortcut for your user directory, the ServerRoot command tells Apache where it should look for any files that are not explicitly named. Since these files are all for its internal use, there's really no need to change the default value.

Listen

Like any server process, Apache listens on a particular port or socket. Normally, it answers any incoming calls on port 80. If you need to change the port for some reason or you want to bind to a specific IP address, you can edit this.

One particular use for Listen is to limit who can see your page. Remember how we said you could load your page by one of several means? What if you don't want people to be able to load your page elsewhere on the network? By binding Apache to 127.0.0.1:80, you will be able to view the page locally only. Dialing in to the actual IP address would simply return an error page.

Another use for the Listen directive is to use a port other than the default. For example, your ISP may block access to port 80 in an effort to prevent you from running a web server from your home. You could instead bind to port 8080.

You can bind to multiple ports and sockets by issuing multiple Listen directives. So, for example, to view the site locally on the standard port but to let others see it only on a secret port, you could say this:

```
Listen 127.0.0.1:80
Listen 1984
```

You could then load your site by simply pointing to 127.0.0.1, but someone else on the network loading your site would get an error unless they knew to append the correct port to the end of your IP address. So, for example, if your IP address were 10.0.0.1, they would have to point their browser to http://10.0.0.1:1984.

Dynamic Shared Object (DSO) Support

Dynamic Shared Object (DSO) is a fancy name for the LoadModule directive. As the name may suggest, LoadModule loads . . . modules, which are plug-in software products that extend the functionality of Apache. Several modules are loaded by default. We will come back to LoadModule when we are ready to add PHP to our web server.

User/Group

Since Apache operates on your system, it needs to be able to access files. You could run it as root, but that would be a security risk. Instead, Apache runs as the user www as part of the group www. Should you want to change this, you would do that here. Honestly, though, you probably don't need to do that.

VirtualHost

If you have a web site running on a host somewhere, chances are you're not on a dedicated server. Lucky for everyone involved, you can run multiple sites on a single machine using a feature called *virtual hosting*.

Virtual hosting is off by default, but if you want to configure multiple sites to run on your machine, perhaps because you work on multiple sites and would like to access them all separately, you can do so.

Incidentally, the different user sites built into Mac OS X, while similar to virtual hosting, are actually a different feature; they're user directories, provided by the UserDir module. User directories are for multiple users on one site, while virtual hosts are for multiple sites on one machine.

ServerAdmin

One of the nice things Apache does is automatically generate index and error pages for you. Since these pages may require action by the server administrator, they will include an e-mail address. That address is given with the ServerAdmin directive.

ServerName

Similarly, the ServerName directive is how the server refers to itself. This would typically be the domain name and port, or possibly the IP address. Since this information can be determined automatically, it's commented out by default. Should you find yourself actually serving web pages to the public, you should define it explicitly.

DocumentRoot

This directive tells Apache where to start serving pages from. That is to say, it defines which directory on the host machine is represented by / in the web address. Directories attached to / will be similarly mapped to directories on the host machine.

By default, the document root is set to `/Library/WebServer/Documents`, so loading `http://127.0.0.1/` loads the contents of `/Library/WebServer/Documents`. Loading `http://127.0.0.1/Site/Welcome.html` loads the file `/Library/WebServer/Documents/Site/Welcome.html`.

If you wanted to change the document root to your user directory, you could change the DocumentRoot directive to the following:

```
DocumentRoot "/Users/username/Sites"
```

You can also redirect the document root using symbolic links, as discussed in the "Tips and Tricks" section later in this chapter.

Permissions

There's no actual Permissions directive, but that's the best term we can think of to describe the several entries that follow. These define the options for directories and files on the system. A notable entry is the Options FollowSymLinks directive, which is on by default and which allows our symbolic link trick to work.

There are several more entries that block web visitors from being able to see certain types of files, such as hidden files that begin with a dot or the Mac OS X resource files.

One thing to keep in mind is that there are permissions entries for every known directory, including the document root. If you change a directory elsewhere in the configuration, you will have to be sure to change its permissions entry as well. This is one of the reasons why using symbolic links is easier than editing the configuration file.

DirectoryIndex

Easily missed amidst all the permissions directives, the DirectoryIndex directive defines the default index file name. That is to say, when a user simply points to a directory, which file do they get? The default is index.html, which is why you don't have to type index.html all the time when you're surfing the Web.

If you decide to start using PHP or some other technology that requires you to use a different file name or extension, you can edit this. By including multiple listings, you can give several possible defaults. Apache will serve up the first one it finds. For example, to serve index.html by default but then serve the old Microsoft FrontPage standard, welcome.html, as a backup, you would say the following:

```
DirectoryIndex index.html welcome.html
```

If nothing listed in DirectoryIndex exists, visitors will see a listing of everything in the directory. To prevent that, you can put a failsafe at the end of the DirectoryIndex directive, such as a reference to a file in your root directory telling people to stop poking around in your directories:

```
DirectoryIndex index.html welcome.html /lost.html
```

Logging

There are several directives related to logging. You can customize where logs are kept, how much logging Apache should do, and what format log messages are in. These are best kept to the default values, but if you spend a lot of time reading your logs and you develop an opinion on some aspect of logging, here is where you can flex your will.

Redirects

Much like the DocumentRoot directive, the Redirect, Alias, and ScriptAlias directives let you map the URLs people request to your file system.

Redirect will actually cause the browser to request a new location. This is useful if you've permanently moved a file to elsewhere on the system. Alias will cause a given path to look outside the normal document root hierarchy.

For example, you might want to give the outside world access to your `Pictures` directory (for some reason) by mapping requests to `www.yoursite.com/pictures` to `/Users/username/Pictures`. You could, of course, also accomplish this with symbolic links, assuming you allow FollowSymLinks on the directory.

ScriptAlias is like Alias, but it applies specifically to directories that contain executable scripts, rather than simple documents.

DefaultType

Most of the Internet uses MIME types to determine how it should deal with files. Since most web servers serve web pages, it's appropriate to leave this set to the default, `text/plain`.

■**Note** MIME stands for Multipurpose Internet Mail Extensions. Like most of the Internet, it has been expanded beyond its original purpose.

What makes this directive interesting is actually the list of AddType and AddHandler directives, which allow you to add support for certain types of files. The list starts with a TypesConfig directive that points to an external list of types, stored by default in `/private/etc/apache2/mime.types`.

Most webmasters meet the `types` section when adding PHP support, because the traditional `php` file extension is not handled by default; however, on Snow Leopard, this is handled for you in the PHP configuration file.

ErrorDocument

If you ever go poking around the coolest sites on the Net, they always seem to have these sexy custom error pages, so pulling a 403: Access Denied doesn't jar you from the overall design of the site. The ErrorDocument directive lets you point to custom pages and scripts.

If you define a custom error document, be sure to actually implement it, lest your users not only be treated to a generic error page but also be blighted with the ever-embarrassing "Additionally, a 404 Not Found error was encountered while trying to use an ErrorDocument to handle the request."

Include

Apache configuration is typically split into multiple files. External files are referred to using the Include directive. For the purposes of scope, you can consider the entire text of an included file to be inserted where the Include directive is used.

This is important, because the general rule with Apache is that the last word is the one that's obeyed. So, if an included file disagrees with the main file, the one farther down the list is going to win. If you find some configuration detail is not working, despite being clearly documented, make sure you're not being overridden by another file.

Of particular importance is this line:

```
Include /private/etc/apache2/extra/httpd-userdir.conf
```

Editing the `httpd-userdir.conf` file reveals two things. First, it uses the UserDir directive to tell Apache that every user's personal root is their `Sites` directory. If, for example, you are old-school and you'd prefer this directory to be called `public_html`, this is where you'd set that up.

Second, this file in turn includes all `.conf` files contained in the directory `/private/etc/apache2/users`. Listing that directory reveals a series of files of the form `username.conf`, where `username` is a username on the system.

Each of these files contains a permissions directive.

```
<Directory "/Users/username/Sites/">
    Options Indexes MultiViews
    AllowOverride None
    Order allow,deny
    Allow from all
</Directory>
```

Again, `username` refers to the actual username dealt with by the file.

By default, all directories on your system are forbidden, except for those explicitly named. This directive makes the named user's `Sites` folder readable and sets up a few options. Were this file to be missing, you would not be able to access your site, regardless of system-level permissions.

When you turn on web sharing, these files are created by default. By editing the files, you can disallow certain users the ability to host sites. You could even remove the main include, disabling all user sites, while giving yourself the document root.

■Note Although disabling the explicit permissions on a user directory will do the job in a roundabout way, the proper way to enable or disable users is with the UserDir directive. See the Apache documents for more information.

Whenever you change Apache's configuration file, you will need to restart Apache. The easiest way to do this is with Terminal, using the special Apache control program, `apachectl`.

```
sudo apachectl -k graceful
```

This will restart Apache gracefully, which is to say, it will let it finish what it's doing, shut down, and then restart.

If you try to restart Apache but it's not already running for some reason, it will just start. If you've messed up the configuration file, it will usually let you know on restart. Otherwise, you should be ready to test your changes.

PHP

PHP is the weapon of choice for many developers for creating dynamic web pages and applications. PHP is a dynamic scripting language that can be embedded in web pages. PHP is processed by the server, outputting normal HTML. Unlike client-side technologies such as JavaScript, PHP developers know their scripts will run with the capabilities they need.

Since it is open source, PHP is the preprocessor of choice on UNIX systems running Apache. Indeed, PHP has been implemented as an Apache module and comes installed, but not activated, by default on Mac OS X.

To properly ensure PHP is installed, you need to have a PHP page. The best test page is a simple PHP Info page. It relies on PHP to be working, so it's a good test, and it gives you a lot of information about your PHP installation, so it's actually useful.

Create a PHP Info page in your favorite text editor, and save it to your document root as `index.php`. All you need to include is a single call to PHP's built-in `phpinfo` function:

```
<?php phpinfo() ?>
```

Then, load the page in your browser of choice by pointing to `http://127.0.0.1/index.php`. You have to point to the page explicitly, because otherwise you'll get the default index page, `index.html`.

■**Note** You can, of course, also save the PHP Info page to your home `Sites` directory.

Loading the page in your browser, you're greeted with the entirety of its source, as written. That's because Apache doesn't know what a `.php` file is, so it's serving it as its default MIME type, `text/plain`.

To enable PHP, you simply need to uncomment a single line of text from the Apache configuration file:

```
#LoadModule php5_module        libexec/apache2/libphp5.so
```

Since it starts with #, it's a comment and is ignored. Delete the # and save. Back in the day, you'd also have to tell Apache how to handle the file type and look for `index.php` by default, but all that stuff is now handled automatically by the included `php5.conf` file. Just restart Apache, and, as the saying goes, there is no step 3. The PHP Info screen should now display properly, as shown in Figure 21-6.

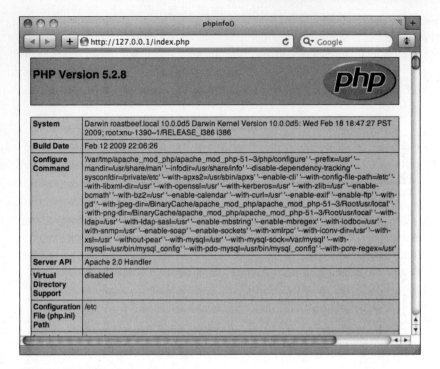

Figure 21-6. *PHP Info page in Safari*

Examining the PHP Info page will tell you a lot about how your server is set up. It's a good idea to run it on both your local machine and your remote host so you can be aware of any differences between versions, features, or configuration options that might affect you.

To learn more about PHP, including an extensive manual with installation and integration guides, visit PHP's official web site at www.php.net.

Database

Many web servers add a database server to the operating system, web server daemon, and scripting engine. You can add several databases to Mac OS X, Apache, and PHP. Choosing a database is a balance between power and effort. Snow Leopard has a database server running and ready, but if you need more features than the default setup provides, it's going to take some doing.

SQLite

Snow Leopard's default database manager is the fast, simple, lightweight SQLite that is quickly gaining popularity with web developers. It's compatible with the same Structured Query Language (SQL) used by nearly every other database in the world. More important, it's directly addressable from PHP.

Aside from the fact that SQLite is already set up for you, it has the major advantage of being the same database server used throughout the system. Applications written with Core

Data can use SQLite as their backing store. That means you can share a database between your Core Data application and your PHP web site without ever having to touch SQL.

■Note For more information on Core Data and other application development topics, see Chapter 23.

If you're serving web pages from your machine or if your remote host has SQLite (and the requisite PHP modules) running, you're good to go. Run `sqlite3` from the command line to access the included management program. You can also learn more by visiting `http://sqlite.org/`.

MySQL

When it debuted in 1995, MySQL was the scrappy alternative to the Tyrannosaur-like Oracle. What it lacked in features and polish, it made up for by being fast and small. It helped that it was free, open source software, quickly establishing itself next to Linux, Apache, and PHP in the standard LAMP stack.

As time went on, MySQL added features to better compete with the name-brand databases. This meant giving up its spot as everyone's favorite nimble, lightweight database to SQLite. If, however, you want to be like everyone else and run MySQL, you're going to have to install it yourself. Fortunately, MySQL maintains a Mac OS X installer package on its web site, `www.mysql.org`. To install MySQL, simply download the disk image that matches your architecture and run it.

■Note Apple also provides a good tutorial on getting up to speed with MySQL, including installation and initial configuration. See `http://developer.apple.com/internet/opensource/osdb.html`.

Although it's available in more traditional tarball format, we downloaded the more Mac-like disk image installer package. This contains an installer for the database server itself and a separate installer if you'd like MySQL to start automatically. If you're running a web server, that's probably a good idea.

Once it's installed, you can start the MySQL server from the command line. It's installed in `/usr/local`, which is not in the default path, so to run any MySQL tools you will have to actually go into the directory, or use the full path:

```
sudo -b /usr/local/mysql/bin/mysqld_safe
```

After entering your password, the server will start. The `-b` flag on `sudo` invokes the server as a background process. At your option, you can eliminate the background flag on your first run just to make sure everything is copacetic.

Alternately, if you installed the startup item, you can use it to start the MySQL database:

```
sudo /Library/StartupItems/MySQLCOM/MySQLCOM start
```

Finally, the installer includes a MySQL preference pane for System Preferences, as shown in Figure 21-7. Double-clicking will install it. The preference pane tells you whether MySQL is running, lets you start and stop MySQL, and includes a setting to automatically start MySQL at boot time.

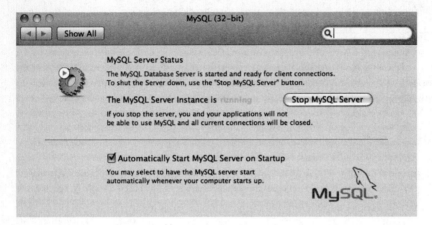

Figure 21-7. *The MySQL pane in System Preferences*

By default, MySQL sets up a root user with full access and no password. In other words, until you do something about it, your MySQL installation is completely unsecured. The first thing to do after starting the server is to lock down that root account. The easiest way to do this is with the MySQL command-line admin tool

```
/usr/local/mysql/bin/mysqladmin -u root password "newpwd"
```

where newpwd is your new password.

■**Note** Aside from the root user, there are also two anonymous accounts with unsecured root access. However, these accounts can access only those databases whose names start with test_, and only from the localhost, so they are not much of a risk. Still, if you are actually planning on serving pages professionally, you should lock or remove these accounts. See the online MySQL manual for more details.

Once it's installed, the default MySQL client program can be invoked from the command line, like so:

```
/usr/local/mysql/bin/mysql -u root -p
```

The -p flag will cause MySQL to prompt you for your password. Once you enter it, the command-line client program will launch. Type help to get a list of available commands, and type quit to exit.

MySQL also makes a set of graphical administrative tools that can be downloaded and installed separately, as shown in Figure 21-8. The graphical package contains a manager, a query tool, and a Dashboard widget for monitoring the health of your database. If you love command-line database management, more power to you. For the rest of us, the GUI is a really nice addition.

Tip To connect to your local machine's MySQL server in the graphical administrator, use the hostname `localhost`.

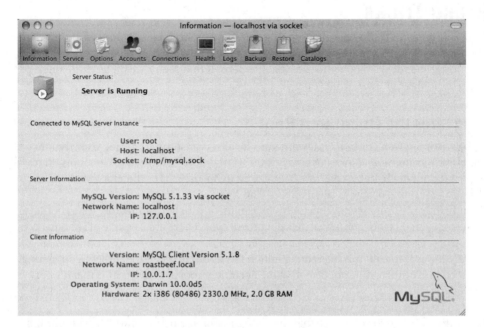

Figure 21-8. *MySQL's graphical database administration tool*

PHP and MySQL are expected to run together, so once you have MySQL running, PHP will notice immediately. Reloading your PHP Info page will confirm this. Beyond that, accessing MySQL in PHP, setting up user accounts in MySQL, and the sometimes maddening, sometimes magical world of database programming are beyond the scope of this book. Fortunately, there is no end of online resources, and there are several excellent books, including *Beginning PHP and MySQL 5* by W. Jason Gilmore (Apress, 2006), *PHP and MySQL Web Development* by Luke Welling and Laura Thomson (Addison-Wesley, 2008), and *MySQL* by Paul DuBois (Addison-Wesley, 2008).

PostgreSQL

While SQLite concentrates on pure performance and MySQL maintains a good mix of performance and added support for advanced features, PostgreSQL has always been conceived as an enterprise-level solution. It has more advanced capabilities (e.g., multiple indexing algorithms) and can be hooked up to the enterprise directory and authentication servers, LDAP, and Kerberos, but it is still free open source software.

Because it is intended for experts, PostgreSQL lacks the handholding niceties of MySQL. Fortunately, Mark Liyanage maintains a Mac OS X installer package of PostgreSQL at www.entropy.ch.

For more information on PostgreSQL, visit its official home page at www.postgresql.org.

Apple also has a page about PostgreSQL at http://developer.apple.com/internet/ opensource/postgres.html.

Tips and Tricks

The joy of running a web server on a personal computer is in mucking around with things. Sometimes a little hackery makes things more convenient; other times, it's just good, clean fun, like mixing chemicals together to see what happens. If that seems to imply a little tingle of danger, so be it. Make of these what you will.

Making Sites the Document Root

If you're developing web content, you want your local server setup to mirror your remote setup as closely as possible. Since ~username sites went out of fashion with Geocities, that means working out of the document root. Compared to the user Sites directory, working out of /Library/WebServer/Documents seems so un-Mac-like.

If you're the only user on your machine, you can unify your Sites directory (or a root-level Sites directory you'd create) with Apache's document root. There are a couple of ways to do this.

The UNIX way is to edit Apache's configuration file, as discussed in the earlier "Configuring Apache" section. The nice thing about setting the document root in httpd.conf is that it's portable. As long as you use the same username, your configuration file will work on any machine. It also doesn't rely on file system trickery, which makes it seem more pure.

The Mac way is to replace the file that the configuration file points to with a symbolic link. This uses the file system to fool Apache into loading a site different than it expects. This is the same method Mac OS X uses to bridge the Finder's view of things to the UNIX beneath.

Creating a symbolic link leaves the configuration file untouched, which makes it that much harder to mess up, but at the end of the day, it really doesn't matter which one you use.

■**Note** A symbolic link is similar to an alias on Mac or a shortcut on Windows. In Mac OS X, links are UNIX file system constructs, while aliases belong to the Finder. Using an alias to redirect your document root will not work.

To redirect your document root using symbolic links, navigate to the /Library/WebServer directory. Move aside the original Documents folder. You could delete it, but simply renaming it to something like OldDocuments will do the trick.

Launch the Terminal application from /Applications/Utilities or, if you're a true power user, from the Dock. Invoke the following command:

```
sudo ln -s ~/Sites /Library/WebServer/Documents
```

This means, "Using superuser privileges (sudo), create a link (ln) that is symbolic (-s) from my local Sites directory (~/Sites) at the path /Library/WebServer/Documents." If your user account does not have administrator privileges, you can invoke your admin user via the –u flag, as follows:

```
sudo -u yourAdminUserName ln –s ~/Sites /Library/WebServer/Documents
```

Since you're using sudo, this will prompt you for your password. After entering it, invoking ls on /Library/WebServer will show a file called Documents. In the Finder, it will appear to be a shortcut. Loading the root site in your browser of choice should show your personal home site.

■**Tip** Your browser may have the old page cached, so you might need to reload or even empty your cache to see the change.

Troubleshooting Permissions

On a clean installation of Snow Leopard, getting your home page to load really is as simple as selecting a check box, but if you've been lugging the same home directory around since 10.0, things can get a little weird. The same is true of site contents. A new site should have no problems, but importing an old site from who-knows-where might leave things broken.

One of the most common problems is seeing a 403 Forbidden message instead of a page on your site. This is caused by having improper permissions settings on Sites or its contents. In general, folders serving web sites need to be readable and executable by everyone, while web documents and files should be readable by everyone.

You can check and fix permissions on your Sites folder and its content using the Finder's Info panel by selecting the folder or file and pressing Command-I. You can also use the chmod command from the terminal—or invoke man chmod to learn more.

Domain Name Tricks

Were you so inclined, you could set up a DNS server, but why? Chances are your registrar has a name server, so providing you have a static outside IP address, you can simply have them point to it and start welcoming visitors to your self-hosted web site.

However, not everyone has the need to spend the money on a static IP address, especially when you consider that the cost of getting one is greater than the cost of professional web hosting. If you're setting up a web host just because it's fun, because you want to save money, or because you're doing local development, paying for a static IP address is overkill.

Custom Domains Without DNS

You can actually override DNS at a local level. Mac OS X maintains a list of known hosts in a file called /private/etc/hosts. Editing this file will let you map web addresses to IP addresses. Why would you do this?

First, looking at IP addresses all day is boring. That's why DNS was invented, after all. It's much more fun to give your local network machines fun names at imaginary top-level domains. Then you can surf over to http://mike.is.awesome.

Second, if you are developing web pages locally, you might run into a problem with absolute paths. That is to say, if you have a link pointing to www.mydomain.com/somefile.php, your browser will want to go to the remote version, rather than the local version you're developing.

The hosts file is the first place your machine looks when it tries to resolve a domain. Rerouting calls to mydomain.com or www.mydomain.com to your local machine is easy. Just open /private/etc/hosts in your favorite text editor, and then add the following line:

```
127.0.0.1 mydomain.com www.mydomain.com
```

Just remember to edit the hosts file back to normal before trying to surf the Web, or strange things might happen. On the other hand, maybe you want strange things to happen. One technique for blocking web content from unwanted domains is to route them to a blank page—for example:

```
128.0.0.1 doubleclick.com
```

For more information on the hosts file, invoke man hosts in Terminal.

■**Caution** It's OK to add things to the hosts file, but don't edit any of the existing entries. The system has that stuff there for a reason.

Dynamic DNS

If you've configured port mapping to reach your machine from the Internet but don't want to spend the money on a static IP address, you can use a dynamic DNS service to keep your domain name pointed to the right place.

There are many cheap to free services, such as No-IP (www.no-ip.com) and FreeDNS (http://freedns.afraid.org/), that will let you point a domain name to your dynamic IP address. Unlike a standard name server, dynamic DNS services keep a very short refresh time on their name servers, so changes propagate quickly.

Other Considerations

Here are a couple more things worth checking out:

Mac OS X Server: If you're running a site as a hobby or as a small business, the standard "client" version of Mac OS X is all you need, but Apple does produce a server version of Mac OS X, aimed at the enterprise. It has some additional administrative features that, while available in UNIX form, have been wrapped in that great Mac OS X user experience. If you're using Mac OS X as a server, you might look into it. Visit www.apple.com/server/macosx/ for more details.

Ruby on Rails: Although PHP is a popular way to create web applications, it's far from the only game in town. One platform that's rising fast is Ruby on Rails. Ruby is an object-oriented programming language, not unlike PHP 5. Rails is a development framework written in and for Ruby. Both are included with Snow Leopard. See http://developer.apple.com/tools/rubyonrails.html for more information.

Summary

With its open source and UNIX roots, Mac OS X is built from the same stuff as the Internet itself. It's no wonder the Mac is such a great platform for web development. Whether you're serving web pages to the public right from your desktop or just building a development environment on your laptop, Mac OS X comes with everything you need, and adding more is easier than ever.

■ ■ ■

Snow Leopard Development and Scripting

CHAPTER 22

■■■

Mac OS X Automation with Automator and AppleScript

If you've been using a computer for a while, you've probably figured out a few basic workflows for getting things done. You even may have committed them to muscle memory because you do them over and over. This is ironic, because computers were designed to spare you from boring, repetitive tasks. It's like tidying your hotel room.

Of course, if the hotel room is in another country, and you don't speak the language, what are you going to do? You could be at the nicest hotel in the world with a staff of thousands standing by 24 hours a day to satisfy your every need, but if you don't know how to ask for help, you'll end up tidying your own room, to say nothing of reusing your towels and foraging for coffee.

If you ever find yourself saying things like, "Why can't I make iTunes Photoshop Safari?," it's time to meet Otto, the friendly automation robot built into Mac OS X, shown in Figure 22-1. Otto isn't like your computer. Otto understands you. You can tell Otto things you want to do with your applications, and he'll do them for you.

Figure 22-1. *Otto, the mascot and application icon for Automator*

To test-drive Automator, let's build something original and cool and kind of dangerous. Mac OS X ships with an amazing photo-slideshow screen saver, but using it to show the same boring vacation photos over and over seems like a waste. Let's solve this problem by asking Otto to build an Automator application that fills our screen saver with fresh pictures it downloads through Google based on some keyword we can change with our mood.

First, just to make sure we're on the same page, let's create a folder to keep our images in and set up the screen saver to use it. Using the Finder, create a new folder in your Pictures folder called Keyword Screensaver, as shown in Figure 22-2.

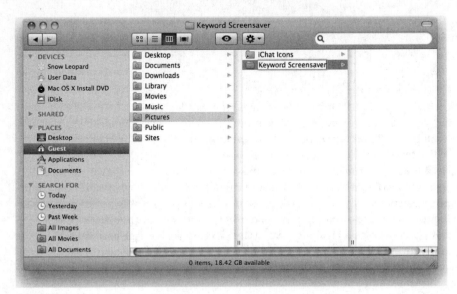

Figure 22-2. *Creating your Keyword Screensaver folder in the Finder*

With the folder in place, select System Preferences... from the Apple menu, select the Desktop & Screen Saver preference pane, and then select the Screen Saver tab. Click the plus button beneath the list of screen savers, then select Add Folder of Pictures..., as shown in Figure 22-3. This presents you with a standard open sheet. Select the Keyword Screensaver folder, and click the Choose button. Select the "falling pictures" display style, which is the second of the three style buttons under the preview.

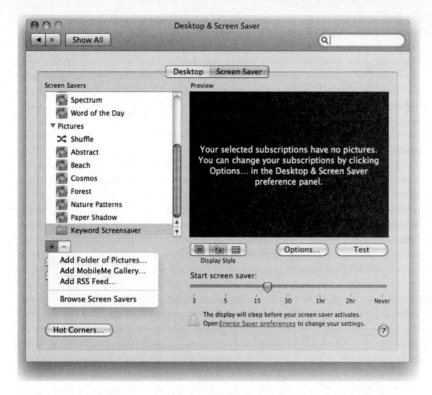

Figure 22-3. *Setting up your photo screen saver in System Preferences*

With the screen saver set up and the Keyword Screensaver folder in place, you can start working on the application. Look for Otto in the Applications folder, then double-click him to launch Automator.

Automator

Like all good document-based applications, Automator greets you with a template picker, as shown in Figure 22-4. The template picker is Otto asking you what you want to do with your workflow. You want an application you can launch from the Dock whenever you want fresh photos, so select Application and click Choose, then save the project as Keyword Screensaver.app.

■**Note** We'll talk about the other types of Automator projects in the upcoming "Advanced Automator Shenanigans" section.

Figure 22-4. *Automator's template picker showcases its expanded role in Snow Leopard.*

Actions

Automator lets you describe your workflow to Otto as a step-by-step list of simple actions, using a graphical drag-and-drop interface. Actions are the basic unit of work in Automator. The typical action takes some piece of data, asks an application to perform some task with that data, and produces the results. The results can then be fed into the next action until the work is done.

All the actions available to you are contained in the Actions library on the left side of your new workflow, as shown in Figure 22-5. You can browse actions, which are grouped in a browser view on the left. Selecting an action pops up a description view that describes what the action does, what the action needs as input, and what the action produces as a result. You can also search for an action using the search field atop the browser view.

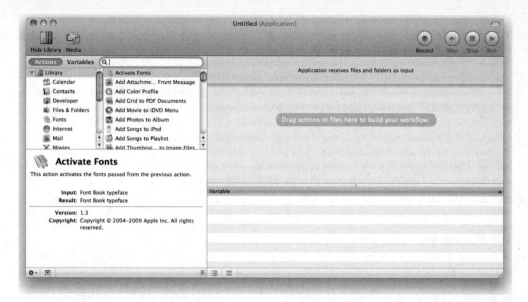

Figure 22-5. *The Actions library gives the empty shell of your new Automator application an air of possibility.*

You can create your own groups and smart groups from the group view's context menu or from the action (gear) menu in the lower-left corner of the Automator window. The default groups are based on the types of data the actions work upon:

Calendar: iCal calendars, events, and To Do items.

Contacts: Address Book contacts and information.

Developer: Xcode, SQL, CVS, and other developer tools.

Files & Folders: Finder items and tasks, including moving, copying, and deleting items; setting the desktop picture; and setting Spotlight comments.

Fonts: Font Book management tasks and metadata.

Internet: Web and RSS data, including extracting, filtering, and loading URLs.

Mail: Mail tasks, such as getting, filtering, displaying, and sending e-mail messages.

Movies: QuickTime, iMovie, iDVD, and DVD Player actions.

Music: iTunes and iPod actions, as well as the cool Text to Audio File action.

PDFs: Preview actions for creating, controlling, or extracting data from PDF documents.

Photos: iPhoto, Preview, and QuickTime actions for getting, manipulating, and organizing photos. This also includes actions for controlling digital cameras and the iSight web camera.

Presentations: Keynote actions for controlling slide-show presentations.

Text: TextEdit actions for creating, editing, and working with text documents.

Utilities: System services and Automator control actions, such as burning a disc and presenting different kinds of dialogs, as well as the powerful Run AppleScript, Run Shell Script, and Run Workflow actions.

Other: Theoretically, this group would contain actions that somehow don't fit into other groups. In practice, it's up to developers to define which groups their actions should be sorted into. If this information is not provided, the action ends up here.

■**Note** Your categories may differ based on which applications you've installed. For example, the Developer category won't exist unless you have installed the developer tools.

Workflows

On the other side of your Automator document, the workflow editor exhorts you to "Drag actions or files here to build your workflow." Heed this advice with a simple exercise to warm up for the Keyword Screensaver app. Find the Get Specified Finder Items action from the Files & Folders group and dragging it into the workflow view. As you drag the action from the sidebar to the workflow editor, it will expand into a small window with its own title bar, content view, and a tabbed details view, as shown in Figure 22-6.

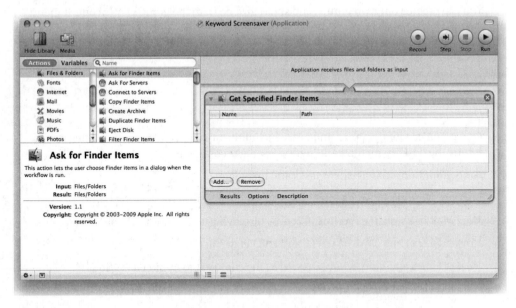

Figure 22-6. *Your first Automator action as it appears in the workflow editor*

The title bar, which has the action's name and icon, has a disclosure triangle on the left that collapses and expands the action. Double-clicking the title bar has the same effect. On the right side of the title bar is an X icon. Clicking this icon removes the action from the workflow.

■**Caution** Clicking the X icon removes the action without warning or confirmation. You can undo this by selecting Undo from the Edit menu or by pressing Command-Z.

The action's content view typically contains preferences or other configuration options in the form of drop-down boxes, text fields, table views, and so forth. The Get Specified Finder Items action contains a list of folders or files you specify, which it returns as its result. To specify the `Keyword Screensaver` folder, click the Add... button, then navigate to the `Keyword Screensaver` folder you created earlier.

■**Tip** To rearrange actions within the workflow, simply drag them around.

To run this simple workflow, click the Run button in the toolbar. Click the Results tab below the content view to see the result of running your first Automator action, as simulated in Figure 22-7.

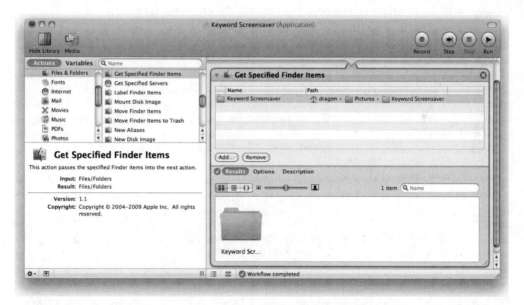

Figure 22-7. *Examining the results of running your first Automator action*

Aside from the Results tab, all actions should have a Description tab. This is the same description you see when you click an action in the Library browser. Some actions have additional options. One option you see a lot is "Show this action when the workflow runs." This is for those actions where you'd rather leave the configuration up the user. If this option is checked, the workflow will pause to present the user with more or less the same interface as the workflow editor, as shown in Figure 22-8.

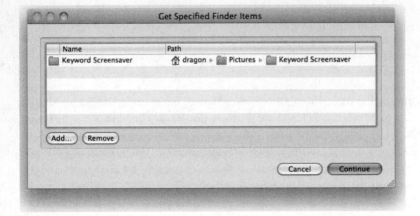

Figure 22-8. *Automator's runtime interface for the Get Specified Finder Items action*

One action isn't much of a workflow, since there's nowhere for the work to flow to. The magic is in connecting the result of one action to the input of another and combining their effects to perform a complicated task. You have a folder; it's time to look inside. Drag the Get Folder Contents action from the Files & Folders group to below the Get Specified Finder Items action. Automator connects these actions automatically, as shown in Figure 22-9.

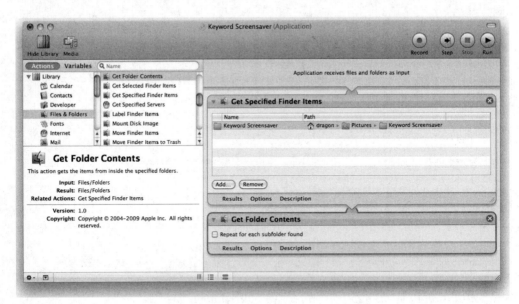

Figure 22-9. *Connecting a second action to your Automator workflow*

This connection indicates that the result of the Get Specified Finder Items action will be the input of the Get Folder Contents action. The Get Folder Contents action takes the folder you specified in the Get Specified Finder Items action and produces a list of the files and folders it contains. Next, drag the Move Finder Items to Trash action from the Files & Folders group to below the Get Folder Contents action. This takes the list of files produced by the Get Folder Contents action as input and deletes them.

Running the workflow produces a warning, as shown in Figure 22-10.

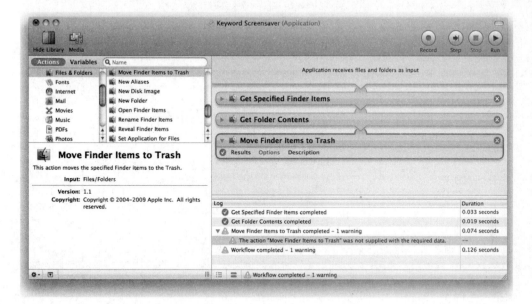

Figure 22-10. *Emptying a folder in Automator*

The warning that the Move Finder Items to Trash action was not supplied with the required data makes sense. You just created the Keyword Screensaver folder, so it doesn't contain anything. If you want to verify that it works, stick some random file in there and run the workflow again. It should run without warnings, and checking the Keyword Screensaver folder should verify that its contents have been deleted.

Deleting the contents of a folder may not seem very exciting, but there's a Mr. Miyagi moment here. Not only have you managed to build something useful, if prosaic, in Automator, but it's actually a necessary component of the Keyword Screensaver application. The first thing the application has to do is remove the old images before it downloads new ones. This forms the second, somewhat more complicated, part of the application.

Using Actions

The first action in the second part of the workflow prompts the user for a keyword. The fact that this requires user interaction should complicate things, but Otto will take care of the details. All you have to do is drag an Ask for Text action to below the Move Finder Items to Trash action. Notice that Automator does not connect these two actions. That's because the Move Finder Items to Trash action destroys its input, so it doesn't produce a result. This broken connection means no data flows between these actions. It does not affect the way the workflow runs. The actions will still run sequentially, regardless of whether the actions are connected.

The Ask for Text action displays a dialog box asking the user a question, and it provides a text area for the user to type an answer, which is this action's result. Fill the Question field with

"What keyword shall I search for?" Leave the Default field blank, and leave the button text as it is, but check the "Require an answer" option, as shown in Figure 22-11.

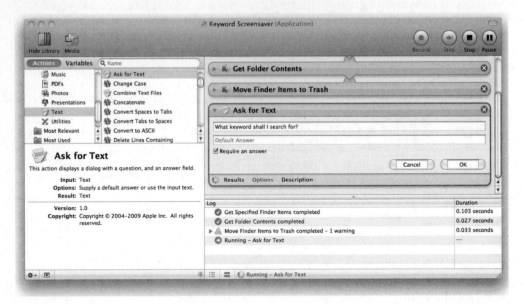

Figure 22-11. *The Ask for Text action in your workflow*

Running the workflow should display a dialog box, as shown in Figure 22-12. The workflow pauses while it waits for an answer. Type a keyword and click OK. The workflow will resume, and the result of the Ask for Text action will be the text you typed.

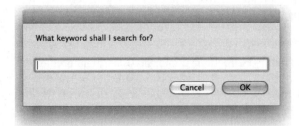

Figure 22-12. *The Ask for Text action in action*

At this point, you have a keyword, but what you really need is a URL to search for that keyword on Google Image Search. This reveals the major difference between using Automator vs. a full programming language. It takes a lot of code to generate a user interface that can ask the user for new input, then convert that input into a usable form. With Automator, that literally comes free with the template. On the other hand, combining two strings to create a URL—among the most basic of programming tasks—is apparently impossible, as there's no "concatenate string" action in the standard Actions library.

Luckily, Automator includes actions like Run Shell Script that let you perform arbitrary tasks. Drag the Run Shell Script action from the Utilities group to below the Ask for Text action. This uses the text the user entered as input to its shell script, and it returns the result of running the script.

The Run Shell Script action has two options. The Shell drop-down lets you select which shell you are scripting for, which affects subtle linguistic differences, analogous to choosing between the US and Canadian keyboard layout. As Bash is perhaps the most common shell, select /bin/bash from the Shell drop-down. The "Pass input" drop-down lets you decide if you want the incoming data (from the Ask for Text action) to arrive as arguments or via standard in. In this instance, it's easier to have the data as arguments, so select "as arguments" from the "Pass input" drop-down.

As for the shell script itself, all you're doing is taking the URL to Google Image Search and appending the first piece of input, represented in Bash as $1. You don't need any processing or anything. You just want the shell to read it back to you, so use the command echo. All together, that looks like this, which you should enter in the action's main text area:

```
echo "http://images.google.com/images?q="$1
```

The output will be the full URL to query Google Image Search, which you can confirm by running the workflow and comparing it to Figure 22-13.

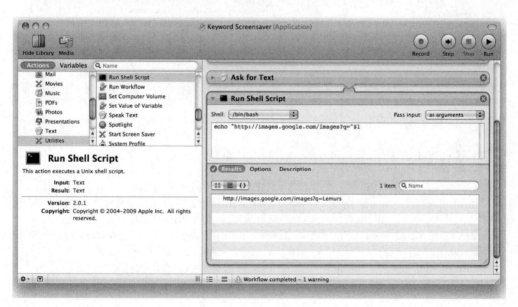

Figure 22-13. *Running a shell script as part of your Automator workflow*

■**Note** Shell scripting is covered in Chapter 17. Apple also provides a shell scripting primer, available online: http://developer.apple.com/documentation/OpenSource/Conceptual/ShellScripting/.

Of course, the URL alone is no good. You need to actually load the URL to run the search, then retrieve the results: a list of URLs pointing to images on the Web. Automator includes the Get Link URLs from Webpages action in the Internet group, which can load the search URL and extract the resulting URLs in one step. Drag the Get Link URLs From Webpages action to below the Run Shell Script action. You're not interested in links to ads or other non-Google content, so check the "Only return URLs in the same domain as the starting page" option. Run your workflow and check the results, as shown in Figure 22-14.

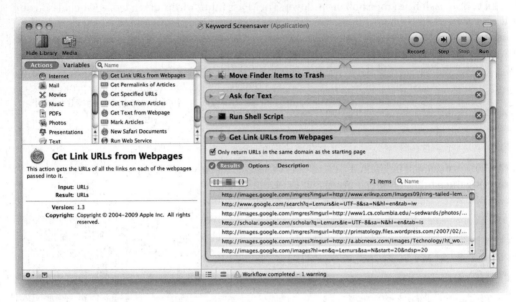

Figure 22-14. *Downloading a page and extracting its link URLs in your Automator workflow*

The Get Link URLs from Webpages action's result contains a few different types of URLs, but you're only interested in the ones that start with `http://images.google.com/imgres?imgurl=`. Automator includes a Filter URLs action in the Internet group. This uses a rule editor, similar to the one used in Mail. The rule you want to define is "Entire URL" "begins with" "`http://images.google.com/imgres?imgurl=`". To do so, drag in the Filter URLs action, then select Entire URL from the first drop-down and "begins with" from the second drop-down. Then enter the text `http://images.google.com/imgres?imgurl=` in the text area.

Running the workflow should show 20 URLs, as shown in Figure 22-15.

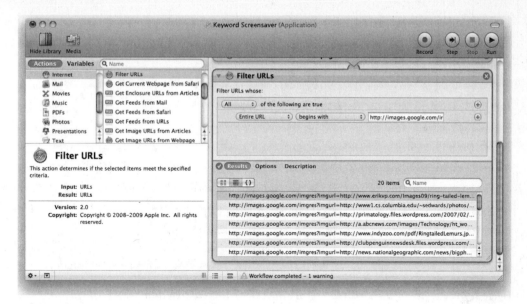

Figure 22-15. *Filtering URLs in Automator*

Frustratingly, plugging one of these URLs into Safari doesn't load the image directly. Rather, it leads to a multiframe Google results page that requires some clicking to get the image. The URL of the image itself is contained within the URL from Filter URLs, but extracting it means going back to the shell for more string manipulation. Drag in another Run Shell Script action, below the Filter URLs action, and enter this script:

```
for url in $@
do
    url=${url##*imgurl=}
    url=${url%%&*}
    echo $url
done
```

This script is a bit more complicated than the previous one. Instead of $1, the first argument, you refer to $@, another built-in variable that represents the list of all arguments. The for...in...do...done construct loops through the arguments, performing the logic between do and done for every item in the list of all arguments. The three cryptic lines of string-manipulation code extract the text between imgurl= and &, which is the direct link to the image result, and return it as its result, as seen in Figure 22-16.

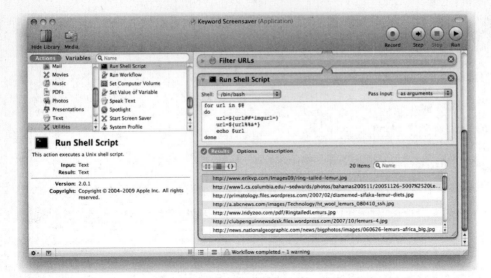

Figure 22-16. *Extracting the direct links from the Google links with a Run Shell Script action*

■**Tip** If you find it confusing having two actions called Run Shell Script, you can rename any action from its contextual menu.

Running the workflow now produces a list of URLs, each one a link to an image. All that's left is to download the images each URL points to. Automator includes the Download URLs action in the Internet group for just this sort of thing. Drag this into your workflow, as shown in Figure 22-17.

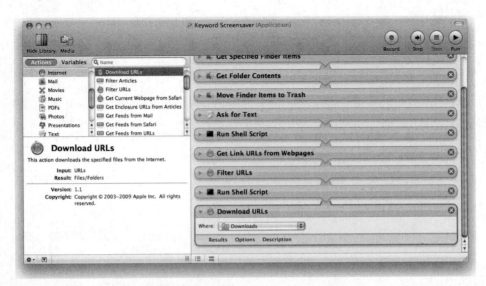

Figure 22-17. *Downloading URLs in Automator*

You could set the download folder directly to `Keyword Screensaver`, but what you'd really like is the same folder reference used way back in the Get Specified Finder Items action. That way, if the folder ever changes, perhaps by user action, you would already know about it. Unfortunately, that information is no longer in the flow, and there's a big separation between the Move Finder Items to Trash and Ask for Text actions. What you really want is for the Get Specified Finder Items action to store its value someplace where you can retrieve it later in the workflow. In the next section, we'll show you how to use Automator's variables to do just that.

Variables

Variables in Automator, as with other programming languages, are a way to store values. Automator provides a wide variety of variables in its Variables library, shown in Figure 22-18. Some are containers for different types of data you provide, but most are values of interest provided by Automator as a convenience for your workflow. To reveal Automator's variables, click Variables at the top of the library view.

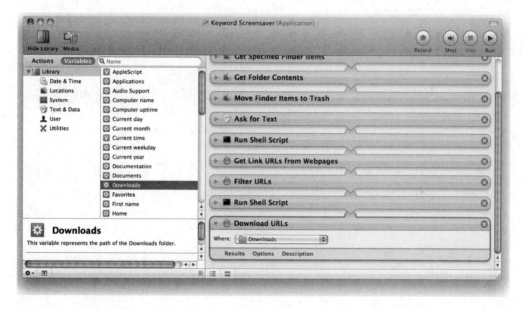

Figure 22-18. *Automator's Variables library shares space with the Actions library.*

Like actions, variables are grouped by category:

Date & Time: The current year, month, day, day of the week, and, of course, the date and time

Locations: Known folders such as `Applications`, `Documents`, `Downloads`, and the current user's home directory

System: System information such as the computer's name, IP address, and operating system version

Text & Data: Generic variables for storing text and data

User: User information such as username, first name, last name, e-mail address, and MobileMe account name

Utilities: Other useful values such as an AppleScript variable or a random number

---

Note Recall that actions can, by user preference, be sorted by the applications that provide them. Variables are not considered part of any application, but rather of Automator itself. Therefore, there is no "group by application" option for variables.

User-definable variables in the sidebar have a blue icon with a V on them. They also appear blue in the workflow. Variables whose contents are predetermined have a purple icon with a gear on it in the sidebar, and they appear purple in the workflow.

There are a number of ways to use variables in Automator. Create a variable to hold the `Keyword Screensaver` folder by selecting "New variable..." from the Where drop-down of the Download URLs action. Name it `Image Folder`, as shown in Figure 22-19.

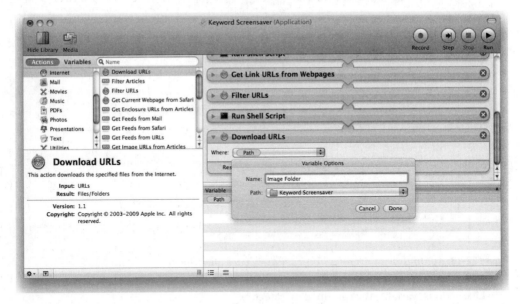

Figure 22-19. *Setting the download folder to a variable in your Automator workflow*

Creating a new variable pops up the variable list below the workflow editor. This list contains every variable in your workflow. You can interact with variables directly in the list, and you can drag variables into this list from the Variables library or out of this list to use in your workflow. To save the `Keyword Screensaver` folder in a variable, drag in a Set Value of Variable action from the Utilities group to between the Get Specified Finder Items action and the Get Folder Contents action. These two actions move apart to make room, as shown in Figure 22-20.

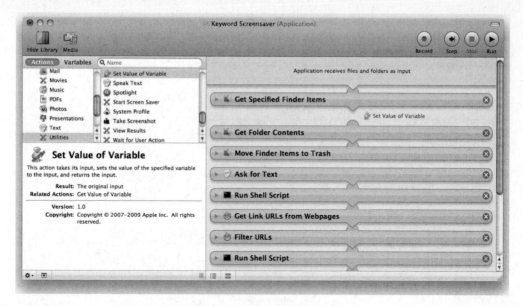

Figure 22-20. *Inserting a Set Value of Variable action in your Automator workflow*

The Set Value of Variable action should automatically set its single option, the Variable pop-up, to the Image Folder variable. If it doesn't, set it manually. The connections between actions are automatically re-established to this inserted action, as shown in Figure 22-21. The result of the Set Value of Variable action will be the value the variable is set to, which is the same as the action's input. In other words, it just passes the value through, so the deletion actions work the same.

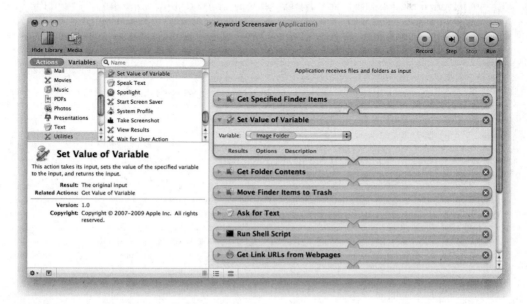

Figure 22-21. *Using a variable in Automator*

Running the workflow now will automatically download the images to the Keyword Screensaver application. The only thing left to do is to actually start the screen saver. Drag a Start Screen Saver action to the end of your workflow to complete the application, as shown in Figure 22-22.

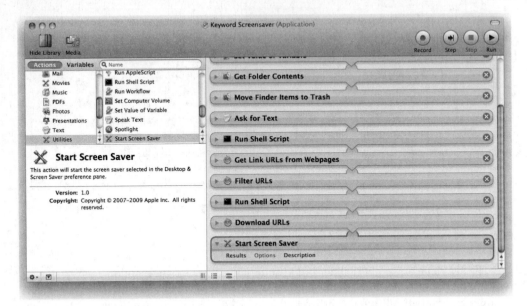

Figure 22-22. *The final action in your Automator workflow launches the system screen saver.*

You can run the workflow from Automator, but since you've built an application, you can also run it from the Dock. Drag the title of your newly minted application directly from the Automator window's title bar into the Dock, then click the Dock icon to launch the application. You may notice that, without the feedback from Automator's workflow editor, it's hard to tell what the application is doing. Fortunately, Otto is there for you. When you run your new application, check out the status (and Stop option) in the menu bar, as shown in Figure 22-23.

Figure 22-23. *Automator workflow status in the menu bar*

Advanced Automator Shenanigans

This brief sojourn into Otto's world is one of an endless array of projects you can build with Automator. It's not just that there's more to Automator than fits in this chapter; there's more to Automator than fits in Automator. There are as many potential workflows as there are types of work, so Automator lets you extend its capabilities by adding new actions.

Extending Automator

Anyone with a modicum of programming skills can write an Automator action. Many software developers include Automator actions with their applications. As you add applications to extend your Mac's abilities, Automator will automatically import their included actions, expanding in turn. If your favorite application lacks the actions you need to incorporate it into your workflows, petition the developer to provide them. Most developers are happy to help you find ways to make their product an indispensable part of your life.

Automator actions don't have to come with an application. You can download new actions individually or in "action packs," as well as whole workflows, from the Internet. Apple provides an official repository of Automator actions at `www.apple.com/downloads/macosx/automator/`. There are also a number of third-party resources; we list several in the "More Information" section.

If you're programmatically inclined, Xcode provides templates for creating Automator actions. If you whip something up for yourself, consider making it available to others. If you wind up shipping an application for the Mac, make sure you include a good set of Automator actions. If you're not programmatically inclined, you may still find a home with AppleScript, but we'll get into that in a moment.

Embedding Automator

Automator is like bacon. It's great on its own, but it's even better when it's combined with other things. Automator started picking up a certain embeddability in Leopard with the introduction of the Automator framework. This lets developers use the step-by-step user interface of Automator's workflow editor in their own applications.

Snow Leopard raises Automator's usefulness by making it easy to extend applications with workflows. Automator now contains templates for creating a folder action, an iCal alarm, a Print plug-in, or an Image Capture plug-in. Most interestingly, however, you can create a service.

A service is an Automator-like construct dating all the way back to NeXTSTEP. The idea was for applications to provide parts of their functionality from anywhere in the system via the Services menu, which is part of the standard main menu set, next to Preferences, Hide, and Quit. By the time Leopard rolled around, there were so many services that the Services menu was overwhelmed with disabled and irrelevant options, as shown in Figure 22-24.

Figure 22-24. *The Services menu in Leopard is filled with disabled options.*

In Snow Leopard, the Services menu now uses contextual information to show only the services that are relevant to what you're doing in an application. If you select some text in Safari, for example, the Services menu will contain only services that make sense given that text, as shown in Figure 22-25.

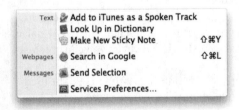

Figure 22-25. *The Services menu in Snow Leopard only shows relevant options.*

Services Made Simple

Your new Keyword Screensaver workflow would make a great service to add to this set. To complete this bonus project, follow these steps:

1. Create a new Automator workflow using the Service template. The workflow's input should be "Service receives selected text in any application," as shown in Figure 22-26.

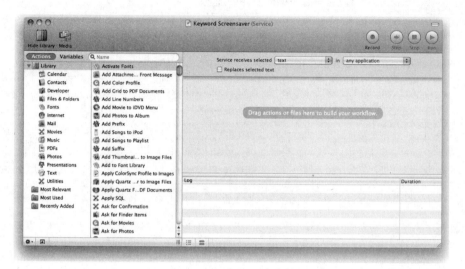

Figure 22-26. *Automator makes it easy to create context-aware Snow Leopard services.*

2. Store the value of the selected text by dragging in a Set Value of Variable action, as shown in Figure 22-27.

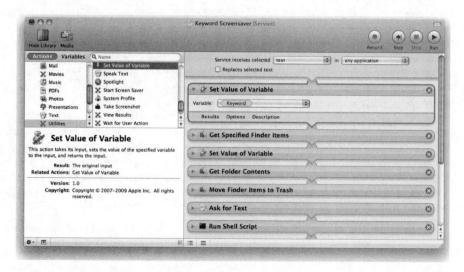

Figure 22-27. *Automator's variables make it easy to make large changes without changing the actual flow of actions.*

3. Select Ignore Input from the Get Specified Finder Items action's contextual menu to disconnect it from the new Set Value of Variable action, as shown in Figure 22-28.

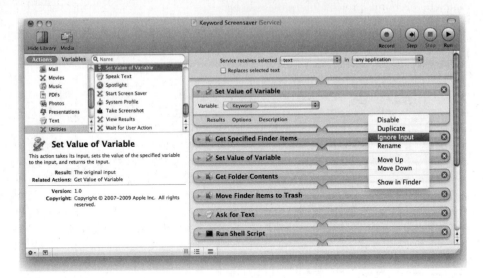

Figure 22-28. *Ignoring input disconnects the action from the results of the action above it.*

4. Replace the Ask for Text action with a Get Value of Variable action using the same variable created in step 2, as shown in Figure 22-29.

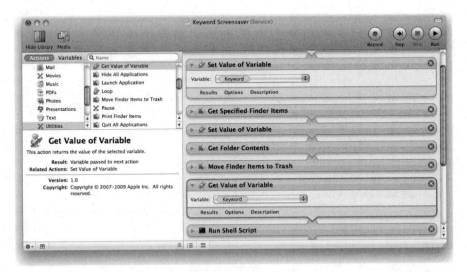

Figure 22-29. *As a service, the Keyword Screensaver gets the keyword as input, instead of asking the user.*

Saving the workflow automatically adds your new service to the Services menu, as shown in Figure 22-30. In Snow Leopard, services also show up in the contextual menu system. That means you can literally click any word anywhere and create a screen saver out of it, all thanks to Automator.

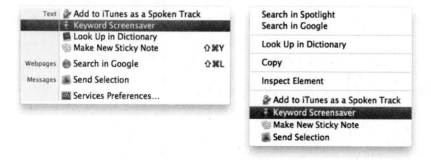

Figure 22-30. *Saving a service in Automator automatically updates the Services menu and contextual menu system.*

How Automator Works

Every Automator action is actually a tiny application. Developers can implement new actions as shell scripts or even full-fledged Objective-C programs. However, many, if not most, of the included Automator actions are simply a drag-and-drop interface on top of some behind-the-scenes voodoo the system uses for controlling other applications. Automator serves as a friendly abstraction from AppleScript, the quirky scripting language that lets you tap into the aforementioned system voodoo.

To look at it from the other direction, controlling other applications from Automator is cool and useful, but more than that, it's easy. That ease of use is inherently limiting. AppleScript is like Automator as a programming language. Learning AppleScript is like putting down your Speak & Spell and learning to type.

■**Tip** We're going to show you AppleScript, but we're not really going to do it justice. For real ultimate power, check out the "More Information" section or just pick up a copy of *Learn AppleScript: The Comprehensive Guide to Scripting and Automation on Mac OS X* by Hamish Sanderson and Hanaan Rosenthal (Apress, 2009).

AppleScript

AppleScript is a simple programming language for controlling applications. Although AppleScript and Automator are different around the edges, it's not a bad metaphor to think of AppleScript as writing Automator workflows in longhand.

To demonstrate that point, here is the Keyword Screensaver application written entirely in AppleScript:

```applescript
-- Remove any existing images
tell application "Finder"
    set _imageFolder to path to pictures folder
    set _imageFolder to folder "Keyword Screensaver" of folder _imageFolder
    delete every file in _imageFolder
end tell

-- Ask for Text
display dialog "What keyword shall I search for?" default answer ""
set _keyword to text returned of result
set _queryURL to "http://images.google.com/images?q=" & _keyword

-- Query Google
tell application "Safari"
    open location _queryURL
    set _timeoutInSeconds to 20
    delay 2
    repeat with _waitInSeconds from 1 to _timeoutInSeconds
        if (do JavaScript "document.readyState" in document 1) is "complete" then
            exit repeat
        else if _waitInSeconds is _timeoutInSeconds then
            number -128
        else
            delay 1
        end if
    end repeat
    set _searchResults to source of document 1
end tell

-- Extract image URLs from page source, then download them
set AppleScript's text item delimiters to "\",\""
set _rawResults to text items in _searchResults
set AppleScript's text item delimiters to ""
repeat with _text in _rawResults
    if _text starts with "http://" and _text does not end with "/images" then
        do shell script "cd ~/Pictures/Keyword\\ Screensaver;
        curl -sO " & quoted form of (_text as string)
    end if
end repeat

-- Activate screen saver
tell application "ScreenSaverEngine"
    activate
end tell
```

To use this script, open the Script Editor application in /Applications/AppleScript. The Script Editor is a basic application that provides a text editor for composing your scripts, simple controls for testing your scripts, and syntax coloring and formatting, which make it easier to read your scripts. Below the text editor is a console for observing the results of running your script.

■Caution In the AppleScript for the Keyword Screensaver application, the `do shell script` command has a carriage return as part of the command. If the shell script portion of the script fails, select the whitespace between the semicolon and the command `curl`, and hit the Return key to replace it with a single carriage return.

AppleScript is a strange language. It tries to look as much like English as possible, which includes having several different ways of saying the same thing. This makes AppleScript readable even by non-programmers. However, many programmers find AppleScript hard to write in, because it's not actually English. You can't just write English and expect AppleScript to understand you. Not only do you still have to deal with the limited comprehension of a programming language, but now you also have to deal with the vagueness of English.

The upshot of all this is AppleScript needs to be written line by line. Don't just rush in, write it all down, and expect it to work. Script Editor is a far cry from the professional tools in Xcode, discussed in Chapter 24. Instead, you must write a line, compile it, test it, then write another and repeat.

Analyzing the Code

Although AppleScript and Automator accomplish similar things, they don't exactly translate back and forth, so you have to do some things a little differently. It's probably best to just run through the code sample and point out some sights along the way.

Comments in AppleScript are preceded by `--`, like so:

```
-- Remove any existing images
```

Since AppleScript is mainly concerned with telling applications what to do, AppleScript programs revolve around the `tell` block:

```
tell application "Finder"
```

Every scriptable application contains a dictionary that lists its vocabulary, which is to say, the functionality it makes available to AppleScript. To examine an application's scripting dictionary from within Script Editor, select Open Dictionary... from the File menu or type Shift-Command-O.

To set a variable to a certain value, use the `set...to` construct:

```
set _imageFolder to path to pictures folder
```

Although AppleScript is meant to read like English, programmers may find it convenient to use a special prefix, or sigil, to mark which words represent variables. We like an underscore combined with standard CamelCase, but this is a personal preference. Script Editor's syntax coloring also helps.

To find the user's Pictures folder, use the path to construct. Note that the literal names of things are enclosed in quotation marks:

```
set _imageFolder to folder "Keyword Screensaver" of folder _imageFolder
```

When something is inside of something else, AppleScript says it is of that thing. You can talk about the third word of a sentence, the last page of a document, or a certain subfolder of a given folder. As in English, this can turned into a possessive relationship by using an apostrophe and then the letter *s*:

```
set _imageFolder to _imageFolder's folder "Keyword Screensaver"
```

In a way, everything in AppleScript is a list. A folder is a list of documents; a document is a list of pages; a page is a list of paragraphs, which are lists of sentences, which are lists of words, and so forth. Anyone familiar with the programming language Lisp will recognize this paradigm. When you think of a folder as a list of files, it makes sense to use a construct like this:

```
delete every file in _imageFolder
```

Like every major language but Python, AppleScript doesn't care about whitespace such as tabs and carriage returns, which are used to give code a readable format. However, it expects sentences to end when you hit Return. This doesn't always work; for example, tell blocks may need to encompass several other lines of code. For this case, you can end the block of code by using an end statement:

```
end tell
```

As a testament to the flexibility of the AppleScript language, you also could have written the entire first tell block as a single line:

```
tell application "Finder" to delete every file in (path to pictures folder)'s ➥
folder "Keyword Screensaver"
```

It's a bit awkward but still understandable. Note the use of parentheses to clear up syntactical ambiguities and the lack of end tell for the single-line version.

Displaying a dialog to ask the user for input uses the quite understandable form:

```
display dialog "What keyword shall I search for?" default answer ""
```

The dialog presents the user with a text field, prefilled with the text appearing after the default answer clause. Since you've defined that text as an empty string, the text area will simply be blank. Simply removing the default answer clause would cause the dialog to appear without any text area at all.

Note Popping up dialogs is part of AppleScript's default functionality. Since you're only telling AppleScript, you don't have to use a tell block.

When a dialog returns, any input from the user appears in a variable named `result`, which you read and store:

```
set _keyword to text returned of result
```

To combine, or concatenate, the Google search URL with the user's keyword, use the & operator:

```
set _queryURL to "http://images.google.com/images?q=" & _keyword
```

As before, this block could have been rendered as a single line:

```
set _queryURL to "http://images.google.com/images?q=" & text returned ➥
of (display dialog "What keyword shall I search for?" default answer "")
```

Automator is a little more polished when it comes to dealing with common Internet tasks, such as fetching results in the background and returning a list of links. Let's start with fetching the results, which is a whole problem in and of itself. Use Safari to load and render the page:

```
tell application "Safari"
    open location _queryURL
```

Using other applications is what AppleScript does best, but there are some problems inherent to this cooperation that remain prosaically manual. For example, the script has to wait for Safari to finish loading the URL. Apple's recommended method is to use a polling loop to ask Safari if it's done loading. Since it might never actually load, start by setting a timeout of 20 seconds:

```
set _timeoutInSeconds to 20
```

Loading will take at least a couple of seconds, so the script will pause for 2 seconds right off the bat:

```
delay 2
```

AppleScript has several ways it can loop. Using the `repeat` commands `from <number> to <number>` construct with a 1-second pause between attempts creates a nice, predictable bit of control logic. The script will poll Safari once per second for 20 seconds, after the initial 2-second pause:

```
repeat with _waitInSeconds from 1 to _timeoutInSeconds
```

To ask the question, use Safari's `do JavaScript` command. This powerful command lets the script speak to Safari in its own language:

```
if (do JavaScript "document.readyState" in document 1) is "complete" then
```

If loading is complete, the script will stop looping and continue building the screen saver:

```
exit repeat
```

If loading is not complete, the script will see if it has timed out, in which case it will return an error:

```
else if _waitInSeconds is _timeoutInSeconds then
    error number -128
```

Error -128 means "User canceled." This basically clicks the Cancel button for you after 20 seconds. If the script has not been running for 20 seconds, it will wait for a second, after which time execution will return to the top of the loop:

```
        else
            delay 1
        end if
end repeat
```

Novice scripters should pay attention to how the logic flows: "If something is true, do something, or else if something else is true, do something else, or else do something else entirely." This is reflected in the code using the `if...else if...else` construct common to most programming languages.

With the power of `do JavaScript`, you could almost write the rest of the script in JavaScript. Navigating a page, finding links, and simple parsing are well within the reach of JavaScript. This being the AppleScript section, we're going to craft a solution using AppleScript:

```
set _searchResults to source of document 1
```

The HTML source of the Google results page is basically one big string. Recall that a string is a list of paragraphs, words, characters, and text items. Wait, text items? What are text items? It turns out text items are kind of complicated.

When you think of a list, you may think of a comma-separated list, where each list item is separated by a comma, followed by a space. This is distinct from the words in the list, which are separated only by a space. Were this list an AppleScript string, the comma-separated list items would be the text items. The comma and space between those items would be the "global text-item delimiter."

Sometimes list items may themselves contain commas, in which case you can use semicolons to separate the list items. In AppleScript, this would be equivalent to changing the global text-item delimiter from comma and space to semicolon and space.

The power of the global text-item delimiter is that you can set it to anything you want, then ask the string for its text items and get custom results based on the delimiter. In the source of the Google results page, the links you want are separated by a comma in quotation marks, which makes the delimiter `"","`". AppleScript will be confused by the quotes inside the quotes, so precede them with backslashes, which tell AppleScript to ignore the next character—in this case, the confusing quotation marks:

```
set AppleScript's text item delimiters to "\",\""
```

■Note Although there is technically a list of delimiters, it's a list of one. Thus, we talk about the text-item delimiter, but the actual keyword is pluralized. We set the delimiter to a single string, but behind the scenes, AppleScript coerces the string into a single-item list.

Retrieving the text items from the string _searchResults now yields a list of substrings, separated by the delimiter you set previously:

```
set _rawResults to text items in _searchResults
```

Since the global text-item delimiter is global and all, it is considered good form to set it back to the default, which is the empty string, "":

```
set AppleScript's text item delimiters to ""
```

Now all that's left to do is loop over the items in the list and decide which ones are URLs. Use the repeat command again, but this time with the form with <item> in <list>:

```
repeat with _text in _rawResults
```

The strings in the list that are URLs will start with the substring "http://", but you don't want all the URLs on the page. Specifically, you want to filter out the ones that end with the substring "/images":

```
if _text starts with "http://" and _text does not end with "/images" then
```

To test for the substrings, you can use the convenient string shortcuts starts with, ends with, and contains. In order to read like grammatical English, AppleScript accepts both singular and plural versions of commands. It also ignores the article the, so you can safely insert it when grammar requires it. As such, you could have written the preceding line with the ungrammatical but nevertheless acceptable

```
if _text start with "http://" and _text does not ends with "/images" then
```

To download the images that the filtered URLs point to, you can use another cool AppleScript command, do shell script. Like the Safari do JavaScript command, do shell script lets AppleScript talk to the UNIX shell in its own language. You can even run UNIX programs, like the URL downloading utility curl:

```
do shell script "cd ~/Pictures/Keyword\\ Screensaver;
curl -sO " & quoted form of (_text as string)
```

Because the name of the directory has a space, but UNIX uses spaces as separators, it has to appear in the shell script as Keyword\ Screensaver. This is the same use of the backslash as AppleScript, which will confuse AppleScript. As such, you must escape the backslash with another backslash, appearing to AppleScript as Keyword\\ Screensaver.

The script will pause while the pictures download to the folder your screen saver is set to, so all that's left is telling the screen saver to activate:

```
tell application "ScreenSaverEngine"
    activate
end tell
```

AppleScript in Context

Given the choice between Automator and AppleScript for your automation needs, which one should you choose? These two tutorials should give you a pretty good idea of the strengths and weaknesses of each. In general, we'd say Automator is easier to use, but AppleScript is more powerful. Even with such features as variables and basic looping, Automator's drag-and-drop ease of use comes at the expense of the flexibility and power that a full written language like AppleScript provides.

Still, for our dollar, we'd pick Automator if at all possible. You can pass things off to shell scripts, just like in AppleScript. You can also call AppleScript from Automator, giving you the best of both worlds. We have to admit a certain bias: when we want to program, we'd rather use Objective-C, which we'll get into in the next few chapters.

For non-programmers, AppleScript may be much more approachable, and even programmers can find AppleScript convenient. Just as C is optimal for communicating with hardware, AppleScript is optimal for communicating with other applications. AppleScript can be used within Objective-C applications, and Xcode has a template for building an entire application out of AppleScript.

In order for the AppleScript party to continue, developers must make their applications scriptable. If you're developing an application, implementing scriptability lets users incorporate your application into their workflows. Snow Leopard's Scripting Bridge framework uses your scripting interface to provide interaction with other programming environments, such as Automator, Ruby, Python, and Objective-C.

Automation saves people time and eliminates wasted effort, and the foundation of automation is interapplication cooperation. The more developers and users can leverage existing applications, the more our platform becomes extensible, flexible, and—that most important of attributes—usable. That makes application developers who write scriptable applications a boon to the platform.

More Information

If you think there's something to the phrase "Cult of Mac," you should see the zealots in the Mac automation community. We don't think we've ever written an AppleScript or a halfway decent Automator action without consulting at least one of the following sources:

Automator home page (`http://automator.us`*):* Sal Soghoian is Apple's product manager for automation and is generally recognized as a, if not the, foremost expert on AppleScript and Automator. We can also personally attest that he is a character. All that aside, Sal's Automator page has everything you need to know, from the whys and wherefores of Automator to a massive collection of free Automator actions and links to other great Automator sites on the Web.

Automator Programming Guide (`http://developer.apple.com/documentation/ AppleApplications/Conceptual/AutomatorConcepts/`*):* This is Apple's official documentation on developing Automator actions. There's less here for the casual user, but the barrier to becoming a power user who can bust out custom actions is really not all that high. If you have any scripting or programming experience, you're practically there already.

Apple Training Series: AppleScript 1-2-3 *by* Sal Soghoian *and* Bill Cheeseman *(Peachpit Press, 2009):* Sal Soghoian's long-awaited book is the ultimate resource for mastering AppleScript. Together with Bill Cheeseman, Sal gives you an understanding of the language that only comes from a lifetime of dedication. Start here, and the rest of these resources will be all the more useful.

Learn AppleScript: The Comprehensive Guide to Scripting and Automation on Mac OS X *by Hamish Sanderson and Hanaan Rosenthal (Apress, 2009)*: This is a definitive reference book on AppleScript, recently updated for Snow Leopard. Hamish and Hanaan's critically acclaimed work walks you step by step from automation neophyte to AppleScript master. It also makes a great footstool, on account of being huge.

*AppleScript Essential Subroutines (*www.apple.com/applescript/guidebook/sbrt/*)*: This page of useful AppleScript functions is the first place we turn when we get stuck trying to figure out how to do something. There's not a lot here, but what is here is solid gold.

*AppleScript Language Guide (*http://developer.apple.com/documentation/AppleScript/Conceptual/AppleScriptLangGuide/*)*: This is Apple's official documentation on AppleScript. It has recently been updated to cover AppleScript 2.0, the latest version of the language, introduced in Leopard. It also includes nostalgic links to older versions of the documentation.

*AppleScript Users Official Mailing List (*http://lists.apple.com/mailman/listinfo/applescript-users*)*: Another official channel for all things AppleScript, the official mailing list is always a good place to get and give help.

*Doug's AppleScripts for iTunes (*http://dougscripts.com*)*: It sounds really specific, but iTunes is probably the most scriptable, and the most scripted, application in the world. As such, Doug's page may well be the largest repository of practical AppleScript on the Web. Having a simple relationship with iTunes, we don't think we've ever actually used one of these scripts for its intended purpose, but we've studied dozens of them. The people who write Doug's scripts are truly some of the cleverest, to say nothing of most dedicated, AppleScript users around.

Summary

If you find yourself doing the same task over and over again, it's time to stop and think about automation. Using Automator or AppleScript might seem like a lot of trouble the first time, but once you learn how to use these powerful tools, your productivity will skyrocket, and you will truly earn the laurels of a power user.

If you've already mastered automation, need more than the OS can provide, or want to contribute to the platform by writing applications, plug-ins, or Automator actions, read on. In the next few chapters, we'll talk about the tools used by professional Macintosh application developers.

■ ■ ■

## CHAPTER 23

Mac OS X Development: The Application Frameworks

What is it about the Mac that makes it so compelling? Almost anyone you ask will surely tell you the same thing: it's the user experience. But what does that mean? What lies at the heart of the Mac OS X user experience?

At the end of the day, it comes down to three things: ease of use, integration, and beauty. It should come as no surprise, therefore, that the major frameworks provided to developers center around these three concepts. We'll tour these frameworks, then see how Snow Leopard covers the whole thing in a thick gravy of performance and concurrency.

■**Note** Many of the things in this chapter have already been discussed from a user standpoint in previous chapters. This chapter, however, will view things from a developer's perspective.

Ease of Use

If you want to build an easy-to-use application, you need to start with an easy-to-use application framework. Smaller code is faster to write and easier to maintain, leading to fewer bugs, more features, and more time to spend optimizing performance and adding all those tiny details that Mac developers always seem to think of.

A framework is the Mac OS X equivalent to a shared code library, but it has a couple of advantages above and beyond simple code reuse:

- It can contain non-code resources like images, documentation, and archived data.
- It can have multiple versions side by side for backward compatibility.
- It can be shared between running applications, saving memory.
- It can contain references to other frameworks, creating umbrella frameworks.

If you want to build an easy-to-use application, therefore, the application framework of choice is Cocoa. Cocoa's motto, mission statement, and design philosophy is "Easy things easy, hard things possible." What makes Cocoa unique, however, is not just that it achieves this simple but powerful idea, but how.

Cocoa applications are better by design. Their graphical user interfaces are designed with a graphical user interface, Interface Builder, as shown in Figure 23-1. Their classes are built with Objective-C, a revolutionary programming language that combines the design advantages of an object-oriented language with the flexibility of a low-level language, the dynamism of a scripting language, and a revolution in readability that almost makes comments obsolete.

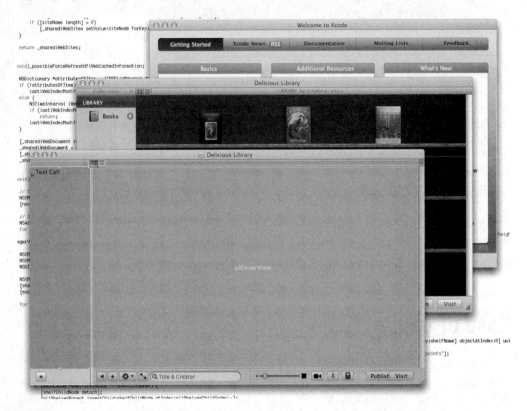

Figure 23-1. *Great applications are built with great tools.*

We'll talk about Interface Builder and Objective-C in the next couple of chapters. For now, let's focus on some of the frameworks that make creating professional applications in Cocoa so easy.

■**Note** Cocoa is only one of several application frameworks on Mac OS X, but you don't have to worry about whether something is technically Cocoa, or a shared framework with a Cocoa interface, or part of another application framework altogether. You can use them all from your Cocoa application, thanks largely to the flexibility of Objective-C.

Application Kit

Just as its name implies, Application Kit (or AppKit, as it is known to its friends) is a collection of prebuilt components common to many applications. Developers can cobble together a completely functional, if uninteresting, application by snapping together components, like those shown in Figure 23-2. Only Swedish furniture rivals the ease of assembly offered by AppKit, and we think you'll be better pleased with the results.

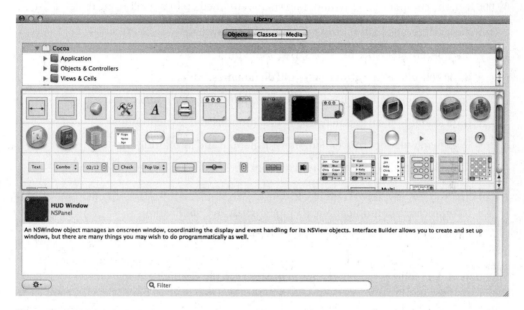

Figure 23-2. *Cocoa components in Interface Builder*

AppKit's components are not just tangible UI widgets like menus, windows, and buttons. Some of the other things AppKit provides are the following:

- Data visualization objects like tables, browsers, and matrices
- Utility objects like controllers, timers, and formatters
- Document creation, management, and persistence
- Text handling, including editing, spell checking, and typesetting
- Graphics handling for images, multimedia, and animation
- Functionality such as event handling, undo management, and threading
- System interaction such as printing, pasteboard (clipboard) operations, and scripting

Most of AppKit's features can be had with little or no code. Customization can be accomplished with simple configuration, either as needed by the developer, or at runtime in accordance with user preferences.

Despite all this simplicity, AppKit is also quite flexible. Because AppKit is object-oriented, developers can write just enough code to customize as much, or as little, as they need.

Foundation

AppKit is a high-level toolkit, so a lot of the basics, and some of the not-so-basics, are taken care of for you. This frees you to write the code that makes your application special. Nothing is better for taking care of business logic than AppKit's fraternal twin, Foundation.

Foundation classes are so legion as to be beyond the scope of this book (Apple's Foundation documentation is more than 2,200 pages long!) However, as you might expect, from 60,000 feet, the components of Foundation can be summed up in the following bulleted list:

- Basic data types such as strings, numbers, and raw data

- Specialized data types like dates, URLs, and time zones

- Basic collections like arrays, sets, and dictionaries

- Specialized collections like character sets, index sets, and pointer arrays

- Data loading—local and networked, synchronous and asynchronous

- Data manipulation, conversion, transformation, and formatting

- XML parsing, editing, and transformation

- System functions like run loops, threads, and timers

- Interprocess communications via pipes, ports, and notifications

- Language services like exceptions, garbage collection, and messaging

It's not called Foundation for nothing. AppKit and the rest of Cocoa are built on top of Foundation. This follows the general trend in Mac OS X development: Apple creates tools and then uses those tools to make easy-to-use frameworks. Then, it gives developers the tools as well, so they can modify or add as they see fit.

Foundation, while extensive, might not seem so different from any other basic library. In practice, however, Foundation is designed with the same ease of use and snap-together design as AppKit. The classes try to maintain similar interfaces, so, for example, if you decide to refactor an array into a set, there's very little effort involved.

Since the interfaces are predictable, it's easy to keep Foundation in your head, despite its breadth. And since it's written in Objective-C, it's extremely easy to figure out how to use a method without having to constantly go back to the documentation.

As with AppKit, Objective-C also makes Foundation classes customizable via subclassing and categorization (one of the many tricks outlined in the section on Objective-C), so no matter what you need to do, you're rarely, if ever, stuck having to roll your own.

Core Data

When Apple transitioned from PowerPC to Intel, a lot of low level-problems, like the fact that the two architectures read bytes of binary code in opposite directions (the so-called endianness issue), ended up not affecting most developers at all.

The reason is abstraction. By using high-level frameworks like AppKit and Foundation, developers are protected from implementation details like byte order. The Core Data framework takes that idea a step further by abstracting applications from even their own data.

Traditionally, the system is ignorant of an application's objects and what they're doing. Whether you've got a word-processing document, a photo album, or a dungeon-roaming adventurer in a mystical land beyond time and space, to the system they're all just ones and zeros. You can ask the system to write those ones and zeros to disk, and you can ask it to read them back, but when it comes to interpreting what they mean and how the user's actions affect them, you're on your own.

Core Data establishes a generalized object model. As long as your objects conform to that model, the system can tell enough about them to handle many aspects of their lives with little or no intervention on your part. For example, undo and redo, traditionally one of the harder problems to deal with, is free in Core Data.

One of the first things you learn in system design is how to plan your objects, their structures, and their relationships in an entity relationship diagram (ERD). Xcode, Apple's integrated development environment, even provides a graphical ERD tool, as shown in Figure 23-3. With Core Data, drawing an ERD doesn't just plan your objects, it also implements them. You can even drag entities out of the ERD into Interface Builder, and Core Data will generate your entire user interface!

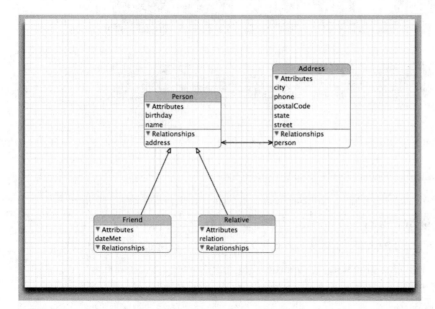

Figure 23-3. *Core Data modeling in Xcode*

Of course, Core Data is best known for persistence. When the user clicks the Save button, you've got to decide if that data is going to be written out in some binary format, converted to human-readable XML, or stored in a relational database. Each has its advantages and disadvantages.

This used to be a hard choice, because changing your mind meant throwing out your old code and rewriting the whole thing—a tremendous waste of time, money, and effort. With Core Data, changing your persistence model is as simple as changing your mind. You haven't written any code to read and write data, nor to communicate with any database. Core Data handles all that dirty business for you, so if you want to develop with easily debugged XML, and then switch to a database for performance, you can.

And if you do decide to use a database, you don't have to worry about installing a database management system onto your users' machines, because all that stuff is already built into Mac OS X. Oh yeah, and you don't have to write, think in, or even be aware of the existence of SQL.

Image Kit

Image Kit is an extremely high-level collection of common components for dealing with images. It has the same functionality you see in Apple's own applications. With Image Kit, you can use the portrait taker from iChat, the filter picker from Photo Booth, or the picture browser from iPhoto, as shown in Figure 23-4.

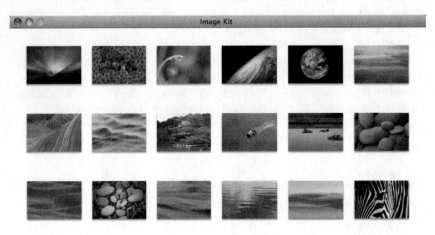

Figure 23-4. *Image Kit's image browser in Interface Builder*

Here are some of the classes provided by Image Kit:

- Browser for viewing a large number of images in a grid view, similar to iPhoto
- Slideshow for viewing and working with multiple images sequentially
- View optimized for images, with controls for zooming, rotating, and cropping
- Edit panel for changing image properties and applying some basic effects
- Filter application and UI elements for browsing and using filters
- Save panel addition that presents specialized options based on the format of the image data
- Picture taker, like the one found in iChat and Photo Booth
- Device manager for handling digital cameras and scanners
- Camera browser and scanner views for browsing image sources

Aside from providing some great functionality, Image Kit is built on the latest Mac OS X graphics libraries. That means, aside from having the animated translucent look of a next-generation application, its interfaces are able to optimize performance for modern graphics cards, using things like hardware acceleration, when available.

Similarly, it uses the same nondestructive Core Image filters found throughout the system, so as Apple or other developers add new filters, your applications pick them up as well, with no extra effort on your part.

That also applies to image formats. Already, Image Kit can also handle icons, movies, PDF documents, and even Quartz Composer compositions. Snow Leopard adds the specialized views to connect and browse devices like digital cameras and scanners.

QuickTime Kit

At the heart of any modern operating system lies the ability to deal with multimedia. In case you're unfamiliar with the term, *multimedia* is a mid-'90s buzzword meaning "the mixture of audio, video, and text, be it local, remote, or streaming." Mac OS X has long been a frontrunner in multimedia. This is largely thanks to a very mature framework known as QuickTime.

Unfortunately, like much that is old, QuickTime had long been a holdout against the paradigm shift offered by Cocoa. This isn't a technical problem, as Cocoa programmers are able to access other frameworks, just as non-Cocoa programmers are able to access Cocoa.

However, having to leave the comfort of Cocoa for the dark recesses of old-fashioned procedural API is so much trouble, even for otherwise brilliant resources like QuickTime. Tiger finally corrected this with a brand-new Cocoa interface to QuickTime, known by the euphonious nickname QTKit.

Here are some of the features of QTKit:

- Access to raw media data from local, remote, and streaming sources

- Object-oriented representations of media, tracks, and time ranges

- View subclass for displaying and controlling media

- Access to iPod media, including content purchased through iTunes

- Interface Builder object, which makes adding a full-featured media player to your applications a zero-code drag-and-drop operation

In addition, QTCapture adds similar functionality for recording media. This includes the ability to control recording devices, such as the iSight camera now built into most Macs. For anyone interested in tapping the power of the iSight, we can attest firsthand: QTCapture will save you thousands of lines of code.

■**Note** For more information on QuickTime, check out Chapter 15.

Integration

Much of what makes the Mac such a compelling experience can be summed up in one word: iLife. This suite of full-featured applications, included free with every new Mac (and the subject of Chapter 16) is not simply the sum of its parts. Rather, it's the integration between those parts.

Make some music in GarageBand. Use it as a soundtrack in iMovie. Burn your movie to disc with iDVD. Then, tell the world with iWeb. This kind of integration, descending from the UNIX world of pipes and scripts connecting specialized tools, extends throughout the operating system.

Your own applications can and should take advantage of this. Not only does this provide an excellent "Mac-like" experience to your customers, but it also saves you the time and trouble of implementing features that are already served quite well by existing applications.

To help you leverage these applications, Apple provides a great number of frameworks. Here is a quick tour of some of the most useful.

Address Book

As strange as it might seem to those of us who spend all our time with machines, many of our users maintain a network of an entirely different sort: friends, family, coworkers, and businesses. To manage this pantheon of people, Apple provides an application called Address Book.

Rather than maintain separate lists for the people you get and receive mail from, call or text via your iPhone, and communicate with via iChat, everything is simply kept in Address Book. Your applications can participate via the framework known, appropriately enough, as Address Book.

In addition to being able to access the contact information stored in Address Book, the framework provides the ability to search, edit, and add contacts. For any social aspects of your application requiring human interaction, the work is already done for you via a prebuilt People Picker, shown in Figure 23-5.

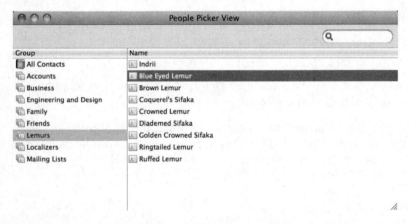

Figure 23-5. *Address Book's People Picker view in Interface Builder*

Finally, Address Book stores a special record known as a Me card, which contains users' own contact information. By programmatically accessing the Me card, you can spare them the trouble of providing their address, phone number, e-mail address, or home page, and simply present those fields for verification and, if necessary, correction.

■**Note** For more information on Address Book, check out Chapter 11.

Automator

Automator gives users the power to create automated workflows using actions (services provided by applications on the system). Automator can be thought of as AppleScript with an easy, drag-and-drop interface. Your applications can use Automator actions and workflows, as well as provide new actions for Automator. Xcode provides an Automator action template to help you get started.

The Automator framework even lets you embed Automator's drag-and-drop interface in your own application, using custom view and controller subclasses. From this interface, users can create standard Automator workflows. Or, if you prefer, you can create your own custom universe of components that just happen to borrow the convenient and familiar workflow concept.

Note For more information on Automator and automation, see Chapter 22.

MobileMe Integration with the DotMac Kit

Behind Apple's slick web-based MobileMe service is an integration framework that allows developers to integrate MobileMe support into their applications. The SDK is overdue for revision, as evidenced by the fact that it's still called the DotMac Kit. What makes MobileMe integration compelling is not what it does, but how.

Normally, publishing things to the Web involves several steps and specialized file transfer programs. Using the WebDAV standard, the DotMac Kit embeds web services directly into applications. A user's MobileMe account becomes less like a server and more like an online extension of his or her home folder.

Integrating with MobileMe is a great way to add value for your users, and it's probably the number-one feature that sets applications designed "for the Mac" apart from applications that are "Mac compatible." Fortunately, the DotMac Kit, also known as the .Mac SDK, makes adding this feature almost as easy as using MobileMe.

The DotMac Kit breaks all operations into transactions. This means checking credentials, making sure a user's account is current, creating a directory, and moving files to and from the server are all encapsulated as transactions.

Transactions allow you to switch between synchronous and asynchronous modes as needed. There are a few places where switching modes is handy, but it's absolutely indispensable for debugging. There's also a compatibility interface for the truly lazy, which mimics the methods used by Cocoa's NSFileManager class. It doesn't have the same flexibility as transactions, but for simple actions or quick prototyping, it's quite convenient.

Calendar Store

As Address Book does for people, iCal does for events. Aside from the standard questions (What's going on? Where? When? Who's going to be there?), iCal events can include things like URLs, notes, and alarms: time-sensitive triggers that can do anything from popping up a reminder to running a script to sending an e-mail. Using a colorful, easy-to-understand interface, iCal lets users manage all their calendar-related information in one place, as shown in Figure 23-6.

Again, just like with Address Book, your application can interact with iCal's data using the Calendar Store framework. Calendar Store frees your application (not to mention your users) from the tedium of dealing with the same information in multiple places.

Calendar Store does more than just accessing, editing, and creating events. It also does the following:

- Manages the system-wide To Do list

- Notifies interested applications of any changes to the calendars

- Provides fast, flexible data-mining services using predicates: high-level, object-oriented queries used throughout Cocoa

In fact, it's better to think of Calendar Store as what it really is: a central database. iCal just happens to be a conveniently prebundled client. Indeed, Calendar Store is based on CalDAV, an open networking standard that lets your users connect with server-side collaboration software, regardless of platform.

It also means your applications' calendaring features need no longer bind users to iCal. Any application can use Calendar Store. In fact, Snow Leopard provides several examples of this kind of integration. The next time you get a piece of e-mail asking if you're coming to the party on Wednesday, try clicking the text and watch iCal add that event, as if your host had sent you an iCal invitation.

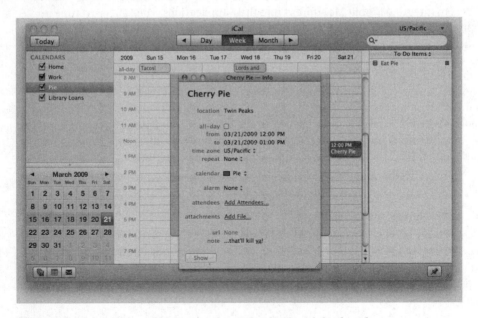

Figure 23-6. *iCal is the bundled front end to Calendar Store's back end.*

Store, by the way, as in storage, refers to the high-performance database that enables Calendar Store to work its magic. If you need a lolcat calendar for your cubicle, you're still going to have to hit the mall.

Note To learn more about iCal, see Chapter 11.

Instant Message

Mac users have long relied on iChat to keep them in constant communication with friends and business partners around the world. This innovative instant messaging client connects users by text, audio, or full-motion video. Your applications can take advantage of iChat using the Instant Message framework.

In basic usage, Instant Message allows you to incorporate iChat data, such as the contents of a user's buddy list and the online status of those buddies. This is how, for example, Mail lets you know that a person you are writing to is currently online, so you can simply chat with them instead.

Enter iChat Theater, which lets users turn their chats into multimedia presentations. Any application, including your own, can use the Instant Message framework to provide audio and video content to iChat Theater, as shown in Figure 23-7.

Figure 23-7. *Sharing a photo with iChat Theater*

Even if your application does not produce video in the traditional sense, the frame-by-frame access afforded by the Core Video framework, discussed later, makes it easy for you to provide static images to the video feed. iChat Theater and the Instant Message framework make it easy to turn your single-user experience into a collaborative multiuser masterpiece.

PDF Kit

Mac users have long been able to take advantage of Adobe's Portable Document Format (PDF). While other systems have required special tools for dealing with this universal format, Mac OS X has PDF support built in. Not only can users view PDFs with the bundled Preview application, but they can also create PDFs from any application via the Print panel.

The PDF Kit framework gives developers the ability to incorporate Preview's high-performance PDF rendering engine in their own applications. If you've ever used Preview, you know this goes far beyond simply displaying PDFs.

Interface Builder includes a PDF view. It has specialized behaviors, like crop, zoom, and rotate. PDF Kit also provides for document navigation, letting users jump to the next or previous page, to the first or last page, or to an arbitrary page.

Here are some other features PDF Kit handles:

- Annotations, which are additions to the page that are not part of the page itself, like sticky notes and editable text fields

- Encryption, including ownership, and permissions, such as limiting the ability to copy or print

- Outlining, which is an interactive table of contents showing the structure of a PDF document

- Pagination, which gives PDFs a familiar, book-like appearance

- Searching a PDF's content, as with Apple's Preview app

- Selection, including the ability to highlight and copy text to the pasteboard

Publication Subscription

Syndication is old technology that's recently taken the Web by storm. It works by letting people subscribe to web feeds—lightweight versions of their favorite web sites. These feeds can then be aggregated using specialized applications, like NewsGator's NetNewsWire, shown in Figure 23-8. Apple and others have expanded on syndication and found novel uses for its technology. In addition to Safari's subscription feature, iTunes's podcasts are implemented using syndication.

Figure 23-8. *NetNewsWire aggregates web content using syndication.*

The bad news about syndication is that it encompasses several competing standards, such as RSS and ATOM. There are also different versions within each standard, such as RSS 0.9, RSS 1.0, and RSS 2.0. The good news is you don't need to care, thanks to the Publication Subscription framework, known simply as PubSub.

PubSub handles the details of monitoring, downloading, and updating feeds, and then notifying interested applications when something changes. Because it's a central database for all syndication information, you can also ask PubSub for other people's feeds. For example, if you're interested in what feeds your user has bookmarked in Safari, PubSub can tell you.

Feeds are typically implemented in XML, and Cocoa's XML framework is quite good. Still, PubSub lets you treat the XML as an implementation detail, giving you a single, object-oriented interface to syndicated data regardless of the vagaries of format. Even if you don't subscribe to a feed, you can still use PubSub to parse it.

Spotlight

If you've been using a Mac (or reading this book), you know about Spotlight: Apple's integrated search utility that reunites users with their data across the vast cluttered landscape of their hard drives. To Mac developers, Spotlight presents a responsibility, as well as opportunity.

Spotlight has built-in support for most common data types, such as JPEG and PDF. If your application has its own document format, you'll want to provide a Spotlight importer—a Spotlight plug-in to translate your document's content into the metadata Spotlight needs to work its magic.

By providing an importer, you can be sure users can always find their stuff. Xcode includes the Spotlight Plug-in template to get you started. There's also a Core Data template that includes a Spotlight importer.

From within your application, you can offer users a standard Spotlight interface. You can also query Spotlight's metadata database programmatically. Spotlight offers an Objective-C interface for building and executing object-oriented queries based on the `NSPredicate` class used throughout Cocoa. You can also set things like sort order, grouping, and whether you want to receive live updates if anything changes behind your back.

Note For more information about Spotlight, see Chapter 3.

Quick Look

Quick Look provides rich previews of files, using a plug-in system similar to Spotlight. Known file types have plug-ins already installed, but custom types must provide a simple thumbnail and an extended preview. Users can then examine the file visually, even if the application used to create it no longer exists on the system.

Quick Look uses a two-level preview system. Documents can provide a thumbnail, which is a simple visual representation of the data. Often, this is just a static image stored in the document bundle.

Once the thumbnail is loaded, Quick Look may present a preview. Unlike the static thumbnail, the preview can be nearly anything. Your preview might be your entire document as a PDF, or perhaps a QuickTime movie of your application in action. You can even generate dynamic content on the fly.

Quick Look is a good chance for your documents to shine, but if you do not provide a preview, users will get disappointing generic icons.

Scripting Bridge

The best way to integrate with other applications is through an official API, but when that nicety is not afforded to you, you can always use AppleScript. As discussed in the last chapter, AppleScript is the high-level language users can use to make applications do their bidding.

Unfortunately, AppleScript is not particularly fast. Using it in your application, while certainly possible, requires you to shift your brain mid-project into another language. When performance is a factor, developers have traditionally turned to Apple events, the low-level system that lets AppleScript work its magic.

Somewhere on Earth we're sure someone understands Apple events, but by now you should know Cocoa programmers hate resorting to low-level programming. Apple, in its inimitable way, has simultaneously solved all these problems at once with Scripting Bridge.

Using Scripting Bridge is so easy it almost defies explanation:

1. Run the command-line tools `sdef` and `sdp` to generate Objective-C headers from another application's AppleScript dictionary.

2. Include the generated headers in your project.

3. There is no step 3.

Using the headers is like using any other header. You instantiate objects and manipulate their properties and methods using the standard Cocoa data types and structures. You can do this even if the program in question was not written in Cocoa and doesn't contain a single line of Objective-C.

Scripting Bridge is also a huge performance win. It's twice as fast as compiled AppleScript and about two orders of magnitude faster than uncompiled AppleScript.

■**Note** Scripting Bridge's underlying technology is also what enables Cocoa to be accessed from Ruby and Python.

WebKit

WebKit is the full-featured, open source, cross-platform, high-performance, web page–rendering engine behind Safari. It's also used in Dashboard and Apple's help viewer. You can also find WebKit in Xcode, and in Mail, as shown in Figure 23-9. In other words, WebKit is everywhere. In fact, WebKit is so ubiquitous that, as a developer, you'll probably manage to use WebKit without even knowing it.

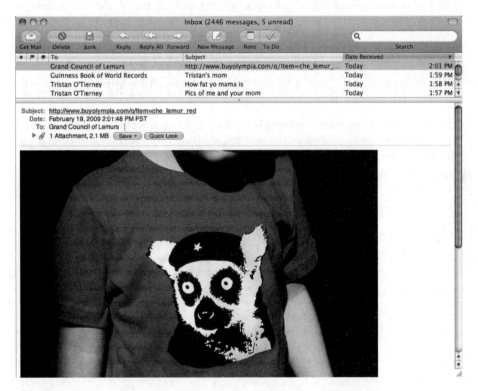

Figure 23-9. *Mail uses WebKit to display rich multimedia messages.*

To understand why WebKit is so ubiquitous, it helps to understand the technical problem of creating a formatted document. Text is easy; it's built into the very lowest levels of any operating system. Text alone, though, is far too boring for most uses.

A good document format will add typesetting information, such as font family, bold and italics, different text sizes and colors, and effects like underlining. You also want structures like bulleted and numbered lists, outlines, and tables. Finally, you want to be able to embed things like images.

This is exactly what a web page is. Content and structure are defined by HTML, and display information is expressed by CSS.

Documents encoded as web pages offer several advantages, and a lot of power, compared to other formats, such as Microsoft Word:

- They include built-in navigation via links (the HT in HTML).

- They are stored in plain text, so they be can created, viewed, and altered using standard tools in any programming language or environment.

- They use open standards that are not owned by, or subject to the whims of, a single company.

- HTML and CSS are free to use and implement without licensing or royalties.

- HTML and CSS are well understood by people all over the world.

- HTML can be made compatible with XML, which makes it extensible, and thus adaptable to myriad purposes.

- Using DOM and JavaScript, web pages can be made into dynamic, interactive, event-driven applications, as with Dashboard's widgets or Google Maps.

- Structure can be separated from style, so display characteristics can easily be changed without creator intervention.

This last point bears exploration. Your best writer can create the document while your best designer creates the style sheet. Every document in your company could exhibit the same style, which could be changed instantly and completely by editing a single style sheet. Your manual could have gorgeous visuals while remaining completely accessible to the blind.

Gaining all this power, thanks to WebKit, is as simple as including a view in Interface Builder. WebKit's extensive API offers low-level access to the various aspects of web pages and rendering behavior. WebKit also provides a bridge between JavaScript and Objective-C, integrating web and desktop technology like never before.

Note For more on Safari, see Chapter 10. For more on Dashboard, see Chapter 3.

Beauty

Mac OS X has always placed a heavy emphasis on design. The operating system itself is beautiful, and the applications written for the Mac inherit the system's aesthetic brilliance for free, whether they are written in modern Cocoa, old-fashioned Carbon, or even a guest platform like Java.

That's because the application frameworks let developers build applications without worrying about any but the highest-level details of the graphics system. Pushing the envelope used to mean dropping into OpenGL and speaking the language of the graphics hardware. Every release of Mac OS X has brought a new graphics API, making it easier than ever to get a lot of whoa for very little dough.

High-level graphics frameworks are not only easier to use, but they also bring the benefit of free improvements. These frameworks take advantage of speed improvements in Snow Leopard, so developers who adopt them will suddenly see their graphics get faster.

General-purpose computing on graphics processing units (so-called GPGPU) lets people tap into the power of the graphics card for general computing tasks. Leopard introduced an operation API to simplify parallelizing tasks to make them efficient for the GPU. Snow Leopard takes operations to a whole other level: the UNIX level. The fast cat also introduces Apple's new open standard for high-performance computing: OpenCL.

■Note For more about Snow Leopard's performance frameworks, see the upcoming "Performance and Concurrency" section.

Core Animation

Core Animation simplifies many advanced graphics techniques, like the eponymous animation. You can use Core Animation in AppKit, or you can use it directly, as a 2.5D layer-based graphics framework.

With Core Animation in effect, changing a view's properties doesn't change the view immediately. Rather, the change animates (or happens gradually), as if the view were a real object. This gives the user feedback that the change is happening, and it gives the interface a natural familiarity.

Core Animation can handle complex animation techniques, such as changing course or following a Bézier path. It also has an API for custom timing and key-frame animation.

Best of all, Core Animation is performant. Its textures are cached, its routines are hardware-accelerated, and its implementation is threaded. That means you're getting OpenGL performance from an API so friendly, you can access it through Interface Builder, as shown in Figure 23-10.

Figure 23-10. *Core Animation's effects panel in Interface Builder*

Core Image

If you've ever used Adobe Photoshop, you know how much fun image filters can be. Core Image takes the idea of image filters and runs with it, for results that are both amazing and amazingly useful.

Filters can range from the very simple, like a blur, to the very complex, like iChat's background replacement effects. Filters can also include operations not typically associated with filtering, such as cropping, resizing, or warping. Best of all, if there's no existing filter to meet your needs, you can write your own.

Core Image filters are nondestructive. Your images are not actually changed on disk. Rather, they are altered before being displayed on the graphics card, so you can undo or alter filters at any time, including runtime.

Core Image filters can be stacked, and the stacks are intelligently optimized to give you the same results with the least processing power possible. For example, if you have a Crop filter later in the stack, Core Image will apply it first, so you don't waste time processing pixels you're never going to see.

Core Image filters are written in OpenGL Shading Language (GLSL) and run directly on the GPU, taking advantage of the latest programmable GPUs. You can write your own Core Image filters to take advantage of the performance and modularity.

Core Image is available system-wide, which means you can apply its filters to anything, including video. Whether you're tidying up your pictures in iPhoto, applying a comic book effect in Photo Booth, pretending to be at work in iChat Theater, or fighting your way through glowing green gas in a video game, Core Image has you covered.

Core Graphics

Also known as Quartz 2D, Core Graphics provides basic drawing services throughout the system. This includes primitive drawing, with paths, shapes, colors, and the like; advanced drawing like shadows, gradients, and patterns; and transforms, bitmaps, transparency, masking, and compositing.

Because the underlying Quartz compositing engine is based on PDF, Core Graphics is also able to deal with PDF directly, including simple file operations like parsing and creation, as well as transforms, metadata access, and conversion from PostScript.

Even if you never use Core Graphics directly, you'll see its influence (and its prefix, CG) everywhere. For example, its width-agnostic floating-point scalar, `CGFloat`, replaces standard float and double types in many applications.

■**Note** In lieu of separate namespaces, frameworks use informal prefixes to give their members unique names. For example, consider three different classes for representing an image: `CGImage`, `CIImage`, and `NSImage`, from Core Graphics, Core Image, and Cocoa (formerly known as NeXTSTEP).

Core Video

When you think about it, video is more of a concept than a thing. When you say you have "a video," you really mean you have a tape, or a disc, or a high-definition digital file. Video, while one simple term, actually encompasses a lot of complexity that the operating system protects us from.

On Mac OS X, this abstraction goes deep. With Core Video, developers can manipulate the individual frames of raw video using a standard buffer to bridge differences between data types, and a pipeline of discrete processing steps for the ultimate in control.

The following are some things Core Video enables:

- Using Core Image filters

- Compositing video streams together

- Editing the content of frames

- Transforming the physical geometry of a video

- Mapping a video onto other surfaces or an OpenGL scene

Core Video also takes care of things most people take for granted, like making sure the picture remains synced with the sound, despite the vagaries of refresh rates, CPU operations, user interactions, and the myriad flavors of lag.

Image I/O

All this image processing is great, but that sort of assumes you have an image to work with in the first place. The formidable task of reading and parsing the myriad image formats out there used to be the job of Core Graphics. Eventually, the size of the task and the ubiquity of its need necessitated spinning off image interpretation into its own framework, called Image I/O.

Despite all the goings-on behind the scenes, the actual use of Image I/O is pretty easy to understand. You've got your I, which is to say, input, and you've got your O, which is to say, output.

For input, Image I/O introduces image sources, an abstraction from the raw data that contains multiple images, thumbnails, metadata, and important but easily overlooked things like color spaces. For output, Image I/O uses image destinations, which are like the same thing, in reverse.

Performance and Concurrency

Apple's focus with Snow Leopard has been on efficiency. Mac OS X is on a diet, and users and developers alike will benefit from its leaner, faster form. To get maximum benefit, developers can learn from Apple's experience—and use its code. Snow Leopard sports APIs, both new and old, to help developers turbocharge their applications.

Intel cofounder Gordon Moore observed that the number of transistors that could be placed in a single integrated circuit doubled every two years. This maxim, called Moore's law, has held true, but even as silicon manufacturing processes improve, the ultimate limit—the width of an atom—looms large.

To ensure the amount of computing power can continue to increase in the spirit of Moore's law, processor designers have turned to multicore and multiprocessor architectures. Graphics code loves a parallel architecture. Big arrays of pixels are easy to parallelize, and graphics hardware has continued to get faster and more programmable.

With concurrency the new frontier, a lot of developers are looking at their code and wondering how they can take advantage of this GPGPU bonanza. While the rewards are tempting, the path is fraught with peril. Threading is a notoriously difficult problem, and actual performance benefits vary wildly.

Gene Amdahl—the computer architect who coined the word *FUD* to describe marketing tactics that instill fear, uncertainty, and doubt—observed that adding processors pays diminishing returns. Amdahl's law means the more processors you add to your pool, the less each one will actually help.

Snow Leopard's performance frameworks abstract away from all these issues. Depending on the level of performance you need, getting the best performance on any system can be as easy as organizing your code the right way.

NSOperation

`NSOperation` and `NSOperationQueue` are Objective-C classes for organizing your code into discrete operations. You can adjust priorities and set dependencies, and the framework handles the rest. Whether your needs are best served on a single thread or on a complicated thread pool across every core on the system, all you need to do is phrase your problem in the form of an operation.

Grand Central Dispatch

Snow Leopard's new Grand Central Dispatch technology brings operations to the UNIX level. Operations are packetized across the user's specific hardware in the way that's most efficient given the capabilities of the system and the demands being placed on it. Blocks, which are central to the Grand Central infrastructure, are covered in Chapter 25.

OpenCL

Deciding what's best executed on the GPU vs. the CPU is difficult, and it begs the question of whether you could use both. OpenCL is a proposed standard developed by Apple for hardware-agnostic parallelization. As OpenGL has done for graphics processing, OpenCL does for general-purpose computing. Now your code can run on any processor that will have it, making the GPU vs. CPU question moot.

Accelerate

Imagine yourself in the future, a happy and productive Cocoa programmer. You've already finished this book, including the section on Apple's optimization tools, so you knew better than to think about performance while you were blasting out your killer new application.

Now, ahead of schedule and under budget, you've carefully profiled away all the major performance bottlenecks, but one tight loop is giving your trouble. You reach for your book on assembly language . . .

Not so fast!

- What if Apple changes processors again?
- What if Intel introduces a new vector library?
- What if some of your users are still on PowerPC?

- What if someone invents a better algorithm?

- What if, somehow, people are still using this in the year 2000?

OK, that last one might not be a problem anymore, but it does illustrate the point: you don't know what's going to happen to your application, to computer science, or to hardware in the future. That's why hand-optimized code is a disaster waiting to happen.

I think you can see where we're going with this. The Accelerate framework, as contradictory as it seems, is a high-level framework for low-level optimizations. That means you can optimize your code in terms of efficient technique, not the implementation details of the machine.

That also means you can answer all the "what ifs" with "who cares." You make one simple optimization, and you're done. No matter where your application ends up in time or space, it will have the best performance available for that particular computer. Even as silicon science progresses, your application will get faster without you even being aware of it.

Here are some of the optimizations available in Accelerate:

- Image processing, including geometric and morphological transformations, histogram operations, and alpha compositing

- Digital signal processing on real and complex data types, including fast Fourier transforms and vector-to-vector and vector-to-scalar operations

- A vectorized analog to the standard math library

- Linear algebra, including simultaneous sets of linear equations, eigenvalue and singular solution problems, and least-squares solutions for linear systems

- Routines that operate on matrices as if they were single variables

Other Application Frameworks

Not everyone who develops on the Mac has the luxury of developing for the Mac, and not everyone writing Mac applications has the luxury of using Cocoa and Objective-C. Fortunately, on Mac OS X Snow Leopard, applications written in any number of languages with any number of frameworks all live and work side by side.

Cocoa

Though primarily intended for development in Objective-C, Cocoa has been bridged to several other languages. Although C and C++ are not completely compatible, they share enough that C++ programmers can mix their native language with Objective-C via a hybrid known as Objective-C++.

The popular scripting languages Ruby and Python are bridged to Cocoa, letting programmers of those languages access Cocoa alongside their own libraries. Xcode includes templates for Ruby and Python Cocoa projects. Indeed, developers have written Apple Design Awards–winning Cocoa applications in languages other than Objective-C, as shown in Figure 23-11.

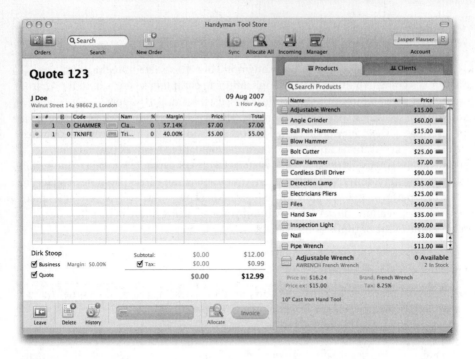

Figure 23-11. *Madebysofa's Checkout was written in Python with Cocoa.*

Carbon

When Apple bought NeXT in 1997, NeXT's operating system, NeXTSTEP, became the new Mac OS X. The old Mac OS, then on its ninth iteration, Mac OS 9, was deprecated but not eliminated. To smooth the transition, the Mac OS 9 operating environment became a part of Mac OS X, called Classic. Mac users could use their old Mac OS 9 applications alongside native applications.

Eventually, everything deemed important became a native Mac OS X application, and Classic went away. For those newer to the platform, this is exactly what is happening with Rosetta, a Classic-like compatibility environment that allows users to run their old PowerPC applications. Eventually, the PowerPC machines will retire, and Rosetta too will go away.

The developer frameworks of Mac OS 9 likewise did not simply vanish. They were rolled into an application framework called Carbon, shown in Figure 23-12. For ten years, Carbon and Cocoa lived side by side. Cocoa continued to expand and mature, and new Carbon development slowed and eventually came to a stop.

That being said, Carbon is not going away any time soon. However, new frameworks are being developed exclusively for Cocoa. For example, while the new 64-bit frameworks include Carbon, there is no Carbon UI. Rather, Carbon developers who wish to take advantage of new development, such as 64-bit, will have to do so with the Cocoa frameworks.

Fortunately, Carbon and Cocoa are compatible, so just as Cocoa developers can dip into Carbon (something that happens less and less as Cocoa has matured), Carbon developers can dip into Cocoa (something that will happen more and more as time goes on).

Figure 23-12. *iTunes was written with Carbon.*

Java

Java is a cross-platform framework and eponymous object-oriented language. If you're a Java programmer, the Mac is a great place to work. The Java implementation on the Mac is the best one out there. It takes almost no effort to package a Java application to launch, look, and behave just like a native Mac application.

That said, with the Java-Cocoa bridge being deprecated, the Java language is not a good choice for writing native Mac applications. Furthermore, when you develop without regard for a particular operating system, you give up all the support that an operating system provides. It is a lot harder to program in Java than it is to program in almost any native application framework.

AppleScript

AppleScript is a language designed for automating tasks that use other applications on the system. It's designed to be friendly to non-programmers, with an English-like syntax and flexible grammar. Apple continues to improve AppleScript, a unique and useful language.

Xcode includes an environment, called AppleScript Studio, that adds graphical interface widgets to AppleScript. This enables power users who dabble in development with AppleScript to bridge the gap to creating full-fledged applications.

■**Note** For more information on AppleScript, see Chapter 22.

WebObjects

A kind of Cocoa for the Web, WebObjects is an enterprise-level product marketed by Apple for creating web-based storefronts and other services. It's included with the developer tools, but not installed by default.

BSD/X11

Lest we forget that Mac OS X has UNIX roots, applications and utilities can be written for and ported to Mac OS X either as command-line BSD applications or as graphical X11 applications. If you're a scientific programmer, a Perl hacker, or have a huge white beard and pipe-scented suspenders, welcome to Darwin.

Note For more on Darwin, see Chapters 17 and 18.

Ajax

Asynchronous JavaScript and XML (Ajax) is the best-known platform of Web 2.0. The basic idea is to extend the concept of a web page into a full-blown application by adding JavaScript—the dynamic, object-oriented language that is not at all related to Java—and background communication with a server, using XML.

While Ajax is hardly specific to the Mac, the Mac is a great platform for Ajax development. There are a lot of great tools for working with Ajax and with other web technologies that you can only use on the Mac, such as Apple's Dashcode, Panic's Coda, and Bare Bones's venerable BBEdit.

Ajax is used to create Dashboard widgets. WebKit allows web technology to be embedded in any application, making Ajax a kind of lingua franca around the platform and beyond. Ajax is used to make web applications for iPhone.

Note For more on iPhone development, check out *Beginning iPhone Development: Exploring the iPhone SDK* by Dave Mark and Jeff LaMarche (Apress, 2008).

Summary

Programming on the Mac is a lot like using a Mac, and how could it be any other way? When you see the thousands of top-notch applications by Apple and others that are available only on the Mac, it's inspiring. Whether you're a student, hobbyist, or professional, the Mac is a great place to live and to code.

Whether you're programming for the Mac, or just a programmer who happens to develop on a Mac, Apple is working hard to keep you happy and productive. The application programming environment is only part of the story. In the chapters ahead, we'll sample some tools of the trade, and we'll meet Objective-C, Apple's secret weapon in the battle against deadlines.

CHAPTER 24

■■■

Mac OS X Development: The Tools

Every copy of Snow Leopard comes with the same set of developer tools used by software engineers both inside and outside Apple to develop applications for the Mac and iPhone. Some of these tools are behemoth environments whose brambles are criss-crossed with the narrow paths cut by tutorials. Some are utilities useful to programmers and non-programmers alike. And some of these tools defy explanation, yet invite exploration. Whether you've bought your Mac to write the next big iPhone game, or whether you're an avid novice looking for more toys to play with, developer tools on Snow Leopard are ready to flex your imagination.

Apple Developer Connection

The tools provided on the installation disc are just a sampling of what Apple has for developers. What Apple would really like is for you to check out `http://developer.apple.com` and sign up for an Apple Developer Connection (ADC) account. The ADC is Apple's official hookup for sample code, documentation, and the latest development kits. It also gives you access to the Bug Reporter, but more on that later. Best of all, it's free.

■**Note** Professional software developers need more support and things like prerelease software. For them, Apple offers Select and Premier ADC memberships for a price. For our purposes, the free online membership is sufficient, but if you decide to make your living this way, it's well worth the cost of upgrading.

Installing Xcode Tools

To install the developer tools, known collectively as Xcode tools, insert your Snow Leopard installation DVD. It doesn't matter if it's the retail upgrade version or the restore version that came with your machine. Navigate to the Xcode Tools folder, and then double-click the Xcode.mpkg package. This launches the installer. Xcode's installer has been simplified to the point where you can pretty well just click through and install without customization.

Xcode includes software development kits for every version of Mac OS X from Tiger on. However, it does not contain the Tiger-era tools, such as Interface Builder 2. You can install them alongside the current versions, but you'll have to dig out your Tiger disks.

■**Note** No discs, no problem. You can always download the latest versions of the developer tools from the ADC web site.

Introduction to Xcode

The installer adds a Developer directory, which contains a treasure chest of goodies in a folder named Applications, some reading material (About Xcode Tools.pdf), and a lot of uninteresting files for use by the star of the show: Xcode.

The Xcode integrated development environment (IDE), known to its friends simply as Xcode, is where all Mac and iPhone developers spend their work day. It is your editor, compiler, and debugger all in one. Much as Mac OS X delivers the power of UNIX in a shiny candy coating, Xcode provides a unified, graphical interface on the same open source tools used by developers all over the world, like the GNU Compiler Collection (GCC).

Xcode also serves as your project manager and research assistant, with integrated access to headers and documentation. It's a beast of an application, sweeping in scope and labyrinthine in architecture. It's also very un-Apple-like in one major way.

Normally, Apple's applications are an exercise in simplicity. If there are five ways to do something, Apple will figure out which one is right 80 percent of the time and use it exclusively. If two options are equally valid, you might get a preference, but that's it. Xcode, on the other hand, replaces a lot of storied tools, like Metrowerks CodeWarrior and Apple's own Macintosh Programmer's Workshop, to say nothing of legendary text editors like Emacs and Vi. Xcode *has* to be all things to all people.

Xcode Preferences

Engineers are a finicky bunch that likes things just so. Xcode accommodates their whims through its preferences. With great configurability comes great complexity. The first time you launch Xcode, it's like being interrogated by a waiter in Paris when you speak terrible French. You may not understand the questions, let alone know the answers. Don't sweat it. You can always use the standard keystroke, Command-comma, to bring up the extensive Xcode Preferences window, shown in Figure 24-1.

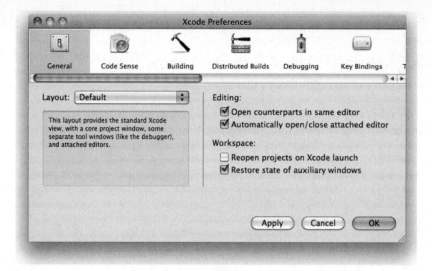

Figure 24-1. *The extensive Xcode Preferences window*

Xcode has several groups of preferences, selectable by scrolling along the top of the window. Here are a few of the preferences Xcode allows you to set:

General:

- Adjust the positioning and grouping of windows.

- Set the behavior of the editor.

Code Sense:

- Code completion is requested with the Esc key, but you can also enable autocompletion and set the delay.

- Decide whether arguments are shown in suggestions or completions.

- Set the display and sorting of the editor's function pop-up list.

Building:

- Set where build products and temp files are located.

- Decide whether and how build, error, and warning logs are displayed.

- Set where and how errors and warnings are displayed.

- Decide whether to compile predictively or in the presence of errors.

■**Note** Predictive compilation builds parts of your application while you edit, to reduce build times.

Debugging:

- Choose the colors used by the debugger.
- Set how and when to display the debugger.
- Adjust symbol and assembly display options.
- Clear the console between runs by checking "Auto Clear Debug Console."
- Decide whether to enable in-editor debugging.

Key Bindings:

- Set customizable shortcuts for menu items and other functions.
- Select prebuilt groups to make Xcode emulate other editors.

Text Editing:

- Toggle editor features like the gutter, line numbers, columns, page guides, code folding, and code focus features.
- Set selection behaviors around braces and default line ending and text encodings.

Fonts & Colors:

- Set fonts and colors used by the editor for every syntax element.
- Enable colored text for printing.
- There are also customizable sets here, but they don't emulate other programs so much as provide mood enhancement.

Indentation:

- Decide whether to use tabs or spaces, and the width and quantity of each.
- Decide whether and how to soft wrap text.
- Decide whether and how to apply automatic indentation.

File Types:

- Set the mapping of file types and which editor to use for each.
- Xcode can be used with any number of external editors.

Opening Quickly:

- Open Quickly is a command that allows you to open a file by selecting or typing its name, rather than by navigating the Open dialog.
- Opening Quickly is the customizable list of directories searched by the Open Quickly command.

SCM:

- Select between CVS, Perforce, and Subversion.
- The Repositories tab is where you add your project servers.
- The Options tab contains preferences such as which editor to use for differencing and whether to autosave.

Documentation:

- Enable and update various documentation sets and publishers.
- Decide the sections and their orders in the Research Assistant.
- Set the documentation's minimum font size.

You might think that the Preferences panel is the only place to set up preferences for Xcode, but in fact Xcode has hidden preferences all over the place. Some of these are based on scope—for example, the different project and target settings. Others are based on tradition, such as right-clicking or Control-clicking the toolbar to edit its configuration.

At the end of the day, while Xcode is much easier to use than traditional command-line tools, it's designed to be powerful, efficient, and endlessly configurable. If there's some way in which you want to exert your will over Xcode, don't assume it doesn't exist just because you can't find it. It's likely it does exist, but is hidden somewhere obscure.

Documentation

After setting up Xcode, you're greeted with the new Welcome to Xcode window, shown in Figure 24-2. Aside from assembling everything you need to start programming with Xcode, the welcome window uses RSS syndication to deliver up-to-the-minute news and documentation. This combines the accuracy and timeliness of web-based documentation with the convenience and accessibility of having the documentation right in Xcode.

Clicking "Getting started with Xcode" is not only a good way to get acquainted with Xcode, but it's also a good way to meet your new best friend, the documentation window, shown in Figure 24-3. This has been radically redesigned again in Snow Leopard.

There are several ways to get to the documentation window, aside from the Welcome to Xcode window. When in Xcode's editor, you can hold Option while double-clicking a term to automatically search for it in the documentation window.

You can also activate the documentation window by selecting Documentation from the Help menu. This means you can also launch it from the keyboard by typing Option-Command-?. That doesn't seem memorable, but it's really easy to type. Press the adjacent Option and Command buttons with your left hand and the adjacent ? and Shift buttons with your right.

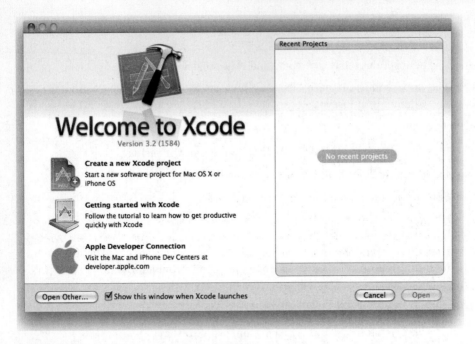

Figure 24-2. *Xcode's Welcome to Xcode window*

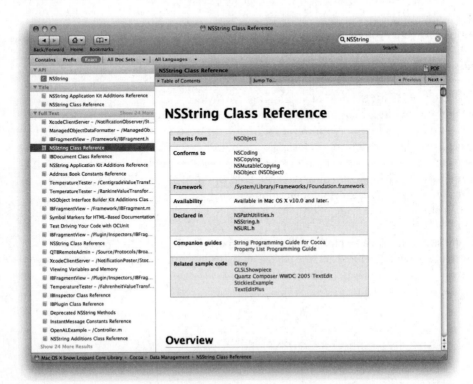

Figure 24-3. *Xcode's documentation window*

The operation of the documentation window should be pretty obvious. Type a search term into the box. Refine your search using the options below the toolbar. Results are displayed, sorted, and selected in the table view. The selected document is shown in the web view below, or in an external editor, as appropriate. The sidebar contains documentation sets and bookmarks.

Finally, there's the Research Assistant, a floating documentation window intended to be kept open as you code (shown in Figure 24-4). As you highlight words in the editor, the Research Assistant provides snippets from the API documentation and links to more information. The nice thing about the Research Assistant is that it gives you just a bit of help in using the frameworks, without taking your focus away from the code. You can activate the Research Assistant from the Help menu, or via an optional toolbar icon.

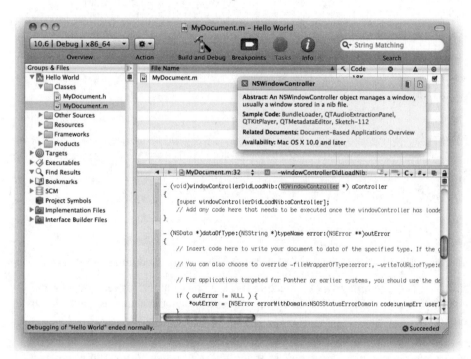

Figure 24-4. *Xcode's new Research Assistant panel*

Project Organization

Xcode organizes your projects into bundles called, appropriately, *projects*. To create a new project in Xcode, select New Project… from the File menu, or type Shift-Command-N. This launches the New Project template chooser, shown in Figure 24-5.

Figure 24-5. *Project templates in Xcode's New Project window*

Xcode presents you with a long list of project templates, organized into several categories:

Application: These templates are for making stand-alone programs against various application frameworks, including Cocoa, Cocoa-AppleScript, Quartz Composer, and the UNIX command line.

Framework & Library: These templates are for making reusable code bundles, including Cocoa frameworks, static and dynamic libraries, BSD C libraries, C++ STL libraries, and Java JNI libraries.

Application Plug-in: These templates are for making non–stand-alone programs for various Apple applications, including Automator actions and plug-ins for Installer, WebKit, Quartz Composer, and Interface Builder.

System Plug-in: These templates are for making non–stand-alone programs for various tasks around the system, including Address Book action plug-ins, Audio Units effects and instruments, C++ plug-ins, kernel extensions, IOKit drivers, preference panes, Quick Look and Spotlight plug-ins, screen savers, and sync schema.

Other: These templates are for other types of projects, including a generic empty template, and a template for using an external build system, as with Ruby or Python applications.

You can't do much in Xcode without a project, so to really see how Xcode works, let's build the traditional Hello World application. To start your first Xcode project from the New Project window, create a new Cocoa application named Hello World. Make sure the "Create document-based application" option is selected, then click the Choose… button.

You will be prompted to give the project a name and a location, as shown in Figure 24-6. We've created a ~/Projects folder in our home folder, adjacent to our ~/Documents folder. We like to subdivide our Projects folder into general categories, but you can adapt this exercise to your own work style.

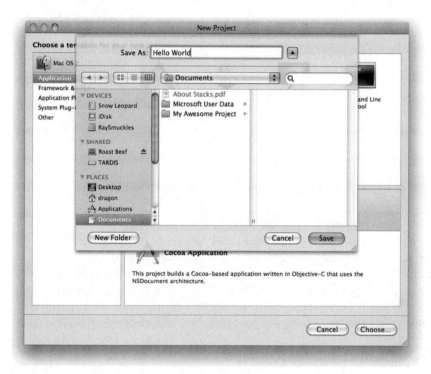

Figure 24-6. *Creating a project in Xcode's New Project window*

Xcode's project window is split vertically into two views. On the left is the Groups & Files sidebar, which organizes your project in a logical, hierarchical way. On the right is a details view that gives you more information on whatever is selected in the sidebar. While it's not immediately obvious at first, the right pane is actually further split horizontally. Centered at the bottom of the view is a small dot. Grabbing the dot with your cursor and dragging reveals the editor view, as shown in Figure 24-7. You can also reveal the editor by selecting a source code file in the sidebar or by clicking the editor toolbar item.

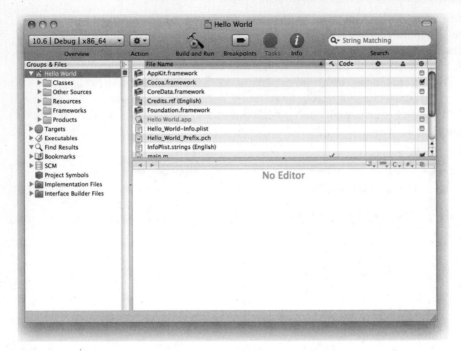

Figure 24-7. *Xcode's project window, with the editor pane revealed*

Your new project already has a lot of content in its sidebar. These are Xcode's smart groups. Like iTunes, some of these are functional and built-in, while others simply serve to demonstrate the kinds of smart groups you can create yourself. You can toggle any of the preset smart groups by right- or Command-clicking the sidebar to bring up its contextual menu, and then selecting Preferences.

Project Structure

The first thing in the sidebar is the Project Structure smart group. Note that this smart group is unique in that its displayed name is the same as your project's. By default, it contains several subgroups, which look and behave like folders. These in turn contain all the source code and resources used by your project.

Groups are created, deleted, and renamed via the contextual menu. (Recall that the contextual menu is what pops up when you Control-click or right-click an item.) You can move or nest the groups by dragging them. You can also move items within the groups by dragging them.

It bears note that the groups within the Project Structure smart group have no actual relevance to your project, nor do they necessarily relate to the actual folders in your project's folder; they are only there for your organizational convenience.

Targets

An Xcode target is the recipe for each product you build in your project. Each project starts with a single target for the main application. You might add additional targets for helper applications, plug-ins, frameworks, command-line tools, or Automator actions. A target is the primary organizational unit of a project. Your Hello World project will contain one target, which will have the build steps for compiling source code, linking, and copying resources to the application bundle.

Executables

Building a project isn't much good unless you can run and debug it. Since Xcode handles these tasks, it needs to know any arguments, environment variables, or debugging attachments you want added when you run. Any executable products of your project, such as the Hello World application, will be kept in the Executables smart group.

Upon selecting an executable in this group, typing Command-I will pull up an executable inspector where you can set things like arguments. As with targets, the default project will only contain a single executable.

Errors & Warnings

Sometimes a change can require so much code that by the time you can compile again, dozens of files have been touched. Even with errors and warnings inline, it's still nice to have a list of all the files that have something wrong with them. The Errors & Warnings smart group is just such a list. Any file with an error or warning on it will be added to this smart group until the next compile.

Find Results

The Edit menu item's Find submenu reveals that Xcode has multiple levels of find. The familiar Command-F launches Single File Find, which does what it says. Typing Shift-Command-F (or clicking the magnifying glass toolbar item) launches Project Find. This is a bit of misnomer, as its focus can be broadened or narrowed from the project.

In any case, all Project Find search results are saved in the Find Results smart group. On large projects, where searches can take several minutes, this is a big time saver.

Bookmarks

Another problem plaguing large projects is navigating the hierarchy of folders to get to the files you're working on. To help you stay organized, Xcode lets you bookmark files. Bookmarked files show up in this smart group. To bookmark a file, right- or Command-click the file in the sidebar, details list, or editor to bring up its contextual menu, and select Add to Bookmarks.

SCM

If you're using version control in Xcode, any file that has been changed will be added to the SCM results details pane, as well as the SCM smart group. Items in the SCM smart group have version control commands in their contextual menu, which makes it easy to commit, revert, or diff a single file.

The SCM smart group's icon turns into a progress indicator during version control operations, so you can keep an eye on how your commit is going while getting ready to break things again.

Project Symbols

Unlike the other smart groups, Project Symbols doesn't have a disclosure triangle revealing a hierarchy of files. Rather, it's just there so you can select it and bring up its details panel. Doing so yields a list of every symbol a programmer could care to see: every method, function, ivar, struct, global, typedef, protocol, property, and macro, as well as anything defined in a Core Data model or Interface Builder file.

Implementation Files/NIB Files

Aside from the built-in smart groups, you can create your own. Although they are functional and potentially useful, the Implementation Files and NIB Files smart groups are really samples of the kinds of things you could do. To create a smart group, select an option from the Project menu's New Smart Group submenu.

To edit an existing smart group, select Get Info from its contextual menu, or select it in the sidebar and type Command-I. Aside from defining a name, filter, and scope for the group, you can also set its icon. Regardless of whether that's useful, it's pretty cool.

Note We explain nib files in the "Interface Builder" section that follows.

Breakpoints

While running your program in the debugger, you may want to stop at a certain line of code to examine the values of variables, test some method calls, or just follow along line by line to see what's happening. To mark lines for the debugger to stop, or break, you set breakpoints. Breakpoints are also handy placeholders in their own right. To help you examine or jump to a certain breakpoint, they are all listed under the Breakpoints smart group.

Tip Xcode also has a Favorites bar, which is similar to the Bookmarks bar in Safari. You can reveal the Favorites bar by selecting Show Favorites Bar from the Layout submenu of the View menu. Dragging files, groups, or smart groups to the Favorites bar will add them. Clicking an item in the Favorites bar will select it in the Groups & Files sidebar.

One thing we've noticed about Apple applications: they always include amazing templates. You can fire up anything in iLife or iWork, and you already have a fully functional, if somewhat boring, web site, movie, song, DVD, presentation, or document. Xcode is the exact same way. Without typing anything, you've already started with a fully functional document-based application.

To see this for yourself, build and run your project by selecting Build and Run from the Build menu, typing Command-R, or clicking the hammer icon on the toolbar. In short order, you'll see a generic document, as shown in Figure 24-8.

Figure 24-8. *Your first Mac application in action*

Traditionally, a Hello World application features the words "Hello World!" whereas yours says, "Your document contents here." Traditionally, you could do a quick search for where in the code the words "Your document contents here" appear, but this application's source code does not include those words. Rather, they're stored in the mysterious nib format. Nibs are edited with a different tool: Xcode's older brother, Interface Builder.

Quit your application like any other—by selecting Quit from its menu or typing Command-Q. Then, from the project's smart group in the sidebar, find the Resources group and double-click MyDocument.xib to open it in Interface Builder.

■**Note** The current nib format is XML-based and uses the file extension .xib to distinguish it from the older file format, which used the .nib extension. Either way, they're all nibs.

Interface Builder

It's fitting that the first development tool for Mac OS X, back when it was still NeXTSTEP, was not a code editor, but an interface editor. Interface Builder made the process of creating a graphic user interface into a graphical experience. It's so much more natural to lay out an interface as it will appear to the user, rather than having to describe an inherently visual concept in programming code.

Even though drag-and-drop user-interface editors are now common, Interface Builder is unique in that it doesn't produce code. Rather, it creates freeze-dried interface objects in NeXTSTEP Interface Builder format, more generally known as nibs. These nibs are literally your application's interface, a precompiled version of what you would get it you wrote it out in code.

The same nibs you create in a project today will be deployed with your shipping application tomorrow.

Later, Interface Builder was joined by a younger sibling, Project Builder, now known as Xcode. Interface Builder remained separate, which is handy for interface designers, translators, and hackers who want to create or alter an application's interface without having to know or care about its source code. It's also handy for localizers who need to make slightly different versions of the interface in other languages.

Interface Builder has four components, as shown in Figure 24-9.

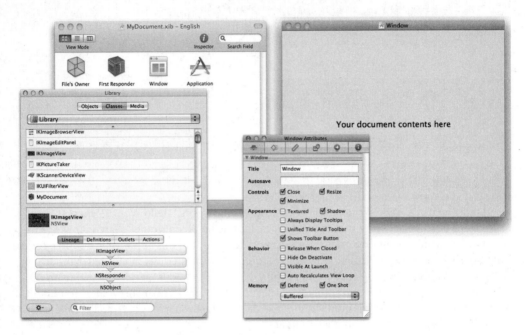

Figure 24-9. *Editing a user interface in Interface Builder*

The Interface

The nib is your interface, so it should come as no surprise that your interface elements are at the center of the nib's contents. When you open your nib in Interface Builder for the first time, you're greeted with the same document window you saw when building and running your nascent application. The window you see in the nib is the same window the user will be greeted with, but editable.

Double-click the words "Your document contents here" to edit the text field. Type the new text, "Hello World!," in its place. Since many interface elements have dynamic content that is difficult to render in edit mode, you can simulate your interface in normal mode by selecting Simulate Interface from the File menu, or by typing Command-R.

This launches your interface in Cocoa Simulator. You can interact with your interface to make sure it does what you expect when, for example, resizing a window. Resizing the window in Cocoa Simulator reveals an unexpected problem. The text area seems to be anchored to the bottom-left corner of the window, rather than doing what we would expect, which is to stay centered. We'll fix that in moment. For now, quit Cocoa Simulator by selecting Quit from the file menu or typing Command-Q.

Testing the interface by itself is OK for some tasks, but it doesn't show how the interface works with your application. For more complicated testing, you'll want to actually build and run your application. There are a few ways to do this. You can save your interface and then quit Interface Builder, or you can switch back to Xcode to build and run, as we did before.

You can also build and run in Xcode from within Interface Builder itself. Save your interface by selecting Save from the File menu or by typing Command-S. Then select Build and Go in Xcode from the File menu, or type Shift-Command-R. This sends a message to Xcode (no doubt using AppleScript) to build and run your application, just like you did earlier.

You should see your document window with your new text. You should also notice we still have that resizing bug. Quit your application in the usual way and return to Interface Builder. Select the text area with a single click. It's time to meet the Inspector.

The Inspector

Like any inspector panel, Interface Builder's Inspector allows you to see and change the attributes of your interface items. The Inspector is open by default, but you can always call it forth by selecting Inspector from the Tools menu or by typing Shift-Command-I. To inspect an item, simply click it, and the Inspector's contents will change as appropriate. The Inspector's functionality is divided into several tabs.

Attributes

As interface objects are reusable, they have several configuration options. Although interface objects can be instantiated and configured in code, it's easier to set up as many attributes as possible in Interface Builder itself. This keeps the attributes with the objects they affect, and presents them in a visual way that often makes their effects easier to understand.

The Attributes tab is divided into subsections based on the object's inheritance. Our text field has several attributes; chief among them is its title, which is the text it displays. Editing the title changes the text, just as you did by double-clicking and editing it in place. You can also set text attributes such as alignment, color, and whether to use rich text, which allows things like bold or italic formatting. You can also set attributes on the text field itself, such as its border, whether it should draw a background, and if so, what color it should be.

Since your text field, as an instance of the class NSTextField, is a subclass of NSControl, the next subsection allows you to edit the attributes of a control. These include the text's direction, how it handles line breaks, and whether it is enabled or dimmed.

As NSControl is in turn a subclass of NSView, you can then edit view attributes like how it draws a focus ring to indicate it's the currently selected item, or whether it's visible at all.

Effects

As discussed in Chapter 23, many Core Animation effects are available from within Interface Builder. These are settable from the myriad subsections of the Effects tab. Since your text field is a view subclass, you can take advantage of Core Animation by activating it in the Rendering Tree subsection.

Note Core Animation was originally called *Layer Kit*, because it uses a lightweight layer-based model. For whatever reason, OS X's architects decided to emphasize the framework's easy animation over its nifty rendering model. Regardless of this change, we still refer to layers and call views that can use Core Animation as *layer-backed*.

Once your view is layer-backed, you can change its transparency and set a custom shadow from the Appearance tab. You can add Core Image filters from the Content Filters, Background Filters, and Compositing Filters subsections. Finally, you can affect the style of animation by setting custom transitions in the Transitions subsection.

Feel free to play with the various Core Animation and Core Image effects later if you like, but since none of this affects resizing (the task at hand), let's move on.

Size

The Size tab would be more properly called Geometry, as it affects more than just size. Nevertheless, this is where you need to go to set the resizing attributes of your text field. Much like the Attributes tab, you'll notice subsections based on inheritance. There are no special text field size attributes, so the first subsection comes from being a control subclass.

All controls come in three standard sizes: regular, small, and mini. Although you can manually change the size of a control and its contents, using one of the predefined sizes ensures that your controls will always match the rest of the system, regardless of design changes down the road. In general, Apple's Human Interface Guidelines suggest using regular controls whenever possible, reserving the use of the smaller controls for when space is at a premium. This is particularly important on iPhone, where buttons must be large enough to press with a finger.

Note Did you think the Mac's usability was an accident? Far from it. Every pixel has been sweated over by design experts and explained in excruciating detail in Apple's Human Interface Guidelines. These are required reading for any Mac developer, and also interesting for any user who'd like to get to know more about what makes using a Mac such a great experience. The guidelines, usually referred to as the HIG (rhymes with dig), are available in Xcode's documentation and online.

Moving down to the View Size subsection, you can set size and location based on any corner or edge, or the view's center. You can also align and center multiple views. What you really want is to change the autosizing behavior, as shown in Figure 24-10.

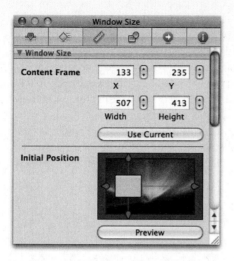

Figure 24-10. *Changing autosizing attributes in the Inspector*

On the left side of the autosizing section is a schematic representation of your view inside its superview. The inner rectangle represents your view. The vertical and horizontal arrows inside your view represent which direction you want your view to resize in. The struts connecting your view to the superview represent which sides of your view you want to be fixed in relation to the superview. The expected results of the settings are animated on the right.

By clicking the resize directions and struts in the schematic, you can change the effects shown in the animation. A little experimentation shows that removing all the struts will enable your text area to remain centered. Save and run the interface to verify that this is so.

Bindings

Applications in Mac OS X generally follow the model-view-controller architecture pattern. The idea is to separate the model (the platform- and application-agnostic data) from the view (the application's interface). The controller layer that connects these two typically consists of a lot of glue code that doesn't do anything particularly new or interesting.

Cocoa bindings eliminate the need for this glue code by letting controls bind their values to other objects. The Inspector's Bindings tab contains a list of bindable attributes. Combined with Interface Builder's controller objects, such as NSArrayController, and especially with Core Data's built-in functionality, it's possible to build an entire functioning application without writing any code. That doesn't mean you should ship such an application, but it does suggest how much technology like bindings frees software engineers from the boring parts of programming, so they can concentrate on innovating.

Connections

Aside from bindings, Interface Builder has two other ways to relate objects to each other and to your code: actions and outlets. Actions are methods called in response to user events, like clicking a button. These methods are marked in code as being of type IBAction. This is an alias for *void*, meaning these methods are one-way, returning nothing. Outlets are instance variables in a class marked with the keyword IBOutlet. When the nib is loaded, these variables will be initialized with the objects connected to them in the nib.

Connecting objects in Interface Builder is really cool. You literally connect them by Control-clicking an object and dragging a line to another object. When you make the connection, a pop-up window of that object's available connections will appear. Selecting a connection will establish the link between the two objects, which will be reflected in the Inspector. All of the connections an object can make are visible in the Inspector's Connections tab.

Control-double-click an object to pop up its connections panel, from which you can create connections, as shown in Figure 24-11. You can also begin connections from the Inspector itself. You can break connections in the Inspector by clicking the small x icon on the connection itself.

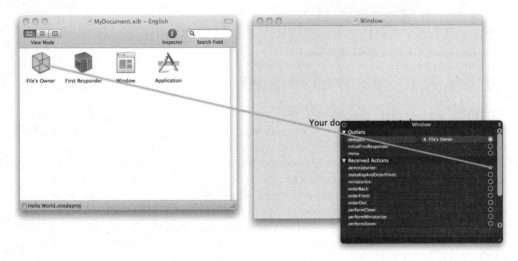

Figure 24-11. *Establishing connections between objects in Interface Builder*

Identity

In addition to attributes, objects also have a lot of metadata, which is configurable via the Inspector's Identity tab. You can change an object's class. If you change it to a class of your own creation, you can add actions and outlets, which you can then add to the class in Xcode with the synchronization options in the File menu.

You can give the item a description, for use by the Accessibility system. That way, for example, a person who has trouble seeing the screen can have the system describe your objects out loud. You can also set tool tips, which are the hints that pop up when a user hovers the cursor over an item for a few seconds. Finally, you can give the object a name, see its object ID, and write notes about it.

AppleScript

The AppleScript tab lets AppleScript users build graphical interfaces in Interface Builder. Much as Objective-C programmers specify action methods in their classes, AppleScript programmers specify event handlers in their scripts.

The Library

When you tire of playing with the default text field, you're ready to check out the plethora of interface elements available in Interface Builder's Library panel, as shown in Figure 24-12.

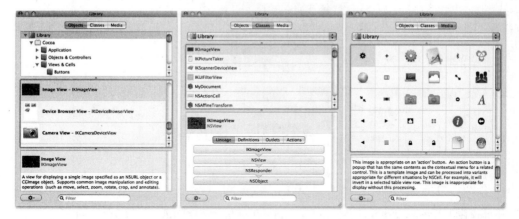

Figure 24-12. *Interface Builder's Library window*

The first section is a group list, which contains groups and sometimes subgroups of objects. The second section is an object list containing the objects available in the selected group. The third section simply contains a description of any object selected in the object list.

The Library panel has a few hidden tricks for power users. By dragging the divider between the group list and the object list all the way to the top of panel, the group list will become a pop-up. You can also group the object list by selecting Show Group Banners from the customization (gear) pop-up menu on the bottom of the panel. You can also set up custom groups from the gear menu.

The gear menu also lets you change the display style of the object list. The default is to simply show representative icons. You can also choose to display the name of the object with those icons, or to display the icon, its name, and a brief description, making the description section unnecessary. You can collapse the description section by dragging the divider between it and the object list all the way to the bottom of the panel.

To use objects in the library, simply drag them from the Library panel to your interface window. A surprising number of objects are at your disposal, as shown in Figure 24-13.

In general, objects in the library fall into several general categories:

Menus: This category includes menus and common menu items used in the application's menu bar. You can also use custom menu items in other menu types, such as pop-up menus.

Toolbars: This category includes toolbars and common toolbar items, as well as a custom toolbar item.

Windows: This category includes standard, textured, and heads-up display windows, auxiliary panels, and a special compound item that creates a window with an auxiliary drawer.

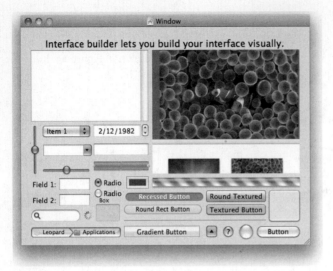

Figure 24-13. *The range of interface items available in Interface Builder's Library panel*

Controllers: Although nibs are typically associated with the view portion of the model-view-controller pattern, nibs can also contain controller objects. These controllers can be completely self-contained, or they can be set to a custom class. A common use for controller objects in the nib is to stand in for collections in the main controller, since the traditional collection classes, such as NSArray, are not compatible with bindings. There is also a special user defaults controller to enable binding directly to the preference system.

Buttons: Interface Builder includes a wide variety of button styles. Technically, these are all the same NSButton object in different configurations. Using preconfigured buttons is a convenience, and it also provides consistency with other buttons in the application and system-wide.

Cells: When Application Kit was being developed, computers were much slower than they are today. As such, a lightweight alternative to views was necessary. Cells are lightweight objects contained and used by views and controls throughout Cocoa. Cells resemble common controls, including text fields, combo boxes, level indicators, and image views.

Formatters: Often the raw data behind a text field and what the user expects to see are two different things. The most common examples of this are dates, times, and currency. Formatters can be attached to text areas to alter the way their values are displayed.

Inputs & Values: The most general group in the library, all these objects have in common is that they display or alter some value. This includes several varieties of text fields, as well as check boxes, combo boxes, sliders, progress indicators, and the color and image wells. This group also contains the text view. In its default configuration, a text view resembles a multiline text field embedded in a scroll view. With a few clicks in the Inspector, you can turn a text view into a self-contained word processor, complete with formatting controls.

Data Views: These objects display and allow interaction with data that is too complicated to be dealt with by the objects in the Inputs & Values group. These include tables, outlines, and multicolumn browsers, as used by the Finder. This group also contains some views new in Leopard: the collection view, which displays a grid of other views, and the predicate editor, which is a visual list of rules like the one used in Mail.

Layout Views: This category includes views that provide layout but don't display data, such as split views, scroll views, tab views, and boxes. There is also a custom view object for adding your own `NSView` subclasses to the nib.

Special: In addition to the standard interface elements, there are many special views, controllers, and other objects provided by various APIs. Special groups included by default include Core Data, WebKit, Address Book, Image Kit, PDF Kit, QuickTime Kit, and Quartz Composer. There is also a special Interface Builder template to integrate custom objects into the library.

The Nib

The main window represents the nib itself. While Interface Builder simply calls it Document, we're going to refer to it as the Nib window. It offers three views: icon, list, and column, as shown in Figure 24-14. With the exception of Cover Flow, these are the same views used by the Finder.

Figure 24-14. *Interface Builder's three nib views*

Although you can navigate your view hierarchy by clicking around the interface itself, some items can be difficult to select. The Nib window's column view is particularly convenient for selecting objects buried deep within subviews, especially as your interface becomes more complicated.

Views are typically contained in other views, but every hierarchy is going to contain an object that is not contained by anything else. The Nib window contains these top-level objects, which are typically windows or panels. The Nib window also contains special components for your convenience:

File's Owner: Although a separate entity in its own right, the nib is not simply floating in space. It's actually owned by your document class, `MyDocument`. In order to communicate with the document class, objects in the nib talk to the `File's Owner` object.

Application: Even though your nib has a direct line to its owner, sometimes its objects need to communicate with the application itself. The `Application` object facilitates that communication.

First Responder: Sometimes an object needs to communicate with whoever is responsible for performing a given action. For times like these, Mac OS X maintains a party line known as the responder chain. To put an event on the responder chain, objects in the nib can send them to First Responder.

Controllers: Controller objects are not views, so they can't be contained as subviews. As such, the Nib window contains any controllers in the nib. Indeed, while windows and panels can simply be dragged anywhere on the screen, controller objects must be dragged into the Nib window directly. The one exception is the user defaults controller, which will automatically be added to the Nib window should you bind an object to it.

Most application projects will require visiting Interface Builder at least once, if not several times. Anything that can be done within Interface Builder probably should be, since it will save a lot of code.

Still, as much as Interface Builder can do, chances are good you're still going to have to write some code. Let's close the interface and check out Xcode's editing and debugging features.

Programming in Xcode

Xcode is Apple's main development environment. If you want to write software for the Mac or iPhone, regardless of the language you use, you'll want to use Xcode. We talked a lot in Chapter 23 about abstraction and how it protects developers from changes to the underlying system. Xcode is a big part of that abstraction. By getting as many programmers on Xcode as possible, Apple has been able to introduce things like universal binaries while minimizing extra work for developers. Since programming is a form of word processing, a lot of effort has been put into making Xcode's text editor efficient for programming.

The Editor

You can invoke Xcode's editor by selecting source code in the sidebar and then adjusting the split pane. Double-clicking the source code launches a new editor in its own window. Clicking the editor icon in the toolbar opens the currently selected source code within the main view itself, filling the entire right side, as shown in Figure 24-15.

Xcode's editor is designed to give you as much information as possible, without getting in the way of the task at hand. It accomplishes this by several different means, which we'll describe in the following sections.

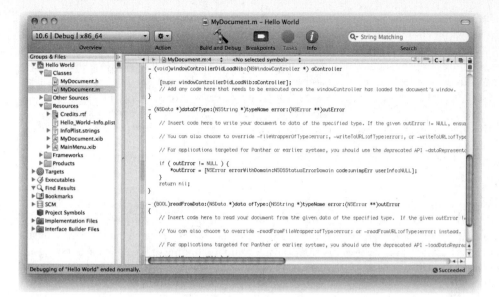

Figure 24-15. *Xcode's built-in editor*

Syntax Coloring

As you type, Xcode analyzes the syntax of your code and automatically colors the text based on what it represents. While the colors can be set to your personal preference, by default, keywords are pink, macros are brown, comments are green, numerical constants are blue, and string constants are red.

Since your code remains black, the colors help it stand out. It also helps you keep your strings and comments closed properly. If, for example, you forget to type a closing quotation mark, the bright pink color of your code will both indicate that something's wrong and give you an immediate idea of where the problem is.

Automatic Formatting

While whitespace remains optional in most languages (the notable exception being Python), no programmer I've ever met would consider forgoing it. Xcode indents your code automatically, and if you like, will even insert closing braces for you. Aside from keeping your code tidy and preventing premature wear on your Tab key, automatic formatting is another trick to help you notice mistakes early. Forgetting a brace or bracket will cause subsequent lines to format improperly.

Autocompletion

Terseness is the enemy of readability, but descriptive member names take longer to type, cramping a coder's mind and hands. Autocompletion combines the best of both worlds. Every variable, method, function, and macro name is indexed by Xcode, usually when you compile. When you type a few letters, Xcode displays possible matches from this index. This produces descriptive, readable code with very little actual typing.

Autocompletion further saves time by inserting replaceable argument tokens in method names. Typing Command-/ highlights the next token. This convenience also prevents errors. Assuming you pick the correct completion, the expanded text will always be correct, while typing out the entire name by hand is prone to human error. It's a good habit to always activate autocompletion, even when you've typed something out, just to make sure you didn't make a mistake.

You can activate the autocompletion suggestions list by pressing Esc. From Xcode's preference window, you can also choose to have autocompletion occur automatically if you pause while typing. Since that could quickly become annoying, the length of the pause is also customizable.

Code Scoping

Note the ribbon bar that runs alongside the main code-editing window. The ribbon shows varying shades of gray depending on the scope of the code beside it. This gives a quick visual check that all your braces and brackets are properly balanced. If you need a little extra indication, hovering your cursor above the ribbon will extend its shading to the code itself, giving an exact indication of scope.

Code Folding

Xcode implements code folding, which collapses a given scope in the editor. For example, a long if statement that doesn't apply to what you're trying to do can be collapsed into a single line. Similarly, functions and sections can be collapsed. The collapsing is syntax-aware, and if you use the line-numbering bar, the appropriate numbers will be skipped, so you won't lose your place.

To fold your code, click the ribbon bar. When code is folded, a disclosure triangle will appear in the ribbon bar. Clicking this disclosure triangle will unfold that section of code.

Navigation

Though they're easy to miss, there are several navigation aids along the top of any editor view (shown in Figure 24-16). These make it easy to move between different areas of a file, or even between files.

Figure 24-16. *Navigation controls on the top of Xcode's editor*

On the left side, there are back and forward buttons; a history menu, which lets you jump between recently edited files; and a function menu. The function menu lists any function, method, or class declarations, as well as macros, typedefs, and pragmas. Selecting an item from the function menu jumps to that item on the page.

You can add navigation aids to your page, which will then show up in the function menu. Perhaps the most common is the mark pragma:

```
#pragma mark This is some text.
```

This causes any text after mark to show up in the navigation menu, like so:

```
This is some text.
```

As with anything else, you can jump to the mark by selecting it. If you group your methods by functionality, marks are a great way to add subheadings to set off the sections. You can also use the mark pragma to add separators to the menu:

```
#pragma mark -
```

You can add comments to the function menu by beginning them with certain special prefixes. Table 24-1 lists these prefixes and some examples of their use.

Table 24-1. *Xcode's Special Comment Prefixes*

Prefix	Example	Result
//???:	//???: Is this really necessary?	???: Is this really necessary?
//!!!:	//!!!: This crashes every 3rd time	!!!: This crashes every 3rd time
//TODO:	//TODO: Implement the edge case	TODO: Implement the edge case
//FIXME:	//FIXME: The image no longer shows	FIXME: The image no longer shows

The editor's upper right has several small buttons. These reveal menus for jumping to bookmarks, breakpoints, includes, and other files that define the current class, including superclasses, subclasses, and categories. There is also a button to jump between the current class's header and implementation files.

■**Tip** You can jump between a class's header and implementation files by typing Option-Command-up arrow.

In the upper-right corner, there is a small lock icon. Clicking this icon locks (or unlocks) the current file, preventing accidental edits. Below the lock is a button that splits the editor horizontally into two independent views of the same file. Halves can be further split, and the split can be adjusted by dragging the divider. When an editor is split, a button appears for rejoining the two halves.

Errors and Warnings

Traditional programming environments separate writing code from building programs. This requires leaving the editor to see the results of a build, and then switching back and forth between modes to handle any errors or warnings from the build system. Xcode merges these two modes with inline error and warning pop-up bubbles, as shown in Figure 24-17. We cannot overstate what a tremendous benefit this is. The time saved by not having to switch contexts is enormous, especially for multifile edits.

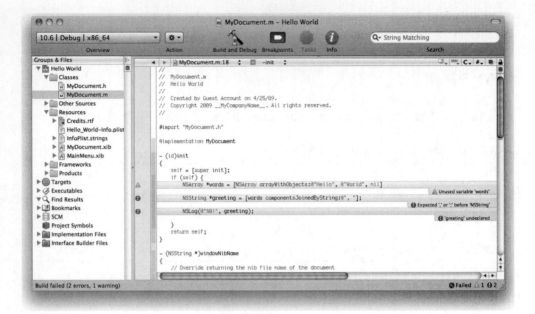

Figure 24-17. *Xcode's inline error and warning bubbles*

You can hide or reveal the bubbles by clicking their icons in the gutter. You can also toggle warning and error bubbles en masse via the View menu. You can use the keyboard shortcut Command-= to move forward through the bubbles and Command-+ (that's Command plus the + key) to move backward.

■**Note** Using = to move forward and + to move backward seems counterintuitive. Shouldn't + move forward and - move backward? However, given the standard keyboard layout, + is actually Shift-=, so these shortcuts make good sense in practice, even if they seem weird in writing.

Debugging

In 1947, operators investigating a problem in the massive electromechanical Mark II computer found a moth stuck in machine's works. Unable to resist making a pun on the well-known engineering term, they taped the moth to their logbook as the first computer "bug." Computer glitches have been called bugs ever since. While it's a cute story, the mental image of bugs as, well, bugs is misleading. Programming bugs are not external pests to be hunted down and squashed. Rather, what we call a bug should really be called what it is: a miscommunication.

As the computer scientist Michael Marcotty once said, "This is essentially what a program was, a love letter from the programmer to the hardware, full of the intimate details known only to partners in an affair." When computers do unexpected things, the solution is to figure out where the hardware's interpretation of code differs from the programmer's intention. This is not a job for poison and fly swatters, but for diplomacy and understanding.

A debugger, then, is a means to slow down, take things step by step, and ask the computer, "When I say this, what do you hear?" Xcode's debugger wraps the power of the command-line tool in the simplicity of its graphical interface, then throws in the flexibility of the Objective-C runtime. The result is an interactive environment that rivals interpreted languages like Lisp, Python, and Ruby.

■**Note** GDB, the GNU Debugger, is part of the free, open source GNU project, along with Xcode's primary compiler, GCC, the GNU Compiler Collection.

Breakpoints

Debuggers, much like vampires, cannot enter uninvited. To invite GDB into your program, set a *breakpoint* by clicking the gutter that runs along the left side of the editor. This adds a blue pointer, representing the breakpoint. To toggle the breakpoint on and off, click it. To remove it, drag it from the gutter; it will vanish in a puff of smoke.

Normally, breakpoints are inactive, and the program runs without paying any attention to them. To activate breakpoints, select Activate Breakpoints from the Run menu, or click the appropriate icon in the toolbar.

When the program reaches the line of code marked by the breakpoint, it usually suspends execution, but this is not the only option. Breakpoints can be set to only break on certain conditions, or to immediately continue after logging something to the console, running other GDB commands, making a sound, or even reading something aloud via text-to-speech. Breakpoints can be set, removed, deactivated, moved, and edited on the fly. This is a major improvement over writing console logs into your code, which requires stopping and re-compiling for every change.

Control-clicking or right-clicking the gutter brings up the breakpoint contextual menu, which has several additional options, including a list of predefined breakpoint behaviors. There is also a Breakpoints window where breakpoints can be set, removed, and edited. To launch the Breakpoints window, select Breakpoints from the Show submenu of the Run menu.

Using the Breakpoints window, you can even set breakpoints outside your own code. A common trick among programmers is to create a breakpoint for the function objc_exception_throw, which the runtime calls right before your program crashes. This causes execution to automatically stop right before a crash, so you can figure out why things are about to fall apart.

Xcode's Debugger Interface

You can always tell a professional, because he or she has three tools that seem to do exactly the same thing. The nuances of a craft dictate a nuance in its tools. You wouldn't expect a blacksmith to own only one hammer, or a painter only one brush. So it is that Xcode comes with not one but three interfaces for debugging your application. These too are nuanced. There's the command-line version of GDB, still lurking beneath the surface, tempting all who crave power. There's the inline debugger: small, nimble, and convenient. Then there's the traditional view, shown in Figure 24-18, which has a little bit of everything.

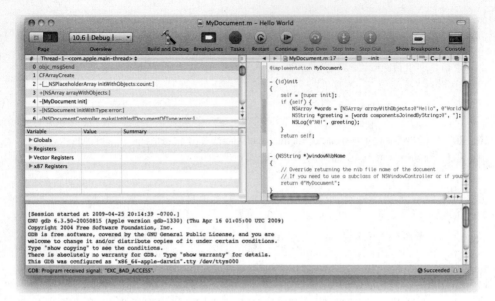

Figure 24-18. *Xcode's traditional debugging environment*

The idea behind the traditional debugging interface is to show a split screen, where one half lists what the programmer said, and the other half lists what the computer heard. To put it another way, half the screen shows the code, and the other half shows the computer's state. Modern programs, and the computers that run them, are quite complicated, so the traditional debugger ends up cramming a lot of information onto the screen.

The code view is straightforward. It's a standard editor window that shows each line of code, with a highlight over the current line. From this view, you can step over each line of code one by one to see what happens. It's like pausing a movie, then advancing it frame by frame to look for tiny details.

The tiny details occur on the other half of the screen: the program's state. Compared to the code, the state is a lot more complicated—so much so, in fact, that the state view must be split into two lists: the stack on the left, and the variables on the right.

The stack is a list of all the method calls it took to get the program to where it is now. Read it from the top down, mentally inserting the words "was called by" between each method name. Clicking a method name on the stack takes you to that method in the code view. If the method is a precompiled framework, the code view will show raw assembly language, which is a good reason to learn assembly. Every thread of execution has its own stack, which you can select from the pop-up menu above the stack view.

The variable list has the name and value of every variable for the selected stack frame. This is typically where you find out some value isn't what it should be, thus resolving the misunderstanding and fixing the bug. You can change the value of a variable by double-clicking it.

■**Note**   You can edit the code in the debugger, but only as a convenience. The changes won't take effect, and the code highlighting won't be accurate, until you recompile.

Console Debugging

Xcode provides a console to interact directly with GDB. You can use the console in conjunction with a traditional debugger by dragging the separator from the bottom of the debugger window or by clicking its icon in the toolbar. The console will display any information being logged from the application or your breakpoints. Any errors or other feedback will also show up here.

More than just a message board, the GDB console is fully interactive. GDB is a whole other world, with its own language and internal politics. You can harness GDB to do all kinds of crazy things. The most basic GDB trick is the print command. If you give it a variable name, it will print its value. If you give it an Objective-C expression, however, it will perform the necessary message sends. You can ask your objects what's wrong with them and try things that might fix them without having to go through the entire build cycle again.

Inline Debugging

Xcode's traditional debugging interface is very powerful, but it suffers from the same problem as the old build results system. That is, it interrupts the programming flow by taking you out of the editor and thrusting you into a different environment. Sometimes you don't need quite as much power as the full interface provides. For times like these, Xcode provides an inline debugging interface, as shown in Figure 24-19.

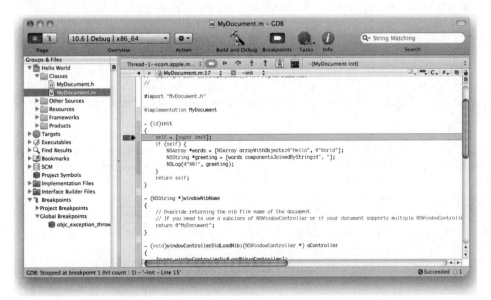

Figure 24-19. *Xcode's inline debugging environment*

Since breakpoints are already built into the editor, those don't change. However, miniature versions of the debugger's toolbar icons appear in the editor window when the application is running. These allow you to pause and continue execution, step from line to line, and so forth. The debugging bar also contains the current stack frame. Clicking it brings up the full stack in a pop-up menu.

Hovering the cursor over a variable pops up its current value in a tool tip window. By using a series of disclosure buttons, the variable's structure can be examined in depth. Highlighting an expression reveals a small i icon. Clicking the icon executes the expression and shows you its return value.

Since the editor still competes with the running application for screen real estate, the inline debugging system includes a small, floating heads-up display that remains visible while you are testing the application. Should you run into a breakpoint that pauses execution, the heads-up display will expand to show the appropriate place in the source code, allowing you to take further action.

Emergent Compiler Technology

When software is new, it offers exciting innovations, but this comes at a cost. New software is often missing features or is rife with undiscovered bugs. As the software matures, these factors are ironed out. The software becomes stable and useful, but this too has a cost. As the user base begins to prize the software for its stability, innovation slows. Major updates become hamstrung by backward-compatibility and confused by the specialized features needed for its growing diversity of users.

Eventually people start looking for a replacement that's faster, that's more focused on their particular needs, and that keeps up the forward march of technological progress. The software that builds software is not an exception. Although the GCC tool chain has served Xcode well, it has started to show its age. Snow Leopard offers developers their first taste of the next generation of compiler technologies.

Users of Xcode can opt to stick with old, reliable GCC, or they can check out the new hotness that is the Low Level Virtual Machine (LLVM). The LLVM compiler is an open source project sponsored by Apple. By using just-in-time technology, LLVM maintains a better picture of your code than GCC. This means better optimization is less time than GCC. Even if your project is too small for the speed of your compiler to be an issue, you will appreciate the smarter errors and warnings.

LLVM is language-agnostic, which means it requires a front-end compiler to deal with specifics, such as programming language and development environment. This modular architecture makes extending LLVM easy. For now, Xcode still uses GCC as the front end but will eventually be replaced by the next-generation front end, Clang.

If you want a taste of Clang, Snow Leopard will not disappoint. Xcode adds the menu item Build and Analyze, which runs your code through the Clang static analyzer, which scans your code for potential bugs so you can fix them without ever having to invoke the debugger. It's like having an expert programmer proofread your code—a major time-saver!

Listing 24-1 shows a contrived example of a typical logic error. The variable windowNibName will have a different retain count depending on which branch of the if statement it follows. This is the kind of subtle bug that can haunt an application for years, manifesting as unreproducible crash reports.

Listing 24-1. *The Simple Code Error Behind a Haunting Bug*

```
NSString *windowNibName;
if (!(windowNibName = [super windowNibName]))
    windowNibName = [[NSString alloc] initWithCString:"My Document"];

return [windowNibName autorelease];
```

It's cool enough that Clang can catch bugs like this, but it's even cooler how it does it. Finding a bug is not the same as fixing a bug. The programmer must first understand what they did wrong, and for complex logic errors, that is easier said than done. Clang will actually take your through the bug step-by-step, drawing arrows to show the faulty code path, as shown in Figure 24-20.

Figure 24-20. *The Clang static analyzer explains exactly what could go wrong*

Other Features

That covers the basics of Xcode and Interface Builder, but what we haven't mentioned could fill a book—specifically, *Learn Cocoa on the Mac* by Dave Mark and Jeff LaMarche (Apress, 2009). Every new version of Xcode brings so many cool new features, it can be hard to keep up. Luckily, Xcode itself is well documented. If you're serious about learning to program on the Mac, make it your goal to learn as much about Xcode as possible. Here are a few nifty features to get you started:

Refactoring: Project-aware find-and-replace and more

Snapshots: A cross between undo and version control

Text macros: Prewritten code snippets

Templates: Allow you to customize Xcode's project templates

Targets: Allow you to leverage the power of Xcode's build system

Project settings: Allow you to customize your project's every minute detail

Class browser: An easy and interesting way to surf the libraries

Data modeling: Allows you to interact with Core Data using entity relationship diagrams

Other Tools

While most application development takes place in Xcode and Interface Builder, the Developer folder contains many more tools. Some of these are complex applications that form entire development environments of their own, while others are simple utilities. Some have very serious and specific purposes, while others are just plain fun. Here are a few favorites.

Instruments

The potential of Instruments to change the way bugs are reported cannot be overstated. Imagine you have a problem with your car. Inevitably, when you take the car to the shop, the mechanic isn't able to reproduce it. Cars and software are equally difficult to fix without being able to reproduce the problem.

Now imagine being able to record yourself driving down the street. When you encounter the problem, you could take the car to the shop, and the mechanic could get into the car and press play. The car would then play back your drive exactly as it occurred. The mechanic could rewind and fast forward, or even pause and disassemble parts of the car frozen in time at the exact moment of the problem.

Once the problem is diagnosed and fixed, it could be played back to confirm that the problem no longer occurs. This is exactly what Instruments does for your applications. Whether you're the programmer who wrote the application, or a user who finds a bug in it, Instruments is exciting.

Most debugging tools are not useful to the general public, but Instruments is a notable exception. It uses an interface that is immediately recognizable to anyone who has used GarageBand. Debugging instruments are arranged into tracks, as shown in Figure 24-21. Several templates are provided, which can be augmented by an extensive library. The Instruments session can then be hooked into any process and recorded.

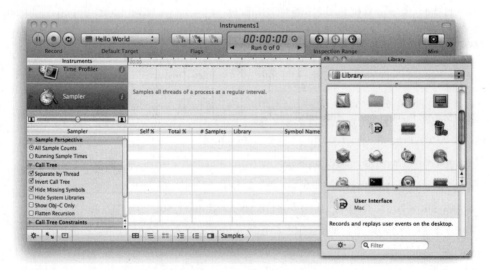

Figure 24-21. *Setting up a session in Instruments*

Not only is it simple enough for mere mortals to use, but specific sessions can be saved as templates and sent to users, who can execute them with minimal instructions. In this vein, perhaps the most exciting instrument is the UI recorder. This "ghost in the machine" uses the Accessibility framework to manipulate an application's interface. Users can record the exact actions they took, then send their recording back to the developer for playback and analysis, as shown in Figure 24-22. It's the next best thing to being there.

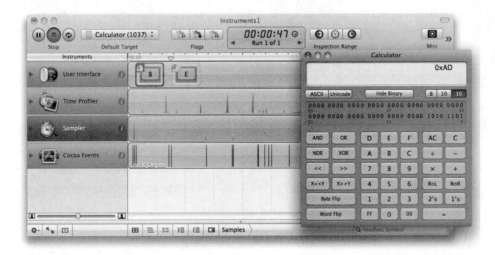

Figure 24-22. *Playing back a session in Instruments*

Under the hood, Instruments runs on DTrace, an OpenSolaris project included in Snow Leopard that provides probes in the very lowest levels of the machine. Thousands of these probes sit idle, causing no performance drain, waiting for the moment they are activated by masters of the arcane arts wishing to see the details of any process.

While using Instruments fortunately doesn't require grimoires, sacrifices, or learning the D scripting language, this open source engine means that the aforementioned arcane masters can create new instruments and share them with the community. As a further testament to the power of Instruments, several developer tools in Apple's toolbox have been replaced with Instruments templates.

Quartz Composer

Playing an electric guitar is a lot like programming. Every amplifier, wah-wah pedal, and fuzz box is a function that alters the guitar's signal data, changing its final sound. That seems to be the theory behind Quartz Composer, one of the strangest, most innovative programming tools ever made. Rather than using pages of code, Quartz Composer uses a graphical interface that looks more like a rock concert than Xcode.

Instead of functions, Quartz Composer uses virtual patch modules. Like their real-life musical counterparts, patch modules take one or more inputs, change them in some way, and produce one or more outputs. You connect patches by dragging and dropping virtual cables, not unlike with Interface Builder. By connecting the different inputs and outputs, users can create complex compositions, as shown in Figure 24-23. Quartz Composer compositions can be rolled into freestanding programs, used as screen savers, or incorporated into other, larger programs. It's also just a fun way to spend an afternoon.

Figure 24-23. *Visual programming in Quartz Composer*

Dashcode

As the name implies, Dashcode was designed to be like Xcode for creating Dashboard widgets. Just as Xcode has expanded to build iPhone native applications, Dashcode has expanded to build iPhone web applications. It contains several templates, including countdowns, maps, RSS feeds, gauges, and podcasts. It also includes a drag-and-drop library of common components, and a WYSIWYG editor for customizing your widget, as shown in Figure 24-24.

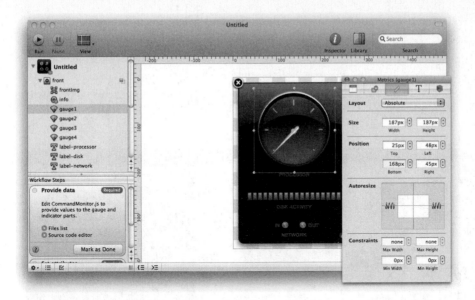

Figure 24-24. *Designing a widget's interface in Dashcode*

Under the hood, a widget is just a web page with HTML, CSS, and JavaScript code. Dashcode provides a code library of common functionality, as shown in Figure 24-25. Even coding neophytes can build complex widgets in Dashcode without ever having to use the keyboard. For the more experienced hands, Dashcode provides a solid JavaScript debugging environment, complete with member lists, breakpoints, and an interactive runtime.

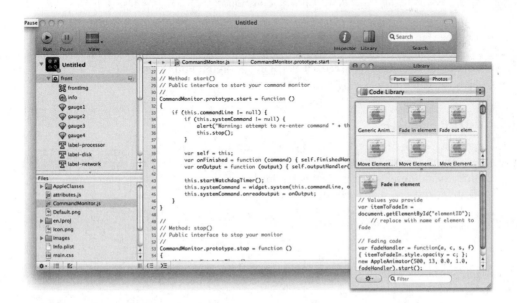

Figure 24-25. *Editing a widget's source code in Dashcode*

Core Image Fun House

When we explain Core Image filters to people, we just say, "You know, like in Photoshop." When Apple's Phil Schiller debuted Core Image during Steve Jobs's 2004 Worldwide Developers Conference keynote address, he needed something a little more tangible. To that end, some clever Apple engineer whipped up a fun demo called Core Image Fun House, shown in Figure 24-26. The demo was so popular it was included with the developer tools.

Figure 24-26. *Testing a filter stack in Core Image Fun House*

Core Image Fun House is a simple application that allows you to load an image and then apply a stack of Core Image filters. If you use Core Image, or an application that makes extensive use of Core Image, like Flying Meat's Acorn image editor, Fun House will save you a lot of time, which you can then waste by continuing to play with Fun House.

FileMerge

FileMerge is one of those tools developed to solve non-programming problems frequently experienced by programmers. It's a stereoscopic text editor that compares two documents, highlighting their differences, as shown in Figure 24-27. You can then select which parts of each you prefer and save a merged copy.

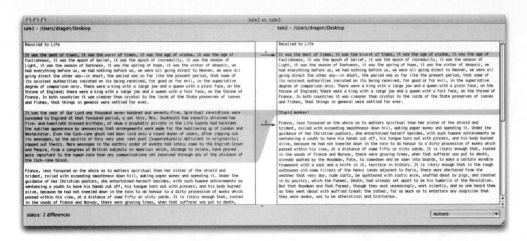

Figure 24-27. *Visual difference management with FileMerge*

Engineering teams use FileMerge to deal with conflicted four-way pileups on multiuser version control systems, but there are plenty of smaller problems for which you might find it useful. A collaboration as simple as proofreading can lead to conflicted documents. Say you get a document back with unknown changes, maybe even after you've made your own changes. Even if you never collaborate and have no friends, how many times have you found multiple copies of the same file and wanted something more reliable than the modification date to tell you what's what? For situations like these, FileMerge is there.

IconComposer

Yeah, you could just set a TIFF file as your project's icon, assuming you're the kind of person who eats peanut butter sandwiches because jelly's too much hassle. The cool kids want real Mac OS X icons in the ICNS format.

As an image gets smaller, its details move closer together, increasing its complexity. This garbles your icon's simple message and often leads to undesirable optical illusions, like the moiré pattern that forms when parallel lines get too close.

An ICNS file is a stack of images in different sizes, representing different levels of detail. The system selects the image best suited for the task at hand. Switch a Finder window from icon to outline view, and an ICNS file switches from a large, three-dimensional, photorealistic masterpiece to a small, flat, simple representation.

IconComposer is a simple tool for editing ICNS files, as shown in Figure 24-28. Creating an icon is a single-step process: drag an image onto the IconComposer window. IconComposer scales the image for smaller representation and extracts any transparency into alpha masks. Most image formats work, including Photoshop files. If a given size looks bad, create a simplified version and drag that onto the appropriate spot.

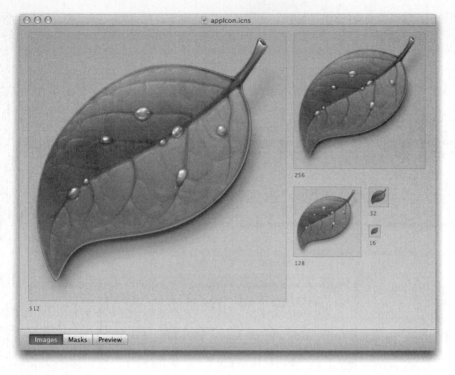

Figure 24-28. *The amazing application icon from Panic's Coda in IconComposer*

___

■**Note**   You don't need IconComposer to set custom icons, but you might use it to customize icons that look bad at small sizes.

___

Property List Editor

Property lists, known colloquially as *plists*, are files originally designed for storing properties, which is to say, preferences. When you set the preferences of a program in its preference panel, or via the command line's `defaults` command, you're editing that application's property list.

However, with the introduction of the XML plist format, these have become a handy way to store standard data structures, such as arrays and dictionaries, in an external, human-readable format. The Property List Editor is a convenient, schema-aware way to create and edit plists. It's also the only way to make heads or tails out of the older, but still useful, binary plist format.

Shark

All developers want their applications to be fast, but the biggest mistake they can make is writing their code for speed. Fast code is optimized code, and the lower a language is, the more opportunity for optimization there will be. Java offers few chances for optimization compared to C, and C is a snail compared to assembly language.

As fast as they might be, low-level languages are harder to read and take much longer to write. Even if you don't change languages, it's a shame to pick a library or function based on it being faster instead of it being easier. Worse than all of that, all those optimizations that took forever to do will probably end up making the program slower.

Why? Because humans are surprisingly bad at guessing where performance bottlenecks are. The only way to know for sure is by using a specialized sampling tool. This tool watches the application and figures out what it's doing and for how long. Shark (shown in Figure 24-29), which comes with the free developer tools, is one of the best optimization programs available.

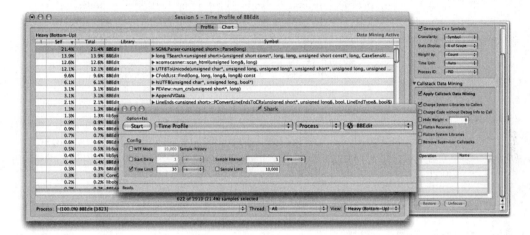

Figure 24-29. *Bare Bones's blazing fast BBEdit profiled by Shark*

Avoiding blind optimizations makes the development cycle faster, because it lets programmers choose code based on ease of writing and readability. That leaves plenty of time for profiling with Shark and then pinpointing bottlenecks and performing optimizations only where they will make the biggest difference.

Note Hard rules are anathema to programmers, but here's one even the most stubborn of hackers should follow: never, ever do something "because it's faster," until you run Shark.

Bug Reporter

Bug Reporter doesn't come with Xcode, but it's one of the most powerful tools available to you as a developer because it allows you to improve Mac OS X itself. The more you use your Mac, the more likely you are to find things about it that annoy you, things that don't work like they're supposed to, or things that Apple could do that would make it even better. These are all kinds of bugs, and they're all filed the same way.

To file a bug, go to Apple Bug Reporter (http://bugreport.apple.com) and sign in with your Apple ID. Click the New Problem tab and simply fill out the form. Apple provides a link to a description format for those unfamiliar with good bug-reporting practices, but here are a few tips for writing good bugs:

- Ninety percent of fixing a bug is reproducing it. Once you can trigger a bug at will, it's relatively easy to find out why it's happening and do something about it. If you notice some unexpected behavior (or lack of behavior), try again to see if it happens again. Try similar things to see if they also trigger the bug. Basically, you want to narrow down the scope of the bug as much as possible, forming a narrative description that an engineer will be able to follow and reproduce, hopefully with the same results.

- Because every system is different, and your system configuration might have something to do with the bug, you should always attach a system profile to your bug reports. To create a system profile, launch the System Profiler application, either by selecting About This Mac from the Apple menu and clicking the More Info... button, or by double-clicking the application icon in /Applications/Utilities. Once in System Profiler, save a profile by selecting Save from the File menu, or by pressing the keyboard shortcut Command-S. There is a special button to attach your system profile in the Bug Reporter form.

- If possible, attach some supporting documentation to the bug report as well. It's one thing to describe how to reproduce a bug. It's quite another to demonstrate it directly. If it's a bug in Apple's frameworks, write a trivial test program that shows the bug. If it's a bug in an Apple application, an Instruments recording of the bug being triggered would be a good use of the tools. Zip up any supporting evidence, and attach it using the appropriate button in the Bug Reporter form.

More Information

There's a lot more that could be said about the Mac's development tools. Aside from Xcode's own documentation, there are a few more online resources worth checking out:

Mac OS X Debugging Magic (http://developer.apple.com/technotes/tn2004/tn2124.html): The complexity of Xcode yields all kinds of obscure tips and tricks. Debugging Magic is Apple's documentation of several dozen. Our personal favorite is the NSZombie class, which turns your deallocated objects into undead monsters that moan horribly if you try to send them messages. As awful as that sounds, believe you me, when you're trying to track down a crash caused by messaging a floating pointer, NSZombie may just save your brain.

Version Control with Subversion (http://svnbook.red-bean.com): Subversion is our favorite version control program. If you want to learn what version control is, how Subversion works, and every possible detail of making Subversion work for you, you could go to the store and buy this book. Or, you could just read the whole thing for free online.

Solaris Dynamic Tracing Guide (http://docs.sun.com/app/docs/doc/817-6223): This is the ultimate guide to DTrace and the D scripting language. With this knowledge, you can create Instruments templates, or head straight to the command line. The reading is a bit dry, but if you've ever seen a demo of what DTrace can do, it's so worth it. This is another real-life book that's available for free online.

Summary

When you bought your Mac, it came loaded with all manner of applications. Some of these you probably use every day. Some of these you not only don't use, but you probably don't even know what they do. The developer tools are the same way. You might use Xcode every day, but never touch Dashcode. You might flex your artistic muscle in Quartz Composer, but never use Interface Builder.

The panoply of developer tools, even more than the bundled applications, is there to ensure that, no matter what kind of development you want to do on your Mac, you'll have the right tools for the job. And as with the `Applications` folder, if you ever find yourself with some free time, we'd encourage you to open one of these mystery tools and find out what it can do. It might not change your life, but it will definitely expand your mind.

Now that you've spent some time with the tools, you're probably ready to write some code. In the next chapter, we'll take a tour of the Objective-C programming language.

CHAPTER 25

■■■

Mac OS X Development: Objective-C

Apple, when its soul was still called NeXT, sought to speak with its beautiful hardware. No crude language like C, nor the insanity of C++, would do. Instead, it adopted an odd little chimera of a thing called Objective-C. ObjC, to friends, was the project of computer scientist Brad Cox, who wanted to rewrite Smalltalk as a dialect of C.

Objective-C is a true superset of C, making it 100 percent compatible with C—a feature sorely missing from C++. That means you can drop into C when it's convenient. It also gives you access to about half the code ever written. And, lest we not forget, Mac OS X is UNIX, and C is the language of UNIX.

■**Note** Objective-C can also host C++, albeit awkwardly (as it always is with C++). Such an arrangement is called Objective-C++.

Being natively compiled like C and C++, Objective-C shares a serious performance advantage over interpreted languages like Python, Ruby, Lisp, Lua, Java, and JavaScript. Unlike C or C++, Objective-C doesn't sacrifice flexibility for speed. It uses a dynamic runtime to give it the same power as an interpreter.

Objective-C is being actively improved. Leopard introduced Objective-C 2.0, which added garbage collection, properties, and fast enumeration. With Snow Leopard, Objective-C adds closures, closing the gap with the newest languages and Lisp.

Now with iPhone dominating the handheld market, Objective-C adds cross-platform to its list of attributes. There's a good chance that if you're reading this chapter, you've already written some code for other platforms but have been lured to the Mac to develop iPhone applications.

This quick tour will demonstrate some of the things that make Objective-C more than just a powerful, performant language, but in fact a genuine pleasure to work with. There's a reason so many polylinguistic programmers make Objective-C their home—it may just be the most fun you've ever had programming a computer.

Objective-C Syntax

Above all else, code must be readable. Elegance, performance, and productivity will follow. The less time you spend figuring out what you wrote yesterday, the more time you'll have to work on it today. The better you can understand what a piece of code is doing, the faster you can add features and fix bugs. If other programmers can understand your code, they can give you constructive criticism, making you and your program better.

The first thing people notice about Objective-C is its syntax. Although standard C syntax remains valid, Objective-C adds new syntax, derived from Smalltalk, the first object-oriented programming language. Many people are at first wary of this alien syntax, but once they get used to it, they can't imagine using anything else. That's because Objective-C is extremely readable. Consider this function call in C syntax:

```
setColor(myObject, 0.4, 0.3, 0.0, 1.0);
```

You can guess it sets a color, but what do those numbers mean? Are those red, green, blue, and alpha? Or alpha, red, green, and blue? Or cyan, yellow, magenta, and black? Or luminosity, hue, and, uh . . . needless to say, most programmers spend a lot of time looking up functions to remember how to write them, let alone ever trying to read them. Now, consider the same thing as an Objective-C method:

```
[myObject setColorWithRed:0.4 green:0.3 blue:0.0 alpha:1.0];
```

It's pretty clear what each of the arguments mean, whether you're writing the code for the first time or you're reading someone else's code three years down the line.

A method's prototype is equally readable, outlining not only the meaning of the method parameters but also their types, the return type, and whether the method belongs to the class or its individual instances:

```
- (void)setColorWithRed:(CGFloat)red green:(CGFloat)green blue:(CGFloat)blue
    alpha:(CGFloat)alpha;
```

This method is of type void, so it returns nothing. All its arguments are of type CGFloat. As detailed in this chapter, CGFloat is a width-neutral, floating-point scalar that is converted at compile time into a float on 32-bit systems or a double on 64-bit systems. In this case, the method is an instance method, as indicated by the starting -. Class methods start with +.

This method is, for all intents and purposes, identical to the following function:

```
void setColor(CGFloat red, CGFloat green, CGFloat blue, CGFloat alpha);
```

In fact, behind the scenes, if this method were implemented on the class MyClass, the language would create a C function with the unlikely name -[MyObject setColorWithRed:green:blue:alpha:]. We'll talk more about this later.

As would be expected by a C programmer, pointers to objects are represented with the * operator. For example, a class method that took an argument of type NSNumber and returned an NSString would look like this:

```
+ (NSString *)stringWithNumber:(NSNumber *)number;
```

In Objective-C, pointers usually point to objects. This is important for a few reasons. Scalar types like NSInteger aren't pointers, so they don't use the star operator. Confusing this point can lead to compiler errors.

Since this is just a pointer, all sorts of interesting things can happen. One common pattern is to use the addressof operator, &, to pass by reference. The typical Objective-C error-handling code demonstrates this:

```
NSError *error = nil;
[myObject someRiskyOperation:&error];
if (error)
    [NSApp presentError:error];
```

Objective-C Improves C

Objective-C was originally implemented as a preprocessor for the C compiler. A quick bit of text replacement later, and all the Objective-C code was translated into straight C. Now Objective-C is compiled natively but remains a true superset of C.

Directions for the C compiler are prefixed by #. Directions for the Objective-C compiler that sits on top of the C compiler are prefixed by the @ sigil. The first parts of Objective-C you meet are the directives @interface, @implementation, and @end. These demarcate the code sections making up a project without being tied to the file itself, which allows the use of separate header and implementation files, but also allows multiple classes to be defined in a single file, as appropriate.

Finally, many parts of the C standard library have new, upgraded versions in Cocoa that should be used instead. The older C features are still there, and the two can be intermixed.

Memory Management

Like a sports car, Objective-C memory management comes in manual and automatic. Most people want an automatic, leaving all that nasty business to Objective-C's excellent garbage collection.

For those who want to micromanage their memory, or for those programming on iPhone where garbage collection fears to tread, Objective-C retains its old-school memory-management system. It's a simple system, but people seem to have a problem with it, particularly around autorelease pools.

Object life cycles and interaction complicate memory management, so the entire C memory system has been abstracted. Although malloc and free are still there, they're not used. Instantiation in Objective-C is actually a four-step process: declaration, assignment, allocation, and initialization. These are usually done on one line:

```
NSObject *object = [[NSObject alloc] init];
```

Here it is again, in slow motion:

```
NSObject *object; // Declaration
object = // Assignment
[NSObject alloc]; // Allocation
[object init]; // Initialization
```

■**Caution** This is just an example. Apple recommends you never call `alloc` and `init` on two different lines.

Once an object is instantiated, memory management gets a bit more complicated, so we'll have to come back to it. The traditional memory-management scheme is discussed in the "Objective-C Memory Management" section. The new garbage collection API is discussed in the "Objective-C 2.0" section.

■**Note** @#*&? Odd sigils got you down? Recall that # means "C compiler directive," and @ means "Objective-C compiler directive." The * means "value of" when dealing with pointers to memory, while the & means "address of."

Scalars

In C, scalars are either width specific or width agnostic, but in general, you want to use scalars with the same width as the architecture for which your application is compiled. In the case of a four-way universal binary—the current recommended configuration in Snow Leopard—the same variable must be compiled as both 32-bit and 64-bit.

To deal with this, Objective-C declares width-agnostic scalars that resolve into the architecture's native width, as shown in Table 25-1.

Table 25-1. *Width-Agnostic Versions of C Scalars*

Objective-C	C	Description
NSInteger	int, long	Signed integer
NSUInteger	unsigned int, unsigned long	Unsigned integer
CGFloat	float, double	Floating-point number

Logging

C's `printf` and friends have no concept of Objective-C objects other than that they are pointers. The function `NSLog` has all the tokens and formatting features of `printf` but adds the %@ token, which calls any object's `description` method.

Strings

In C, a string is just an array of char terminated with NULL. In Objective-C, you should use the NSString class. As an object, NSString provides several built-in methods and a mutable subclass. It also deals with troublesome, modern-day issues like Unicode. NSString constants can be declared inline with a compiler directive in the form @"This is a string". The @ identifies this as an Objective-C string vs. a C string ("This is a C string") or a number of consecutive chars ('These are literal chars').

Arrays

C arrays are just blocks of memory with the convenience of a bracket operator and pointer arithmetic. There is, for example, no standard way of knowing how long an array is, given just the array itself. In Objective-C, use NSArray, which, like NSString, has convenient methods, such as count, and a mutable subclass. Beyond this, NSArray uses behind-the-scenes optimizations to use the data structure most efficient for the length and operations required. It's really quite an amazing class.

Booleans

In C, there is no Boolean type. In operations, zero is considered false, while anything other than zero is considered true. Objective-C maintains this convention and adds the scalar type BOOL, whose values are YES and NO.

Equality

Both C and Objective-C use the = operator for assignment and the == operator to represent equality. However, since objects in Objective-C are represented by pointers, comparing two objects with == will not return true unless both are the same pointer.

To work around this problem, NSObject defines the isEqual: method, which compares the objects' hash values. Although it's possible to override isEqual:, it's not easy, because you also have to override hash, and hashing is tricky. Plus, it's often much faster to disqualify equality based on something like the length of a string or the number of objects in an array than it is to generate a hash. As such, many classes have their own equality methods, as shown in Table 25-2.

Table 25-2. *Class-Specific Equality Methods*

Class	Method
NSArray	isEqualToArray:
NSData	isEqualToData:
NSDate	isEqualToDate:
NSDictionary	isEqualToDictionary:
NSHashTable	isEqualToHashTable:
NSIndexSet	isEqualToIndexSet:
NSNumber	isEqualToNumber:
NSSet	isEqualToSet:
NSValue	isEqualToValue:

It's not as bad as sounds. Aside from the rather obvious naming convention, Xcode's autocomplete is there to help. Whenever you type isEqual, instead of typing the colon and the argument, press the Esc key. This opens the autocomplete list, and you can see whether a more specific completion is available.

■**Caution** Don't be fooled by isEqualTo:, which is part of AppleScript and should not be used directly.

Void

C functions can return nothing by declaring themselves to be of type void and can accept any pointer by declaring arguments that are pointers to void:

```
void nothingFromSomething(void *something)
```

Void return types and void pointers can also be used in Objective-C:

```
- (void)nothingFromSomething:(void *)something;
```

However, any pointer is so rarely what you want, because pointers don't necessarily point to objects. One thing you could do is this:

```
- (void)nothingFromSomeObject:(NSObject *)someObject;
```

Not every object is an NSObject. NSProxy, for example, doesn't inherit from NSObject. Because there's a difference between an object and an NSObject, Objective-C adds the type, id, which is any object:

```
- (void)nothingFromAnyObject:(id)anyObject;
```

> ■**Note** You're probably wondering why, if id is a pointer, it doesn't use the * operator. In general, primitive types from Objective-C itself don't, while user-level objects from the libraries do. Other types that don't use the * operator include selectors (SEL), implementations (IMP), methods (Method), and the class that represents class itself, Class.

Emptiness

C also uses zero to represent emptiness, generally referred to as NULL. Objective-C has NULL, but it also has nil, Nil, and NSNull. As opposed to NULL, which means nothing, nil means no object. In other words, nil has type id. The capitalized form Nil means no class, so it has type Class. Finally, NSNull is a singleton object obtained by calling [NSNull null]. This object is an emptiness placeholder for collections such as NSArray, where actual emptiness is not allowed.

All nothings are not created equal, as shown in Table 25-3. NULL, nil, and Nil are all equal to zero, so they are all equal to each other and also the BOOL value NO. However, by convention, sending a message to nil returns nil, so calling [nil isEqual:nil] returns NO, even though it's true. Since NSNull is an object, its pointer is not equal to zero, so its BOOL value is YES, and it never equals anything but itself.

Table 25-3. *Boolean Operations on Nothing*

Operation	NULL/nil/Nil	NSNull
(BOOL) ____	NO	YES
NULL / nil / Nil == ____	YES	NO
NULL / nil / Nil isEqual: ____	NO	NO
NSNull == ____	NO	YES
NSNull isEqual: ____	NO	YES

Objective-C Memory Management

Objective-C uses a simple memory-management scheme called *retain counting*. Every object has a retain count. When an object is created by calling alloc or copy, the object has a retain count of 1. An object that creates another object is responsible for eventually sending the new object a release message, which reduces its retain count by 1.

When an object's retain count drops to 0, that object will be freed. This poses a problem for any object that tries to access the freed object by dereferencing a pointer to what is now freed memory. This causes the program to crash immediately, as illustrated in Figure 25-1 and explained in the following code.

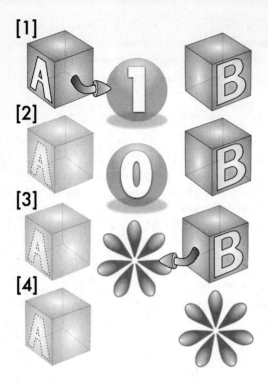

Figure 25-1. *Attempting to dereference a freed object will crash your application.*

1. Cube A creates the sphere, which starts with a retain count of 1:

   ```
   Sphere *sphere = [[Sphere alloc] init];
   ```

2. When Cube A is being freed, it has to release the sphere:

   ```
   [sphere release];
   ```

3. Let's say Cube B were to send the sphere a message:

   ```
   [sphere hello];
   ```

4. In this case, the application would crash:

```
EXC_BAD_ACCESS
```

■Note This section discusses the traditional Objective-C model for manual memory management. You can read more about automatic memory management (a.k.a., *garbage collection*) in the "Objective-C 2.0" section.

To prevent this from happening, objects that are interested in other objects can send them a `retain` message, which increases their retain count by 1. The `retain` method returns the object being retained, so it can be applied as soon as possible, which is to say, within the assignment operation.

When an object is no longer interested in an object it has created or retained, it sends the object a `release` message. When the last `release` message is sent, the object's retain count is 0, and it is freed, as illustrated in Figure 25-2 and explained in the code that follows.

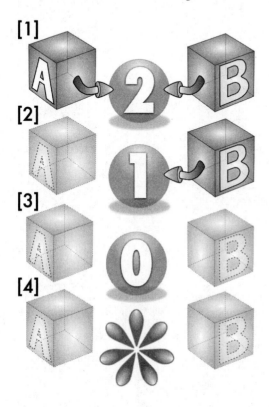

Figure 25-2. *When an object retains another object, the retained object's retain count is increased by 1.*

1. After Cube A creates the sphere, Cube B sends it `retain`, raising its retain count to 2:

   ```
   Sphere *sphere = [[cubeA sphere] retain];
   ```

2. When Cube A releases the sphere, it is not freed, because its retain count is 1:

   ```
   [sphere release];
   ```

3. When Cube B releases the sphere, its retain count is 0:

   ```
   [sphere release];
   ```

4. The sphere is then freed.

Things get more complicated when an object's creator will be out of scope before other objects can send them retain. This problem occurs whenever a method creates an object it wants to return. If the object is sent release within the method, the object may be freed before the method returns, delivering a corrupt pointer, as shown previously. Not sending release, on the other hand, will prevent the object's retain count from reaching 0. The object will never be freed, and the memory will leak, as shown in Figure 25-3.

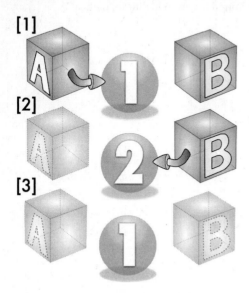

Figure 25-3. *If someone fails to release the object before it leaves scope, the object's retain count will never reach 0 and it will leak.*

1. Within the scope of Cube A, a new Sphere object can be created and returned, but it cannot be sent release before returning:

```
- (Sphere *)sphere;
{
        return [[Sphere alloc] init];
}
```

2. Within the scope of Cube B, the Sphere object is retained during assignment, raising its retain count to 2. Having returned from the method, Cube A is now out of scope and unable to send [sphere release]:

```
Sphere *sphere = [[cubeA sphere] retain];
```

3. When Cube B sends [sphere release], its retain count will be 1. It will be out of scope from any object and will never receive the other release. The memory is thus unrecoverable:

```
[sphere release];
```

For this situation, Objective-C introduces autorelease pools. These are intermediary objects that retain an object on behalf of another object leaving scope, long enough that some other object can retain it, as shown in Figure 25-4.

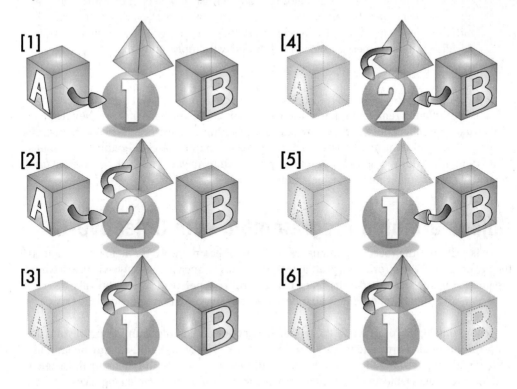

Figure 25-4. *Autorelease pools allow objects to be moved between scopes without being overreleased or leaked.*

1. Cube A creates a Sphere object, which has a retain count of 1:

```
- (Sphere *)sphere;
{
    Sphere *sphere = [[Sphere alloc] init];
```

2. Before Cube A returns sphere, it sends it autorelease. This has the effect of the autorelease pool retaining sphere, then sending it release, in effect transferring ownership:

```
return [sphere autorelease];
}
```

3. Sending autorelease is like sending release in that it relieves Cube A of the obligation of releasing sphere, while not actually letting its retain count drop to 0. Think of autorelease as meaning "release later."

4. Within the scope of Cube B, sphere is returned intact and can be sent retain in time:

```
Sphere *sphere = [[cubeA sphere] retain];
```

5. The autorelease pool will release sphere at a later time, which won't affect Cube B, which has retained sphere.

6. If Cube B sends sphere release before the autorelease pool, it won't matter. The Sphere object will eventually be released twice and freed. Still, to protect against this indeterminate state, it's good practice to set pointers to nil if they will be around for a while. Recall that sending messages to nil is safe and will simply return nil:

```
[sphere release];
sphere = nil;
```

It is important to remember that autorelease pools are not magical, nor are they related at all to garbage collection. Conceptually, they are just arrays. Like arrays, they retain anything added to them. Draining an autorelease pool (or releasing it) releases everything it contains. Unless you have added your own autorelease pool, nothing in your code will be released until the end of the current event loop, which might be a while.

Object-Oriented Programming with Objective-C

Projects written with procedural languages, such as C, become very difficult to understand as they grow larger. Object-oriented programming languages, such as Objective-C, offer a way to organize code into structured units called *classes*. From a C perspective, a class is like a struct, a typedef, and a library of functions all rolled into one. An object is an individual instance of a class.

Other than that broad review, the tenets of object-oriented programming are beyond the scope of this book. Fortunately, it's something most developers should already be familiar with. What's important to the topic at hand are the ways Objective-C implements those tenets and the advantages Objective-C offers, compared to other object-oriented languages.

Declaring an Interface

Let's look at the header of a simple Objective-C class:

```
#import <Cocoa/Cocoa.h>

@interface BMPerson : NSObject {
    NSString *name;
    NSUInteger age;
}

+ (BMPerson *)personWithName:(NSString *)aName age:(NSUInteger)anAge;
- (NSString *)name;
- (void)setName:(NSString *)aName;
- (NSUInteger)age;
- (void)setAge:(NSUInteger)anAge;

@end
```

This looks kind of like C and kind of not. Like C, lines of code end with a semicolon, whitespace is ignored, and scope is opened and closed with curly braces.

The first thing you need to do is import your application frameworks. For convenience, you can just import the entirety of Cocoa:

```
#import <Cocoa/Cocoa.h>
```

The #import directive is an improved version of C's #include directive, which inserts the contents of the named file into the current file. The difference is that #import is smart enough not to insert the same file twice.

Typically, only header files (those ending with .h) are imported. Frameworks use the format <Framework/File.h>, while your own files use the format File.h, as you'll see.

You begin the interface with the Objective-C compiler declaration @interface, name the class BMPerson, and use the : operator to set its superclass to NSObject:

```
@interface BMPerson : NSObject {
```

Note Objective-C class names are in a global namespace, which means if you accidentally name your class the same thing as Apple named one of its, the classes will overlap and cause problems. To avoid such collisions, class names traditionally start with a (usually two-letter) prefix. Since our explorations are taking us beyond the manual, let's go with BM, but you should choose something appropriate, such as your initials, the initials of your company, or something germane to your project.

The brace opens the composition section, where we declare instance variables, also known as ivars. We can use object types by declaring a pointer to the type:

```
NSString *name;
```

We can also use scalars by simple declaration:

```
NSUInteger age;
```

Below the composition section, we declare class and instance methods. A class method is called on the class itself, while an instance method is called on individual instances of that class, which is to say, objects. We start with a common type of class method: a factory method. This is a convenient shortcut in the allocation and instantiation process:

```
+ (BMPerson *)personWithName:(NSString *)aName age:(NSUInteger)anAge;
```

Note that, as a class method, its declaration begins with +.

Following the class methods, we declare instance methods. These begin with - and follow the same form as our class method:

```
- (NSString *)name;
- (void)setName:(NSString *)aName;
- (NSUInteger)age;
- (void)setAge:(NSUInteger)anAge;
```

Finally, you end the interface with @end and save the file following the traditional format. In Objective-C, the file name is usually the same as the class name. The file with the interface uses the extension .h, while the file with the implementation uses the extension .m. So, the BMPerson class has its interface in BMPerson.h and its implementation in BMPerson.m.

Note Although a class's interface typically goes in a header file, and a class's implementation typically goes in an implementation file, this is by no means necessary. For more about the organization of Objective-C classes, read about categories in the "Objective-C Dynamic Runtime" section.

Implementing the Class

The implementation of the class looks like this:

```
#import "BMPerson.h"

@implementation BMPerson

+ (BMPerson *)personWithName:(NSString *)aName age:(NSUInteger)anAge;
{
    BMPerson *newPerson = [[self alloc] init];

    [newPerson setName:aName];
    [newPerson setAge:anAge];

    return [newPerson autorelease];
}

- (id)init;
{
    if (!(self = [super init]))
        return nil;

    name = nil;

    return self;
}

- (void)dealloc;
{
    [name release];
    name = nil;

    [super dealloc];
}
```

```
- (NSString *)name;
{
    return name;
}

- (void)setName:(NSString *)aName;
{
    if (name == aName)
        return;

    [name release];
    name = [aName retain];
}

- (NSUInteger)age;
{
    return age;
}

- (void)setAge:(NSUInteger)anAge;
{
    age = anAge;
}

@end
```

As with the interface, you start by importing

```
#import "BMPerson.h"
```

If you recall, you imported the Cocoa framework differently:

```
#import <Cocoa/Cocoa.h>
```

Note the change in syntax, as mentioned previously. When importing system frameworks, use the path notation and the angle brackets. When importing your own headers, use the quote notation.

Incidentally, you don't have to import Cocoa into this implementation, because the header has already imported it. Importing a header also imports any headers it has imported. As you can imagine, that gets complicated quickly, which is why we use #import and not #include.

You open the implementation with the @implementation directive and the name of the class:

```
@implementation BMPerson
```

You don't have to rename the superclass or redeclare the instance variables, so you can move right into methods.

Class Methods

The list of method declarations in the header—sometimes called *prototypes*—advertise the class's capabilities for the compiler. When it comes time to actually perform the promised service, the machinery looks for an implementation whose signature matches the one listed in the header. As such, you start the methods in the implementation section with the same line as the interface section:

```
+ (BMPerson *)personWithName:(NSString *)aName age:(NSUInteger)anAge;
```

Technically, method declarations in the implementation section don't require semicolons, but the compiler conveniently ignores them. That makes starting an implementation as easy as copying and pasting.

The factory method has a simple implementation. You allocate a new person, set its name and age, and return it. The body of a method begins and ends with curly braces:

```
{
    BMPerson *newPerson = [[self alloc] init];

    [newPerson setName:aName];
    [newPerson setAge:anAge];

    return [newPerson autorelease];
}
```

This is just a convenient shortcut for doing the same thing in code, but there are a few subtle differences that are worth noting.

If you actually instantiated a BMPerson externally, you would do so by sending alloc to the class:

```
BMPerson *newPerson = [[BMPerson alloc] init];
```

From within the class method, however, you send the message to self.

Behind the scenes, every method in Objective-C is converted into a function. When you send a message to an object, the messaging system looks up the appropriate function and calls it. Along with the arguments you provided in the message, a few more arguments are slipped in. The first "secret" argument is a pointer to the object on which the function is being called. That argument's name is self.

As such, whenever an object needs to refer to itself, such as to call one of its own methods, it simply sends a message to self. In an instance method, self refers to the instance, which is to say, the object. Six different objects will get six different results by sending the same message to self. In a class method, self refers to the class. Therefore, when a class calls its own class method, such as alloc, it sends a message to itself, using self. It's a fine point, but one to keep in mind.

Note Objects also have a secret ivar called isa that refers to its class. Class methods can therefore be called by sending a message to isa. However, runtime considerations make calling isa a gamble, so it's better to get your class indirectly, via [self class].

After setting the name and age that were passed in, you return the new object with the standard C keyword `return`. Because you created it, you need to release it, but because you're returning it, you send it an `autorelease` message, as detailed in the previous section on memory management.

To use this method in code, you send a message to the class:

```
BMPerson *worldsToughestProgrammer = [BMPerson personWithName:@"Mike Lee" age:33];
```

This is equivalent to creating an instance on your own, using almost the same code as you used to implement the method:

```
BMPerson *worldsToughestProgrammer = [[BMPerson alloc] init];
[newPerson setName:@"Mike Lee"];
[newPerson setAge:33];
```

The only difference, of course, is that the factory method produces an autoreleased instance, whereas the manually allocated method does not.

■**Note** Why bother with factory methods? There are some edge cases where they are useful. Singleton optimizations are one. Teaching people how to write class methods is another. Mostly, though, it's just a way to save three lines of code. For something you aren't using much, it isn't worth the hassle, but if it's something you use a lot, the savings add up. The foundation classes, such as NSString and NSArray, make frequent use of factory methods. If you multiply three lines of code by the number of times you instantiate NSArray, we're talking thousands of lines of code. That is why it's commonly said that Objective-C programmers hate code.

Init and Dealloc

With the class methods implemented, it's time to fill out the instance methods. The first method declaration you come to looks unfamiliar:

```
- (id)init;
```

A quick visit to the interface reveals no such declaration. Veterans of object-oriented programming are sagely nodding right about now. The `init` method was inherited from the superclass, NSObject.

■**Tip** In Xcode, you can switch between a class's interface and its implementation with the keystroke Command-up arrow.

During the instantiation of an object, you actually call two methods. The first, `alloc`, is sent to the class you want to instantiate. This returns an object—you hope an instance of the class you just called. However, the object is in a dangerous state. Its instance variables have been declared, but any pointers are not actually pointing to anything. Dereferencing or messaging a floating pointer will cause any program to immediately crash. As such, you immediately call the new object's instance method, init.

If a superclass implements a method, you can call the method on any subclass, and the superclass's implementation will be found and executed. However, if that subclass also implements the method, the subclass's implementation will be used instead. In object-oriented programming, you say that the subclass's implementation overrides the superclass's implementation.

Sometimes that's what you want, but sometimes you just want to add something to the superclass's method, rather than replacing it outright. To accomplish this, you call the superclass's implementation from within your own. You do this by sending a message to the superclass via the keyword super.

In Objective-C, as with any language, there are implied contracts. For example, nothing in the language is going to force you to call init right after alloc. You just have to do it to make things work right. Another implied contract is that if you override init, you have to call super, and if that call fails for some reason, you have to return nil. Since nil is equal to the Boolean NO, you can do so with a simple if statement:

```
if (!(self = [super init]))
    return nil;
```

Only then are you safe to do your own initialization, setting your name pointer safely to nil:

```
name = nil;
```

With that accomplished, you can return your newly instantiated self to be assigned to the waiting pointer:

```
return self;
```

Another way to go about this would have been to create an init method that lets the caller pass in the name and age values in one line, not unlike the factory method example earlier:

```
- (id)initWithName:(NSString *)aName age:(NSNumber)anAge;
{
    if (!(self = [super init]))
        return nil;

    [self setName:aName];
    [self setAge:anAge];

    return self;
}
```

A new person could then be initialized with custom values:

```
[[BMPerson alloc] initWithName:@"Mike Lee" age:33];
```

Since someone might still call `init`, it still has to be implemented, but now it can just call the new method:

```
- (id)init;
{
    return [self initWithName:nil age:0];
}
```

Every class typically has one `init` method to which all other `init` methods refer. This is called the designated initializer. Subclasses of that class should call the designated initializer, rather than just calling `init`. The bad news is, you usually can't tell which initializer is the designated initializer without checking the documentation. The good news is, Objective-C doesn't rely on subclassing as much as other languages do, so it's less of a problem in practice.

■**Note** Since this new initializer is not declared in the superclass, you would also have to add its declaration to the header file.

As objects are born, so must they die. Just as `init` gives your objects a chance to get things in order before being used, `dealloc` gives them a chance to get their affairs in order before they're sent off to that big memory heap in the sky:

```
- (void)dealloc;
{
    [name release];
    name = nil;

    [super dealloc];
}
```

In this case, you've got a pointer, `name`, that needs to be released. Whenever releasing an object in `dealloc`, or anywhere else, set the pointer to `nil`. You never know what might happen, especially in the crazy world of multithreaded, multiprocessor computing. You don't want to leave a dangling pointer around for someone to call and crash.

As with `init`, you're overriding your superclass's implementation. Sending a `dealloc` message to `super` gives everyone in the inheritance tree a chance to take care of their final business as well. With `init`, you typically call `super` first. In `dealloc`, you call `super` last.

With the inherited hassle of memory management out of the way, you can finally get back to all those instance methods you declared.

Instance Methods

The whole point of object-oriented programming is to transfer responsibility to your objects. Whereas a functional programmer might say, "I am going to do something with this," an object-oriented programmer would say, "I am going to ask this to do something." The tasks we can ask our objects to do are their instance methods.

The most common instance methods are for directly accessing and mutating an object's instance variables. In technical terms, we call these methods *accessors* and *mutators*, but Apple prefers the more colloquial *setters* and *getters*. Whatever you call them, these methods follow a standard pattern:

```
- (NSString *)name;
- (void)setName:(NSString *)aName;
```

In Objective-C, a getter has the same name and return type as the ivar it's accessing and takes no arguments. The setter adds the prefix set to the name, takes one argument of the ivar's type, and returns nothing. For the special case of Boolean ivars—and Boolean ivars only—the getter may use the prefix is. For example, calling isHidden would access the ivar hidden.

■**Note** Some languages precede the ivar name with the word get, but in Objective-C, you use that pattern for something else.

At its simplest, a getter just returns the value of the ivar:

```
- (NSString *)name;
{
    return name;
}
```

Because of memory management, setters are a bit more complicated:

```
- (void)setName:(NSString *)aName;
{
    if (name == aName)
        return;

    [name release];
    name = [aName retain];
}
```

The first thing you'll notice is that a setter's argument cannot have the same name as its ivar. Looking at the first line explains why that is:

```
    if (name == aName)
```

If you had given the argument the same name, you'd end up with this:

```
    if (name == name)
```

Wouldn't that be confusing?

■**Note** In Java, you can override ivars with arguments, because you can distinguish them with the keyword `this`. So, you could say `this.name == name`. Objective-C doesn't have this nicety (or hassle, depending on your point of view).

In a way, setters are written backward. You're setting the value of the pointer to a new object, which you retain:

```
name = [aName retain];
```

Doing so removes your ability to reach the old object, so you must first release it:

```
[name release];
```

However, if the old object and the new object are the same, you might end up causing the object to be freed, which would cause a crash when you tried to use it. As such, before you can do any of this, you need to check that the two objects are, in fact, not the same, and bail out if they are:

```
if (name == aName)
    return;
```

With all the fuss, it seems like it would be a lot easier to just access the variables directly and not hassle with calling methods. However, there's a good reason not to; it's a violation of encapsulation.

Encapsulation is an important part of object-oriented programming. It states that implementation details should always be hidden. This prevents objects from becoming entangled and making things just as complicated as they were with procedural programming. It also protects programmers from implementation changes.

For example, consider the setter for age:

```
- (void)setAge:(NSUInteger)anAge;
{
        age = anAge;
}
```

Right now, it's very simple. It takes a scalar type rather than a pointer, so you don't even have to worry about memory management. What if you later decide that blithely setting this value is a security risk because of integer overflow exploits? To protect against that, you add some validation logic:

```
- (void)setAge:(NSUInteger)anAge;
{
    if (anAge > 0 && anAge < 100)
        age = anAge;
}
```

If you've been good and respected encapsulation, your work is done. If you've been bad and have been setting the variable directly, you're going to have a lot of implementation work ahead of you. That's why it's always a good idea to use setters and getters, even from within the object itself.

■**Note** In the section on Objective-C 2.0, you'll read about property syntax, which makes writing setters and getters yesterday's hassle.

Protocols

Unlike C++, Objective-C uses a single inheritance model by which a class can inherit only from a single superclass. To overcome the restrictions posed by single inheritance while adding a different sort of flexibility, Objective-C classes may inherit additional interfaces by conforming to any number of protocols.

A protocol is like a class, except it does not contain variables or provide any implementation. Rather, it simply defines an interface, which conforming classes are expected to implement. This same concept was later used in Java but renamed *interfaces*.

What good is this? Recall our discussion about class headers and the method prototypes that tell the compiler what your class can do. A protocol is the exact same thing. The difference is that when you write a class header, you also write its implementation. When you write a protocol, you leave the implementation to whoever adopts the protocol.

This is a handy trick for Apple, because it can define protocols for use with its frameworks that developers such as yourself can implement. For example, some objects can be copied by simply sending them the message copy. You don't really care what class the object is; you just care that it implements the appropriate method. To this end, Foundation defines a protocol, NSCopying. If your BMPerson class implements the copy method, you can add the protocol to your class declaration:

```
@interface BMPerson : NSObject <NSCopying>
```

Nothing else in the interface changes, but now you are expected to implement the copy method.

■**Note** Technically, when you call - (id)copy, you are calling - (id)copyWithZone:(NSZone *)zone with a default value for zone. The concept of zones is largely obsolete, but the upshot is that conforming to NSCopying requires implementing copyWithZone: instead of copy.

You can also define your own protocols. This is great for designing a plug-in architecture, but it's also useful just as a design technique. Say you want a general interface for providing a unique ID. You start by defining your protocol, much as you would a class:

```
@protocol BMIdentifying
    - (NSString *)uniqueIDString;
@end
```

If `BMPerson` implements `uniqueIDString`, you can add that to the protocol list:

```
@interface BMPerson : NSObject <NSCopying, BMIdentifying>
```

Later in your design, you might want to accept some object but need to make sure it complies with your `BMIdentifying` protocol. You can write method signatures that use protocols as types:

```
- (void)addIdentifyingObject:(id <BMIdentifying>)object;
```

To call this method, you can similarly cast to the protocol:

```
[listOfIdentifyingObjects addIdentifyingObject:(id <BMIdentifying>)object];
```

Cocoa uses formal and informal protocols for several class-agnostic patterns:

Plug-ins: By creating a plug-in architecture, a programmer can open his or her application to third-party development. For such an architecture to work, the programmer must define an interface. By using protocols, plug-in writers are given total design freedom, as long as they implement the necessary methods.

Delegates and data sources: To be reusable, an object's behavior and content must be configurable. Languages such as Java rely heavily on subclassing to accomplish this. However, this is often too big a tool for the job. The delegate and data source patterns leave behavioral and content decisions to another object. By implementing the necessary methods, programmers can control these classes without the trouble of subclassing.

Notifications: Often used in conjunction with the delegate pattern, notifications are methods called before and after certain actions occur. By implementing those methods, programmers can synchronize other objects' actions based on what the notifying class is doing. For example, a `didReceiveData` notification might trigger interested objects to act on that data.

Fast enumeration: Objective-C 2.0 introduces a unified, terse, and highly optimized `for...in` loop. Collections become eligible for fast enumeration by conforming to the `NSFastEnumeration` protocol. This makes it easy to add this functionality to existing collection types and lets programmers use fast enumeration with their own collection classes. We discuss fast enumeration in more detail in the "Objective-C 2.0" section.

Key-value coding and key-value observing: In addition to the standard practice of calling explicit methods, objects' properties can be accessed by name. Changes to properties can also be observed, maintaining interobject dependencies with little or no code. We discuss these in more detail in the "Objective-C Runtime" section.

Scripting: To be scriptable, applications require certain additional methods to be implemented. There are also a slew of optional methods that programmers can use to deal with the inherent impedance mismatch between how they use their objects and how a scripter might use them.

Accessibility: By complying with accessibility protocols, applications can not only be used by disabled users but can also participate in user-interface scripting, as used by AppleScript, Instruments, and a slew of third-party applications.

Animation: Like fast enumeration, Cocoa's Core Animation wrappings are implemented by protocol, minimizing the need to change existing frameworks while extending usability to developers' own classes.

Spelling: Among the more renowned features of Mac OS X is system-wide spelling and grammar checking. By implementing the spelling protocols, developers can incorporate these into their own applications, customizing behaviors as necessary.

Locking: The locking protocol simply defines a standard interface for thread-safe classes to let themselves be locked and unlocked.

Pasteboard operations: Drag and drop and copy and paste are two sides of the same coin. Dating back to the very first Macintosh, the pasteboard is at the heart of a modern operating system. Something so basic obviously rises above any class hierarchy. Thus, formal and informal protocols define all parts of a pasteboard operation, from providing data to receiving data to the format of the data itself.

■Note Prior to Leopard, all protocol methods were required. The interface that was considered optional was implemented as an informal protocol, which was really just a category (which we'll get to) on `NSObject`. Objective-C 2.0 uses the compiler directives `@optional` and `@required`, which eliminate the need for informal protocols.

Objective-C Dynamic Runtime

When one says a programming language is dynamic, what does that mean? Dynamism implies the ability to change, but what does that mean in practical terms? It's easier to understand dynamic languages in terms of their opposite: static languages.

In a static language, the programmer defines everything the program does. Things are defined, connected, and welded together. Variables continue to be variable, but only just. In a static language, for example, a variable can be any number, but it must be a number. It cannot be a string, a picture of a lemur, or the color purple.

Dynamic languages let the programmer leave things unsaid. A variable can be a number one moment, and a lemur the next. Methods might perform differently under different circumstances—a practice called *polymorphism*. Things are not welded so much as they are loosely tied.

Objective-C is dynamic, even compared to other dynamic languages. In object-oriented languages such as Java and C++, once classes are compiled, they cease to be dynamic. You can subclass them and do what you like with your subclasses, but you can't change them. Your programming environment is never fully dynamic, because all any programmer can do is create and play in a dynamic sandbox surrounding a static core.

Objective-C doesn't have any such restrictions. Remember that Objective-C is only a very thin layer on top of C. Except for a few compiler directives, notable by their @ prefix, very little above plain C is actually occurring at compile time. With Objective-C, the magic happens at runtime. That means much of what the code is doing is not locked down until right before it happens, and therein lies tremendous power.

At the core of this is Objective-C's unusual messaging syntax. It's not just a readable replacement for dot syntax; it's actually an indirection provided by the runtime that completely separates the act of calling a method from the actual execution of that method.

Consider the previous example:

```
[myObject setColorWithRed:0.4 green:0.3 blue:0.0 alpha:1.0];
```

In the parlance of Objective-C, we call `myObject` the receiver and `setColorWithRed:0.4 green:0.3 blue:0.0 alpha:1.0` the message. Behind the scenes, the runtime separates the message into a method signature and an array of arguments.

Every method signature is resolved into a selector, which is represented by the data type `SEL`. The runtime dynamically pairs selectors with a method implementation, represented by the data type `IMP`. These are tangible data types and can be treated as such. They can be created, examined, changed, and passed around.

■**Note** A method's name is the method declaration, including the colons, but without the argument names or types. So, the name of the method being called in `setColorWithRed:0.4 green:0.3 blue:0.0 alpha:1.0` is `setColorWithRed:green:blue:alpha:`.

So what practical use is all this dynamism? Perhaps the most notable example in Objective-C is the design of the menu system. Every application on the Mac has a menu that contains just about every feature the application has to offer. In a static design, the menu would be the most powerful class in your application, because it would literally have to be tied to just about everything in order to call the methods it needs to call.

In Objective-C, the menu is actually relatively minor. It typically sits in its own file, ignored for most of the development cycle. Rather than being connected to everything, it's connecting to nothing. Menu items send their messages to the first responder, which is literally whoever's listening.

When Objective-C gets a message for the first responder, it sends it to the appropriate place. Key presses go to the currently focused text area, mouse clicks go to whatever is under the cursor—that sort of thing. If the object doesn't respond to whatever method the event is looking for, the next logical object gets the chance.

This dramatically simplifies dealing with how objects connect to each other, which means simpler architectures with fewer bugs. It also makes it possible to coalesce control for a number of views. Imagine a panel with three buttons. You can have all the things those buttons do in one neat package. On the other hand, Java's hideous "anonymous inner functions" bury the functionality inside the views themselves.

Categories

Objective-C gives you the awesome power to modify or extend the behavior of existing classes, even if you don't have the code for those classes. This is important, because it keeps frameworks small and simple. The framework's methods are building blocks with which you can build larger, more complicated things.

Every object-oriented language has a certain version of that power, through subclassing. However, Objective-C categories are way better than subclassing for most situations. Listen, if you will, to the programming version of an old man's rambling tale about hooking an onion on his belt, as was the fashion at the time.

The problem we're going to try to solve is prepending a string. NSString provides a method that takes a string and appends it to the receiver:

```
NSString *greeting = @"Hello";
greeting = [greeting stringByAppendingString:@", world!"];
NSLog(greeting);
```

```
Hello, world!
```

What if you wanted to prepend a string? That is, append it before the receiver? You can't; there's no such method.

Subclassing NSString would create your own string class that inherits the members of its superclass, NSString. You can add methods to your BMString that augment or replace the methods on NSString. When you want to use those powers, you can use BMString instead of NSString.

Creating a subclass is the same as creating any other class, save the : followed by the name of the superclass. In Objective-C, the colon means "inherits from," or as they say in Java, "extends":

```
#import <Cocoa/Cocoa.h>

@interface BMString : NSString
- (NSString *)stringByPrependingString:(NSString *)aString;
@end

@implementation BMString

- (NSString *)stringByPrependingString:(NSString *)aString;
{
    return [aString stringByAppendingString:self];
}

@end
```

Now you can do what you want:

```
BMString *greeting = [BMString stringWithString:@", world!"];
greeting = [greeting stringByPrependingString:@"Hello"];
NSLog(greeting);
```

```
*** initialization method -initWithCharactersNoCopy:length:freeWhenDone: cannot
be sent to an abstract object of class BMString: Create a concrete instance!
```

Or perhaps not. Reading the documentation, there's a lot more to subclassing NSString than you'd think. For one thing, inheritance is not absolute. Members can be marked private by programmers who don't want you mucking up their classes. Also, it turns out that NSString is not an actual class. It's the interface to a class cluster, an implementation detail of the complexities of dealing with strings.

It turns out that subclassing is powerful magic that should be saved for the rarest of occasions. For something as simple as adding a method, there has to be a better way.

Enter Objective-C categories. Categories are extensions of a class. They are the programming equivalent of an addendum, a sticky note, or a "one more thing." You declare them like a class, but with the same name as an existing class, and a category name in parentheses.

You could do it like this:

```
@interface NSString (OneMoreThingPrependingTheString)
```

But this is how *we* roll:

```
#import <Cocoa/Cocoa.h>

@interface NSString (BMString)
- (NSString *)stringByPrependingString:(NSString *)aString;
@end

@implementation NSString (BMString)

- (NSString *)stringByPrependingString:(NSString *)aString;
{
    return [aString stringByAppendingString:self];
}

@end
```

Now prepending a string works as expected:

```
NSString *greeting = @", world!";
greeting = [greeting stringByPrependingString:@"Hello"];
NSLog(greeting);
```

```
Hello, world!
```

Unlike a subclass, we have access to everything in the NSString class, including private members. A category on NSString does not inherit from NSString. It is NSString. There's no calling some special subclass; wherever your category's header is imported, the category is part of NSString.

This is the point at which Objective-C ceases to be as good as or slightly better than other languages. What happens after this paragraph is more or less pure insanity. The authors assume no responsibility for what happens if you continue reading.

Method Swizzling

Categories are nice, safe, respectable folk. Apple uses them all over the place, even just to keep the code organized. They represent the kind of language feature you'd ask to housesit. *Method swizzling*, on the other hand, is drunk and a little bit crazy. It's part of runtime.h, which is essentially Objective-C god mode.

The idea behind method swizzling is to create a bizarro version of some unsuspecting method, then swap the two implementations like a mad scientist switching heads. Anyone who calls the swizzled method will get whatever wackiness you sewed onto it.

Like uranium, method swizzling has peaceful uses. Say you take exception to the way NSXMLNode implements description. It just spits out raw XML, without any whitespace. What is up with that? When we go sticking our noses into our iWeb files, we want to see something like this:

```
<?xml version="1.0" encoding="utf-8"?>
<rss version="2.0">
    <channel>
        <title>My Blog</title>
        <link>http://www.worldofkevin.com/Site/Blog/Blog.html</link>
        <description>Welcome to my blog: Alit, Enit, Laore, Eros Vel, Exer Dolorer,
Niam Lut.</description>
        <generator>iWeb 1.1.2</generator>
        <image>
            <url>http://www.worldofkevin.com/Site/Blog/Blog_files/200206373-3-a.png
</url>
            <title>My Blog</title>
            <link>http://www.worldofkevin.com/Site/Blog/Blog.html</link>
        </image>
        <item>
            <title>Red Vines: the perfect super food</title>
            <link>http://www.worldofkevin.com/Site/Blog/88DD8356-E484-44DD-9419-
AE9F936E8BAD.html</link>
            <guid>http://www.worldofkevin.com/Site/Blog/88DD8356-E484-44DD-9419-
AE9F936E8BAD.html</guid>
            <pubDate>Mon, 20 Aug 2007 10:48:11 -0700</pubDate>
            <description>&lt;a href='http://www.worldofkevin.com/Site/Blog/
88DD8356-E484-44DD-9419-AE9F936E8BAD_files/FD004359-1.jpg'>&lt;img
src='http://www.worldofkevin.com/Site/Blog/Images/FD004359-1.jpg'
style='float:left; padding-right:10px; padding-bottom:10px; width:109px;
height:79px;'/>&lt;/a>Eliquatuero dip numsan vent lam, conum facillum init lut
doloreet ullametuero od tet adit, commod tatummy feug tiam velit praese exer aute
enit alit, veliqua modit dolorer commod niam onul laore. Uptat prat lut lut
iriliquat, quis alisl irilit am irillum at niam zzrit, verosto consequ ismodit
irius</description>
            <enclosure url="http://www.worldofkevin.com/Site/Blog/88DD8356-E484-
44DD-9419-AE9F936E8BAD_files/FD004359-1.jpg" length="101865" type="image/jpg">
</enclosure>
        </item>
```

```
    </channel>
</rss>
```

That's good, clean XML. The tags are on separate lines and indented to show what goes where. If you try to pass an NSXMLNode to NSLog, it will call description on it. This is a method from NSObject that every class may override to provide something useful. The previous XML would be useful. NSXMLNode, on the other hand, craps a brick:

```
NSXMLNode *xmlNode;
// ... load the XML document
NSLog(@"Current node: %@", xmlNode);
```

```
Current node: <?xml version="1.0" encoding="utf-8"?><rss version="2.0"><channel><t
itle>My Blog</title><link>http://www.worldofkevin.com/Site/Blog/Blog.html</link><d
escription>Welcome to my blog: Alit, Enit, Laore, Eros Vel, Exer Dolorer, Niam Lut
.</description><generator>iWeb 1.1.2</generator><image><url>http://www.worldofkevi
n.com/Site/Blog/Blog_files/200206373-3-a.png</url><title>My Blog</title><link>http
://www.worldofkevin.com/Site/Blog/Blog.html</link></image><item><title>Red Vines:
the perfect super food</title><link>http://www.worldofkevin.com/Site/Blog/88DD8356
-E484-44DD-9419-AE9F936E8BAD.html</link><guid>http://www.worldofkevin.com/Site/Blo
g/88DD8356-E484-44DD-9419-AE9F936E8BAD.html</guid><pubDate>Mon, 20 Aug 2007 10:48:
11 -0700</pubDate><description>&lt;a href='http://www.worldofkevin.com/Site/Blog/8
8DD8356-E484-44DD-9419-AE9F936E8BAD_files/FD004359-1.jpg'>&lt;img src='http://www.
worldofkevin.com/Site/Blog/Images/FD004359-1.jpg' style='float:left; padding-right
:10px; padding-bottom:10px; width:109px; height:79px;'/>&lt;/a>Eliquatuero dip num
san vent lam, conum facillum init lut doloreet ullametuero od tet adit, commod tat
ummy feug tiam velit praese exer aute enit alit, veliqua modit dolorer commod niam
onul laore. Uptat prat lut lut iriliquat, quis alisl irilit am irillum at niam zzr
it, verosto consequ ismodit irius</description><enclosure url="http://www.worldofk
evin.com/Site/Blog/88DD8356-E484-44DD-9419-AE9F936E8BAD_files/FD004359-1.jpg" leng
th="101865" type="image/jpg"></enclosure></item></channel></rss>
```

Method swizzling lets you write your own implementation and swap it out:

```
#import <Cocoa/Cocoa.h>
#import <objc/runtime.h>

@interface NSXMLNode (BMPrettyDescriptions)
- (NSString *)prettyDescription;
@end

@implementation NSXMLNode (BMPrettyDescriptions)

+ (void)load;
{
    Method oldMethod = class_getInstanceMethod(self, @selector(description));
    Method newMethod = class_getInstanceMethod(self, @selector(prettyDescription));
    method_exchangeImplementations(oldMethod, newMethod);
```

```
}

- (NSString *)prettyDescription;
{
    return [self XMLStringWithOptions:NSXMLNodePrettyPrint];
}

@end
```

Now when you feed NSXMLNode to NSLog, you get something that looks like XML:

```
NSXMLNode *xmlNode;
// ... load above XML document
NSLog(@"Current node: %@", xmlNode);
```

```
Current node: <?xml version="1.0" encoding="utf-8"?>
<rss version="2.0">
    <channel>
        <title>My Blog</title>
        <link>http://www.worldofkevin.com/Site/Blog/Blog.html</link>
        <description>Welcome to my blog: Alit, Enit, Laore, Eros Vel, Exer Dolorer,
Niam Lut.</description>
        <generator>iWeb 1.1.2</generator>
        <image>
            <url>http://www.worldofkevin.com/Site/Blog/Blog_files/200206373-3-a.png
</url>
            <title>My Blog</title>
            <link>http://www.worldofkevin.com/Site/Blog/Blog.html</link>
        </image>
        <item>
            <title>Red Vines: the perfect super food</title>
            <link>http://www.worldofkevin.com/Site/Blog/88DD8356-E484-44DD-9419-
AE9F936E8BAD.html</link>
            <guid>http://www.worldofkevin.com/Site/Blog/88DD8356-E484-44DD-9419-
AE9F936E8BAD.html</guid>
            <pubDate>Mon, 20 Aug 2007 10:48:11 -0700</pubDate>
<description>&lt;a href='http://www.worldofkevin.com/Site/Blog/88DD8356-E484-44DD
-9419-AE9F936E8BAD_files/FD004359-1.jpg'>&lt;img
src='http://www.worldofkevin.com/Site/Blog/Images/FD004359-1.jpg'
style='float:left; padding-right:10px; padding-bottom:10px; width:109px;
height:79px;'/>&lt;/a>Eliquatuero dip numsan vent lam, conum facillum init lut
doloreet ullametuero od tet adit, commod tatummy feug tiam velit praese exer
auteenit alit, veliqua modit dolorer commod niam onul laore. Uptat prat lut
lut iriliquat,quis alisl irilit am irillum at niam zzrit, verosto consequ
ismodit irius</description>
            <enclosure url="http://www.worldofkevin.com/Site/Blog/88DD8356-E484-
44DD-9419-AE9F936E8BAD_files/FD004359-1.jpg" length="101865" type="image/jpg">
```

```
</enclosure>
        </item>
    </channel>
</rss>
```

What is this sorcery? This is the awesome power of the Objective-C runtime. You wield this power by claiming the Mighty Scepter of Objective-C, which looks a lot less impressive than it sounds:

```
#import <objc/runtime.h>
```

To facilitate just this sort of goings on, the runtime sends the `load` message to any class as it's being loaded but before it's used. This is the perfect place to accomplish what you need to do:

```
+ (void)load;
```

To swap the implementations of the methods, you have to get the methods:

```
Method oldMethod = class_getInstanceMethod(self, @selector(description));
```

The compiler directive `@selector` converts the name of a method into a `SEL`, as required by the function `class_getInstanceMethod`, which returns a `Method`. Recall that the `Method` is a struct that contains a selector of type `SEL`, an implementation of type `IMP`, and some return type encoding information.

With the methods in hand, all you have to do is swap their implementations.

```
method_exchangeImplementations(oldMethod, newMethod);
```

As far as the runtime is concerned, the two methods have literally had their implementations swapped. The message `description` will now call the implementation you defined for `prettyDescription`. The inverse is also true; calling `prettyDescription` will return the original implementation of `description`. So, to "call `super`" from within the new implementation, it has to call itself:

```
- (NSString *)prettyDescription;
{
    NSString *oldDescription = [self prettyDescription];
    ...
}
```

Weird, right?

In Objective-C, nothing is ever written in stone. Even without wandering far from the comforts of object-oriented programming, you have the power to pull off staggering feats of engineering brilliance.

Key Value Coding

In recent years, the designers of Objective-C have begun making use of heretofore informal aspects of the language. For example, given a property `key`, you can assume its getter is `key` and its setter is `setKey:`. Alternately, if `key` is a Boolean property, you can assume its getter is `isKey`.

By making this assumption about the predictability of method names, the system can enable a new level of dynamic behavior known as key value coding (KVC).

KVC treats every property as a named key and introduces a generic form for getting or setting any property by name:

```
id property = [myObject valueForKey:@"property"];
[otherObject setValue:property forKey:@"property"];
```

By allowing you to refer to properties by name, KVC lets you do the following:

- Resolve property names at runtime.

- Deal with unknown or empty keys on the fly.

- Store keys in collections and deal with them en masse without regard to type.

- Create derived properties. For example, you might later decide to derive name from properties called firstName and lastName.

- Create dependent keys, such that a change to one key triggers change notifications in other keys.

- Sync keys to other keys using bindings, the zero-code technology that gives Interface Builder much of its power.

- Bridge properties between Objective-C and other technologies such as Core Data and AppleScript.

Objective-C 2.0

With Leopard, Apple announced it was making major improvements to Objective-C; these improvements are collectively known as Objective-C 2.0. You don't have to do anything to claim this free upgrade. Just be aware that these features were added in Leopard (and iPhone OS), so if you're targeting Tiger for some reason, they won't be available.

Class Extension

One of the most common uses of Objective-C's method categories is the creation of private headers. These define methods that are used by the internal implementation of a class but should not be called from outside the class.

In a way, this is an abuse of the language. Categories are meant to arrange a class's implementation by functionality. Using a category to define private methods creates an artificial separation in the implementation based on visibility rather than function.

Class extensions are a new kind of "anonymous" category. Unlike a standard category, which extends both the interface and the implementation, a class extension extends only the interface. The implementation remains with the main class. Thus, a public method and closely related private methods can remain together.

For example, say you had a contrived class whose public interface declared like this:

```
@interface MyClass : NSObject
- (void)publicMethod;
@end
```

Within your implementation file (or private header), you would declare the following:

```
@interface MyClass ()
- (void)privateMethod;
- (void)privateHelper;
@end
```

Then your implementation would look something like this:

```
@implementation MyClass

- (void)publicMethod;
{
    [self privateMethod];
    // ...
}

- (void)privateMethod;
{
     [self privateHelper];
    // ...
}

- (void)privateHelper;
{
    // ...
}

@end
```

Note Class extensions, unlike protocols, are completely anonymous and cannot be adopted by multiple classes.

Fast Enumeration

Iterating over a collection is one of the most common tasks in programming. Traditionally, C accomplishes this via the standard `for` loop:

```
NSArray *objects = [self methodThatReturnsAnArrayOfObjects];
NSUInteger objectIndex;
for (objectIndex = 0; objectIndex < [objects count]; objectIndex++) {
    NSObject *object = [objects objectAtIndex:objectIndex];
    // ...
}
```

This is effective, but it's a lot to type, it requires an additional method call, and worst of all, it works only for arrays. As such, Cocoa provides the `NSEnumerator` class, which enables the following:

```
NSArray *objects = [self methodThatReturnsAnArrayOfObjects];
NSEnumerator *objectEnumerator = [objects objectEnumerator];
NSObject *object = nil;
while ((object = [objectEnumerator nextObject])) {
    // ...
}
```

For all the object-oriented goodness that enumerators bring, they are slow and require making a copy of every object. They also suffer from the same kind of redundant verbosity as the C iteration loop. Objective-C 2.0 introduces the ultimate solution to the looping problem:

```
NSArray *objects = [self methodThatReturnsAnArrayOfObjects];
for (NSObject *object in objects) {
    // ...
}
```

Fast enumeration is both more concise and more readable than either of the other methods. It is backed by the `NSFastEnumeration` protocol, so it can work with any collection, including your own. It is also highly optimized, so it is not only faster than traditional enumeration, but it is also faster than C iteration.

Finally, fast enumeration adds the benefit of a mutation check, which ensures collections do not change during enumeration. This is part of a general push toward multiprocessor-safe coding practices. With OpenCL and Grand Central Dispatch offering big parallelization opportunities, that's a good practice to have.

Garbage Collection

Aside from the syntax, the scariest thing about Objective-C is manual memory management. Even the most experienced programmers are prone to crashes and memory leaks. Memory problems are also among the hardest to debug, taking up a lot of precious development time.

Other languages have solved this problem with automated memory management, generally known as garbage collection. Unfortunately, garbage collection is synonymous with poor performance. Collection is typically expensive enough to require pausing general operations, frustrating users. Proponents of garbage collection have hoped computers will eventually get fast enough that this won't matter, but it hasn't happened yet.

Objective-C does garbage collection right. The collector in Objective-C 2.0 is built on the collective knowledge of the almost 50 years since garbage collection was invented. It was also designed with a solid foundation in the real world, mindful of the patterns and habits of Objective-C programmers.

CHAPTER 25 ■ MAC OS X DEVELOPMENT: OBJECTIVE-C

613

The designers of Objective-C's garbage collection knew to

- Avoid expensive memory optimization operations such as compacting the heap or moving objects around.
- Concentrate on new objects, which tend to live short lives, rather than old objects, which tend to live forever.
- Avoid stopping all operations for collection. Wait for opportune moments, only collect on the main thread, and yield to user events.
- Retain the dual nature of Objective-C by not breaking compatibility with other frameworks or the use of inline C code.
- Give the programmer control, where needed, to optimize garbage collection, or opt out of it altogether.

This last point is important. It's possible to write your code for both automatic and manual memory management. If you plan on sharing code between your Mac and your iPhone, that will come in handy. There's no garbage collection on iPhone.

Note That's right. There is no garbage collection on iPhone.

Toggling garbage collection is a project option in Xcode, as shown in Figure 25-5. When garbage collection is on, the compiler ignores retain, release, and autorelease operations, except for the NSAutoreleasePool instance method drain, which serves as a hint to the collector. The dealloc method is also ignored, though a finalize method may be implemented if there's somehow something in dealloc that is not made moot by garbage collection.

Tip Switching between automated and manual memory management is a great way to debug crashes. If one mode crashes and the other doesn't, you know there's something wrong in your implementation.

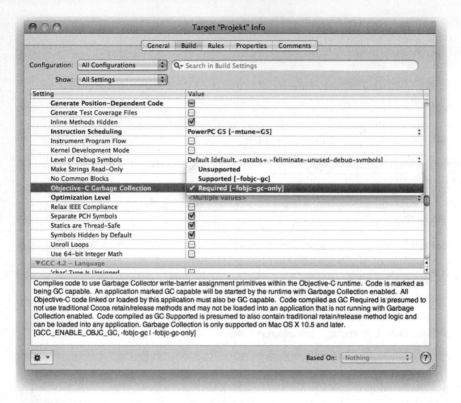

Figure 25-5. *Xcode's garbage collection option*

Properties

Dealing with ivars, getters, and setters takes an enormous amount of time and code. Consider the BMPerson class. All of the instance methods, except for init and dealloc, were concerned with accessing and mutating our instance variables:

```
#import <Cocoa/Cocoa.h>

@interface BMPerson : NSObject {
    NSString *name;
    NSUInteger age;
}

+ (BMPerson *)personWithName:(NSString *)aName age:(NSUInteger)anAge;
- (NSString *)name;
- (void)setName:(NSString *)aName;
- (NSUInteger)age;
- (void)setAge:(NSUInteger)anAge;

@end
```

Every time you add an ivar, you have to add two lines to your interface and as many as 14 lines to your implementation:

```
#import "BMPerson.h"

@implementation BMPerson

+ (BMPerson *)personWithName:(NSString *)aName age:(NSUInteger)anAge;
{
    BMPerson *newPerson = [[self alloc] init];

    [newPerson setName:aName];
    [newPerson setAge:anAge];

    return [newPerson autorelease];
}

- (id)init;
{
    if (![super init])
    return nil;

    name = nil;

    return self;
}

- (void)dealloc;
{
    [name release];
    name = nil;

    [super dealloc];
}

- (NSString *)name;
{
    return name;
}

- (void)setName:(NSString *)aName;
{
    if (name == aName)
        return;

    [name release];
    name = [aName retain];
}
```

```
- (NSUInteger)age;
{
    return age;

}

- (void)setAge:(NSUInteger)anAge;
{
    age = anAge;
}

@end
```

Worse yet, the more ivars you add, the more you're writing the same code over and over again.

Objective-C 2.0 introduces explicitly named properties via a compact header syntax:

```
#import <Cocoa/Cocoa.h>

@interface BMPerson : NSObject {
    NSString *name;
    NSUInteger age;
}

+ (BMPerson *)personWithName:(NSString *)aName age:(NSUInteger)anAge;

@property (retain) NSString *name;
@property (assign) NSUInteger age;

@end
```

That's nice, but what's really amazing is what this does for your implementation:

```
#import "BMPerson.h"

@implementation BMPerson

+ (BMPerson *)personWithName:(NSString *)aName age:(NSUInteger)anAge;
{
    BMPerson *newPerson = [[self alloc] init];
    newPerson.name = aName;
    newPerson.age = age;

    return [newPerson autorelease];
}

- (void)dealloc;
{
    [name release];
    name = nil;
```

```
    [super dealloc];
}

@synthesize name, age;

@end
```

That's a lot less code. For one thing, all the setter and getter method implementations have been replaced by one line:

```
@synthesize name, age;
```

That compiler directive inserts the standard implementations, keeping you from having to type them over and over again. The generated implementations are faster than the hand-written ones and are executed atomically, meaning they are thread-safe. Better results for less work? That's the Objective-C way.

Dot syntax, on the other hand, is decidedly not the Objective-C way, yet when it comes to accessing and mutating property values, the compactness of dot syntax is actually nicer than the readability of Objective-C syntax. Objective-C 2.0 gives you the best of both worlds. Now you can use dot notation and simple assignment to get and set properties:

```
BMPerson *worldsToughestProgrammer = [[BMPerson alloc] init];
worldsToughestProgrammer.name = @"Mike Lee";
NSLog(@"%@ is the world's toughest programmer.", worldsToughestProgrammer.name);
```

```
Mike Lee is the world's toughest programmer.
```

Notably, properties do not prevent you from using standard syntax:

```
[worldsToughestProgrammer setName:@"Mike Lee"];
```

Nor do they prevent you from using KVC syntax:

```
[worldsToughestProgrammer setValue:@"Mike Lee" forKey:@"name"];
```

Properties, like scalars, are automatically initialized to `nil`, so you don't have to do that in `init`, which means, in this case, you don't need `init` at all. You also don't have to explicitly `release` your pointers or remember to set them to `nil`. You can just set the property to `nil`, which will do both.

Should you decide to change the way a property behaves, you can just change the property attributes themselves. The compiler will do the right thing when it comes to the `@synthesize` directive. There are three classes of property behavior; see Table 25-4.

Table 25-4. *Objective-C 2.0 Property Attributes*

Behavior	Values	Notes
Memory management	retain, assign, copy	The default is assign.
Mutability	readonly, readwrite	The default is readwrite.
Thread safety	nonatomic	atomic is assumed.

The Objective-C way is to make things easy but to allow you to do things the hard way if necessary. Properties are the same way. If, for example, you have a property whose instance variable does not have the same name, you can connect the two explicitly. For example, if, in BMPerson, you called the property age but the ivar years, you could note this in your @synthesize directive:

```
@synthesize name, age = years;
```

If you wanted to override the setter of the age property to provide validation, all you would have to do is implement it:

```
- (void)setAge:(NSUInteger)anAge;
{
    if (anAge > 0 && anAge < 100)
        age = anAge;
}
```

Even though you've asked the compiler to synthesize this property, it will see that you've implemented it yourself and do the right thing.

In the converse of assigning an ivar, you can also, if necessary, explicitly assign a setter or getter in the property declaration:

```
@property (assign, getter=ageInYears) NSUInteger age;
```

Properties can be redeclared in subclasses or class extensions to, for example, change a property from readonly to readwrite. Properties can be marked with the garbage collector hints __weak and __strong. Finally, properties can be implemented with the directive @dynamic, which tells the compiler that the implementation will be provided at runtime. Core Data, for example, will dynamically generate property implementations.

64-bit/iPhone Changes

Macintosh processors are capable of operating in both 32-bit and 64-bit modes, and Snow Leopard includes both 32-bit and 64-bit versions of the kernel and system frameworks. Developers can compile their applications as both 32-bit and 64-bit, thanks to the same universal binary technology that allows applications to be compiled for both Intel and PowerPC.

Although many of the improvements of Objective-C 2.0 were able to be added in a completely backward-compatible way, other wish-list items were not possible without breaking binary compatibility. However, since the 64-bit and iPhone versions of the runtime were going to break compatibility anyway, the language designers added them to those versions of Objective-C 2.0.

Some features only available in 64-bit and on iPhone are

- Subclasses are not reliant on the offsets of their superclasses, which is an esoteric issue known as the "fragile base class" problem.

- Instance variables can be synthesized, eliminating the need to explicitly declare them for use in properties.

- The runtime has been improved with an optimized messaging system, which reduces overhead for increased performance.

Blocks

Blocks, known in other languages as closures or lambdas, encapsulate state and functionality into code objects. These objects can be passed to collections for parallel processing, declared statically for performance, or used inline for expressiveness. Though they are optimized for Objective-C, blocks are implemented in C and compatible with C++ and Objective-C++.

Blocks are declared like function pointers, but with ^ instead of *. The following code declares a block called test that takes three parameters and returns a BOOL:

```
BOOL (^test)(id object, NSUInteger index, BOOL *stop);
```

The body of the block is like the body of a function, with scope, parameters, and a return value. Blocks can be assigned to variables or used inline. Blocks can access variables normally according to their enclosing scope. However, should a block persist beyond the life of that scope, those variables will be seamlessly copied to keep the block intact.

To find uses for blocks, look at much of the API added in Snow Leopard. Blocks have found all sorts of uses. For example, you can use them to encapsulate arbitrary test logic for filtering collections:

```
NSArray *lemurNames = [NSArray arrayWithObjects:@"Ringtailed Lemur",
@"Golden Crowned Sifaka", @"Crowned Lemur", @"Coquerel's Sifaka", @"Indrii", nil];
test = ^(id object, NSUInteger index, BOOL *stop) {
    return [(NSString *)object hasSuffix:@"Lemur"];
};
NSIndexSet *lemurIndexes = [lemurNames indexesOfObjectsPassingTest:test];
```

```
<NSIndexSet: 0x100147770>[number of indexes: 2 (in 2 ranges), indexes: (0 2)]
```

As in Ruby, you can also use blocks inline:

```
NSIndexSet *lemurIndexes = [lemurNames indexesOfObjectsPassingTest:
    ^(id object, NSUInteger index, BOOL *stop) {
        return [(NSString *)object hasSuffix:@"Lemur"];
    }
];
```

Many of the classes in Foundation have added methods to take blocks whenever testing, comparing, or callbacks would otherwise be required. For example, NSArray declares the method used previously:

```
- (NSIndexSet *)indexesOfObjectsPassingTest:
    (BOOL (^)(id obj, NSUInteger idx, BOOL *stop))predicate;
```

Learn More

This quick-and-dirty review of Objective-C barely scratches the surface. There are several places to find a more in-depth study of Objective-C and Mac development in general. *Learn Objective-C on the Mac* by Mark Dalrymple and Scott Knaster (Apress, 2009) is a good start.

Apple's own documentation, available online and in Xcode's documentation manager, contains several documents worth reading:

Introduction to the Objective-C 2.0 Programming Language: As the title suggests, this document talks about the language and has been updated with the latest changes brought by Objective-C 2.0. It relates Objective-C to C and C++, including an extensive section on Objective-C++. It also discusses the runtime, the messaging system, and how Objective-C accomplishes much of its magic.

Introduction to Coding Guidelines for Cocoa: This is a style guide of accepted conventions for naming methods, functions, and variables. It also goes over acceptable abbreviations and acronyms and offers tips for developing your own frameworks. Whether you want to produce readable code, read someone else's code, or just generally look like you know what you're doing, this is a must-read.

Object-Oriented Programming with Objective-C: This relates object-oriented programming and Objective-C, giving each a fair explanation in terms of the other. It also discusses the Cocoa frameworks and how and why they relate to Objective-C.

Objective-C 2.0 Runtime Reference: This is detailed and specific documentation of the Mac OS X Objective-C runtime. Rather than discussing the high-level metaphors and philosophies of the runtime, its topics include changes to underlying structure and functions and incompatibilities and deprecations between the 32-bit and 64-bit versions of the application binary interface.

Introduction to Memory Management Programming Guide for Cocoa: This is an in-depth look at manual memory management in Objective-C. It looks at object ownership conventions, autorelease pools, how memory is managed in the API, and how memory management should be implemented in your own classes.

Introduction to Garbage Collection: This is a complete description of automated memory management in Objective-C 2.0. It discusses the essential things any Cocoa programmer must know about garbage collection, the architecture of the garbage collector, issues you're likely to discover while adopting garbage collection, and a summary of the garbage collection API.

Summary

Lots of languages can be used to develop applications for the Mac, and even more can be used to develop applications on the Mac. Yet Objective-C is Apple's choice for the future of native Mac programming. That's because, increasingly, Objective-C has been designed for exactly that purpose.

Since its origins at NeXT, Mac OS X has never been afraid to do things differently in its quest to do things better. Objective-C is an extension of this spirit. Yes, it takes a little bit of extra time to learn to do things this way, but that investment is quickly repaid many times over. Objective-C is to programming languages as the Macintosh is to computers: simply the best combination of speed, power, and productivity.

PART 8

■■■

Cross-Platform
Solutions

CHAPTER 26

■ ■ ■

Working with Microsoft Windows and Other Operating Systems

Occasionally while using Mac OS X, you may find it necessary to utilize resources intended for other operating systems. With Apple's new Intel-based computers combined with Mac OS X's ability to work with different file systems and networks protocols, today your Mac can run just about any software, including entire other operating systems. This chapter will show you how your Mac can do the following:

- Work with a wide range of files and file systems
- Run Microsoft Windows or other operating systems and applications on your Mac
- Access Microsoft Windows systems remotely

Working with Other File Types and File Systems

Long ago, working with files created on another operating system was troublesome. First, the files created by one application were often unreadable in any other application, so if an application were available only on one operating system, that file would be unreadable on another. Second, each operating system stored files in a way that made it difficult to move a file from one operating system to another. (This was back in the days when the most popular way to move a file from one computer to another was with a good ol' floppy disk.)

Today things are significantly better, but they're still not perfect. The most popular applications currently in use have both Microsoft Windows and Mac OS X counterparts that can freely share files back and forth. If a particular application isn't cross-platform, then it's possible either that the host application can save files in a format that is accessible by some other common application or that some native application can import a foreign file type.

File systems are a bit trickier. Although OS X is quite good at reading file systems used by other operating systems, other operating systems aren't quite as capable.

Sharing Files with Windows

With the prevalence of Microsoft Windows computers, unless you work and live in a very enlightened Mac-only universe, it's likely that sooner or later you'll need to share a file or two with a Windows system.

The types of files you can share are fairly vast and inclusive of most situations. For business productivity files, Microsoft Office formats tend to work fine on both Macs and Windows computers with one of the major office suites installed (including, of course, Microsoft Office, but also iWork '09 and OpenOffice.org). Any standard graphics formats, such as JPEG, GIF, PNG, and TIFF files (along with numerous others), will transfer from one system to another just fine. PDF files are also common among most operating systems. When it comes to audio files, MP3, AAC, and WAV are all just fine (FLAC and a number of other audio formats are equally cross-platform but require third-party software to play them).

Video is a bit trickier since video is generally comprised of mixing both audio and video formats. Apple's QuickTime is the best option for cross-platform video with a few important considerations. First, some QuickTime movies created on a Mac must be *flattened* (which means the audio and video are combined in the file in such a way that any external dependencies are removed) to work on the Web or on a Windows computer. This is done by using the Save As... command in QuickTime Player or using the Lillipot utility (www.qtbridge.com/lillipot/lillipot.html). Movies exported from iMovie and most other video-editing software will be flattened automatically. Second, QuickTime must be installed for them to play back properly. This isn't a big issue for most Windows computers, because many computer manufacturers include QuickTime by default, and it's a free and easy install for any Windows computers that don't already have it. QuickTime, however, isn't available for Linux or other alternative operating systems. MPEG-4 files (which is the default video format for QuickTime movies these days) work just fine too.

▌Note Windows Media files are popular; however, they pose a number of tricky problems. First, you will likely need a third-party QuickTime plug-in or stand-alone application to play them on your Mac. Filp4Mac WMV (www.flip4mac.com) is a third-party QuickTime plug-in that today is endorsed by Microsoft for playing Windows Media files, and VLC media player (www.videolan.org/vlc) is an open source stand-alone media player that supports many formats, including WMV. The bigger problem is that at this time neither of these products will support Windows Media protected by DRM (which is quite popular).

▌Note A QuickTime plug-in called Perian (http://perian.org) will greatly enhance QuickTime's abilities to play back a number of media types. QuickTime, combined with Flip4Mac and Perian, should enable you to play back the majority of video files you find on the Internet with the notable exceptions of RealVideo (you can download RealPlayer for the Mac at www.real.com) and protected Windows Media files.

Once you have your file, transferring it from one computer to another is the next trick. Transferring your file over a network circumvents most file system problems. By enabling Windows sharing on your Mac, you can allow a Windows system to simply browse your shared directory and copy the file from your Mac to a Windows computer. Also, your Mac can utilize any Windows file servers or shared directories. If you have MobileMe, you can place your files in your public iDisk folder that is accessible from the Web at http://public.me.com/*mobilemeusername*. Also, you can use any standard Internet file-sharing protocol. If, rather than using the network, you want to use a physical means of file transfer (such as external hard drive, thumb drive, and so on), then you will likely want to format the drive using the FAT32 file system, which will work with both Macs and Windows computers.

■**Tip** You can have easy access to your iDisk from your Windows computers by *mapping* your iDisk to a Windows drive (depending on your version of Windows, the instructions may be slightly different). Select Map Network Drive… from Windows Explorer (right-click the My Network Places or Network icon to reveal this command). This opens a dialog that allows you to select a drive letter and then a text file for the folder. In the text field, enter http://idisk.me.com/*mobilemeusername* and select the "Connect using different credentials" option (Windows 7) or click the "Connect using a different user name" link (Windows XP and Vista). Click the Finish button when everything is filled in and selected. (Windows 7 will prompt you for your login credentials after you click Finish; Windows XP and Vista will prompt you for this info when you click the "Connect using a different user name" link.) Upon success, you will be able to access your iDisk just like any other lettered drive in Windows.

■**Note** Windows computers do not support Apple's default file system (HFS+) without special third-party software. Additionally, Mac OS X currently supports NTFS (the Windows default file system) as read-only only, which makes it a bit limiting for file sharing (without the use of a third-party add-on like MacFUSE or Paragon's NTFS for Mac OS X). The FAT32 file system, however, is the old Windows default file system and has had good Mac support for many years (though FAT32 can't be used for Boot Camp partitions running Vista or Windows 7).

Running Microsoft Windows on Your Mac

Unfortunately, since between 80 and 90 percent of the world's desktops run some version of Microsoft Windows, sometimes you may need to use a Windows-only application or feature (Figure 26-1).

Figure 26-1. *Ugggh! World's best football (a.k.a., soccer) team needs better web developers!*

More than ten years ago, a highly innovative company called Connectix created a product called Virtual PC that allowed your Mac to run an emulated x86 system as a separate application. This x86 system allowed Mac users to run Microsoft Windows on their Macs. Although the performance was notably slow, it worked and ushered in the era of emulation on the Mac. Eventually, Virtual PC was purchased from Connectix by Microsoft (which continues to support Virtual PC but only for running on other Windows systems).

■**Note** Besides Virtual PC, Connectix also invented the QuickCam, which it sold to Logitech. After selling off QuickCam and Virtual PC (as well as selling its Virtual Game Station product to Sony, which promptly killed it), the company effectively called it quits in 2003. During its 15 years of existence, the company also introduced innovative techniques for taking advantage of virtual memory on the pre–OS X Mac platform.

■Note Emulation and virtualization seem similar in many cases but are quite different. Emulation (like the original Virtual PC) requires that the code being run actually be translated before being used. (Virtual PC used dynamic recompilation to translate x86 code to PowerPC code before the code could be run.) Virtualization, on the other hand, allows concurrent computer processes to run using the same hardware by partitioning the hardware's memory and processing power so that each process runs entirely independently of every other. Common "virtualization" software that runs on your Mac today actually is a hybrid of both virtualization and emulation.

■Note Since Tiger, Mac OS X actually contains its own emulation software that, like the original Virtual PC, uses dynamic recompilation. This software (called Rosetta) does the opposite, though. Rather than translate x86 code into PowerPC code, it makes sure old PowerPC code on your Mac runs on the new x86 architecture. Beginning with Snow Leopard, however, Rosetta is an optional component and may not be installed by default.

Upon switching to an Intel-based platform, Apple changed everything. Today not only is it possible to run Windows natively on your Apple computer, but a new range of virtualization products are now available to Mac users that run extremely well with little performance loss.

As a Mac user (provided you are using an Intel-based Mac), you have a number of options for running Windows on your computer. We'll quickly go over each of these and point out the pros and cons of each of them.

Boot Camp

Shortly after Apple started shipping Intel-based computers, it released a utility called Boot Camp (which you had to seek out on its web site and download as a beta). Beginning with Leopard, Boot Camp is included along with Mac OS X. To get it up and running, you can use the Boot Camp Assistant that is located in the Applications/Utilities folder.

Running Boot Camp allows you to effectively turn your Mac computer into a full-fledged Windows machine. The advantage of this is that all your Mac's hardware will become dedicated to running Windows. One significant issue here for most people, which is not available through any current virtualization or emulation methods, is that running in Boot Camp gives you full video acceleration, which is a must for certain applications (including most Windows gaming).

Boot Camp has a few disadvantages as well, though:

- You must reboot your computer to switch between OS X and Windows.

- You must create a dedicated partition on an internal hard drive to install Windows on.

■**Note** You cannot install Windows on an external hard drive using Boot Camp.

- You must have a full version of Windows XP SP2 or newer to install Windows with Boot Camp.

■**Note** When you begin to install Boot Camp with the Boot Camp Assistant, you will be prompted to print out an Installation and Setup Guide. We strongly recommend printing out these 26 pages, as they contain step-by-step installation instructions as well as valuable troubleshooting, usage, and upgrade advice. Also, keep in mind that this information won't be available during the installation process unless you print it out, since your computer will be otherwise occupied (with the installation and all that).

Parallels Desktop and VMware Fusion

Shortly after the release of Intel-based Macs, the buzz started increasing about a company called Parallels (www.parallels.com/products/desktop) that was making a virtualization product for the new Macs that would allow one to run Windows and other x86 operating systems on the new Macs under OS X with exceptional performance. Sure enough, when Parallels Desktop for the Mac was released, it did what it said it would. Soon, VMware, a company that has a long history of virtualization, announced it too was building a product for the Mac; VMware has since released Fusion (www.vmware.com/products/fusion; Figure 26-2) with similar capabilities to Parallels Desktop. These two products, although slightly different, work (from a user's perspective) so similarly that it's hard to pick one to recommend over the other. Overall, they are both excellent.

■**Note** One other virtualization option available today is Sun's VirtualBox (www.virtualbox.org). While it's currently not as feature-rich as either Parallels Desktop or VMware Fusion, it's actively in development and improving at a fast pace. Also, it's an open source product that is free for personal use. (Sun also offers a closed source commercial version of VirtualBox with added features.)

Figure 26-2. *Microsoft Windows 7 running in VMware Fusion*

Running either Parallels Desktop or VMware Fusion has some obvious advantages:

- They run on top of Mac OS X, providing you with the ability to switch quickly and easily from one environment to another without rebooting; in fact, both Parallels Desktop and VMware Fusion have modes that allow you to run Windows applications right next to Mac OS X applications.

- They can both run other operating systems besides Windows, allowing you to run Linux, FreeBSD, Solaris x86, and many other operating systems (Figure 26-3).

- You can run multiple instances of one or many operating systems at the same time.

- They are both reasonably priced, well-supported, easy-to-use products that are quickly evolving with new features and better performance.

Despite the overwhelming advantages, there are a few disadvantages to both of these virtualization products:

- To allow them to run on top of Mac OS X, many hardware devices need to be emulated. Although this largely doesn't affect performance much for most devices, it has a very big effect on video acceleration performance.

Note VMware Fusion 2.0 and Parallels Desktop 4.0 both support DirectX 9, making it possible to use applications that require it. However, there is still a rather significant performance hit. As both of these products evolve, it is likely that video performance will continue to improve, but it's still a big consideration for some (i.e., gamers!).

- You will need a copy of Windows or whatever operating system you choose to run. However, unlike Boot Camp, Parallels Desktop and VMware Fusion allow you to use older products and upgrades.

Figure 26-3. *Ubuntu Linux running in VMware Fusion*

CodeWeavers CrossOver (and Wine)

One other option for running Windows applications (without Windows) is CodeWeavers CrossOver (www.codeweavers.com/products/cxmac). CrossOver is a commercially enhanced and supported product based on the open source Wine (Wine Is Not an Emulator) project (www.winehq.org). What's interesting about this is that rather than rely on Windows to run Windows-based applications, Wine attempts to duplicate the underlying libraries and frameworks used by the applications in order to run them natively on a different host operating system. The advantages of CrossOver over other options are as follows:

- It's a less expensive option that doesn't require you to purchase Windows.

- Nothing is emulated, so the overall performance is very good, even for applications requiring video acceleration. (It's a great way to play supported games like Half-Life 2 on your Mac.)

- It's fairly easy to install and use.

Note The ease-of-use claim is made specifically for the commercial CrossOver product. Wine requires some work to get up and running, and it isn't as easy to use once it's set up either (but it is free and does work).

That said, it has some significant disadvantages. The biggest one is that not all Windows apps will work with CrossOver, and some that do exhibit some significant bugs. So if you need to run one or two Windows applications that are supported by CrossOver (or Wine), then this is a good way to go; if, however, you need to run a wide range of Windows applications, one of the other solutions is likely a better option.

Accessing a Windows Computer Remotely

Another, very different way of using Windows on your Mac is to actually connect to another computer running Windows using Microsoft's Remote Desktop Connection (RDC). With RDC (available for free from www.microsoft.com/mac), you can actually use a remote Windows computer from your Mac as if you were sitting right in front of it (Figure 26-4).

Figure 26-4. *Windows computer accessible from a Mac using RDC*

Not only does RDC allow you to access a remote Windows computer, but it also allows you to copy and paste files and move them back and forth from your Mac to the connected Windows computer. You can even print items on your connected Windows computer to the printer connected to your Mac. Of course, you can also take full advantage of any application installed on the remote Windows computer.

The downside to RDC is that you need to have access to a computer running Windows. And of course, depending on the network connection between your Mac and the Windows computer, your performance may vary.

Summary

As any Mac user will tell you, Macs are just better computers with a better operating system. With the switch to the Intel architecture, a Mac not only can run the best operating system (Mac OS X, of course), but it is more than capable of slipping over into the world of Windows when necessary. Not only do apps such as Boot Camp, VMware Fusion, and Parallels Desktop provide compatibility when necessary, but for people switching from Windows computers to Macs, they provide a way to maintain your investment in Windows software while you discover the advantages of using a Mac.

PART 9

Appendixes

Appendixes

■ ■ ■

What's New in Snow Leopard?

When Steve Jobs got up and announced Snow Leopard at Worldwide Developers Conference back in 2008, we were told that the focus of Snow Leopard would be on performance and efficiency. Most of the changes would be "under the hood," and the end user would see few new features. In general, this holds true today, but a number of differences both in Snow Leopard and the included applications are still worth mentioning.

User Changes in the System

As promised, not a whole lot has changed dramatically in the system as far as how users interact with Mac OS X from Leopard to Snow Leopard. However, some user-focused changes are worth mentioning here.

Overall Appearance

Overall, many interface elements have taken on a slightly darker appearance. It's a subtle but noticeable difference that gives a slightly more professional appearance, and it unifies the overall look a bit more than in the past.

Improved Stacks

Stacks have been improved to provide a few more view options, and most importantly, you can now open subfolders from within each stack's Grid view.

Exposé Refinements

Exposé has seen a number of improvements, including a much more appealing way of showing all the active windows. Most interestingly however, Exposé can now be triggered from the icon of any running application on the dock to reveal all windows for that particular application.

Tweaked System Preferences

Some of the system preferences have changed, and not just a few small options here and there. For example, the International preference pane has been replaced with the Language & Text preference pane, providing a whole set of new text features to OS X. This change and more are covered in Chapter 4.

Application Enhancements

Beyond the changes to the system itself, Snow Leopard introduces a number of application updates and improvements.

Mail, iCal, and Address Book

Mail, iCal, and Address Book have all been updated with native support for connecting with Microsoft's Exchange Server 2007 (and later). This allows Snow Leopard to seamlessly integrate with many corporate environments without additional software.

Safari 4

Snow Leopard ships with Apple's latest version of Safari. Safari 4 offers a faster and overall improved web-browsing experience.

Image Capture

Image Capture has been overhauled in Snow Leopard, making most user tasks easier and faster. On the surface, this comes at the cost of removing the ability to send downloaded images to an application automatically after download (which was a nice, useful feature). However, Image Capture now allows you to create Image Capture plug-ins from the Automator application, so you can add this functionality and much more.

QuickTime

QuickTime has been updated with new features and a new interface. Additionally, there is no longer a separate QuickTime Pro upgrade. All the Pro features are now available by default.

Xcode Tools

Xcode, Interface Builder, and the associated developer tools have all been updated to help developers build better applications faster and easier. These tools include the necessary frameworks and utility additions to allow developers to take advantage of many of the new "under the hood" features introduced in Snow Leopard.

Under the Hood

When Snow Leopard was announced, most of the significant planned changes were said to be "under the hood." Of the many changes, a few are quite significant.

Intel Only

Snow Leopard is written for x86 architectures only. If you have an older PowerPC system, it seems you're going to have to be happy with Leopard for the foreseeable future. Does Apple have a secret version of Snow Leopard running on PowerPC? We can't say for sure, but if it does, it may never leave the secret lab buried deep under 1 Infinite Loop. That said, if you have an Intel system, this means generally better optimization and faster execution of the system, all while occupying less space on your hard drive.

Grand Central

Grand Central is a group of technologies that allows applications to easily and effectively take advantage of the multiple processing cores available in today's computers. Developers utilizing Grand Central technologies are able to greatly increase the performance of their applications.

OpenCL

OpenCL is another Snow Leopard technology that allows developers to increase the performance of their applications. It does this by utilizing the power of today's graphics processing units (GPUs) for specific tasks that usually would be carried out in the CPU.

64-bit

Snow Leopard itself is written to fully take advantage 64-bit processors (Core 2 Duos and higher). This allows Snow Leopard to theoretically utilize up to 16 TB of RAM (though no available Mac hardware currently supports that amount). Still, many servers and high-performance computers will benefit from the ability to use more RAM than they have been able to in the past.

APPENDIX B

■■■

Installing and Setting Up Snow Leopard

Whether you are doing a fresh install or upgrading from an older version of Mac OS X, installing Mac OS X is easier than ever with Snow Leopard. To get started, insert the Mac OS X Snow Leopard Install DVD into your DVD drive on your Mac, and restart your computer from this disc (to start up your computer from a bootable CD or DVD, just hold down the C key on your computer as it starts up). If you simply upgrading, you can just insert the DVD and run the Snow Leopard installer to get started. The installer will walk you through the upgrade process in a few steps and get you taking advantage of the new features of Snow Leopard in no time. If you are looking to do do more then a simple upgrade, or are seeking some specific information about a certain upgrade step just follow along with this chapter.

■**Note** Snow Leopard should run on any of Apple's Intel-based Mac systems, from the Mac mini up to the Mac Pro. However, some behind-the-scenes features are not available on some Intel systems. For example, while Snow Leopard will take advantage of the 64-bit processing power, you need at least an Intel Core 2 Duo processor (initial Intel-based Macs used the Intel Core Duo and Solo without the "2"; these are 32-bit processors). If you are using a PowerPC-based computer, you'll have to stick with Leopard (Mac OS X 10.5), since Snow Leopard is x86 only. (This is a small price to pay for progress, and your PowerPC system should continue to run just as well as it has in the past, just as our old Macintosh with a Motorola 68030 processor still works just fine running Mac OS System 7—of course, that small monochrome monitor from the '90s has a bit of burn-in, ironically left from the After Dark screen saver it runs).

When the system starts from the DVD, you are first presented with a screen (Figure B-1) asking you to select the primary language of your choosing (for the purposes of this book, we chose English). Once you select your language of choice, you're presented with a Welcome screen (Figure B-2).

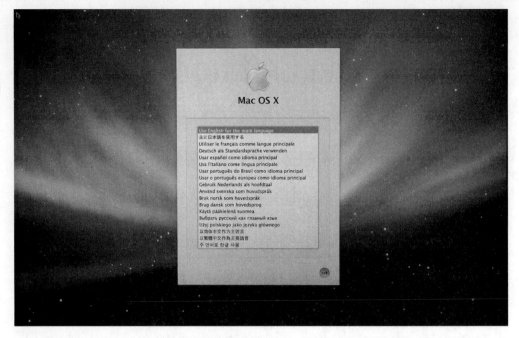

Figure B-1. *The first step when you boot from the DVD is to choose your language of choice. This will be the initial default language of your system.*

Figure B-2. *The Mac OS X Installer screen*

The initial install screen's appearance will depend on whether you booted from the DVD (Figure B-3), or you just ran the installer from the DVD (Figure B-2). If you wish to access the installers Utilities menu you must boot from the DVD (clicking Utilities... button shown in Figure B-2 will walk you through restarting your computer). Two of the utilities available from the Utilities menu (once you restart from the DVD) may be specifically useful as you prepare to install Snow Leopard: Disk Utility… and Restore System From Backup…. You can use the Disk Utility… option to erase, format, or partition a hard drive prior to your install (we cover these tasks in Chapter 6). The Restore System From Backup… utility begins a special installation in which it restores any data from a Time Machine backup during installation. In the unfortunate event of a drive failure, this is the best option to restore your past information into a new hard drive. (If you miss this option, there will be other opportunities to restore information from a Time Machine backup or transfer information from another computer.)

■**Note** If you are planning on restoring your system over your wireless network (i.e., from a Time Capsule backup), you will first need to connect to the wireless network using the AirPort menu on the right side of the menu bar.

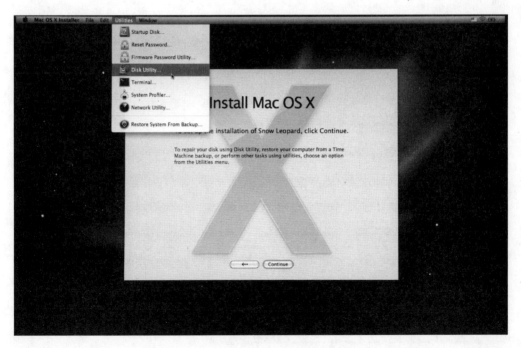

Figure B-3. *The Mac OS X Installer's Utilities menu makes a number of handy utilities available from the install disc.*

Once you are ready to move on with your installation, click the Continue button at the bottom of the Welcome screen, then read through and accept the software agreement (Figure B-4). After accepting the software agreement, you are presented with the Install screen (Figure B-5).

■**Note** The Mac OS X Installer for Snow Leopard has been simplified significantly from previous installers. On one hand, this makes 90 percent of all installations faster and easier, since the default install is usually the right choice. On the other hand, a number of occasionally useful (yet also often confusing) options are no longer available. Two such options are the "Archive and Install" and "Erase and Install" options (these were often referred to as the "clean install" options.) To do an Erase and Install today, you must first pay a visit to Disk Utility to erase your hard drive yourself. As for the Archive and Install option, it seems Apple feels taking advantage of Time Machine and using the Restore System From Backup… utility is a better option (though not quite the same as the Archive and Install).

■**Caution** Installing Snow Leopard on top of a previous Mac OS X system will automatically upgrade the system while preserving user and application data. However, some system-level customizations may be lost during the upgrade process; this is especially true of any changes you have made within the UNIX layer of Mac OS X.

Figure B-4. *You must accept Apple's software agreement to continue.*

Figure B-5. *The Mac OS X Installer's Install screen allows you to choose the volume you wish to install Snow Leopard on.*

At the Install screen, you must first choose which volume you wish to install Snow Leopard upon. Then you can either click the Install button to begin the default install, or select the Customize button to fine-tune which Snow Leopard components get installed (Figure B-6).

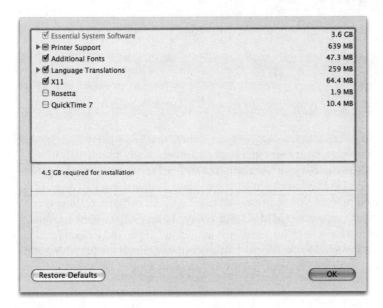

Figure B-6. *Selecting to customize your installation allows you to choose a number of optional items to install.*

If you choose to customize your install, you will have the option of installing a number of Snow Leopard components, including additional drivers for printers, extra fonts, and support for a wide range of languages. Additionally, you can choose to install X11 and Rosetta. X11 is an older GUI system that is necessary to run some UNIX- and Linux-based graphical applications. Rosetta is a technology that allows you to run Mac OS X applications that were written for the PowerPC to run on your x86 (a.k.a., Intel-based) computer.

Once you've finished customizing your install or deciding to use the default options, click the Install button to begin the install (Figure B-7). From start to finish, the actual install takes a bit of time (usually around 30 minutes, but sometimes quicker, sometimes longer; it's easily enough time to go make and enjoy a cup of tea).

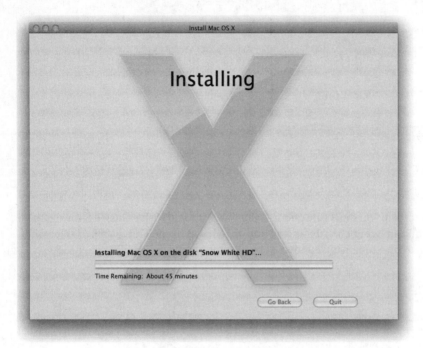

Figure B-7. *The installer shows you the progress of the install. This usually takes awhile to complete.*

After the installation completes, your computer restarts automatically after briefly displaying a short message letting you know your installation completed successfully (Figure B-8).

After the restart, a short movie plays, welcoming you to Snow Leopard in a vast array of languages. Once the movie completes, you're prompted to set up your computer. However, if you're upgrading from a previous version of Mac OS X, many of these steps will be passed over (since this information will have been imported automatically). If you did a *clean install* of Snow Leopard (where you installed Snow Leopard on an empty volume), the first thing you will need to do is select your preferred language (Figure B-9) and the type of keyboard you are using (Figure B-10).

Figure B-8. *When the install is complete, you receive a message letting you know everything installed correctly. After a moment, if you don't click the Restart button, the computer will restart automatically (so if you walk away for too long during your install, you'll miss this).*

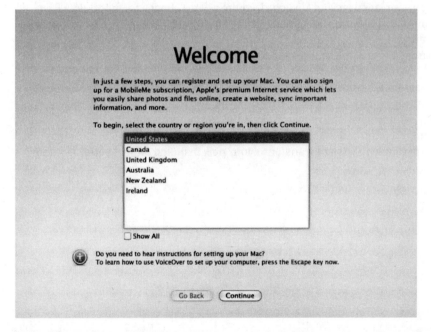

Figure B-9. *After the restart (and a short movie welcoming you to Snow Leopard), you may need to set up a few additional items, beginning with selecting your country and preferred language. (Not all of these steps are necessary if you are upgrading, though.)*

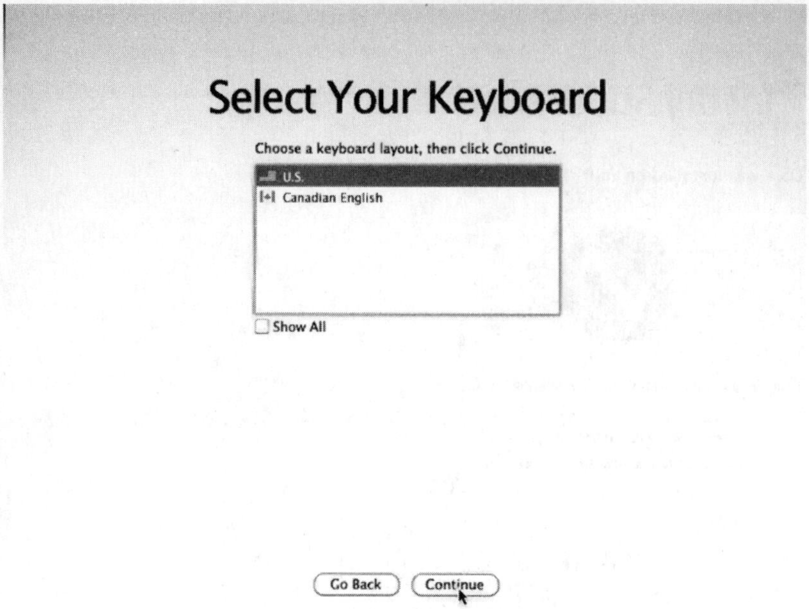

Select Your Keyboard

Choose a keyboard layout, then click Continue.

- U.S.
- ▐◆▌ Canadian English

☐ Show All

(Go Back)   (Continue)

Figure B-10. *After you select your country and language, you're asked what type of keyboard you are using (the options depend on the language you selected).*

After selecting your language and keyboard, you're given a change to import data from another Mac computer, a volume, or a Time Machine backup (Figure B-11). (This is your second chance to import info from a Time Machine volume.) If you wish to bypass this step, you can import info from any of these sources at a later time using the Migration Assistant utility (located in /Applications/Utilities/).

If you choose to import information from another Mac, either you will need to connect the two computers together by using a FireWire cable (Figure B-12), or you will need to connect to another Macintosh over the network. Once the computers are connected (or if you are choosing to import information from another attached volume), you will be prompted to select what information you wish to transfer to your new installed Snow Leopard system (Figure B-13).

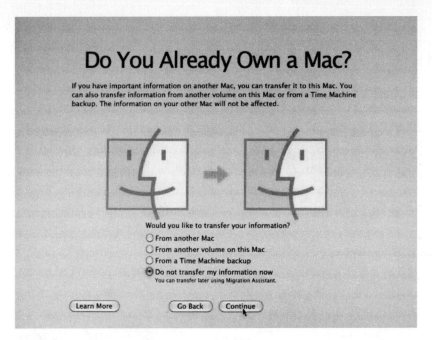

Figure B-11. *This step offers you several options for importing data from a number of different sources.*

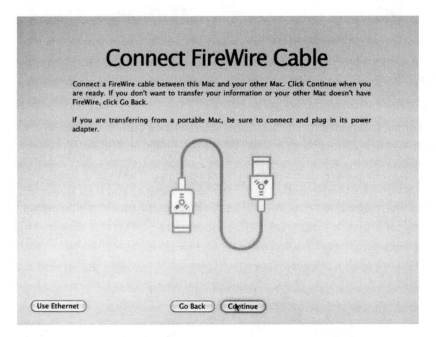

Figure B-12. *If you choose to import information directly from another Mac, you will be prompted to connect the two Macs together using a FireWire cable. (Alternately, you can connect over the network to another computer.)*

Note If you are transferring data from another Mac over the network, you will be given a passcode and instructions to run the Migration Assistant on the other computer. You'll need to enter the code to begin the process.

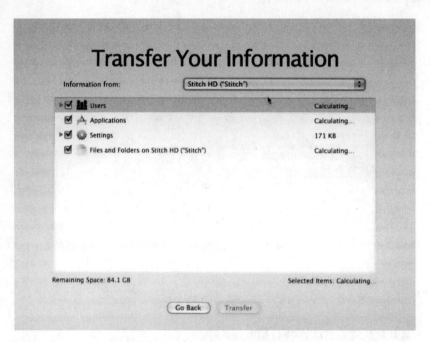

Figure B-13. *After you've established the source of the data you are transferring over to your new install, you're asked what information you want to import.*

If you are importing data from a Time Machine backup (and didn't use the Restore System From Backup… option earlier), you must first select the Time Machine backup you wish to use (Figure B-14).

If you import data from another data source, that information will be used throughout the remaining setup steps (so if you imported your network information, that will be used). Otherwise, unless you have already done so, you will be prompted next to connect to the Internet (Figure B-15).

Figure B-14. *If you wish to import information from a Time Machine backup, you must select the Time Machine volume you wish to use.*

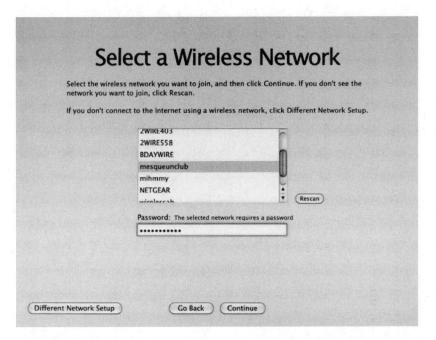

Figure B-15. *If you haven't done so already, you will now be prompted to connect to the Internet (here we're being asked to join a wireless network).*

Once you have connected to the Internet, you can begin the registration process. First, you're asked to enter your Apple ID if you have one (Figure B-16). If you do, your registration information will be filled in based on the information Apple already has. If you don't have an Apple ID, you can simply select Continue to skip this step.

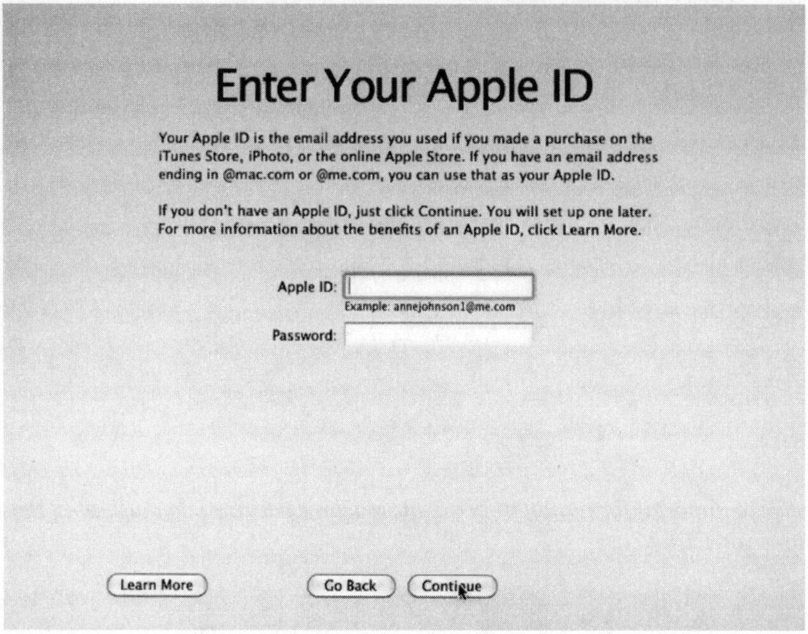

Figure B-16. *Once you have connected to the Internet, you're prompted to enter your Apple ID if you have one.*

The registration is a two-step process. First, you're asked for your name and contact information (Figure B-17). Next, you are asked some general questions about how you will be using your computer (Figure B-18).

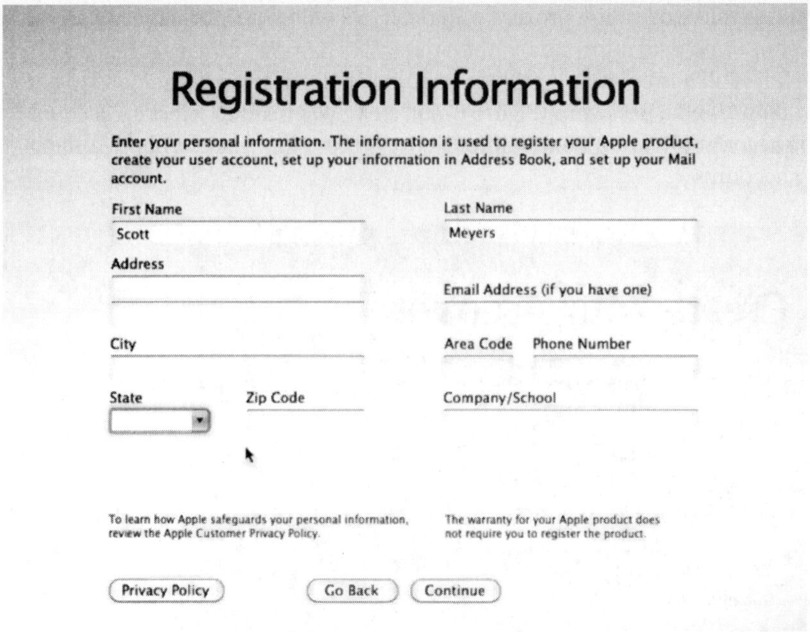

Figure B-17. *The first page of the registration asks you some basic information about you.*

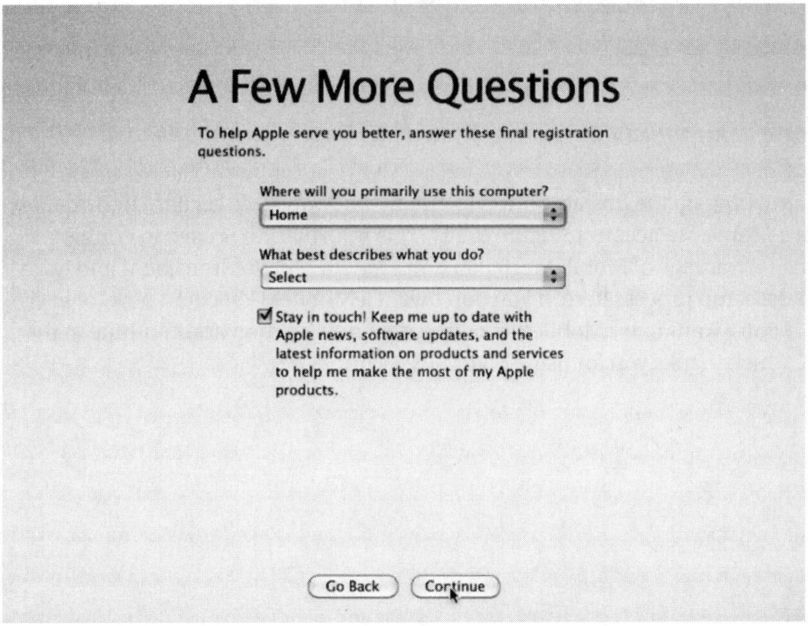

Figure B-18. *Apple also asks some additional questions about how you generally use your computer.*

Once you complete the registration process, you need to set up your primary user account (if you upgraded or imported user information, this step will be bypassed). This initial account that you set up will have full administrator privileges. To create this account, you need to enter a full name, a short name, and a password (Figure B-19). Next, you need to select an account image to use for the account (Figure B-20). Chapter 4 covers more information about adding and setting up user accounts.

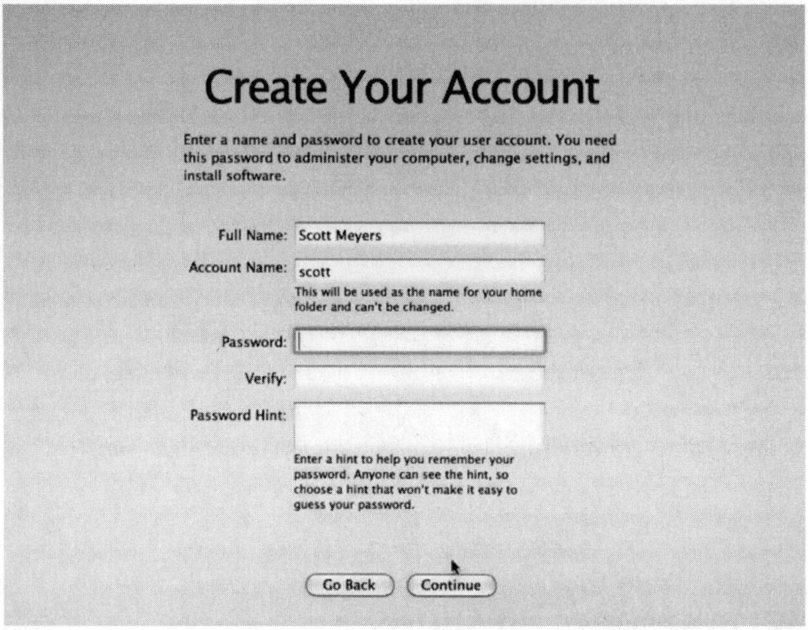

Create Your Account

Enter a name and password to create your user account. You need this password to administer your computer, change settings, and install software.

Full Name: Scott Meyers

Account Name: scott
This will be used as the name for your home folder and can't be changed.

Password:

Verify:

Password Hint:

Enter a hint to help you remember your password. Anyone can see the hint, so choose a hint that won't make it easy to guess your password.

(Go Back)   (Continue)

Figure B-19. *Creating your account during startup if you didn't import user information*

The final step in setting up the first account is to enter your MobileMe account information, if you already have a MobileMe account (Figure B-21). This information is used to configure applications that take advantage of MobileMe. If you don't have a MobileMe account and want one, you can begin the setup process here. If you don't want a MobileMe account now (or ever), you can select the "I don't want to try MobileMe for free right now" option and continue to the final set-up screen, which thanks you for using Mac OS X (Figure B-22).

Figure B-20. *After you select a username and password, you are asked to choose an image for your account. (If you have an iSight camera built in to your computer or monitor, you may use it to capture an account image.)*

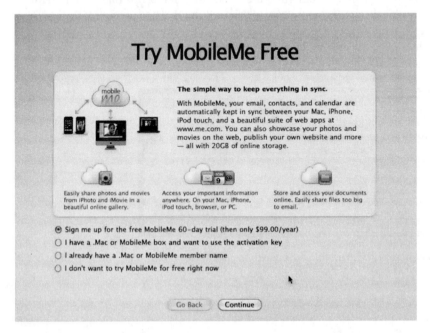

Figure B-21. *The final step in setting up your account is to enter your MobileMe information. If you don't have a MobileMe account, you can set one up from here.*

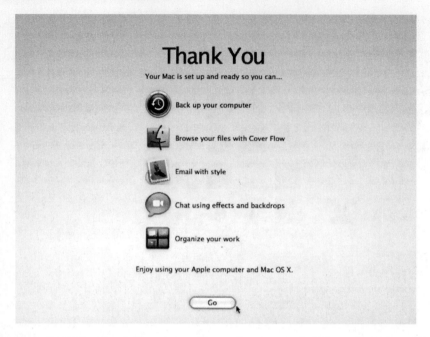

Figure B-22. *The Thank You screen tells you that you made it through the Mac OS X setup.*

After you click Go on the Thank You screen, your computer is all ready to go. If you have more than one volume attached to your computer, one other dialog box may pop up right away: the Time Machine dialog (Figure B-23), which asks if you'd like to use one of the attached volumes as a Time Machine backup location. (If you don't have any extra volumes attached to your computer, this dialog will appear the first time you plug one in.) Either way, you are now ready to go with your freshly installed Snow Leopard operating system (Figure B-24).

Figure B-23. *If you have any additional volumes connected to your computer, you may be asked if you'd like to use one of them as a Time Machine backup.*

Figure B-24. *Snow Leopard, freshly installed and ready to go*

■ ■ ■

Our Favorite Applications

Today, all new Macs come with Snow Leopard (along with its accompanying applications) and iLife '09. In the past, a similar offering has been included with new Macs, and this selection of applications covers many of the tasks that most people use their computers for today. However, people often have tasks that make a different application necessary (or at least desirable).

Table C-1 offers a selection of our recommended applications for various tasks. It's worth pointing out that many more applications are available, and it's quite probable that you'll find an application for a specific task that you like better than the ones listed here.

■**Tip** Many places on the Web offer lists of applications available for your Mac. Here are some good places to start: MacUpdate at www.macupdate.com; Version Tracker at www.versiontracker.com/macosx; and Apple's Downloads site at www.apple.com/downloads.

■**Note** Lists like this are a snapshot in time. New products pop up overnight, and old ones tend to fade away. Because of this, we can't guarantee anything about this list, including the costs, URLs, or even the continued existence of the products mentioned here.

Table C-1. *Our Favorite Applications*

Application	Type	Cost	URL	Notes
Internet				
Camino	Web browser	Free	`http://caminobrowser.org`	Camino is a full-featured, Mac-only web browser based on Mozilla.
Colloquy	IRC	Free	`http://colloquy.info`	Colloquy is a full-featured IRC client for Mac OS X that provides an excellent interface, plug-ins, and AppleScript support.
Cyberduck	FTP and more	Free	`http://cyberduck.ch`	Cyberduck is a free, open source client for FTP, SFTP, WebDAV, and more. It's full-featured and frequently updated.
Firefox	Web browser	Free	`http://firefox.com`	Mozilla Firefox is the most popular, open source, cross-platform web browser on the market. It has a vibrant plug-in community, making it the favorite of power users who want to completely customize their browsing experience.
NetNewsWire	RSS	Free	`www.newsgator.com`	NetNewsWire is an RSS reader that provides a great way to manage and read a large number of RSS feeds.
Skype	Chat	Free download	`http://skype.com`	Skype's VOIP client lets you chat with other Skype users in voice or text, but more importantly, it lets you call any phone number for pennies.
Transmission	BitTorrent	Free	`www.transmissionbt.com`	Transmission is an easy-to-use BitTorrent client for Mac OS X.
Transmit	FTP and more	$29.95	`www.panic.com/transmit`	Transmit is one of the premier, commercial Mac OS X FTP clients with all the features one could ask of an FTP client wrapped in a beautiful interface.
Unison	Usenet	$24.95	`www.panic.com/unison`	Unison, brought to you by the same people who bring you Transmit, is a full-featured application for browsing and contributing to Usenet newsgroups.
Text				
BBEdit	Text editor	$125	`www.barebones.com/products/bbedit/`	In a crowded field of excellent text editors for Mac OS X, BBEdit was one of the first and remains one of the best dedicated text editors available anywhere.
Changes	Diff tool	$49.95	`http://changesapp.com`	Changes is the professional, third-party alternative to Apple's free FileMerge utility for comparing two documents.

Application	Type	Cost	URL	Notes
HexEdit	Hex editor	Free	`http:// hexedit.sourceforge.net`	Hex editors are a specialized form of text editors; they peek into application files and edit them on a very low level. HexEdit is a free, open source hex editor that is under constant development.
Hex Fiend	Hex editor	Free	`http://ridiculousfish.com/ hexfiend/`	Hex Fiend is a fast, efficient hex editor that handles huge files.
TextMate	Text editor	$39 (~$54)	`http://macromates.com`	TextMate is a newer dedicated text editor for Mac OS X; it has a clean interface and lots of power. If you need a powerful text editor, you should definitely give this a try.
TextWrangler	Text editor	Free	`www.barebones.com/ products/textwrangler/`	TextWrangler is BBEdit's little brother. While it lacks many of the features of BBEdit, it is a capable text editor, and it's free.
VoodooPad	Text editor	Free–$49.95	`http://flyingmeat.com/ voodoopad/`	Flying Meat's VoodooPad is a simple, wiki-like document editor. It's like a text editor that makes it easy to branch into new topics. Just highlight a word or phrase to turn it into a link. Every instance of the highlighted text will then link to a new page. This format is convenient for certain types of documents. VoodooPad comes in three versions, from the free Lite version to the $49.95 Pro version.

Web Development and Social Networking

Application	Type	Cost	URL	Notes
Blogo	Blogging tool	$25	`www.drinkbrainjuice.com/ blogo`	Blogo is a multi-account blog editor with a smooth, intuitive interface.
Coda	Web editor	$99	`www.panic.com/coda`	Coda is an application for web developers that provides a number of web-development tools in a single tool. It offers everything you need, from writing and editing HTML, to building style sheets, to managing entire web sites both locally and remotely.
CSSEdit	CSS editor	$29.95 (~$39)	`http://macrabbit.com/ cssedit`	CSSEdit is fantastic tool to help web developers create CSS files for web sites.
Dreamweaver	Web editor	$399	`www.adobe.com/dreamweaver`	Adobe Dreamweaver is one of the premier, commercial web-development tools. It has the added bonus of integrating nicely with the rest of Adobe's graphics and web tools.

Continued

Table C-1. *(Continued)*

Application	Type	Cost	URL	Notes
ecto	Blogging tool	$19.95	http://illuminex.com/ecto	ecto is a desktop blogging tool for creating and managing blog posts for a large number of blogs and blogging platforms.
Espresso	Web editor	$59.95 (~$78)	http://macrabbit.com/espresso	Espresso is a newer web editor that provides excellent, web-centric, text-editing capabilities, along with project-management and FTP capabilities.
MarsEdit	Blogging tool	$29.95	www.red-sweater.com/marsedit	MarsEdit is another excellent desktop blogging tool.
RapidWeaver	Web editor	$79	http://realmacsoftware.com/rapidweaver/	Realmac's RapidWeaver is a web editor and social network in one. You can create your site from one of 40 templates, customize your content with plug-ins, hand-tweak RapidWeaver's standards-compliant XHTML and CSS, and then show off your masterpiece, or find inspiration, with RapidWeaver Showcase.
TweetDeck	Twitter tool	Free	www.tweetdeck.com	TweetDeck is an awesome tool for those who use Twitter a lot. It provides a huge set of features to make browsing, searching, and reading tweets easy and effective. TweetDeck is unique on this list, in that rather than being written for the Mac specifically, TweetDeck is an Adobe AIR application.
Tweetie	Twitter tool	$14.95 (or free with ads)	www.atebits.com/tweetie-mac/	Tweetie is a new desktop Twitter client for Mac OS X. It supports multiple accounts and a host of features, and it looks good too. (There's also a version of Tweetie just for the iPhone.)
Twitterrific	Twitter tool	$14.95 (or free with ads)	http://iconfactory.com/software/twitterrific	If you prefer a full-featured Twitter client with a cleaner, more integrated, experience, then Twitterrific is worth checking out.
Video and Multimedia				
CoverSutra	iTunes add-on	$19.95	www.sophiestication.com/coversutra	CoverSutra is a handy application that allows you to control iTunes from any application. It provides some added features as well, such as music search from your menu bar, and more.

Application	Type	Cost	URL	Notes
Final Cut Express	Video editor	$199	www.apple.com/ finalcutexpress	If you tried iMovie '09 and it just didn't do the job for you, then try Final Cut Studio or Final Cut Express. Final Cut Express provides a lot of video-editing power in a traditional, nonlinear, video-editing environment. For full-on, professional video editing, Final Cut Studio will set you back $1,299.
Flip4Mac	Video player/ plug-in	Free– $179	http:// origin.telestream.net/ flip4mac-wmv/ overview.htm	Flip4Mac is a media player and QuickTime plug-in that allows for the playback of many WMV files (the default movie format for Microsoft Windows). However, it doesn't currently allow playback of WMV files that are protected with DRM. Besides the free Player version, a number of advanced products are available for working with WMV files.
HandBrake	Video converter	Free	http://handbrake.fr	HandBrake is a handy tool for converting DVDs to other video formats, such as MPEG-4, which is suitable for transferring to your iPod or iPhone. One catch here is that HandBrake no longer decrypts encrypted DVDs (most commercial DVDs) natively; however, it works with VLC to accomplish this.
Perian	QuickTime plug-in	Free	http://perian.org	Perian declares itself as the Swiss Army knife for QuickTime by adding support for a wide range of media formats to QuickTime.
VLC media player	Video player	Free	www.videolan.org/vlc	While QuickTime does a great job of playing back media files, occasionally you'll find a file that won't work no matter what you do. In such cases, VLC will manage where QuickTime fails. On top of that, VLC has a number of nice features that QuickTime lacks.
Graphics				
Aperture	Image-management tool	$199	www.apple.com/aperture	Aperture is an image-management application from Apple that is designed for professional, digital-imaging workflow and management. With a sleek interface and powerful RAW editing tools, it has ushered in a new wave of photo-management tools.
Graphic Converter X	Graphic converter	$34.95	www.lemkesoft.com	For light editing and batch conversions, GraphicConverter X is a favorite among many.

Continued

Table C-1. *(Continued)*

Application	Type	Cost	URL	Notes
icns2icon	Graphic converter	Free	http://osxiconeditor.phatcode.net/icns2icon.html	After creating an ICNS file, the first thing you'll notice is that you can't actually set it as an icon. Dropping an ICNS file on this free tool will replace its generic icon with the file itself. You can then use the icon in the usual way: copying and pasting it between info panels.
Illustrator	Illustration tool	$599	www.adobe.com/illustrator	The battle for the top application for creating vector graphics used to be between Macromedia FreeHand and Adobe Illustrator. Since Adobe's purchase of Macromedia, FreeHand is no more.
Inkscape	Illustration tool	Free	www.inkscape.org	Inkscape is a cross-platform vector tool that takes advantage of Mac OS X's UNIX heritage by using X11. Because of this, it doesn't provide quite the same user experience as most native Mac OS X applications, but it's a power application, and the price is right.
Photo Mechanic	Image-management tool	$150	www.camerabits.com	Photo Mechanic is a specialized image-management tool. Rather than focusing on archiving and editing images, it provides professional photographers an excellent tool for quickly viewing and adding important keywords and metadata to images.
Photoshop	Image-editing tool	$699	www.adobe.com/photoshop	Since its inception, Adobe Photoshop has been the leading image-editing tool, and today it's still the best.
Photoshop Lightroom	Image-management tool	$299	www.adobe.com/lightroom	Closing in on Aperture's heels is Adobe Photoshop Lightroom, an image-management tool that's similar and yet different. If you find iPhoto interesting yet lacking in some areas, give both Lightroom and Aperture a try, and pick the one that works best for you.
Pixelmator	Image-editing tool	$59	www.pixelmator.com	While Photoshop is unrivaled in its editing capabilities, sometimes you just want a simple, effective tool for improving images. Pixelmator provides capable image-editing tools at an attractive price.

Application	Type	Cost	URL	Notes
Office				
iWork '09	Office suite	$79	www.apple.com/iwork	iWork '09 provides Mac users an excellent office suite with a powerful word processor (Pages), spreadsheet (Numbers), and presentation tool (Keynote). Each of these programs can read and write popular third-party file formats, including Microsoft Office files.
Microsoft Office	Office suite	$399	www.microsoft.com/mac	Microsoft Office is the leading office suite available. The Mac OS X version provides seamless file-format compatibility with its Windows counterpart.
NoteBook	Outliner/ organizer	$49.95	www.circusponies.com	Circus Ponies NoteBook is, as the name implies, a digital notebook. On top of being an excellent outlining and organization tool, it allows you to add any type of text clipping or media file to your notebook.
OmniGraffle	Flowchart tool	$99	www.omnigroup.com/ applications/ omnigraffle/	OmniGraffle is an excellent tool for creating flowcharts, org charts, or mind-mapping exercises.
OmniOutliner	Outliner	$39	www.omnigroup.com/applications/ omnioutliner	
Project X	Project-management tool	$199.99	http://projectx.com	Project X bills itself as "project management for the rest of us." Project X makes it easy to track progress, generate reports, and collaborate with others via the built-in web app.
Things	Task-management tool	$49.95	http://culturedcode.com	Things, by Cultured Code, is available for Mac and iPhone, and it syncs between the two platforms. Things occupies a unique position between cheap apps that aren't very good, and professional Getting Things Done (GTD) apps that cost much more.
Development and Database				
Bento	Personal database	$49	www.filemaker.com/ bento	Bento, based on FileMaker Pro, is a simple database designed for creating simple personal databases.
Checkout	Point-of-sale tool	$399	http://checkoutapp.com	Checkout is an incredibly gorgeous application that turns your Mac into a smart, multiuser point-of-sale system. It even includes a hardware bundle that adds a cash drawer, barcode scanner, and receipt printer, making this a professional solution at an attractive price.

Continued

Table C-1. *(Continued)*

Application	Type	Cost	URL	Notes
FileMaker Pro	Database tool	$299	www.filemaker.com	FileMaker Pro is a popular database system that provides a nice visual interface for creating and working with databases and reports, and it features a powerful, relational database management system (RDBMS) back end.
MySQL	RDBMS	Free/ $599	http://mysql.com	MySQL is a popular, open source RDBMS. It comes installed on Mac OS X Server, but you'll need to install it on your desktop system if you wish to use it.
Sequel Pro	Database tool	Free	www.sequelpro.com	Sequel Pro allows you to connect to and edit MySQL databases.
SQLEditor	Database tool	$79	www.malcolmhardie.com/ sqleditor	SQLEditor is a tool for designing databases visually. Once you have all of the tables set up, it outputs the SQL necessary to initialize your database.
Versions	Version-control tool	$39 (~$54)	http://versionsapp.com	Versions wraps the power of Subversion in an attractive, user-friendly interface. Versions makes version control with Subversion almost bearable.
Personal/Utility				
1Password	Password-management tool	$39.95	http:// agilewebsolutions.com	1Password is an excellent application for managing passwords and other sensitive data. It integrates with most popular Mac web browsers to provide an easy, efficient way of maintaining strong, unique passwords for all of your web sites and accounts.
AppZapper	Application uninstaller	$12.95	www.appzapper.com	AppZapper provides effective drag-and-drop uninstalls of most applications.
CandyBar	Icon manager	$29	www.panic.com/ candybar	Panic's CandyBar lets you skin your entire system with collections of icons, and it helps you organize them. CandyBar is the only easy way to change some icons, such as the Trash icon.
Delicious Library	Media-management tool	$40	http:// delicious-monster.com	Delicious Library is the personal media-management app that started the trend among third-party Mac apps to have spectacular custom interfaces. Keep track of your books and music by scanning their barcodes using your iSight camera, set due dates while you check items out to your friends, and show off your collection with professionally designed web-publishing templates.

Application	Type	Cost	URL	Notes
huey/hueyPRO	Color-management tool	$89/ $129	www.pantone.com/huey	huey and hueyPRO are a combination of software and hardware that provide effective color management for your Mac's display.
iSale	eBay tool	$39.95	www.equinux.com/us/ products/isale/	equinux iSale is for people who wish the whole world were as easy to use as a Mac. iSale wraps eBay in an easy-to-use application for Mac and iPhone.
Little Snitch	Network monitor	$29.95	http://obdev.at/products/ littlesnitch/	Objective Development's Little Snitch lets you know whenever any running application tries to make a network connection. It's great for web browsing, because you can block connections to specific addresses, like a server with annoying Flash ads.

Index

You Need the Companion eBook